The Psychology of Humor

The Psychology of Humor

A Reference Guide and Annotated Bibliography

Jon E. Roeckelein

GREENWOOD PRESS
Westport, Connecticut • London

Library of Congress Cataloging-in-Publication Data

Roeckelein, Jon E.
    The psychology of humor : a reference guide and annotated bibliography / Jon E. Roeckelein.
      p. cm.
    Includes bibliographical references (p.) and indexes.
    ISBN 0–313–31577–9 (alk. paper)
    1. Wit and humor—Psychological aspects.   2. Wit and humor—Psychological
aspects—Bibliography.   I. Title.
PN6144.P5R64   2002
152.4′3—dc21   2001040554

British Library Cataloguing in Publication Data is available.

Library of Congress Catalog Card Number: 2001040554
ISBN: 0–313–31577–9

First published in 2002

Greenwood Press, 88 Post Road West, Westport, CT 06881
An imprint of Greenwood Publishing Group, Inc.
www.greenwood.com

Printed in the United States of America

The paper used in this book complies with the
Permanent Paper Standard issued by the National
Information Standards Organization (Z39.48–1984).

P

Copyright Acknowledgment

The author and publisher gratefully acknowledge permission to quote several word definitions
from *Webster's Third New International ®Dictionary, Unabridged* © 1993 by Merriam-Webster,
Incorporated.

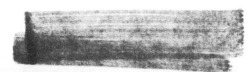

In memory of Don C. Ettore.

To my inlaws—Margie Harris and Don and Pam Ettore—who have always shown me great hospitality, honor, and a deeper aspect of humor: that of joy.

To the "good old days" of the late 1960s, and to my colleagues and the crew at Human Resources Research Office (HumRRO), Division 4 (Fort Benning, Georgia), especially "Jake" Jacobs, Joe Olmstead, and Doug Holmes who each generously provided me with humor, personal friendship, and intellectual stimulation; and to the late James Scoresby—a fellow teacher who knew the true meaning and value of humor and laughter.

Contents

Preface

Recently, in January 2001, I conducted a computer search of the keyword *humor* using the MELVYL Catalog (California Digital Library, CDL) database, and found a total of over 14,015 studies that cut across many different academic disciplines ranging from anthropology to the health sciences to zoology/ethology. [Note: The database WorldCat shows over 75,670 published items worldwide—cutting across many languages and disciplines—for the keyword *humor!*] Also, at about the same time, when I searched *humor* on the more discipline-specific database PsycINFO, I discovered that there are over 3,140 studies on humor in the psychological literature that have been published between 1887 and 2001.

The large number of humor studies published in the field of psychology—as compared proportionately to other discipline areas—indicates that the topic of *humor* is represented strongly in psychology (as well as in a few other discipline areas, such as the fields of literature and history, which include not only the wealth of the writings of the world's humorists themselves, but also of the numerous critiques, commentaries, theses, and dissertations written about humorists and their works). According to the figures here, when contrasting MELVYL with PsycINFO, psychology captures almost one-fourth of the total number of studies published on humor across all disciplines.

The finding that the field of psychology contains such a large number of studies on humor requires that a review, reference, and resource book—such as the present work—set up criteria and boundaries concerning selection of the type of material to be covered. Accordingly, the following parameters serve as the basis for selection of material in this book:

1. The topic of humor as compared and contrasted with a number of humor-related terms such as wit, laughter, comedy, satire/irony, puns, jokes, and cartoons, among others.
2. The topic of humor in a historical context, including the origins and evolution of humor.
3. The topic of humor from theoretical, functional, and differential perspectives.
4. The topic of humor as used in experimental/empirical studies involving various methodologies and measurements of humor.
5. The topic of humor as projected into future research settings and contexts.
6. The topic of humor in the modern psychological literature from 1970 through 2001, including, among others, the rubrics of *humor, wit, laughter, comedy, satire/irony/sarcasm/farce/parody, riddles/puns/jokes,* and *caricature/cartoons/comic strips/slapstick* that comprise a current annotated bibliography of humor studies in psychology.

The goal of this book is to provide a one-volume resource and reference book for the psychology of humor that covers the terminological domains of humor, the origins and evolution of humor, the present and projected future methodological and theoretical concerns of psychologists regarding the study of humor, and a scientific, experimental, and empirical account of the topic of humor as reflected in the recent psychological literature.

In more specific terms, the plan and outline of this book is to cover the following material: the various terminological aspects and domains of humor as distinguished from humor-related terms such as wit, laughter, comedy, satire, irony, sarcasm, farce, parody, riddles, puns, jokes, caricature, cartoons, comic strips, and slapstick (Chapter 1); humor as conceived by ancient/primitive humans, early philosophers, and Jewish and biblical writers (Chapter 2); the various modern theoretical aspects of humor, including prominent nonpsychological and psychological theories of humor (Chapter 3); the differential and functional aspects of humor, including personality, gender, individual, cross-generational, cross-cultural, and ethnic differences, and the functions of humor including humor as a coping mechanism, as a psychotherapeutic aid, as an adjunct in the classroom and the workplace, and the social influences of humor (Chapter 4); the methodological, measurement, and futuristic aspects of humor (Chapter 5); and humor as indicated in a current (1970–2001) annotated bibliography of humor studies in psychology (Chapter 6). Also, this book contains a Name Index and Subject Index to help in the rapid location of particular persons and specific subjects and topics of interest.

Introduction

The topic of humor, including the *psychology* of humor, seems to have gained the reputation over the years of being an elusive and mysterious phenomenon. I suggest that contributing to the elusive nature of humor, perhaps, is the reluctance of the earlier researchers (up to about the 1970s) to "take humor seriously" and to regard it as a proper topic for scientific, empirical, and experimental investigation (cf: Chapman & Foot, 1976, p. 2). Levine (1986, p. 132) maintains that humor has only recently become an area of research interest to behavioral scientists because such states and activities as humor, play, creativity, sports, and curiosity do not fit easily into most motivational theories which emphasize behavior arising from the deprivation of organic needs.

Typically, many human activities lend themselves readily to experimental research where individuals respond because they are aroused by hunger, anger, sex, or anxiety, but humor—in contrast—relates to the environment in nondrive or nondeprivation ways where one's cognitive and interpersonal competence skills and activities are focal points. Harre and Lamb (1983, p. 283) observe that until recently psychologists and other social scientists regarded humor and laughter as either taboo or trivial topics for systematic inquiry, and it is only in the last 10 years or so that psychologists have begun to contribute significantly to the base of knowledge on humor.

O'Connell (1984/1994) notes that humor—while fascinating humanity since recorded history—has not led to the persistent pursuit of crucial knowledge; scientific investigators have approached humor in bits and pieces and their efforts lack both rigor and vigor. As a result, according to O'Connell (1984/1994, p. 187), "there is no comprehensive network of facts about the development and purposes of humor in human existence."

In the first issue (Volume 1) of *Psychological Abstracts*, published in 1927, there are only *two* studies cited concerning the topic of humor: P. Kambouropoulou's "Individual Differences in the Sense of Humor" (see *American Journal of Psychology*, 1926, *37*, 268–278); and an anonymous article, "The Sense of Joy," in *Nation*, 1927, *124*, 468.

In the second issue (Volume 2) of *Psychological Abstracts*, published in 1928, there are *six* entries concerning the study of humor: S. Freud's "On Humor" (a paper given at the Tenth International Psychoanalytic Congress; see *Psychoanalytic Review*, 1928, *15*, 85–107); J. Erskine's "Humor" (see *Century*, 1928, *115*, 421–426); S. Freud's "Humour" (see *International Journal of Psychoanalysis*, 1928, *9*, 1–6); L. Wynn-Jones' "The Appreciation of Wit" (see *Reports of the British Association of the Advancement of Science*, 1927, 373); R. H. Hellyar's "The Meaning of the Comic" (see *Psyche*, 1927, *30*, 78–99); and H. Barry, Jr.'s "The Role of Subject Matter in Individual Differences in Humor" (see *Journal of Genetic Psychology*, 1928, *35*, 112–128).

In the third issue (Volume 3) of *Psychological Abstracts*, published in 1929, there are only *three* studies cited that deal with the topic of humor: T. Reik's "Zur Psychoanalyse des Judischen Witzes (Psychoanalysis of Jewish Wit)" (see *Imago*, 1929, *15*, 63–88); J. Cornelissen's "Vreemde landen en volken in den volkshumor en de spreekwoordentaal (Foreign Lands and Peoples in Popular Humor and Proverbs)" (see *Nederlandsch Tijdschreibe von Volkskunde*, 1928, *33*, 76–91); and D. Murphy's "The Lighter Side of Paul's Personality" (see *Anglican Theological Review*, 1929, *11*, 242–250).

In summarizing the nature of early humor research as indicated in the first three volumes (where each volume contains thousands of citations describing various psychological studies) of *Psychological Abstracts* from 1927 through 1929, there is a total of only 11 studies cited: three are written from a psychoanalytic perspective (Freud and Reik); one is written from a Bergsonian/philosophical point of view (Hellyar), one is a cross-cultural/anecdotal study (Cornelissen); one is a theological apology concerning humor in a biblical character (Murphy); one is a brief homily on the relative merits of a sense of joy versus a sense of humor (anonymous); one is a literary approach to humor (Erskine); one deals with the relationship between wit and personality, and suggests that locality (schools at elementary, secondary, and university levels) plays an insignificant role in the appreciation of wit as compared with some general factor (Wynn-Jones); one describes a two-participant study that employed different types of jokes and a word-association technique, and concludes that humor may be due to change from unpleasantly toned perception to neutrality or pleasantly toned perception wherein incongruity is only an incidental, and not a core, factor (Barry); and one describes the use of humor diaries and joke-ranking to assess individual differences in sense of humor, and suggests that "personal" and "impersonal" types of humor need to be experimentally related to temperament and character in order to advance the study of the sense of humor (Kambouropoulou).

Thus, in the late 1920s—as reflected in these citations—there is barely an empirical emphasis (and virtually *no* experimental emphasis) in the study of the psychology of humor. One may make a weak case, perhaps, that the three early studies of "individual differences in humor" (Barry; Kambouropoulou; and Wynn-Jones) demonstrate a quasi-empirical approach, but even these studies lack the scientific rigor inherent in a truly experimental investigation of humor. Chapter 5 provides further discussion of humor from a methodological and experimental point of view.

Overall interest in the study of humor in the discipline of psychology in the last 114 years from 1887 through 2000 may be assessed quantitatively, decade by decade, by consulting the computer database PsycINFO. This source indicates that three psychological studies on humor were conducted in 1887–1900; three studies were conducted in 1901–1910; four studies in 1911–1920; 45 studies in 1921–1930; 101 studies in 1931–1940; 93 studies in 1941–1950; 105 studies in 1951–1960; 171 studies in 1961–1970; 464 studies in 1971–1980; 945 studies in 1981–1990; and 1,156 studies in 1991–2000. It is apparent that the decade periods of 1921–1930, 1971–1980, and 1981–1990 represent the most dramatic increases in number of humor studies conducted (as compared with the respective adjacent/preceding periods) with an overall positive acceleration in the production curve covering each 10–year period from 1887 through 2000. Thus, the popularity of the psychological investigation of humor seems to have made quantum leaps and gains—decade by decade—and apparently is being studied by more and more psychologists over time.

However, there is one puzzling finding that may reflect the enduring and persistent "old prejudice" against the adoption and inclusion of the topic of humor in mainstream psychology. In a survey of over 136 introductory psychology textbooks (sources within which, presumably, the basic facts and essential features of psychological science reside) that were published between 1885 and 1996 (see Roeckelein, 1996, 1998, pp. 495–529), I found only three books that make reference to humor and humor-related topics: Woodworth (1921) briefly discusses "theories of humor," C.R. Griffith (1929) mentions "theories of laughter," and Titchener (1928) describes a "theory of tickle." Moreover, according to this survey, none of the dozens of post-1929 introductory psychology textbooks published in the 67 years from 1930 through 1996 contain material on humor, theories of humor, or humor-related topics such as wit, laughter, and comedy (cf: Apte, 1985, p. 23, who notes that most introductory *anthropology* textbooks do not even list humor as a significant characteristic of cultural systems). Additionally, there is as yet clearly no scientific "law" (or "laws") of humor extant in psychology [notwithstanding Eastman's (1921, pp. 88–120) attempt to lay down the first eight *laws* of "a code for serious joke-makers"; Eastman's (1937, p. 19) four *laws* of humor which define "all there is in the science of humour as seen from a distance"; or the "law" of laughter cited by Sidis (1913, p. 3)].

Nor, apparently, is there today an organized or systematized body of scientific knowledge on the psychology of humor, although there are a number of promising inroads being made (see Chapters 4 and 5). In all fairness, concerning the striking absence of material on humor in the introductory psychology textbooks, it should be noted that some "specialty area" textbooks published within the field of psychology (e.g., social psychology; child development; child psychology) do contain material on humor varying both in quality and quantity. However, the desideratum yet remains of the scientific and experimental/empirical study of humor for psychology in general, and where, eventually, one seeks to find good theories and strong laws of humor included in the basic introductory textbooks that reflect the science of psychology. Harre and Lamb (1983, p. 283) state that theories on humor abound in the psychological literature today, but they are largely descriptive and taxonomic accounts rather than explanations as to *why* humor occurs and *why* laughter is emitted, and where remarkably few approaches draw on general principles within psychology. According to Harre and Lamb, the quest for a "grand theory" of humor has been abandoned. See Chapter 3, "Modern Theoretical Aspects of Humor," for further discussion on the theories of humor.

It has been two decades since major works, reviews, or bibliographies on the psychology of humor have appeared in the literature (cf: Chapman & Foot, 1976, 1977; Goldstein & McGhee, 1972; McGhee, 1971, 1979; McGhee & Chapman, 1980; McGhee & Goldstein, 1983). While a major article (Wyer & Collins, 1992) and a book (Latta, 1998) on two specific theories of humor, a German-language survey on the psychology of humor (Wicki, 1992), a book on defining sense of humor at a trait level (Ruch, 1998), and many self-help and clinical-application books on humor (e.g., Buckman, 1994; DuPre, 1998; Fry & Salameh, 1987, 1993; Hageseth, 1988; Klein, 1989; LaRoche, 1998; Lefcourt, 2000; Michelli, 1998; Strean, 1994) have appeared recently in the psychological literature, and a number of books, chapters, and a journal on humor from nonpsychological and multidisciplinary perspectives have been published recently (e.g., Barreca, 1991, 1996; Davies, 1990; Davis, 1993; Durant & Miller, 1988; Eckardt, 1992; Gates, 1999; N. Griffith, 1989; Gruner, 1997; Mintz, 1988; Nilsen, 1993, 1996, 1997, 1998, 2000; Raskin, 1988; Rutter, 1998; Seligson & Peterson, 1992; Sloane, 1987; Vaid, 1999; Ziv, 1988; Ziv & Zajdman, 1993), there is yet a great need for a current and comprehensive resource book and annotated bibliography on recent research in the area of the *psychology* of humor. Thus, in consideration of this perceived need, the present book is written for those laypersons, students, teachers, and researchers who are interested in gaining a 21st-century state of the art appreciation of the psychology of humor.

REFERENCES

Apte, M. L. (1985). *Humor and laughter: An anthropological approach.* Ithaca, NY: Cornell University Press.

Barreca, R. (1991). *They used to call me Snow White—but I drifted: Women's strategic use of humor.* New York: Viking.

Barreca, R. (Ed.) (1996). *The Penguin book of women's humor.* New York: Penguin.

Buckman, E. (Ed.) (1994). *The handbook of humor: Clinical applications in psychotherapy.* Malabar, FL: Krieger.

Chapman, A. J., & Foot, H. C. (Eds.) (1976). *Humour and laughter: Theory, research, and applications.* New York: Wiley.

Chapman, A. J., & Foot, H. C. (Eds.) (1977). *It's a funny thing, humour.* Elmsford, NY: Pergamon Press.

Davies, C. (1990). *Ethnic humor around the world: A comparative analysis.* Bloomington: Indiana University Press.

Davis, M. (1993). *What's so funny? The comic conception of culture and society.* Chicago: University of Chicago Press.

DuPre, A. (1998). *Humor and the healing arts: A multimethod analysis of humor use in health care.* Mahwah, NJ: Erlbaum

Durant, J., & Miller, J. (Ed.) (1988). *Laughing matters: A serious look at humour.* New York: Wiley.

Eastman, M. (1921). *The sense of humor.* New York: Scribner's.

Eastman, M. (1937). *Enjoyment of laughter.* Kent, UK: Hamish Hamilton.

Eckardt, A. R. (1992). *Sitting in the earth and laughing: A handbook of humor.* New Brunswick, NJ: Transaction.

Fry, W., & Salameh, W. (Eds.) (1987). *Handbook of humor and psychotherapy: Advances in the clinical use of humor.* Sarasota, FL: PRP/PRE.

Fry, W., & Salameh, W. (Eds.) (1993). *Advances in humor in psychotherapy.* Sarasota, FL: PRP/PRE.

Gates, R. (1999). *American literary humor during the Great Depression.* Westport, CT: Greenwood Press.

Goldstein, J. H., & McGhee, P. E. (Eds.) (1972). *The psychology of humor: Theoretical perspectives and empirical issues.* New York: Springer-Verlag.

Griffith, C. R. (1929). *Introduction to psychology.* New York: Macmillan.

Griffith, N. (1989). *Humor and the old Southwest.* Westport, CT: Greenwood Press.

Gruner, C. R. (1997). *The game of humor: A comprehensive theory of why we laugh.* New Brunswick, NJ: Transaction.

Hageseth, C. (1988). *A laughing place: The art and psychology of positive humor in love and adversity.* Fort Collins, CO: Berwick.

Harre, R., & Lamb, R. (Eds.) (1983). *The encyclopedic dictionary of psychology.* Cambridge, MA: The M.I.T. Press.

Klein, A. (1989). *The healing power of humor: Techniques for getting through loss, setbacks, upsets, disappointments, difficulties, trials, tribulations, and all that not-so-funny stuff*. Los Angeles: Tarcher.

LaRoche, L. (1998). *Relax—You may have only a few minutes left: Using the power of humor to overcome stress in your life and work*. New York: Villard.

Latta, R. (1998). *The basic humor process*. Berlin: Mouton de Gruyter.

Lefcourt, H. (2000). *Humor: The psychology of living buoyantly*. New York: Kluwer Academic/Plenum.

Levine, J. (1986). Humor. In T. Pettijohn (Ed.), *The encyclopedic dictionary of psychology*. Guilford, CT: Dushkin.

McGhee, P. E. (1971). Development of the humor response: A review of the literature. *Psychological Bulletin, 76*, 328–348.

McGhee, P. E. (1979). *Humor: Its origin and development*. San Francisco: Freeman.

McGhee, P. E., & Chapman, A. J. (Eds.) (1980). *Children's humour*. Chichester, UK: Wiley.

McGhee, P. E., & Goldstein, J. H. (Eds.) (1983). *Handbook of humor research. (*Vol. 1, *Basic issues*). (Vol. 2, *Applied studies*). New York: Springer-Verlag.

Michelli, J. (1998). *Humor, play, & laughter: Stress-proofing life with your kids*. Golden, CO: Love and Logic Press.

Mintz, L. (Ed.) (1988). *Humor in America*. Westport, CT: Greenwood Press.

Nilsen, D. (1993). *Humor scholarship: A research bibliography*. Westport, CT: Greenwood Press.

Nilsen, D. (1996). *Humor in Irish literature: A reference guide*. Westport, CT: Greenwood Press.

Nilsen, D. (1997). *Humor in British literature from the Middle Ages to the Restoration: A reference guide*. Westport, CT: Greenwood Press.

Nilsen, D. (1998). *Humor in eighteenth- and nineteenth-century British literature: A reference guide*. Westport, CT: Greenwood Press.

Nilsen, D. (2000). *Humor in twentieth-century British literature: A reference guide*. Westport, CT: Greenwood Press.

O'Connell, W. E. (1984/1994). Humor. In R. J. Corsini (Ed.), *Encyclopedia of psychology*. New York: Wiley.

Raskin, V. (Ed.) (1988). *Humor: International Journal of Humor Research*. Berlin: Mouton de Gruyter.

Roeckelein, J. E. (1996). Citation of *laws* and *theories* in textbooks across 112 years of psychology. *Psychological Reports, 79*, 979–998.

Roeckelein, J. E. (1998). *Dictionary of theories, laws, and concepts in psychology*. Westport, CT: Greenwood Press.

Ruch, W. (Ed.) (1998). *The sense of humor: Explorations of a personality characteristic*. Berlin/New York: Mouton de Gruyter.

Rutter, J. (1998). Laughingly referred to: An interdisciplinary bibliography of published work in the field of humour studies and research. *Salford Papers in Sociology, 21*, University of Salford, UK.

Seligson, M. R., & Peterson, K. (1992). *AIDS prevention and treatment: Hope, humor, and healing*. New York: Hemisphere.

Sidis, B. (1913). *The psychology of laughter*. New York: Appleton.

Sloane, D. (Ed.) (1987). *American humor magazines and comic periodicals.* Westport, CT: Greenwood Press.

Strean, H. (1994). *The use of humor in psychotherapy.* Northvale, NJ: Jason Aronson.

Titchener, E. B. (1928). *A textbook of psychology.* New York: Macmillan.

Vaid, J. (1999). The evolution of humor: Do those who laugh last? In D. Rosen & M. Luebbert (Eds.), *Evolution of the psyche.* Westport, CT: Praeger.

Wicki, W. (1992). The psychology of humor: A survey. *Schweizerische Zeitschrift fur Psychologie, 51,* 151–163.

Woodworth, R. S. (1921). *Psychology: A study of mental life.* New York: Holt.

Wyer, R., & Collins, J. (1992). A theory of humor elicitation. *Psychological Review, 99,* 663–688.

Ziv, A. (Ed.) (1988). *National styles of humor.* Westport, CT: Greenwood Press.

Ziv, A., & Zajdman, A. (Eds.) (1993). *Semites and stereotypes.* Westport, CT: Greenwood Press.

Terminological Aspects and Domains of Humor

DEFINITIONS OF THE CONCEPT OF HUMOR

Hardly a word in the language—and it seems to be exclusively an English word—would be harder to define with scientific precision than this familiar one. It is often used with the greatest degree of looseness, as when a man is endowed with humour because he laughs readily.

—J. Sully, 1902

It is more enjoyable to read a humorous book than to read one explaining humor.

—A. Ziv, 1984

Humor is an enigma. People crave it desperately . . . It is all pervasive; we don't know of any culture where people do not have a sense of humor . . . There is no aspect of our lives that is not open to humor . . . And yet, curiously enough, humor has remained a puzzle to the best minds we have produced.

—A. A. Berger, 1987

It is ironic that we are daily exposed to humor, and the world's literature abounds with examples, yet humor eludes precise definition.

—F. J. MacHovec, 1988

Humor is a genuine mystery . . . In any of its basic applications, there is at present only one way to define the term "humor" adequately, so as truly to convey its meaning, and that is to define it ostensively: here is an example, here is another quite different example, and there is another—that is what "humor" means.

—R. L. Latta, 1998

The noun *humor* (typically spelled "humour" in Australia, Canada, New Zealand, and the United Kingdom) is defined in *Webster's Third New International Dictionary* (1993) as

a normal functioning fluid or semifluid of the body (as the blood, lymph, or bile), especially of vertebrates; a secretion that is itself an excitant of activity (as certain hormones); in *medieval physiology*: a fluid or juice of an animal or plant; specifically: one of the four fluids entering into the constitution of the body and determining by their relative proportions a person's health and temperament; constitutional or habitual disposition, character, or bent; temporary state of mind; a sudden, unpredictable, or unreasoning inclination.

It is only secondarily that *Webster's* (1993) defines *humor* with the meaning that is most modern and relevant for present purposes as

that quality in a happening, an action, a situation, or an expression of ideas which appeals to a sense of the ludicrous or absurdly incongruous; comic or amusing quality; the mental faculty of discovering, expressing, or appreciating ludicrous or absurdly incongruous elements in ideas, situations, happenings, or acts; droll imagination or its expression; the act of or effort at being humorous; something (as an action, saying, or writing) that is or is designed to be humorous.

Other variations on the concept of humor appear in *Webster's* (1993, 1994) and fall outside the purview and purpose of the present book. Such variations—often showing up in computer database searches when the sole keyword *humor* is submitted—include the terms *aqueous humor* (any fluid or fluidlike substance of the body, blood, lymph, bile, etc., especially the watery fluid filling the chambers in front of the lens of the eye; a limpid fluid occupying the space between the crystalline lens and the cornea of the eye); and *vitreous humor* (also called the *vitreous body*, it is the transparent, colorless, jellylike substance that fills the eyeball between the retina and lens). Humor is defined, also, as a secretion that is itself an excitant of activity, as certain hormones; neurohumor (*Webster's*, 1993).

Webster's (1993) also provides definitions of the adjective *humorous*, given in their respective order as

subject to or governed by humor or caprice: capricious, whimsical (archaic); moist, humid, watery (obsolete); full of or characterized by humor: funny, jocular, possessing, indicating, or expressive of a sense of humor; given to the display of or appreciative of humor.

Thus it is observed via the authoritative definitions given by *Webster's* (1993) that the term *humor* originated in ancient theory, most particularly in the early writings of the Greeks. Humor originally referred to any of four bodily fluids

(*Webster's New World Dictionary of American English*, 1994, refers to the four "cardinal humors" under *humor*) that determined human's health and temperament (also, see Harris & Levey, 1975, p. 1288). The Greek physician Hippocrates (c. 460–c. 370 B.C.)—who is well recognized as the father of medicine—maintained that an imbalance among the four fluids or humors (blood, phlegm, black bile, and yellow bile) resulted in pain and disease, and that good health was achieved via a balance of the four humors. This notion of Hippocrates was revered for many centuries and served as the basis of ancient medicine. The teachings of the ancient Hippocratic school attempted to separate medicine from philosophic speculation and superstition, and attempted to place medicine strictly on a scientific level that was grounded in deductive reasoning and objective observation. While Hippocrates conformed to the belief that was current during his time that disease resulted from an imbalance of the four bodily humors, he also advanced the ideas that the bodily disturbance was affected by external forces, that the fluids/humors were actually glandular secretions, and that the body's glands had a controlling influence on the balance of the fluids.

Following Hippocrates, the Greek physician/writer Galen (c. 130–c. 200) introduced a new dimension to the humoral theory. Galen suggested that there are four basic "temperaments" (i.e., moods, natures, frames of mind, or dispositions) that reflect the condition of the four bodily fluids/humors (cf: Roeckelein, 1998, pp. 199–200): the *sanguine* temperament, condition, or type reflects an excess of the blood fluid, the *phlegmatic* temperament indicates an excess of the phlegm fluid, the *choleric/bilious* condition reflects an excess of the yellow bile fluid, and the *melancholic* temperament indicates an excess of the black bile fluid. In this way, Galen effectively tied together the workings of the physical body (fluids/humors) with the corresponding effects on the "psyche" or psychological mind (temperaments). Thus, black bile—secreted from the spleen or kidneys—caused gloominess, irritability, depression, or melancholy; yellow bile—secreted by the intestines—caused anger, irritability, quick temper, or irascibility; phlegm—secreted by the mucous glands of the respiratory tract and throat—caused sluggishness, dullness, apathy, or impassivity; and blood which circulates through the heart, arteries, and veins caused the warm, passionate, cheerful, confident, optimistic, and hopeful temperament.

Galen employed experimentation and animal dissection in making his medical discoveries and emphasized purposive creation in his theories; his work in physiology and anatomy is noteworthy, also, demonstrating that arteries carry blood instead of air. While Galen's work added greatly to knowledge of the structure and functioning of the brain, nerves, spinal cord, and pulse, his authority was virtually undisputed up until the 16th century and, thus, probably slowed medical progress and discouraged much by way of original investigation by others (Harris & Levey, 1975).

Webster's Dictionary of Word Origins (1995) provides further etymological information on the concept of humor. Throughout the Middle Ages (A.D. 476–c. 1450) it was a belief that everything on Earth consisted of different combinations of four elements: earth, air, fire, and water. In turn, these elements were believed to be composed of combinations of what were called the Four Contraries: hot, cold, moist, and dry. It was thought that fire derived from the combination of hot and dry; air from hot and moist; earth from cold and dry; and water from cold and moist.

These same Four Contraries were believed to combine into the four *humors* (blood, phlegm, black bile, yellow bile) in humans where the balance or imbalance of these humors in an individual determined his or her temperament. The four humors were derived from the Four Contraries as follows: choler (yellow bile) from hot and dry, blood (sanguinity) from hot and moist, melancholy (black bile) from dry and cold, and phlegm from cold and moist. Consequently, due to the similarities in their composition, the humors were related metaphorically to the four elements (a *choleric* person is fiery, hot-tempered, irascible, and vindictive; a *sanguine* person is cheerful, confident, and optimistic; a *phlegmatic* person is stolid, sluggish, and dull; and a *melancholic* person is dejected, angry, and depressed). *Webster's* (1995, p. 231) notes that the term *melancholy*—in the Middle Ages—meant more than simply "thoughtful" or "sad." A melancholic person was prone to be extremely dejected and open to protracted anger, as well as being liable to nightmares. The archetypal melancholy character in literature is Shakespeare's Hamlet who complains of his bad dreams and who even diagnoses his own melancholy.

Etymologically, after becoming a general term for "disposition" or "temperament," *humor* came to mean "a mood or temporary state of mind" and from this developed the sense of caprice, whim, or fancy from which are derived the senses of *humor* relating to persons or things that are amusing or comic. The words *temper* and *temperament* originally also referred to the combination and balance within the body of the four humors, as they derive from the Latin *temperare* meaning "to mix, blend, or regulate." The word *complexion*, deriving from the Latin *complexio* meaning "combination" was synonymous originally with *temper* and *temperament*. Inasmuch as an individual's temperament or temper was believed often to be revealed in his or her coloring, the word *complexion* came to mean simply "the appearance or hue of the skin"—a meaning that has endured to this day (*Webster's*, 1995).

Webster's (1995) also notes that the term *humor* itself derives from the Middle English (A.D. 1100–1500) word *humour*, from the Middle French (A.D. 1300–1600) word *humeur*, from the Medieval Latin (A.D. 600–1500) and Latin (to A.D. 200) words *humor* (humor of the body) and *humor/umor* (moisture, fluid), and is akin probably to the Latin word *uvere* (to be moist), to the Middle Dutch word *wac* (damp, wet), to the Old Norse word *vokr* (damp), to the Greek (to A.D. 200) word *hygros* (wet), and to the Sanskrit word *uksati* (he sprinkles, he moistens).

Within the discipline of psychology, various definitions of the concept *humor* have appeared in a number of dictionaries and encyclopedias of psychological and philosophical terms. The following is a brief account of *humor* in some of these books, generally arranged in chronological order (with a few exceptions).

Baldwin (1901–1905, p. 488) defines *humour* and *humorous* as

any disposition of mind, as in good or bad humour; that special disposition which has the feeling of mirth; a complex feeling (or corresponding quality) composed of an element of the comic and an element of sympathy. According to the varying degrees in which these elements are present, it shades from the *comic* on the one hand to the *pathetic* on the other. The humorous was treated as equivalent to the *ludicrous*, or as a species of it. Its complex character was pointed out by those who regarded it as a union of comic and tragic.... It seems desirable to use the term in the sense of a complex feeling composed of an element of the comic and an element of sympathy, although this is not perfectly established.

Baldwin (1901–1905) gives the derivation and linguistic/terminological variations of *humour* as: the derivative Latin *humor* (moisture); the German variations *Stimmung, Laune, Frohlichkeit,* and *Humor* (cf: the interesting German word "Schadenfreude"—receiving joy or glee from someone else's misfortune; see Corsini, 1999; Hall & Allin, 1897, p. 19; Nachman, 1986); the French variations *humeur, bonne humeur; and the Italian variations umore, buon umore,* and *umorismo.* Also included in Baldwin's entry on *humour* are a few references that reflect the historical definitions, usage, and meanings of the term.

Fowler (1926) makes distinctions between *humor* (the "ludicrous") and several humor-related terms (cf: Berlyne, 1969, p. 799)—such as wit, satire, sarcasm, invective, irony, cynicism, and the sardonic—in terms of four features or functional areas (i.e., motive/aim, province, method/means, audience). [Note: See my later section in this chapter on "Humor as Satire/Irony/Sarcasm/Farce/Parody"]. Lilly (1896) lists 21 varieties of humor, including the terms wit, irony, satire, sarcasm, parody, puns, banter, mimicry, and practical joking. Other writers who make distinctions between humor and various humor-related terms (cf: Hayworth, 1928) are Freud (1905/1916/1960), Hazlitt (1819), Kris (1938), and Pearson (1938).

English (1928) defines *humor* in three ways as: moisture, especially fluids of an animal body; temperament (formerly believed to be due to humors in the "moisture" sense); and that which excites mirth or laughter by a sympathetic delineation of human failings.

Warren (1934) defines *humor, humour* in a single entry as

a complex situation which combines an element of the comic and a sympathetic appeal; or, a linguistic or mixed expression on the part of an individual which intentionally portrays such a situation; an emotional attitude which is characteristically pleasant or unpleasant (e.g., good humor); a liquid secretion (e.g., aqueous humor).

In another entry, Warren (1934) defines *humoral theory* (cf: Goldenson, 1970, p. 566, and Roeckelein, 1998, pp. 199–200, for more complete accounts of *humor theory*) as

the theory that the body contains four humors, a mixing of which, in right proportion, constitutes health; while an improper proportion or irregular distribution constitutes disease. (According to tradition, black bile gives rise to the *melancholic* temperament, yellow bile to the *choleric*, blood bile to the *sanguine*, and phlegm to the *phlegmatic*).

In his dictionary of psychology, Drever (1952/1973)—who was born, and lived, in Great Britain—provides an interesting set of entries on the concept of humor. In one entry (p. 123), *humor* (note the American-style spelling) is defined mainly in a *physiological* sense as: "A fluid in the body, particularly one of those which in the older physiology and psychology were supposed to be the basis of the different *temperaments*." In the very next entry, Drever defines *humour* (note the British-style spelling) in a *psychological* sense as: "Character of a complex situation exciting joyful, and in the main quiet, laughter, either directly, through *sympathy*, or (indirectly) through *empathy*." Drever's choices in spelling here seem to be curious and inconsistent, especially in the light of his spelling earlier in his book (p. 19) of the physiological term *aqueous humour* ("transparent fluid occupying the space between the lens and cornea of the eye"). Linguistic consistency (with p. 123) requires that such spelling here (p. 19) would be *aqueous humor* (?). (Or, is my personal interest and penchant here merely pedantic, petty, pesky, priggish, picayunish, and pantagruelistic?).

English and English (1958/1976) define *humor* as

an expression, verbal or otherwise, that portrays a situation with a mixture of sympathy and amusement; a mood, emotional attitude, or tendency to respond favorably or unfavorably to other persons: catch him in a good *humor*; a liquid secretion, e.g., the bile, the *aqueous humor* of the eye. The humoral theory of Galen supposed that temperament depended on the proportion of four bodily *humors*.

Harriman (1959/1966) defines *humor (humour)* simply as: "In ancient medicine, one of the four fluids within the body (blood, phlegm, yellow bile, and black bile); a liquid (e.g., vitreous humor in the eyeball); response to a comic situation.

Goldenson (1970) provides an encyclopedic-type entry on humor and reviews some of the major findings on the *developmental* aspects of humor, the expression of the "sense of humor" from infancy to adulthood (cf: McGhee,

1968, 1971, 1979, 1983, 1986, 1988; McGhee & Chapman, 1980; Wolfenstein, 1954/1978), its functions in the psychic economy, and various theories that seek to explain why people laugh (cf: Svebak, 1974; Wells, 1923). Among the observations here are that the child's first smile may occur during the first week of life and is actually a reflex response, that the child by the age of three months shows pleasure by smiling at other people, and by the end of the first year, most children show some appreciation of the comic. Children not only laugh when tickled (cf: Hall & Allin, 1897), but respond also to unusual sounds, funny faces, and action games such as "peek-a-boo." Goldenson acknowledges that even though humor follows a somewhat predictable developmental pattern there are still considerable individual differences in humor appreciation from person to person (see Chapter 4, this book, section entitled "Individual, Personality, and Gender Differences," for a further discussion of individual differences in humor).

Eysenck, Arnold, and Meili (1972, p. 81) provide a three-part encyclopedic-type entry for *humor* which states initially that "it would not be too extreme to claim that before Freud a real interest in the phenomenon of humor and the use of the term 'wit' were not met with in psychology." Before the publication of Freud's (1905/1916/1960) book on humor (covering the topic of wit/jokes vis-à-vis the unconscious mind), despite a few attempts to define the term previously, it had no precise psychological connotation. The entry by Eysenck et al. on humor includes a Freudian interpretation of it (also see Chapter 3, "Psychodynamic/Psychoanalytic Theories" section, in the present work for an account of the Freudian theory of humor).

In a second part of their discussion of humor, Eysenck et al. report that the concept of humor is derived from Galen's (Latin name: Claudius Galenus) theory of temperaments (in which temperament is a mixture of "humors") and is used today in two ways: in the sense of a cheerful and comprehensive attitude to life or a basic mood; and as a generic term for verbal, graphic, or pantomimic expression designed to excite laughter and mirth (sense of humor). Eysenck et al. indicate that the factor analyses of opinions regarding humorous material show that the sense of humor consists of at least six factors that are correlated partly with certain personality traits. In a third part of their entry on humor, Eysenck et al. describe a distinction between *personal* or *orectic* (affective, conative: for example, sex) and *impersonal* or *cognitive* (formal) aspects of humor (cf: Kambouropoulou, 1926, 1930). It is noted, also, that various studies on humor (e.g., Eysenck, 1947; Williams, 1946) found evidence of a correlation between extraversion and preferences for orectic humor, and between introversion and preferences for cognitive humor.

In her review of the early conceptions of humor, Keith-Spiegel (1972, p. 14)—in a section called "The Brier Patch of Terminology—discusses the difficulty of defining the term *humor*. She suggests that the definitions offered for *humor* are almost as many as the theories themselves, and still one is perplexed and unsure of the complete dimensions of the concept. Moreover, according to Keith-Spiegel, the matter is complicated further by the myriad of other labels that are often used interchangeably with *humor*, and with each other (cf: Morreall, 1987, p. 5). For example, the following words have been used in the literature on humor to characterize humorous events and situations: absurd, amusing, cheerful, comical, corny, derisive, droll, facetious, fanciful, farcical, funny, inane, jocose, jocular, laughable, ludicrous, merry, mirthful, nonsensical, pleasurable, ridiculous, satiric, silly, waggish, whimsical, and witty. Perhaps the most difficult of all the terminology in this area, notes Keith-Spiegel, is the understanding of what it means to have, or *not* to have, a "sense of humor." Such a terminological confusion, and hodgepodge of labels, underscores the extreme difficulty ultimately encountered in comparing and contrasting the various topics and issues related to humor.

Wolman (1973/1989) defines *humor* in the most abridged fashion compared to any of the writers sampled here. According to Wolman, humor is "a positive, pleasant emotional attitude; any liquid secretion; a comical attitude or expression." Wolman also defines *gallows humor* very briefly as "a psychiatric term for humorous behavior under conditions of impending death."

In my survey of many of the published dictionaries of psychological terms, I found that a few writers do not even include the term *humor* in their listings. For instance, Bruno (1986), Statt (1981/1998), and Stratton and Hayes (1993) make no mention of the concept of humor or any of the humor-related terms such as wit, comedy, laughter, puns, satire, and so on. The ninth edition of *The Encyclopaedia Britannica* (1875/1881) has no entries for the terms *humor/humour* or *wit*. However, by the eleventh edition, *The Encyclopaedia Britannica* (1922) does have a very substantial entry on *humour* (Vol. 13, pp. 888–891), but not on *wit*; the entry on *humour* states that it is

a word of many meanings and of strange fortune in their evolution. It began by meaning simply "liquid." It passed through the stage of being a term of art used by the old physicians—whom we should now call physiologists—and by degrees has come to be generally understood to signify a certain "habit of the mind," shown in speech, in literature and in action, and a quality in things and events observed by the human intelligence. The word reached its full development by slow degrees. When Dr. Johnson compiled his dictionary, he gave nine definitions of, or equivalents for, "humour": moisture; the different kinds of moisture in a man's body, reckoned by the old physicians to be phlegm, blood, choler, and melancholy, which as they predominate are supposed to determine the temper of mind; general turn or temper of mind; present disposition; grotesque imagery, jocularity, merriment; tendency to disease, morbid disposition; petulance, peevishness; a trick, a practice; caprice, whim, predominant inclination. The list was not quite complete, even in Dr. Johnson's own time. Humour was then, as it is now, the name of the semi-fluid parts of the eye. Yet no dictionary-maker has been more successful than Johnson in giving the literary and conversational meaning of an English word, or the main lines of its history.

The Encyclopaedia Britannica's (1922) entry on *humour* goes on to describe the various historical and literary aspects of the term, sprinkled here and there with appropriate quotations and definitions from literature. The entry indicates that the word *humour* was "a good thing, but the Elizabethans certainly made it too common. It became a hack epithet of all work, to be used with no more discretion, though with less imbecile iteration, than the modern 'awful.'" (p. 889)

Additionally, *The Encyclopaedia Britannica's* (1922) entry on *humour* includes definitions, examples, and comparisons/contrasts from other writers, critics, and poets, such as Thackeray, Meredith, Bouhours, Moliere, Carlyle, Burney, Cervantes, Goldsmith, Hazlitt, Hobbes, Boswell, Sir Walter Scott, Horace, Chaucer, Rabelais, and Addison ("in whom the place of cheerfulness is taken by humour, and that of mirth by wit") (p. 890).

The 15th edition of *The New Encyclopaedia Britannica* (1997), Vol. 6, *Micropaedia* ("Ready Reference"), has entries on *humor/humour* and *humoresque* ("a type of character piece, generally a short piano composition expressing a mood or a vague nonmusical idea, usually more good-humored than humorous. Robert Schumann is the first composer to use the term as a musical title"). *Humour* is defined as a form of communication in which a complex mental stimulus illuminates or amuses, or elicits the reflex of laughter. Furthermore, the entry states that

most humour, from the crudest practical joke to the most elegant witticism or comic anecdote, comes from the sudden perception of a relation between two consistent but mutually incompatible contexts. The sudden clash between these two different contexts produces the comic effect because it compels the listener to perceive a given situation in two self-consistent but incompatible frames of reference at the same time. This creative type of mental activity seems to be innately delightful to human beings, at least in the context of a humorous appreciation of life.

The entry goes on to indicate that *humour* involves a bewildering number and variety of moods, but the one basic or key ingredient in humor is an impulse (however faint) of aggression, apprehension, or even malice. Sometimes aggressive humor is obvious (e.g., a child's practical joke or an adult's pratfall), whereas other times it is subtle (e.g., a pun makes a serious conversation seem ludicrous). Due to the universality of apprehension and aggression in humor, some theorists have advanced the idea that the function of humor is to discharge these emotional states in socially acceptable ways (e.g., laughter may serve as a "safety valve" for the overflow of redundant tensions). The description of humor here also includes an anthropological observation: the humor of simpler cultures is rather cruel by modern standards (e.g., tribesmen laughing at the pain of wounded animals, or playing painful practical jokes on each other) and such "play" is often too abrasive or divisive for larger or less closely comprised social groups; with increasing urbanization, there is a tendency to produce more verbal humor and less physical humor.

The *Academic American Encyclopedia* (1998) has no actual entry for the term *humor*, except to indicate (p. 303), *Humor*: see *Comedy; Wit*.

The Encyclopedia Americana (1998), Vol. 14 (pp. 563–564), has an entry on *humor* written by Elmer Blistein which states that humor, in modern usage, means the comic or laughable, and its meaning has an interesting historical evolution. Following a brief discussion of the classical "humoral theory," this account of humor focuses primarily on the various theories of humor, especially the theories of superiority/degradation, incongruity/expectation, frustration/bisociation, and tension relief/inhibition release (see my Chapter 3, "Modern Theoretical Aspects of Humor").

The New Columbia Encyclopedia (see Harris & Levey, 1975, p. 1288) gives a brief account of *humor* that includes the ancient humoral theory of Hippocrates and Galen and also states:

In time any personality aberration or eccentricity was referred to as a humor. In literature, a humor character was one in whom a single passion predominated; this interpretation was especially popular in Elizabethan and other Renaissance literature. One of the most comprehensive treatments of the subject was the *Anatomy of Melancholy* by Robert Burton. The theory found its strongest advocates among the comedy writers, notably Ben Jonson and his followers, who used humor characters to illustrate various modes of irrational and immoral behavior. In medicine, the theory lost favor in the 19th century after the German Rudolf Virchow presented his cellular pathology.

Other sources and reviews of psychological terms barely mention humor, or mention it only in a passing or secondary fashion. For example, in an encyclopedia of human behavior, Edelmann (1994) mentions humor merely in passing within the context of the topic of "embarrassment and blushing." In one case, Edelmann states: "A further general strategy involved in coping with embarrassment involves the use of humor or laughter and smiling. Laughter serves to reduce the tension, while joking can turn a potential loss of social approval into a gain in social approval" (p. 244). In the same encyclopedia of human behavior, Dobson and Pusch (1994, p. 632) briefly discuss "humoral theory" within the context of a section on "psychopathology."

In my survey of the Subject Indexes of the 51 volumes of the *Annual Review of Psychology* from 1950 through 2000 (covering over 28,000 pages), I found the following: only one reference to humor from 1991 through 2000, and that was within the context of a chapter on "consumer psychology" (see Tybout & Artz, 1994, p. 148); a section on humor/jokes within the context of a chapter on "cognitive development" (see Ginsburg & Koslowski, 1976, p. 42); and a reference to humor and aggression, and humor concerning feedback mechanisms, in a chapter on "personality" (see Sechrest, 1976, pp. 12, 19–20).

Additionally, the following brief references to humor/laughter (in the context of chapters ranging from behavioral medicine, adult development and aging, personality structure and assessment, facial expressions of emotion, attitudes and opinions, personality, personality dynamics, developmental psychology, mass communication, and psychotherapeutic processes) appear in other volumes/years of the *Annual Review of Psychology* (cited chronologically, from most recent to older here): healing effect of laughter (Vol. 34, 1983, p. 19); humor as an adaptation strategy in aging (Vol. 34, 1983, p. 561); humor and aggression (Vol. 31, 1980, p. 541); expression of humor and presence of others (Vol. 30, 1979, p. 535); laughter and the development of facial expressions in infants (Vol. 30, 1979, p. 534); persuasive effects of humor (Vol. 29, 1978, pp. 526, 537); cartoon humor and sex-role (Vol. 28, 1977, p. 127); laughter in infants (Vol. 28, 1977, pp. 275–277); stimuli in infant laughter (Vol. 25, 1974, p. 54); use of hostile humor (Vol. 22, 1971, p. 320); impact of drive changes on appreciation of humor (Vol. 21, 1970, p. 23); humor and aggression/personality dimension (Vol. 20, 1969, pp. 240–242); humor in psychotherapy (Vol. 14, 1963, p. 373); and humor and anxiety/sex differences in humor (Vol. 13, 1962, p. 506).

Harre and Lamb (1983) give an encyclopedic-type account of the concept of humor, and note that in everyday language "humor" may apply to a number of separate entities: a stimulus, a response, or a disposition (see my Chapter 5, "Methodological and Futuristic Aspects of Humor," for further discussion of the logical and methodological issues involved in the concept of humor). Harre and Lamb observe, also, that in modern times a good sense of humor has come to be recognized as an indication of a healthy personality and that it is a highly desirable trait to nurture. However, historically, a sense of humor was more typically considered as base and degenerate, fit only for the foolish and ignorant. In their discussion, Harre and Lamb also cover a number of developmental aspects regarding humor and cite a variety of social functions ascribed to humor.

O'Connell (1984/1994) discusses humor (cf: O'Connell, 1960, 1964, 1996) in three brief sections in an encyclopedia of psychology. [Note: In the same encyclopedia, Lundin, 1984/1994, authors a brief section on the ancient "humoral theory".] O'Connell notes that—while we have not progressed far from the speculations of the philosopher regarding the study of humor—much of the current interest in humor comes from the area of clinical psychology. O'Connell also raises some interesting questions concerning humor that may be approached empirically [e.g., "Is humor simply one response and, if so, is it measured by inner or outer changes?" (cf: Murray, 1934; Omwake, 1937, 1939, 1942; Wolf, Smith, & Murray, 1934); "What are the relationships in humor between physiological responses, comprehension, production, and simple appreciation?"; "Can humor be analyzed into different types, motivated by different purposes and therefore reflect varying degrees of maturity and pathology?"; "How do physiological responses with their differing latencies, frequencies, and amplitudes relate to social judgments under varying degrees of stress?" (cf: Perl, 1933)]. O'Connell observes that humor is not mentioned in psychological personality theories, as a rule, any more than is death ("the ultimate test of humor"); one exception is Bischoff's (1964) first edition of *Interpreting Personality Theories* in which he speculates on how ten personality theorists might perceive the role of humor in human development. O'Connell suggests that the best way to gain an appreciation of the work on humor of both the clinical psychologist and the experimental psychologist is via Chapman and Foot (1976, 1977), Goldstein and McGhee (1972), Mindess and Turek (1979), M. Stern (1981), and Warkentin (1969).

Petrovsky and Yaroshevsky (1985) provide a brief entry on humor under the rubric *sense of humor*, defining it as

man's ability to note and emotionally respond to the comic sides of events. Sense of humour is inseparably associated with the subject's ability to reveal contradictions in surrounding reality, e.g., to note and, sometimes, exaggerate the contrast of positive and negative traits in a person, somebody's affection of importance accompanied by contrasting behaviour, and so on. In this case, the subject maintains a friendly attitude towards the object of humour, whom he subjects to a kind of emotional criticism. Sense of humour implies the presence in the subject of a positive ideal, without which it degenarates [sic] into a negative trait, e.g, vulgarity, cynicism, etc. One can judge about the presence or absence of sense of humour by how a person takes jokes, anecdotes, friendly jests, and caricatures, and by whether he sees the comic side of a situation and by whether he can laugh not only at others, but also when he himself is made fun of. Lack of or underdeveloped sense of humour is indicative of the individual's declined emotional level and insufficient intellectual development.

Reber (1985/1995) defines *humor* as

any bodily fluid such as the aqueous humor in the eye. Archaic physiological theories assumed that temperament depended on the relative proportions of four cardinal humors in the body. Note that the vestiges of this point of view are still with us in that in common parlance *humor* can be used synonymously with *mood*. The quality of being pleasant, sympathetic, amusing, or funny.

Chapman and Sheehy (1987) note in their encyclopedic-type entry for *humour* that most popular dictionaries—when defining "humour"—include the psychologist's three usages: stimulus, response, and disposition. [Note: In this same encyclopedia, edited by R. L. Gregory (1987), the term *humours* is discussed by Vieda Skultans in an entry with the title, "Insanity: Early Theories," which covers the ancient humoral theory.] Chapman and Sheehy cite the definition of humour in the *Concise Oxford Dictionary of Current English* in its reference to "comicality," "the faculty of perceiving," and "state of mind" as a standard or authoritative source. Chapman and Sheehy also (as I did a few pages back), "pick on" Drever's (1952/1973) account of humor. In Chapman and Sheehy's case, however, it is noted that while Drever's dictionary is one of the best-known specialist dictionaries for psychologists, it provides a very narrow definition of humour, and a "provocative definition of laughter" (p. 320) when compared to other sources. [Note: For an even *narrower* definition of humor, see the title of the first chapter in Escarpit's (1963) book on humor: "On the Impossibility of Defining Humor."] Chapman and Sheehy suggest that today few psychologists—and perhaps no one currently researching humour—would endorse Drever's definition without substantial qualification.

Concerning the overall emphasis, theme, or tenor of Chapman and Sheehy's entry on *humour*, it may be fair to say that their primary focus and interest is on the specific behavior of laughter (a word count/content analysis of their entry shows that the word "laughter"—including "laugh" and "laughing"—occurs 49 times as compared to the 53 instances where the word "humour" is used). However, Chapman and Sheehy (p. 323) conclude generally that "there is now much evidence to the effect that *humour* (italics added) reflects basic underlying trends in emotional, social, and cognitive development."

In his book on the theory, history, and applications of humor, MacHovec (1988, p. ix) provides his own philosophical and clinical psychologist's perspective on the definition of humor:

humor can coldly cut or warmly bind together. It can be cerebral and/or visceral. Advocates can champion any one of these aspects, but humor embraces all of them. Buddha taught this as the nature of truth. . . . The quest for a single, universal definition of humor is reminiscent of the search for personality and intelligence, neither of which has definitions accepted by all.

Finally, in his attempt to answer the question "What's funny?" MacHovec (1988, p. 8) provides a summary of seven "basic elements of effective humor" (cf: his list of the uses of humor and "32 ways of how we are funny," p. 20): *playful mood* (the listener or observer must be in a playful, and therefore receptive, mood), *experiencing pleasure* (the process and its results must facilitate a feeling of pleasure), *transformational* (it changes or elevates the mood), *short-lived* (it has a brief, ephemeral "fairy-shadow" life), *fragile* (it has a delicate, gem-like fragility requiring significant skill to effectively deliver), *universality* (it is a common trait and, therefore, of potentially universal appeal, or appeals to a broad cross-section of people across cultures and languages), and *timeless* (it maintains its humor/funniness for all time).

In his dictionary of psychology, S. Sutherland (1989/1995) apparently equates humor with "humoral theory" when he simply and exclusively defines *humour* as "any fluid in the body (see aqueous humour and vitreous humour); more specifically: the body fluids—blood, black bile, yellow bile, or phlegm—associated by ancient typologists with respectively sanguine, melancholic, choleric, and phlegmatic temperaments."

In a recently published encyclopedia of psychology (Gall, 1996, p. 183), *humor* is defined as "the mental faculty of discovering, expressing, or appreciating the ludicrous or absurdly incongruous" (cf: Raley & Ballmann, 1957). In addition to this brief definition of humor, the entry here provides a short discussion on humor that includes the following: the Freudian approach to humor (a mechanism for "discharging pent up psychic energy"), an observation that since the 1970s, research on humor has shifted from a Freudian focus to an emphasis on its cognitive dimensions including studies on information-processing theory; the part that the concept of "incongruity" (i.e., the disparity between expectations and perceptions) plays in humor study; and the important role that humor plays in both the areas of social interaction (where humor may serve as a coping strategy, as well as to test the status of relationships) and human development (where humor is considered to be a form of "play").

In a style and succinctness that seems satisfying in terms of a good balance between modern and ancient approaches, as well as in terms of theoretical and functional aspects, Corsini (1999) defines *humor* in his dictionary as

the capacity to perceive or express the amusing aspects of situations. There is little agreement on the essence of what is funny and a number of theories abound. Plato and Thomas Hobbes held that situations that make the observer feel superior, such as an elegant person slipping and falling, lead to laughter. Max Eastman took the position that triumphing over adversity was humorous. Sigmund Freud assumed that fear turned around was humorous, such as making jokes about people who were dangerous. Many jokes depend on "punch lines" in which the story preceding ends with an unexpected twist, suggesting delight in being fooled. Humor that degrades some group, such as racial or ethnic jokes, may be based on feelings of superiority, such that a person feels he or she can disparage others with impunity. Humor may also come from disparaging the self. . . . Bodily fluids, especially the semifluid substances that occupy the spaces in the eyeball: aqueous humor, and vitreous humor.

Corsini (1999) also defines other concepts that are variations on the term *humor*, such as *gallows humor* (a macabre or comical type of behavior that is inappropriate at a time of death or disaster; often observed in cases of organic psychosis and delirium tremens), *humor doctrine of diseases*, *humoral theory*, and *humoral reflex* (a vital response caused by a hormone).

R. A. Martin (2000) authored an entry on humor and laughter in a recently published encyclopedia of psychology. In part, this entry defines *humor* as a rather broad range of phenomena associated with the perception, expression, or appreciation of amusing, comical, or absurdly incongruous ideas, situations, or events. Although humor does not always elicit laughter, this is the most common overt behavioral response to humor. Humor is a complex and multifaceted phenomenon, touching on all areas of psychology . . . Humor is also a universal human phenomenon . . . Recent studies indicate that adults laugh an average of about 18 times a day, with no overall differences in frequency between men and women. Smiling appears in human infants during the first month, and laughter occurs by four months of age.

According to Martin (2000), humor has *cognitive* (i.e., mental processes involved in the perception, creation, understanding, and appreciation of humorous incongruity), *emotional* (i.e., pleasurable feelings of amusement, exhilaration, and joy); *behavioral* (i.e., laughter, facial grimaces, teeth-baring, guttural vocalizations, postural/body changes and movements), *social* (i.e., communication/interpersonal contexts in which humorous stimuli occur), and *psychophysiological* (i.e., humor situations involve brain wave pattern changes, autonomic nervous system/respiration/hormone-production and activation) aspects. Moreover, the development of humor in children parallels their growth in other cognitive abilities (e.g., certain verbal jokes may not be appreciated by the child until he or she has entered and mastered the "higher" Piagetian cognitive levels involving the ability to make abstractions and symbolizations).

As a fundamental social phenomenon, humor and laughter are "contagious"—that is, it is difficult to remain composed and "sober" when others around you are laughing and joking; also, a greater proportion of laughter occurs in groups of two or more people as compared to situations involving "canned" laughter or jokes. Martin (2000) maintains that humor and laughter are related closely to "play" and, accepting this connection, infrahuman species may be said to have their own forms of humor/laughter/smiling (e.g., chimpanzees and other apes may laugh in a breathy, panting vocal fashion as they are tickled or as they play; they also have been observed making simple "jokes" by combining newly learned verbal symbols/signs in incongruous or novel ways). Martin (2000, p. 204) states that trait-like individual differences in the perception, expression, or enjoyment of humor are referred to as *sense of humor*. Furthermore, according to Martin, the term *sense of humor* may be used variously to refer to

individual differences in the types of jokes, cartoons, and other humorous stimuli that people find most amusing; the frequency with which the person smiles and laughs and seeks out humor; the ability to perceive or create humor; the tendency to tell jokes and amuse other people; the degree to which individuals understand jokes and other humorous stimuli; the tendency to use humor as a coping mechanism; the tendency not to take oneself too seriously and to laugh at one's own foibles and weaknesses; and so on.

In the remaining sections of this chapter, *humor* is compared and contrasted with the concept of *wit* and, also, various humor-related terms—such as laughter, comedy/ comic, satire/irony/parody, puns/riddles, jokes, slapstick, and cartoons/caricatures—are defined and discussed (cf: Gruner's, 1978, pp. 5–22, discussion and critique of various "categories of humor," such as exaggeration, incongruity, surprise, slapstick, whimsy, ridicule, and such, and his review of Esar's, 1952, seven categories of humor: the wisecrack, epigram, riddle, conundrum, gag, joke, and anecdote), as they delineate the primary domains of humor.

HUMOR VERSUS WIT

What constitutes Wit? Wherein is Wit different from Humor? . . . sufficient evidence may be cited in proof that as yet the Anatomy of Wit and Humor is an unwritten book.

—W. E. Burton, 1872

There are many things which a definition helps us to understand; but there are other things which we understand better than we can any possible definition of them—and among them are that cold, sparkling, mercurial thing which we call wit, and that genial, juicy, unconscious, impersonal thing we call humor.

—W. Mathews, 1888

When I told Bernard Shaw that I was writing this book, he advised me to go to a sanitarium. "There is no more dangerous literary symptom," he said, "than a temptation to write about wit and humor. It indicates the total loss of both."

—M. Eastman, 1921

The history of the word *wit* is a record of a degeneration in meaning.

—J. C. Gregory, 1924

One difficulty inherent in producing a completely logical distinction between wit and humor is the usual lack of *pureness* in most examples of either. Seldom is one dealing with pure humor or pure wit.

—C. R. Gruner, 1978

The term *wit* as a noun is defined in *Webster's* (1993) as

mind, memory; reasoning power: intelligence; mechanical skill: inventiveness (obsolete); sense; mental soundness: sanity; mental capability: pragmatic resourcefulness: ingenuity; astuteness of perception or judgment: acumen, wisdom; creative imagination: intellectual brilliance or subtlety; the ability to discover amusing analogies between apparently unrelated things and to express them cleverly; a talent for banter or persiflage: repartee, satire ("brevity is the soul of wit"); a man [sic] of superior intellectual attainments: thinker, brain; an imaginatively perceptive and articulate individual, especially skilled in banter or persiflage.

Webster's (1993) supplies the following synonyms for the term *wit*: humor, irony, sarcasm, satire, repartee. Furthermore, the entry on *wit* compares and contrasts these terms and states

Wit implies intellectual brilliance and quickness in perception combined with a gift for expressing ideas in an entertaining, often laughter provoking, pointed way, usually connoting the unexpected or apt turn of phrase or idea and often suggesting a certain brittle unfeelingness. *Humor*, in this comparison, can signify a disposition to see the ludicrous, comical, ridiculous, or absurd or to give it expression or can apply to the expression itself, often suggesting a generalness or a greater kindliness or sympathy with human failings than does *wit*. *Irony* applies chiefly to a way of speaking or writing in which the meaning intended is contrary to that expressed on the surface, but in a more literary or dramatic sense it implies a deeper perception of the discrepancies implicit in life and character or applies to the actual discrepancies applying frequently to a situation in which what results is the direct, often tragic, opposite of what was desired, intended, or worked for. *Sarcasm* applies chiefly to a type of humor intended to cut or wound, often employing ridicule or bitter irony; *satire* can apply to any criticism or censure relying on exposure, often by irony and often subtle, of the ridiculous or absurd qualities of something; *repartee* sometimes still applied to a witty or clever retort, applies chiefly to the power or the art of replying quickly and with wit, humor, or, infrequently, sarcasm.

Webster's Dictionary of Synonyms and Antonyms (1992, p. 439) provides further succinct comparisons and contrasts among the terms *wit, humor, irony, sarcasm, satire,* and *repartee* (each of which is "a mode of expression intended to arouse amused interest or evoke laughter"):

Wit suggests the power to evoke laughter by remarks showing verbal felicity or ingenuity and swift perception especially of the incongruous. *Humor* implies an ability to perceive the ludicrous, the comical, and the absurd in human life and to express these usually with keen insight and sympathetic understanding and without bitterness. *Irony* applies to a manner and expression in which the intended meaning is the opposite of the expressed meaning. *Sarcasm* applies to savagely humorous expression frequently in the form of irony that is intended to cut or wound. *Satire* applies to writing that exposes or ridicules conduct, doctrine, or institutions either by direct criticism or more often through irony, parody, or caricature. *Repartee* implies the power or art of answering quickly, pointedly, or wittily or to an interchange of such responses.

Webster's Dictionary of Word Origins (1995) provides a substantial entry on the origins of the term *wit*. Among the ideas presented here are that *wit* is one of our native stock of words and has cognates in such sister languages as Old High

German (*wizzi*—knowledge, understanding, wit), Old Norse (*vit*), and Gothic (*witi*—knowledge). The term *wit* is related via Old English (*witan*—to know) to familiar words such as *wise, wisdom*, and *witness*; it is even cognate with the Greek root (*idein*, meaning "to see") of *idea*. It is acknowledged in the entry that there is little certainty as to which meaning of *wit* is the oldest (one possibility is "the mind"—such as the "mind/wit" of a primitive individual; another possibility is "the faculty of thinking and reasoning, intelligence, or power of reasoning"—such as the phrase "at one's wit's end"). The plural form (*"wits"*) of the term *wit* has early origins, also. For example, among the late medieval theories that relate vaguely to medicine, physiology, and psychology was one that attributed to humans five "inward wits" (known via the English poet Stephan Hawes in 1509 as "common wit/common sense," "imagination," "fantasy," "estimation," and "memory") and five "outward wits" (better known today as the "five senses"). According to the entry, it is not stretching *wit* very far from "mind" and "intelligence" to those attributes characteristic of an active mind or intelligence: intellectual ability, inventive power, talent, cleverness, and ingenuity. Brief examples from the works of writers such as Shakespeare, Shadwell, Dryden, Ben Jonson, Addison, Samuel Johnson, and Alexander Pope are used to explore the various meanings and nuances of the term *wit*. The entry concludes with the observation that the "loftier *wit*" that the 18th-century critics and poets tried to protect from Shakespeare's usage (i.e., as a word-play *wit*) has disappeared, and what earlier critics would have called *false wit* is, for most people today, the only kind of wit.

In his *Cyclopaedia of Wit and Humor*, Burton (1872, p. vii) indicates that "it requires Wit to describe what Wit is"; and states that writers such as Aristotle, Barrow, Dryden, LaBruyere, Bouhours, Montaigne, Locke, Voltaire, Addison, Cowley, Pope, Davison, Leigh Hunt, Hazlitt, Charles Lamb, and Sydney Smith have "enlivened the pensive public with their several definitions, but an acceptable and satisfactory standard of authority has not yet been given." Following his preface (which includes definitions, criticisms, and examples of *wit* from these writers), Burton provides a number of choice and characteristic selections from the writings of the most eminent humorists of America, Ireland, Scotland, and England.

In his book, *Wit and Humor*, Mathews (1888, p. 2) suggests:

The truth is, that, as a jest will not bear explanation, so neither will wit nor humor bear to be anatomized . . . Who can make mathematics out of merriment? Who can postulate a pun? Who can square the circle of a joke? The calculus of cachinnation would be a pleasant kind of cyphering! . . . All the attempts made to explain—and they have been many, and some of them by the acutest thinkers—show that it defies analysis, and cannot be clipped, shaped, or fashioned so as to fit any precise definition or description.

Mathews (1888) also makes the observations that the manner in which a witticism is uttered has much to do with its pungency (the "zest," "relish," look, manner, and voice which the storyteller uses), that the electrical effect of wit or humor is so closely connected with the time, place, and circumstances of its utterance that separated from them it loses much of its significance and force, and that we laugh one day at what would not excite a smile on another day. Although Mathews states that all the attempted definitions of wit have been unsatisfactory, he nevertheless considers some of the principal ones. Originally, the term *wit*—from the Anglo-Saxon *witan* ("to know")—referred to the intellect generally, or to the faculty that perceives, understands, or knows; a "witte" meant a "wise man," and the Saxon parliament was called the "Witenagemot."

Mathews (1888, p. 9) disagrees with Addison's notion that "true wit consists in the resemblance and congruity of ideas; false wit in the resemblance and congruity of words"; on the contrary, asserts Mathews, so far is this from being true that the very essence of true wit consists in bringing dissimilar ideas into juxtaposition, or in suggesting some idea the very opposite of that which the words used were intended to convey when taken literally. According to Mathews, unless the contrast is startling, and the idea evoked unexpected, one should not call it wit. Mathews develops his chapter on "Theories of Wit and Humor" around reviews of the major writers and philosophers concerning their views on wit and humor (including, in one case, Benjamin Franklin); however, the chapter title—using the word "theories"—is, perhaps, a bit misleading by today's standards. [Note: Also see Goodchilds' (1972) chapter titled "On Being Witty: Causes, Correlates, and Consequences" wherein she seems *not* to define the term *wit/witty* in any explicit or satisfactory manner.] Rather than providing systematized sets or connections of statements ("theory"), Mathews gives examples of wit from writers' works and analyzes/critiques them, often from the a priori defining condition that the essence of humor/wit is incongruity. Concerning the issue of "humor *versus* wit," Mathews (1888, pp. 35–36) states that

one great distinction between wit and humor is that wit is artificial and susceptible of culture, while humor is natural. The humorous man is born such; wit may be acquired. Wit is always conscious and personal; humor is generally unconscious and impersonal. The one is allied to the intellect; the other, to the imagination and the affectations. The essence of wit is cleverness, sharpness, hawk-eyed mental cunning; the essence of humor is sensibility . . . As the word originally signified, humor is "moisture"—that is, the very juice of the mind, oozing from the brain, and fertilizing wherever it falls. Wit implies thought; humor, feeling. Wit is analytical, antagonistic, and destructive; it has often the sting as well as the honey of the bee . . . Humor, on the contrary, is genial, kindly, and sympathetic. The former often isolates itself, and watches like a spy in the corner; the latter mingles and fraternizes with men, and keeps them in good spirits. Wit laughs *at* men; humor laughs *with* them.

In addition to his chapter on the theories of wit and humor, Mathews (1888) supplies material in other chapters on the topics of "the uses of wit and humor," "the abuses of wit and humor," "the logic of wit," "the antiquity of wit," "the melancholy of wits," "men who lack the sense of humor," and has separate chapters on the topics of epigrams, parody, puns, repartee, and clerical wit.

In their zealous article on "tickling and laughing," Hall and Allin (1897, p. 27) declare that *wit* "involves elements in the analysis of which there has been the greatest difference of opinion." The chief traits that have been ascribed to *wit* are unexpectedness, suddenness, and descending incongruity. Within the context of their greater discussion on tickling and laughing, Hall and Allin (1897, p. 27) state that

the quick perception of unusual relations, the opening of new brain paths, the unexpected, but not the unpleasant—these and other conceptions and definitions of it suggest some break of continuity in thought. Repartee is wit for two . . . Wit is thus mainly an affair of the intellect, and primarily harmless and without malice. The pun also belongs here . . . Concerning wit also we have a new theory to propose. It has been shown elsewhere that shock tends directly to neuro-psychic disintegration . . . The shock diseases and lesions break up coherence in brains of great plasticity and convulsibility. Now, wit is of the nature of shock, reduced to almost its faintest terms, and is related to it somewhat, as the tickle sensations of minimal contact are related to the more definite forms of touch, or to dermal blows and lesions. Two factors are necessary—suddenness and a light touch.

In attempting to develop an understanding of the two terms *wit* and *humor*, Rapp (1951, p. 150) answers the question "What is the difference between wit and humor?" by stating that "today it is commonly agreed that the question has not been answered." [Notes: For an attempt to answer this question in the field of literature, see R. B. Martin (1974, pp. 25–46); for a bibliography of empirical studies of wit and humor, covering the period 1897–1966, see Treadwell, 1967; also see Chandler & Barnhart, 1938; Holt, 1916; Mahony, 1956; Mikes, 1971; Speroni, 1964.] Moreover, Rapp maintains that the term *humor* is used about half the time to stand for *both* wit and humor, and often is used simply to stand for wit. This type of overlap and ambiguity applies equally well to the terms "sense of humor" and "sense of wit," and in contemporary usage, the term "sense of humor" means both a sense of wit and a sense of humor even though the two concepts cover two substantially different things (Rapp, 1951, p. 150; cf: K. M. Wilson, 1927).

In another place, Rapp (1949) also attacks the problem as one involving the lack of suitable, applicable, and mutually acceptable definitions of the terms *wit* and *humor* (cf: Mercier, 1960); in this case—an article on a phylogenetic theory of wit and humor—Rapp makes two assumptions: all forms of wit and humor which we know derive ultimately from a single prototype; and all families/species which developed out of this prototype contain evidence tending to reveal the transition process (cf: Rapp, 1948). Rapp's "single prototype" is identified subsequently as something he calls "thrashing laughter" (i.e., the laughter of triumph in a primitive physical duel). Gruner (1978, p. 94) points out that *wit* is associated historically with "intellect," while *humor* is linked more with the "emotional activity of feeling" (cf: Eastman's chapter, 1937, pp. 69–78, "The Definition of Wit"). However, according to Gruner, this distinction tends to break down when one considers the behavior of *laughing* to be primarily emotional rather than intellectual (e.g., if a "witty" remark elicits the *emotional* response of laughter, how can it be "purely" intellectual?).

Further, Gruner (1978, pp. 95–98) quotes extensively from Mercier (1960) regarding the differences between wit and humor (e.g., humor connotes kindliness, geniality, and sympathetic amusement, whereas wit is associated with quick, sharp, spontaneous, often sarcastic remarks; wit is intellectual and sarcastic; humor is emotional and kindly; wit is always absurd and true, humor is absurd and untrue; wit is more purely verbal than humor; "unconscious humor" may differ from "unconscious wit"; cf: Freud, 1905/1916/1960; 1959. [Note: Freud also distinguishes between *humor*—the ability to repudiate one's suffering, and *wit*—the release of repressed drives or possible aimless play; cf: O'Connell (1984/1994, p. 188).] However, Gruner disagrees with some of Mercier's distinctions (e.g., Mercier's "untruth" regarding humor is probably "simple exaggeration," and a great deal of exaggeration can appear in a *witticism* without requiring that such witticism be considered "humor" instead of wit).

Moreover, Gruner suggests that *wit* has a stronger grounding in reality than does *humor*, but it is a matter more of degree than of kind. Gruner's (1978, pp. 100–102) review of Rapp's (1951) work indicates five areas or points when differentiating *wit* from *humor*: humorous laughter *must* be accompanied by affection/love/kindness, while wit may be openly hostile/aggressive; wit is intellectual and a "duel of wits," while humor is not; in humor it is nearly always clear who it is you are laughing at/with, but in wit it is not usually clear; wit is artificial and deliberate, whereas humor is more "natural" and spontaneous; the witty person tends to be vain, narcissistic, extrovertish, intellectual, verbal, sadistic, and aggressive, whereas the humorous person tends to be affectionate, tolerant of sin/weakness, sympathetic with sufferers, objective in attitude, patient, masochistic, and mature.

Following his discussion using an extended analogy that views the difference between the terms *rhetoric* and *poetic* (cf: Gruner, 1965) to be equivalent functionally to that between *wit* and *humor*, Gruner (1978) summarizes what he considers to be the major, but relative, differences between *wit* and *humor* (all within the final assessment or conclusion, again, that "wit and humor differ essentially only in degree and not in kind"; cf: Gruner's Figure 5–1, p. 114): humor is based on broad and timeless themes, wit is much more specific and rooted to a particular moment and location; wit is relatively more practical and persuasive in purpose than is humor; wit deals more often with real events while humor more usually deals with fantasy; wit appeals more to the intellect while humor has a more emotional element; wit is addressed often to a more specific audience on a more specific occasion than is humor; and wit appeals more to the events of the here and now, while humor is based broadly on universal human themes (cf: O'Connell's , 1984/1994, distinction between *measures* of wit and those of humor, and his findings of personality differences between the aggressive/competitive wit and the nonjudgmental/ optimistic humorist).

The word *wit* is defined in a small number of dictionaries of psychological terms. [Notes: *Wit* is *not* defined in the dictionaries by Bruno (1986), English (1928), Harriman (1959/1966); Reber (1985/1995); Statt (1981/1998); Stratton & Hayes (1993); and S. Sutherland (1989/1995); English & English (1958/1976) do not define *wit* but do define *wit work*, a psychoanalytic term, as "the psychological processes, mostly unconscious, that produce wit; the processes are similar to those of *dream work*"; and Wolman (1973/1989) also does not define *wit*, but defines *wit-work* exactly—verbatim—as do English & English (1958/1976).] Baldwin (1901–1905) briefly defines *wit* (from the Anglo-Saxon *witt* meaning "knowledge"; and translated into German as *Witz*, French as *esprit*, and Italian as *spirito*) as

the comic so far as it turns upon more formal or intellectual relationships and does not excite real interests and emotions. The wit quality, like that of beauty, includes disinterestedness. Wit, therefore, is more purely aesthetic, humour less. The intellectual quality is seen in the use of the term for intelligence and mental alertness.

Warren (1934) defines *wit* as

an unexpected and ingenious association of ideas, presented usually in spoken language, which causes surprise and pleasant excitement in the hearer unless he is the one against whom it is directed; ready appreciation of any novel complex situation; synonym is *witticism*; is distinguished from *humor*, a more subjective type.

Twenty years later, Drever (1952/1973) states that *wit* is

an unexpected and ingenious turn of thought, or connexion in thought, causing surprise and laughter; Freud distinguishes two kinds, harmless and aggressive, the latter being of the nature of attack directed against another.

In a section of his book called "The Lexicon of Humor," MacHovec (1988, pp. 5–6) provides some entymological information on the term *wit* (cf: Koestler, 1964). The contemporary English word *wit* is derived from the word *witan* which is traceable—via the word *videre*—to the Sanskrit word *veda* meaning "knowledge." [Note: *Webster's*, 1989, defines *witan* as "members of the king's advisory council in Anglo-Saxon England."] The German word for wit is *Witz* (having connotations both as "acumen" and "joke") and has its root in the German word *wissen* meaning "to know." The German word *wissenschaft* (meaning "science") is related to the words *furwitz* and *aberwitz* (meaning "presumption, cheek, or jest"). The French word *spirituel* means "witty" or "spiritually profound," *hue d'esprit* means "a witty remark or a playful and mischievous discovery," and *a-muser* means "to muse" and is the basis for our word "amuse."

MacHovec notes that the search for word origins illustrates how humor cuts across the disciplines of literature, philosophy, history, and psychology; he also provides a sampling of humor-related words (admitting that it is not an exhaustive listing of relational terms): jest, joke/joking around, quip, parody, pun, mockery, ridicule, satire, sardonic, wise crack, wit, witticism, fool, fool around/fooling, tomfoolery, horseplay, sky larking, clown/clowning around, comic/comedic, caricature, cartoon, and "funnin."

MacHovec's discussion of the derivations of the other humor-related words includes: "fun/funny" which comes from the Gaelic *fonn* and the Middle European *fonnen* (meaning to dupe, hoax, or fool); "humor" from the "humoral theory" of the Greek physician Hippocrates—which occasioned the culture-crossing of the term "humor" (bodily fluid) from Greek to Latin. The connotation of "lighthearted joviality"—in addition to "bodily fluid"—to the term "humor" only came into usage in the late 1600s, following William Shakespeare's life (1564–1616); "comedy" derives from the Greek *komoidia* and the Latin *comoedia*, and is a combination of the root word *komos* ("to revel") and *aeidein* ("to sing as in an ode"); "joke" is from the Latin *jocus* ("to say or tell"), and the word "kidding" (having become popular in the early 1800s) is from the Middle European *kide* or the Old Norwegian *kith* ("young goat"—with the probable association that young goats are "easily led").

In his discussion of "neoclassical theories of humor (pleasure-pain and instinct-physiological)," MacHovec (1988, p. 44) observes that various wit-related terms originated with, or were coined by, Sigmund Freud (1856–1939): *wit-work* (the process or mechanics of wit formation), *understanding-work* (wit conception and meaning), *word-wit* (humorous use of words), *thought-wit* (humor from subjects made funny, or funny situations—including the "techniques" of displacement, faulty thinking, absurdity, indirect expression, and representation through the opposite), *harmless-wit* (just for fun), and *tendency-wit* (wit with a hidden agenda or ulterior motive). Freud essentially defined *wit* as "playful judgment" (cf: Brill, 1938), and classified "wit" as a part of "humor" where humor served in a more global capacity (cf: Greig's, 1923/1969, Chapter 10, treatment of Freud's approach to *wit*). Moreover, according to MacHovec, wit may be analyzed by its effect, especially in the differentiation between *harmless-wit* and *tendency-wit*, and wherever wit is not a means to its end (i.e., "harmless"), it is either *hostile wit* (serving as an aggression or satire for defense) or *obscene wit* (serving as a sexual exhibition).

In addition to defining and analyzing wit, Freud considered "humor" to be one of the loftiest of the psychic defense functions that may serve as a means to gain pleasure and to relieve painful affects, and saw humor as a potential weapon against the obstacles to pleasure when it was fused with wit or some other form of the comic. MacHovec (1988, pp. 46–50) cites and discusses 14 varieties/forms of humor (with examples) that Freud (1905/1916/1960, 1938) employed in his treatise on "wit and its relation to the unconscious": puns, displacements, nonsense, false logic, automatic errors of thought, unification, contrast, outdoing-wit, indirect allusion, omission, comparison, peculiar attributes, reproduction of old liberties, and smutty (dirty) jokes.

The 15th edition of *The New Encyclopaedia Britannica* (1997), Vol. 20, *Macropaedia*, has a very substantial entry entitled "Humor and Wit" (pp. 682–688) written by Arthur Koestler. This entry covers the topics of the logic of laughter, laughter and emotion, verbal humour, situational humour, styles and techniques in humour, relations of humour to art and science, the humanization of humour, and humour in the contemporary world; it deals with the changing concepts and practice of humour from the time of Aristotle to the influence of the mass media in the contemporary world; the article also includes a brief bibliography on humor and wit. [Note: The overall impression one gains from this entry is that *humour* and *wit* are equated largely with the term *laughter*, and the concept of *jokes*; indeed, the term *humour* is defined here simply as "a type of stimulation that tends to elicit the laughter reflex" (p. 682).]

Among the ideas presented by Koestler (1997) are the following: laughter is a reflex but unique in that it is an activity that is unrelated to the struggle for survival, and has no apparent biological purpose or utilitarian value (it may be called a "luxury reflex"; its only function seems to be to provide tension-relief); humour is the only form of communication in which a stimulus on a high level of complexity (for instance, telling a "joke") produces a stereotyped, predictable response on the physiological reflex level (i.e., the involuntary contraction of 15 facial muscles resulting in a facial expression ranging from a faint smile to explosive laughter); the key or logic of humour involves a sudden clash between two mutually exclusive codes of rules, or associative contexts, that produces a comic effect by compelling the listener to perceive a situation in two self-consistent but incompatible frames of reference at the same time; and, as long as a potentially humorous condition lasts, the event is not only associated with a single frame of reference but "disociated" with the two. [Note: The term *disociation* was coined originally by Koestler to make a distinction between the routines of disciplined thinking within a single universe of discourse—on a single plane—and the creative types of mental activity that always operate on more than one plane; cf: Koestler (1964).]

Jensen (1998) authored the brief critical/literary type of entry on *wit* that appears in the *Academic American Encyclopedia*. According to Jensen, *wit* is a complex term that during the 17th century became a critical term, equivalent to the current word *genius*, and was used to translate the Latin *ingenium* and the French *esprit* and *genie*. Also, at this time, *wit* was associated more with imagination (poetry) than with judgment (reason and facts), although judgment was thought to keep wit under control.

The qualities associated with the term *wit* were held in lower regard by the end of the 17th century, largely as a result of the popularity of the associative psychology of Thomas Hobbes (1651/1904) and John Locke (1690/1965). To Hobbes and Locke, judgment (i.e., the scientific/historical faculty) discerned differences between things or facts that are similar. Therefore, *wit* (the poetic faculty)—using memory or fancy—discovered similarities between things or ideas that are different, thus functioning as the maker of metaphors. According to Hobbes and Locke, all knowledge derives from the senses, and because memories of such perceptions fade over time, *wit* was considered "decaying sense" and, therefore, less important than judgment.

Jensen notes that Joseph Addison's critical discussions of *true*, *false*, and *mixed wit*, and Samuel Johnson's definition of *wit*, are based on Locke's ideas. The term *wit*, by the early 19th century, was not always an important psychological or elevated critical term, and more often it implied mere cleverness (particularly verbal), a meaning that had always existed parallel to the critical meanings. Jensen also observes that in modern critical writing the kind of wit that is meant is usually qualified, such as *metaphysical wit*, *trenchant wit*, and *satirical wit*. The adjective qualifiers such as *romantic* or *Victorian* would not be used to characterize *wit*, according to Jensen, because neither contains the idea of the conscious manipulation of words and ideas in a clever way, with a satirical intent, or with a purpose of causing delight. The use of the term *wit* in a nonliterary or noncritical manner is similar: *wit* might be described as "sharp," "pointed," or "barbed," but never as "broad"; however, inasmuch as *humor* is of a different origin, one may occasionally encounter the phrase "broad humor."

HUMOR AND LAUGHTER

> The reason man laughs, and animals do not, is because the pericardium is firmly attached to the diaphragm in man, and not in animals.
> —L. Joubert, 1560/1579/1980

> By laughter, society avenges itself for the liberties taken with it. It would fail in its object if it bore the stamp of sympathy or kindness.
> —H. Bergson, 1911

Despite the clever and penetrating theories advanced the essential secret of laughter remains shrouded in mystery.

—S. H. Bliss, 1915

Laughter, according to my view, may be a response to any pleasant stimulus, and to any unpleasant one that can be taken playfully. Since there is no unpleasant thing which can not in some circumstances, or by somebody, be taken playfully, all experiences whatever, except those to which we are indifferent, may become the occasions of laughter.

—M. Eastman, 1937

A distinction can (and indeed should) be drawn between theories of humour and theories of laughter, and clearly theories of laughter need to take into account the numerous types of non-humorous as well as humorous situations which can cause laughter.

—A. J. Chapman and H. C. Foot, 1976

Webster's (1993) defines *laugh* as a verb (from Middle English *laughen*, and Old English *hliehhan, hlehhan, hlaehan*; akin to Old High German *lachen*—to laugh; Old Norse *hlaeja*, Gothic *hlahjan*—to laugh; Old English *hlowan*—to moo, more at "low") as

to give audible expression to an emotion (as mirth, joy, derision, embarrassment, or fright) by the expulsion of air from the lungs resulting in sounds ranging from an explosive guffaw to a muffled titter and usually accompanied by movements of the mouth or facial muscles and a lighting up of the eyes; to find amusement or pleasure in something: enjoy oneself; to become amused or derisive; to produce the sound or appearance of laughter; to be of a kind that inspires joy; to bring to a specified state by laughing; to utter laughingly; to "laugh in one's sleeve," "laugh up one's sleeve," "laugh in one's beard" is to become inwardly elated: congratulate oneself secretly, as on having successfully played a trick on someone; to "laugh on the wrong side of one's mouth" is to cry; to "laugh out of court" is to eliminate from serious consideration by ridicule.

Webster's (1993) defines *laugh* as a noun as

an act or instance of laughing; a disposition to laughter (archaic): hilarity; something that resembles a laugh; a cause for derision or merriment: joke, advantage; an expression of scorn or mockery: jeer; *laughs* (plural) is a means of entertainment: diversion, sport; *laughable* (adjective) is giving rise to mirth or derision: comical, absurd; synonyms for *laughable* are risible, funny, droll, comical, comic, farcical, ridiculous, and ludicrous.

In *Webster's* (1993), the word *laughter*, as British dialect, is defined as "a clutch of eggs"; more commonly, the noun *laughter* is defined as "a sound of, or as if of, laughing; an inclination to laugh: exuberance, amusement; a cause of merriment (archaic)."

Webster's (1994) simply defines *laughter* as "the action of laughing or the sound resulting; an indication of amusement; a matter for or cause of laughter (archaic)." According to *Webster's* (1994), while *laugh* is the general word for the sounds of exhalation made in expressing mirth, amusement, etc., *chuckle* is a soft laugh in low tones, *giggle* and *titter* are half-suppressed laughs (often consisting of a series of rapid, high-pitched sounds; a *titter* may be used to indicate affected politeness), *snicker* is a sly, half-suppressed laugh (often used as in another's discomfiture or a bawdy story), and *guffaw* is a loud, coarse laugh.

The *New Encyclopaedia Britannica* (1997), Vol. 16, *Macropaedia*, contains an entry on *laughter* in a section entitled "Communication" (pp. 623–628) written by G. N. Gordon who observes that although most vocal sounds (other than words) are usually considered "prelinguistic language," the phenomenon of laughter as a form of communication is in a category by itself (with its closest kin being its apparent opposite: crying). A common belief is that laughter either results from, or is related to, the nonconscious reduction of tensions or inhibitions (cf: Freud, 1905/1916/1960, 1959). Laughter develops as a form of self-generated pleasure in the infant and is rewarded both physically and psychologically by feelings of gratification, and it provides an effective, pragmatic, and contagious means of vocal/social communication (cf: Allin, 1903; Kahn, 1975; McComas, 1923; Mukherji, 1935; Myers, 1935). According to Gordon, laughter deals with a wide range of cultural phenomena, often more effectively than speech, in much the same way that crying (initially an instinctive reaction to discomfort) communicates a clear and unambiguous emotional state to others [cf: Young's (1937) study on laughing and weeping where he concludes for college students that the estimated frequency of laughing is more than 400 times that of weeping/crying; also, see Brackett (1933, 1934); Cohn (1951); Davison & Kelman (1939); Ding & Jersild (1932); Edwards (1926); Foss (1961); Justin (1932); Kwang (1921); Lund (1930); Peto (1946); Plessner (1940); Provine (1996, 2000); Sachs (1973); Sroufe & Wunsch (1972); A. Stern (1976); Thomson (1966); Washburn (1929); S. Wilson (1929); Wolff (1963); Zijderveld (1983)].

The theories for laughter (cf: Bliss, 1915; Diserens, 1926; Gregory, 1923; Hayworth, 1928; Piddington, 1933/1963) occurring in complex social situations vary among writers and philosophers [e.g., George Meredith (1897) maintains that laughter serves as an enjoyable social corrective; Henri Bergson (1911) posits that laughter is a form of rebellion against the mechanization of human behavior and nature; Sigmund Freud (1905/1916/1960) advanced the idea that laughter is repressed sexual feeling; Arthur Koestler (1964) considers laughter to be a means of individual enlightenment, revelation, and ultimate freedom concerning unclear information or confusion emanating from the environment].

My survey of dictionaries of psychological terms indicates that *most* of the books in this genre do *not* have an entry for the term *laughter*; exceptions here are the works by Warren (1934) and Drever (1952/1973). Warren (1934) defines *laughter* as

an emotional or social response consisting in violent convulsive movements of the diaphragm and noisy expulsion of air from the lungs (generally stimulated by situations which arouse an idea of incongruity, feeling of superiority, sudden relief of tension or expectation, etc., and a pleasant feeling tone. Also evoked as a social expression of approval, agreement, happiness, or as a means of deception. Usually accompanied by a facial response called *smiling*). (The French term is *rire*, and the German is *lachen*.)

Warren (1934) also defines the laughter-related terms *smile* (cf: Sacks & Wolf, 1955) and *tickle*. [Note: For a brief bibliography of studies on laughter and smiling, see Nilsen (1993, pp. 3–5).] The word *smile* [reflecting the influence of Darwin's (1872/1965), Dearborn's (1900), Spencer's (1860/1891), and Walsh's (1928) expressive and physiological definitions of laughter] is defined by Warren (1934) as

a facial expression chiefly characterized by drawing the corners of the mouth upward and backward, by elevation of the cheeks with or without parting of the lips, and by reduction of the palpebral space with wrinkling of the skin under the eyes; expressive of a variety of sensations, feelings, and emotions. Distinguished from *laughter* which involves greater muscular activity and phonation. (The French term is *sourire*, and the German is *lacheln*.)

The word *tickle* (cf: Claxton, 1975; Hall & Allin, 1897; Hecker, 1873; Leuba, 1941; Tuke, 1892; Washburn, 1929; Willmann, 1940) is defined by Warren (1934) as

a sensory experience involving a complication of contact sensations and a strong feeling tone; an emotional experience involving strong feeling tone and marked by convulsive movements of escape and laughter. Two sorts of tickle are distinguished: *light tickle* (aroused by light pressure in certain regions, e.g., lips), and *deep tickle* (aroused by heavier pressure in other regions, e.g., ribs). (The French term is *chatouillement*, and the German is *kitzel*.)

The relationship between *tickling* and *laughter* is outlined by Crile (1916, p. 330) as follows [cf: Ewald Hecker (1873) who evolved a *theory* of laughter on the basis of tickling; in this case, laughter has the compensatory function of increasing the blood pressure in the brain]:

The laughter excited by adequate stimulation of ticklish areas of the body is a recapitulation of ancestral struggles against the physical attack of biting and clawing foes on these parts. In other words, the laughter excited by tickling is a substitute for the motor act of defense against injury.

Drever (1952/1973) defines *laughter* simply as "an emotional response, expressive normally of joy, in the child and the unsophisticated adult [sic]; the joy in question may vary between wide limits."

Chapman and Sheehy (1987, p. 320) critique Drever's (1952/1973) concept of laughter as defined here. They state that Drever's reference to the "unsophisticated adult" might startle many of us, and some would find it quaint, even amusing, inasmuch as it reflects a long period of history in which laughing was considered to be a low-class, base, or degenerate behavior and was not so universally prized as it is today. For example, Chapman and Sheehy note that in the 18th century Lord Chesterfield (1694–1773)—the English statesman and writer on manners—maintained that there is nothing so ill-bred and illiberal as audible laughter (see Chesterfield, 1901; also, see Vasey, 1877, who attempted to show that laughter was not only ethically and aesthetically objectionable, but medically harmful as well!).

While the term *humor/sense of humor*, simply and strictly speaking, is a "disposition" (or, as the psychologist might say, it is an "intervening variable/hypothetical construct"—much like the term *intelligence*—that is not directly observed, only inferred), and the term *laughter* refers to an observable response or behavior, many writers (especially in works in the early 1900s) in the psychological literature seem to use the two terms interchangeably and to equate the two terms (e.g., Bergler, 1956; Boston, 1974; Diserens, 1926; Diserens & Bonifield, 1930; Eastman, 1921, 1937; Gregory, 1924; Greig, 1923/1969; Kimmins, 1928; Ludovici, 1932; Menon, 1931; Piddington, 1933/1963; Sidis, 1913; Sully, 1902; cf: Flugel, 1954, p. 709; Keith-Spiegel, 1972, p. 16); however, see Dewey (1894–1895) and Potter (1954) who argue that *laughter* may be irrelevant to the study of *humor*, and vice versa, because each may be experienced independently of the other.

Various writers have attempted to clarify the distinctions between *humor* and *laughter*; for example, Chapman and Foot (1976) note that one problem that confuses definitions of humor is whether it is to be considered as a stimulus, a response, or a disposition. Furthermore, say Chapman and Foot (1976, p. 3), "while no one would dispute that laughter is generally a response, it is just as much a response to non-humorous stimuli as it is to humour stimuli; in fact, though not a humour stimulus itself, laughter can act as a stimulus in inducing or augmenting laughter in other persons."

Chapman and Foot observe that a number of articles have offered brief taxonomies of humour and laughter (e.g., Flugel, 1954; Ghosh, 1939; Hall & Allin, 1897; Monro, 1951/1963), but, as yet, no classification has been able to account for the great complexity and diversity of situations that may provoke laughter. [Note: For an ethological approach to laughter and humor, see Weisfeld, 1993.] Apparently, each category of humor or laughter-producing situation has its own antecedents (cf: Berlyne, 1969; Giles & Oxford, 1970). Chapman and Foot (1976, p. 4) state that

no all embracing theory of humour and/or laughter has yet gained widespread acceptance and possibly no general theory will ever be successfully applied to the human race as a whole when its members exhibit such vast individual differences with respect to their humour responsiveness. The paradox associated with humour is almost certainly a function of its being incorrectly viewed as a unitary process.

In the next portion of this section on *laughter*, I sample some of the works (chronologically arranged)—up to the middle 1980s—in the literature (mostly psychological) of various approaches taken to define, describe, and understand the concept of *laughter*.

The 16th-century French physician Laurent Joubert is reputed to have written his best work, the *Traite du Ris (Treatise on Laughter)* in Latin in 1560, even though it was nearly 20 years before the work was published in French in 1579. Joubert (1560/1579/1980) describes the act of *laughter* in words that emphasize features of the human face:

certainly there is nothing that gives more pleasure and recreation than a laughing face, with its wide, shining, clear, and serene forehead, eyes shining, resplendent from any vantage point, and casting fire as do diamonds; cheeks vermilion and incarnate, mouth flush with the face, lips handsomely drawn back.

Concerning his method of attack on the "mystery of laughter," Joubert states that his approach will be as sure as it is simple—a straight path from the effects to the cause, with God's help. In his rather quaint and stylish approach, Joubert employs a "material" strategy (versus a "formal" strategy), and concentrates mainly on the *physiological* mechanisms of laughter (versus the *psychology* of laughter) (cf: Svebak, 1975).

Three centuries following Joubert, Charles Darwin (1872/1965) describes the sound of laughter in physical and expressive terms as something that is produced by a deep inspiration followed by short, interrupted, spasmodic contractions of the chest, and especially the diaphragm in which the mouth is open more or less widely with the corners drawn backwards as well as a little upwards, and the upper lip is raised somewhat. Darwin asserted that laughter is primarily an expression of mere joy or happiness, and cited children's play—with its incessant laughter—as an example of "meaningless" laughter. [Note: See my Chapter 3, section titled "Theories Based in Physiology/Biology" for additional information on Darwin's theory of humor.] Idiots and imbecile persons, according to Darwin, likewise provide good evidence that laughter or smiling primarily expresses mere happiness or joy (Darwin, 1872/1965, Chapter 8). Regarding the issue of whether animals possess laughter and humor, Darwin (1871) contends that dogs show what might be called a "sense of humor" as distinct from mere play. [Note: See other advocates of "humor in infrahuman species": Eastman (1921, 1937); Kohler (1917, 1927); R. A. Martin (2000); Sully (1902); Yerkes & Learned (1925); cf: Douglas (1975).]

Another one of the more modern attempts (following Joubert's 16th–century treatise) to explain laughter on the mere basis of cerebral mechanisms and physiology was made by Herbert Spencer (1860/1891) who suggests that laughter may be aroused by various feelings—not all of which may be pleasant (for example, sardonic or hysterical laughter)—where the surplus nervous energy involved in such feelings may "overflow" in laughter (cf: Spencer, 1916). Such an overflow is not directed by any particular motive, and subsequently follows the most-practiced or most-used channels (i.e., usually those leading to one's speech apparatus where the mouth first becomes active because it has small and easily movable muscles, and followed by activity of the respiratory tract and structures). If this channel is inadequate for the nervous energy to escape, the energy overflows into other motor nerves which, as a consequence, leads to convulsion of the person's entire body. [Notes: For a critique of such an "energy-release" aspect of laughter, see Brody (1950); Hayworth (1928); McDougall (1903, 1922a,b); and Stanley (1898); for a discussion of the *hydraulic theory* (i.e., pressure built up and then released), see Roeckelein (1998, p. 246); and for a summary of McDougall's (1923, 1932) *hormic/ instinct theory*, regarding laughter, see Roeckelein (1998, pp. 319–320).] Such an explanation as Spencer's may apply to laughter that is created by simple feelings; on the other hand, laughter that is aroused by a "ludicrous" (i.e., stimuli that are ridiculous, comic, satirical, absurd, or exaggerated) situation, and involves an element of "incongruity," may be explained in slightly different terms (see Chapter 3, "Theories Based in Physiology/Biology," for additional information on Spencer's theory of humor).

According to Spencer (1860/1891), in general, the ludicrous situation presents something that we initially expect to be great, but discover subsequently that it is actually something small.

Following Spencer, the German psychologist Theodor Lipps—who introduced the notion of "empathy" in psychology, and advanced the movement called "act psychology" (see Peyser, 1994; Roeckelein, 1998, p. 308)—formulated a *psychology* of laughter to correspond with Spencer's *physiology* of laughter (Lipps, 1898). Where Spencer explained why a person laughs in the presence of something ludicrous, Lipps attempted—using slightly different terms—to explain why a person feels happy. Lipps repeated Spencer's definition of the ludicrous/comic in *itself* as a "descending incongruity"—that is, an incongruity in perceiving wherein one's attention passes from great things/expectations to small things. As Greig (1923/1969, p. 268) observes, in Lipps' view, "the comic is something little masquerading as something big . . . It is the little behaving as the big, puffing itself out and playing the role of the big, and then on the contrary appearing as the little, and dissolving into nothingness." Lipps argued that "something little" always is involved in one side of the comic contrast, and it is always the second side—and the goal, not necessarily the starting-point—of one's thought or perceptions that leads to one's appreciation of humor and the comic (cf: Eastman, 1921, p. 183, who asserts that Lipps' sentence—"The feeling of the comic is a feeling of the comic *und weiter nichts!*"—contains his real contribution to the science of humor).

At the turn of the 20th century, the description of the activity of *laughter* in purely physical terms à la Joubert (1560/1579/1980) continues with a contribution by Dearborn (1900, pp. 853–854) that is often quoted (e.g., Keith-Spiegel, 1972, pp. 16–17; Ziv, 1984, p. ix):

There occur in laughter and more or less in smiling, clonic spasms of the diaphragm in number ordinarily about eighteen perhaps, and contraction of most of the muscles of the face. The upper side of the mouth and its corners are drawn upward. The upper eyelid is elevated . . . the nostrils are moderately dilated and drawn upward, the tongue slightly extended, and the cheeks distended and drawn somewhat upward . . . The lower jaw vibrates or is somewhat withdrawn (doubtless to afford all possible air to the distending lungs), and the head, in extreme laughter, is thrown backward . . . fatigue-pain in the diaphragm and accessory abdominal muscles causes a marked proper flexion of the trunk for relief. The whole arterial vascular system is dilated, with consequent blushing from the effect on the dermal capillaries of the face and neck and at times the scalp and hands . . . the eyes often slightly bulge forwards and the lachrymal gland becomes active, ordinarily to a degree only to cause a "brightening" of the eyes, but often to such an extent that the tears overflow entirely their proper channels.

Following Joubert, Darwin, Spencer, and Dearborn, the importance of the purely *physiological* features of laughter is reinforced periodically in the psychological literature; for example, see the relatively more recent works of Lloyd (1938) and Stearns (1972). Taking a brief "chronological digression" here, we discover that in an analysis of respiratory/pneumographic activity during laughter, Lloyd (1938) concludes the following: different persons have different types of laugh; a given individual will vary from time to time in his/her method of laughing; laughter is positively expiratory (rather than inspiratory); the "ha-ha-ha" vocalization in a vigorous laugh (more evident in the abdominal than thoracic recordings) is generally made at the limit of an extreme expiration; after the deep inspiration that generally concludes a period of laughter, there is frequently a long apnea (lasting as long as three or four times as long as a normal breathing cycle) in which there is practically no respiration; and the expiratory movement in laughter is more evident in the abdominal region than in the thoracic region, while in the inspiratory movement in laughter there is more activity in the thoracic than abdominal region. Lloyd (1938) also discusses in detail the "ha-ha-ha" vocalization feature of laughter in physical/anatomical terms as well as contrasting the physical features of crying with those of laughter.

In his book on laughter, Stearns (1972) covers the topics of the physiology of reflex laughing, the evolution of the psychosomatic phenomenon of laughing, the pathophysiology of laughing, the psychology and pathopsychology of laughing, and the biologic development and genetics of laughing. Stearns maintains that laughing is a unique human phenomenon, not having been observed explicitly in other mammals. He asserts that laughter/laughing is unique in humans also because it is both a reflex and a psychosomatic event (distinguished by the "integrant cohesion" of stimulus—informative communication—and response). According to Stearns, laughing may also be a voluntary reaction to conventional situations, a pathophysiological symptom, and the expression of a pathopsychological functional disorder; moreover, the organic development of laughing shows some characteristic chronological physiological and psychological features (cf: Langevin & Day, 1972; Watson, 1972).

The American psychologist Boris Sidis—who is notable for pioneering the study of unconscious motivation, and for experimenting on his own son, pushing him as a youngster to great cognitive feats—declares in his book on the psychology of laughter (Sidis, 1913) that any inquiry into the main psychological principles that underlie laughter presents a number of difficulties. One problem is the wide range of situations that include the ludicrous—from the lowly nursery rhymes of Mother Goose and clowns to the loftier productions in literature such as Shakespeare and Dickens. Another difficulty is the fact that very little satisfactory and systematic work has been done in the area of the psychology of laughter and the ludicrous. A third difficulty, according to Sidis, lies in the disorganized and scattered condition of the material on laughter and the ludicrous. Nonetheless, Sidis (1913) offers his account of the psychology of laughter in 27 chapters, including chapters on the topics of art, religion, and child games; laughter and novelty; ridicule and social decadence; the ludicrous and reserve energy; and freedom and laughter.

Early in his book, along with many quotations from Darwin (1872/1965), Sidis (1913, p. 3) lays down a "law" concerning laughter: "all unrestrained spontaneous activities of normal functions give rise to the emotion of joy with its expression of smiles and laughter." Sidis suggests that *play* is essentially the manifestation of "spontaneous, unrestrained activity" and, therefore, constitutes the beginning in the ultimate understanding of the nature of laughter. Moreover, laughter, smiling, and grinning are the external manifestations of the "play instinct." [Notes: Early in the 20th century, the notion of "instinct" as an explanatory device was popular in psychology, owing chiefly to the work of McDougall (1903, 1922a,b, 1923, 1932). Today, *instinct theory* in psychology is mostly of historic interest vis-à-vis human behavior, aside from a few "holdouts" such as the Freudians. See Roeckelein (1998, pp. 319–320) for a discussion of *instinct/hormic theory*, and Roeckelein (1998, p. 380) for a summary of *theories of play*. Other writers in the early 20th century also have proposed instinct/instinctive behavior theories of humor, including Drever (1917), Eastman (1921), Gregory (1924), Greig (1923/1969), McComas (1923), and Menon (1931).]

Later in his book, Sidis (1913, p. 283) arrives at a definition, of sorts, of the concept of *humor*: In the "higher" forms of ridicule (e.g., various characters in Dickens' novels), the malicious is not only eliminated, but the phenomenon of sympathy seems to emerge; this is called *humor*. Often, it is possible to see through one person's overt ridicule of another person into a covert humaneness and love for human life; in such cases, it is possible to love and sympathize with the individual(s) whom we may have regarded initially as ludicrous.

During the time he was a Registrar at Armstrong College in the University of Durham (UK), and held the M. A. degree, J.Y.T. Greig wrote his book on the psychology of laughter and comedy (Greig, 1923/1969). Greig maintains that study of the earliest laughter of infants leads to the conclusion that the essential element in the situations provoking laughter is personal whereby one's laugh is a response within the "ill-coordinated" behavior of the instinct of *love*. Laughter appears to arise when an obstruction of some kind is first encountered, and then suddenly overcome; it marks the escape of psycho-physical energy mobilized to meet the obstruction, but not acutally required for that purpose and, therefore, for the moment may be considered as "surplus."

Greig asserts that love is a primary (and hate is secondary) development issuing from laughter, and attempts to trace this double strain in laughter from its simplest to its most complex manifestations—from the smile of the infant in his cradle to the highest and most ethereal forms of adult wit and humor. [Note: Monro (1951/1963, p. 210) classifies Greig's approach as an "ambivalence/conflicting emotions" theory of humor.] In addition to his ten chapters covering various topics on the psychology of laughter and comedy, Greig (1923/1969) presents a very substantial appendix (55 pages) on theories of laughter/comedy, and a lengthy bibliography containing over 360 items.

In one place in his book on the nature of laughter, Gregory (1924, p. 222) suggests the relationship between laughter and wit:

Wit attracts the phrase "laughter and wit" because it so often and so competently provides the laughters with occasions. Its decisiveness elicits their fundamental situation of relief and it constantly involves those displays of incongruity that stir the sense of the ludicrous. The alliance between wit and laughter, frequent though not constant, is a reminder of the ubiquity of the laugh.

Gregory (1924) includes the following topics in his book on laughter [an approach that may fairly be characterized as a theoretical position somewhere on the instinct continuum between McDougall's (1903, 1922a,b) "monistic view of laughter" and Eastman's (1921) "modestly pluralistic theory"]: some varieties of laughter (e.g., laughter of triumph/scorn, amused laughter, laughter of play), the humanization of laughter, the laughter of: relief, tickling, pleasure; laughter and: society/civilization, the ludicrous, wit, instinct, repression; and the function and aesthetics of laughter. [Notes: Monro (1951/1963, p. 201) characterizes Gregory's attempt to explain laughter as a "release from restraint" theory; and Berlyne (1969, p. 802) calls Gregory's approach "the most thoroughgoing example of a relief theory."]

One of the reasons that Kimmins (1928) wrote his book on laughter was to review theories of laughter and, especially, to critique the "sudden glory" theory of laughter of the English philosopher Thomas Hobbes (i.e., that the passion of laughter is nothing else but *sudden glory* arising from some sudden conception of some eminency in ourselves, by comparison with the infirmity of others, or with our own formerly). According to Kimmins, the fact that the "sudden glory" theory of Hobbes maintained such a supremacy among the theories of laughter for so long a period indicates that insufficient thought had been given to the earlier stages of child life in the framing of the theory. Additionally, Kimmins asserts that insufficient importance in laughter theories has been given to the following: the child's contribution to the topic; the need for greater emphasis on the play-attitude; the changes in humor appreciation at different ages; and the influence of social attitudes at different epochs of development in human history. Kimmins covers the following subject areas in his book: 17th- and 18th-century theories of laughter; 19th–century theories of laughter; 20th-century theories of laughter; laughter and dreams; laughter and tears; the spirit of the child; the beginnings of laughter; what young children (5–12 years of age) laugh at; the laughter of older (12–18 years of age) children; English and American humour; and the laughter of coloured children.

In his book, Menon (1931) proposes an instinct-type "theory" of laughter that seeks not to create a totally novel or different theory, but to reconcile the theories and observations of other writers such as Hobbes, Bain, Baillie, Bergson, and McDougall. [Notes: In this case, perhaps the term "integrative summary" is a better description of Menon's approach than the term "theory"; Monro (1951/1963, p. 222) classifies Menon's approach as an "ambivalence" theory; cf: the plea by Clubb (1932) for the development of an "eclectic theory of humour"; and Milner's (1972) "semiotic theory of humour and laughter."] Menon (1931, pp. 6–7) states that "my explanation is based on McDougall's conception of the nature of instincts. Those who consider that his conception of the instinctive basis of mind is fundamentally defective or wrong cannot, naturally, find any truth in my explanation of the nature of laughter." However,

Menon asserts that while he is convinced of the truth of McDougall's main contention regarding the nature of instincts and their relation to mind, he is not completely convinced that McDougall's statements about laughter contain the *whole* truth of the matter.

Menon's goal is to "reconcile and harmonize" rather than to "sever and separate"; in his approach, he attempts to establish a consistency, continuity, and unity between the existing diversified views of laughter—to give an integrative account that is a "preliminary condition for a union with the Divine, a reabsorption into the ultimate One" (pp. 8–9). Among the contents and chapters in Menon's book are: laughter as a psychophysical activity; laughter and animals; tickling; the instinctive nature of laughter; types of laughter due to instincts and sentiments; the mental conflict in laughter; the nature of humour; ugliness and beauty; and art and science.

Citing 32 examples of laughter (which, incidentally, are not all mutually exclusive), Ludovici (1932) provides a "new theory of laughter" in which the roots of laughter are seen to lie in the triumph one attains over other people or circumstances. Such an ideational basis for humor/laughter has been incorporated into a genre or rubric called "superiority theories" of humor (e.g., Goldstein & McGhee, 1972; Monro, 1951/1963; cf: Leacock, 1935, 1937). Ludovici asserts that laughter may be traced back to the snarls of triumph or mockery that are made over a defeated adversary, and describes why assertion of superiority takes this particular behavioral form. He maintains that in the specific act of the baring of the teeth—where this behavior evolutionarily carried the functional and nonverbal message in primitives and animals of warding off an enemy or establishing dominance—an interpretation may now be made in modern man, says Ludovici, that involves so-called superior adaptation. Moreover, based upon such an evolutionary pattern involving aggression and attack, Ludovici refers to the audible aspect of laughter as "spiritualized snarling." Ludovici theorizes that human beings also show their teeth (as in a laugh) in all those situations in which they feel themselves "superiorly adapted." Thus, according to Ludovici, the essence of laughter (i.e., "the secret of laughter") is the baring of the teeth; throughout his book he uses the phrase "show teeth" as a synonym for "laugh." On this theoretical connection made by Ludovici between laughter and teeth-baring, Eastman (1937, p. 383) states the following:

Mr. Ludovici asserts that if instead of the word "laugh" we always use the words "show teeth," we shall find that this "explains everything." He then proceeds to remark that "animals show teeth . . . only when they wish to warn a fellow, a foe, or man, of the danger of pursuing certain tactics too far." This he calls an expression of "superior adaptation"—although the fact is that animals unflesh their fangs most often when they are brought into a corner by a power that they fear is superior.

As Monro (1951/1963, pp. 109–110) notes, the phrase (show teeth) is a happy one for Ludovici's purpose, "as it does suggest the hostility and suspicion which he finds lurking in all laughter . . . We may agree with Ludovici that we have not lost the habit of baring our fangs, or snarling. But it hardly seems necessary to look for it in the smile."

In his account of laughter, the anthropologist Ralph Piddington (1933/1963) examines the psychology of the original reaction of laughter and attempts to relate it to the functions it subsumes in society (i.e., the social adaptation of laughter). Piddington observes that one of the difficulties in dealing with the problem of laughter is a verbal one: the word *laughter* refers to a definite physical act, and it may be examined either as the experience that accompanies it or the stimuli that produce it. Moreover, in describing the laughter-producing stimuli, there is no entirely satisfactory term and, even though there are various words available such as "ridiculous," "comic," "satirical," and such, each of these expresses a slightly different shade of meaning. To resolve this semantic problem, Piddington chooses to adopt the word "ludicrous" as his key concept. Among the topics and chapters in his book are the following: review and criticism of previous theories of laughter; the origin of laughter; laughter and play; the ludicrous; the psychology of weeping; laughter as a social sanction and as social compensation; secondary functions of laughter; and forms of the ludicrous. In a lengthy appendix (69 pages), Piddington provides a good historical summary of laughter theories.

Among Piddington's conclusions regarding laughter are that the biological point of view is particularly important in examining laughter, that laughter originally served the function of communicating to parents the contentment of their offspring, that laughter undergoes various modifications (e.g., it comes to be aroused by certain situations that may be described as "ludicrous") when people come to live together in societies, and that the relationship between elementary laughter and laughter at the ludicrous may best be understood via a "principle of psychic compensation," or "compensatory theory," in which laughter serves primarily a social compensatory function whereby any disturbance of the social values of the system may be prevented.

In the first sentence of his book on the enjoyment of laughter, Eastman (1937) warns the reader that "it is not the purpose of this book to make you laugh" (p. 13), and that the book is "a textbook in the science of humour and the art of enjoying it—a book which I invite you to read without mental concentration and in the laziest and most self-indulgent manner of which you are capable" (p. 16). Subsequently, in his "unfunny/funny" book, Eastman presents his material in eight parts; the shortest part of his book (one page in length) is Part 1 (Fun and Funny); in this section, Eastman (1937, p. 19) very briefly presents his *four laws of humor*:

1. Things can be funny only when we are in fun.
2. When we are in fun, a peculiar shift of values takes place.
3. Being in fun is a condition most natural to childhood, and that children at play reveal the humorous laugh in its simplest and most omnivorous form.
4. Grown-up people retain in varying degrees this aptitude for being in fun, and thus may enjoy unpleasant things as funny.

After listing these four "laws," and declaring these laws to be "all there is in the science of humour," Eastman concludes by stating, "That is Part One of our textbook." Eastman includes a supplementary section ("Some Humorists on Humour") at the end of his book in which quotations and ideas about humor of some well-known humorists, past and present, are given (examples: "Laughter always arises from a gaiety of disposition, absolutely incompatible with contempt and indignation"—Voltaire; "I laugh because I must not cry, that's all, that's all"—Abraham Lincoln; "Everything human is pathetic. The secret source of humor itself is not joy but sorrow. There is no humor in heaven"—Mark Twain; "It seems to me people are often sympathetic when they laugh . . . sometimes little children sympathize too much, and have to shut their eyes during a cruel scene"—Walt Disney).

Monro (1951/1963) provides a critical survey of many theories of humor/laughter (excluding "a large number of recent writers who have adopted an experimental laboratory approach to the subject") in which he uses four main classes of theory: superiority theories, incongruity theories, release from restraint theories, and ambivalence theories. In Chapter 2 ("Non-Humorous Laughter"), Monro lists and describes the main types/situations of nonhumorous laughter (tickling, laughing-gas, nervousness, relief after a strain, laughing it off/defence mechanism, joy, play, make-believe, contests), and in Chapter 3 ("Types of Humour") he outlines and describes ten classes/types of humor (e.g., any breach of the usual order of events; anything masquerading as something it is not; word-play, etc.).

At the end of his book, Monro presents his own "synthetic" approach to humor, called the "inappropriate" aspect, whereby laughter is induced by the informational content of external and internal stimulus patterns, or patterns of thought, that contain several items of information in particular kinds of sequence or juxtaposition. Monro (1951/1963, p. 256) admits that there are still many questions to be answered; for example, "If humour is the inappropriate, why should it cause the peculiar manifestations which we call laughter?" and "Why should the same manifestations be called forth by tickling, by laughing-gas, and by nervousness?"

In his book on laughter and the sense of humor, Bergler (1956) suggests that the irony of all the investigations on laughter (wit, the comic, the sense of humor) lies in a contradiction: on the one hand, for all *practical* purposes, laughter is concentrated, split-second *euphoria*; and on the other hand, for *scientific* purposes, laughter consists of concentrated and interminable *dysphoria*. Bergler asserts that laughter is not an inborn instinct and, therefore, the term "sense of humor" is a misnomer. Adopting a psychoanalytic perspective, Bergler states that laughter has a highly complex, individual "case history" that is intimately connected with infantile fears which are perpetuated in the "fantastic severity" of the inner conscience, the superego. Essentially, Bergler's approach to laughter/humor is to describe and understand it within the framework of the superego and the "all-important" defense mechanism of psychic masochism (based on oral regression that is created by the unconscious ego to escape the superego's oppression or tyranny).

Plessner (1961/1970) presents what may be called a "philosophical anthropological" (i.e., a philosophical study of the nature of man) approach to the study of laughing and crying; such an approach (often phenomenological) uses material from several disciplines, including psychology, neurophysiology, physical and social anthropology, and sociology. Plessner's thesis on laughing and crying advances from his notion of the "eccentric position" of man: humans cannot free themselves from their own centered, animal existence, yet they place themselves over against it. As individuals, we stand at a double distance from our own body—we are still animals, but in a peculiar way. We have an inner life that is distinct and inseparable from our external physical existence; we stand over against both of these, holding them apart from each other and yet together. According to Plessner, it is our eccentric position that gives to our existence the ambiguity of freedom, necessity, significance, and contingency. Within this framework, the behaviors of laughing and crying constitute unique expressions of the breakdown of the so-called eccentric position—it is when things are too much with us that we cry, even when we cry for joy, and it is when the ambiguity in our fundamental dilemma becomes incontrollable that we laugh.

Mindess (1971) describes the inner obstacles which block the unfolding of one's humorous potentials and attempts to point out the possibilities of overcoming them. He asserts that a flourishing sense of humor is fundamental to mental health, that it represents a primary source of vitality and excellent means of transcendence, and that it is an agent of "psychological liberation." Mindess' theory, essentially, proposes that the most important function of humor is its power to release the individual from the many inhibitions and restrictions encountered in daily life.

As editors of their book on the psychology of humor—outside of the psychoanalytic framework—Goldstein and McGhee (1972) present original theories and research into the nature and function of humor. The book provides an historical review of early notions of humor, several theoretical papers, and empirical research into various social, structural, motivational, and physiological aspects of humor. More specifically, the following chapters are included, among others: Early Conceptions of Humor: Varieties and Issues (P. Keith-Spiegel); A Two-Stage Model for the Appreciation of Jokes and Cartoons: An Information-Processing Analysis (J. M. Suls); A Model of the Social Functions of Humor (W. H. Martineau); Physiological Correlates of Humor (R. Langevin & H. I. Day); Humor Judgments as a Function of Reference Groups and Identification Classes (L. LaFave); and Humor, Laughter, and Smiling: Some Preliminary Observations of Funny Behaviors (H. R. Pollio, R. Mers, & W. Lucchesi). In Chapter 12 of this book, McGhee and Goldstein attempt to give a systematic summing up and integration of the diverse topics contained in the chapters (cf: Table 1, p. 258); they discuss individually the theoretical, methodological, and empirical advances of each chapter, relate them to other contributors, and point out the implications for future research. In their last chapter, Goldstein and McGhee give a survey of methodology in empirical studies (1950–1971), and provide a valuable bibliography on humor studies (1900–1971) containing nearly 400 items.

Adopting a primarily literary approach to the "anatomy of laughter," Boston (1974) notes that the concept of laughter is an extremely amorphous one, including, among other things, the topics of comedy, humour, wit, mirth, jokes, fun, funniness, smiling, play, games, fooling, clowning, satire, parody, and "Pantagruelism" [i.e., the humorous practice, or fine art, of literary digression from a stated topic; it involves buffoonery or coarse humor with a satirical or serious purpose; cynical humor. The term *Pantagruelism* is derived from a character in Francois Rabelais' (1533/1990) novel *Gargantua and Pantagruel*.] In addition to literary references, Boston also draws from sources relating to various other disciplines such as sociology, anthropology, psychology, zoology, and physiology. Boston's book traces the shifts in attitudes to laughter—both for and against—from the Middle Ages to the present day. At the end of his literary examination of humor, Boston (1974, p. 237) concludes that "there is good laughter and bad laughter—aggressive laughter, obscene laughter, playful laughter. But one thing is clear, and that is that we need laughter."

As editors of a book on humor and laughter, Chapman and Foot (1976) survey the theories, research, and applications of laughter. In general, Section 1 of the book is devoted to showing some of the research currently being conducted that seeks to extend the existing knowledge of the processes involved in the perception of, the appreciation of, and the responsiveness to, humor; Section 2 deals with the impact, use, and applications of humor on/in social settings. More specifically, a sample of some of the topics in Chapman and Foot (1976) includes the following: A Cognitive-Developmental Analysis of Humour (T. R. Shultz); Incongruity and Funniness: Towards a New Descriptive Model (G. Nerhardt); A Disposition Theory of Humour and Mirth (D. Zillmann & J. R. Cantor); Physiological and Verbal Indices of Arousal in Rated Humour (M. Godkewitsch); Social Aspects of Humorous Laughter (A. J. Chapman);

The Social Responsiveness of Young Children in Humorous Situations (H. C. Foot & A. J. Chapman); Wit and Humour in Mass Communication (C. R. Gruner); Freudian Humour: The Eupsychia of Everyday Life (W. E. O'Connell); The Use and Abuse of Humour in Psychotherapy (H. Mindess).

Chapman and Foot (1977) edited another book on humor and laughter which contains material from papers read at the International Conference on Humour and Laughter held in Cardiff, UK on July 13–17, 1976. Ten general topic areas covered in the book are: essays on the nature of humor, laughter, and comedy; approaches to the study of humor; humor as a form of therapy; cross-cultural humor; children's humor; ethnic humor; humor and communication; individual differences in humor; the world of comedy; and miscellaneous studies on humor and laughter. In the book's Foreword (by B. M. Foss), two sets of distinctions—in pithy/aphoristic form—are made between laughter and humor: "laughter has a lot to do with social development, whereas many kinds of humour have more to do with cognitive development," and "laughter is a defence against neurosis, humour is a defence against psychosis" (p. xiv).

Specific articles, among others, in the book are: The Psychoanalytic Theory of Humor and Laughter (P. Kline); A Model of the Origins and Early Development of Incongruity-Based Humor (P. E. McGhee); Cognitive and Disparagement Theories of Humour: A Theoretical and Empirical Synthesis (J. M. Suls); Operationalization of Incongruity in Humour Research: A Critique and Suggestions (G. Nerhardt); Psychological Approaches to the Study of Humour (M. K. Rothbart); Humour and the Theory of Psychological Reversals (M. J. Apter & K. C. P. Smith); Mirth Measurement: A New Technique (M. Mair & J. Kirkland); The Use of Jokes in Psychotherapy (S. A. Grossman); The Place of Humour in Adult Psychotherapy (B. Killinger); Humour in Psychotherapy (H. Greenwald); A Cross-Cultural Study of the Structure of Humour (T. R. Shultz); Children's Humour: A Review of Current Research Trends (P. E. McGhee); Ethnic Humour: From Paradoxes Towards Principles (L. LaFave); Sex Differences in Children's Responses to Humour (H. C. Foot, J. R. Smith, & A. J. Chapman); Uses and Abuses of Canned Laughter (R. Fuller); Suppression of Adult Laughter: An Experimental Approach (K. A. Osborne & A. J. Chapman); Environmental Conditions Affecting the Humour Response: Developmental Trends (F. J. Prerost); and The Measurement of Humour Appreciation (A. Sheehy-Skeffington). Included in the book, is a bibliography on humour, laughter, and comedy ("A Bibliography of Empirical and Nonempirical Analyses in the English Language" by J. H. Goldstein, P. E. McGhee, J. R. Smith, A. J. Chapman, & H. C. Foot) that contains over 1,140 items. [Notes: The typical article length here is 4–6 pages, with a few having one page or less, and a few having 18–24 pages; because there are over 90 articles in the book, and page space is limited here, I've selected only a small representative sample of the titles/authors.]

In his book on laughing and the psychology of humor, Holland (1982)—at one place (Table 1, p. 108)—provides an outline concerning theories of humor and "why do people laugh?" In answering this question, there are five important variables/categories, according to Holland: stimulus aspects/incongruity (involves cognitive, ethical, and formal factors); conditions (factors of playfulness and suddenness); psychology (includes archetype theories, relief theories, superiority theories, psychoanalytic theories, and experiments); physiology (laughter is viewed as an innate action cluster, as physical reflection of mental movements, or as adaptive communication); catharsis (factors of social correction, religious catharsis, and transcendence). Holland (1982, p. 107) summarizes and compresses his whole outline of the theories of laughter, and why we laugh, into a single sentence: "If we perceive a sudden, playful incongruity that gratifies conscious and unconscious wishes and defeats conscious and unconscious fears to give a feeling of liberation, then we laugh." In another place—in his final chapter—Holland (1982, p. 199) suggests a simple answer to the centuries-old and perplexing question of why we laugh: "Why do we laugh? Because we are, as the children's song says, 'Free to be you and me.' Precisely." Holland's (1982, pp. 209–223) "Bibliography of Theories of Humor" contains nearly 300 items.

The philosopher/teacher John Morreall (1983) examines laughter initially by considering the three traditional theories of laughter (i.e., superiority, incongruity, and relief theories) in great length, and then attempts to construct a novel, comprehensive theory based on the older approaches. [Notes: Also see Morreall (1987) which covers the subject areas of traditional and contemporary theories of laughter and humor, amusement and other mental states, and the ethics of laughter and humor; cf: Eckardt (1992, pp. 63–73) for further discussion of Morreall's "comprehensive theory of laughter."] Morreall suggests that three general features of laughter situations should form the basis of any new comprehensive theory: the *change* of psychological state that the laughter undergoes; the *suddenness* of psychological shifts and changes in laughter, and the *pleasantness* of psychological shifts in laughter situations. Subsequently, by putting the three features together into a general "formula" statement for characterizing laughter situations, Morreall (1983, p. 39) states that "laughter results from a pleasant psychological shift." The chapter contents/titles of Morreall's (1983) book include: Can There Be a Theory of Laughter? The Superiority Theory; The Incongruity Theory; The Relief Theory; A New Theory; The Variety of Humor; Humor as Aesthetic Experience; Humor and Freedom; The Social Value of Humor; and Humor and Life. [Notes: Part 1 is on *laughter*; Part 2 is on *humor*. For a further discussion of Morreall's assessments of humor/laughter theories, see my Chapter 3, section titled "Theories Based in Modern Philosophy."]

In taking an anthropological approach to humor and laughter, Apte (1985) divides his book into three parts: humor and social structure, cultural expressions of humor, and behavioral responses to humor. More specifically, Apte's chapter titles include the following: Joking Relationships; Sexual Inequality in Humor; Children's Humor; Humor, Ethnicity, and Intergroup Relations; Humor in Religion; Humor and Language; The Trickster in Folklore; Laughter and Smiling; and Evolutionary and Biosocial Aspects. Apte maintains that anthropologists have generally ignored the topic of humor in their research and, in particular, cross-cultural studies of humor seem to be nonexistent. Apte reviews various definitions of *humor* that have appeared in the literature on humor, and notes that for many scholars the term *laughter* is synonymous with the term *humor* where the phrase "theories of laughter" often means theories of humor (see Armstrong, 1928; Grotjahn, 1957; Hertzler, 1970; Piddington, 1933/1963).

According to Apte, while laughter and smiling are probably the most overt indicators of the humor experience, they differ from humor in being physiologically and anatomically observable, overt activities. Apte notes that some writers use the term *laughter* as a criterion to define the overall domain of humor by others (e.g., Edmonson, 1952, p. 2; Koestler, 1964, p. 31) and, also, that not every instance of laughter results from humor nor does every humorous event necessarily produce laughter (e.g., Berlyne, 1969; Chapman & Foot, 1976; Potter, 1954). "Laughter," says Apte (1985, p. 239), "besides being linked to humor, appears to express the primordial human emotion of sheer joy." Apte uses the term *humor* to refer, first, to a cognitive—often unconscious—experience involving internal redefinition of sociocultural reality and resulting in a mirthful state of mind; second, to the external sociocultural factors that trigger the cognitive experience; third, to the pleasure derived from the cognitive experience labeled "humor"; and fourth, to the external manifestations of the cognitive experience and the resultant pleasure. Apte employs the terms *laughter* and *smiling*, accordingly, to stand for the external manifestations of the humor experience.

Overall, Apte's book is an attempt to explore—by cross-cultural comparison—the interdependence of humor and sociocultural factors in societies around the world, to generate generalizations concerning such cross-cultural investigations, and to formulate theoretical propositions regarding the similar and different ways in which humor is linked to sociocultural factors. While Apte (1985, p. 16) asserts that his book is "the first cross-cultural study of humor in general in anthropology" (cf: anthropological studies of humor within *individual* societies, e.g., Edmonson, 1952; Hill, 1943), the discipline of psychology has generated a number of earlier (pre-1985) studies on cross-cultural humor [e.g., Castell & Goldstein (1977); Goldstein (1977); Handelman (1977);

Hansen (1977); Shultz (1977)]. Apte's (1985) book has a generous references section, containing over 720 items.

HUMOR AND COMEDY

> We shall not aim at imprisoning the comic spirit within a definition. We regard it, above all, as a living thing. However trivial it may be, we shall treat it with the respect due to life . . . the comic spirit has a logic of its own, even in its wildest eccentricities. It has a method in its madness.
> —H. Bergson, 1911

> Whether in the colourful cap and bells of a medieval jester, the spotted silks of a circus clown, or in the immaculate garb of a late night MC, there exists a unique class of people whose very actions and behaviour set them apart from everyone else and these are the comedians . . . we are ever perplexed by the question of whether the clown is melancholic or gay.
> —H. R. Pollio and J. W. Edgerly, 1976

> There is as yet no solid evidence that comics fit a certain personality pattern.
> —S. Fisher and R. L. Fisher, 1983

Webster's (1993) defines the noun *comedy* [Middle English *comedye*, from the Middle French *comedie*, from the Latin *comoedia*, from the Greek *komoidia* and *komos* (revel, village festival, festal procession, ode sung in this procession); from *kome* (village), and *oidia* (from *aeidein*—to sing)] as

a drama of light and amusing character and typically with a happy ending; a mystery play or interlude with a happy ending (obsolete); any medieval narrative that ends happily, especially one written in a vernacular language; any literary composition written in a comic style or treating a theme suitable for comedy; the genre of dramatic literature that deals with the light or the amusing or with the serious and profound in a light, familiar, or satirical manner (compare tragedy); matter suitable for treatment in comedy: a ludicrous, farcical, or amusing event or series of events; the comic element (as in a play, story, or motion picture).

Webster's (1993) defines the adjective *comic* (Latin *comicus*, from the Greek *komikos* and *komos*—festivity with music and dancing) as

dealing or dealt with in comedy as contrasted with tragedy; composing or acting in comedies; showing or conveying an attitude of thoughtful mirth or amused detached reflection rather than sorrow, pain, or resolution; calling forth laughter by intentional wit, humor, or burlesque or by unintentional exaggeration or inappropriateness: comical;

presenting a series of humorous incidents or dramatic adventures in a sequence of pictures usually accompanied by balloons giving conversation.

The term *comic*, as a noun, is defined (*Webster's*, 1993) as

An actor of comic roles: comedian; the element in art or nature that provokes mirth or humorous reflection; the representation of the incongruous (as in character and in conduct or in aim and in method) or amusing; sometimes: the representation of human error and weakness as provocative of amusement; a group of cartoons or drawings arranged in a narrative sequence; *comics*: the portion of a publication (as a daily or Sunday newspaper) devoted to such groups; a motion picture presenting broad comedy or farce . . . *comical*: calling forth often intentionally mirth and easy spontaneous laughter: funny, humorous.

Baldwin (1901–1905, p. 198) defines the term *comic* as "that portion of the laughable which has an aesthetic or semi-aesthetic character. This excludes delight in cruelty (Schadenfreude), although some species of the comic (e.g., satire, ridicule) are complicated with refined forms of that emotion." Moreover, Baldwin maintains that objectively the *comic* usually has a predominating element of incongruity or contrast, while in a subjective sense the *comic* usually involves elements of shock, of tension suddenly released, and of the emotional seizure of laughter. In comparing the *comic* to the phenomenon of beauty, Baldwin cites two main issues: the analysis of the character of the comic (which may be of comic objects, situations, or actions; or of the subjective state of feeling), and the explanation on psychological, physiological, or biological grounds of why people laugh at given objects.

Analyses of the comic object involving some form of error or incongruity include those made by Aristotle, Richter, Schopenhauer, and vonHartmann. Analyses of the comic on subjective grounds include those made by Plato and Hobbes who emphasize the feeling of superiority or "sudden glory." Baldwin also notes that analyses showing the relationship between the comic and the beautiful have been made by Weisse, Vischer, and Bohts, and the successive stages of the comic process analyzed by Zeising involve the processes of tension, discharge, and recovery of poise as the individual frees himself. Other approaches toward analysis of the comic cited by Baldwin are those of Theodor Lipps who treats the comic as a special case of association, by Immanual Kant and Herbert Spencer who looked for the physiological explanations of laughter, by Charles Darwin who investigated the physiological expression involved in comic situations, and by G.S. Hall and A. Allin who attempted to determine the genetic basis for comic experiments. Finally, Baldwin suggests that the word *ludicrous* has been used fully as much as the term *comic* in English, but preference is given to the term *comic* by him because it has a less intensive connotation and also because it is in use in all the other languages (cf: Bawdon, 1910;

Corrigan & Loney, 1971; Helson, 1973; Lilly, 1896; Lynn, 1958; Mandel, 1970; Mikhail, 1972; Olson, 1970; Potts, 1948; W.M. Smith, 1931; Sorrell, 1972; Sypher, 1956; Trachtenberg, 1976).

The Encyclopaedia Britannica (1922) defines *comedy* as a general term that is applied to a type of drama whose chief object—according to modern usage—is to amuse. Comedy is contrasted on the one hand with tragedy and on the other with farce and burlesque; as compared with tragedy, it is distinguished by having a happy ending, by quaint situations, and by lightness of character-drawing and dialogue. As compared with farce, comedy abstains from crude and boisterous jesting and it is associated with some subtlety of dialogue and plot; however, there is no hard and fast line of demarcation between comedy and farce because there is a distinct tendency to combine the characteristics of farce with those of true comedy (e.g., in the "musical comedies" where true comedy is frequently subservient to broad farce and spectacular effects). Following a discussion of the derivation of the word *comedy* from Greek, it is noted that the word comes into modern usage via Latin (*comoedia*) and Italian (*commedia*). The term *comedy* has passed through various shades of meaning (e.g., in the Middle Ages it meant simply a story with a happy ending). The adjective *comic* is confined in meaning—in its modern usage—to the sense of "laughter-provoking" (cf: Sully, 1902), and it is distinguished from "humorous" or "witty" inasmuch as it is applied to a remark or incident that provokes spontaneous laughter without a special mental effort.

It is noted in *The New Encyclopaedia Britannica* (1997, Vol. 3, *Micropaedia*, p. 481) that "the history of comedy shows it to be a form whose complexity cannot adequately be dealt with by any definition that sees it as aiming simply at exciting laughter." The 19th-century notion (e.g., Meredith, 1897) that comedy appeals to the intellect and not to the emotions (and concerns the social group) has been rejected generally today as too narrow in scope.

Different kinds of comedy may be viewed as dependent on the intentions and attitudes of authors; for example, when the intention is to ridicule, "satirical comedy" is the result; when ridicule is turned on persons, the result is the "comedy of character"; a satire of social convention results in the "comedy of manners"; "social comedy" concerns the structure of society itself; "comedy of ideas" derives from the satire of conventional thinking; progress from troubles to the triumph of love in a happy outcome produces "romantic comedy"; the "comedy of intrigue" results from a dominant intention of providing amusement and excitement with an intricate plot of reversals having artificial/contrived situations; "sentimental comedy" is where the author wishes to exploit potentially serious issues merely sentimentally while never really approaching anything like the true emotion of tragedy; "tragicomedy" combines elements of the tragic and the comedic; and "black comedy/absurdism" reflects the existentialists' concerns of the potential meaning, and meaninglessness, inherent in modern life.

Richetti (1998, p. 137) observes that all literary forms contain certain comic elements, but the term *comedy* primarily describes a genre of humorous plays that deal with ordinary or domestic events and end happily. In comparing comedy with tragedy, Richetti notes that comedy depicts people as "worse" than they are, while tragedy depicts people as "better" than they are; and comedy represents inferior people whose actions arouse laughter without causing pain, while tragedy represents the sufferings of noble characters in order to stir pity in the audience (cf: W. Smith, 1910).

Modern theories of comedy include Bergson's notion of the audience's felt superiority over the comic characters in a play or story, and Freud's idea that humor/comedy provides infantile gratification by disrupting the adult world and is often a means of unconscious sexual release. Richetti also describes the various genres, types, and eras of comedy (e.g., Ancient Greek Comedy, Ancient Roman Comedy, Renaissance Comedy, Elizabethan Comedy, 17th- and 18th-Century Comedy, and Modern Comedy) with illustrative works that characterize each era (cf: Herrick, 1964, 1966; Lauter, 1964; Orel, 1961).

Holman (1998) provides a brief description of *comedy* as a form of dramatic literature designed to amuse and frequently to correct or instruct through ridicule; it generally ends happily. Comedy achieves its results by exposing incongruity, absurdity, and foolishness, and its treatment of characters often has elements of caricature and exaggeration (cf: Pollio & Mers, 1974). Holman also notes that comedy—like tragedy—grew out of early Greek religious festivals honoring the god Dionysus in which joyful appreciation was given to the natural world. The greatest Greek writer of comedy was Aristophanes (c. 400 B.C.) who added the element of satire (of institutions and men) to comedy. Later, the Greek playwright Menander, and the Roman playwrights Plautus and Terence, developed the "New Comedy" which was characterized by the use of stock characters to exploit life's absurdities. Holman observes that comedy has taken many forms in Western civilization since the Renaissance period of the 14th to 16th centuries.

Berkowitz (1999) defines *comedy* as a form of drama that deals with humorous or ridiculous aspects of human behavior, has a playful mood, and which ends happily. Berkowitz gives a brief history of the comic play, and defines various types of comedy. There are comedies of: character (humor via the major traits of the characters), ideas (social, moral, or philosophical issues and problems), situation/farce (comic events and actions, usually of everyday life), manners (humorous treatments of the social codes of the upper classes), romance (love relationships), and darkness/absurdity (a mixture of bizarre comic events with serious action).

In Harris and Levey (1975), *comedy* is defined as a "literary work that aims primarily at amusement" (p. 608). Moreover, *comedy* seeks to entertain chiefly through criticism and ridicule of man's customs and institutions (as compared with *tragedy* which seeks to engage profound emotions and sympathies). Harris and Levey note that although comedy is usually used in reference to the drama, the term is applied also to such nondramatic works as Dante's religious poem, *The Divine Comedy*. The origins of dramatic comedy are the boisterous choruses and dialogue of the fertility rites of the feasts of the Greek god Dionysus.

The term "Old Comedy" in ancient Greece referred to a series of loosely connected scenes—using a chorus and individual characters—that depicted particular situations through the literary devices of farce, fantasy, satire, parody, and political propaganda; such scenes usually ended in a lyrical celebration of unity. The epitome of the Old Comedy era was the work/plays of Aristophanes; Middle Comedy—containing social dramas having less vitality and imagination—followed the demise of Old Comedy.

The era of New Comedy (beginning in about the middle of the 4th century B.C.) ushered in plays/dramas that were more "literary," often romantic in style, and less satirical and critical than those of the previous comedy eras. Later, during the Middle Ages (A.D. 470 to c. 1450), the church attempted to minimize the joyous and critical aspects of the drama, but the comic drama survived during that period in the form of medieval folk plays and festivals, in mock liturgical dramas, and in some of the features of the miracle/morality plays.

The Renaissance period (14th to 16th centuries) spawned a novel and vital type of drama (i.e., English plays that blended with the old Latin classic comedy and produced eventually the great Elizabethan comedy form, finding its greatest expression in the plays of Ben Jonson and William Shakespeare; in France, the classical influence was combined with Italian dramatic aspects to find expression in the plays of Moliere—considered by many to be one of the greatest comic and satiric writers in the history of the theater). Harris and Levey (1975, p. 608) discuss in great detail the various historical periods, trends, cycles, and genres of comedy from the early Greeks in the 4th century B.C. up through the comedy plays of the 20th century.

As one may detect from the various authoritative definitions and accounts of the term *comedy*, the word is embedded, historically, in the discipline area of literature and the literary (versus purely psychological) approaches toward humor. Accordingly, the word *comedy* very rarely appears as a separate entity for definition in the standard dictionaries and encyclopedias of psychological terms. [Note: A possible exception here, as indicated earlier, is Baldwin's (1901–1905) entry for the term *comic*.] In psychology, the term *comedy* usually is a variant, derivative, subservient, or secondary term for the more popular terms *humor* and *laughter*.

However, in another regard, there are a few studies and accounts in the psychological literature that focus attention rather directly on the phenomenon of the comic/comedian/comedy. Among such studies are those by Pollio and Edgerly (1976) and Fisher and Fisher (1983). Pollio and Edgerly maintain that comedy makes its appearance in the lived (everyday life) world as well as in the contrived (entertainment, dramatic) world, and any analysis of comedians and their styles must take this complete comic continuum or spectrum into account. [Notes: For "comic figures of speech," "kinds of comic action," and "comic styles," see Eastman (1937, pp. 98–119) and for the "ten commandments of the comic arts," see Eastman (1937, pp. 326–366); also, see Enck, Forter, & Whitley (1960), Esar (1949), Feibleman (1962), Felheim (1962), Prado (1995), Rutter (2000), Swabey (1961), and Wilcox (1947) for various other applied and theoretical accounts of comedy that may serve as a basis for psychological study of this area.]

Pollio and Edgerly note that over and above the specific comedic situation is the larger social context within which comedy occurs, and it is this larger context which is obvious in anthropological and sociological studies and which serves to moderate everything a clown or comedian says and does (cf: Charles, 1945; Levine, 1961, 1986; Welsford, 1935). Pollio and Edgerly describe, and present empirical data for, the following issues and topics: culture, comedy, and the social meaning of what's funny (cf: Pollio, Mers, & Lucchesi, 1972); the specific situations in which people laugh ("the laughing places"); laughter in therapy groups; and the comedian's world (cf: Pollio, Edgerly, & Jordan, 1972, who suggest that there are two different types of comic dimensions of a comedian: the "surface" properties, and the "style" properties).

Pollio and Edgerly (1976) conclude that in social settings most laughter is initiated by men, that women more frequently smile/laugh—but hardly ever joke, that the comedian is not independent of his/her audience (e.g., group cohesiveness is critically important in determining who laughs at what, when, and under what conditions—friends apparently support one another, while strangers can, and often do, inhibit laughter; cf: Murphy & Pollio, 1973, 1975), and that comedians are most often described in negative terms (e.g., "fat," "skinny," "crazy"). Pollio and Edgerly assert that the social event of humor allows for the cathartic release of aggressions, hostilities, and taboos, and provides for a public-private affirmation that such activities are acceptable—providing that an appropriate balance (e.g., between kidding versus hurting, between social commentary versus prejudice, between controlled fantasy versus madness) is maintained.

Fisher and Fisher (1983) attempt to show that the comedians and clowns of today function in ways that are similar to the ceremonial fools, clowns, and court jesters of antiquity (cf: Fisher & Fisher, 1981; Rogers, 1979; Willeford, 1969). Fisher and Fisher (1983) discuss the following topics and questions concerning comedy and comics: Who are the comics of the world? What are their origins? What motivates comics? Do comics have identifiable psychopathologies and personality patterns different from noncomic individuals? Fisher and Fisher conclude that while there are still few systematic studies of comics, enough data have been collected to give a preliminary picture of comedian's/comic's important attitudes and defenses (cf: Charney, 1983; Cohen, 1981; Fry & Allen, 1975; Janus, 1975; Janus, Bess, & Janus, 1978; Lanyi, 1977; Makarius, 1970; Salameh, 1980; Tynan, 1979; Wilde, 1973; Willhelm & Sjoberg, 1958). Specifically, comedians (both in their consciously enunciated values and in their projective fantasies) seem to have a preoccupation with morality and a sense of obligation to do good; when they encounter the tragic, comedians are highly motivated to negate it and transmute it into something pleasant and funny.

Further, the humor of comedians may be seen as a strategy for soothing people and for denying the threats found in life. In terms of developmental-personality dynamics, many comics' mothers seem to have communicated to them the paradoxical notion that although they were children they were not to behave like children; however, Fisher and Fisher (1983) note that there is as yet no good evidence that comedians conform to any particular personality pattern or profile.

HUMOR AS SATIRE/IRONY/SARCASM/FARCE/PARODY

We have somehow to face the undoubted fact that we all resent being laughed at. The surest way to an understanding of this fact lies through an examination of satire . . . Satire is a weapon of offence, used originally for private quarrels. It is a weapon forged by hate.
—J. Y. T. Greig, 1923/1969

The purpose of satire is, through laughter and invective, to cure folly and punish evil.
—G. Highet, 1962

Satire is, like comedy and tragedy, a very ancient form which appears to have its roots in primitive ritual activities such as formulaic curses and the magical blasting of personal and tribal enemies.
—A. P. Kernan, 1971

Humour without satire is, strictly speaking, a perversion, the misuse of a sense. Laughter is a deadly explosive which was meant to be wrapped up in the cartridge of satire, and so, aimed unerringly at its appointed target, deal its salutary wound; humour without satire is a flash in the pan; it may be pretty to look at, but it is, in truth, a waste of ammunition . . . The humorist, in short, is a satirist out of a job; he does not fit into the scheme of things; the world passes him by.

—R. A. Knox, 1971

The emotions that are thought to give rise to satire are generally acknowledged to be the least admirable human emotions—anger, malice, hatred, indignation . . . There is no accepted definition of what satire is, only general dictionary descriptions . . . Satire incorporates into itself such modes as farce, parody, black humor, burlesque, travesty, dadaism, the grotesque, and surrealism, all of which are either inherently comic or contain strong tendencies in that direction.

—G. A. Test, 1991

Webster's (1993) defines *satire* as

an ancient Roman verse commentary on a prevailing vice or folly; a topical literary composition holding up human or individual vices, folly, abuses, or shortcomings to censure by means of ridicule, derision, burlesque, irony, or other method sometimes with an intent to bring about improvement.

The New Encyclopaedia Britannica (1997, Vol. 10, *Micropaedia*) defines *satire* in exactly the same way as does *Webster's* (1993), and adds that although there are examples of satire in ancient Greek literature (notably the comic plays of Aristophanes), the great Roman poets Horace and Juvenal (using different perspectives of form—the satire of Horace is mild, gently amused, yet sophisticated, while that of Juvenal is vitriolic and replete with moral indignation) established the genre known as the formal verse satire that exerted a pervasive influence on all subsequent literary satire.

Webster's New Universal Unabridged Dictionary (1989) defines *satire* as "the use of irony, sarcasm, ridicule, or the like, in exposing, denouncing, or deriding vice, folly, etc.; a literary composition, in verse or prose, in which human folly and vice are held up to scorn, derision, or ridicule."

In *Webster's* (1989), the term *irony* is given as a synonym for *satire*, and a distinction is made between *satire* (a general term that emphasizes the weakness more than the weak person, and usually implies moral judgment and corrective purpose) and the term *lampoon* (refers to a form of satire, often political or personal, characterized by the malice or virulence of its attack).

Webster's (1989) defines *irony* as "a figure of speech in which the literal meaning of a locution is the opposite of that intended, especially as in the Greek sense when the locution understates the effect intended."

The New Encyclopaedia Britannica (1997; Vol. 6, *Micropaedia*) notes that the term *irony* has its roots in the Greek comic character Eiron, a clever underdog, who by his wit repeatedly triumphs over the boastful character Alazon; the

Socratic irony of the Platonic dialogues derives from this comic origin; the nonliterary use of irony is usually considered to be *sarcasm*.

Baldwin (1901–1905) defines *irony* (from the Greek word meaning "a dissembler") as "an assumed ignorance with an implied conscious superiority"; and, also, *romantic irony* as "an aesthetic standpoint which emphasizes the artist's or critic's self-consciousness as the only reality and standard, and from this position of superiority regards the world of so-called reality, with its laws, morality, etc., as futile, unreal, and illusory."

The term *Socratic irony* is defined (*Webster's*, 1989) as "pretended ignorance in discussion" (cf: *Socratic method*—the use of questions, as employed by Socrates, to develop a latent idea, as in the mind of a student, or to elicit admissions, as from an opponent, tending to establish a proposition), and *dramatic irony* is defined as "irony that is inherent in speeches or a situation, understood by the audience but not grasped by the characters of the play." Moreover, the synonymous terms *irony, sarcasm,* and *satire* are compared and distinguished: the essential feature of *irony* is the indirect presentation of a contradiction between an action or expression and the context in which it occurs (in the figure of speech, emphasis is placed on the opposition between the literal and intended meaning of a statement—one thing is said, but its opposite is implied); *irony* differs from *sarcasm* in greater subtlety and wit; in *sarcasm* ridicule or mockery is used harshly, often crudely and contemptuously, for destructive purposes; the distinctive quality of *sarcasm* is present in the spoken word and manifested chiefly by vocal inflection, whereas *satire* and *irony*, arising originally as rhetorical and literary forms, are shown in the organization or structuring of either language or literary material; *satire* usually implies the use of *sarcasm* or *irony* for critical purposes, or censure, and is often directed at institutions, public figures, conventional behavior, or political situations (cf: "satire and irony" in Test, 1991, pp. 250–256; "sarcasm and the irony of fate" in Eastman, 1937, p. 238; "understatement as a weapon: irony" in Eastman, 1937, p. 226; Gruner, 1967, 1971; Kernan, 1965; Smith & White, 1965; J. Sutherland, 1958).

Webster's Dictionary of Word Origins (1995) notes that the term satire is derived from Latin and the Middle French (A.D. 1300–1600) words *satira, satura* (satirical poetry, poetic medley), and *lanx satura* (full plate, plate filled with fruits; mixture, medley). *Webster's* (1995) also notes that when it made its appearance in English in the 16th century, the word *satire* had a meaning closely related to the senses in which it is still used today. It was a term for a literary work holding up human follies and vices to scorn or ridicule, and though no longer necessarily literary, the function of *satire* remains much the same (cf: Feinberg, 1965, 1967; Highet, 1962; Hodgart, 1969; Paulson, 1971). The term *farce* involves a culinary metaphor within a literary context (i.e., "poetic medley"; "a plate filled with various fruits or a dish made from a mixture of many ingredients") that is similar to that of *satire*: in the 14th century, the French word *farce* was borrowed into English as *farse* with its meaning of "force-meat," "stuffing," or "to stuff." The comedic use of *farce* derives from another sense of the word in early French: Latin liturgical texts (e.g., the chanted parts of the Mass) were interpolated often with explanatory or hortatory phrases, frequently in the vernacular language; thus, a similarity may be observed between the culinary stuffing and the interlarding of liturgical texts. Later, in the 15th century, this sense of *farce* was extended to include the impromptu buffoonery that was interpolated by actors into the texts of religious plays; in the 16th century, in England, the *farce* became popular as a short dramatic work whose sole purpose was to provoke laughter, and it has continued to flourish up to today as a broadly satirical comedy with absurdly laughable plots (cf: Ashton, 1968).

Webster's (1989) defines *parody* as "a humorous or satirical imitation of a serious piece of literature or writing; a burlesque imitation of a musical composition; a poor or feeble imitation; travesty."

Dane (1988, p. 4) suggests that "*parody* is the imitative reference of one literary text to another, often with an implied critique of the object text." The imitations found in parodies are seemingly accurate but, in fact, they are distorted with recognizable and conscious efforts toward humor (cf: Eastman, 1937, p. 175). Dane asserts further that *parody* is "parasitic" of its objects (and, thus, cannot be described formally) and, also, that it is a "meta-literary" genre (and, thus, is a form of literary criticism).

Fowler (1971, p. 114) provides a useful tabular statement (a "mechanical device of parallel classification") concerning the distinctions between the words *humour, wit, satire, sarcasm, invective, irony, cynicism*, and the *sardonic*. In terms, respectively, of the four dimensions of motive/aim, province, method/means, and audience, each of the words may be characterized. For example, the motive/aim aspect or feature of *humour* is "discovery," its province is "human nature," its method/means is "observation," and its audience is "the sympathetic." The four aspects of *wit* are "throwing light," "words/ideas," "surprise," and "the intelligent." The four features of *satire* are "amendment," "morals/manners," "accentuation," and "the self-satisfied." The four aspects of *sarcasm* are "inflicting pain," "faults/foibles," "inversion," and "the victim/ bystander." The four features of *invective* are "discredit," "misconduct," "direct statement," and "the public." The four aspects of *irony* are "exclusiveness," "statement of facts," "mystification," and "an inner circle." The four features of *cynicism* are "self-justification," "morals," "exposure of nakedness," and "the respectable." The four aspects of the *sardonic* are "self-relief," "adversity," "pessimism," and "self."

Harris and Levey (1975) note that *satire* is a term applied to any work of literature or art whose objective is ridicule, and suggest that *satire* is more easily recognized than defined (cf: Bergler's, 1956, Chapter 6, pp. 182–191, "Irony,

Sarcasm, 'Life's Little Ironies,' Cynicism, Repartee"; Eastman's, 1937, Chapter 3, Part 7, pp. 262–271, "Satire and Sympathetic Humour"; Elliott's, 1960, Chapter 2, pp. 49–99, "Satire and Magic: Theory"; and Gruner's, 1978, Chapter 6, pp. 119–206, "Humor, Satire, Schmatire: Persuasive?"). Further, Harris and Levey (1975, p. 2430) give a literary history of satire extending from the early Greek dramatist Aristophanes to the 20th-century contemporary satirists Thurber, Huxley, Auden, and Roth (cf: a full treatment of *satire* in *The New Encyclopaedia Britannica*, 1997, Vol. 23, *Macropaedia*, Literature—The Art of, pp. 173–176).

Within the psychological literature, in his book on the psychology of laughter and comedy, Greig (1923/1969, pp. 174–198) includes a chapter on "satire and humour" in which he covers the topics of derision (distinguishing *laughter* which involves both sides of our face from *scorn/sneer* which involves only one side of our face); the genesis of satire (the satirist makes it appear that his private quarrel is really a public one); supplementary laughter in satire (laughter is not the chief aim of the satirist, nor is the effect of great satire to provoke loud laughter); satires on religion (antireligious satires and the "alternative moods" of laughter); caricature and parody (the stock method of caricature is exaggeration; of the two possible kinds of exaggeration—upwards or downwards—only the downwards kind excites laughter; caricature and parody lose their effect when the original, or object of attack, is not well known); irony (of all the methods of satire, none is more effective generally than irony; it is ambivalence reduced to a technique); the sting in laughter (it is when we interpret the laugh as evidence of hostility or hate that it is so bitter); laughter as a corrective (there is only one sure way of avoiding the unpleasantness of being laughed at, and that is to avoid doing the things that the laughter depends on); humour (the great humorists do not laugh, but the possibility of laughter is in them because they gaze steadily on the contradictions of life and its pleasures and distresses).

Also, within the older psychological literature, Hall and Allin (1897) note that *satire* caricatures on a basis of truth much like humor does, but with the opposite effect of destroying sympathy and evoking contempt and aversion from, perhaps, the same qualities that humor inclines one to love. Satire comes into fruition and power much later in life and at a more advanced stage of culture and civilization; its features are more often those of defects or active sins than of mere eccentricities. The laugh that satire evokes is bitter because the associative scorn and contempt are merited; it is a mode in which an old culture, consciousness, or civilization begins to be sloughed off or molted to make room for a better one. Therefore, the laugh of satire is never very hearty, but is somewhat forced, even when brightened by wit. According to Hall and Allin, if satire deepens into cynicism or misanthropy, it may as readily evoke tears as laughter. Another related phenomenon, *sarcasm*, is "one of the stings of satire," and is very rarely observed among younger children—it implies a stronger sense of evil than the young child has yet developed. In applied settings, Hall and Allin (1897, p. 26) maintain that sarcasm should be used very seldomly by parents and teachers on children because "while it very rarely excites laughter, it is very prone to rankle and fester in the soul for a long time afterward."

HUMOR AS RIDDLES/PUNS/JOKES

> The day may come when some insuppressible classificator, a kind of scholastic jocularly entomologist . . . will go about collecting all the different kinds of jokes and puns and whims and twits and follies . . . that the ingenious hand of evolution may unfold, pin them down in a great book with names derived from the all-suffering Latin . . . and so endow the mighty steel-ribbed shelves of the libraries of this world with a new and monumental science.
>
> —M. Eastman, 1921

> First guy: "My dog's got no nose."
> Second guy: "How does he smell?"
> First guy: "Awful."
> —*Monty Python's Flying Circus*, 1969

> Dissecting humor (jokes) is an interesting operation in which the patient usually dies.
> —A. A. Berger, 1976

> The definition of the joke clearly implies that amusement, rather than laughter or smiling or physiological change, is the most significant response to humour.
> —C. P. Wilson, 1979

> Puns are bastards, immigrants, barbarians, extra-terrestrials: they intrude, they infiltrate.
> —W. D. Redfern, 1984

> It is only those unable to pun well who "look down" on punning.
> —C. R. Gruner, 1997

Webster's (1993) defines the word *riddle* (Middle English *redels, redel, ridel*, from Old English *raedels, raedelse*—opinion, conjecture, riddle; akin to Middle High German *ratsel*—riddle; Old English *raedan*—to advise, interpret) as a noun, and linguistic device, as: "A mystifying, misleading, or puzzling question posed as a problem to be solved or guessed often as a game: conundrum, enigma, something or someone difficult to understand: a problematic event, situation, or person: mystery."

Harris and Levey (1975) describe *riddle* as a "puzzling question, specifically one that consists of a fanciful description or definition of something to be guessed" (p. 2324), and offer the following examples of famous/classical riddles: The Sphinx's riddle asks, "What goes on four legs in the morning, on two at noon, on three at night?" (Oedipus answered correctly: "Man—in infancy he crawls; at his prime he walks; in old age he leans on a staff"); Samson's riddle (Judges 14:14) states, "Out of the eater came forth meat, and out of the strong came forth sweetness" (this refers to a lion Samson had just killed, on which he saw bees and honey; he ate some of the lion and the honey); the punning riddle, "When is a door not a door?" is answered, "When it's ajar." Harris and Levey note that there is comparatively little riddle literature (cf: Pepicello, 1989), but riddles do figure prominently in Old English; the "Exeter Book" (compiled about A.D. 975 by Bishop Leofric and given to Exeter Cathedral) contains many English verse riddles of uncertain date, and they vary considerably in subject matter; there are also many riddles in Latin hexameters dating from Anglo-Saxon England (5th–6th centuries A.D.). [Notes: For various articles on the topic of riddles, see the *Journal of American Folklore* and the *Journal of the Folklore Institute*; also, see Garth (1920, 1935); Maranda (1971, 1976); Prentice & Fatham (1975); Roberts & Forman (1971); Scott (1963a,b, 1965); Sein & Dundes (1964); Shultz (1974); Sutton-Smith (1975); Taylor (1943, 1944, 1951).]

The New Encyclopaedia Britannica (1997, Vol. 10, *Micropaedia*) describes the term *riddle*—a form of guessing game that has been a part of the folklore of most cultures from ancient times—as a deliberately enigmatic or ambiguous question requiring a thoughtful and often witty answer. Various types of riddle may be distinguished: the descriptive riddle—which describes an animal, person, or object in an intentionally enigmatic way to suggest something different from the correct answer (e.g., "What runs about all day and lies under the bed at night?" Answer: "a shoe"); the shrewd/witty question riddle (e.g., "What is the strongest of all things?" Answer: "Love; iron is strong, but the blacksmith is stronger, and love can overcome the blacksmith"); the punning riddle (e.g., "What's black and white and red all over?" Answer: "A newspaper"); the paradoxical riddle (e.g., "What grows bigger the more you take from it?" Answer: "A hole"); and the classroom/ "catch" riddle (e.g., "What is in the middle of Paris?" Answer: "r"). Perhaps riddles embody the type of humor that Eastman (1921, p. 86) calls the "nameless little light-winged forms of 'smile talk' that the ingenious hand of evolution unfolds." *Webster's* (1993) defines the noun *pun* (most likely from the Italian *puntiglio*—quibble, fine point) as: "The humorous use of a word in such a way as to suggest different meanings or applications or of words having the same or nearly the same sound but different meanings: a play on words."

Harris and Levey (1975) describe *pun* as the use of words, usually humorous, based on (a) the several meanings of one word; (b) a similarity of meaning between words that are pronounced the same, or (c) the difference in meanings between two words pronounced the same and spelled somewhat similarly (e.g., "They went and told the sexton and the sexton tolled the bell"). Puns have been used, also, in more serious contexts, such as in the Bible [e.g., Matthew 16:18, "Thou art Peter (Greek: *Petros*), and upon this rock (Greek: *petra*) I will build my church"]. In this last regard, Hayford (1991) provides an interesting commentary on Matthew 16:18; he states that the *rock* is not Peter as an individual, because Jesus substituted the word *petra* (a foundation rock or boulder) for *petros* (a fragment of the *petra*). Jesus may have meant that He Himself is the Rock *(petra)* upon which the church is built (cf: 1 Corinthians 3:10, 11; 10:4), and that the church is built out of those stones *(petroi)* that partake of the nature of the *petra* by their confession of faith in Him (cf: 1 Peter 2:5). Peter, therefore, according to Hayford, is the first of many building stones in the church.

Redfern (1984) asserts that the wordplay known as *puns* illuminates the nature of language in general, and that punsters "practise linguistic serendipity" (p. 9). Redfern asks (p. 175), "Why defend wordplay?" and answers, "Play is indefensible; it simply is." According to Redfern, punning is a "free-for-all" available to everyone, and is common property—it is a "democratic trope." Punning is the stock-in-trade of the lowest comedian and, also, of the most sophisticated wordsmith (cf: Eastman, 1937, pp. 133–166; Davis, 1954). Moreover, punning—like laughter itself—is good for the person; it need not involve explosive noise or even movement of the muscles of the eyes, cheeks, lips, chest, or stomach—with puns one may simply and salubriously laugh in the mind (cf: Redfern, 1996). Concerning the writing style of his book on puns, Redfern (1984, p. 183) notes that his approach or tone jumps between academic pedantry, journalese, and the gutter; between a proper pedestrian and a jaywalker ("an approach," says Redfern, "that has, like elephants' foreskins, enormous drawbacks").

Gruner (1997) observes that the Greeks used the word *paronomasia* ("equal word") for what we today call a *pun*. Three major kinds of puns (cf: Lederer, 1988) are: the *homograph* ("same writing") which employs a word or words with two or more meanings (the multiple meanings are represented by the same word, spelled the same way; e.g., "How did Samson die?" Answer: "From fallen *arches*"; or "The girl wished her boyfriend would give her a *ring*"); the *homophone* ("same sound") which combines two words of different meanings *and* spellings but which sound alike (e.g., "The man with a squeaking shoe became a songwriter because he had music in his *sole*"); and the *double-sound pun* which may be a word that *puns* on a *pun* (e.g., the title of Richard Lederer's, 1988, book is *Get Thee to a Punnery*; the word "punnery" is a pun on "nunnery" which, again, is a pun on Hamlet's use of "nunnery" that, in his time, could mean either a "house of ill refute"—as Archie Bunker calls it—or "housing for nuns"). Gruner argues that the pun descended from the *conundrum* ("punning riddle"; e.g., "What kind of doctor does an elephant with a skin disorder go to?" Answer: "a pachydermitologist") which, in turn, descended from the common *riddle* (e.g., the pun, as an abbreviated riddle, may be observed in the query, "Hear about the termite who entered a tavern and asked, 'Is the bar tender here?'"). Gruner's thesis is that all humor, including puns ("the special case of puns: word*play* is a game to be won, too"), is a succession of games; the very idea of games implies fun, leisure, entertainment, recreation, and affable human interaction, but it also implies—according to Gruner—a sort of competition, the notion of keeping score, and a winner/loser outcome (cf: Rapp, 1947, p. 212, who observes that laughter commonly accompanies the solution of riddles, and that the typical riddle is a deliberately staged *contest* of wit in which there is a *winner*—the one who laughs, and a *loser*—the one who is embarrassed).

Webster's (1993) defines the noun *joke* (from Latin *jocus*—jest, joke, game; akin to Old Saxon *gehan*—to say, speak; Old High German *gehan, jehan*—to say, speak; Middle Welsh *ieith*—language; Tocharian A/B *yask*—to demand, beg; Sanskrit *yacati*—he implores; speaking) as: "Something said or done to amuse or provoke laughter: something funny or humorous, especially a brief, usually oral, narrative designed to provoke laughter and typically having a climactic humorous twist or denouement." Synonyms for *joke* include *jest, jape, quip, witticism, wisecrack, crack*, and *gag*, but slight distinctions may be made among these terms.

The term *joke*—when applied to a story or remark—suggests something designed to promote good humor, especially an anecdote with a humorous twist at the end; when applied to an action, it often signifies a practical joke, usually suggesting a fooling or deceiving of someone at his or her expense, generally though not necessarily good humored in intent (e.g., "Did you know that black horses eat more than white horses?" "No, I didn't," "Yes, because there are more black horses!"). The term *jest*, in an older sense, connotes raillery or sarcasm, but generally today suggests humor that is light and sportive, as in banter. The word *jape*, usually of literary occurrence, originally signified an amusing anecdote but today is identical with *jest* or *joke*. Further, according to *Webster's* (1993), the term *quip* suggests a quick, neatly turned, witty remark; the word *witticism* is a bookish/literary term; and *wisecrack/crack* is a more general term for a clever or witty (especially a biting or sarcastic) remark or retort. The term *gag*, originally signifying an interpolated joke or laugh-provoking piece of business, more generally today applies to any remark, story, or piece of business considered funny, especially one written into a theatrical, movie, radio, or television script, and sometimes has its meaning extended to signify any trick, whether funny or not, but usually one considered as foolish (*Webster's*, 1993).

Other synonyms for *joke* (*Webster's*, 1989) are *prank, quirk, sally*, and *raillery* [cf: C. P. Wilson's (1979) account of jokes, including the topics of the theory and form of jokes, amusement and the content/form of jokes, the mechanisms of the joke, and the personal/social functions of joking; and Apte's (1985) anthropological account of jokes in his chapter on "Joking Relationships"; also, see Godkewitsch (1972); MacHovec (1988, pp. 9–12) on "joke-smithing"; Freud (1905/1916/1960) on the functions of jokes; Hall & Allin (1897, pp. 22–24) on "practical jokes"; Handelman & Kapferer (1972) on "comparative forms of joking"; Legman (1968, 1975) on the "dirty joke"; Lundberg (1969) on "person-focused joking"; Shultz & Horibe (1974) on "verbal joke appreciation"; and Wolfenstein (1953) on "children's understanding of jokes"; cf: Oring (1989), Zhao (1988)].

In his notable book on humor, Eastman (1921) includes a chapter called "Good and Bad Jokes"; (cf: Eastman, 1937, Chapter 6, Part 7, "Risque and Ribald Jokes: Freud's Theory") in which he describes eight so-called "laws" of a code for serious joke-makers. Law Number One (p. 88) states that: "There must be a real engagement of the interest of the person who is expected to laugh." Law Number Two (p. 92) says that: "The feelings aroused in the person who is expected to laugh must not be too strong and deep." Law Number Three (p. 96) posits that: "Both the negative and the positive current of feeling must be simply and naturally induced." Law Number Four (p. 99) asserts that: "The identity of the positive current with the negative must be immediate and perfect." Law Number Five (p. 104) states that: "Practical jokes should not be poetically told, nor poetic jokes practically told." Law Number Six (p. 106) states that: "The disappointment involved in a practical joke should be genuine." Law Number Seven (p. 111) declares that: "The interest satisfied must not be too weak in proportion to the interest disappointed." Law Number Eight (p. 116) says that: "The interest disappointed must not be too strong in proportion to the interest satisfied."

Eastman (1921, p. 116) maintains that Law Number Eight is the most significant of all the eight "laws" because its purpose is "to protect the free citizen against sudden aggression and violation in any mortal part of the poetry of his life at the hands of the 'flippant' joker." To Eastman, a "flippant" joker is one who disrupts any strong trend of action or thought/feeling without offering in its place a profound, wise, beautiful, or exciting comment, idea, or vision of life—or even a sincere and contagious contempt of life. In his later book on humor (*Enjoyment of Laughter*), Eastman (1937, pp. 326–363) provides "ten commandments of the comic arts." In this case, Eastman revises his earlier list and adds two missing commandments to the original eight. Briefly, the ten "laws," or commandments, are:

1. Be interesting.
2. Be unimpassioned.
3. Be effortless.
4. Remember the difference between cracking practical jokes and conveying ludicrous impressions.
5. Be plausible.
6. Be sudden.
7. Be neat.
8. Be right with your timing.
9. Give good measure of serious satisfaction (Note: This includes both a *general* and a *specific* "law").
10. Redeem all serious disappointments.

Over two decades ago, a number of articles on the common topic of humor, especially *jokes*, appeared in the same issue of the *Journal of Communication* (1976, Vol. 26), and includes the following selected articles, among others (title of article, authors, and conclusions): "All in the Family: Is Archie Funny?" (S. H. Surlin & E. D. Tate)—concludes that culture, sex, personality, and who is the butt of the joke may all affect audience perception; "Theoretical Notes on Humor" (J. H. Goldstein)—suggests that cognitive balance may explain attitudinal components but self-deprecating jokes indicate a shift in the level of meaning; "Anatomy of the Joke" (A. A. Berger)—presents the use of bipolar oppositions to characterize various approaches involving "incongruity" in humor theories, various techniques of humor (using the dimensions of language, identity, and action), and examples of the structural/analytical elements of a joke (cf: Eastman's, 1937, Chapter 1, Part 8, pp. 315–325, section "To Diagram a Joke"); "Does Ethnic Humor Serve Prejudice?" (L. LaFave & R. Mannell)—concludes that the issues regarding the social psychological functions of ethnic group humor are quite complex, and the evidence appears neither completely on one side nor on the other as to whether ethnic humor serves prejudice; although many ethnic "jokes" exist at the expense of the group, a number of arguments may be made for humanitarian functions of ethnic humor; "The Social Contexts of Humor" (C. Winick)—argues that orally communicated jokes reflect trends in American life and help groups manage social problems of role, power, and conflict; "Joking at Work" (J. A. Ullian)—suggests that the use of banter and joking ("organizational communication") help organizations remain stable in the face of organizational change; "Obscene Joking Across Cultures" (G. A. Fine)—notes that sexual humor often sets and enforces social norms and helps to cope with sexual anxieties; "What is Funny to Whom?" (J. R. Cantor)—concludes from a replication of a 1970 study on the role of gender in humor that it is still funnier to see a woman, rather than a man, as the object or butt of a joke; and "A Process Model of Humor Judgment" (H.

Leventhal & G. Cupchik)—presents a model of humor (cf: Suls', 1972, two-stage model of joke/cartoon appreciation) that incorporates a host of variables simultaneously and allows speculation about their possible interactions and also allows for the evolution of the very same joke in terms of affective or cognitive information depending on the subject and his/her situational set.

HUMOR IN CARICATURE/CARTOONS/COMIC STRIPS/SLAPSTICK

> Caricature may have its root in simple humor, which laughs with the victim, or in satire which laughs at him.
> —G. S. Hall and A. Allin, 1897

> A more immediate precursor of silent film comedy was the knockabout of the music-halls and the clowning of the circus. Indeed, the very word slapstick—most often used to refer to silent film comedy, especially American—comes originally from the theatre.
> —R. Boston, 1974

> Caricature, cartoon (in the satirical sense), and comic strips (including comic books) are related forms. Historically, they arose in the order given, but they all have flourished together. All use the same artistic mediums of drawing and printmaking; caricature and the element of satire are usually present in each.
> —The New Encyclopaedia Britannica, 1997

Webster's (1993) defines the noun caricature (from the Italian caricatura—affectation, caricature; a loading, from caricare—to load, from Late Latin carricare) as "exaggeration by means of deliberate simplification and often ludicrous distortion of parts or characteristics; an instance of such caricature; a representation, especially in literature or art, that has the qualities of caricature; a distortion so gross as to seem like caricature." The synonyms burlesque, parody, and travesty all indicate kinds of grotesque and exaggerated imitation; caricature suggests ludicrous distortion of a particular or peculiar feature; burlesque is likely to imply humor sought or attained in imitation of the dignified, heavy, or grand; parody—like caricature—involves the heightening of a peculiar feature and—like burlesque—is likely to aim at humor; parody may differ from caricature in attempting less obvious and pictorial and more sustained and subtle imitation, and from burlesque in aiming at a quieter, less boisterous effect; travesty is perhaps the strongest word in the group—it may apply to any palpably extravagant imitation designed to mock and is consistently sustained, especially in stylistic matters. All these terms may be used in reference to a situation that contains grotesque distortion (cf: Papp, 1992).

Harris and Levey (1975) describe *caricature* as "a satirical drawing, plastic representation, or description which, through gross exaggeration of natural features, makes its subject appear ridiculous" (p. 457). [Notes: See Paul Gaultier (1906) who gives an account of laughter provoked by caricature; cf: Ashbee (1928); Asher & Sargent (1941); Kris (1936); Kris & Gombrich (1938); Parton (1877); Rosen (1963); Stuart (1964).] Harris and Levey note that although certain 16th-century Northern painters (e.g., Holbein, Bruegel, Bosch) employed various elements of caricature, no comic tradition was established until the 17th century (in the work of the Carracci, a family of Italian painters of the Bolognese school); in the 18th century, caricature flourished in England (in the works of Hogarth, Rowlandson, and Gillray). Subsequently, the genre expanded to include social, political, and personal satire, developing into the art of the "cartoon." In literature, caricature has been a popular form of expression since the ancient Greeks (through verbal distortion and exaggeration the writer achieves an immediate, comic, often satiric, effect; the most notable literary caricaturist of any period, most likely, is Charles Dickens).

Webster's (1993) defines the noun *cartoon* (from the Italian *cartone*—pasteboard, cartoon; augmentative of *carta*—card) as

a preparatory design, drawing, or painting (as for a fresco, painting, mosaic, or tapestry); especially, a drawing in full size, usually on paper which is traced or copied on a surface to be used for a final work; a drawing that is often symbolic and usually intended as humor, caricature, or satire and comments on public, and usually political, matters; comic; animated cartoon.

Harris and Levey (1975) describe *cartoon* as a full-sized preliminary drawing for a final work to be executed subsequently (cf: Ehrle & Johnson, 1961; Fuller, 1972; Harrison, 1981; Hines, 1933). For works of glass/mosaic, the final material is cut exactly according to the patterns taken from the cartoons, while in the case of tapestry the cartoon is inserted beneath the warp to serve as a guide; in fresco painting the lines of the cartoon are perforated and transferred to the plaster surface by "pouncing" (i.e., dusting with powder through the perforations). In England in 1843, a series of drawings appeared in the magazine *Punch* that parodied the fresco cartoons submitted in a competition for the decoration of the new Houses of Parliament. Thus, the term *cartoon*, in journalistic contexts, came to mean any single humorous or satirical drawing employing distortion for emphasis, and often was accompanied by a caption (cf: Eastman, 1937; Reifers, 1981).

Harris and Levey (1975) note that cartoons, particularly editorial or political cartoons, make use of the elements of caricature. The political cartoon first appeared in 16th-century Germany during the Reformation, and this was the first time that such art became an active propaganda weapon having social implications. By the mid-19th century, editorial cartoons had become regular features in American newspapers and were followed soon by humorous cartoons and sports cartoons. Harris and Levey note that humorous nonpolitical cartoons became popular with the development of the color press; in 1893, the first color cartoon appeared in the *New York World*; and in 1896, R. F. Outcault originated *The Yellow Kid*, a large single-panel cartoon with some use of dialogue in balloons.

The *Academic American Encyclopedia* (1998, pp. 140–141) notes that James Swinnerton's cartoon strip "The Little Bears and Tigers," run by the *San Francisco Examiner* in 1892, was the first newspaper comic strip. The first successful comic series was Outcault's "Down in Hogan's Alley," which debuted July 7, 1895, in the *New York World* and depicted life in an urban slum. Its central character was called "The Kid" (a bald, impish tyke with a knowing grin)—later, in 1896, called "The Yellow Kid" when the printer applied yellow ink to the Kid's nightshirt. A subsequent rivalry between the newspapermen William Randolph Hearst (*New York Journal*) and Joseph Pulitzer (*New York World*) inspired the term *yellow journalism* which referred to sensational journalistic practices. The first comic strip to make regular use of "speech balloons" was Rudolph Dirk's "The Katzenjammer Kids," which first appeared in 1897. George McManus pioneered the domestic comic strip in 1904 ("Newlyweds") and 1913 ("Bringing Up Father") with the characters "Maggie and Jiggs." In 1908, Bud Fisher's "Mutt and Jeff" became one of the first comic strips to appear in a daily newspaper.

The *World Book Encyclopedia* (1999, p. 870) notes that the first American *comic books*, such as "Famous Funnies" (first sold in 1934), were collections of popular newspaper strips; "Superman" was the first popular comics "superhero," a character with extraordinary powers (he first appeared in a 1938 comic book called "Action Comics").

Harris and Levey (1975, p. 608) observe that, as a form of communication, the *comic strip* (the "comics") medium goes back to the Middle Ages with the Bayeux Tapestry that retraces the hostilities leading to the Battle of Hastings (October 14, 1066) between the Normans and the Anglo-Saxons. In addition to Harris and Levey's full account and history of the *comic strip*, the section on "Caricature, Cartoon, and Comic Strip" in *The New Encyclopaedia Britannica* (1997, Vol. 15, *Macropaedia*, pp. 539–552) is noteworthy especially, and provides excellent material on these forms of humorous expression. The entries in the *Academic American Encyclopedia* (1998, pp. 140–142), and *The World Book Encyclopedia* (1999, Vol. 4, pp. 869–870), for the terms *comics, comic strip(s)*, and *comic books* are also good sources of information on these topics (cf: Frank, 1944; Hoult, 1949).

The term *slapstick* (from "slap" + "stick"), as a noun, is defined in *Webster's* (1993) as a device consisting of two flat pieces of wood fastened together at one end but loose at the other and sometimes used by an actor in farce to make a loud noise in simulation of a severe blow; any of several similar devices, as two flat pieces of leather sewed together, weighted at the hitting end, and used as a club; a stick hinged on one side to the top of a slate and clapped against the top to mark on a sound track the beginning of a movie take; a comedy that depends for its effect on fast, boisterous, and zany physical activity and horseplay (as the throwing of pies, the whacking of posteriors with a slapstick, chases, mugging) often accompanied by broad obvious rowdy verbal humor; humor, language, or activity like that in slapstick comedy; a flat strip of wood upon which an abrasive (as a piece of emery paper) is fixed for use in polishing or finishing work.

Webster's Dictionary of Word Origins (1995) notes that the term slapstick (a type of broad physical comedy) derives from a device invented in Italy during the 16th century, although this kind of comedy is probably as old as the theater itself. The "rough-and-tumble" school of comedy dates back to the Greco-Roman theater where heavily padded clowns got laughs by boisterously trading blows; the tradition of outrageous mock violence continued into the Renaissance period, when it became a feature of the Italian "commedia dell'arte." [Note: An interesting modern-day variation of this type of activity seems to be manifest in the mock battles of the "wrestlers" who perform regularly on American television.]

One of the favorite "weapons" for making comic mischief in the Italian comedies was a paddle which consisted of two slats of wood fastened together at one end; when wielded with feigned force against some surface (such as the posterior of someone bent over), the two slats slapped together produced a startling "whack" sound suggestive of a powerful blow. In the late 19th century, with the physical ("knockabout") comedy tradition appearing in the English music halls and the American vaudeville and variety shows, the double-slatted paddle became known in English as the *slapstick*. At the turn of the 20th century, the term *slapstick* even came to be applied to literature and other art forms in which the attempt at humor was judged to be lacking in subtlety or delicacy.

The desire in audiences for broad physical/knockabout comedy coincided with the birth of the "silent film," the medium with which *slapstick* is most often associated. *The New Encyclopaedia Britannica* (1997, Vol. 10, *Micropaedia*, p. 872) notes that the best of the *slapstick* comedians (e.g., George Formby, Gracie Fields, Charlie Chaplin, Harold Lloyd, Mack Sennett's "Keystone Kops," Laurel and Hardy, The Marx Brothers, The Three Stooges) may be said to have turned "low humour" into "high art." [Notes: For the employment of *slapstick* movie and cartoon material in a psychological study, see Leventhal & Cupchik (1976); cf: Leventhal & Mace, 1970; and for an extended discussion of *slapstick* comedy, and comedians, see Boston's (1974, Chapter 6) "The Age of Slapstick"; also, see Eastman's (1937, Chapter 5, Part 7) "Slapstick and Aggressive Humour."]

REFERENCES

Academic American Encyclopedia. (1998). Danbury, CT: Grolier.

Allin, A. (1903). On laughter. *The Psychological Review, 10*, 306–315.

Apte, M. (1985). *Humor and laughter: An anthropological approach.* Ithaca, NY: Cornell University Press.

Armstrong, M. (1928). *Laughing: An essay.* New York: Harper.

Ashbee, C. R. (1928). *Caricature.* London: Chapman & Hall.

Asher, R., & Sargent, S. (1941). Shifts in attitude change caused by cartoon caricatures. *Journal of General Psychology, 24*, 451–455.

Ashton, J. (1968). *Humor, wit, and satire of the 17th century.* New York: Dover.

Baldwin, J. M. (Ed.) (1901–1905). *Dictionary of philosophy and psychology.* 4 Vols. New York: Macmillan.

Bawdon, H. H. (1910). The comic as illustrating the summation-irradiation theory of pleasure-pain. *Psychological Review, 17*, 336–346.

Berger, A. A. (1976). Anatomy of the joke. *Journal of Communication, 26*, 113–115.

Berger, A. A. (1987). Humor: An introduction. *American Behavioral Scientist, 30*, 6–15.

Bergler, E. (1956). *Laughter and the sense of humor.* New York: Intercontinental Medical Book Corporation.

Bergson, H. (1911). *Laughter: An essay on the meaning of the comic.* New York: Macmillan.

Berkowitz, G. M. (1999). Comedy. In *The World Book Encyclopedia.* Vol. 4. Chicago: World Book.

Berlyne, D. E. (1969). Laughter, humor, and play. In G. Lindzey & E. Aronson (Eds.), *The handbook of social psychology.* (Vol. 3.) Reading, MA: Addison-Wesley.

Bischoff, L. (1964). *Interpreting personality theories.* New York: Harper & Row.

Bliss, S. H. (1915). The origin of laughter. *The American Journal of Psychology, 26*, 236–246.

Boston, R. (1974). *An anatomy of laughter.* London: Collins.

Brackett, C. W. (1933). Laughing and crying of preschool children. *Journal of Experimental Education, 2*, 119–126.

Brackett, C. W. (1934). Laughing and crying of preschool children: A study of the social and emotional behavior of young children as indicated by crying and laughing. *Child Development Monographs, 14*, 1–91.

Brill, A. A. (Ed.) (1938). *The basic writings of Sigmund Freud.* New York: Random House.

Brody, M. W. (1950). The meaning of laughter. *Psychoanalytic Quarterly, 19*, 192–201.

Bruno, F. J. (1986). *Dictionary of key words in psychology.* London: Routledge & Kegan Paul.

Burton, W. E. (Ed.) (1872). *The cyclopaedia of wit and humor; containing choice and characteristic selections from the writings of the most eminent humorists of America, Ireland, Scotland, and England.* New York: D. Appleton.

Castell, P. J., & Goldstein, J. H. (1977). Social occasions for joking: A cross-cultural study. In A. J. Chapman & H. C. Foot (Eds.), *It's a funny thing, humour.* New York: Pergamon.

Chandler, A. R., & Barnhart, E. N. (1938). *A bibliography of psychological and experimental aesthetics.* Berkeley: University of California Press.

Chapman, A. J., & Foot, H. C. (Eds.) (1976). *Humour and laughter: Theory, research, and applications.* London: Wiley.

Chapman, A. J., & Foot, H. C. (Eds.) (1977). *It's a funny thing, humour.* Oxford, UK: Pergamon Press.

Chapman, A. J., & Sheehy, N. P. (1987). Humour. In R. L. Gregory (Ed.), *The Oxford companion to the mind.* Oxford, UK: Oxford University Press.

Charles, L. H. (1945). The clown's function. *Journal of American Folklore, 58,* 25–34.

Charney, M. (1983). Comic creativity in plays, films, and jokes. In P. E. McGhee & J. H. Goldstein (Eds.), *Handbook of humor research* (Vol. 2. *Applied studies*). New York: Springer-Verlag.

Chesterfield, Lord. (1901). *Letters to his son.* London: Dunne.

Claxton, G. (1975). Why can't we tickle ourselves? *Perceptual and Motor Skills, 41,* 335–338.

Clubb, M. D. (1932). A plea for an eclectic theory of humour. *The University of California Chronicle, 34,* 340–356.

Cohen, J. S. (1981). Personality profiles of American comic art professionals. Unpublished doctoral dissertation, United States International University.

Cohn, R. (1951). Forced crying and laughing. *Archives of Neurology and Psychiatry, 66,* 738–743.

Corrigan, R. W., & Loney, G. M. (1971). *Comedy: A critical anthology.* Boston: Houghton Mifflin.

Corsini, R. J. (1999). *The dictionary of psychology.* Philadelphia, PA: Brunner/Mazel.

Crile, G. W. (1916). *Man—An adaptive mechanism.* New York: Macmillan.

Dane, J. A. (1988). *Parody: Critical concepts versus literary practices, Aristophanes to Sterne.* Norman: University of Oklahoma Press.

Darwin, C. (1871). *The descent of man and selection in relation to sex.* London: Murray.

Darwin, C. (1872/1965). *The expression of the emotions in man and animals.* London: Murray; Chicago: University of Chicago Press.

Davis, H. T. (1954). *The fine art of punning.* Evanston, IL: Principia.

Davison, C., & Kelman, H. (1939). Pathologic laughing and crying. *Archives of Neurology and Psychiatry, 42,* 595–643.

Dearborn, G.V. N. (1900). The nature of the smile and the laugh. *Science, 9,* 851–856.

Dewey, J. (1894–1895). The theory of emotion. *Psychological Review, 1,* 553–569.

Ding, G. F., & Jersild, A. T. (1932). A study of the laughing and smiling of preschool children. *The Pedagogical Seminary and Journal of Genetic Psychology, 40,* 452–472.

Diserens, C. M. (1926). Recent theories of laughter. *Psychological Bulletin, 23,* 247–255.

Diserens, C. M., & Bonifield, M. (1930). Humor and the ludicrous. *Psychological Bulletin, 27,* 108–118.

Dobson, K., & Pusch, D. (1994). Psychopathology. In V. S. Ramachandran (Ed.), *Encyclopedia of human behavior.* San Diego, CA: Academic Press.

Douglas, M. (1975). Do dogs laugh? In M. Douglas (Ed.), *Implicit meanings.* London: Routledge & Kegan Paul.

Drever, J. (1917). *Instinct in man.* London: Cambridge University Press.

Drever, J. (1952/1973). *A dictionary of psychology.* Harmondsworth, UK: Penguin.

Eastman, M. (1921). *The sense of humor.* New York: Scribner's.

Eastman, M. (1937). *Enjoyment of laughter.* Kent, UK: Hamish Hamilton.

Eckardt, A. R. (1992). *Sitting in the earth and laughing: A handbook of humor.* New Brunswick, NJ: Transaction.

Edelmann, R. J. (1994). Embarrassment and blushing. In V. S. Ramachandran (Ed.), *Encyclopedia of human behavior.* San Diego, CA: Academic Press.

Edmonson, M. (1952). Los manitos: Patterns of humor in relation to cultural values. Unpublished doctoral dissertation, Harvard University.

Edwards, S. (1926). The function of laughter. *Psyche, 3,* 22–32.

Ehrle, R. A., & Johnson, B. G. (1961). Psychologists and cartoonists. *American Psychologist, 16,* 693–695.

Elliott, R. C. (1960). *The power of satire: Magic, ritual, art.* Princeton, NJ: Princeton University Press.

Enck, J. J., Forter, E. T., & Whitley, A. (1960). *The comic in theory and practice.* Englewood Cliffs, NJ: Prentice-Hall.

Encyclopedia Americana. (1998). International edition. (Vol. 14.) Danbury, CT: Grolier.

Encyclopedia Britannica. (1875/1881). Ninth edition. Edinburgh: A. & C. Black.

Encyclopedia Britannica. (1922). Eleventh edition. New York: Encyclopedia Britannica, Inc.

English, H. B. (1928). *A student's dictionary of psychological terms.* Yellow Springs, OH: Antioch Press.

English, H. B., & English, A. C. (1958/1976). *A comprehensive dictionary of psychological and psychoanalytical terms.* New York: McKay.

Esar, E. (1949). *Dictionary of humorous quotations.* New York: Doubleday.

Esar, E. (1952). *The humor of humor.* New York: Bramhall House.

Escarpit, R. (1963). *L'humour.* Paris: P.U.F.

Eysenck, H. J. (1947). *Dimensions of personality.* London: Routledge & Kegan Paul.

Eysenck, H. J., Arnold, W., & Meili, R. (Eds.) (1972). *Encyclopedia of psychology.* (Vol. 2.) New York: Herder and Herder.

Feibleman, J. (1962). *In praise of comedy: A study in its theory and practice.* New York: Russell & Russell.

Feinberg, L. (1965). *The satirist.* New York: Citadel.

Feinberg, L. (1967). *Introduction to satire.* Ames, IA: State University Press.

Felheim, M. (1962). *Comedy: Plays, theory, and criticism.* New York: Harcourt, Brace.

Fisher, S., & Fisher, R. L. (1981). *Pretend the world is funny and forever: A psychological analysis of comedians, clowns, and actors.* Hillsdale, NJ: Erlbaum.

Fisher, S., & Fisher, R. L. (1983). Personality and psychopathology in the comic. In P. E. McGhee & J. H. Goldstein (Eds.), *Handbook of humor research* (Vol. 2., *Applied studies*). New York: Springer-Verlag.

Flugel, J. C. (1954). Humor and laughter. In G. Lindzey (Ed.), *Handbook of social psychology*. (Vol. 2.) Reading, MA: Addison-Wesley.

Foss, B. (1961). The functions of laughter. *New Scientist, 11,* 20–22.

Fowler, H. W. (1926). *A dictionary of modern English usage.* London: Oxford University Press.

Fowler, H. W. (1971). Humour, wit, satire, etc. In R. Paulson (Ed.), *Satire: Modern essays in criticism.* Englewood Cliffs, NJ: Prentice-Hall.

Frank, J. (1944). What's in the comics? *Journal of Educational Sociology, 18,* 214–222.

Freud, S. (1905/1916/1960). *Der witz und seine beziehung zum unbewussten.* Leipzig: Deuticke; New York: Moffat Ward/Norton.

Freud, S. (1938). Wit and its relation to the unconscious. In A. A. Brill (Ed.), *The basic writings of Sigmund Freud.* New York: Modern Library.

Freud, S. (1959). Humour. In *The Collected papers of Sigmund Freud.* (Vol. 5.) New York: Basic Books.

Fry, W., & Allen, M. (1975). *Make 'em laugh.* Palo Alto, CA: Science & Behavior.

Fuller, R. E. (1972). Headshrinker: The psychiatrist in cartoons. *Bulletin of the Menninger Clinic, 36,* 335–345.

Gall, S. (Ed.) (1996). *The Gale encyclopedia of psychology.* Detroit, MI: Gale Research.

Garth, T. R. (1920). The psychology of riddle solutions. *Journal of Educational Psychology, 11,* 16–33.

Garth, T. R. (1935). Riddles as a mental test. *American Journal of Psychology, 47,* 342–344.

Gaultier, P. (1906). *Le rire et la caricature.* Paris: Hachette.

Ghosh, R. (1939). An experimental study of humour. *British Journal of Educational Psychology, 9,* 98–99.

Giles, H., & Oxford, G. S. (1970). Towards a multidimensional theory of laughter causation and its social implications. *Bulletin of the British Psychological Society, 23,* 97–105.

Ginsburg, H., & Koslowski, B. (1976). Cognitive development. In L. W. Porter & M. R. Rosenzweig (Eds.), *Annual Review of Psychology.* (Vol. 27.) Palo Alto, CA: Annual Reviews Inc.

Godkewitsch, M. (1972). The relationship between arousal potential and funniness of jokes. In J. H. Goldstein & P. E. McGhee (Eds.), *The psychology of humor: Theoretical perspectives and empirical issues.* New York: Academic Press.

Goldenson, R. M. (1970). *The encyclopedia of human behavior.* Garden City, NY: Doubleday.

Goldstein, J. H. (1977). Cross-cultural research: Humour here and there. In A. J. Chapman & H. C. Foot (Eds.), *It's a funny thing, humour.* New York: Pergamon

Goldstein, J. H., & McGhee, P. E. (Eds.) (1972). *The psychology of humor: Theoretical perspectives and empirical issues.* New York: Academic Press.

Goodchilds, J. (1972). On being witty: Causes, correlates, and consequences. In J. H. Goldstein & P. E. McGhee (Eds.), *The psychology of humor: Theoretical perspectives and empirical issues*. New York: Academic Press.

Gregory, J. C. (1923). Some theories of laughter. *Mind, 32*, 328–344.

Gregory, J. C. (1924). *The nature of laughter*. London: Kegan Paul, Trench, Trubner.

Gregory, R. L. (Ed.) (1987). *The Oxford companion to the mind*. Oxford, UK: Oxford University Press.

Greig, J. Y. T. (1923/1969). *The psychology of laughter and comedy*. New York: Dodd-Mead/Cooper Square.

Grotjahn, M. (1957). *Beyond laughter*. New York: McGraw-Hill.

Gruner, C. R. (1965). Is wit to humor what rhetoric is to poetic? *Central States Speech Journal, 16*, 17–22.

Gruner, C. R. (1967). Editorial satire as persuasion: An experiment. *Journalism Quarterly, 44*, 727–730.

Gruner, C. R. (1971). Ad hominem satire as a persuader: An experiment. *Journalism Quarterly, 48*, 128–131.

Gruner, C. R. (1978). *Understanding laughter: The workings of wit and humor*. Chicago: Nelson-Hall.

Gruner, C. R. (1997). *The game of humor: A comprehensive theory of why we laugh*. New Brunswick, NJ: Transaction.

Hall, G. S., & Allin, A. (1897). The psychology of tickling, laughter, and the comic. *American Journal of Psychology, 9*, 1–42.

Handelman, D. (1977). Play and ritual: Complementary frames of meta- communication. In A. J. Chapman & H. C. Foot (Eds.), *It's a funny thing, humour*. New York: Pergamon.

Handelman, D., & Kapferer, B. (1972). Forms of joking activity: A comparative approach. *American Anthropologist, 74*, 484–517.

Hansen, A. J. (1977). Magnificent liars: Exaggeration in American humour. In A. J. Chapman & H. C. Foot (Eds.), *It's a funny thing, humour*. New York: Pergamon.

Harre, R., & Lamb, R. (Eds.) (1983). *The encyclopedic dictionary of psychology*. Cambridge, MA: The M. I. T. Press.

Harriman, P. (1959/1966). *Handbook of psychological terms*. Paterson, NJ: Littlefield, Adams & Co.

Harris, W., & Levey, J. (Eds.) (1975). *The New Columbia Encyclopedia*. New York: Columbia University Press.

Harrison, R. P. (1981). *The cartoon: Communication to the quick*. Newbury Park, CA: Sage.

Hayford, J. W. (Ed.) (1991). *Spirit-filled life Bible: New King James Version*. Nashville, TN: Thomas Nelson.

Hayworth, D. (1928). The social origin and function of laughter. *Psychological Review, 35*, 367–384.

Hazlitt, W. C. (1819). On wit and humour. In *Lectures on the English writers*. London: Taylor.

Hecker, E. (1873). *Die physiologie und psychologie des lachens und des komischen*. Leipzig: Englemann.

Helson, R. (1973). The heroic, the comic, and the tender: Patterns of literary fantasy and their authors. *Journal of Personality, 41*, 163–184.

Herrick, M. T. (1964). *Comic theory in the 16th century*. Urbana: University of Illinois Press.

Herrick, M. T. (1966). *Italian comedy in the Renaissance*. Urbana: University of Illinois Press.

Hertzler, J. O. (1970). *Laughter: A socio-scientific analysis*. New York: Exposition.

Highet, G. (1962). *The anatomy of satire*. Princeton, NJ: Princeton University Press.

Hill, W. W. (1943). Navaho humor. *General Series in Anthropology, 9*. Menasha, WI: G. Banta.

Hines, E. (1933). Cartoons as a means of social control. *Sociology and Social Research, 17*, 454–464.

Hobbes, T. (1651/1904). *Leviathan*. London: Cambridge University Press.

Hodgart, M. (1969). *Satire*. New York: McGraw-Hill.

Holland, N. N. (1982). *Laughing: A psychology of humor*. Ithaca, NY: Cornell University Press.

Holman, C. H. (1998). Comedy. In *The Encyclopedia Americana*. International Edition. Danbury, CT: Grolier.

Holt, E. (1916). Wit and humor. In D. Robinson (Ed.), *Readings in general psychology*. Chicago: University of Chicago Press.

Hoult, T. (1949). Comic books and juvenile delinquency. *Sociology and Social Research, 33*, 279–284.

Janus, S. S. (1975). The great comedians: Personality and other factors. *The American Journal of Psychoanalysis, 35*, 169–174.

Janus, S. S., Bess, B. E., & Janus, B. R. (1978). The great comediennes: Personality and other factors. *The American Journal of Psychoanalysis, 38*, 367–372.

Jensen, H. J. (1998). Wit. In *Academic American Encyclopedia*. Danbury, CT: Grolier.

Joubert, L. (1560/1579/1980). *Traite du ris (Treatise on laughter)*. Translated by G. D. de Rocher. University, AL: University of Alabama Press.

Justin, F. (1932). A genetic study of laughter-provoking stimuli. *Child Development, 3*, 114–136.

Kahn, S. (1975). *Why and how we laugh*. New York: Philosophical Library.

Kambouropoulou, P. (1926). Individual differences in the sense of humor. *American Journal of Psychology, 37*, 268–278.

Kambouropoulou, P. (1930). Individual differences in the sense of humor and their relation to temperamental differences. *Archives of Psychology, 121*, 1–83.

Keith-Spiegel, P. (1972). Early conceptions of humor: Varieties and issues. In J. H. Goldstein & P. E. McGhee (Eds.), *The psychology of humor: Theoretical perspectives and empirical issues*. New York: Academic Press.

Kernan, A. P. (1965). *The plot of satire*. New Haven, CT: Yale University Press.

Kernan, A. P. (1971). A theory of satire. In R. Paulson (Ed.), *Satire: Modern essays in criticism*. Englewood Cliffs, NJ: Prentice-Hall.

Kimmins, C. W. (1928). *The springs of laughter*. London: Methuen.

Knox, R. A. (1971). On humour and satire. In R. Paulson (Ed.), *Satire: Modern essays in criticism*. Englewood Cliffs, NJ: Prentice-Hall.

Koestler, A. (1964). *The act of creation.* New York: Macmillan.

Koestler, A. (1997). Humour and wit. In *The New Encyclopaedia Britannica, Macropaedia,* (Vol. 20). Chicago: Encyclopaedia Britannica, Inc.

Kohler, W. (1917). *The mentality of apes.* New York: Liveright.

Kohler, W. (1927). *Intelligenzprufungen an anthropoiden.* Berlin: Springer.

Kris, E. (1936). The psychology of caricature. *International Journal of Psychoanalysis, 17,* 285–303.

Kris, E. (1938). Ego development and the comic. *International Journal of Psychoanalysis, 19,* 77–90.

Kris, E., & Gombrich, E. (1938). The principles of caricature. *British Journal of Medical Psychology, 17,* 319–342.

Kwang, L. L. (1921). Theories of laughter. *Chinese Students' Monthly, 17,* 102–111.

Langevin, R., & Day, H. (1972). Physiological correlates of humor. In J. H. Goldstein & P. E. McGhee (Eds.), *The psychology of humor: Theoretical perspectives and empirical issues.* New York: Academic Press.

Lanyi, R. L. (1977). Comic book creativity as displaced aggression. Unpublished doctoral dissertation, University of California at Davis.

Latta, R. L. (1998). *The basic humor process: A cognitive-shift theory and the case against incongruity.* Berlin: Mouton de Gruyter.

Lauter, P. (1964). *Theories of comedy.* Garden City, NY: Doubleday.

Leacock, S. (1935). *Humour: Its theory and technique.* London: J. Lane.

Leacock, S. (1937). *Humour and humanity.* London: Butterworth.

Lederer, R. (1988). *Get thee to a punnery.* New York: Dell.

Legman, G. (1968). *Rationale of the dirty joke.* New York: Grove.

Legman, G. (1975). *No laughing matter: Rationale of the dirty joke.* Breaking Point, NJ: Wharton.

Leuba, C. (1941). Tickling and laughter: Two genetic studies. *The Pedagogical Seminary and the Journal of Genetic Psychology, 58,* 201–209.

Leventhal, H., & Cupchik, G. (1976). A process model of humor judgment. *Journal of Communication, 26,* 190–204.

Leventhal, H., & Mace, W. (1970). The effect of laughter on evaluation of a slapstick movie. *Journal of Personality, 38,* 16–30.

Levine, J. (1961). Regression in primitive clowning. *Psychoanalytic Quarterly, 30,* 72–83.

Levine, J. (1986). Humor. In T. Pettijohn (Ed.), *The encyclopedic dictionary of psychology.* Guilford, CT: Dushkin.

Lilly, W. S. (1896). The theory of the ludicrous. *Fortnightly Review, 59,* 724–737.

Lipps, T. (1898). *Komik und humor: Eine psychologisch-aesthetische untersuchung.* Hamburg: Voss.

Lloyd, E. L. (1938). The respiratory mechanism in laughter. *The Journal of General Psychology, 19,* 179–189.

Locke, J. (1690/1965). *An essay concerning human understanding.* London: Dent.

Ludovici, A. M. (1932). *The secret of laughter.* London: Constable & Co.

Lund, F. H. (1930). Why do we weep? *Journal of Social Psychology, 1,* 136–151.

Lundberg, C. C. (1969). Person-focused joking: Pattern and function. *Human Organization, 28,* 22–28.

Lundin, R. W. (1984/1994). Humoral theory. In R. J. Corsini (Ed.), *Encyclopedia of psychology*. (Vol. 2.) New York: Wiley.

Lynn, K. (1958). *The comic tradition in America*. New York: Doubleday.

MacHovec, F. J. (1988). *Humor: Theory, history, applications*. Springfield, IL: Charles C. Thomas.

Mahony, P. (1956). *Barbed wit and malicious humor*. New York: Citadel.

Makarius, L. (1970). Ritual clowns and symbolic behavior. *Diogenes, 69*, 44–73.

Mandel, O. (1970). What's so funny: The nature of the comic. *Antioch Review, 30*, 73–89.

Maranda, E. K. (1971). Theory and practice of riddle analysis. *Journal of American Folklore, 84*, 51–61.

Maranda, E. K. (1976). Riddles and riddling: An introduction. *Journal of American Folklore, 89*, 127–138.

Martin, R. A. (2000). Humor and laughter. In A. E. Kazdin (Ed.), *Encyclopedia of psychology*. (Vol. 4.) Washington, DC: American Psychological Association; New York: Oxford University Press.

Martin, R. B. (1974). *The triumph of wit: A study of Victorian comic theory*. Oxford, UK: Clarendon.

Mathews, W. (1888). *Wit and humor: Their use and abuse*. Chicago: S. C. Griggs.

McComas, H. C. (1923). The origin of laughter. *The Psychological Review, 30*, 45–55.

McDougall, W. (1903). The theory of laughter. *Nature, 67*, 318–319.

McDougall, W. (1922a). A new theory of laughter. *Psyche, 2*, 292–303.

McDougall, W. (1922b). Why do we laugh? *Scribners, 71*, 359–363.

McDougall, W. (1923). *An outline of psychology*. London: Methuen.

McDougall, W. (1932). *Energies of men: A study of the fundamental dynamics of psychology*. London: Methuen.

McGhee, P. E. (1968). Cognitive development and children's comprehension of humor. Doctoral dissertation, Ohio State University.

McGhee, P. E. (1971). The development of the humor response: A review of the literature. *Psychological Bulletin, 76*, 328–348.

McGhee, P. E. (1979). *Humor: Its origin and development*. San Francisco: Freeman.

McGhee, P. E. (1983). Humor development: Toward a lifespan approach. In P. E. McGhee & J. H. Goldstein (Eds.), *Handbook of humor research* (Vol. 1., *Basic issues*). New York: Springer-Verlag.

McGhee, P. E. (1986). Humor across the lifespan: Sources of developmental change and individual differences. In L. Nahemow, K. McCluskey-Fawcett, & P. E. McGhee (Eds.), *Humor and aging*. New York: Academic Press.

McGhee, P. E. (1988). Introduction: Recent developments in humor research. *Journal of Children in Contemporary Society, 20*, 1–12.

McGhee, P. E., & Chapman, A. J. (Eds.) (1980). *Children's humour*. Chichester, UK: Wiley.

Menon, V. K. K. (1931). *A theory of laughter with special relation to comedy and tragedy*. London: Allen & Unwin.

Mercier, V. (1960). Truth and laughter: A theory of wit and humor. *The Nation, 191*, 74.

Meredith, G. (1897). *An essay on comedy and the uses of the comic spirit.* London: Constable.

Mikes, G. (1971). *Laughing matter: Towards a personal philosophy of wit and humor.* New York: Library Press.

Mikhail, E. H. (1972). *Comedy and tragedy: A bibliography of critical studies.* New York: Whitston.

Milner, G. B. (1972). Homo ridens: Towards a semiotic theory of humour and laughter. *Semiotics, 1,* 1–30.

Mindess, H. (1971). *Laughter and liberation.* Los Angeles: Nash.

Mindess, H., & Turek, J. (1979). *The study of humor.* Los Angeles: Antioch.

Monro, D. H. (1951/1963). *Argument of laughter.* Melbourne, Australia: Melbourne University Press; Notre Dame, IN: University of Notre Dame Press.

Monty Python's Flying Circus. (1969). "The funniest joke in the world" routine. (I. McNaughton, Director). In J. H. Davies (Producer), Python (Monty) Pictures Limited. London: BBC-TV.

Morreall, J. (1983). *Taking laughter seriously.* Albany: State University of New York Press.

Morreall, J. (Ed.) (1987). *The philosophy of laughter and humor.* Albany: State University of New York Press.

Mukherji, N. (1935). The psychology of laughter. *Indian Journal of Psychology, 10,* 95–110.

Murphy, B., & Pollio, H. R. (1973). I'll laugh if you will. *Psychology Today, 7,* 106–109.

Murphy, B., & Pollio, H. R. (1975). The many faces of humor. *Psychological Record, 25,* 545–558.

Murray, H. A. (1934). The psychology of humor. *Journal of Abnormal and Social Psychology, 29,* 66–81.

Myers, H. A. (1935). The analysis of laughter. *Sewanee Review, 43,* 452–463.

Nachman, S. R. (1986). Discomfiting laughter: Schadenfreude among Melanesians. *Journal of Anthropological Research, 42,* 53–67.

New Encyclopedia Britannica. (1997). Fifteenth edition. Chicago: Encyclopedia Britannica, Inc.

Nilsen, D. (1993). *Humor scholarship: A research bibliography.* Westport, CT: Greenwood Press.

O'Connell, W. E. (1960). The adaptive functions of wit and humor. *Journal of Abnormal and Social Psychology, 61,* 263–270.

O'Connell, W. E. (1964). Multidimensional investigation of Freudian humor. *Psychiatric Quarterly, 38,* 97–108.

O'Connell, W. E. (1984/1994). Humor. In R. J. Corsini (Ed.), *Encyclopedia of psychology.* (Vol. 2.) New York: Wiley.

O'Connell, W. E. (1996). Humor: In R. J. Corsini & A. J. Auerbach (Eds.), *Concise encyclopedia of psychology.* New York: Wiley.

Olson, E. (1970). *Theory and comedy.* Bloomington: Indiana University Press.

Omwake, L. (1937). A study of sense of humor: Its relation to sex, age, and personal characteristics. *Journal of Applied Psychology, 21,* 688–704.

Omwake, L. (1939). Factors influencing sense of humor. *Journal of Social Psychology, 10*, 95–104.

Omwake, L. (1942). Humor in the making. *Journal of Social Psychology, 15*, 265–279.

Orel, H. (1961). *The world of Victorian humor.* New York: Appleton-Century-Crofts.

Oring, E. (1989). Between jokes and tales: On the nature of punch lines. *Humor: International Journal of Humor Research, 2*, 349–364.

Papp, J. (1992). Parody: Cognition, rhetoric, and social history. Unpublished doctoral dissertation, University of California, Los Angeles.

Parton, J. (1877). *Caricature and other comic art.* New York: Harper.

Paulson, R. (1971). *Satire: Modern essays in criticism.* Englewood Cliffs, NJ: Prentice-Hall.

Pearson, H. (1938). Humour. In H. Kingsill (Ed.), *The English genius.* London: Eyre & Spottiswoode.

Pepicello, W. (1989). Ambiguity in verbal and visual riddles. *Humor: International Journal of Humor Research, 2*, 207–215.

Perl, R., E. (1933). The influence of social factors upon the appreciation of humor. *American Journal of Psychology, 45*, 308–312.

Peto, E. (1946). Weeping and laughing. *International Journal of Psycho-Analysis, 27*, 129–133.

Petrovsky, A. V., & Yaroshevsky, M. G. (Eds.) (1985). *A concise psychological dictionary.* Moscow: Progress Publishers.

Peyser, C. (1994). Theodor Lipps. In R. J. Corsini (Ed.), *Encyclopedia of psychology.* New York: Wiley.

Piddington, R. (1933/1963). *The psychology of laughter: A study in social adaptation.* London: Figurehead; New York: Gamut.

Plessner, H. (1940). *Laughing and crying: A study of border situations of human behaviour.* Netherlands: Arnheim.

Plessner, H. (1961/1970). *Laughing and crying: A study of the limits of human behavior.* Translated by J. S. Churchill & M. Grene. Bern: A. Franke; Evanston, IL: Northwestern University Press.

Pollio, H. R., & Edgerly, J. W. (1976). Comedians and comic style. In A. J. Chapman & H. C. Foot (Eds.), *Humour and laughter: Theory, research, and applications.* New York: Wiley.

Pollio, H. R., Edgerly, J. W., & Jordan, R. (1972). The comedians' world: Some tentative mappings. *Psychological Reports, 30*, 387–391.

Pollio, H. R., & Mers, R. W. (1974). Predictability and the appreciation of comedy. *Bulletin of the Psychonomic Society, 4*, 229–232.

Pollio, H. R., Mers, R., & Lucchesi, W. (1972). Humor, laughter, and smiling: Some preliminary observations of funny behaviors. In J. H. Goldstein & P. E. McGhee (Eds.), *The psychology of humor: Theoretical perspectives and empirical issues.* New York: Academic Press.

Potter, S. (1954). *The sense of humour.* Harmondsworth, UK: Penguin.

Potts, L. J. (1948). *Comedy.* New York: Putnam.

Prado, C. G. (1995). Why analysis of humor seems funny. *Humor: International Journal of Humor Research, 8*, 155–165.

Prentice, N. M., & Fatham, R. E. (1975). Joking riddles: A developmental index of children's humor. *Developmental Psychology, 11*, 210–216.

Provine, R. (1996). Laughter. *American Scientist, 84*, 38–47.

Provine, R. (2000). *Laughter: A scientific investigation.* New York: Viking.

Rabelais, F. (1533/1990). *Gargantua and Pantagruel.* Translated by B. Raffel. New York: Norton.

Raley, A. L., & Ballmann, C. (1957). Theoretical implications for a psychology of the ludicrous. *Journal of Social Psychology, 45*, 19–23.

Rapp, A. (1947). Toward an eclectic and multilateral theory of laughter and humor. *The Journal of General Psychology, 36*, 207–219.

Rapp, A. (1948). The dawn of humor. *Classical Journal, 43*, 275–280.

Rapp, A. (1949). A phylogenetic theory of wit and humor. *The Journal of Social Psychology, 30*, 81–96.

Rapp, A. (1951). *The origins of wit and humor.* New York: Dutton.

Reber, A. S. (1985/1995). *The Penguin dictionary of psychology.* New York: Penguin.

Redfern, W. D. (1984). *Puns.* Oxford, UK: Basil Blackwell.

Redfern, W. D. (1996). Puns: Second thoughts. *Humor: International Journal of Humor Research, 9*, 187–198.

Reifers, J. (1981). Psychology's evolution in *Playboy* cartoons, 1953–1979. Unpublished doctoral dissertation, The University of Mississippi.

Richetti, J. (1998). Comedy. In *Academic American Encyclopedia.* Danbury, CT: Grolier.

Roberts, J. M., & Forman, M. L. (1971). Riddles: Expressive models of interrogation. *Ethnology, 10*, 509–533.

Roeckelein, J. E. (1998). *Dictionary of theories, laws, and concepts in psychology.* Westport, CT: Greenwood Press.

Rogers, P. (1979). The American circus clown. Unpublished doctoral dissertation, Princeton University.

Rosen, V. (1963). Varieties of comic caricature, and their relationship to obsessive compulsive phenomena. *Journal of the American Psychoanalytic Association, 11*, 704–724.

Rutter, J. (2000). The stand-up introduction sequence: Comparing comedy comperes. *Journal of Pragmatics, 32*, 463–483.

Sachs, L. T. (1973). On crying, weeping, and laughing as defenses against sexual drives, with special consideration of adolescent giggling. *International Journal of Psychoanalysis, 54*, 477–481.

Sacks, R. A., & Wolf, K. M. (1955). The origin of the smiling response. In D. C. McClelland (Ed.), *Studies in motivation.* New York: Appleton-Century-Crofts.

Salameh, W. (1980). La personnalite du comedien. Theorie de la conciliation tragi-comique. Unpublished doctoral dissertation, University of Montreal.

Scott, C. T. (1963a). Amuzgo riddles. *Journal of American Folklore, 76*, 242–244.

Scott, C. T. (1963b). New evidence of American Indian riddles. *Journal of American Folklore, 76*, 236–241.

Scott, C. T. (1965). On defining the riddle. *Genre, 2*, 129–142.

Sechrest, L. (1976). Personality. In L. W. Porter & M. R. Rosenzweig (Eds.), *Annual Review of Psychology*. (Vol. 27.) Palo Alto, CA: Annual Reviews Inc.

Sein, M. T., & Dundes, A. (1964). Twenty-three riddles from central Burma. *Journal of American Folklore, 77*, 69–75.

Shultz, T. R. (1974). Development of the appreciation of riddles. *Child Development, 45*, 100–105.

Shultz, T. R. (1977). A cross-cultural study of the structure of humour. In A. J. Chapman & H. C. Foot (Eds.), *It's a funny thing, humour*. New York: Pergamon.

Shultz, T. R., & Horibe, F. (1974). Development of the appreciation of verbal jokes. *Developmental Psychology, 10*, 13–20.

Sidis, B. (1913). *The psychology of laughter*. New York: D. Appleton.

Smith, E. E., & White, H. L. (1965). Wit, creativity, and sarcasm. *Journal of Applied Psychology, 49*, 131–134.

Smith, W. (1910). Comedy and the comic experience. *The Psychological Bulletin, 7*, 84–87.

Smith, W. M. (1931). *The nature of comedy*. Boston: Gorham.

Sorrell, W. (1972). *Facets of comedy*. New York: Grossett & Dunlap.

Spencer, H. (1860/1891). The physiology of laughter. In H. Spencer, *Essays: scientific, political, and speculative*. London: C. A. Watts; New York: D. Appleton.

Spencer, H. (1916). On the physiology of laughter. In H. Spencer, *Essays on education*. London: Everyman's Library.

Speroni, C. (1964). *Wit and wisdom of the Italian Renaissance*. Berkeley: University of California Press.

Sroufe, L. A., & Wunsch, J. P. (1972). The development of laughter in the first year of life. *Child Development, 43*, 1326–1344.

Stanley, H. M. (1898). Remarks on tickling and laughing. *American Journal of Psychology, 9*, 235–240.

Statt, D. A. (1981/1998). *The concise dictionary of psychology*. New York: Harper & Row/Routledge.

Stearns, F. R. (1972). *Laughing: Physiology, pathophysiology, psychology, pathopsychology, and development*. Springfield, IL: Thomas.

Stern, A. (1976). Laughter and tears as philosophical problems. *Folia Humanistic, 14*, 255–266.

Stern, M. (Ed.) (1981). Humor and illumination. Voices: The art and science of psychotherapy. *Journal of the American Academy of Psychotherapists, 16*, 4.

Stratton, P., & Hayes, N. (1993). *A student's dictionary of psychology*. London: Arnold.

Stuart, I. R. (1964). Iconography of group personality dynamics: Caricatures and cartoons. *Journal of Social Psychology, 64*, 147–156.

Sully, J. (1902). *Essay on laughter*. London: Longmans, Green.

Suls, J. M. (1972). A two-stage model for the appreciation of jokes and cartoons: An information-processing analysis. In J. H. Goldstein & P. E. McGhee (Eds.), *The psychology of humor: Theoretical perspectives and empirical issues*. New York: Academic Press.

Sutherland, J. (1958). *English satire*. Cambridge, UK: Cambridge University Press.

Sutherland, S. (1989/1995). *The international dictionary of psychology*. New York: Crossroad.

Sutton-Smith, B. (1975). A developmental-structural account of riddles. In B. Kirschenblatt-Gimblett (Ed.), *Speech, play, and display*. The Hague: Mouton.

Svebak, S. (1974). A theory of sense of humor. *Scandinavian Journal of Psychology, 15*, 99–107.

Svebak, S. (1975). Respiratory patterns as predictors of laughter. *Psychophysiology, 12*, 62–65.

Swabey, M. C. (1961). *Comic laughter: A philosophical essay*. New Haven, CT: Yale University Press.

Sypher, W. (Ed.) (1956). *Comedy*. Garden City, NY: Doubleday.

Taylor, A. (1943). The riddle. *California Folklore Quarterly, 2*, 129–147.

Taylor, A. (1944). Riddles among the North American Indians. *Journal of American Folklore, 57*, 1–15.

Taylor, A. (1951). *English riddles from oral tradition*. Berkeley: University of California Press.

Test, G. A. (1991). *Satire: Spirit and art*. Tampa: University of South Florida Press.

Thomson, A. A. (1966). *Anatomy of laughter*. London: Epworth.

Trachtenberg, S. (1976). The economy of comedy. *Psychological Review, 62*, 557–578.

Treadwell, Y. (1967). Bibliography of empirical studies of wit and humor. *Psychological Reports, 20*, 1079–1083.

Tuke, D. H. (1892). *A dictionary of psychological medicine*. (Vol. 2.) New York: McGraw-Hill.

Tybout, A. M., & Artz, N. (1994). Consumer psychology. In L. W. Porter & M. R. Rosenzweig (Eds.), *Annual Review of Psychology*. (Vol. 45.) Palo Alto, CA: Annual Reviews Inc.

Tynan, K. (1979). *Show people*. New York: Simon & Schuster.

Vasey, G. (1877). *The philosophy of laughter and smiling*. London: J. Burns.

Walsh, J. J. (1928). *Laughter and health*. New York: Appleton.

Warkentin, J. (Ed.) (1969). Humor in therapy. Voices: The art and science of psychotherapy. *Journal of the American Academy of Psychotherapists, 5*, 2.

Warren, H. C. (Ed.) (1934). *Dictionary of psychology*. Cambridge, MA: Houghton Mifflin.

Washburn, R. W. (1929). A study of the smiling and laughter of infants in the first year of life. *Genetic Psychology Monographs, 6*, 396–537.

Watson, J. S. (1972). Smiling, cooing, and "the game." *Merrill-Palmer Quarterly, 18*, 323–339.

Webster's Dictionary of synonyms and antonyms. (1992). New York: Smithmark.

Webster's Dictionary of word origins. (1995). New York: Smithmark.

Webster's New universal unabridged dictionary. (1989). New York: Barnes & Noble.

Webster's New world dictionary of American English. (1994). Third College Edition. New York: Simon & Schuster.

Webster's Third new international dictionary of the English language unabridged. (1993). Springfield, MA: Merriam-Webster.

Weisfeld, G. E. (1993). The adaptive value of humor and laughter. *Ethology and Sociobiology, 14*, 141–169.

Wells, C. (1923). *Outline of humor*. New York: Putnam.

Welsford, E. (1935). *The fool: His social and literary history*. London: Faber & Faber.

Wilcox, F. B. (1947). *Little book of aphorisms*. New York: Scribner's.

Wilde, L. (1973). *The great comedians*. Secaucus, NJ: Citadel Press.

Willeford, W. (1969). *The fool and his scepter*. Evanston, IL: Northwestern University Press.

Willhelm, S., & Sjoberg, G. (1958). The social characteristics of entertainers. *Social Forces, 37*, 71–76.

Williams, J. M. (1946). An experimental and theoretical study of humour in children. *British Journal of Educational Psychology, 16*, 43–44.

Willmann, J. M. (1940). An analysis of humor and laughter. *The American Journal of Psychology, 53*, 70–85.

Wilson, C. P. (1979). *Jokes: Form, content, use, and function*. New York: Academic Press.

Wilson, K. M. (1927). The sense of humour. *Contemporary Review, 131*, 628–633.

Wilson, S. (1929). Pathological laughing and crying. In *Modern problems in neurology*. New York: Wood.

Wolf, A. A., Smith, C. E., & Murray, H. A. (1934). The psychology of humor. *Journal of Abnormal and Social Psychology, 28*, 341–365.

Wolfenstein, M. (1953). Children's understanding of jokes. *The Psychoanalytic Study of the Child, 9*, 162–173.

Wolfenstein, M. (1954/1978). *Children's humor: A psychological analysis*. Glencoe, IL: Free Press; Bloomington: Indiana University Press.

Wolff, P. H. (1963). Observations on the early development of smiling. In B. M. Foss (Ed.), *Determinants of infant behaviour*. London: Methuen.

Wolman, B. (Ed.) (1973/1989). *Dictionary of behavioral science*. New York: Van Nostrand Reinhold/Academic Press.

World Book Encyclopedia. (1999). Chicago: World Book.

Yerkes, R. M., & Learned, B. W. (1925). *Chimpanzee intelligence and its vocal expression*. Baltimore, MD: Williams & Wilkins.

Young, P. T. (1937). Laughing and weeping, cheerfulness and depression: A study of moods among college students. *The Journal of Social Psychology, 8*, 311–334.

Zhao, Y. (1988). The information-conveying aspect of jokes. *Humor: International Journal of Humor Research, 1*, 279–298.

Zijderveld, A. (1983). The sociology of humor and laughter. *Current Sociology, 31*, 1–100.

Ziv, A. (1984). *Personality and sense of humor*. New York: Springer.

———————————————————————

CHAPTER 2

Origins and Evolution of Humor

ANCIENT/PRIMITIVE HUMOR

Why is man alone, of all creation, the animal that laughs? Readily enough comes the answer: Because man alone has intelligence to perceive the humorous . . . Laughter is born of the exigencies of evolving humanity and it will be long before its joyful echoes die from the earth.

—S. H. Bliss, 1915

Humor is . . . the most philosophic of all the emotions. It is a recognition in our instinctive nature of what our minds in their purest contemplation can inform us . . . that failure is just as interesting as success . . . The sense of humor is a primary instinct of our nature.

—M. Eastman, 1921

Early man is behind us many thousands of years. We can examine his bones, the caves he lived in, the bones of animals he killed. We can examine the rough stone axes, hammers, and chisels. We can piece together some sort of picture of how he lived. But in the life we picture, when did a man laugh?

—A. Rapp, 1947

Paleolithic people were Cro-Magnon stone age people, nomadic hunters and gatherers who lived in caves and used fire, flint blades and bone tools . . . their mentality was similar to that of a bright little contemporary boy of five which would give them the power of laughter at simple things . . . you can also catch a glimpse of Cro-Magnons by talking to a 5–year-old!

—F. J. MacHovec, 1988

Rapp (1947, pp. 208–211) attempts to answer the questions, "What is the place of laughter in primitive man?" and "What type of situation in the days of primitive man evoked laughter?" Rapp maintains that the answers to these questions rest in the notions of "ridicule," "release," and "communication" (cf: Bowman, 1937). As associated with ridicule, laughter was probably directed at other persons at an earlier time than was laughter arising from riddles, jokes, or puns. Moreover, according to Rapp, the derisive type of laughter in the ridicule of other persons probably preceded the more humane and genial laughter more characteristic in modern times. Rapp suggests that we may fairly conjecture that, in earliest times, and as somewhat less often today, when a person saw for the first time some other individual—not connected to him by strong ties—and observed that this person was crippled, ugly, or in any way malformed, for some inexplicable reason he or she burst out into laughter (cf: Rapp, 1949, 1951).

Perhaps the laughter of ridicule is based on a perception of superiority in oneself (e.g., the "sudden glory" thesis of Hobbes, 1651/1839), or perhaps it derives from the observation of a mistake/deformity that is not productive of pain or harm to others (e.g., Aristotle's notion of the ridiculous in his *Poetics*; see Aristotle, 1895; McKeon, 1941; Ross, 1931). As regards the idea of "release" in the origination of humor/laughter, Rapp (1947) suggests that such "relaxation" or "liberty" notions of laughter (e.g., Bain, 1876; Dewey, 1894; Freud, 1905/1916/1960) may be at the foundation of the first laugh of primitive man (cf: Kallen, 1911, p. 156, who asserts that

in the hungry beast of the jungle, that has fought for its life in a double sense, and has triumphed in its struggle, may lie the ultimate parentage of laughter. The explosions of breath, the gurgitations, the throwing back of the head as if to swallow . . . these are actions that beasts still perform when they have their prey completely at their mercy;

and Eastman's, 1921, p. 4, belief that "man's laughter finds its canine equivalent in the wagging of the tail").

Concerning the relationship between "communication" and laughter, Rapp (1947) cites two writers (H. C. McComas and D. Hayworth) who maintain that laughter was a means of communication for primitive man. McComas (1923) concludes that laughter was originally a signal announcing good news; and Hayworth (1928) suggests that laughter was originally a vocal signal to other members of the group that they might relax with safety (cf: Piddington, 1933/1963, who emphasizes the social functions of laughter as communication between parent and offspring; and Wallis, 1922, who suggests that social laughter was expressive of unity in group opinion). In summary, Rapp's analysis of the origins of laughter/humor follows a logical sequence: the triumphant beast of the jungle, the primitive man who has thrashed his foe, the sudden glory at the perception of one's superiority over an antagonist, the triumph over social restraint, and finally, in jokes and riddles, the civilized triumph in an artificial contest deliberately staged and entered into for its attendant relaxation (cf: Radcliffe-Brown, 1965; Schmidt & Williams, 1971).

In her analysis of the early conceptions of humor, Keith-Spiegel (1972, pp. 5–6) discusses biological, instinctual, and evolutionary aspects of humor which hold the common ground that laughter and humor potentials are "built-in" to the nervous mechanism of the organism (presumably including primitive man) and most likely serve some adaptive/evolutionary function (cf: Weisfeld, 1993). The observations that laughter appears early in life before language occurs, and that humor and laughter are universal phenomena, seem to indicate that the human laughter/humor response has survived since earliest times for some utilitarian or adaptive purpose.

Moreover, laughter and humor have been described as being "good" for the body because they restore homeostasis, oxygenate the blood, stabilize blood pressure, stimulate circulation, massage the vital organs, aid digestion, relax the entire system, and produce feelings of "well-being." It is likely, therefore, according to Keith-Spiegel, that ancient/primitive man engaged initially in humor and laughter activities for various biological, instinctual, and evolutionary purposes (cf: Armstrong, 1928; Beerbohm, 1921; Carpenter, 1922; Crile, 1916; Darwin, 1872/1965; Dearborn, 1900; Delage, 1919; Diserens, 1926; Diserens & Bonifield, 1930; Drever, 1917; Dugas, 1902; Dupreel, 1928; Eastman, 1921; Gopala-Swami, 1926; Gregory, 1923, 1924; Greig, 1923/1969; Hayworth, 1928; Hecker, 1873; Kallen, 1911; Kline, 1907; Koestler, 1964; Leacock, 1935, 1937; Ludovici, 1932; McComas, 1923; McDougall, 1903, 1922, 1923; Meerloo, 1966; Menon, 1931; Monro, 1951; Penjon, 1893; Rapp, 1947, 1949, 1951; Spencer, 1860; Sully, 1902; Vasey, 1875; Wallis, 1922; Willmann, 1940).

Eastman (1921) was an enthusiastic proponent of the instinct notion of humor (cf: McDougall, 1903, 1922, 1923, who suggested that an instinct must possess three characteristics: emotional excitement; appearance both in animals and humans; and evidence of morbid exaggeration). To Eastman, laughter is a means of social communication of pleasure that has acquired a kind of identity in humans' nervous systems with a state of satisfaction or joy. Eastman (1921, p. 7) states, "And the smile of dawning welcome, there so eventful, and so clearly demonstrated to be essential to the very warmth and existence of social communion, is the native original of all smiles and all laughter." In terms of Eastman's instinct approach, play and playfulness are a "hereditary gift," and are more spontaneous and instinctive than they are conscious and deliberate.

According to Eastman's analysis, it would be easy to conceive of ancient/primitive mans' initial laughter/humor in a "fighting-glory-laughter" sequence (cf: Ludovici's, 1932, emphasis on "teeth-baring" behavior) in which a primitive hunter would act like ferocious gorillas, gnashing their teeth and thumping their chests, and laughing, after overcoming a formidable human or infrahuman foe in combat (cf: Leacock, 1935, 1937, who suggests that the savage who cracked his enemy over the head with a tomahawk and shouted "Ha! Ha!" was the first humorist. According to Leacock, this begins the so-called "merry ha! ha!" which is the oldest and most primitive form of humor).

MacHovec (1988, p. 157) refers to the "world's first laugh" in his chapter on "Humor in History" (cf: Wells, 1932), and suggests that ancient/primitive humans probably "mimicked" before they could talk; these earliest behaviors were amusing and were reinforced, most likely, by reciprocal grunts or applause which elicited further mimicry. Additionally, the earliest humans probably amused themselves through mockery of their enemies and opponents by laughing at their various weaknesses, physical differences, and deformities. Thus, according to the notions of Wells (1932) and MacHovec (1988), ancient/primitive humans probably had their first laugh in such a reciprocal, nonverbal, mimicry, and mockery scenario. From such beginnings, humorous evolution continued and progresses from mirth through exaggeration perhaps inspired by, and accompanied by, various mirth-provoking or "clownish" painted masks that were popular among the late Paleolithic people. Wells (1932) dates the emergence of the role and function of the clownish "fool" or "buffoon" at about 10,000 B.C.-12,000 B.C.; these individuals were associated with merrymaking, eating, and drinking at the earliest feasts, and won the laughter of the guests by their deformities and idiotic antics (cf: Stanner, 1982).

MacHovec (1988) suggests that the clown is a simple figure—immediately recognized and direct in intent or purpose—that elicits smiles and laughter even without speaking or doing anything, and that exists in the deepest and darkest recesses of the unconscious mind. MacHovec (1988, pp. 159–183) also provides historical samples of the variety and versatility of humor, some of them up to 3,500 years old. For example, the following 3,500–year-old riddles and sayings derive (via archaeological excavations) from the ancient civilization of Sumer in southern Mesopotamia; such riddles, proverbs, and sayings antedate the Biblical book of *Proverbs*, and all of the known Egyptian proverb/precept compilations, by several centuries (cf: Kramer, 1956, pp. 154–159): "Can one conceive without sexual intercourse? Can one get fat without eating?"; and "You can tolerate a lord or a king, but the man to fear is the tax collector." According to Kramer (1956, p. 153), the Sumerian proverbs were compiled and written down (in "cuneiform") more than 3,500 years ago and many had no doubt been repeated by word of mouth for centuries before they were put into written form.

On the other hand, according to Wells (1932, p. 29), there apparently is not a single element of the amusing in the art or literature of the Babylonian and Assyrian civilizations, so "the ancient Babylonians and Assyrians must go down in history as serious-minded folk." The ancient Hebrews were a bit more humorous, frequently engaging in satire and parody of serious matters both of church and state.

MacHovec (1988) presents other riddles, sayings, excerpts, and proverbs from the earliest period ("oldest sources"—prehistoric to 500 B.C.) of the Arabian, Turkish, Indian, Greek, and Chinese cultures; he focuses on the humor of the Greek philosophers in the ancient period ("ancient sources"—500 B.C. to 500 A.D.), and on a number of literary works in the "medieval, Renaissance, modern sources" period (1000 A.D. to 1850 A.D.) (cf: Brown & Kimmey, 1968; Eastman, 1921; McGhee, 1979; Sypher, 1956).

In his anthropological account of humor and laughter, Apte (1985, Chapter 8, pp. 239–260) describes the evolutionary and biosocial aspects of these phenomena in *Homo sapiens*. Humans may be defined as the "laughing animals" because laughter and smiling are considered to be uniquely and exclusively human attributes (along with other traits such as tool-making and language); some higher primates may make use of types of "language" (i.e., communication), and demonstrate "intelligence" (e.g., via rudimentary tool-making), but they do not have the human capability of producing diverse varieties of laughter/smiling and to associate them with symbolic, psychological, and social values. Apte asserts that even though scholars of diverse disciplinary interests have studied humor and laughter from many different perspectives, no single theory has explained satisfactorily the origins of laughter and smiling (cf: Chevalier-Skolnikoff, 1973, p. 82). However, according to Apte, there are promising approaches to understanding such origins, especially in the areas of the physiology/physiognomy (e.g., Darwin, 1872/1965; Eibl-Eibesfeldt, 1972; Ekman, 1973; Ekman & Friesen, 1975, 1976; Spencer, 1860; cf: Flugel, 1954, p. 712) and evolution (e.g., Andrew, 1963, 1965; Eibl-Eibesfeldt, 1975; Loizos, 1967; VanHooff, 1972; cf: Porteous, 1988) of the humor response.

In terms of the evolutionary aspects of facial expressions in humor/laughter/smiling, Apte provides a plausible scenario (in his overall goal of comparing and contrasting, mainly, laughter and smiling) on the origin of these phenomena; the similarities between human smiling and the primate's silent bared-teeth display on the one hand—and between human laughter and primate's relaxed open-mouth display on the other hand—reflect close phylogenetic relationships. In morphological terms, human laughter is considered to be an *intermediate* stage between the classical primate relaxed open-mouth display and the silent bared-teeth face, the human smile being its weaker form (cf: VanHooff, 1967, 1972). Accordingly, the human smile and laughter—though of different phylogenetic origin—began to converge and overlap considerably. Apparently, in the evolutionary process leading from nonprimate mammals to primate, and finally to *Homo sapiens*, the meaning of the teeth-baring display broadened: while it was originally a part of a defensive/protective behavioral strategy, it became a signal of nonhostility and submission. Among primates, the bared-teeth display overlapped with the "lip-smacking" display, while human smiling appears to have resulted from the combination of both with the bared-teeth display almost completely replacing the lip-smacking display.

Gruner (1978, Chapter 3, "Humor's Ancestry," pp. 39–47) addresses the questions, "Where did laughter begin?" "How did laughter begin?" and "Why did laughter begin?" He suggests that it may be quite impossible to determine whether laughter actually *did* have a beginning. Perhaps humans have always had the capacity (instinct) to laugh; in such a case, the questions then become: "When did humans *become* human?" and "At what moment in the evolutionary development did the apelike creatures become more humanlike with the capability of laughter/humor?" Gruner asserts that regardless of when humans *began* to laugh, it had to be before they told jokes, because there was a time when humans did not talk—they had no language, it's that simple: no language, no puns; no gags, punch lines, malapropisms, spoonerisms, bon mots, or witticisms.

Another important question about laughter's beginnings, according to Gruner, is the issue of "How *many* beginnings, or ancestors, of 'humor' can be found?" The kind of answers one gets is more dependent upon the kind of questions one asks than upon the method of investigation—in the case of humor, one may search for *many* beginnings because the varieties or "types" of humorous stimuli are extremely wide, and the English language provides endless descriptions of "different" kinds of laughter. For example, do each of the different types of humor/humorous stimuli (such as wisecracks, epigrams, riddles, conundrums, gags, jokes, anecdotes, tangletalk, spoonerisms, fuddletalk, tongue twisters, wellerisms, transposers, macaronics, malapropisms, boners, bulls, Freudian slips, double blunders, double entendres, biograms, caricatures, repartee, hecklerisms, parkerisms, tricks/practical jokes, satire, irony, parody, sarcasm, burlesque, shaggy dog stories, nonsensisms; cf: Esar, 1952) have a separate, distinct, and unique beginning, or can they be said to have sprung from a common source?

Moreover, do the "different" kinds of laughter (such as rejoicing, exultation, delight, joy, elation, gladness, triumph, jubilation, mirth, merrymaking, giggles, titters, smirks, grins, sniggerings, chuckles, guffaws, cachinnations; sardonic, wry, gay, morose, infectious, and derisive laughter; banter, raillery, chaff, joshing, badinage, buffoonery, fooling, harlequinade, clownery, tomfoolery, farce, jocularity, jocoseness, facetiousness, waggishness, drollery, jesting, jocosity, comicality,) have separate beginnings, or do they derive, also, from a common source?

Gruner (1978) maintains that humans were once very simple creatures (without civilization or language) and it seems likely that laughter (and, by extension, humor) began as something quite simple to early humans, something that was closely related to their simple regimen of keeping body and soul together; laughter's beginning probably had to have a strong connection to the daily tasks of finding—and keeping—food, shelter, and mate(s). Gruner suggests that it makes a great deal of sense to believe that all laughter (humor) had a single, common ancestor, and that all humor forms are closely related, and belong to the same family tree. Furthermore, concerning the question, "What did ancient/primitive man laugh about?," Gruner imagines a primordial scene of combat between our bestial ancestors in which there is success in combat, a sudden victory, and a sudden realization that one has triumphed—that the prize is his, and that his opponent is defeated. The winner in such an imagined scenario bares his teeth, pumps his shoulders, and chops up his breath into grunts and moans, with appropriate grimaces—it is a crude kind of a "horselaugh," a victory shout that permits a rapid return to homeostasis in the winner's body and signals to anyone nearby that victory is his (all this is accompanied by a similar physiological/bodily reaction, and homeostatic recovery, in the "loser" who withdraws and "weeps").

McGhee (1979, pp. 120–123) examines the evolutionary origin of humor and states, in one case, that "the expansion of apes' capacity to assign specific meanings to hand and arm gestures by giving them a ready-made sign language, then, has the pivotal effect of transforming these animals from humorless (although playful) creatures to organisms capable of simple forms of incongruity humor." McGhee emphasizes the distinction between play and humor, and argues that a playful state or "frame of mind" is a necessary prerequisite for humor; he also suggests that the acquisition of language enables apes to experience humor, and this has clear implications for the evolutionary origin of the humor experiences of human beings. McGhee maintains that humor must have been first appreciated soon after the early stages of development of a propositional language system; if the development of language had its origins in a gestural communication system, it is even possible that early humor was similar to that experienced and demonstrated by present-day chimpanzees and apes who have been taught to use a gestural/sign language form of communication.

McGhee is in accord with the anthropological position which asserts that for a long time before the evolutionary appearance of articulate vocal language, the early hominids probably communicated propositionally by means of hand and arm gestures in addition to other nonverbal signs and by primate-like pre-speech vocal calls. McGhee (1979, p. 123) concludes that "regardless of whether initial human communication was vocal or gestural, the question of timing of the evolutionary origin of humor seems to be reducible to the question of the timing of the beginning of language."

Also, along anthropological lines, Butovskaya and Kozintsev (1996) suggest that certain actions which incite humor among humans originated in mock aggressive behaviors and activities of apes such as chimpanzees and orangutans. Analysis of the mock aggressive behaviors of chimpanzees shows that such behaviors are similar to several humor-inducing customs of humans (e.g., ritual clowning that involves excrement or urine throwing during the medieval carnivals of Western Europe is similar to the mock aggressions displayed by apes).

In discussing the "humanization of humor," Koestler (1997) notes that the San (Bushmen) of the Kalahari desert in South-West Africa/Namibia are among the oldest and most primitive inhabitants of the Earth, and may offer an explanation of humor in ancient/primitive humans. Citing Thomas (1959), Koestler provides a picture of prehistoric humour in these people: A springbok was wounded in the stomach (and partly eviscerated), causing him to jump and kick before he finally died. The Bushmen thought that this was extremely funny as they laughed, slapping their thighs, and kicking their heels to imitate the dying animal, showing no pity at all (the Bushmen regard animals with great detachment). In such circumstances, the San are put in good spirits and are pleased with the amusement the wounded animal had given them (cf: Stanner, 1982). Apparently, the San (like most primitive people) do not regard animals as sentient beings, and the dying springbok's anguished kicking is funny to them because, in their view, the animal *pretends* to suffer pain—like a human being.

Koestler observes that the ancient Greeks' attitude toward the stammering barbarian was similarly inspired by the conviction that he is not really human but only pretends to be. Koestler also notes that as laughter emerged from the ancient/primitive form of humor, it was so aggressive that it has been likened to a dagger: In ancient Greece, the dagger was transformed into a quill, dripping with poison at first, then diluted and infused later with amusing lyrical and fanciful elements. The 5th century B.C. evinced the first rise of humor into art, starting with parodies of Olympian heroics and reaching a peak in the comedies of Aristophanes. According to Koestler, from this point onward the evolution of humor/comedy in the Western world merges with the history of literature and art. Thus, the overall trend in humor—from the ancient/primitive to the later sophisticated forms—was away from aggression-based humor and toward the "humanization" of humor (cf: Gregory's, 1924, Chapter 2, pp. 9–19, "The Humanization of Laughter").

HUMOR AND THE EARLY PHILOSOPHICAL THEORIES

One sometimes hears of the philosophy of humor. The phrase itself is most humorous. The philosophy of humor would be truly the humor of philosophy.

—W. Mathews, 1888

It appears that both Plato and Aristotle identified the laughter of the Greek theatre with scorn. Or, to be more scientific, they conceived laughter as the expression of an emotion compounded of complacence, or "positive self-feeling," with a very slight tincture of disgust or anger. And upon the basis of this conception they were inclined to condemn laughter, and advise the philosophers and wise men of the state not to indulge in it.

—M. Eastman, 1921

The history of theories of laughter is of interest mainly because of the varying points of view which different writers have adopted. In Plato and Aristotle we find emphasis placed upon the ethical implications of laughter, while Cicero concentrates upon the use of ridicule in rhetoric. Quintilian's treatment of the subject is of interest as representing the first attempt to produce a psychological analysis of the effects of laughter.

—R. Piddington, 1933/1963

The attributes, "personal" and "incorruptible," as applied to laughter, can be explained by studying the genesis and infantile precursors of this "emotion that hath no name" . . . Laughter wasn't born yesterday, and you can't put anything over on involuntary laughter.

—E. Bergler, 1956

For purposes of the present discussion, the phrase "early philosophical theories" is taken here to mean the notions/theories of humor of the ancient philosophers/writers from the Greek philosophers Plato and Aristotle up to Quintilian in the 1st century. The more "modern philosophical theories" begin in the 17th century when Thomas Hobbes (1651/1904, 1651/1839) put forward the first true *psychological* theory of laughter (cf: Quintilian, 1714/1821–1825; and Quintilian's account of humor in Greig, 1923/1969, p. 227; and Piddington, 1933/1963, pp. 154–155). Chapter 3 of this book ("Theories Based in Modern Philosophy" section) covers the more modern theories of humor, beginning with Hobbes' theory. Thus, the *psychological* ideas of the philosopher Thomas Hobbes concerning laughter and humor serve as a demarcation point between the "early" and "modern" philosophical/ psychological theories of humor.

Material on the early theories of humor in this section is arranged in chronological order, and the main sources consulted here include the following: Bergler (1956), Berlyne (1969), Eastman (1921), Greig (1923/1969), Keith-Spiegel (1972), MacHovec (1988), Morreall (1987), and Piddington (1933/1963).

Among the first "traditional," "classical," or "early" philosophical theories of humor is that of the Greek philosopher Plato (c. 427–c. 347 B.C.). As Morreall (1987, p. 10) states, "As with so many topics, Western thought about humor and laughter begins with Plato." Plato's view on humor is that what we laugh at is vice, particularly self-ignorance, that occurs in people who are relatively powerless; and human amusement is a type of malice toward such people. Plato cautioned that people should be wary of amusement, especially the emotion of amusement, because—under such influences—one tends to lose rational control of oneself. Thus, this *lack of self-knowledge* theory of Plato is the most ancient of the theories of laughter to have come down to us (cf: Bergler, 1956, p. 2).

In his *Philebus 47–50*, Plato is the first to suggest that envy or malice is at the root of comic enjoyment (see Greig, 1923/1969, p. 15; Morreall, 1987, pp. 10–11; Piddington, 1933/1963, p. 152); self-deception—or the vain conceit of beauty, wealth, or wisdom—when it is powerful is to be hated, and when it is feeble and unable to do hurt to others is ridiculous and to be laughed at. Thus, according to Plato, we laugh at the misfortunes of our friends in which we have circumstances with mixed feelings of pain and pleasure.

Plato, thereby, advances a "pleasure-pain" theory of humor. By previously defining lack of self-knowledge as a misfortune, Plato reasons as follows (cf: Bergler, 1956, p. 3): Laughter is a pleasure and to laugh at the conceit of someone is to gloat over his or her misfortune; such gloating implies malice, which is painful. In other terms, Plato compares the appreciation of the ludicrous to the relief that derives from scratching an itch (cf: Piddington, 1933/1963, p. 152). In the case of the itch/scratch, we have a "mixed feeling of the body" (i.e., pain caused by the itch and pleasure evoked by the remedial treatment of scratching). In the case of the appreciation of the ludicrous, we have a corresponding "mixed feeling of the soul" whereby pleasure and pain are combined (e.g., the ludicrous consists of a negation of the Delphic/Socratic precept, "know thyself," or constitutes a lack of self-knowledge). Once again, according to Plato, lack of self-knowledge is a misfortune; because laughter is a pleasure, to laugh at the conceit of one's friends is, therefore, to rejoice in their misfortunes (cf: the German concept of *Schadenfreude*—enjoyment obtained from the mishaps of others), and on that account implies malice which is painful. The logical conclusion follows that laughter involves simultaneously both pleasure and pain. In his *Republic*—when setting up rules for the education of the young Guardians of the "ideal state"—Plato singles out laughter as something to be avoided; the Guardians "must not be prone to laughter, for usually when we abandon ourselves to violent laughter, our condition provokes a violent reaction" (see Morreall, 1987, p. 10). Moreover, Plato goes on to suggest that—in order that the young Guardians are not given bad models to follow—literature should be censored to eliminate all mention of the gods or heroes as overcome with laughter.

The Greek philosopher Aristotle (384–322 B.C.) advanced a theory of humor and laughter (termed the "not too tragic defect" theory by Bergler, 1956, p. 3) that agrees with Plato's notion that laughter basically involves ridicule and malice and is "derisive," and that when we are amused by someone we essentially see that person as "inferior" in some way. [Note: Some writers refer, generically, to such "derisive" theories—as enunciated by Plato and Aristotle—as *superiority* theories of humor; see Berlyne, 1969, p. 800; Blistein, 1998, p. 563; Keith-Spiegel, 1972, pp. 6–7; Martin, 2000, pp. 202–203; thus, such *superiority* theories make humor depend on a comparative sense of one's own superiority, or on a sense of the inferiority of other people.] Our elation/amusement is augmented when we compare ourselves favorably to others as being less ugly, less stupid, less weak, or less unfortunate; the notions of mockery, ridicule, and laughter of the foolish actions of others is central to the *superiority* theories of humor.

In his *Poetics*, Aristotle asserts that the ludicrous is merely a subdivision of the ugly, and it may be defined as a defect or ugliness which is not painful or destructive (see Aristotle, 1895); thus, for example, the comic mask is ugly and distorted, but does not cause pain (cf: Bergler, 1956, p. 3). According to Aristotle, the ludicrous is to be found when characters of a lower moral order are depicted, whereas when men are depicted as better than they are in real life, their imperfections form the subject matter of tragedy.

Piddington (1933/1963, p. 153) notes that Aristotle's view of the ludicrous comes to us from occasional references only, and his specific treatment of the question is lost; Aristotle mentions the topic in his *Poetics, Rhetorica*, and *Nicomachean Ethics* (see McKeon, 1941; Ross, 1931). While Aristotle basically subscribes to Plato's assumption that malice is essential to laughter, he also enlarges the scope of the issue by distinguishing between comedy and irony directed at individuals. Aristotle also introduces the phenomenon of aesthetics in laughter, and maintains that the malicious element—though indispensable to laughter—is undesirable from an aesthetic point of view.

Greig (1923/1969, p. 15) notes that Aristotle's approach toward humor ("To make a jest of a man is to vilify him in a way") is that comedy should avoid satirizing individuals. However, as Piddington (1933/1963, p. 153) observes, Aristotle does not entirely condemn jests, but points out that they may be abused ("most people take more pleasure than they ought in amusement and jesting . . . a jest is a kind of abuse, and lawgivers forbid some kinds of abuse . . . perhaps they ought to have forbidden some kinds of jesting").

In his *Rhetorica* (cf: Harris & Levey, 1975, p. 1110), Aristotle considers jests as being "of some service in controversy"; he subscribes to the opinion of Gorgias (a Greek Sophist, c. 485–c. 380 B.C., who asserted that nothing exists; if anything does exist, it cannot be known; and if it can be known, the knowledge of it cannot be communicated; thus, according to Gorgias subjective truth being impossible, there remains only the Sophists' art of persuasion) who advocated in rhetorics that one "kill the opponents' earnestness with jesting and their jesting with earnestness" (cf: Bergler, 1956, p. 3; Piddington, 1933/1963, p. 154). Thus, though Aristotle did not completely agree with Plato's recommendation that we should suppress laughter generally, he did think that most people overdo laughing and joking (see Morreall, 1987, p. 14). According to Aristotle's view, the moral ideal ("golden mean") is to avoid the extremes of the humorless boor and the buffoon; the ideal is to be ready-witted but tactful.

In addition to his theory of laughter as derision, Aristotle anticipated the later "incongruity" theory (e.g., humor theories by Kant and Schopenhauer) that laughter is a reaction to many kinds of inconsistency/incongruity, and not just human shortcomings. In his *Rhetorica*, Aristotle asserts that a speaker can get a laugh by setting up a certain expectation in the audience, and then jolting them suddenly ("surprise") with something they did not expect (see Morreall, 1987, p. 14). For a thorough analysis of what has been salvaged today of Aristotle's humor/comedy theory, one may consult L. Cooper (1922), as suggested by Keith-Spiegel (1972, p. 7). Finally, according to Eastman (1921, p. 129), the Greek philosophers Plato and Aristotle were "groping toward a real understanding of the complexities of the comic. But they did not labor long enough, and the problem was left at loose ends by them, as it has been by the moderns."

Following Plato and Aristotle, the Roman statesman, orator, and philosopher Cicero (Marcus Tullius, 106–43 B.C.), and the Roman rhetorician Quintilian (Marcus Fabius Quintilianus, c. 35–96 A.D.), advanced what Bergler (1956, p. 3) calls the "two nihilistic theories of laughter." In other words, according to Bergler, the humor theories of Cicero and Quintilian have in common the doubt that anyone has sufficiently explained laughter (i.e., "neither individual adds anything of importance to the body of ancient theory").

Both Cicero (in his *De Oratore*) and Quintilian (in his *De Institutione Oratoria*) echo the Aristotelian aspects or themes of the "deformity" or "baseness" in humor (cf: Greig, 1923/1969, pp. 226–227); Cicero emphasizes that the defeat of expectation causes laughter ("it is by deceiving expectation, by satirizing the character of others, by making merry of our own . . . by talking seeming nonsense, and by reproving follies, that laughter is stimulated"), and Quintilian asserts that laughter is always associated with something low ("humile"), that may take any of six forms: urbanity (urbanitas), gracefulness (venustum), piquancy (salsum), pleasantry (facetum), jesting (iocus), and verbal attacks (dicacitas). In concert with Cicero, Quintilian calls attention to the laughs ("the happiest jokes of all") that arise from surprise, or the deceit of expectation, and from the turning of another person's words to express a meaning not intended by him. In short, says Bergler (1956, p. 3), both Cicero and Quintilian are purely descriptive: "their psychological contribution is a shrug of a toga-draped shoulder."

On the other hand, in a more positive vein, Morreall (1987, p. 17) observes that Cicero follows, in large part, what Aristotle had said, but he adds at least one new (rhetoric) idea of some theoretical importance: the distinction between humor in what is being talked about, and humor arising from the language used.

This distinction, says Morreall, is similar to that made today between the comedian (who says *funny* things) and the comic (who says *things* funny).

Piddington (1933/1963, pp. 154–155) notes that Cicero divides wit into two main types: the cases in which the humor arises from the subject matter (e.g., anecdotes, caricature), and those cases involving verbal form (including ambiguity, surprise, puns, unusual interpretation of names, proverbs, expressions, allegory, metaphor, and irony); and that Quintilian advances and recognizes the rhetorical value of humor as a means of dissipating melancholy, of "unbending" the mind in intense situations, and of humor's power and strength of renewal following fatigue or excesses. Again, Quintilian—like Cicero—notes the effect of surprise and of deceived expectation in producing laughter (cf: Eastman, 1921, pp. 130–132).

BIBLICAL AND JEWISH HUMOR

Thinking on independently and originally, the victims of thought standardization would, moreover, have discovered that there is not a joke in the whole of the New Testament, that even the laughter of the Bible is nearly always an expression of scorn and not of mirth (exceptions: Psalm 126:2, and Job 8:21), and that no saint, prophet, or apostle is ever spoken of as laughing.

—A. M. Ludovici, 1932

The "sin-theory" of laughter is rooted in some deep distrust of all laughter; its theological orientation permits it to dispense with the obligation of explaining laughter as a psychological phenomenon, and to concentrate instead on laughter as an antechamber to, or indication of, sinfulness.

—E. Bergler, 1956

This kind of laugh—indeed, any kind of laugh—is rare in the Bible. Jehovah was a solemn god, little given to gaiety and jollity . . . The New Testament is hardly more hospitable to laughter than the Old. It has often been noted that we are told that Jesus wept, but never that he laughed.

—R. Boston, 1974

The starting points (of this inquiry) are two widely-spread claims: one, by literary critics, that humor is absent in the Hebrew Bible, the other, by social historians, that the Book discriminates against women vis-à-vis men . . . the last who acknowledged that Biblical humor exists at all were, so it seems, the Talmudic sages.

—Y. Radday, 1995

The ancient Hebrews' sense of humour seems to have been no less harsh: it has been pointed out that in the Old Testament there are 29 references to

laughter, out of which 13 instances are linked with scorn, derision, mock-
ing, and contempt and only two are born of joy.

—A. Koestler, 1997

The answer to the question, "Is there humor in the Bible?" perhaps rests on
the answer to a more rudimentary question, "What do you mean by *humor?*"
(cf: Radday, 1991, 1995). If humor means joy, mirth, satire, riddle, and laughter, then one may say "Yes, there is humor in the Bible." On the other hand, if
humor means jokes, puns, comedy, and wit, then one may reply, "No, there is no
humor in the Bible."

In terms of the present terminological domains of humor (see Chapter 1),
Strong (1990) includes in his concordance of the Bible entries for the following
humor-related terms: *laughter/mirth/joy*, and *riddle*. On the other hand, Strong
(1990) does *not* have entries for the following terms: *humor, comedy/wit, farce,
parody, puns, jokes*, and *caricature/cartoons/comics/slapstick*. Also, Strong's
(1990) concordance (in the section, "Universal Subject Guide to the Bible")
shows entries for the terms *satire* ("exposing problems to ridicule"; e.g., Jesus'
devastating use of satire, Matthew 23: 1–33); *irony* ("a pretense of ignorance";
e.g., 2 Samuel 6: 20; 1 Kings 18: 27; 1 Kings 22: 15; Amos 4: 4; Matthew 27:
29; 2 Corinthians 11: 19–20); and *sarcasm* ("a biting taunt, mock"; e.g., Judges
9: 7–19; 1 Samuel 26: 15; 1 Kings 18: 27; 1 Kings 20: 10–11; 2 Kings 14: 8–12;
Job 11: 2–12; Nehemiah 4: 2–3; Matthew 27: 28–29; Acts 23: 1–5; Jeremiah
25: 27).

Ziv (1984, p. 4) notes that humor has a long history as an expression of aggression; he states that if we count the number of times the word *laugh* appears
in the Bible, we find a total of 29 instances, in 13 of which (45%) there is an aggressive connotation. [Notes: In another case, Strong (1990, p. 608) indicates
that in the Bible the word *laugh* occurs 18 times, the word *laughed* occurs 13
times, the words *laugheth* and *laughing* occur once each, and the word *laughter*
occurs seven times. Moreover, the word *mirth* occurs 15 times, the word *riddle*
occurs nine times, the words *joyed/joyful/joyfully/joyfulness/joying/joyous* occur 36 times, and the word *joy* occurs 165 times in the Bible.] Concerning the
humor-aggression connection, for example, Jeremiah 20: 7 (*New Revised Standard Version Bible*, 1991) says: "O Lord, you have enticed me, and I was enticed; you have overpowered me, and you have prevailed. I have become a
laughingstock all day long; everyone mocks me."

In discussing some varieties of laughter, Gregory (1924, p. 3) identifies the
laughter of play, contempt, superiority, self-congratulation, and triumph; he
also identifies the laughter of "scorn" by way of citing the Biblical text in 2
Chronicles 30: 10: "So the runners passed from city to city through the country
of Ephraim and Manasseh, as far as Zebulun; but they laughed them to scorn
and mocked them." Boston (1974, pp. 43–44) observes the type of laughter that

is occasioned by something unusual, citing the Biblical stories of Abram/Abraham and Sarai/Sarah. In the case of Abraham (Genesis 17: 17), the Bible (*Holy Bible: The New King James Version*, 1984) states, "Then Abraham fell on his face and laughed, and said in his heart, 'shall a child be born to a man who is one hundred years old? And shall Sarah, who is ninety years old, bear a child?'" In the case of Sarah (Genesis 18: 11–15), the Bible says:

Now Abraham and Sarah were old, well advanced in age; and Sarah had passed the age of childbearing. Therefore Sarah laughed within herself, saying, "After I have grown old, shall I have pleasure, my Lord, being old also?" And the Lord said to Abraham, "Why did Sarah laugh," saying, 'shall I surely bear a child, since I am old'?" "Is anything too hard for the Lord? At the appointed time I will return to you, according to the time of life, and Sarah shall have a son." But Sarah denied it, saying, "I did not laugh," for she was afraid. And He said, "No, but you did laugh!"

Later, Sarah does conceive and gives birth to a son, and Abraham calls him Isaac (which means "the laughing one").

Boston (1974) notes that the laughter in this Biblical story is of two kinds: first, there are Abraham's and Sarah's laughs of disbelief (which may have been somewhat aggressive and annoying to the Lord); second, there is Sarah's ultimate laughter of joy and delight over being able to bear a child at such an advanced age (which is a sort of Hobbesian "sudden glory" situation wherein Sarah feels "present fertile superiority" over her former "infertile self"). Boston (1974, p. 45) also asserts that most references to laughter in the Bible are disparaging. For example, Proverbs 14: 13 states, "Even in laughter the heart may sorrow, And the end of mirth may be grief"; Ecclesiastes 7: 3, 4, 6 says, "Sorrow is better than laughter, For by a sad countenance the heart is made better; The heart of the wise is in the house of mourning, But the heart of fools is in the house of mirth"; and "For like the crackling of thorns under a pot, So is the laughter of the fool. This also is vanity"; Ecclesiastes 2: 1–2 states, "I said in my heart, 'Come now, I will test you with mirth; therefore enjoy pleasure'; but surely, this also was vanity. I said of laughter, 'It is madness'; and of mirth, 'What does it accomplish?'"

Boston (1974, p. 45) maintains that Jesus had a sense of humor—and that he probably did laugh—because his replies to the Pharisees show a sharp wit and his parables may be interpreted as having a "clear joke structure, complete with punch-line." Boston suggests that "those who admire both Jesus and laughter clearly have a problem on their hands" (pp. 46–47); he also asserts that most people (other than Sir Thomas Browne) instinctively find the idea of Jesus and laughter mutually exclusive. With the exception of Sarah's laugh at the birth of Isaac, neither the Old Testament nor the New Testament shows laughter in a particularly positive or attractive light. A Biblical laugh is usually one of contempt or indignation, rather than of mirth or jocosity. [Notes: Bergler (1956, p.

12) observes that G. K. Chesterton took great pains to prove that Jesus had a sense of humor—he contradicted the conventional biographers, asserting that if Jesus is not reported to have laughed, it was because he deliberately hid his mirth from men, covering it "constantly by abrupt silence or impetuous isolation." Additionally, Ludovici (1932, p. 11) suggests that how much more reverent and more indicative of a profound understanding of laughter is the question (as in Lamennais' protest): "Who could ever imagine Christ laughing?" cf: Wirt, 1991.]

Morreall (1983) also observes that in the Bible laughter has negative connotations; laughter is seldom mentioned in the Bible and when it is, it is almost always the laugh of derision (with the exception of Sarah's laughter that is based initially on her foolishness and failure to believe that God can do all things, and later is based in her joy concerning the bearing of a child). Morreall notes, also, as others have done, that Jesus is never represented in the Bible as laughing or enjoying humor. Historically, the Church Fathers said little about this matter, but St. John Chrysostom (c. 345–407; he was the Archbishop of Constantinople) gave one early Christian view of humor and laughter (cf: Bergler, 1956, p. 12; Boston, 1974, p. 45) when he asserted that to laugh or to speak jocosely does not seem to be an acknowledged sin, but it does *lead* to acknowledged sin. Thus, according to St. John Chrysostom, laughter often gives rise to foul discourse, and foul discourse leads to actions that are still more foul. The logical sequence is that railing and insult derive from words of laughter which, in turn, lead to blows and wounds, and from this come slaughter and murder. St. John Chrysostom counselled in the 4th century that one should avoid foul words, foul deeds, blows, wounds, murders, and even "unseasonable" laughter itself.

Morreall (1983, p. 126) states that it is no accident that Jesus is portrayed in the Gospels as having no sense of humor—Jesus' message is an urgent one, involving the greatest of consequences for the whole human race (cf: Alston & Platt, 1969; Buechner, 1977; Hyers, 1969, 1981, 1987; Jonsson, 1965; Sayward, 1980; Trueblood, 1964; Webster, 1960; Willimon, 1986). His divinity, also, would make him a completely serious person, for the Christian God could have no sense of humor (God knows fully everything and every event in the past, present, and future, and so nothing that happened could surprise Him). The logic here is that God is an all-knowing and changeless being where nothing that happened could amuse Him. He could not experience the psychological shift that is behind laughter. God would recognize incongruities, but as the failures of things to be what He intended them to be, not as events which delight by jolting one's picture of the world but as violations of His divine plan for the world. Thus, according to Morreall, all this explains why (as Baudelaire once suggested) the Incarnate Word was never known to laugh; for God who knows all things, and whose powers are infinite and boundless, the sense of comic does not exist.

In the "Universal Subject Guide to the Bible" section of his concordance, Strong (1990, p. 121) defines *laughter* as "an emotion expressive of joy, mirth, or ridicule," and gives various kinds of, and causes of, laughter. Among the *kinds* of laughter (with the associative Biblical scripture) are: divine laughter (e.g., Psalm 59: 8—"But you laugh at them, O Lord"); natural laughter (e.g., Job 8: 21—"He will yet fill your mouth with laughing"); derisive, scornful, and ridiculing laughter (e.g., 2 Chronicles 30: 10— "But they laughed them to scorn and mocked them"; and Nehemiah 2: 19— "They laughed us to scorn and despised us"); confident laughter (e.g., Job5: 22— "You shall laugh at destruction and famine"); and joyful laughter (e.g., Psalm 126: 2— "Then our mouth was filled with laughter, And our tongue with singing"). Among the *causes* of laughter (with the associative Biblical scripture) are: man's folly (e.g., Psalm 2: 4— "He who sits in the heavens shall laugh; The Lord shall hold them in derision"); something unusual/something untrue [e.g., Genesis 18: 12–15—(Sarah's story) and Matthew 9: 24— "Make room, for the girl is not dead, but sleeping. And they laughed Him to scorn"]; and something highly contradictory (e.g., Psalm 22: 7–8— "All those who see Me laugh Me to scorn; They shoot out the lip, they shake the head, saying, 'He trusted in the Lord, let Him rescue Him; Let Him deliver Him, since He delights in Him!'"

Strong (1990) cites the occasions of, absence of, and inadequacy of *mirth* ("a spirit of gaiety") in Genesis 31: 27; Nehemiah 8: 10–12; Jeremiah 25: 10–11; Hosea 2: 11; Proverbs 14: 13; and Ecclesiastes 2: 1–2. Strong (1990) also cites the numerous references to *joy* ("gladness of heart") in the Bible in his appendix, "Universal Subject Guide to the Bible" (p. 115; also, see pp. 571–572 in the "Main Concordance"); this covers the various kinds, causes, descriptions, contrasts, and expressions of joy in the Bible. The notion of *riddles* ("hidden sayings solved by guessing") is handled by Strong (1990) as well: Samson's famous riddle ("Out of the eater came something to eat. And out of the strong came something sweet")—Judges 14: 12–19; riddle classed as a parable—Ezekiel 17: 2; and riddle/dark sayings avoided by God—Numbers 12: 8.

Further references to *laugh/laughter* in the Bible (see Strong, 1990, p. 608) include: Luke 6: 25— "Woe to you who laugh now, For you shall mourn and weep"; Job 41: 29— "He laughs at the threat of javelins"; Psalm 37: 13— "The Lord laughs at him, For He sees that his day is coming."

Additionally, some individuals living in today's modern world may find humor in the following biblical passages and situations that seem inconsistent, incongruous, surprising, or downright odd: Numbers 22: 22–23 (the "talking donkey" episode in which Balaam has an argument/debate with his donkey); 1 Kings 18: 21–27 (the "busy god" episode in which Elijah mocks the prophets of Baal by saying, essentially, that their god doesn't answer because he is meditating, busy, on a journey, or sleeping!); 2 Kings 2: 23–24 (the prophet Elisha is met by a group of children who taunt him for being bald, and the mauling of 42 of the youths by two female bears as a consequence of Elisha's curse on them in the name of the Lord); 2 Kings 6: 28–33 (the Syria/Samaria "gallows humor" episode in which sons are boiled and eaten); Exodus 3: 2–5 (the surprise of Moses at viewing a "burning bush" that was not actually consumed); Exodus 4: 2–7 (the surprise of Moses at seeing his staff/rod turn into a serpent; and seeing his hand become leprous and then immediately restored by the Lord); Judges 4: 21 (the phraseology of scripture and "gallows humor" of the incident in which Jael, who was Heber's wife, "took a tent peg and took a hammer in her hand, and went softly to him and drove the peg into his temple"); Judges 7: 4–7 (the exchange between the Lord and Gideon regarding the manner in which a person "laps from the water"—with his tongue, as a dog laps, or bends down on his knees to drink); Deuteronomy 25: 1–16 (the perceived oppressiveness and specificity in the many biblical laws and rules; for example, the details given in verses 11–12: "If two men fight together, and the wife of one draws near to rescue her husband from the hand of the one attacking him, and puts out her hand and seizes him by the genitals, then you shall cut off her hand; your eye shall not pity her").

In a discussion of "Christianity," *The New Encyclopaedia Britannica* (1997, Vol. 16, p. 286) states that the roots of a specifically Christian sense of humor lie within the concept of joy, and that joy is a characteristic mark of distinction of the Christian. Joy is the spontaneous result of being filled with the Holy Spirit and is among the main fruits of the Holy Spirit. In congregational gatherings, joy is the basic mood that is often expressed in an exuberant jubilation. Theologically, joy has its origin in the recognition that the dominion of evil is already broken through the power of Christ, that death, devil, and demons no longer possess any claim upon believers, and that the forces of forgiveness, reconciliation, resurrection, and transfiguration are already effective in humankind. The principle of joy of the Christian is most strongly evident in the liturgy of the Eastern Orthodox Church. The peculiarity of the Christian sense of humor consists of the fact that in the midst of the conflicts of life the Christian is capable of regarding all sufferings and afflictions from the perspective of overcoming them in the future or from the perspective of victory over them already achieved in Christ.

In Christian humor, freedom and joy are combined. Christians do not allow themselves to be confused and tempted through suffering but already perceive in suffering, and the cross, a foretaste of eschatological triumph and joy. In this sense, the concept of *joy* has deeper roots in philosophy, theology, and eschatology (but not psychology) than does the concept of *humor*. At one extreme of the joy/humor continuum, the Danish philosopher Soren Kierkegaard is excessively dialectical and bitter and apparently unable to exhaust the entire fullness of the Christian joy. At the other end of the Christian joy/humor continuum, perhaps, is the liturgical approach and the "hallelujahs" of the black spiritual-ists.

Eastman (1921, p. 24) asserts that humor is of all things most *unlike* religion; it fills a similar function, however, in one's moral economy and gives respite to the strengths and intolerabilities of one's will. Humor achieves this by a simple emotional mitigation, says Eastman, whereas religion seems to require a great and heavy process in the heart. Religion magnifies our passions but finds an ob-ject which is impersonal or ideal. According to Eastman, the mystic declares that all the failures and imperfections in time's reality are a part of God's eternal perfection, and so He makes himself happy to suffer them. On the other hand, the humorist declares that the failure and imperfections of life are funny, and he accomplishes the same ends as the mystic. In Eastman's view, both the mystic and the humorist depart in some sense from the poet's pure experience of life, but they depart in opposite directions. Thus, it is not surprising that the mystics should seem wanting in the sacred gift of humor, and that humorists should be wanting in prayerful pursuits. In essense, says Eastman, a prayer is the intense opposite of a comic laugh. Humor is not inherently or necessarily evil or irrev-erent, but it is of a quality incompatible with that fixed concentration of serious feelings that are called "devout"; the nature of humor is flexibility and not fixa-tion, and its food is variety, not unity. Eastman (1921) maintains that humor is a "congenial companion of science" and is superior to religion in humor's "hos-pitality toward the continual arrivals of truth" (p. 25).

Apte (1985) also discusses the relationship between humor and religion (Chapter 5, "Humor in Religion," pp. 151–176). He states that both religion and humor are similar in that they are omnipresent, pervasive, and yet unobtru-sive at the level of individual consciousness in the way they affect the rest of hu-man behavior. Furthermore, anthropological investigations (cf: Malefijt, 1968; Wallace, 1966) show that humor has been intimately connected with religion in many cultures (save the debatable connection already evinced in the Bible and Christianity). Apte notes that after the "joking relationship," the topic of "hu-mor in religion" has received the most extensive attention from anthropolo-gists; the phenomena of clowning and other comical performances have been reported as part of religious ceremonies in ethnographic descriptions of cul-tures from various parts of the world.

Anthropological studies of humor in religion concentrate chiefly on the American Indians, and date from the last quarter of the 19th century to the pres-ent (e.g., Bricker, 1973; Crumrine, 1969; Norbeck, 1974; Parsons & Beals, 1934; Radin, 1914; Steward, 1931). The likely reason for so much data on the American Indian culture is that humor has been a major feature of both rituals and mythologies of American Indian religions. Apte suggests, also, that one reason for the anthropologist's interest in the humorous aspects of religion in preliterate societies may have been the "exotic" nature of the rites, because they often involved scatological and sexual acts that appeared to be a strange mixture of the "sacred" and the "profane" to the Western mind. The purpose and objective of Apte's account is to formulate some hypotheses based on analyses of the interconnections between humor and religion, and to evaluate briefly theories of humor in religion (e.g., a common thread that runs through the *psychological* theories is the emphasis on conflict resolution and on release from tension; however, these theories differ regarding the nature of the tension, its causes, and its release; the *sociological* theories by and large emphasize social criticism and social control as the primary function of ritual humor; however, these theories differ regarding the nature of social criticism). Apte suggests that ritual humor per se is not fundamentally different from humor in other social interactions; rather, the rituals provide a special framework intensifying the degree, mode of exaggeration, and incongruity of humor. Rituals allow humorists to behave outrageously and to have immunity from public ridicule and punishment for such behavior.

Among the theoretical propositions that Apte (1985, p. 176) generates regarding ritual humor are the following: the degree to which humor is integrated in rituals seems to vary not only across cultures but from ritual to ritual within individual cultures; social relationships and membership in specific groups are important criteria in the selection of ritual humorists; ritual clowns play an important role in ceremonials because they not only act as humorists but also carry out other important tasks; and the chief purpose of ritual humor appears to be community entertainment; religious ceremonies are the main events for large group interaction, especially in preliterate societies.

In an extensive account, Eckardt (1992, pp. 131–152) examines the notion of "Jewish humor" (cf: Ziv, 1986a,b, 1988; Ziv & Zajdman, 1993), and suggests that the phrase "humor amongst Jews" may be a better notation than "Jewish humor" because it is less constricting and less stereotyping. Berger (1961, pp. 67–68) accounts for Jewish humor not on the grounds of something peculiarly Jewish, but on the basis of a particular sociohistorical condition called "marginality" which is independent of Jewishness in and of itself (cf: Rosenberg & Shapiro, 1959). That is, the "margins" of society have been the Jewish habitat for many centuries; from a marginal position the individual sees things more clearly and, therefore, more humorously. It is the humorous capacity that allows the placement of oneself in the other's position, to look at oneself critically, and to take all serious matters lightly. Berger (1961) asserts that such characteristics are classically the definition of Jewishness, and such traits may all be seen as the products of social marginality. On the other hand, Eckardt (1992, p. 132) observes that the world contains many marginal peoples (e.g., African-Americans and American Hispanics), but in their contributions to American humor, Jews have become anything but marginalized (indeed, perhaps, in the United States Jews as a people are less and less marginalized).

Eckardt states that the question of the singularity of Jewish humor is thus not answered through the notion of "marginality" as such.

Reik (1929a,b) provides psychoanalytical insight into the Jewish psyche in his essay on Jewish wit. According to Reik, a salient characteristic of Jewish humor is that in so many cases it is directed against the Jews themselves, either as individuals or as a race. In psychoanalytic terms, this aspect of self-effacing humor most likely represents a genuine humorous appreciation of Jewish weaknesses, foibles, and deficiencies where the superego invites the ego in a critical but kindly manner to consider the shortcomings associated with the Jewish attitude and way of life. However, underneath such contemplation there is often the presence of a fierce aggressiveness against the self which, in turn, conceals an aggressiveness against the Gentile world—that world which fundamentally is held responsible for the common deficiencies that Jewish wit seems to understand and to deplore. In their jokes, for instance, the Jews might as well be saying, "Look what miserable, miserly, narrow-minded, and uncouth creatures you have made of us!" Reik asserts that in criticizing themselves, the Jews are really criticizing their enemies and oppressors, much as the self-criticism of the melancholic person is directed not so much against himself or herself as against an introjected object/target that he or she hates.

If the general tendency toward self-criticism as revealed in many Jewish jokes indicates an attitude close to that operating in melancholia—inasmuch as the criticism is really directed against an introjected hostile object—the pleasure momentarily experienced by the joke is reminiscent of the pleasure of mania as it originates from the achievement of a sudden freedom from the hostile introjected object that has so long been a burden and is responsible for so much guilt and self-directed aggression. Reik maintains that such Jewish humor-base pleasure represents a triumph over the oppressor both as introjected and as an outer object. Moreover, according to Reik, the aggression embedded in Jewish jokes need not be limited to human enemies; it may also be directed against what is, perhaps, the greatest tyrant and oppressor of all: the Jewish God himself.

Such an attitude is exemplified by the story of the old Jew (cf: Flugel, 1954, p. 718) who said on his deathbed: "Children, all my life I've worked hard and saved and haven't allowed myself the slightest bit of fun. I've always said to myself that it will all be corrected in the world beyond. However, I will *really* laugh if I find that there's nothing there either!" In such a story containing a superficial element of self-criticism—in which the dying man manifests a doubt as to the wisdom of his abstemious and hardworking way of life—there also appears an attitude of hostile skepticism about his religion and his God who may have fooled His worshippers by promises that would never be fulfilled (cf: Samuel Beckett's, 1952, play, *Waiting for Godot*, which illustrates how the aspiration to a meaningful life—represented by Godot who can be God or the

Revolution or any other significant event that is sought and waited for—cannot be realized because Godot never arrives; and Bertrand Russell's, 1918, essay, "*A Free Man's Worship*," in which God appears as a sadistic humorist, and in which an attitude of cynical humor to the Almighty himself is reflected).

Another view of Jewish humor is provided by Spalding (1969) who asserts that the true Jewish joke mirrors the history of the Jewish people—it is a reflection of their joy and anguish, their aspirations and defects, and their all-too-brief periods of social stability and economic well-being. Jewish humor expresses their age-old desire for a world in which mercy, justice, equality, and understanding will prevail, and it portrays their quest for eternal truths. [Note: Eckardt (1992, p. 149) observes that Jewish humor is, nevertheless, not free of sexism, as in the stereotypes of the "Jewish American Princess" (JAP) and the "Jewish Mother," both of which are male concoctions.] Spalding (1969) describes the various personages often present in Jewish humor stories and jokes. For example, the *schlemiel* may testify as a minor witness in court for his friend and winds up as the convicted party; the *shlimazel* is Jewry's original "hard-luck Harry" whose trousers fall down during his wedding ceremony; the stylish rabbi who demands a mink *yarmulkeh*; the cantor who thinks he's a reincarnated Caruso; and the fancy *mohel* on Park Avenue who insists on using pinking shears for circumcisions. All such cases evoke humor from Jewish listeners because they recognize a little something of themselves in many of the characters.

Another genre of Jewish humor is the "Yiddish droll story " (cf: *The New Encyclopaedia Britannica*, 1997, Vol 22, p. 451); for example: two "sages" went for a walk together, one carrying an umbrella and the other without one. Suddenly it began to rain. "Open your umbrella," said the one without one. "It won't help," answered the other, "it's full of holes." "Then why did you bring it?" rejoined his friend. "I didn't think it would rain," was the reply.

Bermant (1989) recommends the reading of the Yiddish author Sholom Aleichem (1859–1916) to gain an appreciation of the wryness, sharpness, rancor, irony, self-deprecation, cynicism, and pathos which characterize Jewish humor; such humor has a bittersweet quality with rather more bitterness than sweetness, and reflects a sort of resigned stoicism. Bermant suggests that Jewish humor is perhaps a reaction to the soul-searching lamentation required by Jewish tradition, and a defense against the humiliations and torments of their own experience so that in laughing at themselves Jews were able to withstand more readily the scorn of others. Laughter has always been the weapon of the weak against the strong, and the clown is forgiven everything, even—where necessary—his Jewishness.

S. B. Cohen (1987, p. 4) states that Jewish humor is not only based on the masochistic-like characteristics of the Jews expressed in their self-critical jokes, but it also has been a major source of their salvation. In laughing at their tragic conditions, Jews have been able to liberate themselves from those conditions; their humor serves as a balance for dealing with external adversity and with internal sadness.

Novak and Waldoks (1981) maintain that while Jewish humor may be self-critical and somewhat masochistic, it is usually substantive; that is, it is about something—it is infused with the intricacies of the mind and of logic. Novak and Waldoks note that Jewish humor, as a form of social or religious commentary, may be sarcastic, complaining, resigned, or descriptive; it tends to be antiauthoritarian, ridicules grandiosity and self-indulgence, exposes hypocrisy, and is essentially democratic. Jewish humor frequently has a critical edge that tends to create discomfort, and much of it is intended to give offense. Finally, according to Novak and Waldoks, Jewish humor mocks everyone—including God and religion (e.g., Woody Allen's quip that "Not only is there no God, but try getting a plumber on weekends"; McCann, 1990, p. 58)—but it nevertheless seeks a new understanding of the distinction between the mundane and the holy.

Further accounts, examples, and discussions of *Jewish humor* may be obtained from the following sources: Abramson (1991); Afek (1974); Allen (1972, 1978, 1981); Altman (1971); Ausubel (1948, 1967); Avidor-Haccohen (1976); Ben-Amos (1971); Berghahn (1991); Bermant (1986); Bloch (1983); Boyer (1991); Brandes (1983); Chase (1999); J. Cohen (1968); A. Cooper (1987); Cray (1964); Davies (1990, 1991); Dorinson (1981, 1984); Dorson (1960, 1961); Draitser (1994); Dreifus (1999); Dundes (1971); Ehrlich (1979); Eilbirt (1991); Eliach (1982); Glantz (1973); J. Goldberg (1983); M. Goldberg (1993); Goldman (1974); A. Greenberg (1972); I. Greenberg (1988); Grotjahn (1970, 1987); Guttman (1983); Harap (1987); D. A. Harris (1988); Hes and Levine (1962); Hirsch (1981); Howe (1987); Howe and Greenberg (1973); Kalmar (1987); Katz and Katz (1971); Knox (1963); Kristol (1951); Landmann (1962); Lewis (1987); Lieberman (1999); Lipman (1991); Maccoby (1979); McKnight (1983); Menghnagi (1991); Mindess (1972); Mintz (1977, 1989); Nevo (1985, 1986, 1991); Oring (1973, 1981, 1983, 1984a,b); Perelman (1947, 1963); Perlmutter (1991); Rabinowitz (1977); Raskin (1991, 1992, 1997); Reik (1954, 1962); Rivers (1984); Rosten (1959); Rovit (1966–1967); Samuel (1965); Saper (1991a,b); Saposnik (1991); Shechner (1989); Shulman (1980); Silverstein, (1981); Stora-Sandor (1991); Telushkin (1991); Weller, Amitsour, and Pazzi (1976); Wiener (1987); Wilde (1974, 1979); Yacowar (1979, 1981); Zangwill (1965); Ziv (1986a,b, 1988, 1991).

REFERENCES

Abramson, G. (1991). Mightier than the sword: Jewish cartoons and cartoonists in South Africa. *Humor: International Journal of Humor Research, 4*, 149–164.

Afek, Y. (Ed.) (1974). *Israeli humor and satire*. Tel Aviv: Sadan.

Allen, W. (1972). *Getting even*. New York: Warner Books.

Allen, W. (1978). *Without feathers*. London: Sphere Books.

Allen, W. (1981). *Side effects*. New York: Ballantine Books.

Alston, J. P., & Platt, L. A. (1969). Religious humor: A longitudinal content analysis of cartoons. *Sociological Analysis, 30*, 217–222.

Altman, S. (1971). *The comic image of the Jew: Explorations of a pop culture phenomenon*. Teaneck, NJ: Fairleigh Dickinson University Press.

Andrew, R. J. (1963). Evolution of facial expression. *Science, 142*, 1034–1041.

Andrew, R. J. (1965). The origins of facial expressions. *Scientific American, 213*, 88–94.

Apte, M. L. (1985). *Humor and laughter: An anthropological approach*. Ithaca, NY: Cornell University Press.

Aristotle. (1895). The Poetics. In S. H. Butcher (Ed./Translator), *Aristotle's theory of poetry and fine art*. New York: Macmillan.

Armstrong, M. (1928). *Laughing*. London: Jarrolds.

Ausubel, N. (1948). *A treasury of Jewish folklore*. New York: Crown.

Ausubel, N. (1967). *A treasury of Jewish humor*. New York: Doubleday.

Avidor-Haccohen, S. (1976). *Touching heaven, touching earth: Hassidic humor and wit*. Tel Aviv: Sadan.

Bain, A. (1876). *The emotions and the will*. New York: Appleton.

Beckett, S. (1952). *Waiting for Godot*. Paris: Editions de Minuit.

Beerbohm, M. (1921). Laughter. *North American Review, 214*, 39–49.

Ben-Amos, D. (1971). The "myth" of Jewish humor. *Western Folklore, 32*, 112–131.

Berger, P. L. (1961). *The precarious vision: A sociologist looks at social fictions and Christian faith*. Garden City, NY: Doubleday.

Berghahn, K. (1991). Comedy without laughter: Jewish characters in comedies from Shylock to Nathan. In R. Grimm & J. Herman (Eds.), *Laughter unlimited: Essays on humor, satire, and the comic*. Madison: University of Wisconsin Press.

Bergler, E. (1956). *Laughter and the sense of humor*. New York: Intercontinental Medical Book Corp.

Berlyne, D. E. (1969). Laughter, humor, and play. In G. Lindzey & E. Aronson (Eds.), *The handbook of social psychology*. (Vol. 3.) Reading, MA: Addison-Wesley.

Bermant, C. (1986). *What's the joke? A study of Jewish humor through the ages*. London: Weidenfeld & Nicolson.

Bermant, C. (1989). Humor, Jewish. In G. Abramson (Ed.), *The Blackwell companion to Jewish culture: From the eighteenth century to the present*. Oxford, UK: Basil Blackwell.

Bliss, S. H. (1915). The origin of laughter. *The American Journal of Psychology, 26*, 236–246.

Blistein, E. M. (1998). Humor. In *The Encyclopedia Americana, International Edition*. (Vol. 14.) Danbury, CT: Grolier.

Bloch, R. (1983). Fabiaux, fetishism, and Freud's Jewish jokes. *Representations, 4*, 1–26.

Boston, R. (1974). *An anatomy of laughter*. London: Collins.

Bowman, H. A. (1937). The humor of primitive peoples. In G. P. Murdock (Ed.), *Studies in the science of society*. New Haven, CT: Yale University Press.

Boyer, J. (1991). Schlemiezel: Black humor and the shtetl tradition. *Humor: International Journal of Humor Research, 4*, 165–176.

Brandes, S. (1983). Jewish-American dialect jokes and Jewish-American identity. *Jewish Social Studies, 45*, 233–240.

Bricker, V. R. (1973). *Ritual humor in Highland Chiapas*. Austin: University of Texas Press.

Brown, A., & Kimmey, J. L. (1968). *Comedy*. Columbus, OH: Merrill.

Buechner, F. (1977). *Telling the truth: The Gospel as tragedy, comedy, and fairy tale*. San Francisco: Harper & Row.

Butovskaya, M., & Kozintsev, A. (1996). A neglected form of quasi-aggression in apes: Possible relevance for the origins of humor. *Current Anthropology, 37*, 16–17.

Carpenter, R. (1922). Laughter, a glory in sanity. *American Journal of Psychology, 33*, 419–422.

Chase, J. (1999). *Inciting laughter: The rise of "Jewish humor" in nineteenth-century German culture*. Berlin/New York: Walter de Gruyter.

Chevalier-Skolnikoff, S. (1973). Facial expression of emotion in nonhuman primates. In P. Ekman (Ed.), *Darwin and facial expression*. New York: Academic Press.

Cohen, J. (Ed.) (1968). *The essential Lenny Bruce*. New York: Ballantine Books.

Cohen, S. B. (Ed.) (1987). *Jewish wry: Essays on Jewish humor*. Bloomington: Indiana University Press.

Cooper, A. (1987). Jewish sit-down comedy of Philip Roth. In S. B. Cohen (Ed.), *Jewish wry: Essays on Jewish humor*. Bloomington: Indiana University Press.

Cooper, L. (1922). *An Aristotelian theory of comedy*. New York: Harcourt.

Cray, E. (1964). The Rabbi trickster. *Journal of American Folklore, 77*, 331–345.

Crile, G. W. (1916). *Man—An adaptive mechanism*. New York: Macmillan.

Crumrine, N. R. (1969). Capakoba, the Mayo Easter ceremonial impersonator: Explanations of ritual clowning. *Journal for the Scientific Study of Religion, 8*, 1–22.

Darwin, C. (1872/1965). *The expression of the emotions in man and animals*. London: Murray; Chicago: University of Chicago Press.

Davies, C. (1990). An explanation of Jewish jokes about Jewish women. *Humor: International Journal of Humor Research, 3*, 363–378.

Davies, C. (1991). Exploring the thesis of the self-deprecating Jewish sense of humor. *Humor: International Journal of Humor Research, 4*, 189–209.

Dearborn, G. V. N. (1900). The nature of the smile and the laugh. *Science, 9*, 851–856.

Delage, Y. (1919). Sur la nature du comique. *La Revue du Mois, 20*, 337–354.

Dewey, J. (1894). The theory of emotion. *Psychological Review, 1*, 553–569.

Diserens, C. M. (1926). Recent theories of laughter. *Psychological Bulletin, 23*, 247–255.

Diserens, C. M., & Bonifield, M. (1930). Humor and the ludicrous. *Psychological Bulletin, 27*, 108–118.

Dorinson, J. (1981). Jewish humor: Mechanism for defense, weapon for cultural affirmation. *Journal of Psychohistory, 8*, 447–464.

Dorinson, J. (1984). Gold-dust twins of marginal humor: Blacks and Jews. *Maledicta, 8*, 163–192.

Dorson, R. (1960). Jewish-American dialect jokes on tape. In R. Patai, F. Utley, & D. Noy (Eds.), *Studies in Biblical and Jewish folklore*. Bloomington: Indiana University Press.

Dorson, R. (1961). More Jewish dialect stories. *Midwest Folklore, 10*, 133–146.

Draitser, E. (1994). Sociological aspects of the Russian Jewish jokes of the exodus. *Humor: International Journal of Humor Research, 7*, 245–268.

Dreifus, C. (1999). An interview with Mel Brooks and Carl Reiner. *Modern Maturity, 42*, 44–48.

Drever, J. (1917). *Instinct in man*. London: Cambridge University Press.

Dugas, J. (1902). *Psychologie du rire*. Paris: Alcan.

Dundes, A. (1971). A study of ethnic slurs: The Jew and the Polack in the United States. *Journal of American Folklore, 84*, 186–203.

Dupreel, E. (1928). Le probleme sociologique du rire. *Revue Philosophique, 106*, 213–260.

Eastman, M. (1921). *The sense of humor*. New York: Scribner's.

Eckardt, A. R. (1992). *Sitting in the earth and laughing: A handbook of humor*. New Brunswick, NJ: Transaction.

Ehrlich, H. J. (1979). Observations on ethnic and intergroup humor. *Ethnicity, 6*, 383–398.

Eibl-Eibesfeldt, I. (1972). Similarities and differences between cultures in expressive movements. In R. A. Hinde (Ed.), *Nonverbal communication*. London: Cambridge University Press.

Eibl-Eibesfeldt, I. (1975). *Ethology: The biology of behavior*. New York: Holt, Rinehart, & Winston.

Eilbirt, H. (1991). *What is a Jewish joke? An excursion into Jewish humor*. Northvale, NJ: Aronson.

Ekman, P. (Ed.) (1973). *Darwin and facial expression*. New York: Academic Press.

Ekman, P., & Friesen, W. V. (1975). *Unmasking the face*. Englewood Cliffs, NJ: Prentice-Hall.

Ekman, P., & Friesen, W. V. (1976). Measuring facial movement. *Environmental Psychology and Nonverbal Behavior, 1*, 56–75.

Eliach, Y. (1982). *Hasidic tales of the Holocaust*. New York: Avon Books.

Esar, E. (1952). *The humor of humor*. New York: Bramhall House.

Flugel, J. C. (1954). Humor and laughter. In G. Lindzey (Ed.), *Handbook of social psychology*. (Vol. 2.) Reading, MA: Addison-Wesley.

Freud, S. (1905/1916/1960). *Der witz und seine beziehung zum unbewussten*. London: Kegan Paul, Trench, Trubner.

Glantz, R. (1973). *The Jew in early American wit and graphic humor*. New York: KTAV Publishing House.

Goldberg, J. (1983). *Laughter through tears: The Yiddish cinema.* Rutherford, NJ: Fairleigh Dickinson University.

Goldberg, M. H. (1993). *Jewish connection: The incredible, ironic, bizarre, funny, and provocative in the story of the Jews.* Lanthan, MD: Scarborough House.

Goldman, A. (1974). *Ladies and gentlemen—Lenny Bruce!* New York: Random House.

Gopala-Swami, M. V. (1926). The genesis of the laughter instinct. *Psychological Studies/University of Misore, 1,* 1–25.

Greenberg, A. (1972). Form and function of the ethnic joke. *Keystone Folklore Quarterly, 27,* 144–161.

Greenberg, I. (1988). *The Jewish way: Living the holidays.* New York: Summit Books.

Gregory, J. C. (1923). Some theories of laughter. *Mind, 32,* 328–344.

Gregory, J. C. (1924). *The nature of laughter.* London: Kegan Paul

Greig, J. Y. T. (1923/1969). *The psychology of laughter and comedy.* New York: Dodd, Mead/Cooper Square.

Grotjahn, M. (1970). Jewish jokes and their relation to masochism. In W. H. Mendel (Ed.), *A celebration of humor.* Los Angeles: Mara Books.

Grotjahn, M. (1987). Dynamics of Jewish jokes. *American Behavioral Scientist, 30,* 96–99.

Gruner, C. R. (1978). *Understanding laughter: The workings of wit and humor.* Chicago: Nelson-Hall.

Guttman, A. (1983). Jewish humor. In L. D. Rubin (Ed.), *The comic imagination in American literature.* New Brunswick, NJ: Rutgers University Press.

Harap, L. (1987). *Dramatic encounters: The Jewish presence in twentieth century America.* Westport, CT: Greenwood Press.

Harris, D. A. (1988). *Jokes of oppression: The humor of Soviet Jews.* Northvale, NJ: Aronson.

Harris, W. H., & Levey, J. S. (Eds.) (1975). *The new Columbia encyclopedia.* New York: Columbia University Press.

Hayworth, D. (1928). The social origin and function of laughter. *Psychological Review, 35,* 367–384.

Hecker, E. (1873). *Die physiologie und psychologie des lachens und des komischen.* Leipzig: Engelmann.

Hes, J. P., & Levine, J. (1962). Kibbutz humor. *Journal of Nervous and Mental Disorders, 135,* 327–331.

Hirsch, F. (1981). *Love, sex, death, and the meaning of life: Woody Allen's comedy.* New York: McGraw-Hill.

Hobbes, T. (1651/1839). Human nature. In W. Molesworth (Ed.), *Hobbes' English works.* London: Cambridge University Press.

Hobbes, T. (1651/1904). *Leviathan.* London: Cambridge University Press.

Holy Bible: The New King James Version. (1984). Nashville, TN: Thomas Nelson.

Howe, I. (1987). The nature of Jewish laughter. In S. B. Cohen (Ed.), *Jewish wry: Essays on Jewish humor.* Bloomington: Indiana University Press.

Howe, I., & Greenberg, E. (Eds.) (1973). *A treasury of Yiddish stories.* New York: Schocken Books.

Hyers, C. (Ed.) (1969). *Holy laughter: Essays on religion in the comic perspective.* New York: Seabury Press.

Hyers, C. (1981). *The comic vision and the Christian faith.* New York: Pilgrim Press.

Hyers, C. (1987). *And God created laughter: The Bible as divine comedy.* Atlanta, GA: John Knox Press.

Jonsson, J. (1965). *Humour and irony in the New Testament: Illuminated by parallels in Talmud and Midrash.* Reykjavik: Bokautgafa Menningarsjods.

Kallen, H. M. (1911). The aesthetic principle in comedy. *American Journal of Psychology, 22,* 137–157.

Kalmar, I. (1987). Jews on the train. *Journal of Popular Culture, 21,* 139–154.

Katz, N., & Katz, E. (1971). Tradition and adaptation in American Jewish humor. *Journal of American Folklore, 84,* 215–220.

Keith-Spiegel, P. (1972). Early conceptions of humor: Varieties and issues. In J. H. Goldstein & P. E. McGhee (Eds.), *The psychology of humor: Theoretical perspectives and empirical issues.* New York: Academic Press.

Kline, L. W. (1907). The psychology of humor. *American Journal of Psychology, 18,* 421–441.

Knox, I. (1963). Traditional roots of Jewish humor. *Judaism, 12,* 330–331.

Koestler, A. (1964). *The act of creation.* London: Hutchinson.

Koestler, A. (1997). Humour and wit. In *The New Encyclopaedia Britannica. Macropaedia.* (Vol. 20.) Chicago: Encyclopaedia Britannica, Inc.

Kramer, S. N. (1956). *From the tablets of Sumer.* Indian Hills, CO: Falcon's Wing Press.

Kristol, I. (1951). Is Jewish humor dead? The rise and fall of the Jewish joke. *Commentary, 12,* 431–436.

Landmann, S. (1962). On Jewish humor. *Jewish Journal of Sociology, 4,* 193–194.

Leacock, S. B. (1935). *Humour: Its theory and technique.* New York: Dodd, Mead.

Leacock, S. B. (1937). *Humour and humanity.* London: Butterworth.

Lewis, P. (1987). Joke and anti-joke: Three Jews and a blindfold. *Journal of Popular Culture, 21,* 63–73.

Lieberman, L. (1999). *Memories of laughter and garlic: Jewish wit, wisdom, and humor to warm your heart.* Margate, NJ: Comte.

Lipman, S. (1991). *Laughter in Hell: The use of humor during the Holocaust.* Northvale, NJ: Aronson.

Loizos, C. (1967). Play behaviour in higher primates: A review. In D. Morris (Ed.), *Primate ethology.* London: Weidenfeld & Nicholson.

Ludovici, A. M. (1932). *The secret of laughter.* London: Constable Press.

Maccoby, H. (Ed.) (1979). *The day God laughed: Sayings, fables, and entertainments of the Jewish sages.* New York: St. Martin's Press.

MacHovec, F. J. (1988). *Humor: Theory, history, applications.* Springfield, IL: Charles C. Thomas.

Malefijt, A. (1968). *Religion and culture.* New York: Macmillan.

Martin, R. A. (2000). Humor and laughter. In A. E. Kazdin (Ed.), *Encyclopedia of psychology.* (Vol. 4.) Washington, DC: American Psychological Association; New York: Oxford University Press.

Mathews, W. (1888). *Wit and humor: Their use and abuse.* Chicago: S. C. Griggs.

McCann, G. (1990). *Woody Allen: New Yorker*. Cambridge, UK: Polity Press.

McComas, H. C. (1923). The origin of laughter. *Psychological Review, 30*, 45–55.

McDougall, W. (1903). The theory of laughter. *Nature, 67*, 318–319.

McDougall, W. (1922). Why do we laugh? *Scribners, 71*, 359–363.

McDougall, W. (1923). *An outline of psychology*. London: Methuen.

McGhee, P. E. (1979). *Humor: Its origin and development*. San Francisco: Freeman.

McKeon, R. (Ed.) (1941). *The basic works of Aristotle*. New York: Random House.

McKnight, G. (1983). *Woody Allen: Joking aside*. New York: W. H. Allen.

Meerloo, J. A. M. (1966). The biology of laughter. *Psychoanalytic Review, 53*, 189–208.

Menghnagi, D. (1991). Jewish humor in psychoanalysis. *International Journal of Psychoanalysis, 18*, 223–228.

Menon, V. K. (1931). *A theory of laughter*. London: Allen & Unwin.

Mindess, H. (1972). *Chosen people: A testament, both Old and New, to the therapeutic power of Jewish wit and humor*. Los Angeles: Nash.

Mintz, L. E. (1977). Jewish humor: A continuum of sources, motives, and functions. *American Humor, 4*, 4.

Mintz, L. E. (1989). Devil and angel: Philip Roth's humor. *Studies in American Jewish Literature, 8*, 154–167.

Monro, D. H. (1951). *Argument of laughter*. Melbourne: Melbourne University Press.

Morreall, J. (1983). *Taking laughter seriously*. Albany: State University of New York Press.

Morreall, J. (Ed.) (1987). *The philosophy of laughter and humor*. Albany: State University of New York Press.

Nevo, O. (1985). Does one ever laugh at one's own expense? The case of Jews and Arabs in Israel. *Journal of Personality and Social Psychology, 49*, 799–807.

Nevo, O. (1986). Humor diaries of Israeli Jews and Arabs. *Journal of Social Psychology, 126*, 411–413.

Nevo, O. (1991). What's in a Jewish joke? *Humor: International Journal of Humor Research, 4*, 251–260.

New Encyclopedia Britannica. (1997). Fifteenth edition. Chicago: Encyclopedia Britannica, Inc.

New Revised Standard Version Bible. (1991). Grand Rapids, MI: Zondervan.

Norbeck, E. (1974). *Religion in human life: Anthropological views*. New York: Holt, Rinehart, & Winston.

Novak, W., & Waldoks, M. (Eds.) (1981). *The big book of Jewish humor*. New York: Harper & Row.

Oring, E. (1973). "Hey, you've go no character": Chizbat humor and the boundaries of Israeli identity. *Journal of American Folklore, 86*, 358–366.

Oring, E. (1981). *Israeli humor and its oral tradition*. Albany: State University of New York Press.

Oring, E. (1983). People of the joke: On the conceptualization of Jewish humor. *Western Folklore, 42*, 261–271.

Oring, E. (1984a). Jokes and their relation to Sigmund Freud. *Western Folklore, 43*, 37–48.

Oring, E. (1984b). *The jokes of Sigmund Freud: A study in humor and Jewish identity.* Philadelphia: University of Pennsylvania Press.

Parsons, E. C., & Beals, R. L. (1934). The sacred clowns of the Pueblo and Mayo-Yaqui Indians. *American Anthropologist, 36*, 491–514.

Penjon, A. (1893). Le rire et la liberte. *Revue Philosophique, 36*, 113–140.

Perelman, S. J. (1947). *The best of S. J. Perelman.* New York: Modern Library.

Perelman, S. J. (1963). *The most of S. J. Perelman.* New York: Simon and Schuster.

Perlmutter, R. (1991). Woody Allen's "Zelig": An American Jewish parody. In A. S. Horton (Ed.), *Comedy/cinema/theory.* Berkeley: University of California Press.

Piddington, R. (1933/1963). *The psychology of laughter: A study in social adaptation.* London: Figurehead; New York: Gamut.

Porteous, J. (1988). Humor as a process of defense: The evolution of laughing. *Humor: International Journal of Humor Research, 1*, 63–80.

Quintilian, M. F. (1714/1821–1825). *De institutione oratoria.* London: Heinemann; Paris: Lamaire.

Rabinowitz, H. R. (1977). *Kosher humor.* Jerusalem: Mass.

Radcliffe-Brown, A. R. (1965). *Structure and function in primitive society.* New York: Free Press.

Radday, Y. (1991). On missing the humour in the Bible. In Y. Radday (Ed.), *On humour and the comic in the Hebrew Bible.* Sheffield, UK: Academic Press.

Radday, Y. (1995). Sex and women in Biblical narrative humor. *Humor: International Journal of Humor Research, 8*, 363–384.

Radin, P. (1914). Religion of the North American Indians. *Journal of American Folklore, 27*, 335–373.

Rapp, A. (1947). Toward an eclectic and multilateral theory of laughter and humor. *The Journal of General Psychology, 36*, 207–219.

Rapp, A. (1949). A phylogenetic theory of wit and humor. *Journal of Social Psychology, 30*, 81–96.

Rapp, A. (1951). *The origins of wit and humor.* New York: Dutton.

Raskin, R. (1991). God versus man in a classic Jewish joke. *Judaism, 40*, 39–51.

Raskin, R. (1992). *Life is like a glass of tea: Studies of classic Jewish jokes.* Aarhus, Denmark: Aarhus University Press.

Raskin, R. (1997). Far from where? On the history and meanings of a classic Jewish refugee joke. *American Jewish History, 85*, 143–150.

Reik, T. (1929a). Kunstlerisches schaffen und witzarbeit. *Imago, 15*, 200–231.

Reik, T. (1929b) Zur psychoanalyse des judischen witzes. *Imago, 15*, 63–88.

Reik, T. (1954). Freud and Jewish wit. *Psychoanalysis, 2*, 12–20.

Reik, T. (1962). *Jewish wit.* New York: Gamut Press.

Rivers, J. (1984). *The life and times of Heidi Abromowitz.* New York: Delacorte.

Rosenberg, B., & Shapiro, G. (1959). Marginality and Jewish humor. *Midstream, 4*, 70–80.

Ross, W. D. (Ed.) (1931). *The works of Aristotle translated into English.* Oxford, UK: Clarendon Press.

Rosten, L. (1959). *The return of Hyman Kaplan.* New York: Harper.

Rovit, E. (1966–1967). Jewish humor and American life. *American Scholar, 36,* 237–245.

Russell, B. (1918). *Mysticism and logic.* London: Allen and Unwin.

Samuel, M. (1965). *The world of Sholom Aleichem.* New York: Schocken Books.

Saper, B. (1991a). A cognitive-behavioral formulation of the relationship between the Jewish joke and anti-Semitism. *Humor: International Journal of Humor Research, 4,* 41–59.

Saper, B. (1991b). The JAP joke controversy: An excruciating psychosocial analysis. *Humor: International Journal of Humor Research, 4,* 223–239.

Saposnik, I. (1991). The Yiddish are coming! The Yiddish are coming! Some thoughts on Yiddish comedy. In R. Grimm & J. Herman (Eds.), *Laughter unlimited: Essays on humor, satire, and the comic.* Madison: University of Wisconsin.

Sayward, J. (1980). *Perfect fools: Folly for Christ's sake in Catholic and orthodox spirituality.* New York: Oxford University Press.

Schmidt, H. E., & Williams, D. I. (1971). The evolution of theories of humour. *Journal of Behavioural Sciences, 1,* 95–106.

Shechner, M. (1989). Comedy, Jewish. In G. Abramson (Ed.), *The Blackwell companion to Jewish culture: From the eighteenth century to the present.* Oxford, UK: Basil Blackwell.

Shulman, A. (1980). *Adventures of a Yiddish lecturer.* New York: Pilgrim Press.

Silverstein, S. (1981). *A light in the attic.* New York: Harper & Row.

Spalding, H. E. (Ed.) (1969). *Encyclopedia of Jewish humor: From Biblical times to the modern age.* New York: Jonathan David.

Spencer, H. (1860). The physiology of laughter. *Macmillan's Magazine, 1,* 395–402.

Stanner, W. E. H. (1982). Aboriginal humor. *Aboriginal History, 6,* 39–48.

Steward, J. (1931). The ceremonial buffoon of the American Indian. *Papers of the Michigan Academy of Science, Arts, and Letters, 14,* 187–207.

Stora-Sandor, J. (1991). The stylistic metamorphosis of Jewish humor. *Humor: International Journal of Humor Research, 4,* 211–222.

Strong, J. (1990). *The new Strong's exhaustive concordance of the Bible.* Nashville, TN: Thomas Nelson.

Sully, J. (1902). *Essay on laughter.* New York: Longmans, Green.

Sypher, W. (Ed.) (1956). *Comedy.* Garden City, NY: Doubleday/Anchor.

Telushkin, J. (1991). *Jewish humor: What the best Jewish jokes say about the Jews.* New York: Morrow.

Thomas, E. M. (1959). *The harmless people.* New York: Knopf.

Trueblood, E. (1964). *Humor of Christ.* New York: Harper & Row.

VanHooff, J. (1967). The facial displays of the Catarrhine monkeys and apes. In D. Morris (Ed.), *Primate ethology.* London: Weidenfeld & Nicholson.

VanHooff, J. (1972). A comparative approach to the phylogeny of laughter and smile. In R. A. Hinde (Ed.), *Nonverbal communication.* New York: Cambridge University Press.

Vasey, G. (1875). *The philosophy of laughter and smiling.* London: Burns.

Wallace, A. F. C. (1966). *Religion: An anthropological view.* New York: Random House.

Wallis, W. D. (1922). Why do we laugh? *Scientific Monthly, 15*, 343–347.

Webster, G. (1960). *Laughter in the Bible*. St. Louis: Bethany.

Weisfeld, G. E. (1993). The adaptive value of humor and laughter. *Ethology and Sociobiology, 14*, 141–169.

Weller, L., Amitsour, E., & Pazzi, R. (1976). Reactions to absurd humor by Jews of eastern and western descent. *Journal of Social Psychology, 98*, 159–164.

Wells, C. (1932). *An outline of humor*. New York: Putnam's.

Wiener, M. (1987). On Sholom Aleichem's humor. In S. B. Cohen (Ed.), *Jewish wry: Essays on Jewish humor*. Bloomington: Indiana University Press.

Wilde, L. (1974). *The official Jewish/Irish joke book*. New York: Pinnacle Books.

Wilde, L. (1979). *More of the official Jewish/Irish joke book*. New York: Pinnacle Books.

Willimon, W. (1986). *And the laugh shall be first: A treasury of religious humor*. Nashville, TN: Abingdon.

Willmann, J. M. (1940). An analysis of humor and laughter. *American Journal of Psychology, 53*, 70–85.

Wirt, S. (1991). The heresy of the serious: If Jesus is fully human, as orthodoxy insists, then surely he has a healthy sense of humor. *Christianity Today, 35*, 43–44.

Yacowar, M. (1979). *Loser take all: The comic art of Woody Allen*. New York: Ungar.

Yacowar, M. (1981). *The comic art of Mel Brooks*. New York: St. Martin's Press.

Zangwill, I. (1965). *The king of schnorrers*. New York: Dover.

Ziv, A. (1984). *Personality and sense of humor*. New York: Springer.

Ziv, A. (Ed.) (1986a). *First and second international conferences on Jewish humor*. Tel Aviv: Tel Aviv University.

Ziv, A. (Ed.) (1986b). *Jewish humor*. Tel Aviv: Papyrus.

Ziv, A. (1988). Humor in Israel. In A. Ziv (Ed.), *National styles of humor*. Westport, CT: Greenwood Press.

Ziv, A. (1991). Jewish humor: Introduction. *Humor: International Journal of Humor Research, 4*, 145–148.

Ziv, A., & Zajdman, A. (Eds.) (1993). *Semites and stereotypes: Characteristics of Jewish humor*. Westport, CT: Greenwood Press.

Modern Theoretical Aspects of Humor

This chapter is divided into two main sections: Nonpsychological Theories of Humor, and Psychological Theories of Humor. In general, material is presented in chronological order from earliest to more recent theories. Major source and reference materials for these sections include the following: Bergler (1956), Berlyne (1969), Diserens (1926), Eastman (1921), Flugel (1954), Gregory (1923, 1924), Greig (1923/1969), Keith-Spiegel (1972), Kimmins (1928), MacHovec (1988), Monro (1951/1963), Morreall (1987b), Piddington (1933/1963), and Sully (1902).

NONPSYCHOLOGICAL THEORIES OF HUMOR

> Laughter manifests itself in such varied and heterogeneous conditions that the reduction of all these causes to a single one remains a very problematical undertaking. After so much work on such a trivial phenomenon the problem is still far from being completely explained.
> —T. A. Ribot, 1896/1897/1939

> The earnest analysts of laughter become themselves laughable.
> —M. Armstrong, 1928

> In recent years there have been many efforts to design mechanical, electronic, chemical, mathematical, and computer-program models for living organisms . . . But so far, no designer has found it necessary to equip his model with capacities corresponding to human playfulness and sense of humor.
> —D. E. Berlyne, 1969

Comedy may not be a single identifiable subject for which any individual
theory or set of data will be adequate.
                                                                —M. Charney, 1978

Syzygy theory is the first eclectic theory of humor. It includes previous
theories and attempts to integrate them . . . What's funny is a syzygy or convergence of three cluster-like forces: polarity, power, and process. Without
their convergence there is no humor . . . (syzygy theory) appears to be a
good teaching model since it does not exclude previous theories nor favor
one over another.
                                                                —F. J. MacHovec, 1988

Theories Based in Literature

In discussing literary humor theories of the Renaissance period (14th–16th
centuries; the transition from medieval to modern times), Greig (1923/1969,
p. 227) notes that all the Italian literary writers/critics of the Renaissance (e.g.,
Trissino, Maggi, Muzio, Minturno, Scaliger; see Springarn, 1912,
pp. 103–105; cf: "theories of comedy," in *The New Encyclopaedia Britannica*,
1997, Vol. 23, *Macropaedia*, pp. 152–155; Lauter, 1964) derive their notions of
laughter and comedy exclusively from the fragmentary remarks of Aristotle,
and from the works of the Roman writers/comic dramatists Plautus (c. 254–184
B.C.) and Terence (c. 195–159 B.C.) [cf: Piddington (1933/1963, p. 155);
Bergler (1956, p .4)]. At that time, the contemporary *commedia dell'arte* (a
popular Italian form of comedy employing improvised dialogue and masked
characters, and that had an influence on French pantomime and the English harlequinade) was beneath the critics' consideration or notice.

In Greig's (1923/1969) account, Trissino takes a moralistic tone, and makes
the function of the comic poet to be a portrayal of human base actions—so as to
condemn them (i.e., laughter comes from the pleasure one takes in what is
"low"). Maggi's contribution ("the most interesting opinion from the psychological point of view"; Piddington, 1933/1963, p. 155) was in the form of a
modification of the standard Aristotelian maxims by adding the literary element of "surprise," a theoretical supplement to humor theory that had been
noted earlier by Cicero and Quintilian (e.g., one does not laugh at the painlessly
ugly which is familiar, but at the "new" and "unexpected"; cf: T. Wilson,
1560/1909/1994, who confesses his inability to say what laughter is; and Greig,
1923/1969, p. 229).

Greig notes that Muzio expresses regret that the comic poets of his day were
more intent on making people laugh than on correcting the manners of the time;
on the other hand, the writer Minturno adopts a somewhat milder view than
Muzio's and advocated that laughter was not to be deprecated. The great philol-
ogist J. C. Scaliger emphasized the aspect of "form" in humor [cf: the similar

position taken by the Frenchmen Pelletier and DeLaudun; see Springarn (1912, pp. 200, 204)], and defined the comic poem as a dramatic poem that consists of intrigues, is in the popular style, and has a happy ending (cf: Springarn, 1908, 1912, p. 105).

Bergler (1956, p. 4) sums up the contributions to humor theory of the five Italian Renaissance theorists (i.e., Trissino, Maggi, Muzio, Minturno, Scaliger) by stating that these theories of laughter "remind one of the participant in a discussion who finally gets the floor and begins his remarks with the announcement: 'I *also* have nothing to say.' " Bergler also declares that neither the Romans nor the writers of the Renaissance made substantial contributions to the *theory* of laughter.

Coterminous with, and following, the Italian Renaissance, the English literary theorists and critics of the 16th–17th centuries (in "Elizabethan England") were concerned mainly with the low standard of contemporary comedy. For example, the English poet/dramatist George Whetstone (1551?–1587) contrasted the high level of the comedies of Menander, Plautus, and Terence with the low standard of comic drama not only in England, but throughout all of Europe; Whetstone referred to the comedies of the Italians, French, and Spaniards are "lascivious," to those of the Germans as "holy," and to those of the English as "vain," "indiscreet," and "out of order" [see Whetstone (1578/1904, p. 59); Piddington (1933/1963, p. 156); Greig (1923/1969, pp. 229–230)].

Sir Philip Sidney (1554–1586) maintained that the aim of comedy is *not* to excite laughter; it is an imitation of the common errors of life; and it handles the "filthiness of evil" in people's private and domestic lives [see Sidney (1591/1904, pp. 176–177); cf: the similar views of Sir John Harrington (1591/1904, p. 210) who states that "comedies may make men see, and shame at, their own faults"; Hugh Blair (1793/1970, Vol. 3, p. 356) who asserts that comedy proposes for its object the follies, improprieties, and slighter vices of men; R. P. Knight (1805/1808, p. 417) who states that laughter is the expression of triumph over new and uncommon combinations of vices, errors, or frailties; Sir George Ramsay (1848) who classifies the "ludicrous" emotion—along with the emotions of "beauty" and "sublimity"—as the object of taste; the ludicrous emotion is passive, immediate, pleasing, and temporary, and its cause is a combination of novelty and excessive contrast; and Adolph Zeising (1855) who suggests that the comic consists of three phases: a shock—caused by an object that seems to be something and is really nothing; a countershock—caused by a realization of the nothingness of the object; and laughter—caused by a personal assertion of our superiority over the nothingness].

The great English playwright Ben Jonson (1572–1637) produced his first important play, *Every Man in His Humour* in 1598 with William Shakespeare in the cast; the companion play, *Every Man Out of His Humour*, was produced in 1599 (see Harris & Levey, 1975, p. 1430). Ben Jonson carried on the criticism of the earlier Elizabethans in deploring the lack of unity and classic form ("classical role of the unities") in the contemporary English comedy (cf: G. G. Smith's, 1909, Chapter 4, critical/literary exposition of Jonson's "theory of comedy"). Jonson accepted the current theory of the function of comedy (i.e., a criticism of mankind's follies); comedy must be real, must not be confused with farce, and must be distinguished carefully from tragedy. According to Jonson, the primary function of comedy is to correct faults rather than to provoke laughter [cf: Greig (1923/1969, p. 230); Piddington (1933/1963, p. 157)]. Jonson's conception of, and use of, the term *humorous* is derived from the medieval medical doctrine of the "humors/humours" or "humoral theory" (see my Chapter 1, "Definitions of the Concept of Humor" section; and Roeckelein, 1998, pp. 199, 243); the "humorous" character is the person in whom one trait is developed out of proportion to the other traits that go to make up the individual's whole personality; it is the function of comedy to restore the natural balance in the person—similar to the medieval medical therapy/practice of bleedings and purgings—that has been disturbed by the exaggeration of a single character trait.

Jonson asserts that the purpose of comedy is to note those elements in human character that are naturally and permanently dominant in each person (or those that are excessive and overflow) at the expense of other elements, to portray this in a number of characters differently "humoured," and—by showing the clash of contrasts—to indicate with pleasant laughter the "moral" of these disorders. Under such circumstances, according to Jonson, an individual may be said to be "in his humour" or to be "out of his humour" (see Jonson, 1598/1816; 1599/1816). The term *humour*, as employed and "fixed down" by Jonson, retained that meaning for more than a century of literary criticism in England [see Greig (1923/1969, p. 231) and Piddington (1933/1963, p. 157)].

The French playwright/actor Jean Baptiste Poquelin Moliere (1622–1673) theorized about his own art only in self-defense: he accepted the moral aim of comedy (i.e., to correct through amusement). Moliere maintained that ridicule is more effective than condemnation, but he protested against the accusation of singling out particular individuals for ridicule [see Moliere (1662–1664/1817); Greig (1923/1969, p. 233)].

Sir William Temple (1628–1699), English diplomat and author, was the first to suggest that humor is a quality peculiar to the English; the reason Temple gives for this sentiment is that there is less "uniformity of life" in England than on the continent [see Temple (1692/1750, Vol. 2, p. 346); Greig (1923/1969, p. 237)].

The English poet/dramatist/critic John Dryden (1631–1700) was the first to break away from the Jonsonian tradition, and to assert (even though tragedy may secondarily instruct) that the main aim of comedy is to delight [see Dryden (1671/1900, p. 136); cf: Thomas Shadwell's attack on Dryden's view here in

Springarn (1912, Vol. 2, pp. 153–154, "Preface to The Humorists")]. Dryden recognized as the essential elements in laughter the appetite for the unexpected as well as a certain amount of "malicious pleasure" (Piddington, 1933/1963, p. 158).

The English dramatist William Congreve (1670–1729), whose plays are considered to be "the greatest achievement of Restoration Comedy" (Harris & Levey, 1975, p. 627), wrote comedies that dealt with manners and depicted an artificial and narrow world peopled by characters of nobility and fashion—to whom manners, especially gallantry, are more important than morals; his plays are equalled perhaps only by the comedies of Oscar Wilde (1854–1900). According to Greig (1923/1969, p. 234), Congreve cannot, or at the least will not, define *wit* and *humor*, and he can "never care for seeing things that force him to entertain low thoughts of his nature." Thus, by association and implication, Congreve maintains that such things cannot be the proper subject-matter of comedy (cf: Congreve, 1695/1908, p. 244).

Joseph Addison (1672–1719), the English essayist, poet, and statesman, devoted several issues of the famous publication *The Spectator* (1711–1714) to discussions of the topics of humor, laughter, and wit. In these discussions, the psychological problem of laughter was dealt with, in addition to various questions related to the ludicrous in literature (cf: Addison, 1711/1909, especially issues numbered 47, 62, 249, 494, 598). In general, Addison supports both Hobbes' "sudden glory" theory of laughter and Locke's "separation" theory; see section later in this chapter, "Theories Based in Modern Philosophy"). Bergler (1956, p. 7) notes that Addison "adds a proviso to Locke's theory maintaining that the unexpected juxtaposition and resemblance of ideas must produce delight and surprise in order to constitute wit"; and Piddington (1933/1963, p. 162) observes that Addison not only endorses the notion of the resemblance of ideas, but also that the *opposition* of ideas often produces wit.

Moreover, Addison draws a distinction between comedy (which ridicules people by representing them as they are) and burlesque (which ridicules people by representing them as unlike themselves); thus, burlesque attains its objective by representing mean persons in the accoutrements of heroes, or by describing great persons speaking and acting like the lowest among the people. By way of evolution of the relative merits of serious and merry men, Addison comes to the conclusion that either quality—carried to excess—may be detrimental to the personality, and that the ideal condition is to balance the two elements (e.g., a person should not live as though there were no God in the world or, at the same time, as though there were no men in it) (cf: Piddington, 1933/1963, p. 162; Bergler, 1956, p. 7).

The views on humor and comedy of the English statesman and author Philip Dormer Stanhope (1694–1773), the 4th Earl of Chesterfield, seem to be well-known: he considered laughter to be "illiberal" and "ill-bred" (see

Chestefield, 1748/1901/1925, letter 144). According to Chesterfield, loud laughter is the "mirth of the mob" who are only pleased with nonsense, silly things, low buffoonery, and silly accidents; and true wit or good sense never evoked a laugh since the world's creation.

The French author/philosopher Francois Marie Arouet de Voltaire (1694–1778) maintained simply that laughter is a sign of joy just as tears are a symptom of pain, and that anyone who pushes the matter further "is a fool" (Voltaire, 1764/1816/1832/1994; cf: Harris & Levey, 1975, pp. 2910–2911; *The New Encyclopaedia Britannica*, 1997, Vol. 29, *Macropaedia*, pp. 524–528).

The English novelist/dramatist Henry Fielding's (1707–1754) novel *Tom Jones* (because of its memorable characters and episodes, the brilliance of its plotting, and the generosity of its moral vision) is considered to be one of the greatest of English novels (Harris & Levey, 1975, p. 945). Fielding regarded himself to be the founder of a new way of writing—the "comic epic poem in prose" (see Fielding, 1742/1935, "Preface"). The logical sequence in Fielding's theory of comedy is as follows (cf: Greig, 1923/1969, p. 237): The only source of the truly ridiculous is affectation; affectation proceeds from either vanity or hypocrisy; from the discovery of such affectations, the ridiculous arises and always strikes the reader with surprise and pleasure (the surprise/pleasure is in a higher/stronger degree when the affectation arises from hypocrisy than when from vanity). Comedy of the sort that ridicules the vices and follies of society to the result of laughing them out of countenance entered the English novel with Fielding, and his description in *Joseph Andrews* (Fielding, 1742/1935) concerning the function of satire is illustrative of the Neoclassic tradition of comedy as a corrective of mores and manners (cf: *The New Encyclopaedia Britannica*, 1997, p. 157).

The English author Samuel Johnson (1709–1784) is notable primarily for his *Dictionary of the English Language* (1755)—the first comprehensive lexicographical work on the English language ever undertaken. Johnson's view of comedy took on an "anticlassical" aspect when he declared in one of *The Rambler* papers (see Johnson, 1751/1802/1807, number 125) that "any man's reflections will inform him, that every dramatic composition which raises mirth, is comick; and that to raise mirth, it is by no means universally necessary that the personages should be either mean or corrupt, nor always requisite, that the action should be trivial, nor ever that it should be fictitious" (cf: Greig, 1923/1969, p. 239). According to Boswell (1887, Vol. 2, p. 378), Johnson—who was on record saying that his famous literary seniors Jonathan Swift and Alexander Pope never laughed—himself had a different habit altogether: he laughed "like a rhinoceros."

Mark Akenside (1721–1770), English poet and physician, versifies the standard theory of comedy of his day (e.g., "laughter's gay rebuke"; "laughter's gay contempt") in his chief literary work (a didactic poem), *Pleasures of the Imagination* (Akenside, 1744/1810).

The English critic and poet Joseph Warton (1722–1800) compared the ancient writers of comedy (from Aristophanes) with the moderns and found the moderns to be superior in that area of literature (especially in humor and ridicule). Warton maintained that the ancients had more "liberty" and "seriousness," while the moderns have more "luxury" and "laughter." He attributed the superiority of the modern writers, in general, to their more advanced state of conversation in which—by uniting men more closely and frequently—the opportunities are enhanced for observing the absurdities and incongruities of behavior in which ridicule is grounded (cf: Gerard, 1759/1780, p. 66; G. Campbell, 1776/1846, pp. 42, 45, 57–58). Warton's writings (e.g., Warton, 1754/1802/1807, number 133) contribute very little to a *psychological* theory of laughter, but he does cast valuable sidelights on the issue (Piddington, 1933/1963, p. 164). In particular, Warton extols the excellence of the French playwright Moliere as a comic dramatist: "He seems to have hit upon the true nature of comedy . . . to exhibit one singular, and unfamiliar, by such a series of incidents as may best contribute to show its singularities" (Piddington, 1933/1963, p. 164; Greig, 1923/1969, p. 241).

The French critic, dramatist, and storywriter Jean Francois Marmontel (1723–1799) asserted that the elements of surprise and malice form the basis for comedy and laughter, and when we laugh at ourselves there is a "duplicity of character" (Marmontel, 1751/1778; cf: Greig, 1923/1969, p. 240).

The German dramatist, critic, and philosopher Gotthold Ephraim Lessing (1729–1781) wrote a series of critical essays, *Hamburgische Dramaturgie* (1767–1769), in which he attacked the French classical theater, claiming that it had failed to capture the true spirit of Aristotelian dramatic unities. Lessing asserted that comedy corrects by laughter, but not by derision, and it does not correct exactly those failings on which it turns the laugh (nor solely those persons in which it exposes such laughable failings). Comedy, rather, has its true and general utility in laughter itself, and in the exercise it gives one to seize upon the ridiculous both in passion and custom, and in all combinations with bad and good qualities, including solemn earnestness (cf: Greig, 1923/1969, p. 243).

The Anglo-Irish author Oliver Goldsmith (1730?-1774) suggested that the critics of his day made the phenomenon of comedy impossible by refusing to allow the comic poet to deal with what is "low" (Greig, 1923/1969, p. 239). According to Goldsmith, humor is based on the comparison between the absurdity of the character portrayed and one's own character, and on the subsequent triumph via conscious superiority one feels in such a comparison; moreover, the pleasure one receives from wit involves the admiration of another person whereby—through feelings derived from humor—the admiration returns to self-admiration, thus establishing the subject of humor as "low" (Goldsmith, 1750/1854/1858, Chapter 9).

Joseph Priestley (1733–1804), the English theologian and scientist—whose concept of "dephlogisticated air" anticipated Antoine Laurent Lavoisier's discovery of oxygen—asserted that laughter arises from the perception of contrast (Priestley, 1777/1971, pp. 200, 205, 238); also, he surmised, almost any brisk emotion or surprise—suddenly checked and recurring alternately—will result in laughter. Priestley defines the term *risible* as anything in which one perceives a great incongruity or disproportion—provided that the object does not, at the same time, excite a more serious emotion; when the element of contempt is added to the risible, it becomes the ridiculous. Moreover, according to Priestley, men can hardly be the object of a laugh that is *not* more or less a laugh of derision and excited by the ridiculous (Greig, 1923/1969, pp. 245–246).

The longest 18th-century essay on laughter is that by the Scottish poet/essayist James Beattie (1735–1803) who points out that though humor and wit frequently raise laughter, they do not invariably do so. He also makes a distinction between the ludicrous and the ridiculous in which the ludicrous excites "pure laughter" and is free from the element of contempt that is involved in the ridiculous (cf: Diserens & Bonifield, 1930). Moreover, Beattie distinguishes between "natural" and "unnatural/forced" laughter (cf: Laprade, 1861, p. 327, who differentiates between laughter of "gaiety" and laughter of "irony"); natural laughter is subdivided into "animal" laughter (e.g., tickling, gladness) and "sentimental" laughter (e.g., the appreciation of ludicrous ideas).

Beattie discusses Aristotle's views on comedy and observes that Aristotle's approach is intended as a guide to what the comic writer *ought* to write rather than as a theory regarding the nature of the situations that *do* raise laughter. Beattie suggests that Aristotle's theory of comedy is unsound as a general account of laughter because people laugh at things which do not involve faults or depravity of any kind (Beattie, 1776; cf: Piddington, 1933/1963, pp. 165–168). Beattie also reviews and critiques the humor theories of Hobbes, Hutcheson, Akenside, and Gerard. Beattie's own theory of the ludicrous (which Bergler, 1956, p. 9, calls the "unification theory" of laughter) is that laughter arises from the juxtaposition of two or more inconsistent, unsuitable, or incongruous parts or circumstances considered normally to be united in one complex assemblage or object. [Notes: See Victor Courdaveaux's (1875) *four* main headings for the "laughable": slight imperfections—moral, physical, or intellectual; slight annoyances; the unexpected/surprising/extraordinary; and the indecent/vulgar/obscene (cf: Michiels', 1886, *four* categories of comic sources). All these occurring in art or life may result in laughter, but one's enjoyment of them in art is modified by one's appreciation of the ability or cleverness of the artist. Thus, according to Courdaveaux, the pleasures that give rise to laughter are as varied as the objects of laughter and cannot be reduced to any *single* principle. On the other hand, Penjon (1893) regards the element of "liberty/freedom" as the *single* universal cause of laughter (cf: Eastman, 1921, pp. 186–187). Melinaud (1895) suggests that all laughter implies *two* distinct mental acts (appreciation of contradiction, and realization that contradiction is not fundamental) (cf: Piddington, 1933/1963, pp. 185–186; Piddington's spelling here is "Melinand"; cf: Greig, 1923/1969, p. 265, whose spelling is "Melinaud"; and Bergler, 1956, pp. 20–21, whose spelling is "Melinard"). Philbert (1883) asserts that the amusing has *both* an intellectual and an emotional effect—it sets up an oscillation in the intelligence between *two* contrasting ideas. Ribot (1896/1897/1939) considers the two main theories of laughter (incongruity and superiority) as both partially true, but suggests that the attempt to reduce laughter to *one* cause—rather than to many causes—is not possible.]

Beattie also develops what may be regarded as the first thoroughgoing "intellectualist" theory of laughter (cf: Dumont, 1862, who suggests dual intellectual activity in laughter as the person simultaneously affirms and denies a given proposition; and Leveque's, 1863, attack of Dumont's position on the grounds that such dualistic intellectual activities in laughter are psychologically impossible). Beattie examines the various literary devices by which a ludicrous effect may be produced—usually by something that is new and surprising; he also indicates that emotions such as moral indignation, fear, and disgust—as well as good breeding—have the power to inhibit laughter.

The German novelist Johann Paul Friedrich Richter (1763–1825), whose pseudonym was "Jean Paul," maintains that the comic is the opposite of the sublime (Richter, 1804/1813, section 28); the sublime is the infinitely great (and awakens wonder), while the comic is the infinitely small (and awakens the opposite feeling) (cf: Greig, 1923/1969, p. 249).

The English clergyman and writer/wit Sydney Smith (1771–1845) distinguishes between the literary terms "bull" and "wit": a bull is the exact reverse of wit; in the bull, there is a sudden discovery of an apparent congruity and a real incongruity of ideas, whereas wit discovers a real congruity or similarity in an apparent incongruity or dissimilarity; the essence of wit is surprise which must be sudden (S. Smith, 1846/1859; Greig, 1923/1969, pp. 248–249)

The English poet and man of letters Samuel Taylor Coleridge (1772–1834) was one of the most brilliant, versatile, and influential figures in the English literary romantic movement (Harris & Levey, 1975, p. 596). Coleridge made distinctions between the terms *witty, droll, odd,* and *humorous* (Coleridge, 1836, Vol. 1, pp. 131–136): *wit* consists in presenting images or thoughts in an unusual connection with each other for the purpose of exciting pleasure by the surprise; the positive character of the *droll* or ludicrous is impropriety; the true ludicrous or *odd* is its own end; and *humor* depends on some peculiarity of individual temperament; moreover, all *humor* consists in a certain reference to the general and the universal by which the finite great is brought into identity with the little, or the little with the finite great, so as to make both nothing in comparison with the infinite (cf: Greig, 1923/1969, pp. 249–250).

The English essayist William Hazlitt (1778–1830) gives a dual account of the problems of laughter and tears in "On Wit and Humour," the introduction to his *Lectures on the English Comic Writers* (1818/1841/1907). Hazlitt observes that man is the only animal that weeps and laughs, for man is the only animal that is struck with the difference between what things are and what they *ought* to be (cf: Piddington, 1933/1963, p. 170). People weep both at what exceeds or thwarts their desires in serious matters; they laugh only at what disappoints their expectations in trifles. Moreover, laughter is defined—via the same sort of convulsive/involuntary movement as tears—by mere surprise or contrast (in the absence of any more serious emotion), and before it has time to reconcile itself to contradictory appearances. Bergler (1956, p. 10) refers to Hazlitt's humor theory as the "split-second before adaptation" theory of laughter; Hazlitt views laughter as the split-second in adjustment where the essence of the laughable is the incongruous, the disconnecting of one idea from another, or the jostling of one feeling against another. Bergler (1956, p. 11) credits Hazlitt with his novel use of the method of "clinical observation" in describing experiences with children ("an unusual contribution to have made to the study of laughter in 1819").

Hazlitt (1818/1841/1907) argues that the main difference between laughter and tears is the attendant stimulus, circumstance, or emotion attaching to the episode (e.g., a "soft" tickle will make a child laugh, while a "strong/violent" tickle will make the same child cry); the essence of laughter is the incongruous, the disconnecting of one idea from another, or the competition of one feeling against another. Thus, Hazlitt distinguishes between the *laughable* (based in incongruity), the *ludicrous* (based in the contradiction between the object and one's expectation of it), and the *ridiculous* (based on the contradiction between custom, sense, and reason). *Humor*, according to Hazlitt, lies in describing the ludicrous as it is in itself, while *wit* is the exposing of the ludicrous—by contrasting or comparing it with something else (cf: Greig, 1923/1969, pp. 250–251).

The French Roman Catholic apologist/liberal Felicite Robert de Lamennais—or "La Mennais"—(1782–1854) apparently held a poor opinion of laughter—it is an image of evil, the instinctive expression of the sentiment of individuality, and of the joy of belonging to oneself. In all laughter, according to Lamennais, there is secret satisfaction of self-love (Lamennais, 1841, pp. 245, 247). On the other hand, Lamennais maintained that the *smile* is sometimes tender and expresses a tendency opposite to that of the laugh; additionally, a *smile* contains a tendency that moves one towards others and away from the self (cf: Greig, 1923/1969, p. 253).

The French writer Marie Henri Beyle (pseudonym: "Stendhal") (1783–1842) is recognized as one of the greatest of the French novelists; he also wrote a *psychological* analysis of love (*De l'amour*) in 1822 that predates Freud's work (Harris & Levey, 1975, p. 2618). Stendhal distinguishes between the terms "le ridicule" and "le plaisant" (Stendhal, 1823/1907, Chapter 2), and prefers the latter term which connotes an openness, frankness, joyousness, and harmlessness that requires only a society of light- or kind-hearted people who search for happiness (cf: Greig, 1923/1969, p. 252).

The English poet and journalist Leigh Hunt (James Henry Leigh Hunt) (1784–1859) was a noted dramatic/literary critic who was one of the first writers to praise the poetic genius of both Percy Bysshe Shelley and John Keats. Hunt places the cause of laughter in the notion of "triumph" (cf: the "sudden glory" theory of Hobbes, 1650/1839; 1651/1904), wherein people laugh out of a contemptuous sense of superiority). According to Hunt, it is in the reconciliation of perceived disparities (in which surprise is the consequence of a sudden and agreeable perception of the incongruous) that the delightful faculties of humor and wit are exercised (Hunt, 1846/1910/1977, p. 7).

The Scottish-born English author Thomas Carlyle (1795–1881) suggests—in his essay on J. P. F. Richter—that the essence of humor is sensibility ("warm, tender, fellow-feeling with all forms of existence"), and that true humor springs not more from the head than from the heart; humor is not contempt, but its center is love—it results not in laughter but in "still smiles" that lie "far deeper" (Carlyle, 1827/1848/1870, pp. 15–16). According to Carlyle, humor is the bloom and perfume (the "purest effluence") of a deep, fine, and loving nature; it is related to a nature in harmony with itself (cf: Greig, 1923/1969, pp. 252–253).

The American poet/essayist Ralph Waldo Emerson (1803–1882) suggests that the essence of all jokes/comedy is an honest or well-intended "halfness"—a nonperformance of what is pretended to be performed, at the same time that one is giving loud pledges of performance (R. W. Emerson, 1876/1903, pp. 545–546, 645, 647). Moreover, the balking of the intellect, the frustrated expectation, and the break of continuity in the intellect defines comedy; it announces itself in physical terms in the pleasant spasms called "laughter." Emerson also asserts that reason does not laugh because reason sees the whole; the intellect in isolating the object of laughter recognizes in it a disparity with the ideal (cf: Greig, 1923/1969, pp. 259–260).

The French poet and critic Charles Baudelaire (1821–1867) considered laughter to be the mark of man's primeval fall from grace (Baudelaire, 1869/1946, p. 362). In moralistic tones, Baudelaire asserted that until simple innocence is lost, laughter does not occur, for laughter comes from the feeling of superiority over one's fellow humans (cf: Greig, 1923/1969, p. 258).

In taking a comparative approach toward comic literature, the English novelist/poet George Meredith (1828–1909) provides a literary treatment of the corrective function of comedy; he concludes that comedy is the "fountain of sound sense," and the spirit of comedy is the spirit of common sense whose function is to teach the world about the problems that ail it (cf: Piddington, 1933/1963, p. 181; Greig, 1923/1969, pp. 260–261). Moreover, the spirit of comedy tends to equalize the standings of men and women, allowing women to make use of their wit. Thus, the comic spirit, according to Meredith, cannot exist in any civilization in which women occupy an inferior or secluded role (e.g., as in the Arabian culture). [Note: Meredith suggests further that the inferiority of German comedy may be due to the small role that women have in German domestic life which, as a result, limits the possibilities of creating comedies reflecting domestic affairs; see Meredith, 1877/1898/1918, p. 58]. Meredith maintains that comedy must be distinguished from joking, the latter making less of an intellectual appeal for laughter. Also, the sense of the comic is abridged somewhat through the use of the devices of "punning, humoristic phraseology, and verbal tricks which—though they may be humorous—are not truly comic" (Meredith, 1877/1898/1918, p. 65). In the final analysis, according to Meredith, comedy must deal essentially with social values and must examine the degree to which they conform to the dictates of common sense.

Theories Based in Physiology/Biology

In his discussion of laughter, the French physician Laurent Joubert (1529–1582) initially devises categories and examples of the "laughable" (e.g., laughable in deed, actions, words). However, while such categories may be useful to the analysts of laughter, it is Joubert's subsequent emphasis on the *physiological* mechanism causing the convulsions of laughter (cf: my Chapter 1, section on "Humor and Laughter") that are more noteworthy (see Joubert, 1560/1579/1980). Joubert considered laughter to be a mixture of opposite emotions, joy and sorrow, and he set the conflict of emotions—like Plato centuries earlier—clearly in the heart, not in the mind. He asserted that the contrary emotions stirred the heart in alternating contractions and dilations, with sadness causing the contractions and joy causing the dilations. Such an alternating movement is transferred to the pericardium, an organ that is firmly attached by a large tissue to the diaphragm. Moreover, according to Joubert, the diaphragm—which undergoes the same alternations as the heart—causes the breath in the person's lungs to be expelled, and results in what may be called "hearty" laughter. Thus, in such anatomical and physiological terms does Joubert characterize the phenomenon of laughter. Joubert also argues—using rather quaint and unsophisticated rules of evidence—that animals do not laugh because their pericardium is *not* firmly attached to the diaphragm as it is in man.

Greig (1923/1969, p. 228) observes that Joubert—though unable to break away completely from the Aristotelian position—approaches the theoretical problem of laughter from the side of physiology and, in so doing, hits upon some fresh notions of real value (cf: Eastman, 1921, p. 139).

Joubert defines the ridiculous in the orthodox manner as something unseemly or ugly which is simultaneously unworthy of compassion or pity. In his humor theory, Joubert also relates laughter at the ridiculous to the laughter from tickling—whose "strange touch" brings some pain and annoyance to the parts of the body unaccustomed to it but it also causes a kind of "false pleasure" that does not offend (cf: Eastman, 1921, p. 213). Bergler (1956, p. 6) notes that Joubert's theory is "physio-psychological" in nature, and it contains the idea that laughter is based on happiness mixed with pain. Joubert's physiological notions, says Bergler, are totally outdated. [Notes: Allin (1903, pp. 310–312) presents a more modern assessment of the place of physiology in the explanation of laughter ("the real causal ground for laughter must be found in physiological processes"); he asserts that the smile indicates an attitude of the whole organism (in which the inception of food is the most striking characteristic), and that "the laugh is the rehabilitation of function and the rebound to increased metabolism." According to Allin, the sense of joy present in the witticism, and in the "wild atmosphere" of humor, is due seemingly to vasomotor phenomena and a discharge of stored surplus energy where the discharge does not require too much lesion, strain or effort (cf: Greig, 1923/1969, p. 272; Spencer, 1860/1891). Another modern psychologist, J. R. Angell (1904/1905, p. 333) also emphasizes the physiological aspects of laughter as he suggests, "In all these cases" (of laughter in joy, surprise, derision, contempt, and even grief) "the laugh is the motor activity which inevitably accompanies the explosive release from sustained tension with its suspended breathing" (cf: T.G. Brown, 1915; Brownell & Gardner, 1988; Darwin, 1872/1965; Godkewitsch, 1972, 1976; Langevin & Day, 1972; Paskind, 1932).]

The French mathematician/philosopher Rene Descartes (1596–1650) is the "first writer to deal with laughter from the *physiological*, as well as from the *psychological*, point of view." (Piddington, 1933/1963, p. 158; cf: Bergler, 1956, p. 5, who suggests that Descartes may have merely modified the physiological ideas expressed earlier by Joubert in 1597; and, according to Greig, 1923/1969, pp. 231–232, Descartes "marks a great step forward" in the theory of humor). Descartes has nothing to say about comedy, but addresses himself boldly to the more fundamental subject of laughter. He begins with a physiological account of what causes the audible explosion—the blood passing from the right cavity of the heart to the lungs, filling them, and driving out the air (Descartes, 1649/1909). According to Descartes, there are only six *basic* emotions: wonder, love, hatred, desire, joy, and sadness; and laughter is found to accompany three of them: wonder, (mild) hatred, and joy.

Morreall (1987b, p. 21) suggests that had Descartes explored more fully the relation of laughter to wonder itself (considered apart from scorn), he might well have developed a version of the "incongruity theory of laughter" (cf: Berlyne, 1969, pp. 800–801; Keith-Spiegel, 1972, pp. 7–9); Aristotle and Cicero might have done so also, had they not taken ridicule as their paradigm/exemplar case of laughter (cf: Shaftesbury, 1709/1737/1999, who questioned whether ridicule can be taken as the test of truth; he asserts that it can; he advanced the notion that humor is a remedy against vice, and nothing is ridiculous except what is deformed).

Descartes suggests that even though it would seem that laughter is one of the major signs of joy, to cause a laugh the joy must not be too strong, and must be mixed with surprise or hate, and sometimes with both (cf: Piddington, 1933/1963, p. 158). Moreover, any circumstance which suddenly fills the lungs in the physiological manner he describes causes the exterior action of laughter (unless sadness transforms it into cries and groans). Descartes asserts that derision is a kind of joy that is mixed both with surprise and hate. According to Descartes, when laughter is natural (and not artificial or feigned) it appears to be due partially to the joy derived from that which one recognizes as incapable of being injured by the evil that has excited an indignation, and partly to surprise at the novelty of that evil, in such a manner that joy, hatred, and admiration are all contributing causes to the laughter; sometimes, aversion alone may produce laughter. [Note: This last conclusion, notes Piddington (1933/1963, p. 159), which appears to be patently incorrect, seems to rest upon Descartes' unsound physiology rather than upon keen psychological observations.]

By employing somewhat psychological terms, Descartes (1649/1909, articles 178–181) suggests that those who exhibit obvious defects (e.g., the lame, hunchbacks, dwarfs, etc.; cf: Cicero, 1881, who finds personal defects a fit subject for ridicule) are particularly prone to showing or experiencing "malicious joy"; their derision is based on the wish to see other people "disgracie," as they feel themselves to be; the defective individual maliciously cheers every "evil" that befalls another person, for in their view "the other" deserves it.

Bergler (1956, p. 5) suggests that—with some stretching of the point—one could say that Descartes found in his analysis of the defective/afflicted person some hint of the role of the inner conscience. That is, when the deformed person feels that other people "deserve" a misfortune similar to his own, he can only have convinced his conscience—by his suffering—that retaliatory justice is in order; this may explain the absence of any guilt feelings from his gloating behavior. In his theoretical approach to humor, Descartes breaks away from the *literary* tradition that had led all previous thinkers—following the classical writers—to deal with comedy as a literary form rather than with the wider problem of laughter, and though Descartes' account is physiologically inaccurate (e.g., Bergler, 1956, p. 5, calls Descartes' physiological deduction "a museum piece"), it is nonetheless of interest because of the incidental *psychological* aspects contained in it (Piddington, 1933/1963, p. 158).

The English naturalist Charles Darwin (1809–1882) shows a "certain catholicity among conflicting theories" (Greig, 1923/1969, p. 258); in general, he regards laughter as the expression of mere joy or happiness (Darwin, 1872/1965), but the most common cause of laughter is experiencing something incongruous or unaccountable that excites surprise and a sense of superiority in the laugher. Bergler (1956, p. 16) calls Darwin's humor theory the "we don't know" theory because it is the most cautious of them all—past and present.

Darwin maintains that we cannot understand why the sounds expressive of pleasure take the particular reiterated form of laughter, but it is readily seen that they should be different as possible from those screams that express distress. Moreover, the physiological expression of distress takes the form of cries in which the body's expirations are prolonged and continuous, and the inspirations are short and interrupted, while pleasure is expressed by sound production where short and broken expirations together with prolonged inspirations may be observed. Concerning the physical features and shape of the mouth in laughter, Darwin points out that it must not be opened to its utmost extent; the retraction of the corners of the mouth are due to the necessity for a large orifice through which an adequate amount of sound may be issued; thus, because the mouth cannot be opened sufficiently in the vertical plane, the retraction of the corners of the mouth occurs.

According to Darwin, a physical/physiological continuum exists in laughter ranging from the most excessive laughter, through moderate laughter, to the broad smile, and finally to the faintest smile—all these series of movements being expressions of pleasure to different degrees. Darwin maintains that the smile is the first stage in the development of the laugh, and suggests the following origins: the loud reiterated sounds of a certain type are the original expression of pleasure in which the utterance of these sounds implies the retraction of the corners of the mouth; this reaction (the smile) may thus have become a conditioned expression of pleasure when this was not sufficient to excite the more violent reaction to laughter. In the animal kingdom, on the phylogenetic scale, vocal and instrumental sounds like laughter are used either as a call or a charm by one sex for the other, and they may be employed as the means for a joyful meeting between parents and their offspring or between the affiliated members of the same social organization.

Darwin cites a number of authorities to indicate that the reaction of laughter is widespread throughout the world as an expression of satisfaction, although other expressions of this feeling exist (e.g., certain aboriginal or primitive people express pleasure by actions and movements suggestive of eating or of the satisfaction of hunger). Darwin also asserts that laughter—although originally the expression of pleasure—may be used in a forced way to conceal other emotions, such as derision, contempt, shyness, shame, or anger; thus, for example, in derision, a real or feigned smile or laugh is blended with an expression of contempt, the function of which is to show the offending person that he or she evokes only amusement. Darwin observes that there is yet another kind of laughter, a secondary type, that is a result of confronting the ludicrous; however, it is "instinctive" laughter that generally reflects human pleasure and satisfaction that is most primary for him (cf: Averill, 1969; Meerloo, 1966; and MacHovec, 1988, p. 56, who characterizes Darwin's approach as an "instinct-physiological" theory of humor; also, see MacHovec, 1988, pp. 60–64, "The Physiology of Humor").

The 19th-century English philosopher Herbert Spencer (1820–1903) attempted, also (as did Joubert in the 16th century), to explain laughter on the basis of physiology and cerebral mechanisms [cf: Dearborn (1900), Gallivan (1991), Godkewitsch (1976), Lloyd (1938), McGhee (1983), Prigatano & Pribram (1981), and Stearns (1972) for more contemporary attempts to explain the phenomenon of laughter and humor in purely physical/physiological/anatomical/biological terms. Also, see the theory and views of Georges Dumas (1923) who divides the problem of laughter into five separate issues, one of which is the "anatomical and physiological problem"; the other issues for Dumas are the problems of: laughter as an expression of euphoria; the nature of the ludicrous; the psycho-physical mechanism by which the perception of the ludicrous comes to excite the laughter reaction; and the function of laughter as a social language. Dumas stresses two childhood situations that often produce laughter—the sudden relaxation of restraint; and the sudden appearance of some pleasing stimulus; in general, Dumas accepts the theories of Spencer, Darwin, Bergson, and Sully; cf: Piddington (1933/1963, pp. 216–217); Bergler (1956, p. 23); and my Chapter 1, section, "Humor and Laughter"].

Spencer (1860/1891) maintains that laughter, at least all "comic" laughter, is analogous to the operation of a siphon or pump: it is an overflow (along the most available and ready channels) of "nervous energy" from a reservoir that has been filled up too much (Bergler, 1956, p. 16, calls Spencer's theory the "overflow of nervous energy" theory). Laughter, according to this mechanical, energy release, or hydraulic theory, occurs when we have prepared our minds for something large and meaningful, but what follows is something small and insignificant.

Essentially, Spencer advanced the notion that laughter is similar to nervous energy that is active within any part of the nervous system and that must escape through one or more "channels"—channels leading to other nerves not directly connected with motor nerves, motor nerves leading to muscular activity, or efferent nerves leading to the viscera. In the case of the first type of channel, the nervous energy contributes to the production of states of consciousness, while in the other two types of channel, it is used up in the production of movement/activity. Spencer asserts that nervous energy may escape by any one, or all, of these channels, and if any of the three means of escape are blocked, a greater amount of energy must escape via those channels that are open (conversely, if only one channel is capable of allowing for the escape of nervous energy, the other channels will not be used). In laughter, the nervous energy escapes via habitual channels: the speech apparatus and the respiratory mechanism. If these channels do not suffice to carry off the amount of energy present, the entire body is convulsed. In the case of the ludicrous situation, a certain amount of neural energy within the nervous system is deprived of its normal outlet into other neural paths and escapes via arousal of the motor reaction of laughter.

Moreover, Spencer maintains that the incongruity involved in the ludicrous situation must be of a "descending" nature or the state aroused by the inconsistency would be able to relieve the attendant nervous tension; in the case of an "ascending" type of incongruity, the reaction that is produced (e.g., muscular relaxation) is reciprocally inhibitory or prohibitive to the production of convulsions of laughter. Thus, according to Spencer's account, the ludicrous must present a situation in which we expect, or are "keyed up," for something great, but in actuality are confronted with something small.

The British-born American psychologist William McDougall (1871–1938) developed what Bergler (1956, p. 22) calls the "anti-annoyance" theory of humor, what Keith-Spiegel (1972, pp. 5–6) calls an "instinct" theory of laughter/humor, what Gregory (1924, p. 7) calls a "monistic" theory, what Eastman (1921, pp. 224–236) considers to be a "touchstone connection" between instinct and humor, and what Berlyne (1969, p. 802) reluctantly calls a "relief" theory [i.e., "McDougall's (1903, 1923) theory is difficult to place within our classification; it seems best qualified for the relief category, although it comes close to superiority theories regarding misfortunes of other people as a primary cause of laughter"].

The basis of McDougall's (1903, 1922, 1923, 1937) humor theory is the denial that laughter is an expression of pleasure (cf: Piddington, 1933/1963, p. 205); he claims that laughter-provoking situations are all unpleasant, and would be annoying if they were not laughed at. [Note: This viewpoint, notes Bergler, 1956, p. 22, is in contradiction to the scores of theories which see laughter as a proof of joy.] McDougall asserts that the whole misunderstanding concerning this issue began when the smile and the laugh were equated—they actually should be differentiated, because only the smile is a sign of pleasure (cf: the contrary theoretical position of Darwin, 1872/1965, and Sully, 1902, that the smile and the laugh *are* connected in origin). The functions of laughter, according to McDougall, are various *physiological* advantages such as stimulation of circulation and respiration, blood pressure increase, and increase of blood flow to the brain; *psychological* advantages include an increase in euphoria via the interruption of every train of thought and every sustained physical and mental activity.

Greig (1923/1969, p. 276) notes that McDougall reduces the conditions which excite laughter to the following: situations that are mildly unpleasant, except in so far as they are redeemed by laughter; and those things which would excite a feeble degree of sympathetic pain, if we did not actually laugh at them. Accordingly, McDougall (1903, 1922) argues that laughter has evolved in the human race as an "antidote to sympathy," or as a protective reaction that shields one from the depressive influence of others' shortcomings and weaknesses. Monro (1951/1963, p. 146) observes that McDougall's humor theory depends on his assertion that all laughable objects are basically and intrinsically painful. Kimmins (1928, p. 51) notes that McDougall attaches considerable importance to the topic of tickling in the history of laughter, and McDougall suggests that laughter on being tickled is the crudest and earliest form of humor. McDougall (1923), in admitting laughter to the group of "minor instincts," maintains that it differs from all other instincts in that its impulse seeks no goal beyond itself, but secures its own satisfaction by means of bodily processes that affect nothing in the outer environment.

In later years, McDougall accepted a biological theory of laughter (Bergler, 1956, p. 23): there is some special differentiation of instincts that finds expression in playful activity; this came about because it was necessary for humans to develop into social beings and to foster and strengthen their sympathetic tendencies. However, such tendencies would leave a person at a considerable disadvantage (e.g., always depressed about other people) and, therefore, as a countermeasure, nature endowed humans with the ability to laugh on contemplation of the mishaps of others which, according to such an analysis, is actually beneficial to the observing person (McDougall, 1923, p. 168).

In summary, McDougall's instinct theory of humor asserts that laughter was evolved as a necessary corrective of the effects of interpersonal sympathy; without a sense of the ludicrous, nature's antidote for the minor depressing and disagreeable misfortunes confronting humans, the species might not have survived. Keith-Spiegel (1972, p. 6) notes that others who have proposed instinct theories of humor include Drever (1917), Eastman (1921), Gregory (1924), McComas (1923), and Menon (1931).

A more contemporary account of the biology of humor is provided by Fry (1994) who observes that no person or group of persons has been found to be without a sense of humor (except on a temporary basis because of some serious personal or national tragedy—such as terrorists' attacks on the United States on September 11, 2001—which for the time being causes an eclipse of humor). The current view is that humor is bred deeply into human activities. Rather than being regarded as learned (as it was previously), Fry asserts that humor is now considered to be a genetic, biologic characteristic of humankind where each one of us does develop a sense of humor. However, like a kind of psychological fingerprint, each person's sense of humor is distinctive for that individual—even where there are broad overlaps of humor appreciation between people by virtue of family, community, national, or cultural setting. The intimate and complex involvement of the sense of humor with biological heredity and maturational development suggests a very extended history of the presence of aspects of humor in humans' behavioral repertoire—perhaps millions of years, even before humans became human.

Fry cites comparative behavior/primate studies, physiological studies (e.g., Fry, 1992; Fry & Savin, 1998), health and survival evidence, and clinical studies in support of his evolutionary and biological perspective toward humor. Among the implications of his approach, Fry elaborates on the case of mirthful laughter which is intricately involved with crucial physiological functioning (cf: Berk, Tan, Fry, Napier, Lee, Hubbard, Lewis, & Eby, 1989; Fry, 1977) as well as occupying an important role in nonverbal interpersonal/social communication; mirthful behavior became entrenched as a physiological "good thing" and it is now part of the biological "establishment" (cf: Lefcourt, Davidson-Katz, & Kueneman, 1990). Such behaviors as humor, mirth, and laughter are perceived as being generally favorable to the maintenance of biologic health and survival and, ultimately, to improvement of the quality of life itself.

Theories Based in Communications/Culture/Advertising

Fine (1977a, p. 329) makes the point that while researchers agree that humor is preeminently a form of communication, there appears to be little agreement on how to treat humor in terms of its *communicative* aspect. In general, it seems that humor as *communication* may be examined from one of two perspectives: either as *interpersonal* communication/talk (e.g., Bateson, 1969; Fine, 1977b; Hopen, 1977; Linfield, 1977; Ransohoff, 1977), or as *formal* communication spread through the institutions of the mass media (TV, radio, movies) and the publishing industry (e.g., Cantor, 1977; Davies, 1977). It is in this latter sense ("formal communication") that this section deals with humor. [Note: For humor in the former sense, i.e., as "interpersonal communication," see "Theories Based in Sociology/Social Psychology/Anthropology" in a later section of this chapter.]

Davies (1977) emphasizes the notion that the cultural symbols which are associated with joking behavior may change over time (cf: Dundes, 1975), at least as reflected in analyses of jokebooks over time. However, as Fine (1977a) suggests, published humor (as in jokebooks) may be systematically different from spoken humor; for example, if one were to examine humor about blacks/African-Americans as portrayed in American television (comedy programs) to determine the ways in which white society caricatured blacks, one might be misled by the results (cf: Abrahams, 1970). The likely fact is that there still is much spoken humor among whites concerning blacks that relies on the antiquated stereotypes of the past. Thus, the warning is given that it cannot be assumed that a thematic content analysis based upon an institutionally produced or distributed source (mass media) will represent necessarily the extent of those same themes in the "spoken" culture (see Denzin, 1970). Moreover, in noting the spread of certain joke fads in the mass media of a culture (e.g., Polish jokes, elephant jokes, jokes about celebrities' personalities, etc.), one may expect that the joke cycles can start easily and spread rapidly, although their modification or elimination is a much slower process.

Cantor (1977) examines printed humor and broadcast humor, and argues that surface content varies markedly depending on the medium employed. Based upon analysis of research findings in this area ("tendentious humor"), Cantor concludes that a good proportion of what American society is labelling and reacting to as humor is not based upon themes readily identifiable as "tendentious." Fine (1977a) observes that it is not clear if Cantor's operationalization of the term "tendentiousness" is equivalent to Freud's (1905/1916) earlier concept of "tendentious wit," but it is likely that a panel of Freudian analysts would find considerably more "tendentious" (i.e., advancing a definite point of view) jokes than did Cantor's participants. Fine (1977a, p. 330) suggests that Cantor's approach is interesting as an analysis of the ecology of humor, and her work in dealing with overt and implicit themes in media humor is a valuable step in the direction of determining over time the extent of cultural change in humor.

Fine (1977a, p. 333) identifies an area, and a series of questions, for future research that also involves the "formal communication" aspect/perspective: what is the interface between humor in the media and humor in natural settings? For instance, to what extent do scriptwriters, comedians, and jokebook authors utilize humor that already is in popular circulation? When they alter the humor for their particular purposes do they do this in any systematic way? How does one transform a "natural" joke to a "canned" joke? Writers frequently will credit their own experiences with providing them with comic material; however, few writers admit "stealing" jokes from the public domain. Yet by the redundancy that is built into media humor, this situation seems to occur quite often; it is not known if this occurs in a conscious or deliberate fashion. Moreover, according to Fine, the other side of the issue is that often humor in conversation is derived from television. For example, a joke that is told on a popular television program may be spread interpersonally until it becomes so widely known that it is accepted as part of a culture's "jokelore."

It may be assumed that every joke must have had an originator or inventor at some point, although for most of the culture's humor that inventor remains unknown. Apparently, a joke begins to be taken for granted as part of the cultural heritage and is used, changed, or altered as the circumstances require. Further research may study the process by which media jokes are transformed to popular jokes, the process concerning which jokes are most likely to make the transition, and the process of standardization through which any systematic alterations may occur (cf: the discussion by Mintz, 1983, on "Humor and Popular Culture"; Mintz presents a summary of the forms that humor takes in American popular culture, focusing on the prevalence and history of the changing forms of humor).

Brown and Bryant (1983) examine the ubiquitous nature of humor in the contemporary mass media, the strategies for the use of humor (cf: Apter, 1982a,b; Cardiff, 1988; Marc, 1989; Mendelsohn, 1966; Mintz, 1988; Taylor, 1994; Wilde, 1976; Willis, 1967), the ways in which humor is employed in different media (cf: Cantor, 1976, 1977; Gelb & Zinkhan, 1985; Kelly & Solomon, 1975; Sternthal & Craig, 1973; Zillmann, 1977), the social content of humor (cf: Winick, 1976), and the effects of the use of humor on enjoyment, persuasion, learning, and antisocial behavior.

Brown and Bryant note that the most obvious, compelling, and primary reason for employing humor in the American mass media is that humor attracts a large audience—an implicit goal of most media messages that is connected ultimately with the generation of large sums of money for all concerned with the messages. It is estimated that the average American laughs 15 times per day (Feinsilber & Mead, 1980), and a great deal of this laughter is elicited by messages in the mass media. Other secondary reasons for using humor in the mass media include its use in children's educational television to maintain interest and attention to the educational material/messages; and its use in entertainment programs as a relief for consumers from daily problems, frustrations, and boredom. Brown and Bryant observe that normative data on humor use in the mass media generally are missing and that there are only a few studies conducted on the topic of humor in the mass medium of television; conspicuously absent are systematic studies of the way humor is used in magazines, newspapers, and motion pictures.

On the other hand, in marked contrast to the very few investigations into patterns of humor use, Brown and Bryant note that many investigations of the social content (e.g, sexism, racism) of mass media humor have been conducted, as well as numerous critical reviews of the historical developments of media forms. Moreover, much of the work relevant to humor in the area of advertising has developed from a concern with treatment of women and minorities by advertisers. Brown and Bryant note that a few studies have examined the effect of humor on persuasion and learning and have found, generally, that humor is ineffective in promoting either, except with young children; most positive effects of humor tend to relate to humor as an attention-getter. Brown and Bryant

(1983, p. 167) conclude that "even though speculation about the mechanisms of humor is thousands of years old, neither researchers nor mass media practitioners are able to agree completely on how and why people find certain messages funny."

Gruner (1976) reviews theory and research pertinent to the question, "Do wit and humor in mass communication have a particular communicative impact on its audience?" Following a definition of key terms and a discussion of the scope of his study (i.e., he deals only with experimental/empirical/scientific studies, only with wit and humor in American mass communication, and only with material from a communications perspective), Gruner traces the use of humor in persuasive messages, citing several studies involving the use of humor in persuasive speeches. [Note: See the first known empirical study of the effect of humor in persuasive messages by Lull, 1940; cf: Markiewicz, 1974; also, see the earliest known study of satirical materials as rhetoric by Annis, 1939.]

Gruner (1976) makes the following conclusions: the addition of humorous material to otherwise straightforward persuasive message material does *not* result in an increase in persuasiveness; anecdotal evidence suggests that the use of humor in advertising, especially broadcast advertising, can result in increased sales of the product humorously depicted; satire (as differentiated from mere humor) is apparently often not understood by members of the general public—but when the serious point of a satire is understood, it serves to have some persuasive value; and the communicator who chooses to use appropriate humor in his or her discourse is likely to improve his or her image with the audience *only* when the initial perceptual set of the audience members toward the communicator is taken into account.

Martineau (1972) provides a review of the literature on the sociology of humor, presents a *communication* model of the social functions of humor that describes various intragroup and intergroup situations, and gives the social functions in the form of theorems that are related to the sociological literature. The basic premise underlying Martineau's model is that humor is a social mechanism with definite social functions where, more specifically, humor is viewed as a distinctive type of persuasive social process and medium of communication by which acting units in the social system convey information during the ongoing process of interaction. According to Martineau, humor is conceived generically to be any communicative instance which is perceived as humorous by any of the interacting parties, and the humorous communicative instance becomes a vehicle or social mechanism employed for interaction wherein humor may assume different forms and has different functions in various structural settings.

Martineau notes that a number of functions of humor have been emphasized in the literature: consensus, conflict, and control have been studied mainly where the salient variables are the actor, the audience or recipient, the butt of the humor, the judgment of the humor, the cultural context, and the social position of the involved parties. Martineau's model attempts to combine some of the salient variables, to specify combinations of them, and to delineate the functions which humor performs under these combinations. Thus, rather than stressing the functions of humor directly, Martineau's approach reverses the procedure: the model identifies some conditions under which the functions of humor can be further specified (e.g., humor may be analyzed in an intergroup situation with a focus on the internal structure of one group; cf: Barron, 1950).

In summary, Martineau's (1972) model of the social functions of humor derive from three structural situations, each of which is described in terms of four variables which, when combined in sets, are used to delineate theorems representing the social functions. Thus, humor—as a basic medium of *communication*—assumes many forms and its social functions achieve complexity under the influence of other social processes and existing social structures, and Martineau's model attempts to deal with these influences systematically to provide a basis for generating researchable hypotheses, as well as providing a framework for additional theoretical formulations of humor function.

In the field of *advertising/marketing*, the recent studies by Weinberger and Campbell (1990–1991), Scott, Klein, and Bryant (1990), and Chattopadhyay and Basu (1990a,b) may serve to reflect the nature and theory of humor in such an applied setting. Weinberger and Campbell (cf: Weinberger & Gulas, 1992) note that the effect of humor is dependent on the product type that is advertised, and on the relevance of the humor to the specific product [cf: McNamara & Tiffin (1941) who found a negative, or distracting, effect of nearby cartoons on the attention-holding power of advertisements; and Gelb & Zinkhan's (1986) study that tested a model relating humor perceived after repeated exposure to a commercial message to measures of advertising effectiveness; the findings of this study indicate that adding humor to a conventional "hierarchy-of-effects" model does not improve the model's explanatory power; moreover, humor in this study was found to be negatively related to recall of the brand name and advertising copy, and was positively related to attitude toward the advertised brand—both relationships of which are predicted by the theoretical approaches and literature in this area].

According to Weinberger and Campbell (1990–1991), ads that are "humorless" prompt greater consumer recall and persuasion for the high-involvement products that are associated with thinking/cognitive decisions. On the other hand, humor that is relevant and appropriate to the product produces superior recall for the high-involvement products, and superior persuasion for the low-involvement products when decisions are based on emotions and feelings.

Scott et al. (1990) also found that the effectiveness of using humor in product advertising is enhanced when the humor is relevant to the product. Moreover, they suggest that humorous ads are more persuasive than nonhumorous ads when consumers possess favorable preexisting attitudes. In different studies, Chattopadhyay and Basu (1990a,b) report the complementary finding that humor in advertising may be counterproductive when the consumer possesses negative preexisting attitudes. Taken collectively, such studies of humor in advertising indicate that humor effectively increases consumer attention and processing, and that the variables of prior consumer attitudes and product-relevant humor serve to moderate the direction of information processing and personal potential for product purchase and consumption.

Further studies on humor that reflect the theoretical approaches taken in the applied fields of *advertising* and *marketing* include the following: Alden and Hoyer (1993); Alden, Hoyer, and Lee (1993); Alden, Mukherjee, and Hoyer (2000a,b); Allen (1988); Bauerly (1989); Belch and Belch (1984); Bender (1994); Biswas, Olsen, and Carlet (1992); Brooker (1981); Draper (1959); Duncan (1979); Duncan and Nelson (1985); Duncan, Nelson, and Frontczak (1984); Fischer and Thussbas (2000); Friedman (1989); Gelb and Pickett (1983); Gelb and Zinkhan (1985); Kelly and Solomon (1975); Krishnan and Chakravarti (1990); Lammers (1991); Lammers, Leibowitz, Seymour, and Hennessey (1983); Lee and Mason (1999); Lynch and Hartman (1968); Madden and Weinberger (1982, 1984); McCullough and Taylor (1993); Mizerski (1995); Monnot (1981); Nelson (1987); Pharr (1988); Redfern (1982); Scott, Klein, and Bryant (1990); Shama and Coughlin (1979); Shifman (1994); S. M. Smith (1993); Speck (1988, 1991); Spotts, Weinberger, and Parsons (1997); Tanaka (1992); Unger (1995, 1996); Vandeberg (1987); Weinberger and Spotts (1989); Weinberger, Spotts, and Campbell (1995); Wilcox and Moriarty (1984); Wu, Crocker, and Rogers (1989); Zhang (1994, 1996); Zhang and Zinkhan (1991); Zinkhan and Gelb (1987, 1990); and Zinkhan and Johnson (1994).

PSYCHOLOGICAL THEORIES OF HUMOR

> The most difficult question about laughter is to tell in general psychological terms what is the stimulus that arouses it. We have several ingenious theories of humour, which purport to tell . . . One thing is fairly certain: that, while laughing is a native response, we learn what to laugh at, for the most part, just as we learn what to fear.
>
> —R. S. Woodworth, 1921

> The subject of laughter is an intensely interesting study. It has attracted the attention of distinguished philosophers, psychologists, physiologists, educational journalists, and various types of social reformers. The result is that the literature of laughter, in its extraordinary variety, represents an abnormally well-worked field by expert explorers.
>
> —C. W. Kimmins, 1928

Laughter is one of the unsolved problems of philosophy. It is not, indeed, one of the larger and weightier stumbling-blocks, like Being or Knowing; yet some very great men have stubbed their toes upon it. Aristotle, Kant, Hobbes, Bergson, Freud are among them; and there are many lesser names ... They have, of course, contributed a great deal; and yet it can be said that the problem is still largely unsolved.

—D. H. Monro, 1951/1963

If facts do not conform to the theory, they must be disposed of.

—N. R. F. Maier, 1963

Though not wishing to be as disagreeable as McDougall [1922] when he stated that philosophers have given us many ludicrous theories of the ludicrous, we suggest that some of the theoretical notions put forth seem to complicate rather than unravel this Gordian knot. However, humor is a complicated subject, and the early writers have given us a variety of possibilities as to its nature and a host of theoretical issues with which to wrestle.

—P. Keith-Spiegel, 1972

Theories Based in Modern Philosophy

Inasmuch as the discipline of *philosophy* may be characterized as the "linear father," or "direct parent," of the discipline of *psychology*, it is deemed appropriate here to place modern *philosophical* theories of humor under the rubric of *psychological* theories of humor where the former theories often anticipate, or serve as "immediate forerunners" and "ancestors" of, the latter type of humor theories.

According to Greig (1923/1969, p. 232), the most famous English theory of humor/laughter is provided by the "modern" (i.e., post-16th century) English philosopher Thomas Hobbes (1588–1679). Bergler (1956, p. 4) states that Hobbes "sudden glory" theory of humor represents the first systematic *psychological* theory on laughter ever put forward.

Kimmins (1928) discusses the topic of "theories of laughter" in chronological fashion (i.e., laughter in the 17th and 18th centuries; laughter in the 19th century; laughter in the 20th century); he maintains (p. 10) that it is not necessary, in examining theories of laughter, to go further back in history than the 17th century and Hobbes' theory of humor. [Note: Monro (1951/1963, p. 83) states that "there can be no doubt about the claim of Hobbes to be the chief and most vigorous exponent of the superiority theory; and no doubt, either, about the extent of his influence." Monro orders his material on the theories of humor using these five generic/descriptive terms (cf: Berlyne, 1969; Keith-Spiegel, 1972): *Superiority* theories (Hobbes, 1650/1839; Bain, 1859; Leacock, 1935, 1937; Ludovici, 1932); *Superiority/Moral* theories (Bergson, 1911;

Feibleman, 1939, 1949; McDougall, 1903, 1922, 1937); *Incongruity* theories (Kant, 1790/1892/1914; Schopenhauer, 1819/1906; Spencer, 1860/1891; Eastman, 1921); *Release From Restraint* theories (L. W. Kline, 1907; Freud, 1905/1916; Gregory, 1923, 1924); and *Ambivalence* theories (Greig, 1923/1969; Menon, 1931).]

In general, Hobbes' philosophy proceeds from a mechanistic view that life is simply the motions of the organism and that man is by nature a selfishly individualistic animal at constant war with all other men; in a state of nature, men are equal in their self-seeking and live out lives which are "nasty, brutish, and short"; fear of violent death is the principal motive that causes men to create a state by contracting to surrender their natural rights and to submit to the absolute authority of a sovereign power (Harris & Levey, 1975, p. 1251). Concerning his theory of humor, Hobbes (1650/1839, Vol. 4, p. 46; cf: 1651/1839/1904) declares that there is a passion which has no name, the outward sign of which is the distortion of the face known as laughter, which is always joy; and this passion is "nothing else but sudden glory arising from a sudden conception of some eminency in ourselves, by comparison with the infirmity of others, or with our own formerly."

Morreall (1987b, p. 19) notes that the "superiority theory" of laughter—which got its start in Plato and Aristotle—was put into a stronger form by Hobbes (i.e., we are all constantly watching for signs that we are better off than others, or that others are worse off than we are; laughter is nothing but an expression of our "sudden glory" when we realize that in some way we are "superior" to someone else).

Hobbes asserts that those things which cause laughter must be new and unexpected. Furthermore, a man who is laughed at is "triumphed over," and, thus, we do not laugh when we or our friends are made the subjects or the butt of jokes and jests. To be without offense, laughter must be at the absurdities and infirmities abstracted from persons; however, to laugh too much at the defects of others is pusillanimous and, in so doing, we attain superiority only be virtue of the inferiority of others (Hobbes, 1651/1839/1904, Chapter 6).

Piddington (1933/1963, p. 161) notes that a theory similar to Hobbes' is elaborated by Paul Carus (1897–1898). According to Carus, the occasion of laughter is a "petty triumph," which must be sudden. Hobbes disputes the theory that laughter is mere appreciation of wit; men laugh at indecencies and mischances where there is no apparent jest or wit at all. Bergler (1956, p. 4) points out a banality, or perhaps even a logically circular argument, concerning Hobbes' notion of laughter when Hobbes suggests that there must be some *inner* reason in the laughter to account for it. However, on the positive side, it was only after some 2,000 years of recorded theories of laughter that Hobbes' point emerged (cf: Schmidt & Williams, 1971).

Bergler also observes that one may object to the aggressive element in Hobbes' theory of humor as being novel because that aspect of humor was actually clarified by Plato and Aristotle centuries before, and Hobbes' description of the "sudden glory" theory of humor may be nothing but a rehash of past theories. However, once again on the positive side, the presence of the aggressive element in laughter is denied adamantly in more modern theories of laughter (see Bergler, 1956, Chapter 1), and this fact validates the importance of Hobbes' description of the existence of an inner, and aggressive, satisfaction (i.e., the "conception of some eminence in ourselves"; Hobbes, 1650/1839, Vol. 4, p. 46). Bergler (1956, p. 5) concludes that Hobbes' theory of humor was "new" and thought-provoking in that he located the "gravitational center" of the laugh within the laugher himself/herself (even though this, in itself, "did not and does not solve the overall problem").

The British philosopher John Locke (1632–1704) did not deal directly with the problem of laughter, but he did attempt to draw a distinction between "wit" and "judgment"—an issue that is of considerable importance for humor/laughter theory (cf: Piddington, 1933/1963, p. 161). According to Locke (1690/1965), wit lies most in the assemblage of ideas (and putting ideas together with quickness and variety) where one may find a certain resemblance or congruity that allows one to make up pleasant pictures and agreeable visions; judgment, on the other hand, is opposite to wit, and occurs when ideas are separated carefully from one another—finding the smallest differences—and where one avoids being misled by similitude or by the affinity to take one thing for another. [Note: Piddington (1933/1963, p. 161) makes contact with the terminology of modern psychology—via William James (1890/1950, Vol. 1, pp. 483–487)—concerning a parallel between Locke's "wit/judgment" distinction in his humor theory and the modern psychologist's "association/dissociation" distinction regarding the development of experience. While admitting the importance of the distinction in psychology between the two psychic processes of "association" and "dissociation," Piddington tends to doubt whether the literary terms "wit" and "judgment" can be regarded as corresponding exactly to these two psychological concepts.]

Bergler (1956, p. 6) allows the fact that while Locke's tangential "separation theory" of humor is neatly presented (regarding the wit/judgment distinction), Locke seems to avoid completely the real question of "What allows for the 'half-suspension' of judgment in wit?" On the positive side, Bergler also notes that Locke had a vague "inkling" of the influence of unconscious factors in humor (e.g., the "unsought" thoughts that one has—as they often "drop into the mind"—are commonly the most valuable of any that the person has and, therefore, should be "secured" because they seldom return again). Bergler (1956, p. 6) recalls that William Hazlitt (1818/1841/1907) attacked Locke for having "borrowed" from Hobbes; in an interesting section, Bergler presents Hazlitt's material in the form of "side-by-side/comparison" quotations from Locke's *Essays* and Hobbes' *Leviathan* as proof of his (Hazlitt's) contention of Locke's "borrowing" from Hobbes.

The British philosopher Francis Hutcheson (1694–1746), although he was one of the first to write on the subject of aesthetics, is known primary in the field of ethics. According to Hutcheson, man has many senses, the most important of which is the moral sense. Hutcheson's "benevolent theory of morals"—in which man has a desire to do good—was a development of Shaftesbury's natural inclination to benevolent action and was in opposition to Hobbes' theories. The criterion of moral action was the "greatest happiness for the greatest numbers"—an anticipation of the later "utilitarian" philosophers in word as well as spirit (Harris & Levey, 1975, p. 1296). Regarding humor theory, Hutcheson (1750) takes elaborate pains to refute Hobbes' theory [cf: Morreall (1987b, pp. 26–27) who provides excerpts of Hutcheson's (1750) critique of Hobbes]. In his criticism of Hobbes, Hutcheson uses many counterexamples to show that there is no essential connection between having feelings of superiority and laughing or being amused (i.e., having feelings of superiority is neither a "necessary" nor a "sufficient" condition for humor).

In his approach, Hutcheson distinguishes between laughter and ridicule, the latter being only a species of the former; also, according to Hutcheson, the occasion of laughter is the contrast or opposition of dignity and meanness. Greig (1923/1969, p. 239) notes Hutcheson's emphasis on the relativity of laughter to custom and age, and the different manner in which ridicule is received by the person against whom it is directed. Hutcheson's own theory of humor is based on the association of ideas—a phenomenon that was much discussed in the 18th century. Hutcheson (1750) maintains that comic genius is largely the ability to use somewhat inappropriate metaphors and similes to produce ideas that clash with each other. In this sense, according to Morreall (1987b, p. 26), Hutcheson has at least the beginnings of an "incongruity theory of humor." Hutcheson (1750) asserts that the values of humor include the pleasure it occasions, its ability to promote mental flexibility, and its role as a social facilitator (cf: Kallen, 1911, p. 146, who emphasizes that the essential principle in laughter/comedy is the overcoming of "disharmony"; and the range of the comic scene is "no less than the cosmos itself"; Piddington, 1933/1963, p. 204, notes that Kallen attempts to show that laughter has a function similar to that which is involved in the appreciation of beauty, and it is the "directly felt goodness of the environment").

The English physician and philosopher David Hartley (1705–1757) defines laughter as "a nascent cry" (Hartley, 1749, Chapter 4, p. 450); and the first occasion of children's laughter is based in surprise ("stopped of a sudden")—which is momentary fear at first, and then becomes a momentary joy as a result of the removal of the fear (i.e., in the case of tickling, a momentary pain and apprehension of pain is experienced, with the immediate removal of that pain). According to Hartley, young children do not laugh aloud for some months after birth, that they have to learn to laugh, and learn to control or abate their laughter; also, laughter—even in adults—is facilitated by the presence of other laughers. Greig (1923/1969, p. 238) suggests that Hartley, on the whole, has no high opinion of laughter. Hartley asserts that the most natural occasions of laughter and mirth in adults seem to be the little mistakes and follies of children, as well as the smaller inconsistencies and improprieties that happen in conversation, and the daily happenings of life.

Morreall (1987b, p. 41) notes that Hartley's observations on humor/laughter do not, strictly speaking, constitute a new theory of humor, but they are interesting in the way they bring together the elements of traditional theories, and for their rough speculations concerning the ethics, physiology, and sociology of humor. Hartley makes contact with "incongruity theory" when he discusses surprise, inconsistencies, and improprieties as causes of laughter; and contact with "relief theory" (cf: Berlyne, 1969, p. 802; Keith-Spiegel, 1972, pp. 10–11) when he notes that laughter sometimes results from the sudden dissipation of fear and other negative emotions. Morreall (1987b, p. 41) notes that Hartley develops an interesting theoretical/philosophical idea via his notion of an element of "irrationality" to humor; that is, those people who are always looking for the humorous aspects of their experience thereby disqualify themselves from the larger search for truth. Bergler (1956, pp. 7–8) suggests that Hartley's "nascent cry" theory of laughter is important because it represents the first scientific elucidation of the connection between fear or unhappiness and laughter (Bergler notes, also, that the "nascent cry" theory was later echoed by the French dramatist Pierre Augustin Caron de Beaumarchais and by the German philosopher Friedrich Wilhelm Nietzsche). Finally, Bergler (1956, p. 8) observes that Hartley has another "first" to his credit: he was the pioneer in the scientific recording of the development of laughter in children (the only observer to antedate him was the 1st-century Roman naturalist Pliny who simply stated that the child's first laugh takes place 40 days after birth).

The Scottish judge and philosopher Henry Home, Lord Kames (1696–1782) makes logical distinctions between the terms *ludicrous* (the playsome, sportive, or jocular), *risible* (the species of the ludicrous that makes one laugh), and the *ridiculous* (an object that is both mirthful and contemptible) (Kames, 1762/1774/1817, Vol. 1, pp. 245–247; 311–312). Lord Kames invokes Hobbesian theory in attempting to account for the pleasure one takes in the ridiculous; he maintains that ridicule—being corrective of impropriety—is divinely ordered for the greater good of humankind, and asserts that an improper action not only moves one's contempt for the author but also, by means of the element of contrast, increases the good opinion one has of oneself (cf: Greig, 1923/1969, pp. 242–243).

As material for an essay contest in 1749 on the question, "Has the progress of the sciences and arts contributed to the *corruption* or to the *improvement* of human conduct?," the Swiss-French philosopher/author/political theorist/composer Jean Jacques Rousseau (1712–1778) took the negative stand and contended that man was good by nature and had been corrupted by civilization. Rousseau won first prize in the contest, and his essay made him both famous and controversial. Although it is still widely believed today that all of Rousseau's philosophy is based on his call for a "return to nature," this view is an oversimplification, due to an excessive importance usually attached to his famous essay (Harris & Levey, 1975, p. 2365).

Concerning comedy, Rousseau (1758/1826/1926, Vol. 2, p. 26)—also in a negative tone (and much to the chagrin of various men of letters of his day, especially Voltaire)—asserts that comedy performs no useful social function even at its best; at its worst, declares Rousseau, comedy might lead directly to immorality and corruption. [Notes: See the quaint 18th-century treatise by Poinsinet de Sivry (1778/1970/1986) in which an imaginary dialogue—between three of the most famous philosophers of the day, Destouches ("laughter has its origin in a reasoned joy"), Fontenelle ("the principle of laughter is folly"), and Montesquieu ("laughter is the expression of pride")—is recorded on the moral and physical causes of laughter. De Sivry himself identifies *comedy* as a source of pleasure that diverts us with its teachings that are based on a picture of vices and faults, and *laughter* as a respectable means of correcting man while amusing him (cf: Greig, 1923/1969, pp. 246–247; Bergler, 1956, p. 13).]

In one instance, Rousseau opposed the establishment of a theater of comedy at Geneva (cf: Piddington, 1933/1963, pp. 164–165). His well-reasoned argument contends that because public performances are always adapted to the civilization in which they are produced, they must reflect the dominating characteristics of the civilization, and their nature is necessarily determined by the pleasure which they produce rather than by their usefulness. Moreover, because the theater thus appeals to the sentiments of the public, it only condemns those things that are already regarded as immoral, whereas it encourages the dominating characteristics of the people, which it tends to increase. Thus, because exaggeration of this type is, in general, a bad thing, the theater cannot be said to exert a beneficial effect upon morals. Piddington (1933/1963, p. 165) notes that Rousseau's view of comedy seems to have influenced the attitude of Victor de Laprade—a writer concerned with moral values—who asserts that the essence of laughter is eventually to turn against the good itself, and who declares that without evil in the world there would be neither laughter nor tears (cf: Greig, 1923/1969, p. 256). Thus, regarding humor and comedy, Rousseau presents more of a moralistic diatribe against comedy than of a legitimate theoretical position on the issue of humor.

The German philosopher Immanuel Kant (1724–1804) proposes a theory of jokes (that may be taken for a general theory of humor) in his work on aesthetics in the *Critique of Judgment* (1790/1892/1914) (cf: Morreall, 1987a, pp. 45–50). Kant's approach to humor is a kind of "incongruity theory," although he emphasizes the physical, over the mental, side of amusement. According to Kant (1790/1892/1914), the pleasure one takes in humor is not as great a pleasure as one's delight in beauty or in moral goodness. Furthermore, even though amusement is caused by the play of ideas, it is a type of sensory gratification based on feelings of health and well-being. Kant asserts that in listening to a joke the person develops a certain expectation as to how it will turn out; then, at the "punch line," the expectation suddenly vanishes. The sudden mental activity is not enjoyed by one's reason, and the desire to understand is frustrated. Moreover, accompanying the mental movement and gymnastics at the punch line is the activity of the person's internal organs (this bodily motion produces the resultant feeling of health). Thus, in this way, according to Kant, the incongruity one experiences in humor gives the body a "wholesome shock" (cf: Morreall, 1987a, p. 45).

In other terms, Kant maintains that the *transformation* accompanying laughter (i.e., the sudden transformation of a strained expectation into "nothing") must be into nothing, and not into the positive opposite of expectation. This is because it is not enjoyable to one's understanding directly, but only indirectly, by throwing the body's organs into a state of oscillation, restoring them to equilibrium, and thus promoting health (Greig, 1923/1969, p. 247; cf: Piddington, 1933/1963, pp. 168–169).

Bergler (1956, p. 9) calls Kant's theory of humor the "nothing theory," in which the "nothing" stands for holes that are *not* filled with explanations concerning laughter and wit; many a "strained expectation" which fails to materialize leads to a letdown, and not to laughter, in the listener. Bergler notes that if this situation—as Kant describes it—were *not* so, there would be no disappointments in life; he also suggests that the only important contribution that Kant made to humor theory was the idea of "transformation," although Kant's observations—of the material supposedly used in the "nothing" transformation process—are incorrect.

The Scottish philosopher Dugald Stewart (1753–1828) asserted that the natural and proper objects of ridicule are the small improprieties in character and manners that do not arouse one's feelings of moral indignation or give a sense of human depravity (Stewart, 1828/1849/1866, Vol. 1, p. 316). The ludicrous, on the other hand, does not necessarily imply immorality because minor defects of reasoning or behavior produce laughter; however, one may laugh at a defect only in contrast to some moral imperfection which makes the person ignorant of his defects or causes him to conceal it from others. Moreover, according to Stewart, laughter serves both to cause amusement and to discipline others and, though it may occasionally be contrary to the interests of morality, it is generally a useful aid to one's sense of duty. Stewart maintains that an appreciation of the ludicrous implies not only the ability to reason, but also the capacity to recognize right and wrong. Additionally, one of the major functions of education, according to Stewart, is to regulate properly the sense of ridicule (cf: Piddington, 1933/1963, pp. 170–171). Greig (1923/1969, p. 253) observes that Stewart advances the ideas of the salutary effect on mankind of the ridiculous, and that the ridiculous is not always immoral but it always implies some kind of imperfection and often arouses contempt.

The German philosopher Georg Wilhelm Friedrich Hegel (1770–1831) developed a unified philosophy around an absolute idealism that envisioned a world-soul that emerges out of, and is known through, the dialectical logic. In this approach (known universally as the "Hegelian dialectic"), one concept (thesis) inevitably generates its opposite (antithesis), and the interaction of these leads to a new concept (synthesis); this, in turn, becomes the thesis of a new triad (Harris & Levey, 1975, p. 1216). It is only incidentally that Hegel (1820/1886/1920/1975) mentions laughter in dealing with comedy, maintaining that every contrast between what is essential and its appearance (the object and its instrument) may be ridiculous where the merely ridiculous is distinguished from the truly comic (Piddington, 1933/1963, p. 169, regards this distinction as an aesthetic, rather than a psychological, difference). In general, Hegel considers laughter to be little more than an expression of self-satisfied shrewdness, a sign that one has sufficient wit to recognize, and be aware of, such a fact. Piddington suggests that this view of Hegel's must be distinguished carefully from the "sudden glory" theory of Hobbes in which arousal occurs via the perception of one's superiority to the "ludicrous object," and not by one's triumph in "seeing the point." Piddington (1933/1963, p. 169) states that it is regrettable that Hegel did not elaborate this theoretical approach which might be said to have the same fundamental motif as that of Hobbes—that is, that the pleasure aroused by the ludicrous arises from a feeling of superiority.

Leigh Hunt (1846/1910/1977) propounded a similar view 26 years later; however, Hunt deals more fully with the issue than Hegel (Hunt recognizes that in the case of wit and humor the "jar" against the person is not so violent as to hinder one from recurring to a habitual idea of fitness, or adjustment, by which the shock of the surprise is mitigated). Greig (1923/1969, p. 247) confesses that it is with "great diffidence" that he attempts a summary of Hegel's views on laughter and comedy, and that he "cannot pretend to know exactly what Hegel means." Moreover, in this regard, Greig states that a reading of J. B. Baillie (1921) has helped him understand better Hegel's position on humor.

Hegel (1820/1886/1920/1975, pp. 303, 328) asserts that the true comic occurs when the person attempts to realize ends that are at variance with reality ("the substantive being"; "the realized divine nature of the world"), but when the contradiction is exposed, the person feels no serious loss because he or she is conscious that what was attempted to achieve was really of no great importance. Hegel maintains that in the *resolution* of comedy neither the substantive being, nor the personal life as such, must be abolished or repealed and, therefore, it is only when the persons in the play are aware that they are comic that genuine comedy really occurs.

The German philosopher Arthur Schopenhauer (1788–1860) considered himself to be the true successor of Immanuel Kant; however, he interpreted Kant's "unknowable thing-in-itself" as a blind, impelling force that is manifest in individuals as a "will to live" in which intellect and consciousness arise as instruments in the service of the will (Harris & Levey, 1975, p. 2447). Also, Schopenhauer (like Kant) has an "incongruity theory" of humor; while Kant located the essence of humor in the evaporation of an expectation, Schopenhauer locates it in a mismatch between one's sensory knowledge of things and the abstract knowledge of those same things (Morreall, 1987a, p. 51).

Schopenhauer (1819/1906) asserts that what one perceives through the senses are individual things with many characteristics, but when the person organizes his or her sense perceptions under abstract concepts the focus is on only a few characteristics of any individual thing; this allows one to lump very different things under the same concept, and to refer to very different things by the same word. Schopenhauer suggests that humor arises when one is struck by some clash between a concept and a perception that are "supposed" to be of the same thing. Bergler (1956, p. 11) refers to Schopenhauer's approach to humor as the "sudden contrast" theory of laughter in which the cause of laughter in every case is simply the sudden perception of the incongruity between a concept and the real objects that have been thought through in some relation, and laughter itself is just the expression of this incongruity. Piddington (1933/1963, p. 171) notes that Schopenhauer claims to have solved once and for all the problem of laughter: Abstract rational knowledge—though a reflex of ideas of perception—never corresponds to them exactly (Schopenhauer, 1819/1906); abstract knowledge approximates to sensuous knowledge (much like mosaic approximates to painting).

According to Schopenhauer, it is in such a principle as this that one may find the ultimate explanation of laughter. Additionally, the ludicrous may be divided into two species: wit and folly. Wit is the case in which one has previously known two or more very different real objects (ideas of sense-perception) and have identified them intentionally through the identity of a concept that comprehends them both. On the other hand, folly is the case in which one starts with a concept under which two objects were subsumed, the difference between which the person suddenly perceives. Thus, according to Schopenhauer, everything ludicrous is either a flash of wit or a foolish action—based on whether the procedure has been from the discrepancy of the objects to the identity of the concept, or vice-versa. [Notes: In their definition of the "ludicrous," C. Renouvier & L. Prat (1899, pp. 214–215) follow Schopenhauer, generally. However, they differ somewhat from him on the issue of the cause of one's enjoyment of the ludicrous: they contend that this arises from the "liberty in the play of ideas" that is aroused by contradiction in the ludicrous situation. Essentially, Renouvier & Prat (1899) regard laughter as a form of "play" in which incoherence is fundamental in the comic and the amusing; additionally, there is another type of laughter situation in which the smile and the laugh reflect sympathy and friendship (cf: Greig, 1923/1969, p. 269; Piddington, 1933/1963, pp. 188–189). C. C. Everett (1888/1893, p. 177) also follows Schopenhauer on the issue of the comic: the ludicrous is simply the incongruity between the elements that are subsumed under a single generalization, or the incongruity of any one fact with the generalization under which one would bring it. Everett asserts that the tragic is also the incongruous, and the difference between the tragic and the comic lies in the fact that the comic is found in an incongruous relation—considered merely as to its "form," while the tragic is found in an incongruous relation—taken in this case as to its "reality." Moreover, according to Everett, the tragic has objective existence, the comic is purely subjective, and the pleasure one takes in the comic is probably due to the freedom one finds in it (cf: Greig, 1923/1969, pp. 263–264).]

Schopenhauer (1819/1906) cites examples to illustrate his humor theory; one of these examples, as Piddington (1933/1963, p. 173) notes, is widely discussed in the literature on laughter. Schopenhauer suggests, in this example, that if we contemplate the tangent of a circle, we are faced with the incongruity between our abstract conviction of the impossibility of an angle between the circumference of a circle and its tangent, and the fact that such an angle lies visibly before us on paper will—says Schopenhauer—easily excite a smile. Piddington observes that such a result or conclusion may be unwarranted: most people, he suggests, would not find such a situation amusing (Schopenhauer himself admits that the ludicrous, in this case, is rather weak). However, in general, Schopenhauer maintains that the reason for one's enjoyment of the ludicrous lies in the primacy of the *will*. Schopenhauer (1819/1906, Vol. 1, p. 531) sums up this notion epigrammatically as: "No will: no idea, no world." Essentially, according to Schopenhauer, one's pleasure at the ludicrous arises from the victory of knowledge of perception over thought (cf: Greig, 1923/1969, pp. 253–254).

The dominant theme in the writings of the Danish philosopher Soren Kierkegaard (1813–1855) is that "truth is subjectivity"; Kierkegaard argued that in religion the important thing is not truth as objective fact but rather the individual's relationship to it; thus, for example, it is not enough to believe the Christian doctrine, one must also live it (Harris & Levey, 1975, p. 1477).

Kierkegaard (1846/1941) presents another version of the "incongruity" theory of humor in which he analyzes humor in terms of the "comical" and suggests that the primary element in the comical is "contradiction." Morreall (1987b, p. 83) notes that Kierkegaard, in his examples, has in mind something that is weaker than logical or formal contradiction—rather, he is thinking of "incongruity." Kierkegaard (1846/1941) examines humor, and its close relative "irony," for their relations to the three "spheres of existence" or the three "existential stages of life"—the aesthetic, the ethical, and the religious spheres. Kierkegaard claims that irony marks the boundary between the aesthetic and ethical spheres, while humor marks the boundary between the ethical and religious spheres; he asserts that humor is the last stage of existential awareness before faith. Kierkegaard also indicates a strong connection between having a religious view of life and possessing a sense of humor; he maintains that the humorous is present throughout Christianity, and that Christianity is the most humorous view of life in world history (cf: Morreall, 1987b, p. 83).

The Scottish philosopher/psychologist Alexander Bain (1818–1903) made major contributions in the newly emerging field of psychology, including the establishment of new directions in psychological study via his emphasis upon a greater recognition of the importance of the will and emotions (Bain, 1859). He deals with the topic of laughter under the headings of "The Emotion of Power" and "The Aesthetic Emotions" (Bain, 1859, Chapters 10 and 14). Essentially, Bain's theory of humor is an elaboration of Hobbes' "sudden glory" humor theory. According to Bain, one of the causes of laughter is triumph over an enemy or a challenging or fatiguing task, e.g., after a period of intense activity, when one's work is completed, the person needs to "let off steam" via the spasmodic outburst of laughter (cf: Spencer's, 1860/1891, "overflow of nervous energy" theory of humor). Piddington (1933/1963, p. 174) observes that, according to Bain, laughter becomes so intimately related to the pleasure aroused by victory that it has become a sign of pleasure in general; for the same reason, a person may feel intense pain whenever he or she is made the target of ridicule.

Bain (1859) asserts that the first causes of laughter are physical (such as coldness, acute pain, tickling, or hysteria); also, among the mental causes of laughter are "animal spirits" or "hilarity" (such as an outburst of liberty after a period of restriction); and the smile is an outward sign of the existence of certain tender sentiments. In addition to critiques of the theories of Aristotle and Hobbes, Bain provides criticism of those theories that regard "incongruity" as the essential or sole element of the ludicrous (e.g., many situations exhibit incongruity, but do not provoke laughter). Fundamentally, according to Bain, there are two elements in laughter: a feeling of superiority and a sudden release from constraint; the truly comic nature arises from a natural inability for expression of the serious, the solemn, or the dignified (cf: Greig, 1923/1969, pp. 255–256; Piddington, 1933/1963, pp. 174–176). Bergler (1956, p. 18) refers to Bain's humor theory as the "degradation theory" of laughter.

The German philosopher/psychologist Harald Hoeffding (1843–1931) asserts that laughter—as an expression of pleasant feeling—is possible at a lower stage of consciousness than is involved in the appreciation of the ridiculous (Hoeffding, 1887/1891/1896, pp. 291–298). Also, laughter may be aroused by certain physical conditions without being the expression of any emotion (e.g., intense cold may produce laughter as well as shivering). According to Hoeffding, smiling does not appear until the fourth week after birth, when it is accompanied by various "bleating" sounds; such sounds, together with the smile, later develop into laughter which is considered originally as an expression of satisfaction (Piddington, 1933/1963, p. 183 notes that this is the case with idiots who—without intellectual comprehension—burst into peals of laughter on hearing music, when caressed, or when given food).

Hoeffding arrives at Hobbes' position regarding laughter when he examines how laughter is aroused by the perception of the ludicrous: laughter is primarily an expression of pleasure in general, but—because in the struggle for existence—self-preservation plays a leading role, laughter comes to be the *specific* expression of the satisfaction of the "instinct of self-preservation," which Hoeffding identifies with the love of self. Thus, according to Hoeffding, the original sentiment of pure superiority may be tempered by contempt, or by sympathy; in the latter case, one observes humor. Additionally, laughter may be an expression not so much of superior power as of deliverance; in this case, the sublime has a powerful enemy in the ridiculous, and one is ever ready to detect the ludicrous in any authority, especially one that has partially lost its power.

Piddington (1933/1963, p. 184) suggests that probably the most significant feature of Hoeffding's theory of the ludicrous is his insistence on the affective, rather than the cognitive, nature of the contrast involved (i.e., one's feeling of the ludicrous—like one's feeling of the sublime—depends upon contrast); they both rest on one and the same fundamental relation—on the relation between greatness and insignificance—looked at from opposite sides). Greig (1923/1969, p. 262) observes that, according to Hoeffding, in humor one feels great and small at the same time, and sympathy makes laughter humorous, just as it changes fear into reverence.

Bergler (1956, p. 19) designates Hoeffding's humor theory the "Hobbes plus" theory of laughter in which the pure superiority emphasis of Hobbes may be colored or augmented by the "plus" element of sympathy. Bergler (1956, p. 19) also notes that Hoeffding's "deduction" (i.e., theory) is a blend of many other theories and concepts: Hobbes plus Penjon plus injection of the "instinct of self-preservation" into the phenomenon of laughter; Bergler states that

blend or not, the sum total of the deduction amounts to very little; as in so many of the attempts at explanation . . . the basic question is circled but never approached, and we still do not know why the specific reason ('liberty' or 'self-preservation' or 'superiority' or what not) produces the specificity of the reaction—laughter.

Bergler concludes that "One cannot but suspect that many authors have been so eager to find a theory which would distinguish them from their precursors that their success in turning up a difference blotted out all interest in the main question, why laughter is produced" (pp. 19–20).

The German-born American philosopher Paul Carus (1852–1919) held a monistic philosophical position, and also attempted to establish religion on a scientific basis. In his article, "On the Philosophy of Laughing," Carus (1897–1898) claims that the secret of the problem of laughter is in the concept of "triumph"; one laughs only at "petty triumph"; and nothing is in itself ridiculous, but anything may become so as soon as it produces a "harmless triumph." Moreover, according to Carus, every joke must have a point—it must be directed against someone or something, otherwise there is nothing at which one may laugh. Carus (1897–1898, p. 263) emphasizes in his theoretical approach toward humor that the triumph involved must be of a sudden nature (cf: Greig, 1923/1969, pp. 267–268).

The American philosopher/educator John Dewey (1859–1952) treats the topic of laughter only incidentally in an article on the theory of emotion (Dewey, 1894–1895). Dewey asserts that laughter is not to be viewed from the standpoint of humor, because its connection with humor is only secondary; the laugh is of the same general character as the sigh of relief. According to Dewey, laughter marks the ending (i.e., the attainment of a unity) of a period of suspense, or expectation, and an ending that is sudden and sharp (cf: Greig, 1923/1969, p. 265). In one case, Dewey attacks Darwin's view of laughter (i.e., that it is simply an expression of pleasure). [Note: Piddington (1933/1963, pp. 186–187) suggests that Dewey has difficulty in understanding why pleasure—as feeling—should express itself in laughter, and presents a brief analysis of this issue.]

The French philosopher Henri Bergson (1859–1941) developed a humor theory that has been in vogue for a long time (Bergler, 1956, p. 21, refers to Bergson's theory as the "mechanization" theory of laughter—that is, the ludicrous is something mechanical that is "encrusted on the living"). Bergson (1911, p. 4) opens his famous essay on laughter by pointing out that the ludicrous must necessarily be *human* (animals or inanimate objects become laughable only insofar as they remind us of something human). According to Bergson (1911, p. 5), a necessary condition of laughter is absence of feeling, because the "greatest foe" for laughter is emotion. [Note: John Palmer (see Piddington, 1933/1963, p. 195) attacks Bergson's postulation here of an unemotional attitude in laughter (cf: Sharpe, 1987, pp. 208–211, who gives "seven reasons why amusement *is* an emotion," and Morreall's, 1987b, pp. 212–224, rebuttal to Sharpe's position; also, see DeSousa, 1987, pp. 226–249, who—like Bergson—stresses the social nature of humor, but also revives the older Platonic-Hobbesian idea of a malicious element in humor; and Boskin, 1987, pp. 250–263, who shows how humor depends on shared beliefs and attitudes, and how it tends to perpetuate those beliefs and attitudes); Palmer himself emphasizes the importance of national and individual differences in sensibility to various types of comic situation.]

In Bergson's view, the essence of the comic involves a kind of "momentary anaesthesia" of the heart—its appeal is to one's intelligence, pure and simple. Bergson attacks the intellectualist definitions of the comic with the reasoning that—even if they did give a true and complete account of the comic—they still cannot explain *why* the comic excites laughter. In order to understand the *why* of humor, Bergson (1911, p. 8) asserts that one must determine the *social* function of laughter.

Bergson's logical sequence of reasoning concerning the social basis of humor goes as follows (cf: Greig, 1923/1969, pp. 269–270): Life and society today demand from the individual both elasticity and tension, adaptability and alertness; life sets a lower standard than does society; a moderate degree of adaptability enables one to live; to live well—which is the aim of society—requires much greater flexibility; society is compelled to be suspicious of all tendencies towards the inelastic, and for this reason has devised the social gesture of *laughter* to serve as a "corrective" of all unsocial deviations. [Note: Piddington (1933/1963, p. 190) declares that Bergson does not suggest this as a definition or explanation of the comic, but regards it as applying only to cases which are elementary, theoretical, and perfect; it is, rather, the *leitmotiv* that accompanies all of Bergson's explanations; cf: Bergson, (1911, p. 21).] Bergson maintains that the comic is always something rigid, inelastic, and inflexible and usurps the place in human activities of the fine tension and adjustment that society requires (i.e., "something mechanical encrusted on the living"; Bergson (1911, p. 37). According to Bergson, laughter is corrective in purpose, whether consciously or unconsciously applied; in laughter and humor, one always finds an intention to humiliate and, consequently, to "correct" one's neighbor, if not in his will, at least in his deed.

Comedy and the comic stand midway between art and life—in the zone of artifice: on one hand, the comic in life is appealing because we watch it in a detached/disinterested manner; on the other hand, comedy is not (like art) disinterested—it has a social function. Bergson asserts that the social function of comedy is not to be confounded with morality, and it is a failure to distinguish the immoral from the unsocial that has misled those writers on humor who have centered (theoretically) the comic in the trivialities, foibles, and faults of humans. Moreover, a virtue as well as a vice may be the target of the comic because the comic relies on the prejudices and conventions of a particular social group, and not upon any more stable moral standard; laughter is the "revenge of society" on the unsocial.

Laughter, says Bergson (1911, p. 200), is a "froth with a saline base; like froth it sparkles; it is gaiety itself. But the philosopher who gathers a handful to taste may find that the substance is scanty, and the after-taste bitter." Additionally, laughter is not kindly nor is it strictly just; it breaks out in a spontaneous way, and is just only in a somewhat rough form—it punishes certain failings as disease punishes others, not always distinguishing the innocent from the guilty; laughter is an averaging process, always aiming at an average result (cf: Greig, 1923/1969, p. 270). Bergson (1911, p. 23), in dealing with the simplest form of the comic (i.e., physical deformities which are ludicrous rather than ugly) formulates the following "law" (cf: Piddington, 1933/1963, p. 190): "A deformity that may become comic is a deformity that a normally built person could successfully imitate." The reasoning behind this principle is that the deformity suggests a certain rigidity that is acquired as a habitual feature of a normal person. For example [Bergson, (1911, p. 23)], the figure of a hunchback suggests a "person who holds himself badly"; there is always in such cases (including "comic physiognomy") the suggestion of a certain "rigidity" or "automatism" that produces the effect (this applies, as well, to the comic's body movements where, Bergson suggests, "the attitudes, gestures, and movements of the human body are laughable in exact proportion as that body reminds us of a mere machine"). Further, Bergson (1911, p. 23) observes, "by a kind of physical obstinacy, by *rigidity*, in a word, it persists in the habit it has contracted. Try to see with your eyes alone. Avoid reflection, and above all, do not reason. Abandon all your prepossessions; seek to recapture a fresh, direct, and primitive impression."

Morreall (1987b, p. 117) notes that some philosophers have developed theories of laughter and humor that had little connection with the rest of their philosophy. This, however, is *not* the case with Bergson whose account of humor is an extension of his ethics and metaphysics; many of Bergson's notions spring from his opposition to materialism/mechanism, especially as grounded in the theories of evolution of his day. Bergson's own theory of "creative evolution" suggested the existence of a nonmaterial "vital force" (*elan vital*) that drives social and biological evolution. The purpose of laughter—according to Bergson, once again—is to remove the "mechanical encrustation on the living" through humiliation and, thereby, promote free, well-adapted behaviors. Morreall suggests that Bergson's theory is in the tradition of "superiority theories of humor" (although he does not treat amusement as an emotion as most superiority theories do); what Bergson adds to superiority theories is a perspective about the object of the mockery (i.e., "mechanical inelasticity") and the social function/aspect of laughter. [Note: Both Bergler (1956, Chapter 7) and

Piddington (1933/1963, pp. 189–195) provide excellent extensive accounts of Bergson's theory of humor.]

The Spanish-born American philosopher and poet George Santayana (1863–1952) enunciated in his 1896 work, *The Sense of Beauty*, a qualified hedonism that placed high value on aesthetic pleasure; it was a pleasure that was understood to be an irrational expression of vital interests but was distinguished from direct, sensual pleasures. In that same work, Santayana (1896/1904) challenges both the "incongruity" and "superiority" theories of humor; he asserts that amusement (i.e., the feeling prompting laughter) is more directly a physical thing than incongruity and superiority theories claim—it depends on a certain amount of nervous excitement (e.g., a person may be amused merely by being tickled, or by hearing other people laughing). According to Morreall (1987b, p. 90), Santayana does not totally reject the incongruity and superiority theories, however, for he agrees that people often laugh in situations involving incongruity or degradation. For example, when we react to a comic incongruity or degradation, it is never those things in themselves that give us pleasure; it is, rather, the excitement and stimulation caused by the individual's perception of those things.

Santayana (1896/1904) asserts that the shock that they bring may sometimes be the occasion of a subsequent pleasure, but the incongruity and degradation, as such, always remain unpleasant. Moreover, Santayana insists that it is impossible to enjoy the incongruity itself (as some versions of the incongruity theory provide) because, as rational animals, humans are averse constitutionally to incongruity, absurdity, or nonsense in any form (we endure such things only for the pleasure of stimulation that they afford). Morreall (1987b, p. 90) suggests that Santayana would agree with Plato that amusement is a pleasure that is mixed with pain, and that is why people prefer to get their mental stimulation with *no* incongruity—as in wit, rather than with incongruity—as in humor.

Greig (1923/1969, pp. 266–267) confesses that although he has read, several times, Santayana's accounts of wit, the comic, humor, and the grotesque, he still doubts his understanding of Santayana and "what he would be at." It would seem (in Greig's view) that Santayana considers the essentially fictitious nature of the comic as the important matter. In this regard, Santayana (1896/1904, p. 249) maintains that the pleasure one derives from comic effects comes from the inward rationality and movement of the fiction, not from its inconsistency with anything else ("we enjoy the stimulus and the shaking up of our wits"). According to Santayana, it is not disorder that we like, but expansion; we put up with the "disorderliness" of the comic for the sake of the freedom that it gives to us. With wit, one can dispense with absurdity altogether because wit is "purer" amusement. The essence of humor, says Santayana

(1896/1904, p. 254) , is that "amusing weakness should be combined with an amicable humanity."

The modern-day philosopher John Morreall provides a section in his book, *The Philosophy of Laughter and Humor* (1987b), on contemporary theories of laughter and humor that includes the views and approaches of Michael Clark, Roger Scruton, Mike W. Martin, and John Morreall.

In his essay, "Humor and Incongruity," Clark (see Morreall, 1987b, pp. 139–155) characterizes the superiority, relief, and incongruity theories as theories of *humor*, rather than as theories of *laughter*. Clark asserts that in their classical forms and versions all three types of theories are open to counterexamples, although the incongruity theory may be properly modified to accommodate such instances and examples. Clark develops his own version of the incongruity theory and proceeds by looking for the "formal object" of amusement (i.e., the description under which anything must be thought if it is to cause amusement in us); this "formal object" is that which is seen as incongruous. To capture the complete essence of amusement, Clark (p. 150) offers the following generalization: "Amusement is the enjoyment of (i.e., the perceiving, thinking of, or indulging in) what is seen as incongruous, partly at least because it is seen as incongruous."

In his essay, titled "Laughter," Scruton (see M. Morreall, 1987b, pp. 156–171) discusses laughter *at* humor. Scruton agrees with Clark in that it would be useful to find a "formal object" of humorous laughter (i.e., "the description under which anything must be thought if it is to amuse us"), but he disagrees with Clark's claim that incongruity is the formal object. Ultimately, Scruton offers not a formal object of amusement, but a "pattern of thought" that is characteristic of amusement; this pattern consists of the enjoyable devaluing and demolition of something human. Additionally, Scruton asserts that amusement is a kind of aesthetic interest, and it differs significantly from standard accounts of emotions.

In his essay, "Humor and Aesthetic Enjoyment of Incongruities," M. Martin (see Morreall, 1987b, pp. 172–187) challenges two common perspectives about humor: that amusement is the enjoyment of incongruity, and that amusement is a type of aesthetic experience. According to Martin, both views require qualification; he challenges the first view by discussing Clark's "Humor and Incongruity," and challenges the second view by showing that only *some* amusement is aesthetic (e.g., when the basis for humor enjoyment is aggressive or sexual, amusement is not aesthetic enjoyment; it is only when the basis for the amusement is in the enjoyment of incongruity for its own sake that amusement defines aesthetic enjoyment). Martin maintains that the enjoyment of incongruity for its own sake is a *necessary* condition for amusement, but it is not a *sufficient* condition; he argues that to develop a sufficient condition (for at least the central cases of amusement), one needs to add a condition based on the tendency of amusement to result in laughter.

In one of his essays, Morreall (1987b, pp. 128–138) presents a "new theory of laughter" (cf: Morreall, 1982; 1983, Chapter 5) wherein he examines the three traditional theories of laughter (incongruity, relief, and superiority theories), and shows that none explains all cases of laughter; however, by drawing on features shared by the three theories, Morreall creates a new formula (pp. 133–134) which states that "laughter results from a pleasant psychological shift (sudden change)"; Morreall argues that his new theory of laughter does account for all cases of laughter (cf: Pfeifer, 1994, for a rebuttal of Morreall's approach). In another essay, Morreall (1987b, pp. 188–207) suggests that one may better understand amusement if it is contrasted with two other reactions to incongruity: negative emotion and "reality assimilation" (i.e., puzzlement at the strange).

According to Morreall, when we react to the incongruity with emotions such as fear or anger (or else when we try to make sense out of the incongruity), it disturbs us and we feel uneasy about it. Such uneasiness derives in part from a feeling of loss of control, and acts as a motivator to regain control by doing something. In the case of negative emotion, the person tries to change the incongruous situation, while in the case of reality assimilation, the individual attempts to change his or her understanding of it. Morreall argues that amusement contrasts sharply with both negative emotion and reality assimilation; when amused, one is not disturbed by the incongruity, one does not feel a loss of control, and one is not motivated to change the incongruous situation in any way. Morreall concludes that once we see the special nature of amusement as a reaction to incongruity we can better appreciate its value in human life.

Behavioral Theories

The word "behavioral," as used in this section, is employed in a broader and more general way than that of the "behaviorists" or "Behaviorism" (e.g., Skinner, 1938, 1953, 1963, 1974, 1979; Watson, 1913, 1919/1929, 1925/1958, 1928; Watson & McDougall, 1929; cf: MacHovec, 1988, pp. 54–56, "Behaviorism—A Parting Shot!"). For example, within the context of humor theory analyses, the phenomenon of *play* may be considered as a behavior in the present more expansive sense. Several writers have attempted to define *play*, and to offer criteria for play behavior (cf: Berlyne, 1969, pp. 813–814). Beach (1945) gives the following aspects and characteristics most often attributed to "playful behavior": contains an emotional element of pleasure; is demonstrated more frequently in the immature, than in the adult, animal; has no immediate biological effect that results in the continued existence of the individual or the species; outwardly, it has species-specific forms and features; and the amount, duration, and diversity of play is related to the position of the species on the phylogenetic scale. Piaget (1945/1951), also, lists several criteria that define the behavior of *play* and which distinguish it from "non-ludic" activities: it is overmotivated; it shows freedom from conflicts; it is relatively unorganized; it is directed toward pleasure; it is spontaneous; and it is an end in itself.

Meyer-Holzapfel (1956) cites the following features among the hallmarks of animal play (cf: Eibl-Eibesfeldt, 1975): it contains both instinctive and learned actions without subsuming their functions; it is repeatable at will and often takes the form of a rhythmic reiteration of one action; it shows outward manifestations of a pleasurable condition; it includes the search for a playmate that may be conspecific, a human being, or an object; all species-specific social inhibitions are suspended in "playful fighting"; and there is an "appetite for play" in animals. In his definition, Valentine (1942) states simply that play is any activity that is carried out entirely for its own sake (cf: Schlosberg, 1947). Berlyne (1969, p. 814) notes that some authorities have been content to define "play" widely enough to include activities such as "exploration" and "esthetic" behavior, among other things. [Note: For a comprehensive account of the "theories of play," see Berlyne, 1969, pp. 829–843.]

The English psychologist James Sully (1842–1923) held an overriding interest in the playful behavior of children and even founded a society for studying children. In his approach to humor, Sully (1902) provides "situations" or "content" descriptions that give rise to laughter (cf: Boston, 1974, pp. 50–51; Keith-Spiegel, 1972, p. 15; Kimmins, 1928, p. 36). More specifically, Sully gives the following 12 behavioral classes of laughter-provoking circumstances: novelties, physical deformities, moral deformities and vices, disorderliness, small misfortune, indecencies, pretenses, desire for knowledge or skill, the incongruous and absurd, word play, the expression of a merry mood, and the outwitting or getting the better of another person. Bergler (1956, p. 22) refers to Sully's humor theory as the "play-mood" theory of laughter. Sully (1902) assumes that the enjoyment of the laughable is rooted in a sudden arousal of the behavior of "play-mood" which involves a refusal to take the current situation seriously (one of the key features of play); of course, it must be mentioned—for present purposes—that the concept of a "play-mood" here may refer both to *overt* and externally expressive playful behavior, as well as to *covert* mental, intellectual, or "cognitive" manipulations (such as in "word-play"). In this regard, it may be said that Sully's position is that laughter is an *overt* expression of an already existent *covert* pleasurable state.

Kimmins (1928, p. 34) suggests that students of the history of laughter are under a great debt of gratitude to Sully who gives an admirable summary of views held—concerning laughter—at the beginning of the century; Monro (1951/1963, p. 83) observes that Sully regards all theories of humor as variants of two main ones: the moral/degradation theory and the intellectual/incongruity theory; to this classification, Monro adds two more: the release from restraint theory, and the ambivalence theory. In his account of humor and laughter, Sully gives full recognition to the "evidence of the child" in the matter; he confirms Darwin's (1872/1965) conclusion that there is a series of gradations from the smile to the laugh and that the laugh, in fact, is a "grown-up" smile. Moreover, Sully—also like Darwin—attaches great importance to the behavior of tickling in the early stages of development. As regards the physiological value of laughter, Sully is in complete agreement with Spencer (1860/1891).

Greig (1923/1969, p. 271) observes that Sully (like M. L. Dugas, 1902/1910, 1906) makes the principle of *play* fundamental in his theory of laughter (cf: Stanley, 1898, for an account of another "play" theory); Greig states that it is impossible to do justice to Sully's admirable book (*An Essay on Laughter*) in any summary—the "mere theory it happens to contain is the least valuable thing in it." Sully (1902, p. 149) declares that much of the laughable "may be regarded as an expression in persons or things of the play-mood which seizes the spectator by way of a sympathetic resonance . . . and by a sweet compulsion forces us to play with it rather than to consider it seriously." Sully (1902, p. 153) asserts that the feeling out of which laughter comes, and its accompanying behavioral expression, is highly complex, "containing something of the child's joyous surprise at the new and unheard of; something, too, of the child's gay responsiveness to a play-challenge; often something also of the glorious sense of expansion after compression which gives the large mobility to freshly freed limbs of young animals and children."

In summary, according to Sully, laughter expresses pleasure, and its bodily activity further provokes a condition of physiological euphoria within the organism; laughter at laughable situations may serve as a corrective *social* function (see Sully, 1902, pp. 255–257, 261, 272 for the important *social* aspects of laughter), but its chief *psychological* function is related to more elementary forms and is essentially an activity or behavior that is analogous to play. Bergler (1956, p. 22) notes that far-reaching conclusions are deduced from the idea that reality can be viewed as a playful game; moreover, Bergler, suggests that one may search in vain for a passage in Sully (1902) explaining how the "play-mood" is achieved or where it comes from; he also makes the observation that children take their play seriously more often than not, but this fact is not touched upon by Sully.

More contemporary/modern approaches that employ the *behavioral* paradigm to humor analysis are found in studies that investigate the "drive-reduction/stimulus-response learning" aspects of humor, and the effects of "experimental arousal" on humor responses (e.g., Levine, 1969, Chapters 7–10). The following writers and researchers have used classical behavior principles and theory to study and/or explain humor appreciation: Berlyne's (1960) "theoretically versatile" proposal that humor springs from an "arousal jag" that stems from an experience of threat, discomfort, uncertainty, unfamiliarity, or surprise that is followed by some factor that signifies safety, readjustment, release, or clarification (according to Berlyne, the arousal found in the humor experience is more of a neurophysiological event than a psychological state; however, also see Berlyne, 1960, in the next section, "Cognitive/Perceptual Theories"); Kant's (1790/1892/1914) definition of humor as an affection arising from a strained expectation being suddenly reduced to insignificance, and his emphasis on humor as a sudden relief from tension or a reduction in anxiety; and Tomkins' (1962) model of positive effects (e.g, joy) that combines a reduction of tension component ("neural firing") with a cognitive approach in which the smiling response, for instance, is activated by a steep or sudden reduction of tension (in this way, according to Tomkins, sudden relief from negative stimulation such as pain, fear, distress, or aggression produces the smile of joy; also, the sudden reduction of positive affect, such as excitement, activates similarly the smile of joy.

Recently, the behavioral scientists have conducted experiments to test the applicability of the drive-reduction model of human behavior as the basis for the gratification obtained from humor. The basic experimental premise here is that the enjoyment of humor takes on the function of a "secondary reinforcer" (in learning theory terms) because humor reduces the sexual or aggressive drives; such an assumption is consistent with Freud's (1905/1916, 1928) theory of humor (i.e., the notion that humor gives pleasure because it gratifies prohibited aggressive or sexual "wishes" which operate as unconscious psychological forces that constantly seek to be discharged. As Levine (1969, p. 8) observes, the behavioral drive-reduction theory—in a restricted sense—is a simplification of the psychoanalytic theory because it omits the mediating processes between the stimulus and response; whether such mediating responses are necessary or not has been an enduring issue between the behavioral theorists and the psychoanalysts.

In their approach (an "approach-avoidance" formulation of the drive-reduction model), Dollard and Miller (1950) have incorporated psychoanalytic concepts as mediating processes between stimulus and response; and Porr (1961) has applied this "neo-Hullian" formulation to the humor situation, reasoning that sexually aroused persons will prefer sexual humor—and even if the individual is too anxious to show such preferences he or she will express sexual feelings and thoughts more freely because the humor serves to reduce anxiety. Other relatively recent works on the effects of "experimental arousal" on humor responses include: Dworkin and Efran (1967), Shurcliff (1968), Singer (1968), Singer, Gollob, and Levine (1967), and Strickland (1959).

In an amalgamation of behavioral theory and physiology, Koestler (1964, p. 31) observes that "humor is the only domain of creative activity where a stimulus on a high level of complexity produces a massive and sharply defined response on the level of physiological reflexes." Also, in behavioral theory overtones, Diserens (1926, p. 254) describes the many sides of laughter as a "complex form of behavior, unlearned yet highly susceptible to conditioning in the presence of psychic stimuli. It is at once a biological mechanism of adjustment, a physiological safety-value, a psychological exhilarant and a regulator of social relations." The relationship between the acts of laughing and smiling (cf: Keith-Spiegel, 1972, pp. 18–19) may be viewed in terms of behavioral tendencies along a continuum, and where different laughs (e.g., giggle, titter, belly laugh, chuckle, snigger, roar, etc.) and different smiles (e.g., smirk, grin, sneer, the "Mona Lisa," etc.) occupy various positions on the behavioral "pleasure dimension."

The tenets and concepts of classical behavioral theory are indicated, also, in the famous "nature versus nurture" controversy that has permeated psychology since its earliest days. The issue at hand is whether humor-related behaviors are learned ("nurture") or are innate ("nature"). Most psychologists have safely assumed that laughter/humor is a maturational process having individual differences in frequency and time of onset. However, some psychologists label laughter as an "instinct" (e.g., Greig, 1923/1969; McComas, 1923; McDougall, 1922), an "unconditioned mechanism" (e.g., Mones, 1939), and a "reflex" (e.g., Koestler, 1964). McComas (1923), Washburn (1929), and Justin (1932) argue that laughter becomes increasingly conditioned as the individual matures. Other writers accept the inborn nature of the laughter response, but maintain that what is laughed at is extended increasingly through learning, habit, and experience (e.g., Allport, 1924; Koestler, 1964; Mones, 1939; Woodworth, 1921). Furthermore, Hartley (1749) proposed that laughter itself is a learned behavior; Guthrie (1903) argued that the smile is inborn but the act of laughter is learned; and Byrne (1958b), Fisher (1964), and Keith-Spiegel (1968) have applied the behavioral theory/Hullian model (e.g., Hull, 1943, 1951, 1952) to expectancies involved in the humor experience and humor appreciation.

More current studies reflecting the influence of behavior analysis and behavioral theory on humor appreciation are those by Deckers and Hricik (1984), Harris and Christenfeld (1997), Strack, Martin, and Stepper (1988), and Deckers and Hricik present behavioral/cognitive evidence for the hypothesis that a humor response is an instance of a more general orienting response (cf: Kimmel, VanOlst, & Orlebeke, 1979; Lynn, 1966; VanOlst, 1971). Although their subjective components may differ, the two types of responses (orienting and humor) both occur to stimulus novelty or incongruity, and are behaviorally and physiologically identical. Dimensions on which the two types of responses show strong parallels are the effects of habituation, and the degree of stimulus change; also, weaker parallels have been observed for such parameters as direction of stimulus change, number of habituation trials, stimulus complexity, salience, intensity, and the participants' level of arousal. Deckers and Hricik assert that the subjective component may be the major distinguishing feature between orienting responses and humor responses. Accordingly, the occurrence of humor instead of some other emotion may be determined by the cognitive level attached to the facial responses or any concomitant arousal. The cognitive label, in turn, depends on the degree of incongruity, arousal, stimulus intensity, and context.

Strack, Martin, and Stepper (1988) investigated the behavioral hypothesis that people's facial activity influences their affective/humor responses in a study designed to manipulate facial expressions with a new methodology (i.e., participants were induced to hold a pen with their lips only, with their teeth only, or with their nondominant hand as they rated the funniness of cartoons; such a procedure either inhibits or facilitates the facial muscles typically associated with smiling without requiring participants to pose in a smiling face) that avoids a cognitive interpretation of the facial action. The results obtained lend support to the "facial feedback hypothesis" (i.e., feedback from one's facial expressions affects one's emotional experience and behavior; cf: Buck, 1980; Darwin, 1872/1965; Roeckelein, 1998, p. 180).

The findings of Strack et al. are consistent with those of earlier studies in which the manipulation of the facial activity associated with particular emotional expressions influenced persons' affective experiences in the presence of an emotional stimulus; in particular, the rated funniness of cartoons depended on the possibility of producing the behavioral/muscle action involved in smiling. The results of the Strack et al. studies suggest that the affective reaction toward an emotional stimulus is intensified when the facial expression is facilitated and "softened" (cf: Darwin, 1872/1965), and when this expression is inhibited by an irrelevant task; their findings suggest, also, that cognitive processes that imply the recognition of the emotional meaning of one's facial expression are not necessary to influence resulting emotional experiences. Moreover, the results obtained by Strack et al. are inconsistent with the following typical or "traditional" mechanisms: compliance with "experimental demand of the situation"; intentional mood manipulation; priming of emotion-relevant concepts; and "self-perception" theory (e.g., Bem, 1967). Thus, Strack et al. suggest that recognizing the emotional meaning of the facial response is *not* a necessary precondition for the effect; rather, it seems that the interplay between an emotional stimulus and an innate motor program (e.g., Leventhal & Scherer, 1987)—such as the smile—is the determinant of the emotional experience.

In a third study indicating the influence of behavioral theory/factors on humor, Harris and Christenfeld (1997) maintain that laughter induced by tickling and by humor share common underlying mechanisms—a view that was suggested much earlier by Darwin (1872/1965) and Hecker (1873). Participants in Harris and Christenfeld's study were tickled before and after viewing comedy and control videotapes (cf: the "warm-up effect" found by Deckers, Buttram, & Winsted, 1989; L. Martin, 1905); the participants who exhibited more pronounced laughter to comedy also laughed more vigorously to tickle (cf: Fridlund & Loftis, 1990). However, Harris and Christenfeld found no evidence that comedy-induced laughter increased subsequent laughter to tickle nor that ticklish laughter increased laughter to comedy; they suggest that humor and tickle may be related only in that the two behaviors share a final threshold for elicitation of their common behavioral response (i.e., smiling and laughing). Harris and Christenfeld conclude that their results do not rule out the possibility that humor develops ontogenetically from tickling (e.g., Fridlund, 1994; cf: Hoshikawa, 1991; Leuba, 1941; Newman, O'Grady, Ryan, & Hemmes, 1993), but that after such a development has taken place, the two behaviors may share only a final common pathway. Also, according to Harris and Christenfeld, their results leave open the possibility that tickle shares an internal state with other emotions such as social anxiety, and that ticklish laughter might be more similar to nervous, rather than mirthful, laughter.

Other works that invoke—wholly or partially—the classical behavioral theory principles are those of: Baron and Ball (1974); Berkowitz (1970); Brackbill (1958); Bush (1989); Byrne (1956, 1958a, b, 1961); Campbell (1968); Cantor, Bryant, and Zillmann (1974); Chapman (1973, 1974, 1975, 1976); Chapman and Wright (1976); Coulter, Wundeleigh, Ball, and Canary (1973); Cupchik and Leventhal (1974); Eckerman and Whatley (1975); Ellis and Sekyra (1972); Etzel and Gewirtz (1967); Eysenck (1942); Feshbach (1955); Foot and Chapman (1976); Fuller (1977); Fuller and Sheehy-Skeffington (1974); Gerber and Routh (1975); Godkewitsch (1976); Goldstein (1970); Goldstein, Suls, and Anthony (1972); Groch (1974); Gutman and Priest (1969); Hetherington and Wray (1964, 1966); Hom (1966); Kenny (1955); Kirkland (1976); Kole and Henderson (1966); Laffal, Levine, and Redlich (1953); LaGaipa (1968); Lamb (1968); Landy and Mettee (1969); Leak (1974); Lefcourt, Antrobus, and Hogg (1974); Leventhal and Cupchik (1975); Levine and Abelson (1953, 1959); Lieberman (1976); Main and Schillace (1968); Malpass and Fitzpatrick (1959); Mussen and Rutherford (1961); Nerhardt (1970, 1975); Nosanchuk and Lightstone (1974); Pollio and Swanson (1995); Prerost (1975, 1977); Prerost and Brewer (1974); Redlich (1960); Roberts and Johnson (1957); Roeckelein (1969); Rosenwald (1964); Salzen (1963); Schachter and Wheeler (1962); Schick, McGlynn, and Woolam (1972); Schmidt (1957); Schmidt and Williams (1971); Schwartz (1972); Sheehy-Skeffington (1977); Singer (1968); Smith (1973); Smith, Ascough, Ettinger, and Nelson (1971); Smyth and Fuller (1972); Spitz and Wolf (1946); Sroufe and Waters (1976); Stephenson (1951); Suls (1975); Ullmann and Lim (1962); Ventis (1973); Ware (1999); Weiner and

Lorenz (1994); Williams and Cole (1964); Zelazo (1971); Zillmann and Bryant (1974).

Cognitive/Perceptual Theories

The German-British personality psychologist Hans J. Eysenck (1916–1998) generally distinguishes among *cognitive* theories (which emphasize elements such as "incongruity" and "contrast between ideas," i.e., "thinking"), *conative* theories (which stress the satisfaction of desire for superiority, self-glory, etc.), and *affective* theories (which emphasize emotional components); the conative and affective theories, when paired together, comprise what Eysenck (1942) and Eysenck, Arnold, and Meili (1972, p. 81) call *orectic* (i.e., involving "personal" or "feeling" components) aspects of humor [cf: Scheerer (1966) who similarly divides the basic theoretical approaches in humor study into those that localize the experience of humor *objectively* in the overt/external content of the situation, and those that explain humor *subjectively* in terms of the covert/internal motive or emotional aspects. According to both Eysenck and Scheerer, the humor theory of Freud (1905/1916) managed to include both approaches].

Flugel (1954, p. 710) adopts—as a "convenient working model" for his review of humor and laughter—the classical tripartite division of mental states/processes into "cognitive," "conative," and "affective" classes (cf: McGhee's 1979, p. 9, "General model of qualities accounted for in psychological theories of humor"). The elements of all three classes are involved in any given psychological state or process—although their relative predominance may vary greatly from one case to another; this same condition holds true for jokes and the mental concomitants of laughter. Accordingly, Flugel describes the cognitive, conative, and affective aspects of the mental processes at work in the humorous situation. Eysenck (1947), also, suggests the classification of the numerous theories of laughter according to whether the authors stress the cognitive, conative, or affective elements involved in humor. In the first class of those theorists who emphasize the *cognitive* factors, Eysenck places the names of Cicero, Quintilian, Dryden, Locke, Beattie, Kant, Schopenhauer, Spencer, Lipps, Sidis, Renouvier and Prat, and Willmann, among others. In the *conative* class may be found the names of Plato, Aristotle, Hobbes, Hegel, Bain, Bergson, Kimmins, and Ludovici. The *affective* class would include the names of Descartes, Hartley, Hoeffding, and McDougall. Eysenck (1947) admits that the humor theories of some authors (e.g., Ribot, Sully, and Santayana) have recognized at least two of the three aspects of humor, while Freud has recognized all three aspects.

Eysenck suggests, furthermore, that the distinctions between the comic, the witty, and the humorous may be viewed in terms of a predominance of cognitive, conative, and affective elements, respectively (cf: Flugel, 1954, p. 711).

For present purposes of the discussion of humor theories in this section, primary consideration is given to the *cognitive* (i.e., mental, thinking, or intellectual), and the *perceptual structure/transformation* (i.e., overall cognitive-perceptual organization of a complex stimulus; percept modification due to additions/deletions/alterations/novel interpretations of the physical stimulus; cf: Reber, 1995, pp. 551–552) aspects and types of humor theories.

Keith-Spiegel (1972, p. 31) notes that the "thinking-based" type of humor theories are most likely to be found in the "incongruity" and "Gestalt" domains (cf: Berlyne, 1969, p. 805, who states that "the influence of Gestalt psychology has produced interpretations of humor, as of so many other psychological phenomena, as a perceptual process"). In the "cognitive/perceptual/intellectual/thinking" approach toward humor analysis, the structure of jokes in particular is emphasized and the suddenness with which a joke is so often "gotten" is related to the abrupt restructurings that occur when perceptual patterns are reorganized or when problems, puns, word-play, and such are solved through insight.

Examples of other general areas of humor that involve mental operations are the following: the reconciliation of the possible with the impossible (e.g., Shaw, 1960); the matching of true and feigned values leading to a revelation of the counterfeit (e.g., Mones, 1939); the recognition of the unusual and the unexpected (e.g., Wallis, 1922); the attitudinal judgment of a situation as ludicrous ("intellectualist theory"), and comparing judgment to mere apprehension or comprehension (e.g., Baillie, 1921); the relationship between laughter and cognitive strategies (e.g., Kreitler & Kreitler, 1970); cognitive development and children's humor appreciation (e.g., McGhee, 1971a,b, 1972, 1974, 1977; McGhee & Johnson, 1975; Shultz, 1976); the order of cognitive processing in humor (e.g., Shultz, 1974; Tsur, 1994); the perception of smiles (e.g., Simpson & Crandall, 1972); cognitive similarity and group laughter (e.g., Wolosin, 1975); the cognitive aspects of smiling and vocalizing (e.g., Zelazo, 1972); conceptual tempo and joke appreciation (e.g., Brodzinsky, 1977); children's jokes and emotional conflicts (e.g., Yorukoglu, 1974, 1977); the phenomenology of joy (e.g., Meadows, 1975); the playful realization of the multiplicity of meaning and coincidence (e.g., Scheerer, 1966); and studies of the relationship between humor and intelligence/reasoning ability (e.g., Carpenter, 1922; Dearborn, 1900; Feibleman, 1949; Hellyar, 1927; Koestler, 1964; Levine & Redlich, 1960; Lilly, 1896; Menon, 1931; Schiller, 1938).

In offering the basics of a Gestalt theory of humor, Maier (1932) observes that the sudden change in interpretation that occurs when a joke is understood implies that the meaning of particular elements changes because the meaning of an element depends on the nature of the configuration in which it operates. Also, humor implies objectivity in that the attitude with which one approaches the content of a joke is one in which emotions and sympathies are "unengaged"

(Maier, 1932). The two aspects of jokes/humor—objectivity and sudden change in configuration—are equally characteristic of productive thinking, so the essence of the ridiculous, according to Maier, must be found elsewhere; for example, found in the isolation of a humorous situation in which humorous configurations are not to be taken seriously and not to be judged by tests used in extrahumorous situations (cf: Bateson, 1953, who views the appreciation of a joke as analogous to the sudden perceptual/cognitive shifts that occur with the relevant figure-ground relationships).

Another cognitive/perceptual area of humor analysis is discussed in a section Berlyne (1969, p. 806) calls "collative motivation." In an earlier work, Berlyne (1960, Chapter 9) gives an interpretation of humor that is based on the similarities between jokes and works of art, as well as on some findings on exploratory behavior and cognate phenomena. In general, Berlyne attempts to combine the *motivational* factors of psychoanalytic theory with the *structural* factors of Gestalt theory, based upon the evidence that *motivation* (i.e., reward/drive sources) and *structure* (i.e., relations among simultaneously occurring processes in the nervous system) are often interdependent, particularly in the ideational and perceptual spheres [cf: the "stimulus contrast" notion of Andrew (1963a,b, 1964) that involves other similar perceptual/cognitive determinants of laughter; also, see McCall (1972)]. More specifically, Berlyne (1960) invokes the notions of "arousal," "arousal jag," "arousal-increasing factors," and "arousal-decreasing factors" as operative in humorous situations (cf: Byrne, 1958a,b; Rickwood & Price, 1988; Tierney, 1991). Moreover, the arousal-raising aspect of a joke or comical situation often depends on certain collative variables (whether acting singly or in conjunction with other drive conditions) such as novelty, surprise, puzzlement, incongruity, ambiguity, strangeness, complexity, and apparent contradiction—all of which presumably affect arousal via conflict. Such collative-variable arousal is mitigated when ideational understanding/reorganization occurs; e.g., upon supplying the "punch line" of the joke.

Inasmuch as the concepts of superiority, incongruity, surprise, and ambivalence serve as the basis for classifying and systematizing humor theories in the literature (e.g., Berger, 1987; Berlyne, 1969; Blistein, 1998; Holland, 1982; Keith-Spiegel, 1972; R. A. Martin, 2000; Monro, 1951/1963; Morreall, 1983), such types of theories may be viewed, also, as being predominantly *cognitive/perceptual* in nature. That is, the "superiority theories" are characterized by one's cognitive comparison of self against others on the bases of intelligence, beauty, strength, wealth, and so on, and on a subsequent personally experienced elation, triumph, or victory as the result of such self-others comparisons. According to the principle of superiority, one's laughter, mockery, and ridicule—at the expense of others—is central to the humor experience (see Bain, 1859; Beerbohm, 1921; Carpenter, 1922; Carus, 1897–1898; Dunlap,

1925; Hunt, 1846/1910/1977; Knight, 1805/1808; LaFave, Haddad, & Maesen, 1976; Leacock, 1935, 1937; McDougall, 1922; Rapp, 1947, 1949; Sidis, 1913; Stanley, 1898; Wallis, 1922).

The "incongruity theories" are characterized by cognitions involving disjointed ideas, ill-suited ideational pairings of ideas or situations, and/or presentations of ideas/situations that diverge from habitual or expected customs (cf: Flugel, 1954, p. 722, who subsumes the notion of incongruity under the rubric "cognition"). According to the principle of incongruity, the perception of contrast, contrariness, incompatibility of contexts, expectancy violations, inconsistency, incongruity, and/or uncommon mixtures of relations is central to the humor experience (see Baillie, 1921; Beattie, 1776; Bergson, 1911; T. Brown, 1820; Byrne, Terrill, & McReynolds, 1961; Carpenter, 1922; Deckers & Buttram, 1990; Deckers, Edington, & Van Cleave, 1981; Deckers & Salais, 1983; Delage, 1919; Eastman, 1921; Everett, 1888/1893; Forabosco, 1992; Gerard, 1759/1780; Gerber & Routh, 1975; Guthrie, 1903; Hazlitt, 1818/1841/1907; Hunt, 1846/1910/1977; Kallen, 1911; Kant, 1790/1892/1914; Kimmins, 1928; Leacock, 1935; Lipps, 1898; McGhee, 1972, 1979; Menon, 1931; Morreall, 1989; Nerhardt, 1970, 1975, 1976, 1977; Nilsen, 1990; Priestley, 1777/1971; Rothbart, 1976; Schopenhauer, 1819/1906; Shultz, 1972; Sinnott & Ross, 1976; Spencer, 1860/1891; Staley & Derks, 1995; Stanley, 1898; Willmann, 1940).

The "surprise theories" are characterized by "unexpectedness/surprise," "shock," or "suddenness" in cognitions or perceptions where such elements are considered by many theorists to be *necessary* (though not necessarily *sufficient*) conditions for the humor experience (cf: Flugel, 1954, p. 724). The concepts of "surprise" and "incongruity" overlap often in which there is an instantaneous breaking up of the normal or routine course of ideation, thought, or action (see Carpenter, 1922; Courdaveaux, 1875; Darwin, 1872/1965; Desai, 1939; Descartes, 1649/1909; Feibleman, 1939; Gerard, 1759/1780; Hartley, 1749; Hobbes, 1651/1839/1904; Hollingworth, 1911; Masson, 1925; Priestley, 1777/1971; Quintilian, 1714/1821–1825; Ramsay, 1848; Stanley, 1898; Sully, 1902; Willmann, 1940).

The "ambivalence theories" are characterized by "oscillation," "conflict-mixture," and "simultaneously experienced incompatible emotions/feelings." The notions of "ambivalence" and "incongruity" overlap often and possess common features. However, the incongruity theories tend to emphasize cognitions/ideas/perceptions whereas the ambivalence theories emphasize feelings/emotions as central to the humor experience (see Descartes, 1649/1909; Dessoir, 1923; Eastman, 1921; Gregory, 1924; Greig, 1923/1969; Hecker, 1873; Hellyar, 1927; Hoeffding, 1887/1891/1896; Joubert, 1560/1579/1980; Knox, 1951; Lund, 1930; Menon, 1931; Monro, 1951/1963; Plato, 1871; Willmann, 1940; Winterstein, 1934).

The "configurational theories" (which are closely allied to Gestalt psychology) are characterized by the perceptual experience of originally unrelated elements as suddenly falling into the "proper" place; both the configurational theories and the incongruity theories possess the common features of cognitive and perceptual attributes of humor; however, the incongruity approach emphasizes the perception of "disjointedness" in humor, whereas the configurational approach stresses "perceptual figure-ground shifts," the "falling into place," and "sudden insight" of originally ambiguous elements as the basis for the humor/amusement experience (see Bateson, 1953; Maier, 1932; Scheerer, 1966; Schiller, 1938; Wallis, 1922).

Modern versions of the *cognitive/perceptual* approach to humor analysis are found in Levine (1969), especially in his section titled "Cognition and Humor" (pp. 139–158). Also, see Giles, Bourhis, Gadfield, Davies, and Davies (1976); Gollub and Levine (1967); Hillson and Martin (1994); Hofstader and Gabora (1989); Karnick (1991); Littman (1980); McGhee (1979); McGhee and Panaoutsopoulu (1990); Nerhardt (1977); Oring (1975); Schrempp (1995); Shultz (1976); Suls (1977); G. A. Wilson (1989); Zigler, Levine, and Gould (1966a,b, 1967); cf: Deckers and Kizer (1974, 1975).

Levine (1969, p. 2) notes that theories of humor based on experimental evidence have employed three basic research models to explain motivational (including the cognitive) sources of humor: *cognitive-perceptual* theory—which emphasizes the successful and surprising resolution of an incongruity, paradox, or double entendre; *behavior* theory—which stresses the reduction of base drives and stimulus-response learning; and *psychoanalytic* theory—which focuses on the gratification of the primary unconscious drives of aggression and sex in conjunction with the pleasures of mental activity, sometimes involving regression to infantile modes of cognition/thinking. Levine observes that experimental evidence, so far, has neither confirmed nor disproved any theory, and apparently the advocates of each model remain unmoved. Levine also notes that the most comprehensive theory—psychoanalysis—has been the richest source of ideas for experimentalists who have employed parts of the theory to support either cognitive-perceptual hypotheses or drive-reduction assumptions. In discussing the "Cognitive-Perceptual Models of Humor," Levine (1969, pp. 4–6) states that

to the theorist who favors the cognitive-perceptual model, "getting the joke" is the real source of pleasure in humor. In comprehending the point of a joke we are able to master the symbolic properties of the event with the multiple meanings and the figurative and allegorical allusions. It is like solving a complex puzzle or problem. The sudden discovery achieved by the reshuffling of the symbols and meanings into a surprisingly new relationship is the source of gratification.

Other modern writers and researchers who employ the *cognitive/perceptual* approach in their work include: Kagan (1967) who describes one form of the general cognitive model for humor analysis (i.e., the creation of a schema for an event is one major source of pleasure where schema is the representation of an external pattern); Bateson (1953) and Fry (1963) who present another cognitive-perceptual approach to humor in which it is argued that the pleasure in humor comes from the unexpected cognitive resolution of a series of paradoxes climaxed by a "punch line" (i.e., humor, here, is initiated by the metacommunication, "this is a joke," which is itself a paradox); McGhee (1977, 1979) who defines humor as a form of "intellectual play," and suggests, also, that the cognitive experience of humor has other characteristics associated with it—such as underlying physiological (arousal) changes and overt behavioral reactions (smiling and laughter)—but which are only byproducts of the basic fantasy-play processes of humor; and Koestler (1964) who combines creativity, artistic creation, humor, and scientific discovery into one cognitive/perceptual/mental process which he calls "bisociation" [i.e., the perceiving of a situation or idea in two self-consistent—but habitually incompatible—frames of reference, and in which there is routine ("single-minded") and creative ("double-minded") thought that involves a transitory state of cognitive instability and disequilibrium where there is an imbalance in both emotional and cognitive domains].

In another case—concerning another issue (i.e., whether laughter and humor are strictly human affairs, or whether they are shared with infrahumans and the higher animals/mammals)—Koestler (1964) again invokes cognitive-intellectual factors when he contends that laughter can only occur in a biologically secure species that possesses "intellectual autonomy," that is, in humans (cf: Walsh, 1928, who views laughter curiously—in physical terms—as essential to the "upright" human because he is so poorly engineered that he needs the accompanying diaphragm movement to massage the vital organs). According to Lilly (1896), animals have no sense of the ludicrous because they lack the cognitive and reasoning ability to engage in the phenomena of abstract knowledge which characterizes humans' thought processes during the humor experience (cf: McGhee, 1979, p. 86, "Humor in Animals"; McGhee, p. 103, states that "humor is the logical result of an extension of playful forms of behavior to the more abstract intellectual sphere of ideas").

Thus, a number of cognitive explanations of humor have appeared in the literature, ranging from purely Gestalt approaches (e.g., Maier, 1932) to cybernetic (e.g., Bateson, 1953) and information-processing analyses (e.g., Jones, 1970; Shultz, 1972; Suls, 1972, 1983). Such cognitive humor theories, as well as others (e.g., Berlyne, 1960, 1972; Koestler, 1964), have the following two-stage process, or characteristics, in common: the perception of some complexity, incongruity, discrepancy, ambiguity, or novelty in the humor stimulus;

and the resolution (i.e., cognitive integration or understanding) of the stimulus. According to such a cognitive approach to humor analysis, it is implied that humor is a process involving the interaction between the recipient and some structural aspect of the stimulus and that a joke, cartoon, or riddle may be understood and appreciated by assimilation of the humor stimulus into the individual's existing cognitive structures.

The following older (pre-1970), and also more current, humor studies (given in chronological order)—that reflect the influence of cognitive approaches and theories in psychology—may be examined in more detail concerning their procedures and results: Zigler, Levine, and Gould (1967), Deckers and Kizer (1974), McGhee (1974), Goldstein, Harman, McGhee, and Karasik (1975), Kuhlman (1985), Wyer and Collins (1992), Latta (1998), and Veatch (1998). Zigler et al. (1967) advanced the hypothesis that an important ingredient in humor appreciation is the degree to which the humor stimulus makes a cognitive demand on the individual; they specifically tested the prediction that cartoons at the upper limit of the child's ability to comprehend would evoke the greatest degree of laughter as well as the greatest preference; their participants were children in the third, fifth, and seventh grades who were given groups of cartoons varying in difficulty level from easy to nearly impossible. Results confirmed the Zigler et al. prediction and showed that at all three grade levels the mirth and preference scores peaked at the moderately difficult range of the difficulty dimension; they discuss their findings in relation to the child's motive of cognitive mastery, as well as to a motivation-free information-processing approach; children appear to laugh at those cartoons which make appropriate demands on their cognitive structure, and not at those which are either too easy or too difficult (i.e., the mirth response is greatest when the complexity of the humor stimulus and the complexity of the child's cognitive structure are congruent and, in a larger sense, this indicates that children enjoy most that which lies at the growing edge of their capacities).

Deckers and Kizer (1974) tested the discrepancy/incongruity hypothesis of humor (i.e., that a cognitive inconsistency or discrepancy between two ideas or events produces humor) by employing weights in a psychophysical-like task (cf: Deckers & Devine, 1981; Deckers, Edington, & VanCleave, 1981; Deckers & Kizer, 1975; Nerhardt, 1970). Participants in Deckers and Kizer's (1974) study used the method of constant stimuli and evaluated "comparison" weights against a "standard" weight; it was predicted that lifting the standard and comparison weights in the first eleven trials would produce an adaptation level (AL) having a value less (88 grams) than the standard weight (90 grams). On the twelfth and thirteenth trials, the comparison weights were identical to, much lighter than, or heavier than, the AL value. It was expected that laughing and smiling responses would occur more frequently to the lighter and heavier comparison weights because they were discrepant from the AL value. According to the discrepancy-incongruity hypothesis, smile and laugh responses are the result of the discrepancy between the weight the participant expects and the weight actually lifted; the person expects a weight near the standard and lifts one equal to that or one much lighter or heavier. Deckers and Kizer's results indicate that a greater frequency of smile and laugh responses occur for participants who lift the discrepant weight; however, after lifting the first discrepant weight, the participant's AL (or "expectancy") shifts; thus, in the second presentation, these weights are no longer as discrepant from the person's expectation and, hence, there is a decline in the number of smile and laugh responses from the twelfth to thirteenth trials (cf: Suls, 1972, who presents a cognitive model of humor which posits that discrepancy is only the first stage in a two-part process; the second stage consists of the participant's solution of the discrepant situation; in this case, discrepancy is a necessary—but not sufficient—condition for humor; in such a setting—because the participants found the light and heavy weights funny—it may be inferred that they were able to resolve the incongruity or discrepancy).

McGhee (1974) reviews the theoretical approaches and research dealing with the cognitive aspects of children's humor (cf: McGhee, 1968; Rothbart, 1976; Shultz, 1972, 1976; Wolfenstein, 1954), and suggests that a Piagetian theoretical framework may offer the most promising approach to studying the relationship between cognitive mastery and the appreciation and comprehension of humor. McGhee gives special attention to the operation of the cognitive congruency principle in children's humor.

In an attempt to study humor as a problem-solving process, Goldstein, Harman, McGhee, and Karasik (1975) monitored participants' heart rates and skin conductance (cf: Langevin & Day, 1972) as they responded to riddles and problems that cognitively were structurally similar; hypotheses based on cognitive problem-solving models of humor were tested by assessing changes occurring during problem solving against those occurring during riddle solving. Goldstein et al. found that heart rate accelerated once a riddle or problem was presented and decelerated once the answer/punch line was given, and also found differences between skin conductance measures during riddle-versus-problem-solving tasks which suggested that a purely problem-solving model of humor may not be promising. Moreover, in testing Berlyne's (1960, 1972) arousal-change hypothesis as applied to humor appreciation, Goldstein et al. found—as predicted—that humor responses were greatest for participants who indicated a moderate amount of change in arousal.

Kuhlman (1985) designed a study to test the cognitive-salience model (e.g., Goldstein, Suls, & Anthony, 1972) versus the motivational theory approach (e.g., Freud, 1905/1916) of humor analysis. Motivational content theories emphasize thematic properties of cartoons, jokes, etc.; Freud (1905/1916) viewed sexual and aggressive humor as important release valves in the "psychic economy"; he called this situation "tendentious humor" inasmuch as humor functions as a defense mechanism in which the acute, fleeting pleasure of laughter stems from gratifying a drive that otherwise would have remained pent up in the individual. Generally, studies of the motivational theory of humor have yielded inconsistent relationships between experimentally induced drive states and the enjoyment of sexual and aggressive humor (e.g., Baron, 1978a,b; Dworkin & Efran, 1967; Goldstein, 1970; Lamb, 1968; Landy & Mettee, 1969; Mueller & Donnerstein, 1983; Singer, 1968; Trice, 1982), and has led to the development of micro-theories that link humor and aggression to situation-specific variables (e.g., Zillmann & Bryant, 1974, 1980; Zillmann & Cantor, 1972).

The cognitive-salience model of humor (e.g., Goldstein et al., 1972) assumes that in the experimental manipulations of materials in humor studies that a cognitive set for processing sexual and aggressive stimuli occurs more easily than that assumed by motivational theories in which a drive state is modified. In his experiment, Kuhlman (1985) had participants assign humor ratings to three sets of jokes containing salient themes (examination content), taboo themes (sex and violence content), and neutral themes; the salience of examination content was manipulated by requiring the participants to rate jokes under one of three conditions: control (normal classroom setting), before taking an examination, and 20 minutes after beginning an examination. Kuhlman's overall results do not confirm the hypotheses derived from the cognitive-salience model; he found that motivational factors (taboo content, mastery theme) were associated with high humor ratings. Subsequently, Kuhlman suggests that a conceptual integration of *both* cognitive and psychoanalytic mechanisms of humor would be most fruitful.

In addition to reviewing existing theories of humor (motivational theories; arousal and arousal-reduction theories; superiority and disparagement theories; incongruity resolution theories; and Apter's, 1982b, reversal theory), Wyer and Collins (1992) present a general theory ("comprehension-elaboration theory" containing eight postulates) of humor elicitation (cf: Long & Graesser, 1988, for definition of a "humor-eliciting stimulus") that specifies the conditions in which humor is experienced in both social and nonsocial situations. The factors which the theory takes into account are: the interpretation of a stimulus event that is necessary to elicit humor; the difficulty of identifying the humor-eliciting features of the interpretation; and the cognitive elaboration of the implications of the event. The influence of such factors on one's humor response is seen as dependent on the person's information-processing objectives at the time a stimulus event occurs. Wyer and Collins' theory is used also to conceptualize the humor elicited by jokes, witticisms, and social events (cf: Apter, 1982a) that initially are neither expected nor intended to be humorous; special attention is given to the cognitive underpinnings of responses to ethnic humor and to the humor of self-behavior in social settings. Thus, according to Wyer and Collins, it is reasonable to suppose that the perception of something as humorous involves processes similar to those that more generally underlie the comprehension and elaboration of social information in terms of previously acquired concepts and general knowledge and, if so, the much-studied situational and individual difference variables that affect the perception of humor may be thought of in terms of their mediating influences on these processes.

Two final theories or versions of the *cognitive/perceptual* approach toward humor analysis are provided by Latta (1998) and Veatch (1998). Latta (1998)—in logical and syllogistical terms—proposes a "cognitive shift" theory (cf: Cetola, 1988; Koestler, 1964; Morreall, 1983, 1987b) of humor (which he calls "Theory L," named after himself) that is intended to be an argument against the traditional "incongruity theory" of humor. Latta's theory may be classified as a "response-side" theory: it states that the response aspect of the basic humor process shows a certain pattern. Essentially, the person responds (to stimuli) in a way that entails "unrelaxation"; he or she responds (to stimuli) by making a cognitive shift which implies relaxation, and then he or she responds—to the situation this shift creates—by relaxing again through the mechanism of laughter. Latta asserts that his Theory L meets the challenges often raised against "relief theories" of humor, that it allows for the occurrence of a very wide variety of humor processes, that it incorporates the genuine insights of other theories of humor, that it explains the psychodynamics of many diverse examples of humor, that it provides a basis for plausible answers to many questions about the global phenomenon of humor, that it squares with evolutionary theory, that it accounts for the specious appeal of "incongruity theory," and that it explains why humor has remained mysterious for such a long time (cf: Oring, 1999).

Veatch (1998) proposes that humor is characterized fully by certain conditions which individually are necessary, and jointly sufficient, for humor to occur. The conditions of Veatch's humor theory (cf: Raskin's, 1985, "linguistic-semantic theory of verbal humor") describe a subjective state of apparent emotional absurdity where the perceived situation is viewed as normal, and where, simultaneously, some affective commitment of the perceiver—to the way something in the situation *ought* to be—is violated. In other terms, humor occurs when a perceiver views a situation simultaneously as being normal and, at the same time, as constituting a violation of the "subjective moral order" where such an order is defined as the set of principles to which an individual both has an affective commitment and a belief that he or she ought to hold those principles. Veatch explains the logical properties and empirical consequences of his theory, and explores the often-recognized aspects and features of humor (e.g, incongruity, surprise, aggression, emotional transformation, apparent comprehension, difficulty, etc); he also accounts for a wide variety of biological, social/communicational, and other classes of humor-related phenomena, as well as suggesting practical applications of the theory.

Psychodynamic/Psychoanalytic Theories

The term "psychodynamic" refers to all those psychological systems and theories that emphasize processes of change and development, and/or those systems/theories that make motivation and drive their central concepts; occasionally, "psychodynamic" is a synonym for the term "psychoanalytic" (Reber, 1995, p. 614).

The most famous, and most-referenced (cf: Roeckelein, 1995, 1996a,b, 1998, p. 195), of the psychodynamic/psychoanalytically-oriented theorists on humor is the Austrian physician/psychiatrist (and founder of psychoanalysis) Sigmund Freud (1856–1939). Essentially, Freud's (1905/1916, 1928, 1960) laughter/humor theory is based on the "hydraulic theory of psychic energy" that was popular in the 19th century. In a manner similar to Spencer's (1860/1891) theoretical position (i.e., overflow of surplus energy, and "descending incongruity"), Freud regarded laughter as an outlet for nervous or psychic energy (cf: Marshall's, 1894, pp. 329–331, "pleasure/pain" and "surplus energy" notions). Freud's humor theory may be classified as a "relief/tension release" theory (Morreall, 1987b, p. 111), but his theory is more complicated than previous relief theories of humor (cf: Berlyne, 1969, p. 802; Keith-Spiegel, 1972, pp. 10–11).

The "relief/tension release" class of theories places main weight on the relief from stress and on relaxation that accrues from the sudden removal of a threat or discomfiture (cf: Shurcliff, 1968). For example, Descartes (1649/1909) asserts that laughter results from the joy that comes when an indignation at some evil has been mitigated by the realization that it does not cause harm; Hartley (1749) declares that laughter is an expression of pleasure at the elimination of something alarming or painful; Sully (1902) indicates that laughter may be produced by relief from strain or by the sudden induction of a playful mood; L. W. Kline (1907) holds that the humorous process involves a disruption of orderly thought processes due to a sudden triumph of good and pleasurable values, and which involves a release from the tension produced by controlled thought; and Gregory (1924) points out that among the many different occasions for laughter, relief/tension release is the most common factor of all.

Other theorists who have incorporated the notion of relief/tension release into their humor theories include: Allin (1903), Bergson (1911), Bliss (1915), Dewey (1894–1895), Lipps (1898), Marshall (1894), Patrick (1916), Penjon (1893), Rapp (1947, 1949, 1951), and Sidis (1913). Keith-Spiegel (1972, p. 12) notes that in a "ponderous but highly influential work," Freud (1905/1916) distinguishes among three kinds of laughter situations: wit/jokes, humor, and the comic. [Note: Grieg (1923/1969, p. 273) cautions that it is a mistake to take Freud's (1905/1916) "theory of wit" for a "complete theory of laughter," cf: O'Connell, 1976; Oring, 1975. Also Note: It is interesting, as Bergler (1956, p. 42) points out, that Freud's humor theory was formulated *before* he developed his other celebrated notions/theories of: the three psychic provinces (id, superego, unconscious ego); the duality of instincts (Eros and Thanatos) which fuse and defuse in clinically visible libidinous and aggressive tendencies; the existence of pre-Oedipality; and the whole gamut of inner defense mechanisms (including psychic masochism).]

Each kind of laughter situation (wit/jokes, humor, the comic), according to Freud (1905/1916), involves a saving of psychic energy that is available for a given task but is subsequently not needed for that purpose; thus, according to this theory, the superfluous energy is that which is discharged via the muscular movements of laughter. Freud asserts that in the joking situation the energy saved is that which would normally be used to repress sexual/hostile thoughts and feelings (cf: Kelling, 1971; Plass, 1972; Strickland, 1959).

In Freud's view, joking—like dreaming—functions as a "safety valve" for forbidden thoughts and feelings, and when the person expresses what is normally inhibited, the energy of repression is released in the form of laughter (cf: Bear, 1992). In the case of the comic, moreover, the energy saved is energy of thought; the person is spared some mental/cognitive processing (which normally involves energy that is called up for performance) and the surplus energy now is discharged in laughter. In the case of humor, the energy that is saved is energy of emotion; the person prepares for feeling a negative emotion (such as pity or fear), but with the subsequent realization that there is no real need for concern, the energy summoned up for the emotion is suddenly superfluous and is now available for discharge in the form of laughter (cf: Sidis, 1913, p. 68, who—although he objects to Freud's idea that economy is at the root of all laughter—adopts a view of laughter as a "discharge of surplus energy" that is very similar in appearance to Freud's notion).

Morreall (1987b, p. 111) observes that Freud's definition and use of the term "humor" is much narrower in scope than that normally expressed today (contemporary usage includes both joking and the comic situations). Keith-Spiegel (1972, p. 13) employs psychoanalytic jargon in summarizing Freud's theoretical position concerning humor (cf: Berlyne, 1960, p. 256; 1969, pp. 803–804): according to Freud (1905/1916, 1960), the ludicrous always represents a saving in the expenditure of psychic energy; when energy that accumulates for use in certain psychic channels (cathexis) is not utilized (due to the censoring action of the superego), it may be discharged pleasurably in the form of laughter.

In this regard, Freud could be characterized as the most eminent of the "release" and "economy" theorists. The pleasure in the *comic* situation is due to economy in the expenditure of *thought*; in the *wit* situation, there is economy in the expenditure of *inhibition*; in the *humor* situation, there is economy in the expenditure of *feeling*. Furthermore, in the comic situation, some contrast or deceived expectation is involved; in the case of wit, social restrictions (introjected in the form of the superego) prevent the acting out directly of "regressive infantile sexual and aggressive behavior"; the wit is a camouflage that functions to "deceive the superego" temporarily as repressions are being released suddenly; in the case of humor, an event that would ordinarily cause suffering is turned into something of less significance—energy is displaced onto the superego, and the ego is allowed thereby to return to an infantile state. In a later work, Freud (1928, p. 3) elaborated on this psychic mechanism that involves a "triumph of narcissism"—humor signifies the triumph both of the ego and of the pleasure principle where the individual may function adequately in aversive conditions.

Berlyne (1969, p. 804) notes that later "depth psychologists" have built on the Freudian/psychoanalytic humor theory foundation. For example, Kris (1938) compares the pleasure of laughter (involving a *past* time frame) with the pleasure received in mastering the environment and in children's play (involving a *present* time frame). Grotjahn's (1957) version of Freudian humor theory asserts that witticisms always contain "latent aggressive content," and that laughter is "creative communication" between the conscious and the unconscious which results in happiness over fulfilling one's potentialities; Grotjahn argues that the humorist reveals traits of melancholy and masochism, while the wit reveals sadistic tendencies. Other theoretical positions and studies related to Freud's notions of humor, the comic, and wit include: Bergler (1937), Brody (1950), Christie (1994), Collier (1960), Dooley (1934, 1941), Eidelberg (1945), Feldmann (1941), Frankel (1953); Gerst (1992); Higgins (1981); Hill (1991); Jekels (1952), Kantha (1999); Kline (1977), Korb (1988); Levine (1956), Levine and Redlich (1955), Lewin (1950), Liu (1995); Modol and Hortal (1995); O'Connell (1958, 1960, 1964a,b, 1968), Pereda (1994); Reik (1954), Rosenbaum (1976); Schalkwijk (1996); Schimel (1989); Tarachow (1949), Wildavsky (1994); Winterstein (1934), and Wolfenstein (1954).

Bergler (1956, pp. 31–41) provides a relatively lengthy section on the Freudian approach toward humor; he also notes (p. vii) that

the language of the typical scientific theories of laughter is more careful, more complex, more highbrow than that of the popular explanation. None the less, typical scientific theory on laughter also works on the level of rationalizations. And all of these theories, including the contemporary ones, are dwarfed to insignificance by Freud's famous theory on wit.

[Cf: Kimmins' (1928, p. 40) assessment that Freud's (1905/1916) book "has probably aroused more adverse criticism than any other contribution to the subject of wit and humour . . . In some cases it is abnormally difficult to understand exactly what the author means, and, moreover, how some of his conclusions are reached." Kimmins also refers to Freud's fundamental principle of "economy of psychic expenditure" as a modern variant on the literary slogan "brevity is the soul of wit".]

Bergler (1956) observes that Freud's theory of wit is an outgrowth and sequel to his studies of dreams; Freud was taken by the similarity between "dream-work" and "wit-work" (cf: Piddington, 1933/1963, pp. 200, 202). Freud's research on wit introduced a new element into the traditional literature on the issue: previous writers on aesthetics considered wit to be a subdivision of the comic, but Freud reversed the case and claimed autonomy for the topic of wit. In his approach, Freud investigated various techniques and literary devices that are applied in wit (cf: Bergler, 1956, pp. 31–33), such as "mixed words" (which involve condensation with substitutive formation; e.g., Bill Gates treated me just like an equal, quite *famillionaire*); "word division," "manifold application of same material," "ambiguity," "puns," "displacement," "sophistic faulty thinking," "automatic errors of thought," "unification," "representation through the opposite/through trifles/minutiae," "outdoing wit," "indirect expression with allusion," "omission," "comparison," "peculiar attributions," and "double meaning/play on words" (e.g., "an undertaker is one who always carries out what he undertakes"). Freud (1905/1916), who made much of the "disturbing dynamics" behind humor, notes that along with this "tendency wit" there is "harmless wit." However, as Keith-Spiegel (1972, p. 20) suggests, most subsequent psychoanalytic writers have emphasized the more "displeasing" or "disturbing" element behind humor and have either ignored or renounced the "harmless/benign" type of humor.

Freud (1905/1916, 1960, p. 269) concludes that the three situations (wit/jokes, humor, the comic) have one point in common: they all represent ways of bringing back from the psychic realm/activity a state of pleasure that is lost in the development of that very activity (in which the sought-after euphoria is a mental state of bygone times involving psychic work having a minimum of energy expenditure)—it is the state of one's childhood in which one did not know the comic, was incapable of wit, and did not need humor to achieve personal happiness.

Employing a "counterpoint," "contrarian," or "counterissue" technique, Bergler (1956, pp. 30–31) provides a useful summary concerning the main distinctions among the traditional *nonpsychoanalytic* humor theories; the list includes the following dozen strategic differences on which the various nonpsychoanalytic theories *cannot* agree:

1. Whether laughter is of a *pleasurable* nature or not (Plato, Descartes, et al. versus McDougall).

2. Whether laughter is an inborn *instinct* or an individually acquired ability (Eastman and McDougall versus nearly all other theorists).

3. Whether of not laughter contains *aggressive* components (Plato, Hobbes, Bergson, Ludovici, et al. versus Voltaire, Eastman).

4. Whether laughter contains *moralistic* notions of goodness/spontaneous appearance (Ben Jonson versus John Dryden).

5. Terminology (the terms wit, the comic, grim humor, self-derision, and humor are *confused* invariably).

6. Whether a laughter theory must explain (in addition to the *causes* of laughter) the *transformation of energy* (Spencer, Freud versus Eastman, et al.).

7. Whether the use of laughter for *social purposes* is secondary or primary (Bergson, Dupreel, and Piddington promote the "primary" position).

8. Whether laughter is a purely *aesthetic* issue or is a *psychological* problem (Richter, Lipps, and Fischer promote the "aesthetic" position).

9. Whether laughter is exclusively a *human* (versus inclusion of infrahuman animals) attribute (Darwin and Eastman versus nearly all other theorists).

10. The reasons and mechanisms that *produce* laughter (which leads to innumerable theories that magnify only one aspect of the problem and, thereby, mistakenly take it for *the* essential reason/mechanism).

11. The *mood* that precedes a "belly laugh" (Bergson says that all emotion must be absent; Greig says that emotion is present; Eastman maintains that a "playful mood" must exist).

12. Whether the *unconscious* plays any role in laughter at all (Freud versus almost all other writers).

Further material concerning the influence of the psychodynamic/psychoanalytic theoretical orientation vis-à-vis the *functions* of humor is given in Chapter 4 of this book in the sections titled "Humor as a Coping Mechanism," and "Humor and Psychotherapy."

Theories Based in Sociology/Social Psychology/Anthropology

Adopting an extreme sociological position, Dupreel (1928) argues that laughter/humor is purely a sociological problem and does not concern psychology or metaphysics (cf: Piddington, 1933/1963, pp. 218–220). Bergler (1956, p. 26) refers to Dupreel's theory of humor as the "theory of pure sociology" in laughter, and notes that Dupreel's approach is so exclusively sociologically-oriented that Dupreel classifies the humor theories of Bergson and Sully as "half-sociological." Dupreel (1928) suggests that there are two kinds of laughter: the laughter of *companionship/solidarity/inclusion* (the prototype of which is the substitution of laughter for cries of distress and woe; for example, when the infant is separated or "deserted" by its mother for a moment, sees her reappear, and the consequent pleasure of "group solidarity" of the infant-mother relationship); and the laughter of *exclusion/opposition* (see Piddington, 1933/1963, footnote, pp. 218–219)—such as being a member of an exclusive, restricted, or "in" group (e.g., being a "white, Anglo-Saxon, Protestant," and where a social group unites or reunites itself upon the exclusion of one or more individual members). Often in the laughter of opposition, if the members of one group laugh at the actions of another group, it serves to integrate the first group; such laughter need not only apply to oppressed groups but can be a cohesive device for any social group (Fine, 1983, p. 173; cf: Davies, 1982; Dresser, 1967; Miller, 1967).

In effect, Dupreel's two types of laughter are part of his general acceptance of Bergson's "mechanization" view of the cause of laughter. Piddington (1933/1963, p. 218) notes that Dupreel attempts to harmonize the "demisociological" views of Sully and Bergson with the nonsociological theories. Moreover, Dupreel (1928) points out an important difference between the views of Sully (1902) and Bergson (1911) concerning the place of laughter/humor in society: for Sully, the social function of laughter is merely an incident in its evolution, whereas for Bergson its social nature is fundamental and central. Dupreel also critiques Bergson's approach that all automatism is comic, and suggests that to produce laughter there must be the fact of a lack of the laugher's adaptation to the group. Additionally, Dupreel asserts that his humor theory includes the salient features of earlier approaches (e.g., Melinaud's, 1895, theory), and that he accepts Bergson's view that the ludicrous always involves something mechanical (some automatism) but that this is the consequence (rather than the cause) of ridicule which excludes someone (the consequence of which is that the "victim" appears to be "mechanical" and badly adjusted to the standards of the group of the laughers).

On the other hand, Dupreel does not accept Sully's view that there is a "presocial" laugh, and points out that no one has taken the trouble to observe (in the tickle-laughter situation) whether a child laughs when tickled if the tickler himself does *not* laugh. That is, unless it can be demonstrated that such "tickle-laughter" is *not* imitative, this case cannot be used in opposition to the view of laughter as being a social product (cf: Piddington, 1933/1963, p. 220). Dupreel suggests that it is important to note that both types of laughter may coexist in which "humor" is the product of such a fusion or composite.

Keith-Spiegel's (1972, p. 33) review of humor theories also includes the perspective that humor and laughter are primarily social phenomena (cf: Meredith, 1877/1898/1918). One of the social features of humor is its use as a communication device (e.g., Hayworth, 1928; McComas, 1923; Wallis, 1922); another feature of humor is its "social corrective" aspect and its value in maintaining group standards, norms, and mores. Wallis (1922) proposes a theory of laughter that combines Hobbes' view with the "corrective" interpretation of laughter; Wallis cites various anthropological data from which he concludes that laughter universally serves as a social corrective mechanism (e.g., he notes certain Australian initiation ceremonies in which the novice is forbidden to laugh at the ridiculous antics of the old men because by so doing he would be asserting his superiority over them). Wallis also gives evidence to show that among other primitive peoples the fear of ridicule is very important and argues that the social function of laughter is corrective but that the pleasure one derives from it is due to a feeling of superiority (cf: Piddington, 1933/1963, p. 210).

Hayworth's (1928) view is that laughter was originally a vocal signal to other members of the social group that they might relax with safety. According to Hayworth's theory, it is not correct to say that laughter originally caused joy or that joy caused laughter; rather, the two (joy and laughter) became associated because they were produced by the same set of circumstances—that is, a condition of safety. Piddington (1933/1963, p. 220) observes that a simpler type of "communication theory" than Hayworth's is given by McComas (1923) for whom laughter is simply a means of communicating "joy."

Other early writers and researchers who view humor/laughter mainly as a *social corrective*, as a maintenance device for *group* roles, standards, and values, or as a *social conflict resolution* mechanism are: Armstrong (1928), Bergson (1911), Bliss (1915), Bogardus (1945), Bowman (1939), Burma (1946), Dennis (1935), Gregg, Miller, and Linton (1929), Hazlitt (1890), Honigmann (1942), Horowitz and Horowitz (1949), Klapp (1950), Mace (1927), Mones (1939), Piddington (1933/1963), Shadwell (1671), Spitz and Wolf (1946), Stephenson (1951), Thomson (1927), and K. M. Wilson (1927). Martineau (1972, p. 104) observes that the first major article to deal with humor in a *sociological* framework was Obrdlik's (1942) work on "gallows humor" (i.e., ghoulish or macabre humor); another early investigation of humor in *anthropology* was Radcliffe-Brown's (1940, 1949) research on the "joking relationship" (i.e., a major manifestation of kinship, and an institutionalized form of interpersonal behavior that includes joking, teasing, banter, horseplay, and obscenity); Radcliffe-Brown's interest in humor dates back to the early 1900s (see Martineau, 1972, footnote, p. 105). Keith-Spiegel (1972, p. 33) notes that the "contagion" of laughter (the fact that humans rarely laugh when alone), and the audible sounds emitted in laughter (calling attention to the laugher), are points that have been made to substantiate the social aspect/function of laughter.

More recent writers and investigators also emphasize the *social, cultural, social psychological*, and *sociological* aspects of humor and include the following: Appelo (1989), Borsos (1990), Bricker (1973), Buckalew and Coffield (1978), Burnand (1977), Cameron (1963), Castell and Goldstein (1977), Chapman (1973, 1974, 1976), Chapman and Chapman (1974), Chapman and Wright (1976), Coates (1972), Coser (1959, 1960, 1966), Cross (1989), Daniels and Daniels (1964), Davis and Farina (1970), Dines (1995), Douglas (1968), J. P. Emerson (1969), Fine (1976), Foot and Chapman (1976), Fuller and Sheehy-Skeffington (1974), Giles, Bourhis, Gadfield, Davies, and Davies (1976), Goldman (1960), Goldstein (1977), Goodchilds and Smith (1964), Hertzler (1970), Hess and Mariner (1975), Hetherington and Wray (1966), Kaplan and Boyd (1965), LaFave (1967, 1972), LaGaipa (1977), Leventhal and Cupchik (1975), Lindeman (1969), Malpass and Fitzpatrick (1959), Markiewicz (1974), Marlowe (1989); Martineau (1967, 1972), McGhee (1973), Mettee and Wilkins (1972), Mettee, Hrelec, and Wilkins (1971), Nosanchuk and Lightstone (1974), Pitchford (1960), Pollio (1983), Priest (1966, 1972), Priest and Abrahams (1970), Sherman (1975, 1985), Shultz (1977), Smith and Goodchilds (1959, 1963), Smyth and Fuller (1972), Svebak (1974, 1975), Wilson and Brazendale (1973), Winick (1976), Wolosin (1975), Worthen and O'Connell (1969), Zelazo (1971), Zijderveld (1968), Zillmann and Bryant (1974, 1980), Ziv (1979).

Kane, Suls, and Tedeschi (1977) refer to humor as a tool of *social* interaction in their examination of the question, "why is humor initiated?" Traditionally, psychologists have assumed that persons do not initiate actions unless there is an anticipation of something to be gained from it, either in the "pull" of an incentive or in the "push" of a punishment. Accordingly, in the case of humor, it is assumed that a person (source) does not emit humorous statements unless he or she expects to achieve some interpersonal goal by such behavior. Kane et al. suggest that humor is unique to humans, and it is fundamentally a social psychological phenomenon—not merely a biological release or only a cognitive process.

Kane et al. give an account and analysis of the social-influence functions of humor that differs somewhat from Martineau's (1967, 1972) prototypical model; Martineau's approach focuses on how humor is used to initiate and facilitate communication and how it encourages the development of social relationships (e.g., via esteeming one's "ingroup" and disparaging the "outgroup"). However, according to Kane et al., Martineau's model fails to explain or to take into account why humor should be used in cases where praise or criticism would serve, presumably, just as well. Moreover, Martineau's theory focuses on the importance of humor for group behavior, while the approach taken by Kane et al. is equally applicable to the relationship between the person and his or her group, as well as with the relationship between the person and another separate individual. Kane et al. assert that the use of humor (as an instrument of social influence) can help the source to claim or disclaim responsibility for his or her actions, can reveal courage or relieve embarrassment, and may invoke normative commitments or release the person from commitments. In essence, the source can decide, to some extent, how she wishes her statements or behavior to be interpreted if she couches it in humorous terms (e.g., if the source wishes to disclaim the action, she may simply say, "after all, it was only a joke"). Kane et al. also consider some of the social functions that may be achieved by the use of humor precisely because of its "ambiguous" nature (i.e., humor carries with it a potential nonserious cue or "play" aspect, and may be interpreted in several different ways at the same time).

Among humor's social functions (Kane et al., 1977) are the following: self-disclosure and social probing (cf: Davis & Farina, 1970; J. P. Emerson, 1969); conflict and control (cf: Stephenson, 1951); decommitment; face-saving; an unmasking tactic; an antecedent of interpersonal attraction (cf: Mettee, Hrelec, & Wilkins, 1971; Mettee & Wilkins, 1972; Tedeschi, 1974); and an ingratiation tactic. Kane et al. conclude that the source's use of humor serves as a rather safe way of self-disclosing taboo interests or values and to probe the values, intentions, and motives of others; that as a decommitment tactic it allows the source to dissociate himself from responsibility for performing a prior action; that as a face-saving device it helps preserve a person's identity after the occurrence of an embarrassing incident; and that as an unmasking tactic it reveals the hypocrisy and pretensions of persons, groups, institutions, and nations. In each case, laughter/humor may be used to initiate a cognitive transformation of a situation into a nonserious one, or it may indicate acceptance of the meanings conveyed by a source of humor.

Chapman (1983) examines humor and laughter in social interaction terms (cf: Berlyne, 1972, who is critical of laughter's prime significance as a social factor versus Hertzler's, 1970, approach which gives laughter primary significance as being social in its origin, in its functions, and in its effects); and reviews the empirical work on humor that employs children as participants (cf: the early studies of children by Brackett, 1933, 1934; Enders, 1927; Kenderdine, 1931; C. O. Wilson, 1931). The early studies of children's humor largely employed a naturalistic-observation technique in which children's laughter was recorded as it occurred in situ (during the child's free-play and routine activities); as a result, most of the early studies provide weak theoretical and empirical foundations, and may be faulted for their weak conception and execution (cf: Chapman, 1972; Ransohoff, 1975).

Chapman (1983) observes that behavioral measures, particularly duration and frequency of laughing and smiling, have been evident in only a small portion of humor studies (cf: the amplitude and latency measures of Holmes, 1969). Moreover, the two common types of humor measures (expressive behaviors and subjective ratings) are not always well correlated (cf: Leventhal & Cupchik, 1975; Leventhal & Mace, 1970; Young & Frye, 1966). Chapman suggests that new and more refined behavioral measures should be developed in humor research that are more sensitive than the common duration and frequency varieties (cf: the oscillographic recordings of laughter by Pollio, Mers, & Lucchesi, 1972). (Note: For a more detailed account of measurement issues in humor research, see my Chapter 5, section on "Measurement of Humor"). Chapman (1983) also directs attention to the problems of the generalizability of humor research results (i.e., the valid "carry-over" from laboratory to real life, and from small samples to larger populations), and to the great potential for "experimenter" and "companion" effects in humor research, especially in the area of the social psychological study of children's humor (cf: McGhee & Chapman, 1980).

Fine (1983) discusses sociological approaches to the study of humor, and notes that humor traditionally has not been the legitimate subject area in sociology that it has been in psychology (part of this reason is that psychologists study the reaction of the individual to humorous stimuli, whereas sociologists typically study the social context and social forces that influence the creation and experience/appreciation of humor). Fine (1983) examines the major traditions of sociological research on humor, and finds that—with the growth of, and increased specialization within, sociology—there has been a modest increase in the number of humor studies (most recently by writers who may be classified as belonging to the "symbolic interactionist" tradition; cf: Denzin, 1983).

However, at the same time, according to Fine, there have been fewer studies dealing with humor in the leading sociological journals (e.g., in the period 1942–1959, there were six articles on humor in the *American Sociological Review* and the *American Journal of Sociology*—the two leading American sociological journals; since 1959, there has not been an article primarily on humor published in either journal). Apparently, in Fine's view, the sociology of humor is not identified as a topic of general interest for scholars in sociology. Part of the problem may lie in the fact that the few humor researchers in sociology typically take established sociological traditions and attempt to apply them to the topic of humor, rather than generating new theories.

Fine discusses the following diverse areas where humor research has been conducted in sociology: the relationship between humor and social roles (e.g., the "clown," the "wit and joker," the "comedian," and the "fool"; Daniels & Daniels, 1964; Klapp, 1950, 1962; cf: Salutin, 1973); the nature of joking relationships (e.g., Roy, 1959–1960); the contextual rules of humor performance (e.g., J. P. Emerson, 1969; Zijderveld, 1968); ethnomethodological approaches to humor and laughter in conversation (e.g., Jefferson, 1979; Sacks, 1975, 1978; Schenkein, 1972; cf: Garfinkel, 1967; Heritage, 1984); humor and group culture (e.g., Adams, 1971; Fine, 1977a,b); reference group theory (e.g., LaFave, 1961, 1972; LaFave, Haddad, & Maesen, 1976; Middleton, 1959; Wolff, Smith, & Murray, 1934); and social cohesion, conflict, and control (e.g., Burma, 1946; Coser, 1956; Davies, 1982; Dresser, 1967; Dupreel, 1928;

Martineau, 1967, 1972; Stephenson, 1951; Zenner, 1970). Fine (1983, p. 176) concludes his analyses by indicating that most sociologists of humor agree with the sentiment of LaFave, Haddad, and Maesen (1976) that jokes only become jokes because of the *social* responses to them.

Mulkay (1988) also offers an empirically based sociological view of humor (cf: the sociological overviews of humor by Fry, 1963; Hertzler, 1970; Zijderveld, 1983; and the review of theories by Paulos, 1980) in two main parts: the dynamics of humorous interchange in small-scale social settings along with the basic features of humorous conduct; and the role of humor in society at large. In separate chapters, Mulkay provides material on the following topics: an analysis of humorous exchange among a group of American adolescent young men; the organizing principles of the serious mode and the humorous mode; the semantics of humor and the ways in which the linguistic resources of the serious domain may be redeployed to create multiple meanings; the ways in which standardized jokes are connected to the surrounding serious discourse; the description of several kinds of applied humor; analyses of sexual humor and the prominence of sexual themes and obscenity within humorous discourse; an analysis of men's sexual humor; the relationship between humor and socially formalized structures; humor as a commodity; and the differences between static and dynamic representations of the political system and differences between the political sitcom and political cartoons.

In one case, Mulkay (1988, p. 216) speculates on the social origins of laughter: "It seems likely that laughter, or something like laughter, was once employed by our ancestors as a sign of deference and submission in the course of serious interaction." In his approach, Mulkay argues for a connection between deference/submission and humor that is based on the assumed characteristic features of humorous language (i.e., that it tends to create conflict and misunderstanding when encountered unexpectedly in the course of serious interaction). According to Mulkay, it is likely that when such difficulties arose during the early evolution of ordinary, everyday language, they were experienced as disturbing and as potentially threatening by those involved in the social interaction. Consequently, when contradictions, ambiguities, and incongruities occurred inadvertently—and when the "serious mode" seemed to be in danger of breaking down—participants in the interaction made use of the customary sign of nonaggression to indicate that no offense was meant and that the apparent breech of the "unitary mode" should be accepted as having no serious consequences. Thus, in Mulkay's view, it may be that laughter and smiling came to be employed to identify such discourse as being not intended in the usual way and, on the contrary, it is "nonserious"; with the passage of time, people came to realize that this subordinate/derivative mode of discourse was available permanently and could be adopted at will.

Mulkay (1988) asserts that his approach provides an alternative to Koestler's (1964) account of the function of laughter and humor whereby laughter comes to be viewed not as a physical mechanism (in which aggressive energies are released), but as a signal that accompanies and facilitates adoption of an alternative form of discourse. Mulkay's alternative view of humor contains certain functional properties in that it provides participants with an enjoyable release from the restrictions of serious discourse, and also that it helps them to deal effectively with various kinds of recurrent interpersonal, social, and interactional problems and difficulties. Mulkay concludes by suggesting that if we are to deal successfully with the "multiple realities" of the social world, we will have to devise a new kind of analytical language or discourse that resembles in certain critical respects what is called the "humorous mode" (cf: Mulkay, 1985; 1987; Woolgar, 1988).

The anthropologist Ralph Piddington essentially reduces humor and laughter to a *social* problem in his major work, *The Psychology of Laughter* (1933/1963). In the second edition of that work, Piddington (p. 6) states that since his book was first written, two important theoretical developments occurred—both of which are consistent with his original viewpoint; that is, Piddington's approach may be described as a reaction against the one-sided views of the French sociologist Emile Durkheim (1858–1917) and the British anthropologist Alfred Reginald Radcliffe-Brown (1881–1955), both of whom insisted on the isolation of "social facts" and on the irrelevance of psychology for the study of society. [Notes: Piddington (1933/1963, pp. 6, 40) asserts that "every *social* fact is at the same time a *biological* fact and a *psychological* fact, and this must be recognised in any adequate treatment of human social behaviour"; cf: Piddington, 1950. Moreover, Piddington gives credit to Sully (1902) as recognizing the social function of laughter "more clearly than any other observer," but Sully does not recognize the important principle that the psychological function and the sociological function are actually the *same* function (but which is approached from different points of view). In this sense, also, Piddington considers Sully (as well as Durkheim and Radcliffe-Brown) as being "one-sided" in approaching the problem of laughter; in the case of Sully, however, the assumption is that the psychological function is primary and the sociological one is secondary.] The two "theoretical developments" to which Piddington refers are: Malinowski's (1944) "theory of needs" and Warner's (1959/1975) "theory of species behaviour." Both Malinowski and Warner take into account the biological needs *and* the psychological drives upon which social behaviors such as kinship/family are founded—both viewpoints of which are in concert with Piddington's theoretical approach toward humor analysis. Piddington's treatment of laughter is neither entirely psychological nor entirely sociological; he attempts to examine the psychology of the original reaction of laughter, and to relate this to the various functions that it subserves in society.

Piddington (1933/1963, p. 148) refers to his approach as the "compensatory theory" which is a concept derived from the relationship between elementary laughter and laughter at the ludicrous in which the principle of "psychic compensation" is invoked; according to Piddington, this laughter serves a social function by a process that is analogous to "exaggeration of the opposite character." The reasoning behind this theory is that all ludicrous situations are potentially subversive to the social order, and that the reaction of laughter—affirming as it does the entirely satisfactory nature of the situation, breaking up all trains of thought, and producing an effect of bodily euphoria—is the socially appropriate response to the stimulus of the ludicrous. Moreover, it is the response which expresses the "suitable" attitude for members of society to take up towards ludicrous situations, and its primary function is to prevent any disturbance of the system of social values upon which the society depends for its existence and strength. Piddington (1933/1963, pp. 149–151) compares his "compensatory" approach against various other intellectualist, degradation, corrective, kathartic [sic], play-mood, biological, and aesthetic theories. Bergler (1956, p. 27) refers to Piddington's theory of laughter as the "two contradictory social situations" theory; that is, the ludicrous essentially involves two contradictory social evaluations whereby the laughter that is aroused is basically a socially conditioned reaction signifying satisfaction under socially disturbing conditions. Thus, laughter at the ludicrous arises fundamentally from the presence of the multiplicity of social evaluations and the potential for conflict that exists among/between them.

More recently, the anthropologist Mahadev L. Apte (1983, 1985) discusses his approach to the topic of humor/laughter. In one case, Apte (1983) examines the methodological issues involved in the general area of anthropological research and their impact on humor research, and suggests the contributions that anthropology can make to theoretical developments in humor research. Apte notes that anthropology is a broad discipline which includes the specialty areas of archaeology, linguistic anthropology, physical anthropology, and sociocultural anthropology; his emphasis is on humor research in sociocultural anthropology [archaeology has no direct relevance to humor study, and physical anthropology has only made contributions to humor research in the area of the phylogenetic aspects of laughter and smiling as expressions of emotions among higher primates (cf: Andrew, 1963a,b, 1965; Eibl-Eibesfeldt, 1975, 1989; VanHooff, 1972)].

Apte (1983) provides an overview of existing research in the major areas of humor so far investigated by anthropologists including: institutionalized joking within the context of kinship and other types of social relationships (e.g., Bradney, 1957; Howell, 1973; Moreau, 1943; Sykes, 1966); humor in religion or "ritual humor" (e.g., Codere, 1956; Crumrine, 1969; Norbeck, 1961, 1974; Steward, 1930); description and analysis of tricksters—that is, the mythological and folkloristic figures considered to be ludicrous (e.g., Carroll, 1981; Radin, 1956/1969; Ricketts, 1964); linguistic humor (especially verbal banter, riddles, insults, etc.); and the nature of play and games. Additionally, Apte covers brief/sporadic descriptive accounts of humorous episodes, types of humor, attitudes toward techniques used in humor, and appropriate/inappropriate humor in various social interactions as scattered in the ethnographies of many cultures. In most of these cases, the focus is on humor's relevance to other aspects of culture and not on the direct analysis of humor itself. Apte notes that there is an absence in the anthropological literature of systematic/thorough analyses of the multifaceted nature of humor in terms of its development, the various techniques used in its development, its different genres, its appreciation as expressed in overt behavior, its relevance to—and functions within—the context of individual cultures, general theories designed to explain its nature and scope, and systematic comparative studies of its substantive and formal aspects across cultures.

Apte (1983, p. 194) also observes that "the lack of significance attached to humor in anthropological studies is reflected in introductory textbooks of sociocultural anthropology, which do not even mention humor as an aspect of individual cultures worthy of investigation" (cf: Jacobs, 1964, as an exception here). The term *humor* "does not appear in the indexes of some popular sociocultural anthropology texts . . . The lack of interest in humor in general is also reflected in its absence in historical and evolutionary studies of human cultural development." Apte indicates that anthropological theories of humor appear to emphasize its contextual basis and aspects (i.e., in explaining humor, there is a focus on humor's interrelationship to other sociocultural traits) and, in this sense, the theories are both functional and structural in orientation. Moreover, there seems to be fewer theoretical explanations of humor in terms of its textual, symbolic, or substantive nature. A major theme recurring in anthropological humor theories, according to Apte, is that expressions of humor are the result of attempting to resolve ambivalence in social situations, roles, statuses, cultural values, and ideologies (e.g., ambivalence may occur because of a conflict between social obligations and self-interest; the use of humor via institutionalized joking, ritual clowning, and/or listening to trickster tales may provide a relief from such ambivalence).

According to Apte (1983), there is frequently a psychological orientation to many anthropological humor theories that characterizes them as speculative for the reason that they cannot be confirmed or validated by empirical and experimental methods (cf: Edgerton & Langness, 1974; Ford, 1967; Honigmann, 1976; McCall & Simmons, 1969; Moore, 1961; Naroll & Cohen, 1970; Pelto & Pelto, 1978). At present, in Apte's view, there are no studies specifically devoted to the elaboration of methods for ethnographic and comparative anthropological research on the topic of humor (cf: Apte, 1985, p. 9).

In the discipline areas of anthropology, ethology, and sociobiology, Weisfeld (1993) attempts to apply evolutionary theory and previous research results to the issue of the adaptive value of humor (cf: Vaid, 1999, for an attempt to apply the paradigm of *evolutionary psychology* to the analysis of humor). Weisfeld asserts that it would be desirable to identify a single, parsimonious, and original evolutionary function for humor, one that would be consistent with most evolutionary explanations of particular emotions. According to Haig (1988), no such unitary explanation has been advanced that includes all the major examples of humor, including tickling, ridicule, word play, agonistic play, and humor in apes. Weisfeld (1993) proposes the tentative explanation that humor evolved to induce the individual to seek out informative social stimulation and to reward others for providing such information; his approach distinguishes the derivative effects of humor (such as group solidarity, competition, courtship, and relaxation) from the fundamental adaptive value of humor.

Weisfeld's (1993) explanation of humor is intended to be consonant with modern evolutionary theory, and it does not rest on the traditional assumptions of humor theory concerning tension-release or pleasure-seeking. Weisfeld's theory avoids group-selection reasoning; it addresses the fitness benefits of the humorist as well as the laugher; it accounts for the fact that laughter is a means of social influence; and it applies to chimpanzees as well as humans. Inasmuch as Weisfeld's approach is an ethological theory, it recognizes both the motivational and affective properties of humor, and not just its cognitive characteristics. Moreover, Weisfeld's proposal is consistent with the available psychological and anthropological research on humor; for example, it helps to explain why aggressive, sexual, and competitive content is particularly funny; why a "playful mood" is necessary for appreciating humor (cf: P. K. Smith, 1982); why intelligent and socially competent children and adults tend to make good humorists; and why the condition or state of incongruity is humorous. Finally, Weisfeld's adaptive theory of humor appears to contain elements that are in touch with existing biological explanations for various "esthetic" emotions (e.g., olfaction, music appreciation, visual art appreciation). Weisfeld (1993, p. 162) admits that one potential drawback of his explanation for humor may be that it is not very different from the leading evolutionary explanations for the emotion of "interest," namely, that of motivating practice in skills that enhance fitness.

SUMMARY: A CONCISE DICTIONARY OF HUMOR THEORIES

A number of writers (e.g., Bergler, 1956; Greig, 1923/1969; Kimmins, 1928; MacHovec, 1988; Monro, 1951/1963; Morreall, 1987b; Piddington,

1933/1963) have presented extensive discussions of humor theories. The purpose of this section is to give a condensed account of the theories of humor in what may be called a "concise dictionary" of humor theories and to provide the reader with a summary via "one eye's gulp" of the richness and diversity of laughter/humor theories across writers and theorists across time. Accordingly, the following nine sets of listings, chronologically arranged by author's publication date, indicate various accounts of the theories of humor/laughter.

1. Greig (1923/1969, pp. 225–279) describes the theories of: Addison, Akenside, Allin, Angell, Aristotle, Baillie, Bain, Baudelaire, Beattie, Bergson, Blair, Bliss, Brown, G. Campbell, Carlyle, Carus, Cicero, Coleridge, Congreve, Courdaveaux, Darwin, DeLaprade, DeLaudun, DeMarmontel, Descartes, DeSivry, Dewey, Dryden, Dugas, Dumont, Earl of Chesterfield, Earl of Shaftesbury, Eastman, R. W. Emerson, Everett, Fielding, Freud, Gaultier, Gerard, Goldsmith, Hall, Harrington, Hartley, Hazlitt, Hecker, Hegel, Hobbes, Hoeffding, Home, Hunt, Hutcheson, Johnson, Jonson, Joubert, Kallen, Kant, Knight, Lamennais, Lessing, Leveque, Lipps, Locke, Maggi, Marshall, McDougall, Melinaud, Meredith, Michiels, Minturno, Moliere, Muzio, Pelletier, Penjon, Philbert, Plato, Prat, Priestley, Quintilian, Ramsay, Renouvier, Ribot, Richter, Rousseau, Santayana, Scaliger, Schauer, Schopenhauer, Shadwell, Sidis, Sidney, S. Smith, Spencer, Stendhal, Stewart, Sully, Temple, Trissino, Voltaire, Warton, Whetstone, T. Wilson, and Zeising.

2. Kimmins (1928, pp. 10–52) gives an account of the various theories of laughter under the following general chronological headings: "Laughter in the 17th and 18th Centuries," "Laughter in the 19th Century," and "Laughter in the 20th Century."

3. Piddington (1933/1963, pp. 152–221) examines the theories of: Addison, Allin, Aristotle, Baillie, Bain, Beattie, Bergson, Bliss, Cicero, Darwin, Descartes, Dewey, Dryden, Dumas, Dumont, Dupreel, Eastman, Freud, Gregory, Greig, Hall, Hartley, Hayworth, Hazlitt, Hegel, Hobbes, Hoeffding, Jonson, Kallen, Kant, Kimmins, Leveque, Locke, Maggi, McDougall, Melinand, Meredith, Minturno, Muzio, Palmer, Penjon, Plato, Prat, Quintilian, Renouvier, Rousseau, Schopenhauer, Sidis, Sidney, Spencer, Stewart, Sully, Wallis, Warton, Whetstone, and T. Wilson.

4. Monro (1951/1963, pp. 83–234) uses the following rubrics in his analyses of the theories of humor: Superiority Theories (Hobbes, Bain, Leacock, Ludovici); Bergson; Feibleman and McDougall; Incongruity Theories (Kant, Schopenhauer, Spencer, Eastman); Release from Restraint (Kline, Freud, Gregory); and Ambivalence Theories (Greig, Menon).

5. Bergler's (1956) particular descriptive style (which involves slogan-like labels) in discussing the theories of laughter and humor allows easy access to the whole range and variety of theories and theorists; Bergler (1956, pp. 1–41)

describes over six dozen theories of humor/laughter in the following terms (I've alphabetized them here):

Anti-annoyance theory or "laughter is nature's antidote for sympathy" theory of William McDougall (1871–1938).

Appendix to the separation-theory theory of Joseph Addison (1672–1719).

Bull-wit theory of laughter reflected by Sydney Smith (1771–1845).

Combined oscillation and contrast theory of Wilhelm Wundt (1832–1920).

Communicating joy theory of laughter by H. C. McComas (c. 1923).

Contrast/contradiction between two ideas theory of Theodor Vischer (1807–1887).

Correction of human follies theory of Ben Jonson (1572–1637) and John Dryden (1631–1700).

Degradation theory of Alexander Bain (1818–1903).

Deliverance from the constraint of rationality theory of Charles Renouvier (1815–1903).

Division theory (separating derision from laughter) of Baruch Spinoza (1632–1677).

Double affirmation theory of A. W. Bohtz (c. 1844).

Double-feature theory of "wise and foolish" laughter of Oliver Goldsmith (c. 1730–1774), John Ray (c. 1705), Wyndham Lewis (1886–1957), and Lord Chesterfield (1694–1773).

Duality theory of Charles Leveque (c. 1863).

Economy of psychic expenditure/saving of psychic energy theory of wit by Sigmund Freud (1856–1939).

Elevation theory of Christian W. Weisse (c. 1830).

Esthetic dead-end theory of laughter by Jean Paul Richter (1763–1825).

Expectation theory of Theodor Lipps (1851–1914).

Extension theory of laughter by C. W. Kimmins (c. 1928).

Five Italian Renaissance theories of laughter by Trissino (1478–1550), Maggi (c. 1560), Muzio (c. 1551), Minturno (c. 1564), and Scaliger (1484–1558).

For-each-otherness theory of R. Hermann Lotze (1817–1881).

Fountain of sound sense theory of George Meredith (1828–1909).

Goodness of the environment theory of laughter of Horace M. Kallen (c. 1909).

Good-old-times theory of laughter of Stephen Leacock (1869–1944).

Gymnastic exercise theory of laughter of G. W. Crile (1864–1943).

Hobbes plus theory of Harald Hoeffding (1843–1931).

I'm ashamed of my ancestors theory of laughter of George Eliot (1819–1880).

Insolence theory of La Rochefoucauld (1612–1680).

Instinctive enjoyment theory of laughter of Max Eastman (1883–1969).

Interrupted love reaction theory of J. Y. T. Greig (c. 1923).

Lack of fundamentality in contradictions theory of laughter of Camille Melinaud (c. 1895).

Lack of self-knowledge theory of Plato (427–348 B.C.).

Liberty theory of Lord Shaftesbury (1671–1713) and A. Penjon (c. 1893).

Mechanization theory of Henri Bergson (1859–1941).

Meeting of extremes theory by Leigh Hunt (1784–1859).

Midwife theory of laughter by Alexander Pope (1688–1744).

Minimal-touch theory of G. Stanley Hall (1844–1924) and Arthur Allin (c.1896).

Moral contrast theory of Johann Wolfgang von Goethe (1749–1832).

Nascent cry theory of laughter of David Hartley (1705–1757).

Nascent cry-echoed theory by Pierre-Augustine Beaumarchais (1732–1799).

Not too tragic defect theory of Aristotle (384–322 B.C.).

Nothing theory of Immanuel Kant (1724–1804).

Occult resemblance theory of Samuel Johnson (1709–1784) and Mme. de Stael (1766–1817).

Oscillation theory of laughter by Ewald Hecker (c. 1873).

Overflow of nervous energy theory of Herbert Spencer (1820–1903).

Perception of unreality theory of laughter of Herbert Barry (c. 1928).

Perfection-imperfection theory of Moses Mendelssohn (1729–1786) and G. E. Lessing (1729–1781).

Physio-psychological blend theory of Rene Descartes (1596–1650).

Playful judgment theory of wit by K. Fischer (c. 1889).

Play-mood theory of laughter by James Sully (1842–1923).

Primeval fall from grace theory of laughter of Charles Baudelaire (1821–1867).

Pure sociology theory of laughter by E. Dupreel (c. 1928).

Rationalization theory of laughter of E. F. Carritt (c. 1923).

Reason theory of laughter by Marie-Joseph Blaise Chenier (1764–1811).

Relax in safety theory of laughter of Donald Hayworth (c. 1928).

Relief theory of laughter by J. C. Gregory (c. 1924).

Restfulness theory of K. W. F. Solger (c. 1829).

Roar-of-triumph in an ancient jungle duel theory of laughter by Albert Rapp (c. 1951).

Separation theory of John Locke (1632–1704).

Show-teeth theory of laughter by A. M. Ludovici (c. 1933).

Sin theory of laughter reflected by St. John Chrysostom (c. 345–407).

Split-second before adaptation theory of laughter by William Hazlitt (1778–1830).

Sudden contrast theory of laughter advanced by Arthur Schopenhauer (1788–1860).

Sudden glory theory of Thomas Hobbes (1588–1679).

Sudden relaxation of strain theory endorsed by John Dewey (1859–1952).

Sympathy theory of Voltaire (1694–1778) and Thomas Carlyle (1795–1881).

Tragic contradiction theory of J. Bahnsen (c. 1877).

Trio of philosophical authorities substituting for a theory theory of wit imagined by Poinsinet de Sivry (c. 1778), who cites Destouches (laughter originated in a "reasoned joy"), Fontanelle ("the principle of laughter is folly"), and Montesquieu (laughter is "the expression of pride") as the "authorities."

Two Charlie Chaplin theories on laughter reported by Max Eastman (1883–1969).

Two contradictory propositions theory of Leon Dumont (1837–1876).

Two contradictory social situations theory of laughter elaborated by Ralph Piddington (c. 1933).

Two nihilistic theories of laughter by Cicero (106–43 B.C.) and Quintilian (c. 35–c. 95).

Two-types-of-laughter theory of George Dumas (1886–1946).

Unexpected intellectual contrast theory of Emil Kraepelin (1856–1926).

Unification theory of James Beattie (1735–1803).

We don't know theory of Charles Darwin (1809–1882).

Will-to-laugh theory by E. F. Allen (c. 1941).

6. Keith-Spiegel (1972, pp. 5–33) employs the following "varieties" and "issues" rubrics that serve stylistically as her organizational strategy and "dichotomy device" for discussing humor theories: Biological/Instinct/Evolution Theories; Superiority Theories; Incongruity Theories; Surprise Theories; Ambivalence Theories; Release/Relief Theories; Configurational Theories; Psychoanalytic Theory; Monistic versus Pluralistic Bases; Relationship of Laughter to Humor; Relationship of Laughter to Smiling; The Order of Pleasure and Laughter; Pleasure versus Displeasure Disguised; Role of Nervous Energy Release; Animals versus Humans; Inborn versus Acquired Aspects; Universality versus Selectivity; Nomothetic versus Idiographic Aspects; Good versus Evil; Reality versus Unreality; Levels of Control/Awareness; Healthy versus Unhealthy Attributes; Creative Expression versus Defensive Repression; Good Mood versus Bad Mood; Effort versus Economy of Effort; Intellectual versus Emotional Aspects; and Self-Serving versus Social Serving.

7. Morreall (1987b, pp. 10–186) describes the theories of: Aristotle, Bergson, Cicero, Clark, Descartes, Freud, Hartley, Hazlitt, Hobbes, Hutcheson, Kant, Kierkegaard, Martin, Morreall, Plato, Santayana, Schopenhauer, Scruton, and Spencer.

8. MacHovec (1988, pp. 27–105) employs time/period and functional rubrics in his account of humor. The following main headings, under which various specific theories of humor are examined and critiqued, are used by MacHovec: *classical* theories/historical-cultural context: derision/superiority theory (e.g., Plato), disappointment/frustrated expectation (e.g., Aristotle); *neoclassical* theories: pleasure-pain (e.g., Freud) and instinct-physiological

(e.g., Darwin) theories; *neoclassical* theories: sympathy and empathy (e.g., Rogers) and creativity-change (e.g., Bergson) theories; *modern* theories: semantics/content analysis/script-based semantic theory (e.g., Raskin), bisociative theory (e.g., Koestler), and syzygy/eclectic theory.

9. Brown and Keegan (1999, pp. 67–68) identify "eight main streams of theory about humor": *relief theory* (Kant, Freud); *conflict theory* (Greig, Menon, Freud, Hobbes); *incongruity theory* (Freud); *dualistic* theory (Bergson, Feibleman, Leach); *gestalt* theory (Maier); *piagetian* theory (Piaget, Kagan, McGhee); *masterly* theory (Hobbes, Kris, Zigler); and *cognitive appraisal* theory (Mandler).

REFERENCES

Abrahams, R. D. (1970). *Positively Black*. Englewood Cliffs, NJ: Prentice-Hall.

Adams, C. C. (1971). *Boontling: An American lingo*. Austin: University of Texas Press.

Addison, J. (1711/1909). *The Spectator*. 8 Vols. London: Tonson, Draper/Everyman's Library.

Akenside, M. (1744/1810). Pleasures of the Imagination. In S. Johnson (Ed.), *The lives of the poets*. (Vol. 14.) London: World's Classics.

Alden, D., & Hoyer, W. (1993). Examination of cognitive factors related to humorousness in television advertising. *Journal of Advertising, 22*, 29–37.

Alden, D., Hoyer, W., & Lee, C. (1993). Identifying global and culture specific dimensions of humor in advertising—A multinational analysis. *Journal of Marketing, 57*, 64–75.

Alden, D., Mukherjee, A., & Hoyer, W. (2000a). Effects of incongruity, surprise, and positive moderators on perceived humor in television advertising. *Journal of Advertising, 29*, 1–15.

Alden, D., Mukherjee, A., & Hoyer, W. (2000b). Extending a contrast resolution model of humor in television advertising: The role of surprise. *Humor: International Journal of Humor Research, 13*, 193–217.

Allen, N. (1988). Semantics and Madison Avenue: Application of the semantic theory of humor to advertising. *Humor: International Journal of Humor Research, 1*, 27–38.

Allin, A. (1903). On laughter. *Psychological Review, 10*, 306–315.

Allport, F. H. (1924). *Social psychology*. Boston: Houghton Mifflin.

Andrew, R. J. (1963a). Evolution of facial expressions. *Science, 142*, 1034–1041.

Andrew, R. J. (1963b). The origin and evolution of the calls and facial expressions of the primates. *Behaviour, 20*, 1–109.

Andrew, R. J. (1964). Vocalization in chicks, and the concept of "stimulus contrast." *Animal Behavior, 12*, 64–76.

Andrew, R. J. (1965). The origins of facial expressions. *Scientific American, 213*, 88–94.

Angell, J. R. (1904/1905). *Psychology*. New York: Holt.

Annis, A. D. (1939). The relative effectiveness of cartoons and editorials as propaganda media. *Psychological Bulletin, 36*, 628–633.

Appelo, T. (1989). Comic relief. *The Sciences, 29*, 44–49.

Apte, M. L. (1983). Humor research, methodology, and theory in anthropology. In P. E. McGhee & J. H. Goldstein (Eds.), *Handbook of humor research* (Vol. 1., *Basic issues*). New York: Springer-Verlag.

Apte, M. L. (1985). *Humor and laughter: An anthropological approach.* Ithaca, NY: Cornell University Press.

Apter, M. (1982a). Fawlty Towers—A reversal theory analysis of a popular television comedy series. *Journal of Popular Culture, 16*, 128–138.

Apter, M. (1982b). *The experience of motivation: The theory of psychological reversals.* San Diego, CA: Academic Press.

Armstrong, M. (1928). *Laughing.* London: Jarrolds.

Averill, J. R. (1969). Autonomic response patterns during sadness and mirth. *Psychophysiology, 5*, 399–414.

Baillie, J. B. (1921). *Studies in human nature.* London: Bell.

Bain, A. (1859). *The emotions and the will.* London: Longman.

Baron, R. A. (1978a). Aggression-inhibiting influence of sexual humor. *Journal of Personality and Social Psychology, 36*, 189–197.

Baron, R. A. (1978b). The influence of hostile and nonhostile humor upon physical aggression. *Personality and Social Psychology Bulletin, 4*, 77–80.

Baron, R. A., & Ball, R. L. (1974). The aggression-inhibiting influence of nonhostile humor. *Journal of Experimental Social Psychology, 10*, 23–33.

Barron, M. L. (1950). A content analysis of intergroup humor. *American Sociological Review, 15*, 88–94.

Bateson, G. (1953). The role of humor in human communication. In H. von Foerster (Ed.), *Cybernetics.* New York: Macy Foundation.

Bateson, G. (1969). The position of humor in human communication. In J. Levine (Ed.), *Motivation in humor.* New York: Atherton Press.

Baudelaire, C. (1869/1946). *Curiosites esthetiques.* Paris: Aubry.

Bauerly, R. J. (1989). An experimental investigation of humor in television advertising: The effects of product type, program context, and target of humor on selected consumer cognitions. Unpublished doctoral dissertation, Southern Illinois University at Carbondale.

Beach, F. A. (1945). Current concepts of play in animals. *American Naturalist, 79*, 523–541.

Bear, G. (1992). A Freudian slip? *Teaching of Psychology, 19*, 174–175.

Beattie, J. (1776). *Essay on laughter and ludicrous composition.* Edinburgh: Creech.

Beerbohm, M. (1921). Laughter. *North American Review, 214*, 39–49.

Belch, G., & Belch, M. (1984). Investigation of the effects of repetition on cognitive and affective reactions to humorous and serious television. *Advances in Consumer Research, 11*, 4–10.

Bem, D. (1967). Self-perception: An alternative interpretation of cognitive dissonance phenomena. *Psychological Review, 74*, 183–200.

Bender, J. (1994). Gender differences in the recall of humorous advertising material. *Dissertation Abstracts International, 54 (11–A)*, 4178.

Berger, A. A. (1987). Humor: An introduction. *American Behavioral Scientist, 30*, 6–15.

Bergler, E. (1937). A clinical contribution to the psychogenesis of humor. *Psychoanalytic Review, 24*, 34–53.

Bergler, E. (1956). *Laughter and the sense of humor.* New York: International Medical Book Corporation.

Bergson, H. (1911). *Le rire. (Laughter: An essay on the meaning of the comic).* New York: Macmillan.

Berk, L., Tan, S., Fry, W., Napier, B., Lee, J., Hubbard, R., Lewis, J., & Eby, W. (1989). Neuroendocrine and stress hormone changes during mirthful laughter. *The American Journal of the Medical Sciences, 298*, 390–396.

Berkowitz, L. (1970). Aggressive humor as a stimulus to aggressive responses. *Journal of Personality and Social Psychology, 16*, 710–717.

Berlyne, D. E. (1960). *Conflict, arousal, and curiosity.* New York: McGraw-Hill.

Berlyne, D. E. (1969). Laughter, humor, and play. In G. Lindzey & E. Aronson (Eds.), *The handbook of social psychology.* (Vol. 3). Reading, MA: Addison-Wesley.

Berlyne, D. E. (1972). Humor and its kin. In J. H. Goldstein & P. E. McGhee (Eds.), *The psychology of humor: Theoretical perspectives and empirical issues.* New York: Academic Press.

Biswas, A., Olsen, J., & Carlet, V. (1992). Comparison of print advertisements from the United States and France. *Journal of Advertising, 21*, 73–81.

Blair, H. (1793/1970). *Lectures on rhetoric and belles-lettres.* London: Unwin.

Bliss, S. H. (1915). The origin of laughter. *American Journal of Psychology, 26*, 236–246.

Blistein, E. M. (1998). Humor. In *The Encyclopedia Americana: International Edition.* (Vol. 14.) Danbury, CT: Grolier.

Bogardus, E. (1945). Sociology of the cartoon. *Sociology and Social Research, 30*, 139–147.

Borsos, D. P. (1990). An investigation of humor use and sociometric position. Unpublished doctoral dissertation, Temple University.

Boskin, J. (1987). The complicity of humor: The life and death of Sambo. In J. Morreall (Ed.), *The philosophy of laughter and humor.* Albany: State University of New York Press.

Boston, R. (1974). *An anatomy of laughter.* London: Collins.

Boswell, J. (1887). *Life of Samuel Johnson.* Oxford: Clarendon.

Bowman, H. A. (1939). *Studies in the science of society: The humor of primitive people.* New Haven, CT: Yale University Press.

Brackbill, Y. (1958). Extinction of the smiling response in infants as a function of reinforcement schedule. *Child Development, 29*, 115–124.

Brackett, C. W. (1933). Laughing and crying of preschool children. *Journal of Experimental Education, 2*, 119–126.

Brackett, C. W. (1934). Laughing and crying of preschool children. *Child Development Monographs*, No. 14.

Bradney, P. (1957). The joking relationship in industry. *Human Relations, 10*, 179–187.

Bricker, V. R. (1973). *Ritual humor in highland Chiapas.* Austin: University of Texas Press.

Brody, M. W. (1950). The meaning of laughter. *Psychoanalytic Quarterly, 19,* 192–201.

Brodzinsky, D. M. (1977). Children's comprehension and appreciation of verbal jokes in relation to conceptual tempo. *Child Development, 48,* 960–967.

Brooker, G. (1981). Comparison of the persuasive effects of mild humor and mild fear appeals. *Journal of Advertising, 10,* 29–40.

Brown, D., & Bryant, J. (1983). Humor in the mass media. In P. E. McGhee & J. H. Goldstein (Eds.), *Handbook of humor research* (Vol. 2, *Applied studies*). New York: Springer-Verlag.

Brown, R., & Keegan, D. (1999). Humor in the hotel kitchen. *Humor: International Journal of Humor Research, 12,* 47–70.

Brown, T. (1820). *Lectures on the philosophy of the human mind.* Edinburgh: Tait.

Brown, T. G. (1915). Note on the physiology of the basal ganglia and mid-brain of the anthropoid ape, especially in reference to the act of laughter. *Journal of Physiology, 49,* 195–207.

Brownell, H. H., & Gardner, H. (1988). Neuropsychological insights into humour. In J. Durant & J. Miller (Eds.), *Laughing matters: A serious look at humour.* Essex, UK: Longman House.

Buck, R. (1980). Nonverbal behavior and the theory of emotion: The facial feedback hypothesis. *Journal of Personality and Social Psychology, 38,* 811–824.

Buckalew, L., & Coffield, K. (1978). Relationship of reference group to perception of humor. *Perceptual and Motor Skills, 47,* 143–146.

Burma, J. H. (1946). Humor as a technique in race conflict. *American Sociological Review, 11,* 710–715.

Burnand, G. (1977). Teasing and joking in isolated societies. In A. J. Chapman & H. C. Foot (Eds.), *It's a funny thing, humour.* Oxford, UK: Pergamon Press.

Bush, L. K. (1989). On facial mimicry and facial feedback. Unpublished doctoral dissertation, Dartmouth College.

Byrne, D. E. (1956). The relationship between humor and the expression of hostility. *Journal of Abnormal and Social Psychology, 53,* 84–89.

Byrne, D. E. (1958a). Drive level, response to humor, and the cartoon sequence effect. *Psychological Reports, 4,* 439–442.

Byrne, D. E. (1958b). Response to humor as a function of drive arousal and psychological defenses. Unpublished doctoral dissertation, Stanford University.

Byrne, D. E. (1961). Some inconsistencies in the effect of motivation arousal on humor preference. *Journal of Abnormal and Social Psychology, 62,* 158–160.

Byrne, D., Terrill, J., & McReynolds, P. (1961). Incongruity as a predictor of response to humor. *Journal of Abnormal and Social Psychology, 62,* 435–438.

Cameron, W. B. (1963). *Informal sociology: The sociology of humor and vice versa.* New York: Random House.

Campbell, G. (1776/1846). *The philosophy of rhetoric.* London: Strahan.

Campbell, P. A. (1968). The effects of role playing and verbal conditioning in humor preference. Unpublished doctoral dissertation, University of Illinois.

Cantor, J. R. (1976). Humor on television: A content analysis. *Journal of Broadcasting*, *20*, 501–510.

Cantor, J. R. (1977). Tendentious humour in the mass media. In A. J. Chapman & H. C. Foot (Eds.), *It's a funny thing, humour*. Oxford, UK: Pergamon Press.

Cantor, J. R., Bryant, J., & Zillmann, D. (1974). Enhancement of humor appreciation by transferred excitation. *Journal of Personality and Social Psychology*, *30*, 812–821.

Cardiff, D. (1988). Mass middlebrow laughter—The origins of BBC comedy. *Media, Culture, and Society*, *10*, 41–60.

Carlyle, T. (1827/1848/1870). *Critical and miscellaneous essays: Jean Paul Friedrich Richter*. London: Fraser.

Carpenter, R. (1922). Laughter, a glory in sanity. *American Journal of Psychology*, *33*, 419–422.

Carroll, M. P. (1981). Levi-Strauss, Freud, and the trickster: A new perspective upon an old problem. *American Ethnologist*, *8*, 301–313.

Carus, P. (1897–1898). On the philosophy of laughing. *Monist*, *8*, 261–265.

Castell, P. J., & Goldstein, J. H. (1977). Social occasions for joking: A cross-cultural study. In A. J. Chapman & H. C. Foot (Eds.), *It's a funny thing, humour*. Oxford, UK: Pergamon Press.

Cetola, H. (1988). Toward a cognitive-appraisal model of humor appreciation. *Humor: International Journal of Humor Research*, *1*, 245–258.

Chapman, A. J. (1972). Some aspects of the social facilitation of "humorous laughter" in children. Unpublished doctoral dissertation, University of Leicester, UK.

Chapman, A. J. (1973). Social facilitation of laughter in children. *Journal of Experimental Social Psychology*, *9*, 528–541.

Chapman, A. J. (1974). An experimental study of socially facilitated "humorous laughter." *Psychological Reports*, *35*, 727–734.

Chapman, A. J. (1975). Eye-contact, physical proximity, and laughter: A re-examination of the equilibrium model of social intimacy. *Social Behavior and Personality*, *3*, 143–155.

Chapman, A. J. (1976). Social aspects of humorous laughter. In A. J. Chapman & H. C. Foot (Eds.), *Humour and laughter: Theory, research, and applications*. London: Wiley.

Chapman, A. J. (1983). Humor and laughter in social interaction and some implications for humor research. In P. E. McGhee and J. H. Goldstein (Eds.), *Handbook of humor research* (Vol. 1, *Basic issues*). New York: Springer-Verlag.

Chapman, A. J., & Chapman, W. (1974). Responsiveness to humour: Its dependency upon a companion's humorous smiling and laughter. *Journal of Psychology*, *88*, 245–252.

Chapman, A. J., & Wright, D. S. (1976). Social enhancement of laughter: An experimental analysis of some companion variables. *Journal of Experimental Child Psychology*, *21*, 201–218.

Charney, M. (1978). *Comedy, high and low*. New York: Oxford University Press.

Chattopadhyay, A., & Basu, K. (1990a). Does brand attitude moderate the persuasiveness of humor in advertising? *Advances in Consumer Research*, *17*, 442.

Chattopadhyay, A., & Basu, K. (1990b). Humor in advertising: The moderating role of prior brand evaluation. *Journal of Marketing Research, 27*, 466–476.

Chesterfield, Earl of. (1748/1901/1925). Letters 144–147. In C. Strachey (Ed.), *The Earl of Chesterfield's "Letters to his son."* London: Methuen.

Christie, G. L. (1994). Some psychoanalytic aspects of humor. *International Journal of Psychoanalysis, 75*, 479–489.

Cicero. (1881). *De oratore.* Oxford: Clarendon.

Coates, J. F. (1972). Wit and humor: A neglected aid in crowd and mob control. *Crime and Delinquency, 18*, 184–191.

Codere, H. (1956). The amiable side of Kwakiutl life: The potlatch and the play potlatch. *American Anthropologist, 58*, 334–351.

Coleridge, S. T. (1836). *The literary remains.* London: W. Pickering.

Collier, M. J. (1960). Popular cartoons and prevailing anxieties. *The American Imago, 17*, 255–269.

Congreve, W. (1695/1908). Essay upon Humour in Comedy. In J. E. Springarn (Ed.), *Critical essays of the seventeenth century.* (Vol. 3.) Oxford: Clarendon.

Coser, R. L. (1956). *The functions of social conflict.* Glencoe, IL: Free Press.

Coser, R. L. (1959). Some social functions of laughter. *Human Relations, 12*, 171–182.

Coser, R. L. (1960). Laughter among colleagues. *Psychiatry, 23*, 81–95.

Coser, R. L. (1966). Role distance, sociological ambivalence, and transitional status systems. *American Journal of Sociology, 72*, 173–187.

Coulter, S. K., Wundeleigh, R. A., Ball, M. F., & Canary, J. J. (1973). Humor ratings as a function of weight and food deprivation. *Psychological Reports, 32*, 1099–1105.

Courdaveaux, V. (1875). *Le rire dans la vie et dans l'art.* Paris: Remque.

Cross, M. J. (1989). Leadership perceptions: The role of humor. Unpublished doctoral dissertation, University of Pittsburgh.

Crumrine, N. R. (1969). Capakoba, the Mayo Easter ceremonial impersonator: Explanations of ritual clowning. *Journal for the Scientific Study of Religion, 8*, 1–22.

Cupchik, G. C., & Leventhal, H. (1974). Consistency between expressive behavior and the evaluation of humorous stimuli: The role of sex and self-observation. *Journal of Personality and Social Psychology, 30*, 429–442.

Daniels, A. K., & Daniels, R. R. (1964). The social function of the career fool. *Psychiatry, 27*, 218–229.

Darwin, C. (1872/1965). *The expression of the emotions in man and animals.* London: Murray.

Davies, C. (1977). The changing stereotype of the Welsh in English jokes. In A. J. Chapman & H. C. Foot (Eds.), *It's a funny thing, humour.* Oxford, UK: Pergamon Press.

Davies, C. (1982). Ethnic jokes, moral values, and social boundaries. *British Journal of Sociology, 33*, 383–403.

Davis, J. M., & Farina, A. (1970). Humor appreciation as social communication. *Journal of Personality and Social Psychology, 15*, 175–178.

Dearborn, G. V. N. (1900). The nature of the smile and the laugh. *Science, 9*, 851–856.

Deckers, L., & Buttram, R. (1990). Humor as a response to incongruities within or between schemata. *Humor: International Journal of Humor Research, 3*, 53–64.

Deckers, L., Buttram, R., & Winsted, D. (1989). The sensitization of humor responses to cartoons. *Motivation and Emotion, 13*, 71–81.

Deckers, L., & Devine, J. (1981). Humor by violating an existing expectancy. *The Journal of Psychology, 108*, 107–110.

Deckers, L., Edington, J., & VanCleave, G. (1981). Mirth as a function of incongruities in judged and unjudged dimensions of psychophysical tasks. *The Journal of General Psychology, 105*, 225–233.

Deckers, L., & Hricik, D. (1984). Orienting and humor responses: A synthesis. *Motivation and Emotion, 8*, 183–204.

Deckers, L., & Kizer, P. (1974). A note on weight discrepancy and humor. *Journal of Psychology, 86*, 309–312.

Deckers, L., & Kizer, P. (1975). Humor and the incongruity hypothesis. *Journal of Psychology, 90*, 215–218.

Deckers, L., & Salais, D. (1983). Humor as a negatively accelerated function of the degree of incongruity. *Motivation and Emotion, 7*, 357–363.

Delage, Y. (1919). Sur la nature du comique. *La Revue du Mois, 20*, 337–354.

Dennis, W. (1935). An experimental test of two theories of social smiling in infants. *Journal of Social Psychology, 6*, 214–233.

Denzin, N. K. (1970). Problems in analyzing elements of mass culture. *American Journal of Sociology, 75*, 1035–1038.

Denzin, N. K. (Ed.) (1983). *Studies in symbolic interaction.* (Vol. 5). Greenwich, CT: JAI Press.

Desai, M. W. (1939). Surprise: A historical and experimental study. *British Journal of Psychology Monograph Supplement*, No. 22.

Descartes, R. (1649/1909). *Les passions de l'ame.* Paris: Le Gras.

DeSousa, R. (1987). When is it wrong to laugh? In J. Morreall (Ed.), *The philosophy of laughter and humor.* Albany: State University of New York Press.

Dessoir, M. (1923). *Asthetik und allgemeine kunst wissenschaft.* Stuttgart: Enke.

Dewey, J. (1894–1895). The theory of emotion. *Psychological Review, 1*, 553–569.

Dines, G. (1995). Toward a critical sociological analysis of cartoons. *Humor: International Journal of Humor Research, 8*, 237–255.

Diserens, C. M. (1926). Recent theories of laughter. *Psychological Bulletin, 23*, 247–255.

Diserens, C. M., & Bonifield, M. (1930). Humor and the ludicrous. *Psychological Bulletin, 27*, 108–118.

Dollard, J., & Miller, N. (1950). *Personality and psychotherapy.* New York: McGraw-Hill.

Dooley, L. (1934). A note on humor. *Psychoanalytic Review, 21*, 50–57.

Dooley, L. (1941). Relation of humor to masochism. *Psychoanalytic Review, 28*, 37–46.

Douglas, M. (1968). The social control of cognition: Some factors in joke perception. *Man, 3*, 361–376.

Draper, D. (1959). *The copywriter's guide: Humor in advertising*. New York: Harper.

Dresser, J. W. (1967). Two studies on the social function of joking as an outlet for aggression. *Dissertation Abstracts, 28*, No. 2, 778A-779A.

Drever, J. (1917). *Instinct in man*. London: Cambridge University Press.

Dryden, J. (1671/1900). Preface to "An Evening's Love." In W. P. Ker (Ed.), *Essays of John Dryden*. (Vol. 1). Oxford, UK: Clarendon.

Dugas, M. L. (1902/1910). *Psychologie du rire*. Paris: Alcan.

Dugas, M. L. (1906). La fonction psychologique du rire. *Revue Philosophique, 62*, 576–599.

Dumas, G. (1923). *Traite de psychologie*. Paris: Alcan.

Dumont, L. A. (1862). *Des causes du rire*. Paris: A. Durand.

Duncan, C. (1979). Humor in advertising: A behavioral perspective. *Journal of the Academy of Marketing Science, 7*, 285–306.

Duncan, C., & Nelson, J. (1985). Effects of humor in a radio advertising experiment. *Journal of Advertising, 14*, 33–40.

Duncan, C., Nelson, J., & Frontczak, N. (1984). Effect of humor on advertising comprehension. *Advances in Consumer Research, 11*, 432–437.

Dundes, A. (1975). Slurs international: Folk comparisons of ethnicity and national character. *Southern Folklore Quarterly, 39*, 15–38.

Dunlap, K. (1925). *Old and new viewpoints in psychology*. St. Louis, MO: Mosby.

Dupreel, E. (1928). Le probleme sociologique du rire. *Revue Philosophique, 106*, 213–260.

Dworkin, E. S., & Efran, J. S. (1967). The angered: Their susceptibility to varieties of humor. *Journal of Personality and Social Psychology, 6*, 233–236.

Eastman, M. (1921). *The sense of humor*. New York: Scribner's.

Eckerman, C. O., & Whatley, J. L. (1975). Infants' reactions to unfamiliar adults varying in novelty. *Developmental Psychology, 11*, 562–566.

Edgerton, R. B., & Langness, L. L. (1974). *Methods and styles in the study of culture*. San Francisco: Chandler & Sharp.

Eibl-Eibesfeldt, I. (1975). *Ethology: The biology of behavior*. New York: Holt, Rinehart & Winston.

Eibl-Eibesfeldt, I. (1989). *Human ethology*. New York: Aldine de Gruyter.

Eidelberg, L. (1945). A contribution to the study of wit. *Psychoanalytic Review, 32*, 33–61.

Ellis, G. T., & Sekyra, F. (1972). The effect of aggressive cartoons on the behavior of first grade children. *The Journal of Psychology, 81*, 37–43.

Emerson, J. P. (1969). Negotiating the serious import of humor. *Sociometry, 32*, 169–181.

Emerson, R. W. (1876/1903). *Letters and social aims*. Boston: Osgood.

Enders, A. C. (1927). A study of the laughter of the preschool child in the Merrill-Palmer Nursery School. *Papers of the Michigan Academy of Science, Arts, and Letters, 8*, 341–356.

Etzel, B. C., & Gewirtz, J. L. (1967). Experimental modification of caretaker-maintained, high-rate operant crying in a 6– and 20–week-old infant:

Extinction of crying with reinforcement of eye-contact and smiling. *Journal of Experimental Child Psychology, 3*, 303–317.

Everett, C. C. (1888/1893). *The philosophy of the comic: Poetry, comedy, and duty.* Boston: Houghton Mifflin.

Eysenck, H. J. (1942). The appreciation of humor: An experimental and theoretical study. *British Journal of Psychology, 32*, 295–309.

Eysenck, H. J. (1947). *Dimensions of personality.* London: Kegan Paul.

Eysenck, H. J., Arnold, W., & Meili, R. (Eds.) (1972). *Encyclopedia of psychology.* (Vol. 2). New York: Herder & Herder.

Feibleman, J. K. (1939). *In praise of comedy.* New York: Macmillan.

Feibleman, J. K. (1949). The meaning of comedy. In J. Stolnitz (Ed.), *Aesthetics.* Chicago: Meredith.

Feinsilber, M., & Mead, W. (1980). *American averages.* Garden City, NY: Dolphin.

Feldmann, S. (1941). A supplement to Freud's theory of wit. *Psychoanalytic Review, 28*, 201–217.

Feshbach, S. (1955). The drive-reducing function of fantasy behavior. *Journal of Abnormal and Social Psychology, 50*, 3–11.

Fielding, H. (1742/1935). *Joseph Andrews.* London: Dent.

Fine, G. A. (1976). Obscene joking across cultures. *Journal of Communication, 26*, 134–140.

Fine, G. A. (1977a). Humour and communication: Discussion. In A. J. Chapman & H. C. Foot (Eds.), *It's a funny thing, humour.* Oxford, UK: Pergamon Press.

Fine, G. A. (1977b). Humour in situ: The role of humour in small group culture. In A. J. Chapman & H. C. Foot (Eds.), *It's a funny thing, humour.* Oxford, UK: Pergamon Press.

Fine, G. A. (1983). Sociological approaches to the study of humor. In P. E. McGhee & J. H. Goldstein (Eds.), *Handbook of humor research* (Vol. 1, *Basic issues*). New York: Springer-Verlag.

Fischer, K., & Thussbas, C. (2000). The effect of humorous-episodic element in television commercials on memory performance and brand evaluations. An experimental study. *Medienpsychologie: Zeitschrift fur Individual- und Massenkommunikation, 12*, 51–68.

Fisher, G. M. (1964). Response to aggressive humor by depressive, sociopathic, and normal persons. Unpublished doctoral dissertation, University of Utah.

Flugel, J. C. (1954). Humor and laughter. In G. Lindzey (Ed.), *Handbook of social psychology.* (Vol. 2). Reading, MA: Addison-Wesley.

Foot, H. C., & Chapman, A. J. (1976). The social responsiveness of young children in humorous situations. In A. J. Chapman & H. C. Foot (Eds.), *Humour and laughter: Theory, research, and applications.* London: Wiley.

Forabosco, G. (1992). Cognitive aspects of the humor process: The concept of incongruity. *Humor: International Journal of Humor Research, 5*, 45–68.

Ford, C. S. (1967). On the analysis of behavior for cross-cultural comparisons. In C. S. Ford (Ed.), *Cross-cultural approaches.* New Haven, CT: HRAF Press.

Frankel, E. B. (1953). An experimental study of psychoanalytic theories of humor. Unpublished doctoral dissertation, University of Michigan.

Freud, S. (1905/1916). *Der witz und seine beziehung zum unbewussten (Wit and its relation to the unconscious)*. New York: Moffat Ward.

Freud, S. (1928). Humor. *International Journal of Psychoanalysis, 9*, 1–6.

Freud, S. (1960). *Jokes and their relation to the unconscious*. New York: Norton.

Fridlund, A. (1994). *Human facial expression: An evolutionary view*. San Diego, CA: Academic Press.

Fridlund, A., & Loftis, J. (1990). Relations between tickling and humorous laughter: Preliminary report for the Darwin-Hecker hypothesis. *Biological Psychology, 30*, 141–150.

Friedman, M. (1989). Commercial expressions in American humor: An analysis of selected popular cultural works of the post war era. *Humor: International Journal of Humor Research, 2*, 265–283.

Fry, W. (1963). *Sweet madness: A study of humor*. Palo Alto, CA: Pacific Books.

Fry, W. (1977). The respiratory components of mirthful laughter. *The Journal of Biological Psychology, 19*, 39–50.

Fry, W. (1992). The physiologic effects of humor, mirth, and laughter. *Journal of the American Medical Association, 267*, 1857–1858.

Fry, W. (1994). The biology of humor. *Humor: International Journal of Humor Research, 7*, 111–126.

Fry, W., & Savin, W. (1988). Mirthful laughter and blood pressure. *Humor: International Journal of Humor Research, 1*, 49–62.

Fuller, R. (1977). Uses and abuses of canned laughter. In A. J. Chapman & H. C. Foot (Eds.), *It's a funny thing, humour*. Oxford, UK: Pergamon Press.

Fuller, R., & Sheehy-Skeffington, A. (1974). Effects of group laughter on responses to humorous material: A replication and extension. *Psychological Reports, 35*, 531–534.

Gallivan, J. (1991). Is there a sex difference in lateralization for processing of humorous materials? *Sex Roles, 24*, 525–530.

Garfinkel, H. (1967). *Studies in ethnomethodology*. Englewood Cliffs, NJ: Prentice-Hall.

Gelb, B., & Pickett, C. (1983). Attitude toward the ad: Links to humor and to advertising effectiveness. *Journal of Advertising, 12*, 34–42.

Gelb, B. D., & Zinkhan, G. M. (1985). The effect of repetition on humor in a radio advertising study. *Journal of Advertising, 14*, 13– 20.

Gelb, B. D., & Zinkhan, G. M. (1986). Humor and advertising effectiveness after repeated exposures to a radio commercial. *Journal of Advertising, 15*, 15–20.

Gerard, A. (1759/1780). *An essay on taste*. London: Menston, Scolar.

Gerber, W. S., & Routh, D. K. (1975). Humor response as related to violation of expectancies and to stimulus intensity in a weight-judgment task. *Perceptual and Motor Skills, 41*, 673–676.

Gerst, M. (1992). Humor and suffering. Unpublished doctoral dissertation, California School of Professional Psychology at Berkeley/Alameda.

Giles, A., Bourhis, R. Y., Gadfield, N. J., Davies, G. J., & Davies, A. D. (1976). Cognitive aspects of humour in social interaction: A model and some linguistic data. In A. J. Chapman & H. C. Foot (Eds.), *Humour and laughter: Theory, research, and applications*. London: Wiley.

Godkewitsch, M. (1972). The relationship between arousal potential and funniness of jokes. In J. H. Goldstein & P. E. McGhee (Eds.), *The psychology of humor: Theoretical perspectives and empirical issues*. New York: Academic Press.

Godkewitsch, M. (1976). Physiological and verbal indices of arousal in rated humour. In A. J. Chapman & H. C. Foot (Eds.), *Humour and laughter: Theory, research, and applications*. London: Wiley.

Goldman, M. (1960). The sociology of Negro humor. Unpublished doctoral dissertation, New School for Social Research.

Goldsmith, O. (1750/1854/1858). Inquiry into the present state of polite learning. In P. Cunningham (Ed.), *Works*. London: Bell.

Goldstein, J. H. (1970). Repetition, motive arousal, and humor appreciation. *Journal of Experimental Research in Personality, 4*, 90–94.

Goldstein, J. H. (1977). Cross-cultural research: Humour here and there. In A. J. Chapman & H. C. Foot (Eds.), *It's a funny thing, humour*. Oxford, UK: Pergamon Press.

Goldstein, J. H., Harman, J., McGhee, P. E., & Karasik, R. (1975). Test of an information-processing model of humor: Physiological response changes during problem and riddle-solving. *The Journal of General Psychology, 92*, 59–68.

Goldstein, J. H., Suls, J. M., & Anthony, S. (1972). Enjoyment of specific types of humor content: Motivation or salience? In J. H. Goldstein & P. E. McGhee (Eds.), *The psychology of humor: Theoretical perspectives and empirical issues*. New York: Academic Press.

Gollub, H. F., & Levine, J. (1967). Distraction as a factor in the enjoyment of aggressive humor. *Journal of Personality and Social Psychology, 5*, 368–372.

Goodchilds, J. D., & Smith, E. E. (1964). The wit in his group. *Human Relations, 17*, 23–31.

Gregg, A., Miller, M., & Linton, E. (1929). Laughter situations as an indication of social responsiveness in young children. In D. S. Thomas (Ed.), *Some new techniques for studying social behaviour*. New York: Teachers College.

Gregory, J. C. (1923). Some theories of laughter. *Mind, 32*, 328–344.

Gregory, J. C. (1924). *The nature of laughter*. London: Kegan Paul.

Greig, J. Y. T. (1923/1969). *The psychology of laughter and comedy*. New York: Dodd, Mead/Cooper Square.

Groch, A. S. (1974). Generality of response to humor and wit in cartoons, jokes, stories, and photographs. *Psychological Reports, 35*, 875–838.

Grotjahn, M. (1957). *Beyond laughter*. New York: McGraw-Hill.

Gruner, C. R. (1976). Wit and humour in mass communication. In A. J. Chapman & H. C. Foot (Eds.), *Humour and laughter: Theory, research, and applications*. London: Wiley.

Guthrie, W. N. (1903). A theory of the comic. *International Quarterly, 7*, 254–264.

Gutman, J., & Priest, R. F. (1969). When is aggression funny? *Journal of Personality and Social Psychology, 12*, 60–65.

Haig, R. A. (1988). *The anatomy of humor: Biopsychosocial and therapeutic perspectives*. Springfield, IL: Thomas.

Hall, G. S., & Allin, A. (1897). The psychology of tickling, laughter, and the comic. *American Journal of Psychology, 9*, 1–42.

Harrington, J. (1591/1904). A brief apology for poetry. In G. G. Smith (Ed.), *Elizabethan critical essays*. (Vol. 1). Oxford: Clarendon.

Harris, C., & Christenfeld, N. (1997). Humour, tickle, and the Darwin-Hecker hypothesis. *Cognition and Emotion, 11*, 103–110.

Harris, W. H., & Levey, J. S. (Eds.) (1975). *The new Columbia encyclopedia*. New York: Columbia University Press.

Hartley, D. (1749). *Observations on man, his frame, his duty, and his expectations*. London: Johnson.

Hayworth, D. (1928). The socal origin and function of laughter. *Psychological Review, 35*, 367–385.

Hazlitt, W. (1818/1841/1907). *Lectures on the English comic writers*. London: Bell.

Hazlitt, W. (1890). *Studies in jocular literature*. London: Stock.

Hecker, E. (1873). *Die physiologie und psychologie des lachens und des komischen*. Berlin: Dummler.

Hegel, G. W. F. (1820/1886/1920/1975). *The philosophy of fine art*. London: Paul, Trench.

Hellyar, R. H. (1927). Laughter and jollity. *Contemporary Review, 132*, 757–763.

Heritage, J. (1984). *Garfinkel and ethnomethodology*. Cambridge, UK: Polity Press.

Hertzler, J. O. (1970). *Laughter: A socio-scientific analysis*. New York: Exposition.

Hess, A. G., & Mariner, E. A. (1975). On the sociology of crime cartoons. *International Journal of Criminology and Penology, 3*, 253–265.

Hetherington, E. M., & Wray, N. P. (1964). Aggression, need for social approval, and humor preferences. *Journal of Abnormal and Social Psychology, 68*, 685–689.

Hetherington, E. M., & Wray, N. P. (1966). Effects of need aggression, stress, and aggressive behavior on humor preferences. *Journal of Personality and Social Psychology, 4*, 229–233.

Higgins, D. J. (1981). A study of the relationship of Freud's theory of comic and hostile wit appreciation with anxiety. Unpublished doctoral dissertation, Ohio University.

Hill, C. D. (1991). The soul of wit: Freud's joke book as the analysis of a social psyche. Unpublished doctoral dissertation, Stanford University.

Hillson, T., & Martin, R. A. (1994). What's so funny about that? The domains-interaction approach as a model of incongruity and resolution in humor. *Motivation and Emotion, 18*, 1–29.

Hobbes, T. (1650/1839). Human nature. In W. Molesworth (Ed.), *Hobbes' English works*. Cambridge, UK: Cambridge University Press.

Hobbes, T. (1651/1839/1904). *Leviathan*. Cambridge, UK: Cambridge University Press.

Hoeffding, H. (1887/1891/1896). *Outlines of psychology*. London: Macmillan.

Hofstader, D., & Gabora, L. (1989). Synopsis of the workshop on humor and cognition. *Humor: International Journal of Humor Research, 2*, 417–440.

Holland, N. H. (1982). *Laughing: A psychology of humor*. Ithaca, NY: Cornell University Press.

Hollingworth, H. L. (1911). Experimental studies in judgment: Judgment of the comic. *Psychological Review, 18*, 132–156.

Holmes, D. S. (1969). Sensing humor: Latency and amplitude of responses related to MMPI profiles. *Journal of Consulting and Clinical Psychology, 33,* 296–301.

Hom, G. L. (1966). Threat of shock and anxiety in the perception of humor. *Perceptual and Motor Skills, 23,* 535–538.

Honigmann, J. J. (1942). An interpretation of the social psychological functions of the ritual clown. *Character and Personality, 10,* 220–226.

Honigmann, J. J. (1976). The personal approach in cultural anthropological research. *Current Anthropology, 17,* 243–261.

Hopen, E. C. (1977). Tracking the intractable—The analysis of humour in the study of value systems. In A. J. Chapman & H. C. Foot (Eds.), *It's a funny thing, humour.* Oxford, UK: Pergamon Press.

Horowitz, M. W., & Horowitz, L. S. (1949). An examination of the social psychological situations of the physically disabled as it pertains to humor. *American Psychologist, 4,* 256–257.

Hoshikawa, T. (1991). Effects of attention and expectation on tickle sensation. *Perceptual and Motor Skills, 72,* 27–33.

Howell, R. W. (1973). *Teasing relationships.* Reading, MA: Addison-Wesley.

Hull, C. (1943). *Principles of behavior.* New York: Appleton-Century-Crofts.

Hull, C. (1951). *Essentials of behavior.* New Haven, CT: Yale University Press.

Hull, C. (1952). *A behavior system.* New Haven, CT: Yale University Press.

Hunt, L. (1846/1910/1977). *Wit and humour.* London: Smith, Elder.

Hutcheson, F. (1750). *Reflections upon laughter.* Glasgow: Urie.

Jacobs, M. (1964). *Pattern in cultural anthropology.* Homewood, IL: Dorsey.

James, W. (1890/1950). *The principles of psychology.* New York: Dover.

Jefferson, G. (1979). A technique for inviting laughter and its subsequent acceptance declination. In G. Psathas (Ed.), *Everyday language: Studies of ethnomethodology.* New York: Irvington.

Jekels, L. (1952). *Selected papers: On the psychology of comedy.* London: Imago.

Johnson, S. (1751/1802/1807). The Rambler. In *British Essayists.* (Vol. 21). London: J. Johnson.

Johnson, S. (1755). *Dictionary of the English language.* London: Strahan & Knapton.

Jones, J. M. (1970). Cognitive factors in the appreciation of humor: A theoretical and experimental analysis. Unpublished doctoral dissertation, Yale University.

Jonson, B. (1598/1816). Every man in his humour. In W. Gifford (Ed.), *Works.* London: Unwin.

Jonson, B. (1599/1816). Every man out of his humour. In W. Gifford (Ed.), *Works.* London: Unwin.

Joubert, L. (1560/1579/1980). *Treatise on laughter.* Translated by G. D. de Rocher. University, AL: The University of Alabama Press.

Justin, F. (1932). A genetic study of laughter-provoking stimuli. *Child Development, 3,* 114–136.

Kagan, J. (1967). On the need for relativism. *American Psychologist, 22,* 131–143.

Kallen, H. M. (1911). The aesthetic principle in comedy. *American Journal of Psychology, 22,* 137–157.

Kames, Lord. (1762/1774/1817). *Elements of criticism.* Edinburgh: Kincaid.

Kane, T. R., Suls, J., & Tedeschi, J. T. (1977). Humour as a tool of social interaction. In A. J. Chapman & H. C. Foot (Eds.), *It's a funny thing, humour.* Oxford, UK: Pergamon Press.

Kant, I. (1790/1892/1914). *Critique of judgment.* London: Macmillan.

Kantha, S. (1999). Sexual humor on Freud as expressed in limericks. *Humor: International Journal of Humor Research, 12,* 289–299.

Kaplan, H. B., & Boyd, I. H. (1965). The social functions of humor on an open psychiatric ward. *Psychiatric Quarterly, 39,* 502–515.

Karnick, K. (1991). Playing in prime time: Narrative and humor in fictional series television. Unpublished doctoral dissertation, The University of Wisconsin-Madison.

Keith-Spiegel, P. (1968). The relationship between overtly aggressive behavioral modes and reactions to hostile humor. Unpublished doctoral dissertation, Claremont Graduate School and University Center.

Keith-Spiegel, P. (1972). Early conceptions of humor: Varieties and issues. In J. H. Goldstein & P. E. McGhee (Eds.), *The psychology of humor: Theoretical perspectives and empirical issues.* New York: Academic Press.

Kelling, G. W. (1971). An empirical investigation of Freud's theory of jokes. *Psychoanalytic Review, 58,* 473–485.

Kelly, J., & Solomon, P. (1975). Humor in television advertising. *Journal of Advertising, 4,* 31–35.

Kenderdine, M. (1931). Laughter in the pre-school child. *Child Development, 2,* 228–230.

Kenny, D. I. (1955). The contingency of humor appreciation on the stimulus-confirmation of joke-ending expectations. *Journal of Abnormal and Social Psychology, 51,* 644–648.

Kierkegaard, S. (1846/1941). *Concluding unscientific postscript.* Princeton, NJ: Princeton University Press.

Kimmel, H., VanOlst, E., & Orlebeke, J. (Eds.) (1979). *The orienting reflex in humans.* Hillsdale, NJ: Erlbaum.

Kimmins, C. W. (1928). *The springs of laughter.* London: Methuen.

Kirkland, J. C. (1976). Interest, and smile perception. Unpublished doctoral dissertation, University of Missouri-Columbia.

Klapp, O. E. (1950). The fool as a social type. *American Journal of Sociology, 55,* 157–162.

Klapp, O. E. (1962). *Heroes, villains, and fools.* Englewood Cliffs, NJ: Prentice-Hall.

Kline, L. W. (1907). The psychology of humor. *American Journal of Psychology, 18,* 421–441.

Kline, P. (1977). The psychoanalytic theory of humour and laughter. In A. J. Chapman & H. C. Foot (Eds.), *It's a funny thing, humour.* Oxford, UK: Pergamon Press.

Knight, R. P. (1805/1808). *An analytical enquiry into the principles of taste.* London: T. Payne.

Knox, I. (1951). Towards a philosophy of humor. *Journal of Philosophy, 48,* 541–548.

Koestler, A. (1964). *The act of creation.* New York: Macmillan.

Kole, T., & Henderson, H. L. (1966). Cartoon reaction scale with special reference to driving behavior. *Journal of Applied Psychology, 50,* 311–316.

Korb, L. (1988). Humor: A tool for the psychoanalyst. *Issues in Ego Psychology, 11,* 45–54.

Kreitler, H., & Kreitler, S. (1970). Dependence of laughter on cognitive strategies. *Merrill-Palmer Quarterly, 16,* 163–177.

Kris, E. (1938). Ego development and the comic. *International Journal of Psychoanalysis, 19,* 77–90.

Krishnan, H. S., & Chakravarti, D. (1990). Humor in advertising: Testing effects on brand name and message claim memory. In W. Bearden & A. Parasurama (Eds.), *Proceedings of the Summer Educators' Conference.* Chicago: American Marketing Association.

Kuhlman, T. L. (1985). A study of salience and motivational theories of humor. *Journal of Personality and Social Psychology, 49,* 281–286.

LaFave, L. (1961). Humor judgments as a function of reference groups: An experimental study. Unpublished doctoral dissertation, University of Oklahoma.

LaFave, L. (1967). Comment on Priest's article: "Election jokes: The effects of reference group membership." *Psychological Reports, 20,* 305–306.

LaFave, L. (1972). Humor judgments as a function of reference group and identification classes. In J. H. Goldstein & P. E. McGhee (Eds.), *The psychology of humor: Theoretical perspectives and empirical issues.* New York: Academic Press.

LaFave, L., Haddad, J., & Maesen, W. (1976). Superiority, enhanced self-esteem, and perceived incongruity humour theory. In A. J. Chapman & H. C. Foot (Eds.), *Humour and laughter: Theory, research, and applications.* London: Wiley.

Laffal, J., Levine, J., & Redlich, F. C. (1953). An anxiety reduction theory of humor. *American Psychologist, 8,* 383.

LaGaipa, J. J. (1968). Stress, authoritarianism, and the enjoyment of different kinds of hostile humor. *Journal of Psychology, 70,* 3–8.

LaGaipa, J. J. (1977). The effects of humour on the flow of social conversation. In A. J. Chapman & H. C. Foot (Eds.), *It's a funny thing, humour.* Oxford, UK: Pergamon Press.

Lamb, C. W. (1968). Personality correlates of humor enjoyment following motivational arousal. *Journal of Personality and Social Psychology, 9,* 237–241.

Lamennais, F. (1841). *De l'art et du beau.* Paris: Mandar.

Lammers, H. (1991). Moderating influence of self-monitoring and gender on responses to humorous advertising. *Journal of Social Psychology, 131,* 57–69.

Lammers, H., Leibowitz, L., Seymour, G., & Hennessey, J. (1983). Humor and cognitive responses to advertising stimuli: A trace consolidation approach. *Journal of Business Research, 11,* 173–185.

Landy, D., & Mettee, D. (1969). Evaluation of an aggressor as a function of exposure to cartoon humor. *Journal of Personality and Social Psychology, 12,* 66–71.

Langevin, R., & Day, H. I. (1972). Physiological correlates of humor. In J. H. Goldstein & P. E. McGhee (Eds.), *The psychology of humor: Theoretical perspectives and empirical issues.* New York: Academic Press.

Laprade, Vide. (1861). *Questions d'art et de morale*. Paris: Didier.

Latta, R. L. (1998). *The basic humor process: A cognitive-shift theory and the case against incongruity*. Berlin: Mouton de Gruyter.

Lauter, P. (1964). *Theories of comedy*. Garden City, NY: Doubleday.

Leacock, S. B. (1935). *Humour: Its theory and technique*. London: Lane.

Leacock, S. B. (1937). *Humour and humanity*. London: Butterworth.

Leak, G. K. (1974). Effects of hostility arousal and aggressive humor on catharsis and humor preference. *Journal of Personality and Social Psychology, 30*, 736–740.

Lee, Y., & Mason, C. (1999). Responses to information incongruency in advertising: The role of expectancy, relevancy, and humor. *Journal of Consumer Research, 26*, 156–169.

Lefcourt, H. M., Antrobus, P., & Hogg, E. (1974). Humor response and humor production as a function of locus of control, field dependence, and type of reinforcements. *Journal of Personality, 42*, 632–651.

Lefcourt, H., Davidson-Katz, K., & Kueneman, K. (1990). Humor and immune system functioning. *Humor: International Journal of Humor Research, 3*, 305–321.

Lessing, G. E. (1767–1769). *Hamburgische dramaturgie*. Berlin: Hempel.

Leuba, C. (1941). Tickling and laughter: Two genetic studies. *Journal of Genetic Psychology, 58*, 201–209.

Leventhal, H., & Cupchik, G. C. (1975). The informational and facilitative effects of an audience upon expression and evaluation of humorous stimuli. *Journal of Experimental Social Psychology, 11*, 363–380.

Leventhal, H., & Mace, W. (1970). The effect of laughter on the evaluation of a slapstick movie. *Journal of Personality, 38*, 16–30.

Leventhal, H., & Scherer, K. (1987). The relationship of emotion to cognition: A functional approach to a semantic controversy. *Cognition and Emotion, 1*, 3–28.

Leveque, C. (1863). Le rire, le comique, et le risible, dans l'esprit et dans l'art. *Revue des Deux Mondes, 47*, 107.

Levine, J. (1956). Responses to humor. *Scientific American, 194*, 31–35.

Levine, J. (Ed.) (1969). *Motivation in humor*. New York: Atherton.

Levine, J., & Abelson, R. (1953). An anxiety reduction theory of humor. *American Psychologist, 8*, 383.

Levine, J., & Abelson, R. (1959). Humor as a disturbing stimulus. *Journal of General Psychology, 60*, 191–200.

Levine, J., & Redlich, F. C. (1955). Failure to understand humor. *Psychoanalytic Quarterly, 24*, 560–572.

Levine, J., & Redlich, F. C. (1960). Intellectual and emotional factors in the appreciation of humor. *Journal of General Psychology, 62*, 25–35.

Lewin, B. (1950). *The psychoanalysis of elation*. New York: Norton.

Lieberman, J. N. (1976). Playfulness in play and the player: A behavioral syndrome viewed in relationship to classroom learning. *Contemporary Educational Psychology, 1*, 197–205.

Lilly, W. S. (1896). The theory of the ludicrous. *Fortnightly Review, 65*, 724–737.

Lindeman, H. (1969). Humor in politics and society. *Impact of Science on Society, 19,* 269–278.

Linfield, E. G. (1977). The function of humour in the classroom. In A. J. Chapman & H. C. Foot (Eds.), *It's a funny thing, humour.* Oxford, UK: Pergamon Press.

Lipps, T. (1898). *Komik und humor.* Hamburg: Voss.

Littman, J. (1980). A theory of humor. *Dissertation Abstracts International, 40* (*11–B*), 5410–5411.

Liu, F. (1995). Humor as violations of the reality principle. *Humor: International Journal of Humor Research, 8,* 177–190.

Lloyd, E. L. (1938). The respiratory mechanism in laughter. *The Journal of General Psychology, 19,* 179–189.

Locke, J. (1690/1965). *An essay concerning human understanding.* London: Dent.

Long, D., & Graesser, A. (1988). Wit and humor in discourse processing. *Discourse Processes, 11,* 35–60.

Lull, P. E. (1940). The effects of humor in persuasive speeches. *Speech Monographs, 7,* 26–40.

Ludovici, A. M. (1932). *The secret of laughter.* London: Constable & Co.

Lund, F. H. (1930). Why do we weep? *Journal of Social Psychology, 1,* 136–151.

Lynch, M., & Hartman, R. (1968). Dimensions of humor in advertising. *Journal of Advertising Research, 8,* 39–45.

Lynn, R. (1966). *Attention, arousal, and the orientation reaction.* Oxford, UK: Pergamon Press.

Mace, C. A. (1927). *Sibylla: Or the revival of prophecy.* New York: Dutton.

MacHovec, F. J. (1988). *Humor: Theory, history, applications.* Springfield, IL: Thomas.

Madden, T., & Weinberger, M. (1982). The effects of humor on attention in magazine advertising. *Journal of Advertising, 11,* 8–14.

Madden, T., & Weinberger, M. (1984). Humor in advertising—A practitioner's view. *Journal of Advertising Research, 24,* 23–29.

Maier, N. R. F. (1932). A Gestalt theory of humour. *British Journal of Psychology, 23,* 69–74.

Maier, N. R. F. (1963). Maier's law. In R. A. Baker (Ed.), *Psychology in the wry.* Princeton, NJ: D. Van Nostrand. [Note: Also see *American Psychologist,* 1960, *15,* 208–212.]

Main, D. C., & Schillace, R. J. (1968). Aversive stimulation and the laughter response. *Psychonomic Science, 13,* 241–242.

Malinowski, B. (1944). *A scientific theory of culture and other essays.* Chapel Hill: University of North Carolina Press.

Malpass, L. F., & Fitzpatrick, E. D. (1959). Social facilitation as a factor in reaction to humor. *Journal of Social Psychology, 50,* 295–303.

Marc, D. (1989). *Comic visions: Television comedy and American culture.* Boston: Unwin Hyman.

Markiewicz, D. (1974). Effects of humor on persuasion. *Sociometry, 37,* 407–422.

Marlowe, L. (1989). A sense of humor. In R. K. Unger (Ed.), *Representations: Social constructions of gender.* Amityville, NY: Baywood.

Marmontel, J. F. (1751/1778). Comedie and Comique. In *Encyclopedie ou dictionnaire raisonne des sciences, des arts, et des metiers*. Geneve: Pellet.

Marshall, H. R. (1894). *Pain, pleasure, and aesthetics*. London: Macmillan.

Martin, L. (1905). Psychology of aesthetics: Experimental prospecting in the field of the comic. *American Journal of Psychology, 16*, 35–116.

Martin, R. A. (2000). Humor and laughter. In A. E. Kazdin (Ed.), *Encyclopedia of psychology*. (Vol. 4). Washington, DC: American Psychological Association; New York: Oxford University Press.

Martineau, W. H. (1967). A model for a theory of the function of humor. *Research Reports in the Social Sciences, 1*, 51–64.

Martineau, W. H. (1972). A model of the social functions of humor. In J. H. Goldstein & P. E. McGhee (Eds.), *The psychology of humor: Theoretical perspectives and empirical issues*. New York: Academic Press.

Masson, T. L. (1925). Humor and the comic journal. *Yale Review, 15*, 113–123.

McCall, G. J., & Simmons, J. L. (Eds.) (1969). *Issues in participant observation*. Menlo Park, CA: Addison-Wesley.

McCall, R. B. (1972). Smiling and vocalization in infants as indices of perceptual-cognitive processes. *Merrill-Palmer Quarterly, 18*, 341–347.

McComas, H. C. (1923). The origin of laughter. *Psychological Review, 30*, 45–55.

McCullough, L., & Taylor, R. (1993). Humor in American, British, and German ads. *Industrial Marketing Management, 22*, 17–28.

McDougall, W. (1903). Theory of laughter. *Nature, 67*, 318–319.

McDougall, W. (1922). Why do we laugh? *Scribner's, 71*, 359–363.

McDougall, W. (1923). *Outline of psychology*. London: Methuen.

McDougall, W. (1937). New light on laughter. *Fortnightly Review, 148*, 312–320.

McGhee, P. E. (1968). Cognitive development and children's comprehension of humor. Doctoral dissertation, Ohio State University.

McGhee, P. E. (1971a). Cognitive development and children's comprehension of humor. *Child Development, 42*, 123–138.

McGhee, P. E. (1971b). The role of operational thinking in children's comprehension and appreciation of humor. *Child Development, 42*, 733–744.

McGhee, P. E. (1972). On the cognitive origins of incongruity humor: Fantasy assimilation versus reality assimilation. In J. H. Goldstein & P. E. McGhee (Eds.), *The psychology of humor: Theoretical perspectives and empirical issues*. New York: Academic Press.

McGhee, P. E. (1973). Birth order and social facilitation of humor. *Psychological Reports, 33*, 105–106.

McGhee, P. E. (1974). Cognitive mastery and children's humor. *Psychological Bulletin, 81*, 721–730.

McGhee, P. E. (1977). A model of the origins and early development of incongruity-based humour. In A. J. Chapman & H. C. Foot (Eds.), *It's a funny thing, humour*. Oxford, UK: Pergamon Press.

McGhee, P. E. (1979). *Humor: Its origin and development*. San Francisco: Freeman.

McGhee, P. E. (1983). The role of arousal and hemispheric lateralization in humor. In P. E. McGhee & J. H. Goldstein (Eds.), *Handbook of humor research* (Vol. 1, *Basic issues*). New York: Springer-Verlag.

McGhee, P. E., & Chapman, A. J. (1980). *Children's humour*. Chichester, UK: Wiley.

McGhee, P. E., & Johnson, S. F. (1975). The role of fantasy and reality cues in children's appreciation of incongruity humor. *Merrill-Palmer Quarterly, 21,* 19–30.

McGhee, P. E., & Panaoutsopoulu, T. (1990). The role of cognitive factors in children's metaphor and comprehension. *Humor: International Journal of Humor Research, 3,* 379–402.

McNamara, J. J., & Tiffin, J. (1941). The distracting effect of nearby cartoons on the attention holding power of advertisements. *Journal of Applied Psychology, 25,* 524–527.

Meadows, C. M. (1975). The phenomenology of joy: An empirical investigation. *Psychological Reports, 37,* 39–54.

Meerloo, J. A. M. (1966). The biology of laughter. *Psychoanalytic Review, 53,* 189–208.

Melinaud, C. (1895). Pourquoi rit-on? Etude sur la cause psychologique du rire. *Revue des Deux Mondes, 127,* 612.

Mendelsohn, H. (1966). *Mass entertainment*. New Haven, CT: College & University Press.

Menon, V. K. (1931). *A theory of laughter*. London: Allen & Unwin.

Meredith, G. (1877/1898/1918). *An essay on comedy and the uses of the comic spirit*. London: Constable.

Mettee, D. R., Hrelec, E. S., & Wilkins, P. C. (1971). Humor as an interpersonal asset and liability. *Journal of Social Psychology, 85,* 51–64.

Mettee, D. R., & Wilkins, P. C. (1972). When similarity "hurts": Effects of perceived ability and a humorous blunder on interpersonal attractiveness. *Journal of Personality and Social Psychology, 22,* 246–258.

Meyer-Holzapfel, M. (1956). Uber die bereitschaft zu spiel- und instinkthandlungen. *Zeitschrift fur Tierpsychologie, 13,* 442–462.

Michiels, A. (1886). *Le monde du comique et du rire*. Paris: Alcan.

Middleton, R. (1959). Negro and White reactions to racial humor. *Sociometry, 22,* 175–182.

Miller, F. C. (1967). Humor in a Chippewa tribal council. *Ethnology, 6,* 263–271.

Mintz, L. E. (1983). Humor and popular culture. In P. E. McGhee & J. H. Goldstein (Eds.), *Handbook of humor research* (Vol. 2, *Applied studies*). New York: Springer-Verlag.

Mintz, L. E. (1988). Broadcast humor. In L. Mintz (Ed.), *Humor in America: A research guide to genres and topics*. Westport, CT: Greenwood Press.

Mizerski, R. (1995). The relationship between cartoon trade character recognition and attitude toward product category in young children. *Journal of Marketing, 59,* 58–70.

Modol, R., & Hortal, M. (1995). Humor and its relation with external reality. *Revista Catalana de Psicoanalisi, 12,* 67–79.

Moliere, J. B. P. (1662–1664/1817). *Oeuvres*. Paris: Didot.

Mones, L. (1939). Intelligence and a sense of humor. *Journal of Exceptional Child Psychology, 5,* 150–153.

Monnot, M. (1981). *Selling America: Puns, language, and advertising*. Washington, DC: University Press of America.

Monro, D. H. (1951/1963). *Argument of laughter*. Melbourne: Melbourne University Press.

Moore, F. W. (Ed.) (1961). *Readings in cross-cultural methodology*. New Haven, CT: HRAF Press.

Moreau, R. E. (1943). Joking relationships in Tanganyika. *Africa, 14*, 386–400.

Morreall, J. (1982). A new theory of laughter. *Philosophical Studies, 42*, 243–254.

Morreall, J. (1983). *Taking laughter seriously*. Albany: State University of New York Press.

Morreall, J. (1987a). Funny ha-ha, funny strange, and other reactions to incongruity. In J. Morreall (Ed.), *The philosophy of laughter and humor*. Albany: State University of New York Press.

Morreall, J. (Ed.) (1987b). *The philosophy of laughter and humor*. Albany: State University of New York Press.

Morreall, J. (1989). Enjoying incongruity. *Humor: International Journal of Humor Research, 2*, 1–18.

Mueller, C., & Donnerstein, E. (1983). Film-induced arousal and aggressive behavior. *Journal of Social Psychology, 119*, 61–67.

Mulkay, M. (1985). *The word and the world: Explorations in the form of sociological analysis*. London: Allen & Unwin.

Mulkay, M. (1987). Humour and social structure. In W. Outhwaite & M. Mulkay (Eds.), *Social theory and social criticism*. Oxford, UK: Basil Blackwell.

Mulkay, M. (1988). *On humour: Its nature and its place in modern society*. Oxford, UK: Polity Press.

Mussen, P., & Rutherford, E. (1961). Effects of aggressive cartoons on children's aggressive play. *Journal of Abnormal and Social Psychology, 62*, 461–464.

Naroll, R., & Cohen, R. (Eds.) (1970). *A handbook of method in cultural anthropology*. Garden City, NY: Natural History Press.

Nelson, J. (1987). Humor and advertising effects after repeated exposures to a radio commercial. *Journal of Advertising, 16*, 63–65.

Nerhardt, G. (1970). Humor and inclination to laugh: Emotional reactions to stimuli of different divergence from a range of expectancy. *Scandinavian Journal of Psychology, 11*, 185–195.

Nerhardt, G. (1975). Rated funniness and dissimilarity of figures: Divergence from expectancy. *Scandinavian Journal of Psychology, 16*, 156–166.

Nerhardt, G. (1976). Incongruity and funniness: Towards a new descriptive model. In A. J. Chapman & H. C. Foot (Eds.), *Humour and laughter: Theory, research, and applications*. London: Wiley.

Nerhardt, G. (1977). Operationalization of incongruity in humour research: A critique and suggestions. In A. J. Chapman & H. C. Foot (Eds.), *It's a funny thing, humour*. Oxford, UK: Pergamon Press.

New Encyclopedia Britannica (1997). Fifteenth edition. Chicago: Encyclopedia Britannica, Incorporated.

Newman, B., O'Grady, M., Ryan, C., & Hemmes, N. (1993). Pavlovian conditioning of the tickle response of human subjects: Temporal and delay conditioning. *Perceptual and Motor Skills, 77*, 779–785.

Nilsen, D. (1990). Incongruity, surprise, tension, and relief: Four salient features associated with humor. *Thalia: Studies in Literary Humor, 9*, 22–27.

Norbeck, E. (1961). *Religion in primitive society*. New York: Harper & Row.

Norbeck, E. (1974). *Religion in human life: Anthropological views*. New York: Holt, Rinehart & Winston.

Nosanchuk, T. A., & Lightstone, J. (1974). Canned laughter, public and private conformity. *Journal of Personality and Social Psychology, 29*, 153–156.

Obrdlik, A. J. (1942). Gallows humor: A sociological phenomenon. *American Journal of Sociology, 47*, 709–716.

O'Connell, W. E. (1958). A study of the adaptive functions of wit and humor. Doctoral dissertation, The University of Texas.

O'Connell, W. E. (1960). The adaptive functions of wit and humor. *Journal of Abnormal and Social Psychology, 61*, 263–270.

O'Connell, W. E. (1964a). Multidimensional investigation of Freudian humor. *Psychiatric Quarterly, 38*, 1–12.

O'Connell, W. E. (1964b). Resignation, humor, and wit. *Psychoanalytic Review, 51*, 49–56.

O'Connell, W. E. (1968). Humor and death. *Psychological Reports, 22*, 391–402.

O'Connell, W. E. (1976). Freudian humour: The eupsychia of everyday life. In A. J. Chapman & H. C. Foot (Eds.), *Humour and laughter: Theory, research, and applications*. London: Wiley.

Oring, E. (1975). Everything is a shade of elephant: An alternative to a psychoanalysis of humor. *New York Folklore, 1*, 149–159.

Oring, E. (1999). Book review: Robert L. Latta's "The basic humor process: A cognitive-shift theory and the case against incongruity." *Humor: International Journal of Humor Research, 12*, 457–470.

Paskind, H. A. (1932). Effect of laughter on muscle tone. *Archives of Neurology and Psychiatry, 28*, 623–628.

Patrick, G. T. W. (1916). *The psychology of relaxation*. New York: Houghton.

Paulos, J. A. (1980). *Mathematics and humor*. Chicago: University of Chicago Press.

Pelto, P. J., & Pelto, G. H. (1978). *Anthropological research: The structure of inquiry*. New York: Cambridge University Press.

Penjon, A. (1893). Le rire et la liberte. *Revue Philosophique, 36*, 113–140.

Pereda, L. (1994). On humor. *Revista de Psicoanalisis, 51*, 159–170.

Pfeifer, K. (1994). Laughter and pleasure. *Humor: International Journal of Humor Research, 7*, 157–172.

Pharr, J. M. (1988). The moderating influence of humor and program context on the relationship between attitude-toward-the-ad and brand attitude. *Dissertation Abstracts International, 49 (3–A)*, 556–557.

Philbert, L. (1883). *Le rire: Essai litteraire, moral et psychologique*. Paris: Alcan.

Piaget, J. (1945/1951). *Plays, dreams, and imitation in childhood*. New York: Norton.

Piddington, R. (1933/1963). *The psychology of laughter: A study in social adaptation*. London: Figurehead.

Piddington, R. (1950). *An introduction to social anthropology*. Edinburgh: Oliver & Boyd.

Pitchford, H. G. (1960). The social function of humor. Unpublished doctoral dissertation, Emory University.

Plass, P. (1972). Freud and Plato on sophistic joking. *Psychoanalytic Review, 59*, 347–360.

Plato. (1871). Philebus (c. 355 B.C.). In B. Jowett (Ed.), *The dialogues of Plato*. London: Clarendon.

Pollio, H. R. (1983). Notes toward a field theory of humor. In P. E. McGhee & J. H. Goldstein (Eds.), *Handbook of humor research* (Vol. 1, *Basic issues*). New York: Springer-Verlag.

Pollio, H. R., Mers, R., & Lucchesi, W. (1972). Humor, laughter, and smiling: Some preliminary observations of funny behaviors. In J. H. Goldstein & P. E. McGhee (Eds.), *The psychology of humor: Theoretical perspectives and empirical issues*. New York: Academic Press.

Pollio, H. R., & Swanson, C. (1995). A behavioral and phenomenological analysis of audience reactions to comic performance. *Humor: International Journal of Humor Research, 8*, 5–28.

Porr, R. (1961). An experimental investigation of the function of sexual impulses and anxiety in humor. Unpublished doctoral dissertation, Yale University.

Prerost, F. J. (1975). The indication of sexual and aggressive similarities through humor appreciation. *Journal of Psychology, 91*, 283–288.

Prerost, F. J. (1977). Environmental conditions affecting the humour response: Developmental trends. In A. J. Chapman & H. C. Foot (Eds.), *It's a funny thing, humour*. Oxford, UK: Pergamon Press.

Prerost, F. J., & Brewer, R. E. (1974). The common elements of sex and aggression as reflected in humor preferences. *Personality and Social Psychology Bulletin, 1*, 189–191.

Priest, R. F. (1966). Election jokes: The effects of reference group membership. *Psychological Reports, 18*, 600–602.

Priest, R. F. (1972). Sexism, intergroup conflict, and joking. American Psychological Association, J. S. A. S., *Catalog of Selected Documents in Psychology, 2*, 15.

Priest, R. F., & Abrahams, J. (1970). Candidate preference and hostile humor in the 1968 elections. *Psychological Reports, 26*, 779–783.

Priestley, J. (1777/1971). *A course of lectures on oratory and criticism*. London: J. Johnson.

Prigatano, G., & Pribram, K. (1981). Humor and episodic memory following frontal versus posterior brain lesions. *Perceptual and Motor Skills, 53*, 999–1006.

Quintilian, M. F. (1714/1821–1825). *De institutione oratoria*. London: Heinemann.

Radcliffe-Brown, A. R. (1940). On joking relationships. *Africa, 13*, 195–210.

Radcliffe-Brown, A. R. (1949). A further note on joking relationships. *Africa, 19*, 133–140.

Radin, P. (1956/1969). *The trickster*. New York: Greenwood Press.

Ramsay, G. (1848). *Analysis and theory of the emotions*. London: W. Pickering.

218   THE PSYCHOLOGY OF HUMOR

Ransohoff, R. (1975). Some observations on humor and laughter in young adolescent girls. *Journal of Youth and Adolescence, 4*, 155–170.

Ransohoff, R. (1977). Developmental aspects of humour and laughter in young adolescent girls. In A. J. Chapman & H. C. Foot (Eds.), *It's a funny thing, humour*. Oxford, UK: Pergamon Press.

Rapp, A. (1947). Toward an eclectic and multilateral theory of laughter and humor. *Journal of General Psychology, 36*, 207–219.

Rapp, A. (1949). A phylogenetic theory of wit and humor. *Journal of Social Psychology, 30*, 81–96.

Rapp, A. (1951). *The origins of wit and humor*. New York: Dutton.

Raskin, V. (1985). *Semantic mechanisms of humor*. Boston: D. Reidel.

Reber, A. S. (1995). *The Penguin dictionary of psychology*. New York: Penguin.

Redfern, W. (1982). Guano of the mind—Puns in advertising. *Language and Communication, 2*, 269–276.

Redlich, F. C. (1960). Intellectual and emotional factors in appreciation of humor. *Journal of General Psychology, 62*, 25–35.

Reik, T. (1954). Freud and Jewish wit. *Psychoanalysis, 2*, 12–20.

Renouvier, C., & Prat, L. (1899). *La nouvelle monodologie*. Paris: Colin.

Ribot, T. A. (1896/1897/1939). *Psychologie des sentiments*. Paris: Alcan.

Richter, J. P. F. (1804/1813). *Vorschule der aesthetik*. Stuttgart: Cotta.

Ricketts, M. L. (1964). The structure and religious significance of the trickster-transformer-culture hero in the mythology of the North American Indians. Unpublished doctoral dissertation, University of Chicago.

Rickwood, L., & Price, G. (1988). Hedonic arousal, time intervals, and excitation transfer. *Current Psychology: Research and Reviews, 7*, 241–256.

Roberts, A. F., & Johnson, D. M. (1957). Some factors related to the perception of funniness in humor stimuli. *Journal of Social Psychology, 46*, 57–63.

Roeckelein, J. E. (1969). Auditory stimulation and cartoon ratings. *Perceptual and Motor Skills, 29*, 772.

Roeckelein, J. E. (1995). Naming in psychology: Analyses of citation counts and eponyms. *Psychological Reports, 77*, 163–174.

Roeckelein, J. E. (1996a). Citation of *laws* and *theories* in textbooks across 112 years of psychology. *Psychological Reports, 79*, 979–998.

Roeckelein, J. E. (1996b). Contributions to the history of psychology: CIV. Eminence in psychology as measured by name counts and eponyms. *Psychological Reports, 78*, 243–253.

Roeckelein, J. E. (1998). *Dictionary of theories, laws, and concepts in psychology*. Westport, CT: Greenwood Press.

Rosenbaum, R. J. (1976). Toward a symbolic theory of humor: A Jungian perspective. Unpublished doctoral dissertation, California School of Professional Psychology, San Diego.

Rosenwald, G. C. (1964). The relation of drive discharge to the enjoyment of humor. *Journal of Personality, 32*, 682–698.

Rothbart, M. K. (1976). Incongruity, problem-solving, and laughter. In A. J. Chapman & H. C. Foot (Eds.), *Humour and laughter: Theory, research, and applications*. London: Wiley.

Rousseau, J. J. (1758/1826/1926). *Lettre a M. d'Alembert*. Paris: Garnier.

Roy, D. F. (1959–1960). "Banana time": Job satisfaction and informal interaction. *Human Organization, 18*, 158–168.

Sacks, H. (1975). An analysis of the course of a joke's telling in conversation. In R. Bauman & J. Sherzer (Eds.), *Explorations in the ethnography of speaking*. Cambridge, UK: Cambridge University Press.

Sacks, H. (1978). Some technical considerations of a dirty joke. In J. Schenkein (Ed.), *Studies in the organization of conversational interaction*. New York: Academic Press.

Salutin, M. (1973). The impression management techniques of the burlesque comedian. *Sociological Inquiry, 43*, 159–168.

Salzen, E. A. (1963). Visual stimuli eliciting the smiling response in the human infant. *Journal of Genetic Psychology, 102*, 51–54.

Santayana, G. (1896/1904). *The sense of beauty*. New York: Scribner's.

Schachter, S., & Wheeler, L. (1962). Epinephrine, chlorpromazine, and amusement. *Journal of Abnormal and Social Psychology, 65*, 121–128.

Schalkwijk, F. (1996). Humor and psychoanalysis: Horse and carriage. *Tijdschrift voor Psychotherapie, 22*, 115–128.

Scheerer, M. (1966). An aspect of the psychology of humor. *Bulletin of the Menninger Clinic, 30*, 86–97.

Schenkein, J. N. (1972). Towards an analysis of natural conversation and the sense of "heheh." *Semiotica, 6*, 344–377.

Schick, C., McGlynn, R. P., & Woolam, D. (1972). Perception of cartoon humor as a function of familiarity and anxiety level. *Journal of Personality and Social Psychology, 24*, 22–25.

Schiller, P. (1938). A configurational theory of puzzles and jokes. *Journal of Genetic Psychology, 18*, 217–234.

Schimel, J. L. (1989). Some notes on nuance and subtlety in psychoanalysis: Humor. In A.-L. Silver (Ed.), *Psychoanalysis and psychosis*. Madison, CT: International Universities Press.

Schlosberg, H. (1947). The concept of play. *Psychological Review, 54*, 229–231.

Schmidt, H. E., & Williams, D. I. (1971). The evolution of theories of humour. *Journal of Behavioural Sciences, 1*, 95–106.

Schmidt, W. (1957). The analysis of laughter by means of paper-model experiments: A contribution to the solution of the problem of communicative functions of human expression. *Psychologische Beitrage, 3*, 223–264.

Schopenhauer, A. (1819/1906). *The world as will and idea*. London: Routledge & Kegan Paul.

Schrempp, G. (1995). Our funny universe: On Aristotle's metaphysics, Oring's theory of humor, and other appropriate incongruities. *Humor: International Journal of Humor Research, 8*, 219–228.

Schwartz, S. (1972). The effects of arousal on appreciation for varying degrees of sex-relevant humor. *Journal of Experimental Research in Personality, 6*, 241–247.

Scott, C., Klein, D., & Bryant, J. (1990). Consumer response to humor in advertising: A series of field studies using behavioral observation. *Journal of Consumer Research, 16*, 498–501.

Shadwell, T. (1671). *The humorists*. London: Herringman.

Shaftesbury, A. A. C. (1709/1737/1999). *Characteristics of men, manners, opinions, times*. London: Clarendon.

Shama, A., & Coughlin, M. (1979). An experimental study of the effectiveness of humor in advertising. *Educators' Conference Proceedings, American Marketing Association, 44*, 249–252.

Sharpe, R. (1987). Seven reasons why amusement is an emotion. In J. Morreall (Ed.), *The philosophy of laughter and humor*. Albany: State University of New York Press.

Shaw, F. J. (1960). Laughter: Paradigm of growth. *Journal of Individual Psychology, 16*, 151–157.

Sheehy-Skeffington, A. (1977). The measurement of humour appreciation. In A. J. Chapman & H. C. Foot (Eds.), *It's a funny thing, humour*. Oxford, UK: Pergamon Press.

Sherman, L. W. (1975). An ecological study of glee in small groups of preschool children. *Child Development, 46*, 53–61.

Sherman, L. W. (1985). Humor and social distance. *Perceptual and Motor Skills, 61*, 1274.

Shifman, R. B. (1994). Take my brand . . . please: Attitudinal effects of functional relationships among type of humorous appeal, context, and seriousness of salient product attributes in print advertisements. Unpublished doctoral dissertation, Temple University.

Shultz, T. R. (1972). The role of incongruity and resolution in children's appreciation of cartoon humor. *Journal of Experimental Child Psychology, 13*, 456–477.

Shultz, T. R. (1974). Order of cognitive processing in humour appreciation. *Canadian Journal of Psychology, 28*, 409–420.

Shultz, T. R. (1976). A cognitive-developmental analysis of humour. In A. J. Chapman & H. C. Foot (Eds.), *Humour and laughter: Theory, research, and applications*. London: Wiley.

Shultz, T. R. (1977). A cross-cultural study of the structure of humour. In A. J. Chapman & H. C. Foot (Eds.), *It's a funny thing, humour*. Oxford, UK: Pergamon Press.

Shurcliff, A. (1968). Judged humor, arousal, and the relief theory. *Journal of Personality and Social Psychology, 8*, 360–363.

Sidis, B. (1913). *The psychology of laughter*. New York: Appleton.

Sidney, P. (1591/1904). An apology for poetry. In G. G. Smith (Ed.), *Elizabethan critical essays*. (Vol. 1). Oxford: Clarendon.

Simpson, W. E., & Crandall, S. J. (1972). The perception of smiles. *Psychonomic Science, 29*, 197–200.

Singer, D. (1968). Aggression arousal, hostile humor, catharsis. *Journal of Personality and Social Psychology Monographs Supplement, 8*, 1–14.

Singer, D., Gollob, H., & Levine, J. (1967). Mobilization of inhibitions and the enjoyment of aggressive humor. *Journal of Personality, 35*, 562–569.

Sinnott, J. D., & Ross, B. M. (1976). Comparison of aggression and incongruity as factors in children's judgments of humor. *Journal of Genetic Psychology, 128*, 241–250.

Sivry, L. P. (1778/1970/1986). *Traite des causes physiques et morales du rire, relativement a l'art de l'exciter.* Geneva: Slatkine.

Skinner, B. F. (1938). *The behavior of organisms: An experimental analysis.* New York: Appleton-Century.

Skinner, B. F. (1953). *Science and human behavior.* New York: Macmillan.

Skinner, B. F. (1963). Behaviorism at fifty. *Science, 140*, 951–958.

Skinner, B. F. (1974). *About behaviorism.* New York: Knopf.

Skinner, B. F. (1979). *The shaping of a behaviorist.* New York: Knopf.

Smith, E. E., & Goodchilds, J. D. (1959). Characteristics of the witty group member: The wit as a leader. *American Psychologist, 14*, 375–376.

Smith, E. E., & Goodchilds, J. D. (1963). The wit in large and small established groups. *Psychological Reports, 13*, 273–274.

Smith, G. G. (1909). *English men of letters: Ben Jonson.* London: Bell.

Smith, P. K. (1982). Does play matter? Functional and evolutionary aspects of animal and human play. *Behavioral and Brain Sciences, 5*, 139–184.

Smith, R. E. (1973). The use of humor in the counterconditioning of anger responses: A case study. *Behavior Therapy, 4*, 576–580.

Smith, R. E., Ascough, J. C., Ettinger, R. F., & Nelson, D. A. (1971). Humor, anxiety, and task performance. *Journal of Personality and Social Psychology, 19*, 243–246.

Smith, S. (1846/1859). *Works.* London: Unwin.

Smith, S. M. (1993). Does humor in advertising enhance systematic processing? *Advances in Consumer Research, 20*, 155–158.

Smyth, M. M., & Fuller, R. G. C. (1972). Effects of group laughter on responses to humorous material. *Psychological Reports, 30*, 132–134.

Speck, P. S. (1988). On humor and humor in advertising: I and II. *Dissertation Abstracts International, 49 (3–A)*, 557–558.

Speck, P. S. (1991). The humorous message taxonomy: A framework for the study of humorous ads. *Current Issues and Research in Advertising, 13*, 1–44.

Spencer, H. (1860/1891). The physiology of laughter. In H. Spencer, *Essays: Scientific, political, and speculative.* London: Watts.

Spitz, R. A., & Wolf, K. M. (1946). The smiling response: A contribution to the ontogenesis of social relations. *Genetic Psychological Monographs, 34*, 57–125.

Spotts, H., Weinberger, M., & Parsons, A. (1997). Assessing the use and impact of humor on advertising effectiveness: A contingency approach. *Journal of Advertising, 26*, 17–32.

Springarn, J. E. (Ed.) (1908). *Critical essays of the seventeenth century.* Oxford: Clarendon.

Springarn, J. E. (1912). *Literary criticism in the Renaissance.* New York: Harcourt, Brace.

Sroufe, L. A., & Waters, E. (1976). The ontogenesis of smiling and laughter: A perspective on the organization of development in infancy. *Psychological Review, 83,* 173–189.

Staley, R., & Derks, P. (1995). Structural incongruity and humor appreciation. *Humor: International Journal of Humor Research, 8,* 97–134.

Stanley, H. M. (1898). Remarks on tickling and laughing. *American Journal of Psychology, 9,* 235–240.

Stearns, F. R. (1972). *Laughing: Physiology, pathophysiology, psychology, pathopsychology, and development.* Springfield, IL: Thomas.

Stendhal (Marie Henri Beyle). (1823/1907). *Racine et Shakespeare.* Paris: Larousse.

Stephenson, R. M. (1951). Conflict and control functions of humor. *American Journal of Sociology, 56,* 569–574.

Sternthal, B., & Craig, C. S. (1973). Humor in advertising. *Journal of Marketing, 37,* 12–18.

Steward, J. (1930). The ceremonial buffoon of the American Indian. *Papers of the Michigan Academy of Science, Arts, and Letters, 14,* 187–207.

Stewart, D. (1828/1849/1866). *The philosophy of the active and moral powers of man.* Boston: Wells, Lilly.

Strack, F., Martin, L., & Stepper, S. (1988). Inhibiting and facilitating conditions of the human smile: A nonobtrusive test of the facial feedback hypothesis. *Journal of Personality and Social Psychology, 54,* 768–777.

Strickland, J. F. (1959). The effect of motivation arousal on humor preferences. *Journal of Abnormal and Social Psychology, 59,* 278–281.

Sully, J. (1902). *Essay on laughter.* New York: Longmans, Green.

Suls, J. (1972). A two-stage model for the appreciation of jokes and cartoons: An information-processing analysis. In J. H. Goldstein & P. E. McGhee (Eds.), *The psychology of humor: Theoretical perspectives and empirical issues.* New York: Academic Press.

Suls, J. (1975). The role of familiarity in the appreciation of humor. *Journal of Personality, 43,* 335–345.

Suls, J. (1977). Cognitive and disparagement theories of humour: A theoretical and empirical synthesis. In A. J. Chapman & H. C. Foot (Eds.), *It's a funny thing, humour.* Oxford, UK: Pergamon Press.

Suls, J. (1983). Cognitive processes in humor appreciation. In P. E. McGhee & J. H. Goldstein (Eds.), *Handbook of humor research* (Vol. 1, *Basic issues*). New York: Springer-Verlag.

Svebak, S. (1974). A theory of sense of humor. *Scandinavian Journal of Psychology, 15,* 99–107.

Svebak, S. (1975). Styles in humour and social self-images. *Scandinavian Journal of Psychology, 16,* 79–84.

Sykes, A. J. M. (1966). Joking relationships in an industrial setting. *American Anthropologist, 68,* 188–193.

Tanaka, K. (1992). Puns in advertising—A pragmatic approach. *Lingua, 87,* 91–102.

Tarachow, S. (1949). Remarks on the comic process and beauty. *Psychoanalytic Quarterly, 18,* 215–226.

Taylor, R. (1994). *Guinness book of sitcoms.* London: Guinness.

Tedeschi, J. T. (1974). Attributions, liking, and power. In T. Huston (Ed.), *Foundations of interpersonal attraction*. New York: Academic Press.

Temple, W. (1692/1750). *Works of Sir William Temple: Of poetry*. London: T. Woodward.

Thomson, M. C. (1927). *The springs of human action*. New York: Appleton.

Tierney, W. (1991). The influence of arousal and positive affect on humor perception and response. Unpublished doctoral dissertation, City University of New York.

Tomkins, S. (1962). *Affect, imagery, consciousness* (Vol. 1, *The positive affects*). New York: Springer.

Trice, A. (1982). Ratings of humor following experience with unsolvable tasks. *Psychological Reports, 51,* 1148.

Tsur, R. (1994). Droodles and cognitive poetics: Contribution to an aesthetic of disorientation. *Humor: International Journal of Humor Research, 7,* 55–70.

Ullmann, L. P., & Lim, D. T. (1962). Case history material as a source of the identification of patterns of response to emotional stimuli in a study of humor. *Journal of Consulting Psychology, 26,* 221–225.

Unger, L. (1995). A cross-cultural study on the affect-based model of humor in advertising. *Journal of Advertising Research, 35,* 55–71.

Unger, L. (1996). The potential for using humor in global advertising. *Humor: International Journal of Humor Research, 9,* 133–168.

Vaid, J. (1999). The evolution of humor: Do those who laugh last? In D. Rosen & M. Luebbert (Eds.), *Evolution of the psyche*. Westport, CT: Praeger.

Valentine, C. W. (1942). *The psychology of early childhood*. London: Methuen.

Vandeberg, M. (1987). Puns in Spanish advertising—An Americanized cultural addition to the Spanish classroom. *Hispania—A Journal Devoted to the Teaching of Spanish and Portuguese, 70,* 684–690.

VanHooff, J. A. R. A. M. (1972). A comparative approach to the phylogeny of laughter and smiling. In R. A. Hinde (Ed.), *Nonverbal communication*. New York: Cambridge University Press.

VanOlst, E. (1971). *The orienting reflex*. The Hague: Mouton.

Veatch, T. C. (1998). A theory of humor. *Humor: International Journal of Humor Research, 11,* 161–215.

Ventis, W. L. (1973). Case history: The use of laughter as an alternative response in systematic desensitization. *Behavior Therapy, 4,* 120–122.

Voltaire, F. M. A. (1764/1816/1932/1994). Le Rire. In *Dictionnaire philosophique*. Paris: Klincksieck.

Wallis, W. D. (1922). Why do we laugh? *Scientific Monthly, 15,* 343–347.

Walsh, J. J. (1928). *Laughter and health*. New York: Appleton.

Ware, A. P. (1999). What is a sense of humor?: Identification of behavioral content, cognitive templates, and cue utilization patterns in judgments of the construct of humor. *Dissertation Abstracts International, 60 (3–B),* 1342.

Warner, W. L. (1959/1975). *The living and the dead: A study of the symbolic life of Americans*. New Haven, CT: Yale University Press.

Warton, J. (1754/1802/1807). Adventurer. In *British Essayists*. (Vol. 25). London: J. Johnson.

Washburn, R. W. (1929). A study of the smiling and laughing of infants in the first year of life. *Genetic Psychology Monographs, 6*, 397–535.

Watson, J. B. (1913). Psychology as the behaviorist views it. *Psychological Review, 20*, 158–177.

Watson, J. B. (1919/1929). *Psychology from the standpoint of a behaviorist.* Philadelphia, PA: Lippincott.

Watson, J. B. (1925/1958). *Behaviorism.* New York: Norton.

Watson, J. B. (1928). *The ways of behaviorism.* New York: Norton.

Watson, J. B., & McDougall, W. (1929). *The battle of behaviorism.* New York: Norton.

Weinberger, M. G., & Campbell, L. (1990–1991). The use and impact of humor in radio advertising. *Journal of Advertising Research, 30*, 44–51.

Weinberger, M., & Gulas, C. (1992). The impact of humor in advertising—A review. *Journal of Advertising, 21*, 35–39.

Weinberger, M., & Spotts, H. (1989). Humor in U. S. versus U. K. TV advertising—A comparison. *Journal of Advertising, 18*, 39–44.

Weinberger, M., Spotts, H., & Campbell, L. (1995). The use and effect of humor in different advertising media. *Journal of Advertising Research, 35*, 44–56.

Weiner, E., & Lorenz, A. (1994). Initiation of a behavioral scientist: Lessons learned from a boy who wouldn't poop. *Family Systems Medicine, 12*, 73–79.

Weisfeld, G. E. (1993). The adaptive value of humor and laughter. *Ethology and Sociobiology, 14*, 141–169.

Whetstone, G. (1578/1904). Dedication to Promos and Cassandra. In G. G. Smith (Ed.), *Elizabethan critical essays.* (Vol. 1). Oxford: Clarendon.

Wilcox, G., & Moriarty, S. (1984). Humorous advertising in the Post, 1920–1939. *Journalism Quarterly, 61*, 436–439.

Wildavsky, A. (1994). Freud on jokes: A postconscious evaluation. In L. B. Boyer & R. M. Boyer (Eds.), *Essays in honor of George A. DeVos.* Hillsdale, NJ: Analytic Press.

Wilde, L. (1976). *How the great comedy writers create laughter.* Chicago: Nelson-Hall.

Williams, C., & Cole, D. L. (1964). The influence of experimentally induced inadequacy feelings upon the appreciation of humor. *Journal of Social Psychology, 64*, 113–117.

Willis, E. (1967). *Writing television and radio programs.* New York: Holt, Rinehart & Winston.

Willmann, J. M. (1940). An analysis of humor and laughter. *American Journal of Psychology, 53*, 70–85.

Wilson, C. O. (1931). A study of laughter situations among young children. Unpublished doctoral dissertation, University of Nebraska.

Wilson, G. A. (1989). Towards a computational model of humor. *Dissertation Abstracts International, 50 (2–B)*, 774.

Wilson, G. D., & Brazendale, A. H. (1973). Sexual attractiveness, social attitudes, and response to risque humour. *European Journal of Social Psychology, 3*, 95–96.

Wilson, K. M. (1927). Sense of humor. *Contemporary Review, 131*, 628–633.

Wilson, T. (1560/1909/1994). *The art of rhetorique*. Oxford: Clarendon.

Winick, C. (1976). The social contexts of humor. *Journal of Communication, 26,* 124–128.

Winterstein, A. (1934). Contributions to the problem of humor. *Psychoanalytic Quarterly, 3,* 303–316.

Wolfenstein, M. (1954). *Children's humor: A psychological analysis*. Glencoe, IL: Free Press.

Wolff, H. A., Smith, C. E., & Murray, H. A. (1934). The psychology of humor. I. A study of responses to race-disparagement jokes. *Journal of Abnormal and Social Psychology, 28,* 341–365.

Wolosin, R. J. (1975). Cognitive similarity and group laughter. *Journal of Personality and Social Psychology, 32,* 503–509.

Woodworth, R. S. (1921). *Psychology: A study of mental life*. New York: Holt.

Woolgar, S. (Ed.) (1988). *Knowledge and reflexivity*. London: Sage.

Worthen, R., & O'Connell, W. E. (1969). Social interest and humor. *International Journal of Social Psychology, 15,* 179–188.

Wu, B., Crocker, K., & Rogers, M. (1989). Humor and comparatives in ads for high-involvement and low-involvement products. *Journalism Quarterly, 66,* 653.

Wyer, R. S., & Collins, J. E. (1992). A theory of humor elicitation. *Psychological Review, 99,* 663–688.

Yorukoglu, A. (1974). Children's favorite jokes and their relation to emotional conflicts. *Journal of Child Psychiatry, 13,* 677–690.

Yorukoglu, A. (1977). Favorite jokes of children and their dynamic relation to intrafamilial conflicts. In A. J. Chapman & H. C. Foot (Eds.), *It's a funny thing, humour*. Oxford, UK: Pergamon Press.

Young, R. D., & Frye, M. (1966). Some are laughing: Some are not—why? *Psychological Reports, 18,* 747–754.

Zeising, A. (1855). *Aesthetische forschungen*. Frankfurt: Meidinger.

Zelazo, P. R. (1971). Smiling to social stimuli: Eliciting and conditioning effects. *Developmental Psychology, 4,* 32–42.

Zelazo, P. R. (1972). Smiling and vocalizing: A cognitive emphasis. *Merrill-Palmer Quarterly, 18,* 349–365.

Zenner, W. (1970). Joking and ethnic stereotyping. *Anthropological Quarterly, 43,* 93–113.

Zhang, Y. (1994). Audience involvement and persuasion in humorous advertising. *Dissertation Abstracts International, 54 (11–A),* 4182.

Zhang, Y. (1996). Responses to humorous advertising: The moderating effect of need for cognition. *Journal of Advertising, 25,* 15–32.

Zhang, Y., & Zinkhan, G. (1991). Humor in television advertising—The effects of repetition and social setting. *Advances in Consumer Research, 18,* 813–818.

Zigler, E., Levine, J., & Gould, L. (1966a). Cognitive processes in the development of children's appreciation of humor. *Child Development, 37,* 507–518.

Zigler, E., Levine, J., & Gould, L. (1966b). The humor response of normal, institutionalized retarded, and noninstitutionalized retarded children. *American Journal of Mental Deficiency, 71,* 472–480.

Zigler, E., Levine, J., & Gould, L. (1967). Cognitive challenge as a factor in children's humor appreciation. *Journal of Personality and Social Psychology, 6,* 332–336.

Zijderveld, A. C. (1968). Jokes and their relation to social reality. *Social Research, 35,* 286–311.

Zijderveld, A. C. (1983). The sociology of humour and laughter. *Current Sociology, 31,* 1–99.

Zillmann, D. (1977). Humour and communication. Introduction to symposium. In A. J. Chapman & H. C. Foot (Eds.), *It's a funny thing, humour.* Oxford, UK: Pergamon Press.

Zillmann, D., & Bryant, J. (1974). Retaliatory equity as a factor in humor appreciation. *Journal of Experimental Social Psychology, 10,* 480–488.

Zillmann, D., & Bryant, J. (1980). Misattribution theory of tendentious humor. *Journal of Experimental Social Psychology, 16,* 146–160.

Zillmann, D., & Cantor, J. R. (1972). Directionality of transitory dominance as a communication variable affecting humor appreciation. *Journal of Personality and Social Psychology, 24,* 191–198.

Zinkhan, G., & Gelb, B. (1987). Humor and advertising effectiveness re-examined. *Journal of Advertising, 16,* 66–68.

Zinkhan, G., & Gelb, B. (1990). Humor repetition and advertising effectiveness. *Advances in Consumer Research, 17,* 438–441.

Zinkhan, G., & Johnson, M. (1994). Use of parody in advertising. *Journal of Advertising, 23,* 3–8.

Ziv, A. (1979). Sociometry of humor: Objectifying the subjective. *Perceptual and Motor Skills, 49,* 97–98.

CHAPTER 4

Differential and Functional Aspects of Humor

This chapter is divided into two main sections: Differences in Humor Appreciation, and Functions of Humor. Major source materials for these sections are taken from early classical studies and current books, periodicals, and journals with an emphasis on the *psychological* literature.

DIFFERENCES IN HUMOR APPRECIATION

The core of humor can be best abstracted by the fundamental scientific method of concomitant variations, and, if the same content is humorous to one person and less so (or not at all) to another, we have, not only the interesting fact of an individual difference, but also the possibility of inquiring further into other individual differences that may perhaps come to be regarded as the "reason" for the difference and thus the "explanation" of the humor when it occurs.

—H. Barry, 1928

The aim (of this study) . . . is two-fold: to determine whether or not certain individuals show a preference for certain classes of funny things consistently enough to justify the supposition that there are individual differences in the sense of humor; and to determine whether or not differences in the sense of humor correspond with certain temperamental tendencies.

—P. Kambouropoulou, 1930

Take my wife . . . please.

—H. Youngman, 1981

There seems to be general agreement, among humor researchers and laypersons alike, that there is considerable variability across individuals in the degree to which they possess a sense of humor; however, when we begin to ask what, exactly, researchers and laypeople mean by "sense of humor," and how they conceptualize individual differences in this trait, we encounter a great deal of disagreement.

—R. A. Martin, 1998

Individuals behave differently in humor experiments and this can not be ascribed only to failure to keep the conditions equal for everybody.

—W. Ruch, 1998

Individual, Personality, and Gender Differences

One of the earliest investigations of individual differences in humor (cf: "nomothetic versus idiographic aspects" in Keith-Spiegel, 1972, pp. 24–25) published in the psychological literature is by Polyxenie Kambouropoulou (1926, 1930) who analyzed the material in "humor diaries" made by female participants over a seven-day period (students were asked to record in their diaries the things they laughed at and the things that amused them each day, and to mark these things as A, B, or C according to the degree of laughter or amusement that accompanied them).

In one study (Kambouropoulou, 1930), 100 diaries containing 4,217 humorous events/episodes were collected and analyzed (it was noticed that there was a tendency for the diary student-authors of higher academic standing to write the longer diaries, and this may have been due either to their actual observation of a greater number of funny things, or to their concern and conscientiousness regarding the academic assignment). In another study (Kambouropoulou, 1926), the material contained in 70 student-authored "humor diaries" was analyzed and classified.

Based upon the use of such a methodology involving "humor diary" content analyses, Kambouropoulou (1926, 1930) concludes that there is a fair degree of consistency to types of humor shown by the diary authors, and that these types may be characterized primarily as the "personal" and the "impersonal." The former type may be subdivided into "passive personal" and "directed personal," and the latter type subdivided into the perceptions of "incongruity in situations" and "incongruity in ideas" (or the perception of "nonsense"). Moreover, the "personal" class of humor (also called the "superiority" class) is that type of humor that involves the enjoyment of the frailty, weakness, or inferiority of another person, and the "impersonal" class involves the enjoyment of the incongruity/nonsense aspect of humorous events. Further, Kambouropoulou (1930) found that preference for personal ("superiority") humor goes together with greater extraversion and greater "confidence in social intercourse." Kambouropoulou also asserts that the personal and impersonal types of differences in humor appreciation need to be related experimentally to temperament and character, and the relative influence of these—along with the influence of mental ability—needs to be determined before the phenomenon of sense of humor can be understood completely.

Another early study in the psychological literature on individual differences in humor was conducted by Barry (1928) who attempted to show that humor may be approached from the aspect of meaningful content in which some topics are humorous to some persons and not to others. [Note: Barry presents an extensive table of the humorous materials used in his study.] The following are among Barry's conclusions: there are marked individual differences in humor; humor may be classified into types according to meaningful content; topics that evoke a humorous reaction from an individual seem to be "loaded" frequently for that person with an unpleasant emotional affect; it is likely that the humor is due to a change of affective tone of the original perception from unpleasant to neutral or pleasant; incongruity and suddenness seem to be incidental rather than primary factors; and introspections tend to be unreliable because of the repressions induced by the unpleasant component of the perception and because of an apparent tendency for the participant to rationalize.

In another early study of individual differences in humor—in this case, relating humor to *other* personality traits—Landis and Ross (1933) asked participants (390 female and male students) to rate and classify jokes that were presented in a standardized fashion. Additionally, all participants took the following tests: a humor test containing seven categories of humor (humor based on: quantity, incongruity, the unexpected, truth, superiority, repression, and the ridiculous), an introversion-extroversion scale, and an intelligence test. Landis and Ross found that those students scoring high as "extroverts" had a greater tendency to place jokes in a "truth" category and to value such jokes, whereas those students scoring high as "introverts" were more prone to place jokes in a "repression" category and to prefer this category. Landis and Ross (1933, p. 174) also state that "the judgments which assign the jokes at various categories of humor reflect true differences in performance both between individuals, between different social groups, and between the sexes" (cf: Stump, 1939).

A series of studies on humor was conducted in the late 1930s and early 1940s by Omwake (1937, 1939, 1942). In one case (Omwake, 1937, p. 692), she admits to being impressed by the subjective nature of the study of sense of humor and by the importance of elements apart from the humor stimulus (e.g., the time and place, the previous experience and knowledge of the participant, and the participant's physical and mental set); accordingly, she offers only a comparison of humorous tastes of groups of people having certain characteristics in common, such as age, sex, education, etc. Among Omwake's (1937) findings are (cf: R. Wells, 1934): when 12 heterogeneous jokes were ranked with respect to humor by over 400 high school and college students, no single joke was marked consistently as "best" or "poorest"; adolescent boys show a significantly greater liking for the "shady" jokes than do the girls of the same age and the older college students; and there is a tendency for students to rate themselves high on: possession of a sense of humor, ability to understand the point of a joke, acceptance of an unconventional joke without being shocked, and enjoyment of a good pun. In later studies, Omwake (1939) found that measured levels of intelligence failed to show up as a determining factor in the comprehension of jokes; however, she also found (Omwake, 1942) that sense of humor was modified more by differences in participants' grade levels than by the variations due to sex/gender.

In an early doctoral dissertation on individual differences and the psychology of humor, Sears (1934) identified two major factors determining the appreciation of jokes in different types of *personality*: the schematic/cognitive and the thematic/orectic. Sears employed joke materials having themes dealing with some degree of social inhibition, such as sexuality, scatology, and superiority. In another early dissertation on humor, J. M. Williams (1945) found two groups of factors, somewhat similar to those of Sears (cf: Kambouropoulou, 1930), which she called "personal" and "impersonal" attitudes; the former type was associated more with joke appreciation in which some emotional tendency (especially "superiority") played the major part, and the latter attitude type of individual preferred jokes depending largely on humor of "incongruity" and "the fantastic"; moreover, the "personal" type showed a tendency to extraversion, and the "impersonal" type showed a tendency to introversion.

In a series of factorial analysis studies on the relationship between *personality* and sense of humor, R. B. Cattell and L. B. Luborsky (see Cattell & Luborsky, 1946, 1947; Luborsky & Cattell, 1947) found—in one case (Luborsky & Cattell, 1947)—that some of Guilford-Martin's Personality Factors correlated significantly with some of their own derived "humor clusters" (cf: Yarnold & Berkeley, 1954). In another case, Cattell and Luborsky (1947, pp. 417–418) use the following contingent labels to define their 13 "humor clusters": debonair sexuality, derision-superiority, blunt reality, disregard of conventions, anti-authoritarian ridicule of customary deference-receiving persons, repressed male passivity versus resigned male dominance, sturdy irony/dominance, playfulness, bringing surprise/discomfiture to well-meaning people, extravert aggression, cynicism, naïve self-composure, and unsophisticated/good-natured play. Also, they identified *five* general personality factors corresponding to the following: good-natured self-assertion/assurance, rebellious dominance, easy-going sensuality versus sex-repressed aggressiveness, passive/resigned derision, and urbane sophistication (cf: Andrews, 1943, who suggested *six* factors based upon his participants' humor responses: derision-superiority, reduction to debauchery, subtlety, play on words/ideas, sexual, and ridiculous wisecracks).

Eysenck (1942, 1943, 1947) made empirical investigations of individual differences in sense of humor and discovered little conformity in the sense of general agreement regarding the relative humor values of various individual jokes or different kinds of humorous material (e.g., cartoons, limericks, verses); this finding is in agreement with studies by Stump (1939), Heim (1936), and Omwake (1939). According to Eysenck (1942, 1947), the three aspects of cognition, conation, and affection are stressed by theories of humor that give preeminence to incongruity (e.g., contrast between ideas, deceived ideational expectation, conflict; cf: Bruner & Postman, 1949), to superiority/disparagement, and to emotionality (e.g., positive laughter; relief from tension).

Eysenck's factor analyses produced a single factor that represents the total amount of "fun" that a participant derives from comic verses, jokes, and cartoons, and a bipolar factor that reflects preferences for "cognitive" (sudden, insightful integration of contradictory or incongruous ideas, attitudes, or sentiments) versus "orectic" (sexual/aggressive content) jokes (cf: Sordoni, 1980); evidence from studies of humor with child, normal adult, and neurotic adult participants indicates that the tastes/preferences of introverts tend toward "cognitive" humor, while those of extraverts tend toward "orectic" humor (cf: Grziwok & Scodel, 1956; Lynn, 1981; Ruch, 1992; Wilson & Patterson, 1969). Additionally, Eysenck's analyses indicate three specific factors that could be used to classify a person's sense of humor along three dimensions of humor preference: liking for sexual versus nonsexual jokes, liking for simple versus complex jokes, and liking for personal versus impersonal jokes.

Leventhal and Safer (1977) note that there are two broadly different strategies for the study of individual differences in humor appreciation: the *traditional* individual differences search for factors comprising the humor domain; and the *theory-directed* personality factors. Leventhal and Safer discuss the traditional individual differences approach, as well as three types of theory (social-cultural, cognitive, and affective), as guides for the study of individual differences in humor appreciation. Based upon their review of the two approaches, Leventhal and Safer conclude that the traditional approach has not been fruitful for both methodological and conceptual reasons and, instead, suggest that humor research should apply personality models to the sociocultural, cognitive, and affective factors in humor. Also, they suggest that the personality models provide: a sequential theory of the humor experience, the social situation establishing the conditions (initial perception and readiness) for the action of cognitive processes that construct incongruity units (perceptual interpretation), and the integration of these units at a second stage with an affective category; these factors, then—taken together—make up the humor experience.

Leventhal and Safer assert that individual differences exist in each of these domains: in sociocultural background, in roles and role relationships, in cognitive factors for the understanding of rule structures, in intellectual tempo responsible for forming incongruity units, and in expressiveness and willingness to enjoy or sustain emotional experience. Further, Leventhal and Safer maintain that the study of individual differences in each of these areas will require the development of refined measuring devices and the use of these measures in an experimental setting where situational factors are varied; only when one can predict which participants will be affected by specific situational variables, and not by others, can psychologists be sure that the individual difference measures are assessing a specific, underlying, conceptual factor.

Other studies which discuss *individual and personality differences* in humor include the following: M. Andrews (1990), T. Andrews (1943), Avant (1982), Bartholomew (1984), Bell, McGhee, and Duffey (1986), Bergen (1998), Berger and Wildavsky (1994), Bobo (1989), Brisland, Castle, and Dann (1977), Brodzinsky (1977), Brodzinsky and Rightmyer (1980), W. Carpenter (1925), Carroll (1989), Cattell and Tollefson (1963), Cetola (1980), Cleary (1991), Craik and Ware (1998), Darmstadter (1964), Deckers (1998), Dooley (1941), Elbert (1961), Fern (1989), Fine (1975), Fine and Martin (1990), Fisher and Fisher (1983), Foot, Smith, and Chapman (1977), Forabosco and Ruch (1994), Fry and Allen (1975), Galinkin (2000), Gavanski (1986), Goldstein (1970a), L. Graham (1958), Grossman (1966), Haggard (1942), Hampes (1999), Hehl and Ruch (1985), Hirt and Genshaft (1982), Honeycutt and Brown (1998), Hoppe (1976), Janus (1975), A. M. Johnson (1990b), Juni (1985), Kelling (1971), Khoury (1978), P. Kline (1977a), Korotkov and Belicki (1989), Kuiper and Martin (1993, 1998), Kuiper, McKenzie, and Belanger (1995), Lamb (1980), Lee and Griffith (1960, 1963), Lefcourt (1996), Lefcourt and Davidson (1991), Lefcourt, Davidson, Shepherd, Phillips, Prkachin, and Mills (1995), Lefcourt and Shepherd (1995), Lundy (1999), Manke (1998), Marek (1989), Martin and Kuiper (1999), Martin, Kuiper, and Westra (1989), Martin and Lefcourt (1984), Masten (1989), McClure (1989), McFadden (1984), McGhee (1968, 1979, 1983a), McGhee, Ruch, and Hehl (1990), Miller and Bacon (1971), Monson (1966), Muir (2000), Nevo, Aharonson, and Klingman (1998), J. K. Newton (1993), Nias and Wilson (1977a,b), Nilsen (1988), O'Connell (1964a,b, 1977), O'Connell and Peterson (1964), J. Olson (1992), Olson and Roese (1995), O'Neill, Greenberg, and Fisher (1992), Oring (1984, 1994), Overlade (1954), Pearson (1982), Petry and Meyer (1987), Pollio, Edgerly, and Jordan (1972), Pollio and Mers (1974), Prerost (1982, 1984b, 1993a,b), Redlich (1960), Reutener and Kazak (1976), A. F. Roberts (1958), Roberts and Johnson (1957), V. Rosen (1963), Rosenfeld, Giacalone, and Tedeschi (1983), Ruch (1988, 1994, 1998), Ruch, Busse, and Hehl (1996), Ruch and Deckers (1993), Ruch and Hehl (1983, 1987, 1988), Ruch and Kohler

(1998), Shade (1990), Shapiro, Biber, and Minichin (1957), Shepherd (1990), Sheppard (1977a), Sherman (1977), Shultz (1974), Silverman (1995), Suls (1975), Tanner (1989), Thorson and Powell (1993a,b,c, 1994), Tollefson (1961), Trice (1985), Turner (1980), Verinis (1970a,b), Vitulli and Barbin (1991), Vogel (1958), Wanzer, Booth-Butterfield, and Booth-Butterfield (1996), Whissell (1998), Wicker, Thorelli, Barron, and Ponder (1981), Wicker, Thorelli, Barron, and Willis (1981), Williams and Cole (1964), Ziv (1992).

R. A. Martin (1998) notes that a great many theories of humor, laughter, and comedy have been advanced by philosophers, psychologists, and theorists over the centuries, but the great majority of the theories have not specifically examined individual variability in sense of humor (cf: Berlyne, 1969, pp. 809–811; Flugel, 1954, pp. 725–732). [Note: Martin (1998, pp. 16–17) observes a distinction between the terms *humor* and *sense of humor* where *humor* is "that quality of action, speech, or writing that excites amusement; oddity, jocularity, facetiousness, comicality, fun"; and *sense of humor* refers, more specifically, to "a personality trait or individual difference variable—or, more likely, a family of related traits or variables"; in this sense, *sense of humor* is viewed as a construct within the domain of personality psychology.] Traditionally, humor theorists have attempted to explain why we laugh at certain situations and not at others, and what kinds of mental, emotional, and motivational processes are involved in the perception and experience of humor. Martin notes that, by and large, the theorists have had little (in systematic, theoretical, or empirical ways) to say about why it is that some people laugh and engage in humor more than others, or why people differ in the sorts of things that amuse them (cf: Weaver, Masland, Kharazmi, & Zillmann, 1985, for the influence of *alcohol* on humor).

Martin discusses individual differences in humor within the framework of three main types of humor theories: psychoanalytic, incongruity, and superiority/disparagement. According to Martin, the implications of psychoanalytic theory (wherein Freud referred to the release of libidinal drive as the "tendentious" element of jokes, and the cognitive aspects as the "nontendentious" elements) for individual differences in sense of humor are very limited when seen through Freud's actual writings (Freud did not discuss, specifically, "individual differences," but rather emphasized processes assumed to occur in all people).

However, some post-Freudian psychoanalytic and nonpsychoanalytic writers have obtained results and derived hypotheses about individual differences based on Freud's work (e.g., Abelson & Levine, 1958; M. Berkowitz, 1954; Hom, 1966; Juni, 1982; Laffal, Levine, & Redlich, 1953; Lamb, 1968; Levine & Abelson, 1959; Levine & Rakusin, 1959; Levine & Redlich, 1955, 1960; O'Connell, 1960, 1976; Redlich, Levine, & Sohler, 1951; Rosenwald, 1964; Wilson & Patterson, 1969; however, for contrary findings, see: Byrne, 1956, 1958, 1961; Doris & Fierman, 1956; Epstein & Smith, 1956; Groch, 1974a,b; Hammes, 1962; Hammes & Wiggins, 1962; Holmes, 1969; Prerost, 1983a,

1984b; Ruch & Hehl, 1988; Sands, 1983; Spiegel, Keith-Spiegel, Abrahams, & Kranitz, 1969; Ullmann & Lim, 1962; cf: P. Kline, 1977b, who suggests that individuals finding sexual jokes funniest are those whose sexuality is normally repressed, that individuals finding aggressive jokes funniest are those whose aggression is normally repressed, that those individuals with a strong superego and whose main defense mechanism is repression won't laugh at jokes, that witty individuals—who most likely are more neurotic than the normal population—tend to have powerful unconscious aggression, and that individuals who are highly repressed are likely to prefer jokes with complex structure to simple jokes).

The implications of incongruity theory for individual differences in sense of humor (Martin, 1998) is that sense of humor may be viewed as being closely associated with creativity, with perceptual expectations, and, perhaps, with intelligence (cf: Babad, 1974; Bleedorn, 1982; Brackett, 1934; Brodzinsky & Rubien, 1976; Brumbaugh, 1939; Byrne, Terrill, & McReynolds, 1961; Clabby, 1980; Cunningham, 1962; Derks, Staley, & Haselton, 1998; Ding & Jersild, 1932; Fabrizi & Pollio, 1987a; Feingold & Mazzella, 1991; Ferris, 1972; Gregg, 1928; Kenny, 1955; Koppel & Sechrest, 1970; Levine & Redlich, 1960; Mones, 1939; Murdock & Ganim, 1993; O'Connell, 1969; Omwake, 1939; Piret, 1940; Rouff, 1975; Sordoni, 1980; Terry & Ertel, 1974; Treadwell, 1970; Webb, 1915; Wicker, 1985; Wynn-Jones, 1927, 1934; Ziv, 1980). Martin notes that the association of humor with creativity is most congenial with definitions of sense of humor that stress humor production/comprehension rather than appreciation, and with measurement approaches that emphasize ability, performance, and behavioral observation rather than the method of self-report. Another implication for incongruity theory for individual differences in humor is the increased focus on differences in cognitive style vis-à-vis sense of humor that includes ancillary concepts such as "cognitive complexity" (cf: Grove & Eisenman, 1970), "tolerance of ambiguity," "cognitive appraisal" (e.g., Kuiper, McKenzie, & Belanger, 1995), and "need for certainty." In this latter way, sense of humor may be regarded as a form of cognitive trait and, in contrast to the creativity-related approach, this approach places more emphasis on humor appreciation rather than on humor production (and, further, in contrast to the psychoanalytic approach, the cognitive approach stresses the structure of the preferred humorous stimuli rather than their thematic content). The measurement of sense of humor in the context of the cognitive style approach focuses on "typical performance" rather than a "maximal performance/ability" approach (e.g., Ruch & Hehl, 1998).

The few implications of the superiority/disparagement theories for individual differences in sense of humor are similar to the paucity of material found in Freud's work; the proponents of the superiority/disparagement approach typically have not discussed individual differences in sense of humor, but instead emphasize the dynamics presumed to exist in all individuals as they exhibit humor and laughter (cf: LaFave, Haddad, & Maesen, 1976, who assert that there is no such thing as "sense of humor," and refer to the concept as a "myopic illusion"). Researchers who study and advance the superiority or disparagement approaches to humor tend to focus on group—rather than individual—differences; a possible implication of this practice is that sense of humor is related predictably to general negative traits such as aggesssion, dominance, or hostility (e.g., Middleton, 1959; Middleton & Moland, 1959; Wolff, Smith, & Murray, 1934; cf: Byrne, 1956; Hetherington & Wray, 1964; Rosenwald, 1964; Ullmann & Lim, 1962; Zillmann, Bryant, & Cantor, 1974; Zillmann & Cantor, 1972, 1976).

One of the individual difference- and personality-related concepts that has been given a good deal of attention in the psychological literature on humor appreciation is that of *creativity*. Several theoretical and empirical studies of humor and creativity focus on the characteristics of creative people, finding that humor is related to creative personality (e.g., Amabile, 1987; F. Barron, 1982; Brodzinsky & Rubien, 1976; Clabby, 1979; Getzels & Jackson, 1962; Hauck & Thomas, 1972; Koestler, 1964; Kris, 1952; Lieberman, 1977; McGhee, 1976, 1980a; Rouff, 1975; Singer & Berkowitz, 1972; Thorson & Powell, 1993b; Weisberg & Springer, 1961). Other studies suggest that humor is a facilitator of the creative process, or vice-versa (e.g., Babad, 1974; M. Bruner, 1988; Cornelius & Casler, 1991; Derks & Hervas, 1988; O'Connell, 1969; Schoel & Busse, 1971; Treadwell, 1970; Ziv, 1976).

Humke and Schaefer (1996) note that although relationships have been found between *creativity* and humor, research has not led to definite conclusions because the definitions and measures of both constructs have considerable variation. One of the problems associated with humor measures is that they focus too narrowly on distinct aspects of the humor construct (cf: Thorson & Powell, 1993a, who developed a comprehensive measure, the Multidimensional Sense of Humor Scale, that includes various aspects of humor such as recognition of humor, appreciation of humor, playfulness, and use of humor as an adaptive coping mechanism).

The following selected studies indicate the relationships between *creativity* and humor. Smith and White (1965) conducted a study to test the following hypotheses: wit and creativity are positively correlated; defensiveness and creativity are negatively correlated; witty persons are effective leaders; and witty persons could be effective under stress; also, effects of sarcastic versus nonsarcastic wit were explored. The first two hypotheses were supported by Smith and White's data; there was a significant positive correlation between wit and creativity (cf: Koestler's, 1961, description of a witticism as a "creative act"); and there was a significant negative correlation between defensiveness and creativity. Also, it was found that less joking occurred under conditions of stress, and that there was a positive effect of sarcastic wits on group performance (cf: Fry, 1963).

Fabrizi and Pollio (1987a) assessed the relationships among measures of humor, creativity, and self-concept in early and late adolescents via use of observational, rating, and psychometric procedures (including direct observation of humorous events, and teachers', peers', and raters' judgments of humorousness and creativity). Their results provide a partial confirmation for, and a partial contrast with, previous findings concerning the relationship of humor to creativity. Consistent with previous studies, they found a number of positive relationships between measures of humor and creativity, but only for eleventh-grade students. However, their results do not show clear cut patterns between measures of humor and creativity for seventh-grade students. Moreover, Fabrizi and Pollio's results suggest that seventh-graders who are humorous are neither the most creative nor the most self-satisfied students; eleventh-graders who are humorous tend to score well on tests of creative ability as well as on teachers' ratings of creativity. Thus, for the seventh-grader, humor seems to be a sign of relatively low self-esteem, while for the eleventh-grader, it seems to be a sign of potential creative ability (cf: Fabrizi & Pollio, 1987b; Fisher & Fisher, 1981). Finally, in answering the question, "Are funny teenagers creative?," Fabrizi and Pollio (1987a) suggest that it seems to depend on the developmental level of the individual: during early adolescence, making one's peers laugh is a matter of going against authority, of being silly, or of acting out—there is little need for originality; during later stages of adolescence, however, making one's peers laugh is a more complex matter, and there is some requirement—within a secure sense of self—to be original and/or creative.

Ziv (1988c) presents theoretical and empirical evidence relating the concept of divergent thinking/creativity to humor. Ziv views humor as a two-dimensional concept that involves both appreciation and creativity. Creativity, according to Ziv, currently has a different meaning from that of almost all psychological writing prior to the 1960s (cf: Freud, 1950); until then, creativity was conceptualized as a rare talent and creative people were considered to be those able to produce something valuable in the fields of art and the sciences. The first widely accepted psychological theory of creativity was given by Wallas (1926) who described the creative process/act in four stages: preparation, incubation, illumination, and verification; thus creativity was formerly considered to involve long and tortuous mental operations, a high level of special skills and motivational aspects such as perseverance, need for achievement, and willingness to engage in hard work. However, as Ziv notes, psychological research on the relationship between creativity and humor uses a different meaning of creativity and special tests to measure it. For example, in contemporary thought, the concept of "divergent thinking" (cf: Guilford, 1956,

1959) has come to be considered as an important element in creativity where the unique feature of divergent thinking/production is that a variety of responses is exhibited, and the creative product is not completely determined by the given information. Most creativity tests today measure the following variables: fluency of thinking (including word, associational, expressional, and ideational fluency), flexibility, originality, and elaboration (cf: Torrance, 1974; Wallach & Kogan, 1965, for current and popular tests of creativity). In humor research, creativity is judged by the simple and obvious criteria of creating something judged by others to be humorous. Ziv (1988c) provides a description of humor measurement in humor research to help in understanding the relationship between creativity and humor; he gives conceptual and operational definitions of humor, and discusses the theoretical relation between humor and creativity. Ziv notes that while most research on humor focuses on humor appreciation, he describes a project developed at Tel Aviv University aimed at exploring and enhancing humor creativity among adolescents, as well as a project whose goal is to train teachers to use humor in the classroom (cf: Ziv, 1976, 1979, 1980, 1981, 1983, 1984, 1988b). Ziv concludes—based on experimental findings—that humor seems to be an efficient tool or device to use in developing creative thinking in adolescents.

Murdock and Ganim (1993) describe a study that examines the relationship between creativity and humor (13 definitions of humor and 11 theories of humor are identified and analyzed; cf: Figures 1, 2, pp. 62–65). Murdock and Ganim observe that the literature on creativity has been characterized by diversity in its definitions and theories as well as its approaches and methodologies; and humor has been included as an aspect of creativity by a number of researchers (e.g., Amabile, 1987; Arieti, 1976; Barron, 1982; Koestler, 1964; Maslow, 1954; VanGundy, 1982, 1984; cf: Ganim, 1992; MacHovec, 1988, pp. 75–79, 91). During the creative process, individuals go through a series of stages and steps that involve humor in some way, and the experience or manifestation of humor becomes a part of this overall creative activity (cf: Blatner, 1988; Cousins, 1979a; Freud, 1905/1916; Gordon, 1961; Koestler, 1964; Moody, 1978; Osborn, 1953; Parnes, 1967; Runco, 1996; VanGundy, 1984).

Murdock and Ganim assert that a lack of conceptual clarity about the relationship between creativity and humor has resulted in limitations in developing humor theory itself, and also has hindered the legitimacy of the study of humor as well. If creativity as a multidimensional phenomenon has credibility (cf: Isaksen & Murdock, 1990), then humor as one multifaceted aspect of it should be viewed more seriously as well. In this study, Murdock and Ganim found that in contrast to the diversity of content illustrated in the selected humor *definitions*, the content of humor *theories* was more integrated. Based on commonalities of definitions and key concepts, the 11 theories (i.e., ambivalence, arousal, biological/instinct/evolution, configurational, gallows, incongruity, psychoanalytic, release/relief, superiority, play/spontaneity, and surprise) were collapsed into three basic categories: play/spontaneity, release/relief, and incongruity/unexpected relationships. As with their collapsing of the definitional themes into the core category of integration and incongruity, Murdock and Ganim note that the collapse of humor theories into three categories indicates sufficient content commonality to encompass the other eight theories (the three theoretical core categories may provide a starting point for future research concerning the conceptual organization of the construct of humor).

Murdock and Ganim conclude that their analysis of creativity and humor definitions and theories indicates that there is a highly integrated relationship between both constructs; within the selected literature and parameters of their study which combines humor and creativity, they maintain that humor is sufficiently integrated to be considered a subset of creativity (cf: Harrington, 1990), and—in that respect—both humor and creativity may be productively studied within similar conceptual frameworks (e.g., one of the conceptual frameworks could be based on the three theoretical categories of play/spontaneity, incongruity/unexpected relationships, and release/relief).

Other studies that describe the relationships between *creativity* and humor include the following: Behrens (1974), Berg (1980), Bleedorn (1982), B. Cade (1982), Calvert (1968), Charney (1983), Cleland (1957), Colell and Domino (1980), Corbett (1990), Couturier, Mansfield, and Gallagher (1981), Derks (1987), Dimmer (1993), Escarpit (1969), Feingold and Mazzella (1991), Galloway (1994), Hampes (1993), Holt and Willard-Holt (1995), Kovac (1999a,b), Kuznetsova (1990), McGhee (1980a), Muthayya and Mallikarjunan (1969), Newman and Fiordalis (1985), Nilsen and Nilsen (1987), Reynolds (1989), Russo (1987), Shade (1991), Shibles (1979), K. Smith (1996), Stypulkowska (2000), Townsend, Torrance, and Wu (1981), Valett (1981), Westcott (1983), Wicker (1985), M. P. Wilson (1968), and Ziv and Gadish (1990a).

Although joking and humor appreciation have traditionally been considered an essentially masculine preserve in Western culture, particularly in the domains of sexual and aggressive humor (e.g., E. Fine, 1976; Freud, 1905/1916; Grotjahn, 1957, 1972), conflicting evidence has been found in research on *gender* differences in humor appreciation (see Wilson & Molleston, 1981). Also, although the majority of studies have produced data to support the notion of gender differences in preference for sexual and aggressive humor (e.g., Brodzinsky, Barnet, & Aiello, 1981; Cantor, 1976; Chapman & Gadfield, 1976; Hassett & Houlihan, 1979; Losco & Epstein, 1975; O'Connell, 1960; Terry & Ertel, 1974), several other studies have reported no gender differences (e.g., Boyer, 1981; M. Greenberg, 1979; Ingrando, 1980). It has been found that gender differences, when they occur, usually emerge when the humor contains material relevant to gender differences in general—in terms of motives, attitudes, and interests (Wilson & Molleston, 1981). Henkin and Fish

(1986) note that there have been few consistent gender differences experimentally obtained for nonsexual, nonhostile humor with the exception of consistently greater female appreciation of nonsense or absurd humor (e.g., Groch, 1974a; Hassett & Houlihan, 1979; Terry & Ertel, 1974).

Studies on the relationship between *gender/sex/sexuality* and humor appreciation also indicate the following generalizations (cf: Henkin & Fish, 1986; A. M. Johnson, 1992; Myers, Ropog & Rodgers, 1997). In general communicative interactions, men's humor is characterized by aggression, hostility, and competition (e.g., Palmer, 1994; Walker & Dresner, 1988) that often target women for disparagement (e.g., Cantor, 1976; Crawford & Gressley, 1991; Palmer, 1994). Women, on the other hand, are more inclined to employ self-deprecation, understatement, and irony (e.g., Walker & Dresner, 1988) as forms of humor (cf: Booth-Butterfield & Booth-Butterfield, 1991; Chapman & Gadfield, 1976; Cupchik & Leventhal, 1974; Rowe, 1995; Stillion & White, 1987; White, 1988). Men exceed women in their *preference* for aggressive humor, and men rate aggressive humor more highly than they do nonsense humor (e.g., More & Roberts, 1957; O'Connell, 1969; Svebak, 1975b). Women rate nonsense humor more highly than men do, and more highly than they rate aggressive humor (e.g., Gadfield, 1977; Groch, 1974a; Hassett & Houlihan, 1979; Malpass & Fitzpatrick, 1959; Terry & Ertel, 1974). Sex differences in lateralization may affect humor appreciation (e.g., Leventhal & Cupchik, 1975; A. M. Johnson, 1990a, 1992; cf: Gallivan, 1991, 1997; Gardner, 1981). It appears likely that the differences in one's sexual perspective influence one's perception of sexual and aggressive humor (e.g., Green, 1977; Mitchell, 1977, 1978).

Henkin and Fish (1986) suggest that the lack of consideration of *gender* in choice of humor stimuli constitutes one of the most prevalent sources of bias in humor research, and may be an important factor in explaining why researchers have often found women to be less amused than men by the humor presented to them. Typically, in humor research, male and female participants have been presented with cartoons or jokes created by men, depicting a male viewpoint (cf: Levine, 1976; Mitchell, 1977), and often employing aggressive or sexual humor. [Note: The journal *Medical Aspects of Human Sexuality* periodically carries sexual joke material under the heading of "Psychodynamics of Sexual Humor" (e.g., see 1985, Vol. *19*: February, pp. 196–201; March, pp. 168–174; June, pp. 210–214; November, pp. 80–84).]

In jokes depicting both genders, women are more frequently the victims of aggressive humor and the objects in sexual humor than are men (e.g., Cantor & Zillmann, 1973; Sheppard, 1977b). Women's failure to respond to these humorous stimuli as positively as men has been interpreted as support of a view of limited female interest in, and appreciation of, both sexual and aggressive humor in particular, and humor in general. Henkin and Fish (1986) note, also, that in those few studies where attempts have been made to depict both male and female viewpoints (e.g., Boyer, 1981; Brodzinsky, Barnet, & Aiello, 1981), other factors (e.g., lack of equal numbers of male- and female-oriented stimuli, lack of control for rated level of funniness of humor stimuli, and lack of control for degree of aggression or sexual victimization in the humor stimuli) have often not been well controlled (cf: Chapman & Gadfield, 1976; Hassett & Houlihan, 1979).

Apparently, what is needed to control such variables is an equal number of humor items (e.g., cartoons) that are identical except for the sex of the person who is the object/victim, and the sex of the person who is the subject/aggressor. The development of such a humor instrument has been attempted with aggressive humor, and has produced mixed results (cf: Cantor, 1976; Losco & Epstein, 1975; A. J. Williams, 1979). In light of the findings on humor in the context of participants' tendency to align themselves with characters in cartoons and jokes (e.g., members of various groups—including race, nationality, religion, and political affiliation—have tended to find jokes in which the "out-group" is disparaged to be more amusing than jokes in which members of the "in-group" are the butt of the humor; cf: LaFave, Haddad, and Marshall, 1974; Priest, 1972), it is reasonable to assume that the same findings should hold for the sexes. That is, men should prefer jokes in which women are the butt of the humor, and women should find jokes in which men are the butt to be funnier.

This type of pattern has been clearly established for men, but the picture for women is more complicated. A number of studies have indicated that women respond as expected: they either prefer jokes disparaging the opposite sex or show no gender preference (e.g., LaFave, 1972; Priest & Wilhelm, 1974). Other studies, however, have found that women prefer jokes in which women are disparaged (e.g., Cantor, 1976; Losco & Epstein, 1975). Henkin and Fish (1986) observe that such results have been interpreted in a number of ways, ranging from female masochism (e.g., Blanch, 1974), to female fear of disclosing male-directed aggression (e.g., Wyer, Weatherly, & Terrell, 1965), to greater conventionality and so greater acceptability of the more prevalent male-oriented, female-disparaging humor (e.g., Chapman & Gadfield, 1976); however, the notion that has been most productive in predicting results is the concept of the "reference group." Thus, in terms of humor appreciation, a joke would be predicted to be humorous to the extent to which it enhances a positive reference group ("in-group") or disparages a negative reference group ("out-group"), and nonhumorous to the extent that it does the opposite.

The following selected studies, chronologically arranged, also indicate the relationships between *gender/sex/sexuality* and humor appreciation/preferences. Felker and Hunter (1970) studied differences in responses to cartoon humor both from the aspect of differences in respondents' characteristics (i.e., gender and age differences) and differences in cartoon characteristics. Felker and Hunter's results indicate that women see cartoons as funnier than men, and adults see them as funnier than do adolescents; it was also discovered that cartoon subject material (i.e., adolescent male, adolescent female, adult male, adult female) did not differentially influence the ratings of the cartoons' humor. Felker and Hunter conclude that there are sex differences in the responses to cartoon humor, and such differences are not limited to the period of adolescence.

McGhee (1979, p. 201) asserts that the greatest single source of individual differences in humor may be whether the person is male or female. According to McGhee, the most obvious difference between adult male and female humor is that a man is more often than not the joke-teller, whereas a woman is typically in the position of reacting to humor (cf: Coser, 1959). Inasmuch as this difference does not appear until the end of the preschool years, it may be related to certain sex-role expectations in our society. Moreover, in occupational settings where a clear status difference exists between employees, individuals in positions of higher status initiate more jokes and other witty remarks than do people in low-status positions (cf: Coser, 1960); this finding supports the view that the humorist tends to have more social power than do others and, when sex differences are taken into account in such an occupational setting where women are assumed to occupy a lower status than men, women might be expected to initiate joking less frequently than men, and also to be more self-disparaging in their humor as well.

McGhee makes the common observation that humor which is sexual or aggressive is more popular among men than women (cf: Malpass & Fitzpatrick, 1959; Mulkay, 1988, pp. 134–151; Spiegel, Brodkin, & Keith-Spiegel, 1969; Terry & Ertel, 1974; Thomas, Shea, & Rigby, 1971), but he cautions that such a conclusion may be misleading because of the faulty research methods used in studies on the relationship between gender and humor. Consequently, McGhee suggests that there are no valid grounds for the assumption that adult men respond more to sexual humor than do women (cf: Chapman & Gadfield, 1976). According to McGhee (1979), we continue to know little about the development of sexual humor in children; moreover, there appears to be a pervasiveness of hostility in young boys' humor (cf: Groch, 1974b; King & King, 1973)—both in their appreciation, and initiation, of humorous events—that requires closer study.

Prerost (1984b) notes that experimental investigations of male and female responses to sexual stimuli have primarily been conducted during the decade 1974–1984. This empirical research focuses on nonhumorous pictorial and narrative stimuli; and results consistently indicate wide individual differences in the quality and magnitude of affective responses elicited by erotic stimuli. Individuals showing a positive affective pattern of response also typically oppose the restriction of erotica and engage in increased eye contact with persons of the opposite sex when sexually aroused (e.g., Griffit & Kaiser, 1978). On the other hand, those individuals showing a negative affective pattern when exposed to erotica are likely to label sexual stimuli as pornographic (as well as show disgust, anger, or nausea) and, when sexually aroused, avoid those of the opposite sex (e.g., Griffit & Kaiser, 1978); also, such patterns in this case are characteristic in individuals who possess conflicts, repressions, or maladjustments in the area of sexual functioning (e.g., Mosher, 1973).

Prerost attempted to relate participants' reactions to humorous erotic stimuli to sexual experience and satisfaction. Adult participants, both male and female, gave appreciation ratings of pictorial humorous sexual and aggressive stimuli following assessment of sexual activity. Results indicate that participants' reactions to stimulus material were significantly affected by the frequency of sexual expression and the degree of satisfaction with sexual experience. Further, although the men showed appreciation of all humor content to higher levels than the women, no differential pattern of preference emerged (cf: Prerost, 1975, 1980a; Prerost & Brewer, 1974) for the sexes. Prerost suggests that the similar patterns of humor appreciation found among men and women in his study indicates that the divergence of traditional sex-role expectations has relaxed as women here show a responsiveness to sexual stimuli traditionally afforded only to men.

Neuliep (1987) examined the influence of gender on perceived funniness of sexist and nonsexist jokes. Neuliep tested three hypotheses which argue that perceived funniness is, in part, a function of joke type (sexist and nonsexist), joker gender (male and female), and receiver gender (male and female). His results indicate that two of the three hypotheses are supported where: men perceive sexist humor as funnier than do women, and women perceive nonsexist humor as funnier than sexist humor (cf: Pearson, Miller, & Senter, 1983); also, it was found that joker gender had no significant impact on perceived funniness by men or women. Neuliep discusses his results within the framework of "muted group" theory (i.e., subordinate cultural groups may be muted within their society because the language they use has been created by a dominant cultural group; in American society, it is assumed here that women are a muted group).

Mundorf, Bhatia, Zillmann, Lester, & Robertson (1988) asked female and male participants to judge humorous jokes and cartoons representing three humor types: sexual, hostile, and nonsense. Results include the following observations: within the sexual and hostile humor category of material, the disparagement of men and women was balanced; men rated the sexual humor funnier than did the women (cf: Burns & Tyler, 1976); there was a parallel rating tendency for women and men for the hostile humor material; no gender difference was found for the enjoyment of nonsense humor; men enjoyed hostile humor more when women were victimized than when men were victimized (women showed a reversed tendency, contrary to previous research findings: they enjoyed hostile humor more when men were victimized than when women were victimized); a gender-specific enjoyment was indicated for jokes versus cartoons—while there was no gender difference for jokes, the men enjoyed the cartoons more than did the women (cf: Groch, 1974a; Malpass & Fitzpatrick, 1959). Mundorf et al. conclude that their results are consistent with predictions based upon the "disposition theory of humor" (e.g., Zillmann, 1983; Zillmann & Cantor, 1976; cf: other studies which support the dispositional theory of humor include: Chapman & Gadfield, 1976; LaFave, 1972; LaFave, Haddad, & Marshall, 1974; LaFave, McCarthy, & Haddad, 1973; Nevo, 1985).

Butland and Ivy (1990) briefly review research on humor and note the presence of a number of contradictions. For example, concerning the effects of humor on the recall of a message: two studies indicate that humor tends to enhance recall (Kaplan & Pascoe, 1977; Zillmann, 1980); four studies suggest that humor has a negative effect on recall (Cantor & Venus, 1980; Markiewicz, 1974; Sutherland, 1982; P. M.Taylor, 1972); other studies indicate that humor does not seem to affect recall (Bryant, Brown, Silberberg, & Elliott, 1981; Gruner, 1967, 1970; A. Kennedy, 1970; P. M. Taylor, 1964). Butland and Ivy observe a similar trend in the analyses of humor and source perception: four studies conclude that the use of humor enhances the perception of the source of a message (Gruner, 1967, 1970; A. Kennedy, 1970; Zillmann, 1980); four studies find that humor has a negative effect on source perception (Bryant, Brown, Silberberg, & Elliott, 1981; Markiewicz, 1972, 1974; P. M. Taylor, 1972); two studies support the notion that humor does not actually change source perception (Cantor & Venus, 1980; Lampton, 1971). In the context of *biological/sex* factors vis-à-vis humor (cf: Zillmann, 1983, who suggests that biological sex may not be the best predictor of humor appreciation; he advances the notion that psychological factors—such as an individual's psychological gender predisposition—offer a more fruitful approach), Butland and Ivy note that a provocative generalization stems from the dispositional theory of humor to the effect that *gender* of the disparaged victim affects the appreciation of humor (cf: Cantor, 1976; Groch, 1974a, b; Landis & Ross, 1933; Losco & Epstein, 1975; McGhee & Duffey, 1983b; Neuliep, 1987; O'Connell, 1960; Terry & Ertel, 1974; Zillmann & Stocking, 1976). Typically, men appreciate the disparagement of women over men and, based on such findings, it might be expected that women should appreciate the disparagement of men over women. However, some studies have shown that women enjoy humor that disparages women more than that which disparages men (e.g., Brodzinsky, Barnet, & Aiello, 1981; Cantor, 1976; Losco & Epstein, 1975; McGhee & Duffey, 1983b; Zillmann & Stocking, 1976).

Butland and Ivy's (1990) research was conducted in an attempt to clarify the sex differences concerning the dispositional theory and, in particular, to replicate and extend Cantor's (1976) study. In their study, Butland and Ivy take into account not only the participants' biological sex but their psychological sex role attitudes as well. Their results indicate that the hypothesized effects for biological sex and manipulations of disparaged roles in jokes (as based on Cantor's 1976 research) were not significant. In the case of one joke (cf: Wood, 1985), however, men had significantly greater appreciation for female-disparaging humor than did women. Further, results for male participants support the dispositional theory of humor (which is consistent with Cantor's research); also, a new trend was observed in women's responses to disparaging humor where there appears to be a shift in women's humor away from female-disparagement and toward male-disparagement (cf: Pearson, Miller, & Senter, 1983). Butland and Ivy conclude that their study underscores the lack of predictive value on humor appreciation of either biological sex or psychological sex role attitudes when examined alone; rather, a combination of these variables in humor studies is more likely to increase predictive power.

Lampert and Ervin-Tripp (1998) observe that—despite Freud's (1905/1916) early characterization of the three-way relationships between tellers, audiences, and targets—researchers on humor today generally focus on two-way relationships involving either tellers and the targets of their jokes, or audiences and their reactions to jokes with systematically varied targets, structures, and themes. In the area of *gender* differences and humor, this trend has resulted in a body of research centered around the presentation of published jokes and cartoons to men and women within a laboratory setting to see whether the two sexes differ in their preferences for humor with, typically, aggressive and sexual content and themes. However, as Crawford (1989, 1992) and Marlowe (1984–1985) note, this particular research paradigm carries with it a number of inherent problems, including: an absence of a social context, the use of nonrepresentative materials, and a lack of parallel between the public humor of the laboratory and the private humor of men and women in everyday life.

Thus, although men and women differ in their liking for a laboratory joke, the reason for the divergence may have nothing to do with differences in the personal enjoyment of the structure or theme of the joke, but rather may have to do with the fact (as Freud, 1905/1916, p. 179, noted over 90 years ago) that the meaning of a joke is often constructed within a social context, and without this context, men and women are forced to rely on their prior experiences to aid their understanding. Consequently, according to Lampert and Ervin-Tripp, to the extent that the experiential worlds of men and women are different, the two sexes may differ in their enjoyment of a joke, not simply because one group likes it more than the other, but because they are actually reading two different jokes.

Lampert and Ervin-Tripp (1998, pp. 235–245) provide an excellent literature review of the study of humor and *gender* (1970–1996), and explore the ways in which researchers over the last 25 years have attempted to look at gender differences through the use of experimental procedures as well as behavioral reports and natural observation methods. Following an analysis of how the "humor appreciation" paradigm has accounted for gender differences in humor, Lampert and Ervin-Tripp offer alternative methods and paradigms, including the use of observer- and self-assessment procedures, and the natural conversation (discourse research) method. Lampert and Ervin-Tripp agree that investigators in the area of *gender* differences in humor need to employ more multidimensional techniques when making statements about humor appreciation and use. The use of unidimensional measures—or measures that collapse behavioral ratings into one or two scales—may obscure subtle differences especially when the dimensions are constructed around a single humor-related activity; in contrast, the use of multidimensional measures allows the varied and stylistic differences of women and men to reveal themselves more completely (cf: Craik, Lampert, & Nelson, 1993, 1996; Crawford & Gressley, 1991; Lampert & Ervin-Tripp, 1993).

Other studies that explore the relationships between *gender/sex/sexuality* and humor appreciation/preferences include the following: Abel (1998), Apte (1985, pp. 67–81), Bauer and Geront (1999), Bender (1994), Bergmann (1986), Borges, Barrett, and Fox (1980), Brennanparkes, Goddard, and Wilson (1991), Connelly and Kronenberger (1984), Cox, Read, and VanAuken (1990), Crawford (2000), E. M. Davis (1983), Derks and Arora (1993), Deutsch (1990), Ehrenberg (1995), Feingold (1992), Ford (2000), Frauenglass (1967), Gallivan (1992, 1994, 1999), Gravley (1983), Greenberg (1979), Halberstadt, Hayes, and Pike (1988), Hall (1993), Hay (2000), Herzog (1999), Herzog and Hager (1995), Hickson (1977a), Janus (1981), A. M. Johnson (1991), Khoury (1977), Kleinke and Taylor (1991), Kotthoff (2000), Lampert (1996), LaRossa, Jaret, Gadgil and Wynn (2000), Legman (1968), Lewin (1980), Love and Deckers (1989), Lundell (1993), Lundy and Tan (1994), Mitchell (1977), Morse (1982), Neitz (1980), Parisi and Kayson (1988), Prerost (1995b), Sev'er and Ungar (1997), Shirley and Gruner (1989), Thompson and Zerbinos (1995, 1997), Thorson and Powell (1996), VanGiffen (1990), VanGiffen and Maher (1995), Vitulli and Tyler (1988), Walker and Dresner (1988), W. Wilson (1975), Wilson, Nias, and Brazendale (1975), Winkel (1993), Zippin (1966).

Ethnic, Cross-Cultural, and Cross-Generational Differences

MacHovec (1988, p. 116) defines *ethnic humor* as humor based primarily on "racial, religious, national, regional, local, social, sex/sexist, age characteristics, or other differences." (cf: "humor in ethnohistory," Axtell, 1990; Isajiw,

1974). Ethnic jokes are almost always simplistic and stereotypical in their content, and involve bias, prejudice, and a condescending attitude (e.g., consider the following example of ethnic humor: A patient seeks a brain transplant and is offered a Jewish brain for $5,000 or a Polish brain for $10,000. Asked why the difference in price, the patient is told: "The Polish brains have never been used"; cf: Bier, 1988).

Most ethnic humor is disparaging and derisive, although there may be sympathetic support for the joke teller if she or he shares the same ethnic background as the listener(s); almost any group can be the victim of the "ethnic put-down" (cf: Wilde, 1983). Arieti (1976) points out the "relativity" of the ethnic put-down: Jewish and Italian ethnic humor are examples of "self-deprecation" when used by someone from within those groups, but are "anti-Semitic" and "anti-Italian" when imposed on the groups from someone outside the groups (cf: discussion of an experiment with Jewish jokes in Wolff, Smith, & Murray, 1934, pp. 351–359; and development of racial-ethnic differences in children in McGhee & Duffey, 1983a). According to Arieti, Jewish jokes told by Jews are different from Jewish jokes told by non-Jews. Freud (1905/1916) maintained that when Jews joke about themselves they are sincere acknowledgements and admittances of one's real shortcomings (cf: Nevo, 1985). However, Arieti (1976) asserts that the habit of Jewish jokes being told by Jews is paradoxically an unconscious defense against anti-Semitism; after living for centuries in hostile environments, the Jews make relatively harmless jokes about themselves and, thereby, preempt or disarm any potential enemy—it is better to be laughed at than to be massacred. Arieti claims that laughter extinguishes anger, hostility, and various allied affects at least for the period during which the laughter continues (cf: Schutz, 1989); many comedians use masochistic techniques to elicit laughter, especially when the audience is being unresponsive.

In regard to national or ethnic differences in humor, Flugel (1954) suggests that there is little clear evidence concerning national differences in humor appreciation (cf: Ziv, 1988a). He asserts that the existence of such differences has often been implied and they have sometimes been related to supposed differences in the personality types prevalent in different countries. For example, Egner (1932) indicates that German humor is full of sympathetic feeling, English humor attempts to fight off the seriousness of life, American humor is primitive and delights in an exaggeration which the Germans find silly, and French humor/wit is cruel and hostile. According to Flugel, however, other investigators have so far found practically nothing to support these or any comparable formulations (cf: McCullough, 1993). Kimmins (1928) found little difference between American and English humor, and Kinnosuke (1927) discovered little difference between American and Japanese humor (cf: Wolff, Smith, & Murray, 1934, who suggest that laughter may be raised more readily by the foibles of other nations, cultures, or races than by one's own; humor in such cases may be due merely to surprise and quaintness of different customs and unfamiliar mannerisms of speaking which may seem unusual or incongruous and, hence, funny to some individuals; also, to some degree such humor may reflect a subtle intergroup aggressiveness).

Eysenck (1944) conducted an extensive investigation of national differences in sense of humor and found corroborating evidence for the strongly held views as to the relative "goodness" and particular characteristics of the humor of various nations. However, he could find little evidence for the soundness or validity of these views (in one case, the observed differences in humor that Eysenck found between his American and English participants could be attributed chiefly to differences in educational and cultural status).

McCullough (1993) asserts that research on perceptions of humor for the two nations of Finland and America indicates that individuals of both countries enjoy "aggressive-sexual" and "nonsense" humor. Finnish humor has been characterized as liking nonsense and also as being wry and self-deprecating (e.g., Nickels & Kallas, 1973); and the American sense of humor has been described as prone to heavy use of exaggeration, is anti-intellectual, and is inclined to poke fun at ethnic and dialectic differences (e.g., Nilsen, Nilsen, & Donelson, 1988). Based on the results of her own study, McCullough draws three conclusions regarding national differences in humor: a two-part humor typology (i.e., aggressive/sexual and nonsense) is too simplistic and does not fully represent the humor perceptions of the participants of either nationality; a two-part typology generally is not useful for identifying national differences; and a two-part typology probably represents a more reductive humor *structure* that may exist across cultures.

Apte (1985, pp. 108–148) discusses humor, ethnicity, and intergroup relations from an anthropological perspective. He explores the nature of ethnic humor and its relationship to sociocultural systems; the relevant theoretical concepts; the forms and techniques of ethnic humor; and the sociocultural bases of the text, context, and function of ethnic humor (cf: Apte, 1987, pp. 27–41). Apte (1985) maintains that intercultural contacts and interactions have led societies to formulate opinions, beliefs, and attitudes about peoples who are culturally "different"; the "images" developed, in turn, become the bases of "ethnic humor." Apte operationally defines the concept of "ethnic humor" as a type of humor in which fun is made of the perceived behavior, customs, personality, or any other traits of a group or its members by virtue of their specific sociocultural identity. Although the phrase "ethnic humor" may be of recent origin, humor that disparages other groups is probably as old as is the contact between cultures; the tendency to ridicule and to mock groups other than one's own (cf: the exception provided by the self-disparaging type of humor of the Jews) is widespread in human societies (e.g., Dundes, 1971, 1975; Roback, 1944).

Researchers have investigated the sources, forms, types, contents, and functions of ethnic humor, and responses to it in intragroup and intergroup interaction as well as its relevance to ethnic identity. Different disciplines have formulated diverse goals, methodologies, and perspectives. For example, psychologists show an interest in developing theoretical models (which are validated through controlled experimental studies) that predict motivational factors which encourage individuals to engage in ethnic humor or the variables that determine their differential responses to ethnic humor (e.g., Gadfield, Giles, Bourhis, & Tajfel, 1979; Issar, Tsang, LaFave, Guilmette, & Issar, 1977; LaFave, 1972, 1977; LaFave, Haddad, & Marshall, 1974; LaFave, McCarthy, & Haddad, 1973; Mutuma, LaFave, Mannell, & Guilmette, 1977; Wolff, Smith, & Murray, 1934); on the other hand, sociologists, folklorists, and anthropologists are typically concerned with content analyses and typologies of themes extracted from ethnic jokes (e.g., Abrahams, 1970; M. Barron, 1950; Clements, 1969; Dundes, 1971, 1975; Kravitz, 1977; Rosenberg & Shapiro, 1959; Rosenthal, 1956; Zenner, 1970).

Apte notes that the research on ethnic humor in the United States of America in the 1940s and 1950s was concerned mainly with white-Negro or Jewish-Gentile interactions and with the images these groups had of each other as reflected in their respective senses of humor. In particular, the studies included content analyses of intergroup humor to discover attitudes (e.g., M. Barron, 1950); investigations of racial humor in relation to ethnic and social class background (e.g., Middleton, 1959; Middleton & Moland, 1959; Simmons, 1963); research into the use of humor to establish dominance in interethnic relations (e.g., Burma, 1946); and analyses of the self-image that minority ethnic groups expressed in their humor as it indicates their status in, and relating to, dominant groups in the society at large (e.g., Rinder, 1965; Rosenberg & Shapiro, 1959). Moreover, jokes involving different ethnic groups have also been collected and analyzed in recent years to discover the underlying stereotypes (e.g., Abrahams & Dundes, 1969; Barrick, 1970; Birnbaum, 1971; Clements, 1969; Dundes, 1971, 1975; W. Ferris, 1970; Klymasz, 1970; Kravitz, 1977; Simmons, 1963).

According to A. Greenberg (1972), ethnic humor may have developed as an urban form due to the concentration of different ethnic groups in large cities; despite the current popularity of the phrase "ethnic humor," it was not used widely in the literature on humor until the 1970s. Rather, expressions were used such as: "race-conscious humor," or simply "race" humor (Burma, 1946); "racial humor," or "racial jokes" (Middleton, 1959); "intergroup humor" (M. Barron, 1950); and "interethnic humor" (Zenner, 1970). Generally, today, "ethnic humor" is the phrase commonly used in the psychological and social science literature; it is also well-established in popular writings and humor anthologies (e.g., J. Adams, 1975; Larkin, 1975; Wilde, 1973a,b).

Among Apte's (1985) theoretical propositions derived from his extensive discussion of ethnic humor are the following: certain "pan-human primoridal" emotions and attitudes (e.g., ethnocentrism, in-group adulation, out-group resentment, prejudice, intolerance of the lifestyles of others) constitute a broad base for the development and popularity of ethnic humor; ethnic humor tends to reflect negative attitudes toward certain sociocultural traits (e.g., excessive sexuality, uncleanliness, gluttony) that are projected onto other groups in order to make them the butt of such humor; stereotypes constitute a significant basis for ethnic humor; overgeneralization is a characteristic feature of ethnic humor whereby groups are seen as totally homogeneous and where intracultural variation is ignored; textual factors define the domain of ethnic humor, while contextual factors establish its specific categories, types, forms, and functions; ethnic humor is less likely to occur in highly homogeneous/small-scale societies, and more likely to occur in heterogeneous/large-scale complex societies; and major historical events (e.g., war, migration, social/religious movements) may modify ethnic groups' perceptions of each other and, thereby, change the stereotypes and the ethnic humor based on these stereotypes.

Ziv (1988a, p. ix) defines *humor* as "a social message intended to produce laughter or smiling." Consistent with the aspects of any social message, humor fulfills certain functions, uses certain techniques, has a content, and is used appropriately in certain situations (i.e., it covers *why* people use humor—its functions; *how* it is transmitted—its techniques; *what* it communicates—its content; and *where* and *when* it is communicated—the situation). Ziv notes that some of these aspects of humor are universal, and characterize humor everywhere; others are more influenced by culture. At the present state of knowledge, the aspects of humor theoretically may be placed on a continuum ranging from universal to culturally relative; on such a continuum, the *techniques* of humor may be considered as most universal—there is no society in which humor has not been reported to exist. In anthropological research in which cultures are compared, the *techniques* of humor have a commonality where incongruity, surprise, and local/contextual logic are the chief elements in all humor. These elements are cognitive, and because cognitive processes are universal (similar to the universal physiological aspects of laughing and smiling), there is little reason to expect national/cultural differences.

According to Ziv, next on the continuum are the *functions* of humor—these are universal because they reflect humor needs (however, certain functions are probably more dominant in some cultures than in others). Closer to the cultural end of the continuum, one finds the *contents* of humor which are more likely to be influenced by the particular society in question; societies probably differ most in the *situations* in which humor is used and considered to be appropriate.

Inasmuch as Ziv suggests that there are no differences in humor *techniques* between nations and cultures, he looks more fully into the functions (cf: Ziv, 1984), the contents, and the situations of national humor. The authors of the articles in Ziv's (1988a) edited book used Ziv's (1984) theory concerning the functions of humor—as they present and analyze the humor in their respective countries; as a result, one may note the differences among national styles of humor in using one or another of Ziv's (1984) functions. Thus, again, although the functions may be universal, a nation's cultural history and background likely influence them. Some cross-cultural research on humor has pointed out such relative differences; for example, hostile jokes were found to be more appreciated by American students than by Japanese, Belgians, Chinese, or Senegalese students because aggression and violence are more prevalent and salient to Americans (e.g., Castell & Goldstein, 1977; Goldstein, 1977); Chinese jokes deal more with social interaction (as compared to the sexual and aggressive nature of American jokes); and nonliterate cultures have more jokes about the physical environment (e.g., Shultz, 1977). Ziv asserts that national differences in humor clearly exist, and this is most likely due to language, historical, and traditional differences across nations; inasmuch as humor reflects a nation's life, differences among national forms of humor can be expected to be found. The nations that are covered in Ziv's account of national styles of humor include: Australia, Belgium, France, Great Britain, Israel, Italy, Yugoslavia, and the United States of America.

Davies (1998b) discusses a new sociological approach to the cross-cultural study of humor that is positioned—theoretically—between two already-established methods of investigation: the quantitative studies of humor appreciation (e.g., Eysenck, 1944; Ruch, Accoce, Ott, & Bariaud, 1991; Ruch & Forabosco, 1996) and the qualitative approach toward humor analysis (e.g., Ziv, 1988a; cf: Davies, 1990, 1991a; Oring, 1991). The approach of Ruch and his colleagues (which goes back to the pioneering work of Eysenck, 1944) has led to an empirically based taxonomy of humor consisting of three categories: two of them are structural—*incongruity resolution* humor and *nonsense* humor, and one is content-based—*sexual* humor. According to Davies (1998b), Ruch's major findings for the comparative study of humor are that the *same* basic humor categories have been found in each of the studied cultures, and consistent correlations have emerged between patterns of humor preference and particular personality traits (such as "conservatism" or "sensation-seeking"). Thus, Ruch and his co-workers have been able to produce a relatively "culture-free" psychology of humor that is likely to have applications throughout Western Europe and North America. Apparently, the peoples of these cultures perceive and respond to humor in a common manner, with differences being shaped by individual personality traits rather than merely by membership in a particular society.

The qualitative approach to study differences in the sense of humor of nations—as opposed to the quantitative approach—has tended to focus on the unique qualities of the humor created within each nation, to examine the literary works (as well as smaller items such as jokes and cartoons) of each nation, and to draw on the products and works from the humanities as well as on the methodologies of the social sciences. Davies (1998b) proposes a new methodological approach to cross-cultural humor which takes jokes as the basic units of analysis and treats them as aggregates, not separate individual items; Davies characterizes his key methodological principle as "the dog that didn't bark in the night" (adapted from a bit of ratiocination made by the fictitious literary character Sherlock Holmes). That is, Davies systematically asks the question: "What are the jokes that could easily be told in a particular society but, in fact, are *not?*" Thus, if jokes move easily between two sets of societies (say, Culture A and Culture B), but a particular genre of jokes is common and popular in Culture A but absent/rare in Culture B, then this indicates a significant difference between the sense of humor of the two cultures or two sets of societies. On this basis, finding such a difference indicates a "social fact" that calls for an explanation in terms of another "social fact" (such as differences between the social *structure* or cultural *values* of the sets of societies in which the jokes are present and absent, respectively).

Davies maintains that such a postulate/methodology is compatible with the findings of humor researchers such as Ruch and that the mechanisms posited by Ruch and his colleagues may be incorporated into Davies' proposed sociological model. Davies asserts that his approach defines a sociological technique that cannot be reduced to aspects of individual psychology, and that its validity lies in a rationale that is similar to the traditional hypothesis-testing notion of "falsifiability." In particular, in the present context, should it be discovered that the supposedly absent jokes have, in fact, gone into circulation in Culture B, then the model either collapses or it has to be shown that they are told in Culture B only in a specific and restricted context that is congruent with the social and cultural differences between Culture A and Culture B that have been used to explain why the senses of humor of the peoples of Culture A and Culture B differ. Davies suggests that the key test of whether a genre of jokes is present or absent is to determine whether or not a particular set of jokes is being *spontaneously* generated and transmitted *orally* within a culture/society. Moreover, studies that are based only on *written* and published material may be misleading for several reasons (e.g., jokebook censorship by a government; pressure to change material from powerful or "politically correct" minorities, etc.).

In summary, Davies' approach to the cross-cultural study of humor/jokes is empirical (data-driven) and binary ("absent" versus "abundant") in character; the crucial evidence to be collected is the absence (or rare and highly specific existence) in one culture/society of a genre of jokes that is abundantly present in another culture/society; and the empirically based data may be subjected to the concept of "falsifiability" and openness to refutation (i.e., the data would be shown to be incorrect if it were demonstrated that sets of jokes exist where the investigator has suggested that they do not exist and should not exist). Davies concludes that the method he proposes, and that he calls "the dog that didn't bark in the night," is of value as a means of demolishing theories of humor and the supposedly rational taxonomies of humor derived from them, as well as being a good method of producing new, empirically grounded, sociological generalizations and theories about the nature of the spontaneous order produced by mass joking. Davies' approach toward the study of humor provides a useful addition to the longer-established approaches in the disciplines of quantitative psychology on one hand, and of the historical/literary/linguistic study of texts on the other hand.

Other studies that explore the relationships between *ethnic/national/cross-cultural* factors and sense of humor include the following: J. Adams (1975), Adelson (1947), Alperin (1989), J. Anderson (1986), P. M. Anderson 1988–1989), Apte (1987), Attardo (1988), Austin (1978), Baghban (1977), Bendelac (1988), Bier (1968, 1976), Blair (1937, 1987), Blair and Hill (1978), Bleustein (1981), Blyth (1959), Boatright (1949), Boskin (1986, 1997), Boskin and Dorinson (1985), Bourhis, Gadfield, Giles, and Tajfel (1977), Bradley (1937), Cerf (1954), Chun (1977), Clark and Turner (1984), Clements (1979, 1986), S. B. Cohen (1978), Cong (1986), Cook (1985), Dance (1977), Davidson (1987), C. Davies (1982, 1987, 1990, 1991b, 1998a, b), Deren (1989), Dorinson and Boskin (1988), Dormon (1985), Draitser (1998), Dundes and Hauschild (1983), Easthope (2000), Ehrlich (1979), Farzen (1973), Feinberg (1971), Ferro-Luzzi (1990, 1992), Gallois and Callan (1985), Gardiner (1972), Gelazis (1994), Griffith (1989), Grow (1991), Hughes (1966), Husband (1988a,b), Jaret (1999), Jordan (1988), Kao (1946), Keough (1990), Kuipers (2000), LaFave and Mannell (1976), Leacock (1936), Linneman (1974, 1984), Lowe (1986), Mintz (1977a,b, 1988), Modlin (1988), R. Morris (1991), Murray (1997), Nickels (1993), Nilsen (1991, 1993, 1996, 1997, 1998), Oring (1988), Oshima (2000), Pratt (1996), Rodrigues and Collinson (1995), M. Rosen (2000), Rourke (1931), Rubin (1983), Sackett (1987), Saper (1991), Schechter (1970), Schulman (1992), J. Siegel (1995), M. Siegal (1987), Sikov (1986), Spencer (1989), Thurston (1991), Turcotte (1989), H. Wells (1971), Wickberg (1993, 1998), Zavala (1989), Zilberg (1995), Ziv and Zajdman (1993).

The study of *cross-generational* or *age* differences in humor appreciation may be approached initially and most properly by analysis of the *development* of humor in children. In this regard, Bariaud (1988) discusses developmental changes in children's humor between ages two and eleven years; she maintains that the developmental study of children's humor—in the Piagetian sense—may be used to improve psychologists' understanding of the complexity of the higher forms of humor found in adolescence and adulthood, through an analysis of the simpler forms and a reconstruction of their progressive complexification during the course of childhood. In defining the phenomenon of humor, Bariaud notes that humor generally makes people laugh or smile, but not all laughs or smiles are manifestations of humor; laughter and smiling are ambiguous in terms of meaning, and they may result from highly varied types of emotional experiences (cf: Dumas, 1923, who distinguished between laughter which indicates a state of general excitement of pleasure, and laughter which indicates the pleasure of comic experience; Bariaud focuses on the latter type of laughter which often arises from the specific experience of the perception of, or evocation of, a "funny" or "amusing" event). Bariaud asserts that there is almost total consensus among researchers that humor is related to comprehending (humor reaction) or producing (humor creation) an "incongruity" where incongruity refers to the simultaneous occurrence of normally compatible elements (i.e., elements that are not ordinarily associated with each other in a given context; cf: Koestler's, 1964, term "bisociation" which refers to the ability to see things on two levels at the same time).

Moreover, according to Bariaud, incongruity—although it is necessary to describe the humor experience—is not sufficient in itself to account for it and must be supplemented by other explanatory components; for example, humor cannot really be understood without placing it in the framework of social exchange, an exchange based on mutual complicity and not on exclusion. In this regard, people are usually cued to the intent to amuse through certain communicative signals which are invitations, essentially, to take the incongruous event in a "playful mode" (cf: the term "fantasy assimilation" used by McGhee, 1972, in this context). Children seem to need these cues more than adults do in order to be sure that they are encountering humor and not something bizarre; children's ability to recognize such cues likely has its roots in early experience, in the first play-exchanges with familiar adults. Ten- or 12–month-olds are able to perceive the playful, nonthreatening character of unexpected or incongruous events that, in other circumstances, would provoke fear rather than laughter. On the basis of this early "social intelligence," children gradually familiarize themselves with a whole variety of humor in other forms (e.g., television cartoons, pictures in books, etc.) and, thus, learn how to decode the "rules" behind what is humorous and what is not (cf: Mahony & Mann, 1992).

Some humor theorists (e.g., Bateson, 1953; Berlyne, 1960; Freud, 1905/1916; Maier, 1932) suggest that once the initial incongruity has been grasped, a second process involving the reassessment of the situation as a whole takes place (cf: Nerhardt, 1977; Rothbart, 1973, 1976). Wit and humor begin with a puzzling status which then becomes intelligible, thus allowing the incipient surprise to give way to clarity; theoretically, this produces the comic effect. Such a notion regarding this sequence of events is central to the theory of incongruity-resolution posited by Jones (1970), Shultz (1970, 1972), and Suls (1972). Following an initial phase of contradiction between what the person encounters and his or her original expectations, the humor-receiver engages in a second phase of "resolution" of incongruity in which the two initially incompatible elements are reconciled; thus, resolution gives a particular coherency to incongruity without rendering it more serious. Also, resolution is the complement of identification of incongruity, and they together make up comprehension—the intellectual aspect of the humor response which is a necessary basis for amusement.

It has been argued (e.g., Malrieu, 1967; McGhee, 1977b, 1979; Tower & Singer, 1980) that humor has its origin in the "pretend play" of children which develops at about the age of 18 months as a manifestation of a significant change in cognitive development (i.e., the emergence of capacities for symbolic thought through which individuals may mentally represent objects, people, places, or events with which they have had prior experience). There are ramifications and theoretical reasons for linking later forms of humor with these early forms of "make-believe" play. For example, in later humor we momentarily free ourselves from the binds of reality and accept in fantasy the incongruities which we don't take literally because we are cognizant that they are erroneous; to "play the game" in humor (as in pretend play) amounts to acting *as if* the incongruities were not erroneous. Thus, in humor, as in pretend play, there is a certain "distancing" from the norms of reality, and a combination of being fooled and complicity required from another individual; this suggests that there may be a positive relationship between humor and pretend play (cf: Lieberman, 1965; Wolfenstein, 1954).

In discussing preschool humor, Bariaud (1988) refers to McGhee's (1977a, 1979) model which views humor essentially as a cognitive experience; such a model accounts for humor development in preschoolers, and older children, in terms of several phases that are related to the Piagetian stages of intellectual development (transitional ages from one stage to another may vary across individuals, but the sequence is thought to be identical for all individuals).

At the foundations of humor, the first stage, as already indicated, is characterized by incongruities in pretend play behaviors. The emergence of language in the child at the end of the second year of life opens up new and wide perspectives for humor: the child may now share her or his incongruous perceptions and actions with others by substituting one object designation for another, thus discovering the social enjoyment inherent in these exchanges.

In the second stage of the model (McGhee, 1977a, 1979), incongruous labels for objects or events may be combined with incongruous actions directed toward objects, or the child may also create purely verbal incongruities. The phase of enjoyment derived from incorrect labeling may extend over several years with great differences observed between children, depending on their personalities and the responses or feedback (e.g., punishment, reinforcement, or neutral consequences) of those around them.

At about the age of three, a new advance in humor accompanies the emergence of conceptual thought—children begin to understand that a word does not refer necessarily to a single object, but rather to a category of objects sharing common distinctive features that differentiate them from other objects (e.g., the *concept* of "cow"). This development of conceptual categories makes children between the ages of three to six particularly amused by incongruities that bear on distinctive category features (e.g., a cartoon of a cow shown tap dancing with shoes on and holding an umbrella). The third stage of humor development, then, may be characterized as the "violation of conceptual representations"; the child's mode of thought during this period is based exclusively on the *perceptual* characteristics of objects or events.

In the fourth stage of humor development, the humor changes and begins to be centered around incongruities related to *appearance*; in its verbal expression, it consists of the invention of nonsense words, enjoyment of rhymed sequences, and laughter upon hearing words having unexpected pronunciations. [Note: See Wolfenstein's, 1954, discussion and psychoanalytic model of humor development which analyzes dominant themes in children's humor at different ages and stages of childhood. According to this approach, humor is a way of subtly getting around prohibitions through the use of increasingly complicated disguises; this skill reflects underlying cognitive development as well as a need arising from the progressive internalization of morals. As a result of such developments, according to this approach, an important change in joking style takes place at about six years of age; prior to this time, children's productions are spontaneous, original, and relatively crude involving sexual, scatological, or aggressive themes. At about age six, children begin to show a keen interest in ready-made jokes, and this interest continues to develop between the ages of seven and ten.]

Bariaud (1988) notes that in order to study humor creation—not only at the age of three, but through the whole course of childhood—the ideal conditions would be to catch its products in their natural and spontaneous context. However, due to various inconveniences, restrictions, and difficulties with this method, many researchers opt to study humor reactions of children rather than the more difficult study of humor creation. The more popular and convenient method usually involves the experimental presentation of humorous products (e.g., jokes, riddles, cartoons) that are analyzed subsequently concerning the individual's understanding and appreciation of the humor involved (cf: L. Graham, 1958; Harms, 1943). Bariaud examines various conditions and materials regarding children's humor appreciation, including humor in actions, humor in pictures and drawings, distortion of sizes, transfer of features, disguises and masks, anomalous behaviors and situations, mishaps and pranks, and verbal humor (play with word sounds—phonological level, and play with word shapes—morphological level).

In terms of McGhee's (1977a, 1979) approach, the age of seven marks the attainment of the fourth stage in humor development that is associated with new abilities concerning the emergence of concrete operational thinking (Piaget, 1947); the child now becomes able to understand more abstract and implied incongruities and not just those that can be immediately perceived. Shultz's (1970, 1972) experiments conducted with children between seven and 12 years of age support the incongruity-resolution theory in that the degree of humor appreciation follows an ordered sequence: it was weaker when the stimulus material (cartoon) had no incongruity, stronger when it contained one without the resolution information, and even stronger when the incongruity and resolution information were both available. However, Shultz's data failed to confirm a hypothesis concerning two developmental stages; while the 11- to 12–year olds were more likely to detect "pertinent" or intended resolution, the seven- to eight-year-olds also tended to find some other ways of resolving the incongruity. That is, the preference for the "incongruity with resolution" form (versus a form lacking incongruity and a form including incongruity but no resolution) was comparable in both age groups. [Notes: See Shultz & Horibe, 1974, who found a transition stage in children at seven years of age regarding incongruity plus resolution; also see Pien & Rothbart, 1976, who conclude that four- to five-year-olds are capable of appreciating the resolution information in humor; and Zigler, Levine, & Gould, 1966a, 1967, who posit a "cognitive congruency principle" where the child's appreciation of humor in jokes or drawings should be greater if the stimulus material presents a "challenge" to the child's capacity for understanding, and finds a fit with the "complexity level" of her/his cognitive development or appreciation.]

McGhee (1979, p. 149) cautions that we still know very little about the reasons why children's preferences for humor change as they get older. There can be no doubt about the fact that progressive changes in cognitive development have a strong influence on the kinds of humor a child can understand—and there must be some level of comprehension before the humor can be appreciated—but not all children show the same changes in preferences as they get older. What this means is that other important personality or experiential factors must also have a strong effect on the child's developing sense of humor.

Turning from the stage, age, maturational, and *developmental* analyses of humor appreciation in children (e.g., Bariaud, 1988; McGhee, 1977a, b, 1979; Shultz, 1970, 1972), we now examine various other selected studies concerned with other variables in the context of the *cross-generational/age* aspects of humor. Variables that interact with one's perception of the incongruities, absurdities, and mirthful events of life include age, gender, and educational level.

Vitulli and Barbin (1991) suggest that the *value* one places on humor should vary, in part, as a function of such demographic variables; they examine how participants from among four levels of education (eighth-grade, high school, college, and postcollege adults) respond to a humor rating scale. Their rating technique ("Vitulli's Humor Rating Scale") measures attitudes toward male-oriented humor, female-oriented humor, general humor values, and an index of "differentiation of humor by gender."

Vitulli and Barbin found significant interactions between sex and humor scales, and between educational levels and humor scales; also, they found significant differences between educational levels on the male- and female-oriented scales, as well as on the differentiation scale (cf: Vitulli & Tyler, 1988). Vitulli and Barbin reason that if (as McGhee, 1979, notes) the limited evidence on sex differences in humor at different ages suggests that boys and girls do not differ in their attempts at verbal humor during the preschool years, then their present data indicate the following hypothesis: the large eighth-grade and high school differences in male-oriented humor, and the large eighth-grade differences in differentiated humor, are due to reinforcement of *stereotyped* humor roles in the early school years and continuing through high school. Moreover, according to Vitulli and Barbin, it is not until the college years that a more "egalitarian" relationship (cf: McGhee's, 1979, "egalitarian hypothesis") exists between the sexes regarding the *value* and role of humor (cf: Vitulli & Tyler, 1988, who describe this convergence with the concept of "androgyny" in relation to humor to focus on the behavioral orientation of men's and women's life styles).

Thus, in effect, Vitulli and Barbin suggest an "egalitarian-androgyny" hypothesis to describe converging changes toward humor at the higher levels of education such that "egalitarian" indicates *value*-convergence, and "androgyny" indicates *behavioral*-convergence; however, Vitulli and Barbin state that while the data on the male-oriented humor scale support such a combined "egalitarian-androgyny" hypothesis *cross-generationally* (across years of education), the data from the differentiation scale do not (i.e., after the eighth-grade, both men and women alike perceive large differences in the manner in which humor will be *responded* to as a function of whether a joke is told by a woman or a man). Consequently, while both sexes may *value* humor similarly ("egalitarian" view), the sexes do not believe equally that the elicitation of laughter will be the same regardless of the gender of the joke-teller. Such a finding suggests that the term "androgyny" may not be the most appropriate way to describe educational influences on expression of humor as perceived by women and men. The data from the women indicate that *young* women view humor as more important for women (than for men), yet *older* women view the joke-teller as having a different effect depending upon gender (cf: Carroll, 1989).

Yoder and Haude (1995) examine the notion that a jocular nature and an ongoing appreciation of humor may facilitate successful survival into older adulthood (cf: studies that suggest an *inverse* relationship between humor and longevity; e.g., Friedman, Tucker, Tomlinson-Keasey, Schwartz, Wingard, & Criqui, 1993; Rotton, 1992). Their participants—who ranged in age from 66 to 101 years—completed the Multidimensional Sense of Humor Scale (Thorson & Powell, 1993a); the participants were selected on the basis of having a sibling who died of natural causes, and they also provided ratings on sense of humor for their deceased siblings (cf: G. A. Fine, 1975, who used a similar methodology); siblings mean age at death was 64.6 years. Yoder and Haude found a significant mean difference between the two groups of ratings on the subscale measuring humor appreciation; this suggests that there may be a possible positive relationship between humor appreciation and longevity. [Note: For a critical reaction to this study, see Ridley & Harrison, 1996, who suggest that Yoder & Haude did not acknowledge other alternative explanations for their results; for example, since the deceased siblings at death were generally younger than the raters' current ages, developmental differences may be influential; or the loss of a sibling may be accompanied by grieving that affects participants' recollections of positive and valued characteristics such as sense of humor, and the passage of time since a sibling's death which might result in memory loss concerning sibling's actual characteristics or traits.]

Other studies that explore the relationships between humor and *cross-generational/developmental/age* variables include the following: Ackerman (1983), Anisfeld (1982), Athey (1977), Bariaud (1977, 1989), Barrick, Hutchinson, & Deckers (1990), Bjorkqvist and Lagerspetz (1985), Boyd (1991), Brodzinsky and Rightmyer (1980), I. Brown (1993), Bryant and Meyer (1977), Capelli, Nakagawa, and Madden (1990), Casertano (1992), Celso (1999), Chapman (1973, 1975b), Chapman and Speck (1977), G. D. Cohen (1995), Collins (1988), Creusere (2000), Curran (1973), Czwartkowski and Whissell (1986), Datan (1986), L. Davies (1977), Demos and Jache (1981), Dupont and Prentice (1988), Elliott (1989), Fabrizi and Pollio (1987b), Farling (1996), Ferraro (1981), Fichtenbaum (1993), Fry (1986), Giachin (1989), Giora and Fein (1999), Hancks (1980), Harwood and Giles (1992), C. Hill (1996), Hindman (1994), Horgan (1989), Hummel (1992), Jacoby (1988), Jaffe (1995), Kelly, Knox, and Gekoski (1987), Krogh (1988), Laing (1939), LaPointe, Mowrer, and Case (1990), Leitner (1992), Manke (1995), Masten (1989), Mayes, Klin, and Cohen (1994), Mazick (1990), McDowell (1979), McGhee (1971a, b, 1974, 1977b, 1980b, 1986, 1988, 1989), McGhee, Bell, and Duffey (1986), McGhee and Kach (1981), McGhee and Lloyd (1982), Miles (1989), Nahemow (1986), Nahemow, McCluskey-Fawcett, and McGhee (1986), Nahemow and Raymon (1986), Nwokah and Fogel (1993), Owens and Hogan (1983), Palmore (1986), Parisi and Kayson (1988), Pfeifer (1992), Pien and Rothbart (1977), Pita (1984), H. Pollio (1988), Prentice and Fatham (1975), Ransohoff (1975, 1977), Rothbart (1973), Ruch, McGhee, and Hehl (1990), Schaier and Cicirelli (1976), Seltzer (1986), Shaeffer and Hopkins (1988), Shakun (1995), Sheppard (1977a, 1981), Sherman (1988), Shultz and Robillard (1980), Simon (1990), Simons and McCluskey-Fawcett (1986), Sinnott and Ross (1976), Sletta, Sobstad, and Valas (1995), D. Smith (1994), Sobol (1999), Solomon (1996), Spector (1996), Tamashiro (1979), Tansey (1989), Tennison (1994), Thorson and Powell (1996), Toda and Fogel (1993), Vitulli and Parman (1996), R. Wells (1934), Whitt and Prentice (1982), M. H. Williams (1993), Winner (1988), Wright (1977), Yorukoglu (1974), M. M. Young (1989), Ziff (1982), Zinger (1988), Zink (1989).

Aggression as a Variable in Humor Studies

Ziv (1984, p. 2) maintains that humor is created and enjoyed because it allows individuals to express fundamental needs in ways that are both pleasurable and socially acceptable. One of the needs of individuals deals with social taboos: when the content of jokes is analyzed, it is found that most deal with aggression and sex—two topics that happen to be main taboos of our society. Ziv asserts that aggression is probably part of human nature, whether one likes it or not (e.g., just look at the *history* of humankind!). However, in the preservation of, and the functioning of, a healthy and viable society, the human tendency toward aggression has to be controlled and regulated in special ways. One way of controlling individuals' aggression is through the use of humor.

Early theories of humor as an aggression-related device go back to the basic theories of Plato and Aristotle who held that laughter occurs (as a subtle attack) when one person detects a weakness in another person, and when one derives pleasure from humiliating or belittling someone else (cf: Epstein & Smith, 1956, who observed that hostile cartoons were generally preferred by their participants; Highet, 1954, who explains how the Arabs consider humor—via satire—to be a dangerous, aggressive, and destructive weapon; McCauley, Woods, Coolidge, & Kulick, 1983, who found that more aggressive cartoons are funnier; Mikes, 1970, who insists that *all* humor is aggressive; and Rapp, 1949, who proposed a theory of the development of humor as an aggressive expression, connecting it with the physical aggression of primitive humans, and who claimed that laughter first appeared in warfare—at the end of the battle, the victor relieved his tension with audible laughter, while the loser relieved his tension by crying; thus, laughter came to symbolize victory; a modern version of Rapp's theory is given by Gruner, 1978).

Ziv (1984) notes that with the evolution of civilization, intellectual warfare began to replace physical warfare where words were exchanged rather than physical blows. However, even in intellectual battle (such as in "joke competition"), there is a competition between/among individuals or groups in which questions may be asked and the ones who answer correctly are the winners, and the others are the losers; the winners laugh and the losers are sad. Ziv observes that aggressive behavior takes on many forms; an individual's original instinctive impulse toward aggression may be modified by learning processes, and different theories have emphasized different aspects of aggression vis-à-vis humor.

For example, Freud (1905/1916) suggests that humor preferences are an expression of repressed drives and that individuals with repressed aggressive tendencies should enjoy aggressive humor; however, when a hostile person expresses aggression directly, catharsis may result through the release of tension with a consequent reduction in aggressive drive level and lessening of pleasure in aggressive humor; Adler's (1959) theory stresses the universality of inferiority feelings where persons attempt to compensate for such inferior feelings by trying to achieve and prove superiority over others; humor that may be directed at a person of high or superior position is actually an expression of aggression toward that person; and Dollard and Miller (1939) proposed a behavioral theory based on the relationship between frustration and aggression: a sense of frustration is produced when we come across an obstacle that prevents us from achieving our important goals; according to this approach, when other people are the sources of frustration, there is a tendency to react aggressively toward them; since direct aggression against frustrating individuals is not permitted, typically, in our society, it may take a hidden form—humor is one form that allows one to express aggressive feelings in a socially acceptable way. Also, aggressive humor itself may take on many forms, ranging from a direct and insulting attack to a clever and gentle play on words (cf: Ziv, 1984, p. 10, for a theoretical framework concerning the dimension of aggressive humor).

Summaries and results from the following selected studies (chronologically arranged) taken from the early and more recent psychological literature indicate the relationship between humor and *aggression/hostility*. H. A. Murray (1934) conducted experiments in which jokes of an aggressive, disparaging, or derisive nature were presented to participants, as well as tests of social sentiments. Results indicate that the enjoyment of derisive humor is associated with the possession of egocentric, individualistic, aggressive, and world-derogatory sentiments. Murray's results suggest, also, that intense enjoyment of crudely disparaging jokes is an indication of repressed malice—that is, of an unconscious need for destruction (cf: Wolff, Smith, & Murray, 1934).

Byrne (1956) conducted a study to help resolve the conflict between Freudian theory and previous experimental findings by exploring the relationships among the expression of hostility in behavior, the extent to which hostile cartoons are judged funny, and the ability to recognize hostility in cartoons (cf:

Holzberg, Bursten, & Santiccioli, 1955). Using neuropsychiatric participants (cf: Brill, 1940), Byrne found the following results: those individuals who frequently express hostility, either overtly or covertly, find hostile cartoons significantly more amusing than do persons who fail to express hostility; that there is a significant positive correlation between ability to differentiate hostile versus nonhostile cartoons and estimated IQ, but there is no significant correlation between IQ and finding the hostile cartoons amusing; that those individuals who frequently express hostility are significantly better able to differentiate hostile and nonhostile cartoons than are those persons who fail to express hostility (if the effects of intelligence are controlled statistically); and that there is a significant positive correlation between ability to differentiate hostile and nonhostile cartoons and finding hostile cartoons amusing only if the effects of intelligence are partialled out.

Hetherington and Wray (1964) studied the humor preferences of participants who had extreme scores on scales indicating "need aggression" (NA) and "need for social approval" (NSA) under nonalcohol and alcohol conditions. Their results indicate that high NA participants (college students) rate aggressive cartoons as funnier than do low NA persons; also, nonsense cartoons were rated higher by high NSA participants than by low NSA individuals. Moreover, alcohol seems to facilitate the expression of repressed aggressive needs in humor because the ratings of aggressive cartoons by high NA/high NSA persons was greater under alcohol than nonalcohol conditions; however, such a difference was not found for high NA/low NSA persons, nor for individuals with low NA. In a related study, Hetherington and Wray (1966) explored the effects of stress and the commission of an aggressive act on ratings of aggressive, sexual, and nonsense cartoons by high NA and low NA participants (college students). In this case, stress had little influence on ratings of aggressive cartoons; however, ratings of aggressive cartoons by high NA individuals increased, and ratings of aggressive and sexual cartoons by low NA persons decreased, following aggressive behavior (cf: L. Berkowitz, 1962a,b). Hetherington and Wray's (1966) results concerning low NA persons are compatible with a "cathartic hypothesis," while those of high NA persons are not; these researchers give an interpretation of their findings in terms of "aggression-anxiety" and "inhibition of aggressive responses."

Dworkin and Efran (1967) investigated the relationship between anger and humor using an independent index of arousal, orally presented humor stimuli, and a measure of the effect of humor on aroused anger. Angered participants in this study listened to tape recordings of hostile humor, nonhostile humor, or documentary/musical recordings; a control group of participants listened to the various recordings without having been angered. Results indicate that anger seems not to have a general effect on humor preferences; rather, there is an interaction between anger and the content of the humor. In particular, individuals who are angry respond more positively to hostile humor than do people who are not angry; also, exposure to humor seems to decrease reported feelings of anger and anxiety.

Gollob and Levine (1967) had participants give humor ratings of cartoons before and after they had their attention focused on the cartoon content by being asked to explain the joke. Based on Freud's (1905/1916) argument that successful aggressive humor distracts a person so that she or he is not fully aware of the content of what is being laughed at (e.g., if a person focuses attention on the fact that the humor expresses aggressive impulses, that person's inhibitions become mobilized and is then relatively unable to enjoy the humor), Gollob and Levine hypothesized that cartoons depicting a high degree of interpersonal aggression (although selected to be the most humorous on the pretest) would on a posttest be rated significantly less funny than either low-aggressive or nonsense/innocent cartoons. Results from ratings of cartoons by female participants under such conditions showed that—although initially highest in humor— high-aggressive cartoons received significantly lower ratings on a posttest than either low-aggressive or nonsense cartoons. Thus, Gollob and Levine attempted to "mobilize" participants' inhibitions surrounding aggression by having them focus their attention on the aggressive content of the cartoons (cf: an analogous study using male participants by Singer, Gollob, & Levine, 1967, who found that aroused inhibitions interferred specifically with the appreciation of aggressive cartoons, with most interference occurring for cartoons highest in aggressive content). Thus, the studies by Gollob and Levine (1967), and Singer, Gollob, and Levine (1967), complement each other in giving experimental support for the notion that mobilization of strong inhibitions surrounding aggression interferes with the enjoyment of aggressive humor.

Singer (1968) reports on a study conducted by Negro experimenters where Negro participants first heard either a recording that mobilized aggressive impulses towards segregationists or a control recording. Subsequently, they heard Negro performers deliver hostile antisegregationist humor, neutral humor, or a benign speech. Results indicate that aggression arousal does not significantly affect humor appreciation. Moreover, for participants who were moderately aroused/involved, both hostile and neutral humor reduced aggression and tension as measured by a mood checklist, but posthumor tension and aggression levels were not related to humor appreciation. Singer found that when participants were highly aroused/involved, however, hostile humor reduced aggression (only the hostile humor reduced tension, and only hostile humor appreciation was related significantly with low residue aggressive tension and motivation). Generalizing from the findings of his study, Singer maintains that under appropriate conditions the gratification of fantasy (via hostile humor) may have profound cathartic effects without in any way altering external reality (cf: Singer, 1964), and highlights the importance of symbolic processes in the moment-to-moment fluctuations of feeling and motive state that characterize normal psychological functioning. Singer's findings also support the view that symbolic processes (such as fantasy and the humor response) may serve as mediators which affords the possibility of delay between one's impulse and one's action, and provides a satisfying alternative to action on one hand and rigid suppression on the other hand.

L. Berkowitz (1970a) examines the notion that witnessing aggressive humor can produce a cathartic purge of the observer's aggressive inclinations. Participants in Berkowitz's study were female (university) students who were first either angered or not aroused by having them hear a job applicant's statements concerning university women; participants then listened to a tape recording either of a nonhostile comedian or a hostile comedian. When the participants subsequently rated the job applicant on several measures (knowing that their comments might affect the applicant's chances of getting the job), the women who had heard the aggressive humor were more aggressive toward the applicant than were the women who had listened to the neutral humor. Berkowitz concludes that however "hostility catharsis" is defined (cf: Berkowitz, 1970b), his results place severe restrictions on the alleged beneficial effects of hostile humor; his results suggest that angry people will display a lowered intensity of attacks upon their tormentor after encountering hostile jokes, stories, or cartoons only if this humor is regarded as belittling the anger-instigator (cf: Byrne, 1961; Singer, 1968), or if the aggressive content of the humor is not clearly detected (cf: Landy & Mettee, 1969). Berkowitz states that if the hostile material of the comic routine is very recognizable (as was the case in his study), however, the humor could well stimulate enhanced aggressiveness, and—just like other stimuli having aggressive meaning—it can elicit aggressive responses from those persons who are ready or set to act aggressively.

Cantor and Zillmann (1973) studied the notion that aggression aimed at those who possess authority is more amusing than aggression aimed at someone of similar status (cf: Cantor, Bryant, & Zillmann, 1974; Cantor, Zillmann, & Bryant, 1975). Participants were presented with a series of cartoons to be rated. In some of the cartoons, the "victim" held a position of authority (e.g., banker, policeman); in other cartoons, the "victim" was an ordinary person, similar to the participants (e.g., student). All the cartoons suggested that something unpleasant was about to happen to the "victim"; in each case, the "assailant" was either an animal or a child. Participants were asked to rate the cartoons in terms of their "facetiousness." Results indicate that the cartoons in which the "victims" held a position of authority were considered to be funnier than the others. Cantor and Zillmann conclude that their results support Hobbes' hypothesis: one's need to feel superior is stronger when a person who possesses high authority and a higher position than one's own is questioned or evident; or, in simple terms, the suffering of authority figures amuses us.

Prerost and Brewer (1974) conducted a study whose results support the hypothesis that aggressively aroused men and women prefer sexual humor over nonsexual humor; however, their hypothesis that aggressively aroused individuals will prefer aggressive humor over sexual humor was not supported (cf: Baron, 1978a). Their data indicate that both types of humor (aggressive and sexual) were rated as more funny after aggression arousal, with only women showing a preference for the sexual humor; apparently, the two types of humor are very closely related, especially for the male participants (cf: Prerost, 1975, 1976). Prerost and Brewer assert that their study shows that humor is a natural vehicle for expression of an aggressive mood where—when consistently under states of aggression—both women and men demonstrate greater humor appreciation. Further, although both women and men show this use of humor, the female participants apparently cognitively differentiate the humor types to a greater degree, leading to definite humor preferences under all experimental conditions; women seem to prefer other forms of humor to sexual humor when in nonaggressive moods, but once aroused the preferred choice is sexual humor (cf: Prerost, 1980a,b). Prerost and Brewer suggest that perhaps the women were following the dictates of standard female social roles (i.e., "passive-submissive"), and they unconsciously reject sexual humor under nonarousal moods; however, once aggression is aroused, the women act upon this mood and reject their role-expectant behavior, specifically attending to the sexual humor content; the sexual aspects of humor must fit the nature of their aggressive mood. Prerost and Brewer conclude that the two arousal states of sex and aggression may have similar components and internal emotional cues; sexual and aggressive humor may have similar elements of messages both relating to an aggressive mood (cf: Prerost, 1995a, and Prerost & Brewer, 1977, for the influence of humor content in the humor-aggression paradigm; and Prerost, 1983b, 1987, for the influence of "locus of control" on aggression-reduction; for other studies on the influence of "locus of control" on humor appreciation, see Lefcourt, Antrobus, & Hogg, 1974; Lefcourt, Gronnerud, & McDonald, 1973; Lefcourt, Sordoni, & Sordoni, 1974; and Sordoni, 1980).

Leak (1974) tested hypotheses derived from psychoanalytic theory regarding humor and catharsis following a hostility-arousal manipulation. Previous experimental studies relating the interaction of motivational factors with humor preferences have yielded inconsistent results. For instance, various researchers have found that anger arousal creates a preference for hostile humor (e.g., Berkowitz, 1970a; Dworkin & Efran, 1967), while other researchers have found that humor preferences are *not* affected by temporary motivational states (e.g., Byrne, 1961; Young & Frye, 1966). Similarly, with regard to the influence of the "catharsis effect" on the humor-aggression connection, there are inconsistent results: several studies have found an *increase* in hostility after an experience with aggression (e.g., Berkowitz, 1965, 1970a), while other studies have found a *decrease* in hostility after an experience with aggression (e.g., Landy & Mettee, 1969; Singer, 1968). Leak found, as predicted, that aroused participants who were given aggressive humor rated the experimenter significantly less negatively than the aroused individuals who were not given the aggressive humor. However, according to Leak, contrary to expectation it was found that aroused participants did *not* show an increased preference for either hostile or racial wit/jokes when compared to nonaroused controls. Leak concludes that hostile-wit/jokes has a cathartic value in mitigating participants' hostility toward the experimenter, and gives support to the notion that under certain conditions a catharsis effect may be obtained with humorous stimuli (cf: Berkowitz, 1970a).

Baron and Ball (1974) hypothesized that prior exposure to nonhostile humor markedly reduces the level of aggression directed by angry individuals against the person who had previously provoked them. Participants were first angered or not angered by a confederate of the experimenter, then exposed to either humorous cartoons or nonhumorous pictures, and subsequently given an opportunity to aggress against this individual by means of electric shock. Results show that exposure to the nonhostile cartoons significantly reduced the duration of the shocks delivered to the confederate by participants in the angry condition, but failed to influence the level of aggression shown by participants in the nonangry group. Baron and Ball discuss their findings in terms of the elicitation by the cartoons of responses and emotional states that are incompatible with anger or overt aggression (cf: Berkowitz, 1970a; Dworkin & Efran, 1967; Lamb, 1968; Singer, 1968; Strickland, 1959). They assert that the implications of their findings suggests that exposing angry individuals to nonhostile humor may serve often as an effective means of reducing the strength of their subsequent attacks against the anger instigator and, insofar as the control of aggressive behavior is concerned, "laughter is the best medicine" (cf: Baron, 1978a, for a study on sexual humor's aggression-inhibiting properties, and Baron, 1978b, for findings which show that exposure to nonhostile humor reduces, and exposure to hostile humor increases, subsequent aggression).

Mueller and Donnerstein (1977) hypothesized that humor serves two functions: arousal and attentional shift (i.e., various stimuli, such as erotic, aggressive, or humorous presentations, may serve to divert a participant's attention away from some earlier instigation of anger)—with regard to its influence on the relation of prior anger arousal and aggression. Specifically, they attempted to determine under what conditions humor stimuli act to facilitate or inhibit aggression in angered individuals. The results of their study indicate that the effect of humor stimuli tend to depend on the arousal level of the stimuli, on attentional shift, and possibly on the gender of the participant. When the arousal is mild but the attentional shift is large, the subsequent aggression is decreased (cf: Baron & Ball, 1974). When the arousal is high and the attentional shift is similarly large, the subsequent aggression is greater than that following mildly arousing humor stimuli (e.g., Berkowitz, 1970a), and could conceivably facilitate aggression beyond a control rate. Mueller and Donnerstein found that female participants reduced their aggression after exposure to low-arousing humor while maintaining aggression at a high level for high-arousing stimuli; male participants, on the other hand, were not influenced by humor exposure.

Nevo (1980, 1984) tested both Jewish and Arab men in Israel concerning their production and appreciation of humor. In the appreciation condition, participants rated jokes that included aggressive themes, nonaggressive jokes, and jokes with a Jewish/Arab butt; in the production condition, participants gave humorous responses to a frustration scale. Nevo compared two sets of hypotheses: one derived from the "cathartic" approach which postulates that Israeli Arabs—being more frustrated—will express more aggression in humor and more aggression toward a Jewish butt; and another one derived from the "social" approach which postulates that social status determines the expression of aggression in humor—members of a minority (Arabs) will express less aggression in humor, despite being more frustrated. Nevo's results support hypotheses derived from the social approach both in appreciation and in the production of humor. Nevo's results which indicate that the preferred butt of humor by Jews is an Arab (and Arabs that feel positively toward Israel preferred it also) is in accordance with previous arguments concerning Jewish humor. For example, Rosenberg and Shapiro (1959) and Reik (1962) note that Jews traditionally prefer jokes about Jews, and the Jewish minority identifies with the aggression and internalizes negative stereotypes. Nevo suggests that the Jews in Israel have changed their humor habits: they laugh more at the minority (Arabs) than at themselves; the Arabs have now replaced Jews as the butt of the latter's humor; and Arabs now prefer humor about themselves. Nevo (1985), and Nevo and Nevo (1983), provide further discussions on the phenomenon of "self-aimed" humor.

McDonald and Wooten (1988) designed a study to test an alternative explanation for the results of Baron's (1976) study regarding the reduction of aggression via incompatible responses. The incompatible response strategy/paradigm is one possible means of reducing aggression in persons disposed to behave in such a manner (cf: Baron, 1976, 1983). Specifically, "stimuli or conditions serving to induce reactions among aggressors which are incompatible either with anger or overt aggression may be highly effective in reducing the occurrence of such behavior" (Baron, 1976, pp. 261–262). A number of studies have used stimuli to elicit such incompatible responses; for example, the use of humor (e.g., Baron & Ball, 1974; Landy & Mettee, 1969) has provided results that are consistent with the incompatible response hypothesis (cf: Mueller & Donnerstein, 1977, for alternative explanations of such results; they propose that "attentional shift" or "distraction" may serve as an explanation where stimuli that distract an individual from her or his previous provocation may reduce subsequent aggression). In McDonald and Wooten's study, before being detained at an intersection after the signal turned green, participants were exposed to one of the following stimulus conditions: control, humor, aggression, or sexual arousal. According to the incompatible response hypothesis, the humor and sexual arousal conditions should increase the latency of horn-honking (i.e., reduce aggression), whereas the aggression condition should not show such a result. However, results obtained by McDonald and Wooten give no support for the incompatible response hypothesis; rather, their results are congruent with the attentional shift/distraction hypothesis (all three treatment groups—humor, aggression, and sexual arousal—yielded longer horn-honking latencies than did the control group). McDonald and Wooten conclude that the introduction of distracting stimuli, including humor stimuli, may be a viable means of reducing the occurrence of aggression.

Palmer (1993) examined the patterns of anger, aggression, and humor that occurred during floor hockey games in Newfoundland (cf: Alexander, 1986). Results and observations confirm predictions—based on evolutionary theory—that anger and aggression are more frequent among male players at the age (late teens, early twenties) when mate competition is most intense; also, aggression was seen to be combined with humor most frequently in interactions among players attempting to form social relationships [this finding is consistent with the hypothesis that combining humor (e.g., smiling and laughing) with what could otherwise be viewed as aggressive behavior is a way of establishing trusting relationships between players]. Palmer suggests that although his study applied an evolutionary perspective to the relatively unimportant subject of sports violence, his findings have implications for the larger and more general phenomenon of anger and aggression among young men which is a major social problem in many societies.

Other studies that explore the relationships between *aggression* and humor include the following: Askenasy (1976), Bjorkqvist and Helenelund (1985), Bryant (1977), J. M. Davis (1966), Deckers and Carr (1986), Dunn (1975), Fisher (1962), Gutman (1967), Gutman and Priest (1969), Hogman (1969), Jablonski and Zillmann (1995), King (1995), Kuhlman (1988), LaGaipa (1957, 1968), Mannell (1977a, b), Raeithel (1988), Rubinstein (1965), Sprafkin and Gadow (1987), Ziv and Gadish (1990b).

FUNCTIONS OF HUMOR

The psychical function of humor is to delicately cut the surface tension of consciousness and to increase the pliancy of its structure to the end that it may proceed on a new and strengthened basis . . . Perhaps its largest func-

tion is to detach us from our world of good and evil, of loss and gain, and
enable us to see it in proper perspective.

—L. W. Kline, 1907

Postcard message from a patient to his analyst, "Dear doctor, Having a
wonderful time. Wish you were here to tell me why."

—H. Mindess, 1971

The healing power of nature is the response of an organism to stress. It is a
creative adaptation achieved by a change in the body, mind, or both. Humor functions as one of the "assist devices" in this adaptation.

—I. N. Silberman, 1987

Humor is a multidimensional construct that seems to be intimately related
to quality of life.

—J. Thorson, F. Powell,
I. Sarmany-Schuller, and W. Hampes, 1997

Humor as a Coping Mechanism

Since the 1980s, there has been a surge of interest in the potential benefits of
humor as a means of coping with stress (R. A. Martin, 2000). Partially responsible for this increased interest in humor as a coping mechanism is Cousins'
(1977, 1979a, 1982) anecdotal account of his recovery from a life-threatening
disease through laughter (cf: MacHovec, 1988, pp. 188–192), along with massive doses of Vitamin C. Subsequently, a number of correlational and experimental studies in psychology and other health-related sciences have provided
some evidence that a sense of humor may mitigate the harmful effects of
psychosocial stress on various outcome variables such as mood, physical
health, and some aspects of one's immune system functioning.

Martin (2000) notes that there are several possible mechanisms by which
humor may moderate or buffer stress: it may serve as an appraisal-focused coping strategy—where the cognitive-perceptual shifts associated with a humorous outlook permit the individual to achieve an alternate perspective and make
more salubrious appraisals of an otherwise stressful situation; it may
strengthen interpersonal relationships—which yield enhanced feelings of
closeness and increased social support that, in itself, has been shown to be an
important buffer against stress; it may counteract negative stress-related emotions via the pleasurable emotions inherent in humor and laughter—which is
similar to the manner in which relaxation and other emotion-focused coping

strategies function; and it may have a direct beneficial effect on the body via the physiological changes accompanying laughter.

A number of studies have shown evidence of the health-enhancing physiological effects of laughter (including changes in respiration, muscle tension, blood pressure, cardiovascular, pain tolerance, and neuroendocrine and immune functions), and of the beneficial psychological effects of laughter/sense of humor when coping with life's stresses (e.g., M. A. Andrews, 1990; Arroyo, Lesser, Gordon, Uematsu, Hart, Schwerdt, Andreasson, & Fisher, 1993; Averill, 1969; Berk, Tan, Fry, Napier, Lee, Hubbard, Lewis, & Eby, 1989; Berk, Tan, Napier, & Eby, 1989; Berk, Tan, Nehlsen-Cannarella, Napier, Lewis, Lee, Eby, & Fry, 1988, Bizi, Keinan, & Beit-Hallahmi, 1988; Brownell & Gardner, 1988; Bushnell & Scheff, 1979; Carroll, 1990; Carroll & Shmidt, 1992; Dillon, Minchoff, & Baker, 1986; Dillon & Totten, 1989; Dixon, 1980; Doskoch, 1996; Frey, 1980; W. Fry, 1992b, 1994; Fry & Salameh, 1987; Fry & Stoft, 1971; Godkewitsch, 1976; Goldstein, 1970b, 1982; Goldstein, Mantell, Pope, & Derks, 1988; Harrison, Carroll, Burns, Corkill, Harrison, Ring, & Drayson, 2000; Itami, Nobori, & Teshima, 1994; Kamei, Kumano, & Masumura, 1997; Langevin & Day, 1972; Lefcourt, Davidson-Katz, & Kueneman, 1990; Lefcourt & Martin, 1986; Lefcourt & Thomas, 1998; Martin & Dobbin, 1988; McClelland & Cheriff, 1997; Nezu, Nezu, & Blissett, 1988; Overholser, 1992; Paskind, 1932; Rim, 1988, 1990; Safranek & Schill, 1982; Saper, 1988; Schachter & Wheeler, 1962; Schill & O'Laughlin, 1984; Silberman, 1987; Sumners, 1988; Svebak, 1975a, 1977; Thorson, Powell, Sarmany-Schuller, & Hampes, 1997; Vardi, Finkelstein, Zlotogorski, & Hod, 1994; Welander-Hass, 1990; Wise, 1989; Yoder & Haude, 1995).

Chafe (1987) hypothesizes that humor's basic, evolutionary, and adaptive function is a "disabling" one (cf: Fry, 1992a): the humor state arises in an individual in the first instance in order to keep the person from doing things that would be counterproductive. According to Chafe, the things that humor keeps a person from doing are things that her or his natural, schema-based human reasoning might lead the person into, but which—given the larger reality of a particular situation—would be undesirable, bad, or sometimes even disastrous. Thus, humor is the "safety valve" that saves the individual from the consequences of one's natural reasoning when it would get the person into trouble; that is, humor is an adaptive mechanism whose function is to keep the person from taking seriously those things that she or he ought not to take seriously (cf: Fry, 1987). Chafe suggests that it is instructive to look at the main physiological and psychological manifestations of humor in light of his "disabling hypothesis"; the physiological properties of the humor state have not generally been viewed as having this function, but it is consistent with current knowledge about them to say that the humor state is one in which the individual simply is physically disabled.

Various physiological studies have emphasized what happens when a person laughs (it is possible, of course, to be in the humor state without manifesting overt signs of laughter). Fry and Rader (1977) assert that laughter is the "end point of humor," representing the climax of humor, and indicates that the level of mirth has exceeded a critical threshold value; that is, the humor state is manifested prototypically in laughter, and to be in the humor state without overtly laughing is an indication of failure to have entered the state completely (cf: Clark & Schultz, 1981; Wagoner & Sullenberger, 1978). Current knowledge of the physiology of humor suggests that its most salient physiological component is its interference with normal respiration (e.g., Fry & Rader, 1977; Lloyd, 1938; Svebak, 1977; cf: Feleky, 1916; Meerloo, 1966). While there are distinct individual differences in the respiratory component of laughter, for all persons there is a marked increase in the frequency and magnitude of both expiratory and inspiratory movements, indicating a major deviation from normal breathing (cf: Lloyd, 1938, who found that expiration predominates over inspiration, and laughter is positively expiratory, rather than inspiratory; and Fry & Rader, 1977, who assert that laughter is averaged into a "tidal gas exchange position" that is on the expiratory side of the midline of the respiration cycle).

In terms of Chafe's (1987) "disabling hypothesis," a paroxysmal interruption of normal respiration might alone be considered as sufficient to disable the human organism and to deny it the possibility of any type of effective behavior (the fact that laughter tends to involve a stronger component of expiration than of inspiration suggests the operation or existence of a "disabling function" even more strongly). Accordingly, there is a clear interference with any activities requiring a stable body and, simply put, while you are laughing, you cannot do anything else.

Contrary to the supposition that the decrease in available air to a person's body via laughter might cause a lowering of the oxygen level of the blood, Fry and Stoft (1971) found that a decreased air supply is compensated for by a higher heart rate. Also, Fry (1971) suggests that the heart rate increase appears to be a secondary effect of the respiratory disturbance, not a primary component of laughter. Thus, the available evidence indicates that laughter is designed to keep the individual from acting by radically interrupting normal respiration and grossly disturbing the body's stability (cf: Paskind, 1932, who found that laughter involved a decrease in muscle-tension). In essence, the body has learned to cope with a potentially damaging drop in oxygen level by simultaneously increasing the heart rate and, thus, laughter "disables" the person physically without causing her or him the more serious distress that results from oxygen depletion.

In summarizing Chafe's (1987) position, it is suggested that laughter physically disables the individual—a person in the midst of laughter cannot physically perform other activities. Additionally, the sound of laughter overtly communicates to other humans the fact that one is in the humor state and cannot, at least for the moment, be expected to think or act seriously; also, the sound of laughter may be contagious or infectious (cf: Freedman & Perlick, 1979), producing the humor state in others (i.e., "carriers" of the humor state not only disable themselves, but also—via the sound of laughter—may contribute to the disablement of others). Finally, in addition to its physiological and social components, humor has a psychological or phenomenological aspect: the humor state is pleasing, which also may serve as a disabling mechanism by its diversion of attention and effort away from any decisive action the individual might take. In short, humor has two principal effects: physiologically it incapacitates, and psychologically or socially it directs attention to itself and away from effective action.

Current physiological, neuroendocrinological, and immunological studies have provided evidence for the coping effects of humor on stress situations (see Lefcourt & Thomas, 1998). For example, the following researchers report the positive effects of humor on various aspects of the immune system: Dillon et al. (1986) found increased salivary-immunoglobulin A (IgA); Berk et al. (1988) found increased spontaneous lymphocyte blastogenesis with decreased cortisol; and Berk, Tan, Napier, & Eby (1989) found increased natural "killer cell" activity. Also, Berk, Tan, Fry, et al. (1989) suggest that mirthful laughter may attenuate some classical stress-related hormones; Martin and Dobbin (1988) found that a sense of humor moderates immunosuppressive effects of stress (cf: Kamei, Kumano, & Masumura, 1997, who correlated measures of both "stress" and "humor" with immune responses of the same participants); Dillon and Totten (1989) report that salivary-IgA scores (one of two measures they studied concerning immune function) are correlated with coping-humor scores; and Lefcourt, Davidson-Katz, and Kueneman (1990) obtained results that support the link between humor orientation and total salivary-IgA protein levels.

Other studies provide further *psychological* evidence for the coping effects of humor in stress situations. For example, the following selected studies, chronologically arranged, give a representative cross-section of researchers' interests in the area, and indicate the influence and importance of a number of psychological variables in the supposed humor-coping relationship. O'Connell (1960) tested the possible adaptive values of the Freudian mechanisms of humor, hostile wit, and nonsense/harmless wit on participants grouped as to self-ideal discrepancies, sex difference, and presence/absence of external stressors; he concluded that the Freudian distinction between wit and humor is a valid one, with wit possibly operating to reduce tension under various conditions depending upon the interaction of adjustment, stress, and sex factors. LaGaipa (1968) found that the effects of stress on hostile humor preference differ by humor stimulus type (e.g., cartoons), and by degree/level of participants' authoritarianism.

McGhee (1979, pp. 227–238) discusses humor as a health-promoting coping mechanism and observes that humor facilitates attempts to master sources of anxiety or distress, as well as helps to release sexual and aggressive impulses in a socially acceptable way. Robinson (1983, pp. 116–119) explores the psychological and physiological functions of humor and the individual's ability to cope with internal stress; also, Robinson (1977) summarizes the functions of humor as: a coping mechanism to relieve anxiety, stress, and tension; an outlet for hostility and anger; an escape from reality, and a means of lightening the heaviness related to crisis, tragedy, chronic illness, disabilities, and death (cf: Moody, 1978; Walsh, 1928; also, see Friedman, Tucker, Tomlinson-Keasey, Schwartz, Wingard, & Criqui, 1993, regarding the relationship between humor and longevity, and whose findings are contrary to their expectation: cheerfulness—optimism and sense of humor—was found to be *inversely* related to longevity).

Blank, Tweedale, Cappelli, and Ryback (1983) obtained results that do not support their initial directional hypothesis that participants high in anxiety will give higher positive responsiveness to, and appreciation of, humor; however, their data do support the contention that anxiety does interact to influence an individual's appreciation of humor (i.e., rather than supporting the view that humor acts as a cathartic mechanism which alleviates anxiety, they found that responsiveness to humor is an external reflection of inner perceptions of control and competence; low-state anxiety correlates with positive perceptions of humor). McCrae (1984) studied different kinds of coping situations (e.g., those involving losses, threats, and challenges) and found that participants who faced challenges, in particular, often turn primarily to the use of the coping mechanisms of humor, rational action, positive thinking, escapist fantasy, self-blame, restraint, and self-adaptation (cf: R. A. Martin, 1989). Nezu, Nezu, and Blissett (1988) report that humor serves as a moderator of stress for depressive (but not anxiety) symptomatology, regardless of the measure of humor used in their analyses (i.e., Coping Humor Scale or Situational Humor Response Questionnaire; cf: Lefcourt & Martin, 1986; R. A. Martin, 1996; Martin & Lefcourt, 1983, 1984).

Rim (1988) investigated the relationship between sense of humor and coping styles, and found that most humor scales correlate negatively with age for men, and positively for women; Rim reports that, as in other studies on coping, sex/gender proved to be a major moderating variable (cf: Lefcourt & Martin, 1986, who conclude in their review of several theoretical approaches to humor that by combining them one gains a comprehensive theoretical foundation for understanding the stress-buffering effects of humor). Bizi, Keinan, and Beit-Hallahmi (1988) note that humor as rated by one's peers (but not by self-report) is positively related to performance under stress (this is especially true for active—self-produced—humor as opposed to reactive humor); no differences were found between participants characterized by self-directed humor and other-directed humor in performance under stress (cf: G. A. Fine, 1975; Turner, 1980). R. A. Martin (1988) presents a theoretical model of stress and coping, and discusses the ways in which nonhostile, self-accepting, realistic humor, and laughter may represent a healthy broad-spectrum coping strategy (cf: Porterfield, 1987); also, Martin provides some practical suggestions for encouraging the development of a healthy sense of humor in children.

Grumet (1989) observes that the development of modern civilization seems to have been accompanied by a functional ascendancy of humans' frontal lobes, and with it repression of one's instinctive and emotional behaviors; humor is viewed as a symbolic means of circumventing such inhibitions. According to Grumet, the laugh reflex is a species-specific motor automatism that dissipates nervous energy by momentarily freeing the ancient diencephalic and brain stem centers from cortical inhibition and, in so doing, serves to control the individual's most incorrigible emotions. [Note: For anatomical and cerebral influences and anomalies vis-à-vis humor/laughter, see: Ashkenasy, 1987; Bihrle, Brownell, & Powelson, 1986; I. Brown, 1994; T. G. Brown, 1915; Brownell, Michel, & Powelson, 1983; Bruno, Johnson, & Simon, 1987, 1988; Docking, Jordan, & Murdoch, 1999; Docking, Murdoch, & Jordan, 2000; Duchowny, 1983; Fischman, 1999; Gallagher, Happe, Brunswick, Fletcher, Frith, & Frith, 2000; Gardner, 1981; Gardner, Ling, Flamm, & Silverman, 1975; Gascon & Lombrosco, 1971; Gelkopf, Kreitler, & Sigal, 1993; Grieg, 1985; Heath, 1999; L. Horowitz, 1957; Ironside, 1956; A. M. Johnson, 1990a; Kramer, 1954; Leekman & Prior, 1994; J. P. Martin, 1950; McGhee, 1983b; Pickering, Pickering, & Buchanan, 1987; Prigatano & Pribram, 1981; Rogers, Gittes, Dawson, & Reich, 1982; Shaibani, Sabbagh, & Doody, 1994; Shammi & Stuss, 1999; Siegel & Hirschman, 1985; Starer, 1961; Stern & Brown, 1957; Svebak, 1982; Swash, 1972; Weil, Nosik, & Demmy, 1958; Weiner, 1981; cf: Ekman & Davidson, 1993; Niethammer, 1983.]

White and Camarena (1989) studied the effectiveness of laughter as a stress-reducer in three groups of participants: laughter, control, and relaxation training; they found that while the laughter group did not experience significantly reduced stress, it did show consistent decreases in stress levels as compared to the control group for the two psychological measurements (mood-adjective checklist, and state-trait anxiety inventory) that were made (cf: Cogan, Cogan, Waltz, & McCue, 1987; Prerost, 1993a).

Yovetich, Dale, and Hudak (1990) designed a study to test the hypothesis that humor enhances both psychological and physiological indices of coping by participants exposed to an anxiety-provoking threat (cf: Perlini, Nenonen, & Lind, 1999); they found that individuals with a high sense of humor had lower anxiety ratings than persons with a low sense of humor, and suggest further research to study the humorist's ability to make "rapid cognitive-perceptual shifts" (cf: O'Connell, 1976) to find the humor in an otherwise threatening situation (cf: Hudak, Dale, Hudak, & DeGood, 1991).

Overholser (1992) explored sense of humor in participants and their capacity to cope with life stress; he found that humor was associated with lower levels of loneliness, lower depression, and higher self-esteem; however, these relationships differed according to participant's sex and the frequency with which they used humor to cope (cf: Deaner & McConatha, 1993). Kuiper, Martin, and Dance (1992) studied the relationship between sense of humor and *positive* quality of life indicators, including personal role evaluations and positive affect in response to life events. [Note: This approach is distinct from studies which indicate that a good sense of humor buffers the *negative* effects of stressful life events; see Martin & Dobbin, 1988; Martin & Lefcourt, 1983; Nezu, Nezu, & Blissett, 1988.] The findings of Kuiper et al. support the notion that greater humor facilitates a more positive orientation towards life (cf: Kuiper & Martin, 1993; Martin, Kuiper, Olinger, & Dance, 1993). Nilsen (1993) discusses the functional aspects of humor, and concludes that there are four basic functions: *physiological* (includes exhilaration, relaxation, healing), *psychological* (includes relief, ego defense, coping, and gaining status), *educational* (includes factors of alertness, arguing and persuading, effective teaching, and long-term memory/learning), and *social* (includes in-bonding, out-bonding, and promotion of social stability).

Zillmann, Rockwell, Schweitzer, and Sundar (1993) investigated the mediation of superior coping with physical discomfort following humorous stimulation; among their findings is the observation that exposure to comedy is capable of elevating an individual's threshold for physical discomfort (cf: Cogan, Cogan, Waltz, & McCue, 1987). Interestingly, Zillmann et al. also found, unexpectedly, that there was an elevation of participants' thresholds for physical discomfort following exposure to *tragedy* stimulus material, as well as to the *comedy* material (cf: Weaver & Zillmann, 1994; and the endocrinological research by Levi, 1965, and Carruthers & Taggart, 1973, which suggests that *both* comedy and tragedy may produce comparable increments in sympathetic nervous system activity; exposure to highly amusing comedy and suspenseful drama in these studies resulted in similarly high levels of catecholamine release).

Thorson, Powell, Sarmany-Schuller, and Hampes (1997) studied participants' scores on the Multidimensional Sense of Humor Scale (MSHS) and found, generally, that scores were related positively to various factors associated with psychological health such as self-esteem and optimism, and negatively correlated with factors such as depression and other signs of psychological distress. Thorson et al. conclude that humor is a multidimensional construct that appears to be related closely to the psychological notion of quality of life. Furthermore, in particular, they conclude that the MSHS correlates *positively* with the personality traits of exhibition, dominance, warmth, gregariousness, assertiveness, excitement-seeking, creativity, intrinsic religiosity, arousability, positive emotions, extraversion, and cheerfulness; and the MSHS correlates *negatively* with traits of neuroticism, pessimism, avoidance, negative self-esteem, deference, order, endurance, aggression, depression (cf: Thorson & Powell, 1994), death anxiety (cf: Thorson, 1985; Thorson & Powell, 1992, 1993b), seriousness, perception of daily hassles, and bad mood.

In an excellent review of the area, R. A. Martin (1998) discusses sense of humor and individual differences, psychological health, and coping strategies. According to Martin, the idea that humor is associated with feelings of mastery, liberation (cf: Mindess, 1971), and increased self-esteem has led researchers to focus on the importance of a sense of humor as a sign of psychological health. Many studies have implicated the cognitive, psychodynamic, and personal aspects of humor as the basis for its salubrious effects (e.g., Allport, 1961; Christie, 1994; Kuiper & Martin, 1993; Kuiper, Martin, & Olinger, 1993; Kuiper, Martin, Olinger, Kazarian, & Jette, 1998; Lefcourt & Martin, 1986; Lefcourt & Thomas, 1998; Martin & Lefcourt, 1983, 1984; Maslow, 1954; Mishkinsky, 1977; O'Connell, 1976; Priest & Wilhelm, 1974; cf: Apter & Smith, 1977, who proposed a theory of humor based on "reversal theory" which is a more general model of personality and motivation; also, see Apter, 1982).

In a longitudinal/historical assessment of the construct of sense of humor, Martin notes that much of the humor research prior to the 1970s focused on humor *appreciation*; these studies—largely based on psychoanalytic theory, examined individual differences in the *content* of humorous stimuli. The assumptions of this earlier approach were that the types of humor people enjoy reveal certain aspects of their personality or repressed impulses. Martin asserts that overall these studies give little support for Freudian hypotheses (cf: Gelkopf & Sigal, 1995), but rather confirm the notion that individuals tend to enjoy and laugh at humor that reflects themes and attitudes which are in agreement with their own attitudes, behavior, and interests (cf: Wilson, Rust, & Kasriel, 1977). Later research in humor appreciation emphasized the factor analytic approach which indicated that aspects of the *structure* of the humorous material (incongruity-resolution versus nonsense) are at least as important as content in understanding individual differences in humor, and various personality traits (e.g., conservative social attitudes) have been found to correlate with preferences for one type of humor structure over another. Most recently, in the past two decades, research in humor has broadened and moved beyond humor appreciation to humor *production* and individuals' tendencies to create, express, and enjoy humor in daily life, and to employ humor as a coping mechanism/strategy in stress situations. Martin cautions that systematic work on the psychometric refinement of current measures of humor is inadequate or lacking, often leading to questions regarding their reliability and/or validity. Martin concludes that there is yet no standard conception of the construct of sense of humor (cf: Herzog & Bush, 1994; Herzog & Karafa, 1998; A. M. Johnson, 1992) or theoretical framework upon which investigators generally agree (cf: R. A. Martin's, 1998, own proposed three-dimensional model which includes cognitive, emotional, and motivational dimensions, pp. 58–59), and suggests that there is much more work to be done in the research and understanding of humor.

Other studies that focus on the functional relationships between humor/laughter and its *healthful/stress-coping* aspects include the following: Abel (1998), Adams (1984), Adams and McGuire (1986), Anderson and Arnoult (1989), Astedt and Liukkonen (1994), P. Barry (1999), Bischoff (1990), Bosker (1995), Burns (1996), Carroll (1990), Chandler (1988), Danzer, Dale, and Klions (1990), Dienstbier (1995), Doris and Fierman (1956), Frecknall (1988), Frio (1991), P. Fry (1995), Fry and Salameh (1987, 1993), Gillikin and Derks (1991), Goldin (1994), Goldsmith (1979), Gottschalk (1986), Grant (1987), Holden (1993), Holt (1994), Hunt (1993), Johnston (1990), Kant (1942), Keavney (1993), Kimmel (1987), A. Klein (1989), M. A. Klein (1992), Koppel (1969), Kuhlman (1993), Kwandt (1992), Labott and Martin (1987), Lehman (1995), Lieber (1986), Lodico (1997), Long (1987), Mager and Cabe (1990), R. A. Martin (1984), Martinez (1989), McGhee (1991), Mealyea (1989), Minasian (1990), Moran (1996), Moran and Massam (1999), Mueller (1988), Nevo, Keinan, and Teshimovsky-Arditi (1993), Nevo and Shapira (1989), Noriega (1995), Parse (1994), Phillips (1992), Poole (1991), Prerost (1988), Prerost and Ruma (1987), Richman (1995), Ritz (1996), Rosenberg (1990), Rotton and Shats (1996), Safranek (1981), Seligson and Peterson (1992), Silverman (1995), Smith, Ascough, Ettinger, and Nelson (1971), Spruill (1993), Svebak (1994), P. Thomas (1986), Townsend and Mahoney (1981), Viti (1995), Vitulli (1978), Weisenberg, Tepper, and Schwarzwald (1995), Wender (1996), Whaley (1991), White and Winzelberg (1992), Wiklinski (1994), Wilder (1995), Williams (1986).

Humor and Psychotherapy

Salameh (1983) discusses the use of humor in the psychotherapeutic context and examines specific therapeutic theories and techniques that explicitly incorporate humor into their treatment programs; for instance, "provocative therapy" (e.g., Farrelly & Lynch, 1987; Farrelly & Matthews, 1981) focuses on the current experiences and the context of the therapeutic process in terms of patient/client-therapist interactions, and employs the humor techniques of exaggeration, mimicry, ridicule, irony, distortion, sarcasm, and joke-telling to help amplify the client's maladaptive behaviors while simultaneously provoking the client's worst fears and thoughts about themselves; and "natural high therapy" (e.g., O'Connell, 1981) employs a didactic-experiential format that combines individual and group therapy, and often includes "humordrama" in which participants soliloquize their feelings and thoughts while acting out their stressful situations, and in which "doubles" subsequently use brief sudden switches, verbal condensations, understatements, and overstatements to generate humorous attitudes in order to pursue the process of self-actualization in the individual.

Other therapeutic approaches that employ humor-related techniques are "logotherapy" (e.g., Frankl, 1966; Shaughnessy, 1984) in which "paradoxical intentions" encourage the client to exaggerate her or his symptoms to the point of absurdity and self-laughter; and "rational-emotive therapy" (e.g., A. Ellis, 1977) in which puns, witticisms, and evocative language may be used to facilitate clients' cognitive restructuring, self-acceptance, and a responsible and pragmatic assessment of her or his interpersonal realities. Yet other approaches involving humor in the therapeutic processes are provided by Greenwald (1975, 1977) who used humor in his "direct decision therapy" to exaggerate maladaptive patterns in clients' behavior and perceptions, Haley (1963) and Whitaker (1975) who employ humor within the context of "family therapy," and Mindess (1971), Grossman (1977), Grotjahn (1970, 1971), and Zwerling (1955) who use situationally generated humor to help clients gain emotional liberation to project potential psychodynamic problems onto the humorous material, and to overcome therapeutic resistance.

Salameh (1983) also explores the existing research on the therapeutic uses of humor, noting two trends in the area: studies that are largely psychoanalytically oriented, anecdotal, and/or speculative and lacking either in methodological systematization or theoretical conceptualization; and more recent studies that are characterized by a nonpsychoanalytic and empirical approach (cf: Goldstein & McGhee, 1972)—that include a number of important doctoral dissertations in the field dealing with various problems such as methodological/theoretical issues (e.g., Burbridge, 1978; Kaneko, 1971); humor's effect on the therapeutic process (e.g., Huber, 1974; Killinger, 1977), client's reactions to the use of humor in therapy (e.g., Golub, 1979; Labrentz, 1973), therapist-related variables in using humor (e.g., Buckman, 1980, 1994a; Schienberg, 1979), and the use of humor in group therapy (e.g., Childs, 1975; Peterson, 1980; Taubman, 1980).

Salameh (1983) discusses some future research perspectives and suggests a third trend in the study of humor's use in psychotherapy (involving the study of the characteristics of the therapist, the client, the therapist-client interaction, treatment stages, the institutional setting, the social context of the client's life, and overall treatment outcome; cf: Levinson, 1962). Salameh also discusses ethical problems in therapy in general, and he identifies and examines various other problem areas in the use of humor in psychotherapy (cf: Kubie, 1971), including: problem-definition factors, environmental factors, motivational factors, creativity factors, and outcome factors. Salameh concludes that humor represents a relatively new emphasis that may significantly benefit the field of psychotherapy (cf: Fry & Salameh, 1987, 1993; Salameh & Fry, 2001), and may be expected to make important contributions to the treatment of *mental* illness.

For the relationship between the use of humor and *physical illnesses, disabilities*, and *disorders*, see the following: Allman (1994), D. Black (1982), K. Black (1994), Brill (1940), Broden (1994), I. Brown (1991), Buffum (1992), Burbach and Babbitt (1993), Chatterji (1952), Coriat (1939), D'Adamo (1989), D'Antonio (1988), Derks, Leichtman, and Carroll (1975), Druckman and Chao (1957), Duchowny (1983), Elitzur (1990a,b), Forsythe (1985), Gardner, Ling, Flamm, and Silverman (1975), Gascon and Lombrosco (1971), Gelkopf and Sigal (1995), Gillikin and Derks (1991), Haig (1990), Harrelson and Stroud (1967), Hehl (1990), Hetherington (1964), Horowitz and Horowitz (1949), Ironside (1956), Ivan and Franco (1994), Kawasaki, Shimizu, and Kawasaki (1982), Kizner (1994), Kramer (1954), Krents (1982), Levin (1957), Lindsey and Benjamin (1979), J. P. Martin (1950), Miller (1956), Nevo and Shapira (1988), Olin-Jarvis (1990), Panzer and Mellow (1992), Pines (1964), Robinson, Parikh, and Lipsey (1993), Rosin and Cerbus (1984), Roubicek (1946), Sanders (1983, 1986), Savell (1983), Scott (1989), Senf, Houston, and Cohen (1956), Shimizu, Kawasaki, and Kawasaki (1986), Signer (1988), Spector (1990, 1992), St. James and Tagerflusberg (1994), Starer (1961), Stern and Brown (1957), Swash (1972), Tait (1986), Tait and Ward (1982), Trutt (1983), VanBourgondien and Mesibov (1987), Welch (1999), Wessell (1975), Wise (1989), Witztum, Briskin, and Lerner (1999), Zigler, Levine, and Gould (1966b).

Robinson (1983, p. 111) notes that there has been much support for the emotionally therapeutic value of humor as an adaptive, coping behavior (e.g., Fink & Walker, 1977), as a catharsis for, and relief of, tension, as a defense against depression, as a sign of emotional maturity, and as a survival mechanism. However, others have stressed the destructive aspects of humor, such as the sadistic, masochistic, guilt-arousing, and anxiety-producing effects, and its inappropriate use in psychotherapy (e.g., Brody, 1950; Grotjahn, 1957; Kubie, 1971; Mindess, 1976), even while extolling its virtues and benefits. Robinson views the issue of healthy versus unhealthy use of humor in psychotherapy as comparable to the years of struggle in psychology and other health-related fields to define the concepts of "health" and "mental health"; she adopts the model of a continuum across which the notion of health/mental health ranges, and becomes an individual state involving optimum functioning. Humor, according to

Robinson, is also a complex construct that ranges on such a continuum from healthy to unhealthy (cf: Robinson, 1977).

Other studies that explore (either directly or indirectly) the use of humor in the *psychotherapeutic/counselling/mental health* setting include the following: Amada (1993), Avant (1982), Bader (1993), Baker (1993), Banmen (1982), Bennett (1996), Berger (1988), Bernstein (1986), Birbilis (1990), Bloch, Browning, and McGrath (1983), Bloomfield (1980), Brooks (1994), P. E. Brown (1980), Buckman (1994a,b,c), Cade (1986, 1992), Carozza (1986), Cassell (1974), Chapman and Chapman-Santana (1995), Chasseguet-Smirgel (1988), Chubb (1995), Cousins (1985), Dana (1994), Davidson and Brown (1989), Dewane (1978), Dimmer, Carroll, and Wyatt (1990), Dowd and Milne (1986), Driscoll (1987), Dunkelbau (1987), Eisenman (1992), Epstein (1996), Fabian and Vonbulow (1994), Falk and Hill (1992), Fisher and Fisher (1987), Forabosco (1998), Foster (1978), Foster and Reid (1983), Francis, Monahan, and Berger (1999), Furman and Ahola (1988), Gelkopf, Sigal, and Kramer (1994), Golan, Rosenheim, and Jaffe (1988), Goldin and Bordan (1999), Goldstein (1987), M. J. Greenberg (1995), Greenwald (1987), Haig (1986, 1988b), Herring and Meggert (1994), Heuscher (1980, 1993), Hickson (1976, 1977a,b), Hirdes (1988), Hutchison (1976), Jackson and King (1982), L. Kennedy (1991), Kerrigan (1983), Killinger (1987), J. Klein (1974, 1976), Koelin (1988), Konig (1995), Korb (1988), Kropiunigg (1985), Kuhlman (1984), Lacroix (1974), Lederman (1988), Lemma (1999), Levine (1977, 1980), Loewald (1976), Lynch (1987), MacHovec (1988), Madanes (1987), Maher (1993), Mahrer and Gervaize (1984), Mango and Richman (1990), Marcus (1990), J. F. Martin (1983), McBrien (1993), McGhee (1979), McGuire (1992), Mc Kiernan (1993), Megdell (1984), Minden (1994), Mooney (2000), W. Moore (1992), Morris (1996), Mosak (1987), Mosak and Maniacci (1993), Murgatroyd (1987), Nagaraja (1985), Ness (1989), Neto (1984), Newton (1988), Newton and Dowd (1990), Nussbaum and Michaux (1963), H. Olson (1976), L. Olson, (1996), O'Maine (1994), Pasquali (1987), Pauluk (1999), Pelusi (1991), Peterson and Pollio (1982), Pinegar (1984), Poland (1971, 1990), Pollio (1995), Potter and Goodman (1983), Praver, DiGiuseppe, Pelcovitz, Mandel, and Gaines (2000), Prerost (1981, 1984a, 1985, 1989), Pritzker (1999), Ravella (1988), Rayl (2000), Reynes and Allen (1987), A. K. Roberts (1994), Rose (1969), Rosenheim (1974), Rosenheim and Golan (1986), Rosenheim, Tecucianu, and Dimitrovsky (1989), Rossel (1981), Rutherford (1994), Ruvelson (1988), Salameh (1987a,b, 1993), Salisbury (1990), Sandberg (1992), Sands (1984), Saper (1987, 1988), Savell (1983), Schienberg (1979), Schimel (1993), Schnarch (1990), Schwarz (1974), Scogin and Merbaum (1983), Shapiro (1995), Shaughnessy and Wadsworth (1992), Shlien and Wachs (2000), Shurte (1992), Simon (1988), Sloshberg (1996), Squier (1995), Strean (1994), Streff (1994), Szafran (1981), Titze (1987),

Turek (1992), Tuttman (1991), Ventis (1973, 1987), Ventis and Ventis (1988), Vergeer and Macrae (1993), Volcek (1994), VonWormer (1986), Walter (2000), Weiss (1984), Wells (1983), Wigginton (1992), Yorukoglu (1993), F. Young (1988), Zalis (1980), Zall (1994), Zuk (1964, 1966), Zuk, Boszormenyi-Nagy, and Heiman (1963).

Humor in the Classroom and the Workplace

Zillmann and Bryant (1983) caution that any unqualified generalizations regarding the use of humor for teaching and learning in the *classroom*—especially in educational television programming—are tenuous at best, and should take into account factors such as: the differences between types of humorous stimuli (such varied forms of stimuli may uniquely impact on teacher-student rapport, attention to educational materials, and learning), differences in respondents' acceptance of humor in the educational setting, and situational/contextual variables and differences. However, based on their research and review of the area, Zillmann and Bryant are able to offer the following tentative generalizations concerning the use of humor in educational settings.

For child audiences: dense distributions of *brief* humorous events have stronger effects on selective exposure than the less frequent use of *larger* humorous events/episodes; the interspersion of humor that is unrelated to the educational message is related to superior attention to information acquisition (however, as the child grows older, the positive effect of the use of unrelated humor on attention and information acquisition grows weaker); the use of humor that is well-integrated with the educational message (in particular, in forms such as irony) may be confusing and minimize information acquisition; and the funniness of humorous stimuli involved in the educational materials seems inconsequential.

For adult audiences: in an educational setting (such as the classroom), the use of humor that is unrelated/irrelevant to the educational message seems to have detrimental effects on information acquisition; and the use of unrelated/irrelevant humor in educational messages (via textbooks or in the classroom) is detrimental to teacher-student rapport.

Bryant and Zillmann (1988, p. 49) note the "curious contradiction" that appears when the professional trade literature on the effects of using humor in the classroom is compared with the scholarly research literature on that topic. For example, teachers who use humor in the classroom typically praise its pedagogical benefits and characterize humor as an effective teaching tool (e.g., Cornett, 1986); on the other hand, empirical investigations of the effects of using humor in teaching have indicated results that are mixed, and scholars in their state-of-the-art reviews on the issue typically indicate the potentially detrimental aspects of humor use in addition to citing the benefits that may be accrued from using humor in teaching (e.g., Davies & Apter, 1980; Zillmann & Bryant, 1983). Bryant and Zillmann (1988) attempt to give an integrative and conciliatory account of the apparent contradictions and oversimplifications in this area by positing several specific questions (along with relevant research findings for each question) concerning the use of humor in teaching: Does teaching with humor enhance students' *attention?* Does using humor improve the classroom environment and make learning more *enjoyable?* Does using humor in the classroom help children *learn?* Does using humor in the classroom improve students' *creativity?* Does using humor in testing situations lower students' *anxiety* and promote improved test performance? Should teachers *avoid* certain types of humor?

Bryant and Zillmann conclude that the judicious use of humor has been found to facilitate students' attention to educational messages, to make learning more enjoyable, to promote students' creativity (cf: Ziv, 1976, 1980, 1988c), and, under some conditions, to improve information acquisition and retention. Bryant and Zillmann suggest that success in teaching with humor depends on employing the right type of humor—under the proper conditions, at the right time, and with properly motivated and receptive students.

The following studies provide further discussions regarding the use of humor in *classroom/educational* settings: W. Adams (1974), Alberghene (1988), Bahr (1978), Barnhart (1984), Berk (2000), Berk and Nanda (1998), Bradford (1964), Brownlee (1992), Bryant, Brown, Silberberg, and Elliott (1981), Bryant, Comisky, and Zillmann (1979), Bryant, Crane, Comisky, and Zillmann (1980), Bryant, Gula, and Zillmann (1980), Bryant, Hezel, and Zillmann (1979), Burke, Peterson, and Nix (1995), Carlson (1990), Casper (1999), Chapman and Crompton (1978), Clinton (1994), Conkell (1994), Cornett (1986), Curran (1973), A. Davies (1977), Davies and Apter (1980), Deneire (1995), Dixon, Willingham, Strano, and Chandler (1989), Downs, Javidi, and Nussbaum (1988), Dritz (1983), Droz and Ellis (1996), Earls (1972), Ellermeier (1991), Endlich (1993), Fabrizi (1982), Forbes (1997), Geller (1981), M. G. Gilbert (1990), Gill (1976), Gilliland and Mauritsen (1971), Good (1977), Gorham and Christophel (1990), Hauck and Thomas (1972), Hibbs (1995), Hill (1988), Holt and Willard-Holt (1995), Houndoumadi (1977), J. M. Hunter (1991), Idar (1984), Javidi and Long (1989), Kaplan and Pascoe (1977), Kaywell (1984), Klein, Bryant, and Zillmann (1982), Kuhlig (1983), Lippold (1977), Loomis and Kolberg (1993), Lott (1990), MacAdam (1985), Markiewicz (1972, 1974), McGhee (1980c), McMorris, Urbach, and Connor (1985), McNamara (1980), McNinch and Gruber (1995), Morkes (1999), Morkes, Kernal, and Nass (1999), Mowrer and D'Zamko (1990), Nelson (1974), Park (1977), Porcella (1979), Prosser (1997), Sadowski, Gulgoz, and LoBello (1994), Satterfield (1988), Sev'er and Ungar (1997), Shannon

(1993), Sherman (1988), Smith, Ascough, Ettinger, and Nelson (1971), Spindle (1989), Stopsky (1992), Stuart and Rosenfeld (1994), Sullivan (1992), Tamaoka and Takahashi (1994), Tamborini and Zillmann (1981), Taylor (1971), Tennison (1994), Terry and Woods (1975), Teslow (1995a,b), Townsend and Mahoney (1981), Vance (1981, 1987), Varga (2000), Wakshlag, Day, and Zillmann (1981), Wakshlag, Reitz, and Zillmann (1982), Weaver and Cotrell (1987), Weaver, Zillmann, and Bryant (1988), Weinberg (1973), Welker (1977), D. Wells (1974), Whisonant (1999), Wiberg (1993), Wong-Leonard (1992), Yoder (1989), Yuill (1996), Zillmann and Bryant (1988), Zillmann, Masland, and Weaver (1984), Zillmann, Williams, Bryant, Boynton, and Wolf (1980), Ziv (1987, 1988b).

Morreall (1991) explores three benefits of humor in the *workplace*: its advancement of health, its promotion of mental flexibility, and its facilitation of social relations. Traditionally, the common viewpoint toward humor was that it is a frivolous and unproductive type of play activity, and the phrase "humor in work" was considered to be an oxymoron; as dictated by our ancestry and the "Puritan work ethic," the workplace is for labor and work exclusively and not a place for play/humor. However, in the past few decades, the positive functions of humor in the workplace have come to outweigh the traditional negative biases and prejudices against humor in work. Morreall notes that of all the health benefits of humor in the workplace, perhaps the most important is its relaxing function; the need for periodic relaxation on the job is indicated by the increasingly stressful character of most jobs in today's unstable and fast-paced business climate. A great deal of tension is created for the average modern worker by foreign competition, by dependence on foreign goods and energy sources (e.g., oil, petroleum), and by corporate takeovers, layoffs, and "restructurings." Morreall observes that such workplace stress is reflected in the personal consumption of prescription drugs in the United States, where the three best-selling drugs are Tagamet (to treat ulcers), Inderal (to treat hypertension), and Valium (a tranquilizer), and by the statistics concerning office visits to family doctors: two-thirds of such visits are prompted by stress-related problems.

Morreall asserts that humor's opposition to (workplace) stress may be seen both physiologically and psychologically: in laughter there are lower levels of three chemicals associated with stress—plasma cortisol, epinephrine, and DOPAC; (see Berk, Tan, Fry, Napier, Lee, Hubbard, Lewis, & Eby, 1989; Berk, Tan, Napier, & Eby, 1989; and Berk, Tan, Nehlsen-Cannarella, Napier, Lewis, Lee, Eby, & Fry, 1988); and the activity of the autoimmune system (which is suppressed in stress) is enhanced in laughter (see Lefcourt, Davidson-Katz, & Kueneman, 1990). When an individual reacts to a potentially stressful situation with laughter rather than with fear or anger, she or he avoids these unproductive emotions along with their physiological damage. Morreall also explores the value of humor (especially in the enjoyment of incongruity) in the workplace via its ability to give the worker a greater tolerance for novelty, ambiguity, and change, as well as fostering higher levels of divergent thinking, creative problem-solving, and risk-taking. Finally, Morreall discusses how humor helps groups to work together more smoothly and productively (cf: Consalvo, 1989); in many cases, the ability of humor to reduce feelings of interpersonal hostility makes it important for workers' morale in the workplace.

Decker and Rotondo (1999) examine business school graduates' self-reported sense of humor, their use of humor at work, and their perceptions of their supervisors' use of humor. Decker and Rotondo note that few data are available regarding age and sex differences (cf: Ehrenberg, 1995) in the use of humor and its appreciation in the work environment; they hypothesized that in addition to the role that individual differences play, it seems likely that superiors and subordinates influence each other with respect to the use of humor in the workplace. Decker and Rotondo found that the Multidimensional Sense of Humor Scale (a measure of the individual's use and enjoyment of humor) is significantly associated with the use of both positive humor and negative humor at work; the supervisors' uses of both positive and negative humor are associated also with the subordinates' similar uses of humor. In effect, subordinates perceive their own use of negative humor to correspond more closely to their supervisors' use of negative humor than is the case for positive humor; consequently, if such perceptions are accurate, it is likely that the use of positive humor is more a function of one's personality and less often stimulated by the humor used by others. Inasmuch as negative humor may be seen as "socially risky," its use may be more dependent on cues supplied by others to verify its appropriateness in a given setting, for instance, with a superior in the workplace.

A potential application of Decker and Rotondo's findings is that managers should be aware that their use of humor could have significant effect on subordinates' behavior (cf: Decker, 1987, who found that subordinates rating their supervisors as having a good sense of humor reported higher job satisfaction and rated other supervisors' qualities more positively than did those who rated their supervisors as being low in sense of humor; and Decker, 1996, who observed that the use of positive humor seems to be beneficial to female supervisors' ratings even more than to those of males). Such studies as those of Decker and Rotondo (1999) and Decker (1987, 1996), suggest that the use of humor by supervisors may affect subordinates' use of humor, as well as affecting the subordinates' attitudes, generally, toward the work setting.

Other studies that emphasize the functions, advantages, and uses of humor in the *workplace* include the following: Barnette (1992), Basso and Klosek (1991), Blackburn (1984), Blumenfeld and Alpern (1994), Boman (1996), Boverie, Hoffman, Klein, McClelland, and Oldknow (1994), Bradney (1957),

Braham (1988), Carrell (1994), Cleese (1990), Clouse and Spurgeon (1995), Collinson (1988), Consalvo (1986), Cox, Read, and VanAuken (1990), Duncan (1982, 1985), Duncan and Feisal (1989), Duncan, Smeltzer, and Leap (1990), Dwyer (1991), Ellis (1991), Franzini and Haggerty (1994), Gibson (1994), Greenberg (1995), Hemmasi, Graf, and Russ (1994), Hunter (1978), Iapoce (1988), C. A. Johnson (1997), Kahn (1989), Kaufman (1995), Kaupins (1989), Kendall (1984), Kushner (1990), Linstead (1985), Locke (1996), Mackoff (1990), Malone (1980), Meissler-Daniels (1990), Mougenot (1999), Nolan (1986), Oertel (1990), Parsons (1989), Paulson (1989), Philbrick (1989), Pierson (1990), Reece (1998), Ross (1989), Roy (1960), Russell and Calvacca (1991), Scogin and Pollio (1980), Smeltzer and Leap (1988), Sykes (1966), Ullian (1976), Vinton (1989), Ziegler (1982), Zirlott (1999).

Social Influences/Aspects of Humor

This section examines the separate issues of both the social *functions of* humor, as well as the social *influences on* humor (also see Chapter 3, section on "Theories Based in Sociology/Social Psychology/Anthropology").

As early as the first two decades of the 1900s, writers have indicated a wide consensus of opinion that humor performs useful *social functions*, even though there has been disagreement as to the precise nature of these functions. For example, Bergson (1911) views laughter as a social corrective regarding harmful "automatisms" (by making people aware of their absurdity) and it serves as a factor which is conducive to social progress (cf: Flugel, 1954, p. 731); McComas (1923) suggests that laughter was originally a social signal announcing good news and, similarly, Hayworth (1928) views laughter within the domain of communication theory, and it serves as a social signal to the group ("my theory is that laughter was originally a vocal signal to other members of the group that they might relax with safety"; p. 370; cf: Lorenz, 1963, who claims that laughter—ever since primitive times—has indicated a situation of security for group members, that danger is no longer expected, and that they may continue their enjoyment together without suspicion). Baillie (1921), Bliss (1915), and Wallis (1922)—all with slightly different emphases—view laughter as a social corrective that preserves the mental stability and social unity of the group in the face of the incongruous, the unexpected, or the socially disruptive. Other writers (e.g., Armstrong, 1928; Carpenter, 1922; K. Wilson, 1927) have stressed the potentialities of humor for good outcomes if it could be aroused in connection with social situations; for instance, in cases involving intergroup suspicions, prejudices, or hatreds.

Additional social functions of humor are indicated by Stephenson (1951) who analyzes the utility of humor in social life under the rubrics "control" and "conflict"; as a means of social control, humor may be used to communicate approval or disapproval, to develop common attitudes, or to indicate friendship and safety; as a factor during times of social discomfort, humor may serve to express agreement and to strengthen group members' morale. Radcliffe-Brown (1940, 1949) has provided another social function of humor in the anthropologists' analysis of a "joking relationship," which is a social relation that exists between two persons, one of whom is permitted (and, in some instances, required) to tease or make fun of the other—who, in turn, is expected to take no offense. The parties to such a social joking relationship are persons generally who are brought into close/frequent contact but who have divergent interests that could lead to tension, conflict, or clashes (cf: Bradney, 1957; Coser, 1959, 1960, Daniels & Daniels, 1964; Klapp, 1950).

Chapman (1983a) notes that humor—through smiling and laughter—may serve a wide variety of social functions, among which are assistance in the communication flow of an interpersonal interaction, the indication of social and interpersonal attitudes with relative impunity, the communication of social/group allegiances, the induction of changes in group esteem/morale, the formation of a group coping strategy to aid in times of conflict, the assistance in the maintenance of a social status hierarchy, and the testing of the conditions and standings of relationships (cf: Gall, 1996, p. 183; Martineau, 1972). Chapman also observes that humor is multidimensional and, in particular social contexts, and single instances, may cause multiple and diverse effects among the relevant initiators, recipients, and bystanders; the dynamic social effects of humor on the recipients are mediated partly by the perceived values and motives of the initiator who, in turn, is influenced by the social responses made to the humor (cf: Goode, 1996).

Chapman (1983b) suggests that humor's social functions may be its most crucial aspect for modern humans (cf: Berlyne, 1972, p. 51, on one hand, who asserts that it is doubtful that laughter's major significance is a social one; and Hertzler, 1970, and Fine, 1983, on the other hand, who maintain that laughter is a socially important phenomenon both in its processural occurrence, and in its functions). Moreover, Chapman and his colleagues found various nuances in the humor situation where smiling and laughing serve *different* functions in social interaction: smiling most directly reflects the congeniality of the social situation, while laughter reflects tension within the individual (cf: Chapman, 1973, 1975a,b; Foot & Chapman, 1976; and Foot, Smith, & Chapman, 1977; for a test of the classroom social distance/social facilitation theory that humor facilitates social attraction, see Sherman, 1988; cf: Sherman, 1985).

Ziv (1984, Chapter 3, "The Social Function of Humor") suggests that the social function of humor may be considered as having two aspects: the relationships *within* a group (involving the social system within which personal acquaintances and interactions between and among group members exist), and social phenomena (involving society as a *whole* where humor functions as a social corrective). Ziv notes that various aspects of group life (e.g., formation of group atmosphere or character, lessening of tension and narrowing of conflicts, cohesion, hierarchy, and the maintenance of group norms) are connected with one another and appear in an interlocked and dynamic fashion in which the multifaceted phenomenon of humor is an important aspect of each component of a group's life. Ziv also suggests that humor and laughter may serve as a tool for correcting, ameliorating, or improving society (cf: Obrdlik, 1942, who studied the social function of humor as a way of facing oppressive political/social power).

Other studies that indicate the *social functions* and *social aspects* of humor include the following: Barrett (1992), Berger (1995), Chapman, Smith, and Foot (1980), Davies (1988), Davis and Farina (1970), Dews, Kaplan, and Winner (1995), Dresser (1967), Flaherty (1990), Goodchilds (1959, 1972), Goodchilds and Smith (1964), Hackman (1988), Haig (1988a), Kane, Suls, and Tedeschi (1977), Katz (1996), Knutson (1989), McGhee (1988), Morreall (1994), Murstein and Brust (1985), Pierson (1990), Salmons (1988), Smith and Goodchilds (1963), Smith, Harrington, and Neck (2000), Swartz (1995), Weise (1996), K. E. Williams (1997), Wimmer (1994), Zapinsky (1978).

Concerning the question/issue of the social *influences* on humor, Chapman (1976) describes experiments (within the framework of social facilitation theory, social intimacy theory, and laughter-arousal theory) which demonstrate that the social aspects of situations are crucial determinants of "humorous laughter." For example, given the same humor stimuli, there are great differences in a child's laughter and smiling according to the following factors: whether another person/companion is present, the role that is occupied by that companion, and how the individual responds to the subject and humor. Moreover, in one series of experiments, Chapman cites the following as some of the important features of the companion's presence and responsiveness: the amount of time she or he spends laughing or engaging in humorous smiling; the amount of time he or she looks at the participant's face; how close the companion sits to the participant and her or his seating orientation relative to that of the participant; and whether or not the companion encroaches on the participant's psychological/personal body space while laughing; also, the simple addition of a second companion is not sufficient to increase laughter and smiling, but the degree to which two companions look at one another may be an important determinant of responsiveness to humor.

Other experiments with children demonstrate that a two-year age/status difference between seven-year old participants and nine-year old confederates has no effect on humor responsiveness. Studies with adult participants indicate that canned laughter facilitates overt expressive responses; also, the presence of an unresponsive adult companion inhibits humorous smiling and laughter (this finding is in opposition to results with children for whom the effect of the presence of a companion—no matter how taciturn she or he may appear—is to enhance the participant's laughter). The behavioral effects of such "social influence" experiments are explicable in terms of the sharing of social situations and the companion's variable psychological presence, in terms of reflexive, disinhibiting, motivational, and perceptual models of social facilitation, and in terms of social conformity and social desirability processes.

Chapman (1976) was able to extract two major social functions of laughter from the experiments that he reviewed: humor serves as a "safety valve" against excessive "social arousal," and it alleviates various forms of motivational arousal in a manner that is socially acceptable and physically harmless to other individuals; moreover, other secondary aspects of humor include its ability to attract attention and to convey information. Chapman concludes that a thorough examination of humor is not possible unless it incorporates studies on the social dimensions and social variables of humor (cf: Chapman, 1973, 1974, 1975a,b; Chapman & Chapman, 1974; Chapman & Wright, 1976; Paton, Powell, & Wagg, 1996).

Foot and Chapman (1976) explore the ways in which the social situation modifies by enhancement or inhibition the expression of laughter in response to humor stimuli; in such a context, the laughter of a child may be simultaneously a function of both "humorous" and "social" laughter [cf: the early studies by Ding & Jersild (1932) who found that the presence of another child or an adult enhances laughter more with older than younger preschool children; Enders (1927) who found that young children's laughter is enhanced more by the presence of other children than by the presence of adults; Kenderdine (1931) who found that her nursery school children/participants very seldom laughed except when in the presence of others; and various other studies (e.g., Brackett, 1933, 1934; Gregg, Miller, & Linton, 1929; Wilson, 1931) which suggest that laughter is rarely elicited from children unless there is some form of social stimulation present to accompany the more obvious laughter-provoking stimuli]. Foot and Chapman's own research examined a wider range of social variables than did the earlier studies of the social influence on humor; their emphasis was on the responsiveness of children to *each other* rather than on responsiveness to the humor *per se*.

Among the results of Foot and Chapman's (1976) empirical studies are the following: children are sensitive (i.e., both their laughter and smiling are enhanced) to the presence of a companion of either sex; girls are more affected by the sex of their companion than are boys (girls laughed and smiled more in the presence of a boy than in the presence of a girl companion); children's humor responsiveness is a function of an adult companion's responsiveness; distance between pairs of children (up to one meter) does not seem to influence children's responsiveness to each other, nor does the distance of the adult companion from the children; results with films accompanied or unaccompanied by a soundtrack suggest (with qualifications regarding the equality of the mirth-provoking material in both silent and sound films) that children laugh more in response to a silent film than in response to a sound film; there appears to be no warm-up effects upon the measures of laughter and smiling; and while the relationships between the total durations of laughter, smiling, and looking behaviors generally was very low, partial evidence indicates that children rarely look at their companion without smiling at some stage of interaction.

Foot and Chapman conclude that if they are to advance theory in the area of *social influence* on humor, they need to advance *measurement*. They note that with the exception of the work of Pollio, Mers, and Lucchesi (1972), the most sophisticated forms of measurement typically used have been cumulative measures of duration and total frequencies of particular behavioral events. Foot and Chapman assert that such measurements, however, are no more than summary data, and are useful only for comparing *amounts* of one form of activity or another between or within the experimental conditions.

Other studies that focus on the *social influences of*, and *social influences on*, humor include the following: Alberts (1990), Angel (1990), Burrs (1967), Dale, Hudak, and Wasikowski (1991), Dresser (1967), Emerson (1963), Francisco (1990), Fuller and Sheehy-Skeffington (1974), Giles and Oxford (1970), Graham (1995), Hampton (1973), Janes and Olson (2000), Kronik and Kronik (1989), LaFave (1961), Malpass and Fitzpatrick (1959), Marini (1992), Markiewicz (1974), Meguiar (1988), Meyer (2000), Moore (1992), Mullaly (1981), Nosanchuk and Lightstone (1974), O'Quin and Aronoff (1981), Pretorius (1990), Raniseski (1998), Rosenfeld, Giacalone, and Tedeschi (1983), Rust and Goldstein (1989), Ryan, Kennaley, Pratt, and Shumovich (2000), Sletta, Sobstad and Valas (1995), Smyth and Fuller (1972), Socha and Kelly (1994), Suls and Miller (1976), Warners-Kleverlaan, Oppenheimer, and Sherman (1996), Williams and Cole (1964), Word (1960), Young (1989), Young and Frye (1966), Zajdman (1995), Zelvys (1990), Zink (1989), Ziv and Gadish (1989), Zolten (1982).

REFERENCES

Abel, M. (1998). Interaction of humor and gender in moderating relationships between stress and outcomes. *Journal of Psychology, 132*, 267–276.

Abelson, R., & Levine, J. (1958). A factor analytic study of cartoon humor among psychiatric patients. *Journal of Personality, 26*, 451–466.

Abrahams, R. (1970). The Negro stereotype. *Journal of American Folklore, 83*, 229–249.

Abrahams, R., & Dundes, A. (1969). On elephantasy and elephanticide. *Psychoanalytic Review, 56*, 225–241.

Ackerman, B. (1983). Form and function in children's understanding of ironic utterances. *Journal of Experimental Child Psychology, 35*, 487–508.

Adams, E., & McGuire, F. (1986). Is laughter the best medicine? A study of the effects of humor on perceived pain. *Activities, Adaptation, and Aging, 8,* 157–175.

Adams, J. (1975). *Ethnic humor.* New York: Manor.

Adams, J. (1984). *Live longer through laughter: How to use a joke to save your health.* New York: Stein and Day.

Adams, W. (1974). The use of sexual humor in teaching human sexuality at the university level. *Family Coordinator, 23,* 365–368.

Adelson, J. (1947). Ethnocentrism and humor appreciation. *American Psychologist, 2,* 413.

Adler, A. (1959). *Understanding human nature.* New York: Premier Books.

Alberghene, J. (1988). Humor in children's literature. *Journal of Children in Contemporary Society, 20,* 223–245.

Alberts, J. K. (1990). The use of humor in managing couples' conflict interactions. In D. D. Cahn (Ed.), *Intimates in conflict: A communication perspective.* Hillsdale, NJ: Erlbaum.

Alexander, R. (1986). Ostracism and indirect reciprocity: The reproductive significance of humor. *Ethology and Sociobiology, 7,* 253–270.

Allman, P. (1994). Post-stroke pathological laughing and crying. *American Journal of Psychiatry, 151,* 291.

Allport, G. (1961). *Pattern and growth in personality.* New York: Holt, Rinehart & Winston.

Alperin, M. (1989). JAP jokes: Hateful humor. *Humor: International Journal of Humor Research, 2,* 411–416.

Amabile, T. (1987). The motivation to be creative. In S. G. Isaksen (Ed.), *Frontiers of creativity research: Beyond the basics.* Buffalo, NY: Bearly Limited.

Amada, A. (1993). Role of humor in a college mental health program. In W. Fry & W. Salameh (Eds.), *Advances in humor and psychotherapy.* Sarasota, FL: P. R. E.

Anderson, C., & Arnoult, L. (1989). An examination of perceived control, humor, irrational beliefs, and positive stress as moderators of the relation between negative stress and health. *Basic and Applied Social Psychology, 10,* 101–117.

Anderson, J. (1986). *Scandinavian humor and other myths.* New York: Perennial Library.

Anderson, P. M. (1988–1989). American humor, handicapism, and censorship. *Journal of Reading, Writing, and Learning Disabilities International, 4,* 79–87.

Andrews, M. A. (1990). The positive humorous attitude. *Dissertation Abstracts International, 50 (7–B),* 3142–3143.

Andrews, T. G. (1943). A factorial analysis of responses to the comic as a study in personality. *Journal of General Psychology, 28,* 209–224.

Angel, M. H. (1990). The roles of humor and laughter in marital issue engagement. Unpublished doctoral dissertation, Vanderbilt University.

Anisfeld, E. (1982). Onset of social smiling in pre-term and full-term infants from two ethnic backgrounds. *Infant Behavior and Development, 5,* 387–395.

Apte, M. (1985). *Humor and laughter: An anthropological approach.* Ithaca, NY: Cornell University Press.

Apte, M. (1987). Ethnic humor versus "sense of humor": An American sociocultural dilemma. *American Behavioral Scientist, 30,* 27–41.

Apter, M. (Ed.) (1982). *The experience of motivation: The theory of psychological reversals.* London: Academic Press.

Apter, M., & Smith, K. (1977). Humour and the theory of psychological reversals. In A. J. Chapman & H. C. Foot (Eds.), *It's a funny thing, humour.* Oxford, UK: Pergamon Press.

Arieti, S. (1976). *Creativity: The magic synthesis.* New York: Basic Books.

Armstrong, M. (1928). *Laughing: An essay.* London: Jarrolds.

Arroyo, S., Lesser, R., Gordon, B., Uematsu, S., Hart, J., Schwerdt, P., Andreasson, K. & Fisher, R. (1993). Mirth, laughter, and gelastic seizures. *Brain, 116,* 757–780.

Ashkenasy, J. (1987). The functions and dysfunctions of laughter. *Journal of General Psychology, 14,* 317–334.

Askenasy, G. (1976). Humor, aggression, defense, and conservatism: Group characteristics and differential humor appreciation. *Social Behaviour and Personality, 4,* 75–80.

Astedt, P., & Liukkonen, A. (1994). Humor in nursing-care. *Journal of Advanced Nursing, 20,* 183–188.

Athey, C. (1977). Humour in children related to Piaget's theory of intellectual development. In A. J. Chapman & H. C. Foot (Eds.), *It's a funny thing, humour.* Oxford, UK: Pergamon Press.

Attardo, S. (1988). Trends in European humor research: Toward a text model. *Humor: International Journal of Humor Research, 1,* 349–369.

Austin, J. (1978). *American humor in France: Two centuries of French criticism of the comic.* Ames: Iowa State University Press.

Avant, K. (1982). Humor and self-disclosure. *Psychological Reports, 50,* 253–254.

Averill, J. (1969). Autonomic response patterns during sadness and mirth. *Psychophysiology, 5,* 399–414.

Axtell, J. (1990). Humor in ethnohistory. *Ethnohistory, 37,* 109–125.

Babad, E. (1974). A multi-method approach to the assessment of humor: A critical look at humor tests. *Journal of Personality, 42,* 618–631.

Bader, M. (1993). Analysts' use of humor. *Psychoanalytic Quarterly, 62,* 23–51.

Baghban, H. (1977). The context and concept of humor in Magadi theater. (4 volumes). Unpublished doctoral dissertation, Indiana University.

Bahr, J. D. (1978). A comparison of learning and retention as functions of three levels of humorous emotional arousal, humor augmentation, and verbal repetition of facts. Unpublished doctoral dissertation, University of Southern California.

Baillie, J. (1921). *Studies in human nature.* London: Bell.

Baker, R. (1993). Some reflections on humor in psychoanalysis. *International Journal of Psychoanalysis, 74,* 951–960.

Banmen, J. (1982). The use of humour in psychotherapy. *International Journal for the Advancement of Counseling, 5,* 81–86.

Bariaud, F. (1977). Comprehension and emotional adhesion in the genetics of humour. In A. J. Chapman & H. C. Foot (Eds.), *It's a funny thing, humour*. Oxford, UK: Pergamon Press.

Bariaud, F. (1988). Age differences in children's humor. *Journal of Children in Contemporary Society, 20*, 15–45.

Bariaud, F. (1989). Age differences in children's humor. In P. E. McGhee (Ed.), *Humor and children's development: A guide to practical applications*. New York: Haworth.

Barnette, J. R. (1992). Humor in preaching: The contributions of psychological and sociological research. Unpublished doctoral dissertation, The Southern Baptist Theological Seminary.

Barnhart, N. C. (1984). The humor found in basal readers appropriate to second and fourth grade students. Unpublished doctoral dissertation, University of Maryland.

Baron, R. (1976). The reduction of human aggression: A field study of the influence of incompatible reactions. *Journal of Applied Social Psychology, 6*, 260–274.

Baron, R. (1978a). Aggression-inhibiting influence of sexual humor. *Journal of Personality and Social Psychology, 36*, 189–197.

Baron, R. (1978b). The influence of hostile and nonhostile humor upon physical aggression. *Personality and Social Psychology Bulletin, 4*, 77–80.

Baron, R. (1983). The reduction of human aggression: An incompatible response strategy. In R. G. Geen & E. Donnerstein (Eds.), *Aggression: Theoretical and empirical reviews*. New York: Academic Press.

Baron, R., & Ball, R. (1974). The aggression-inhibiting influence of nonhostile humor. *Journal of Experimental Social Psychology, 10*, 23–33.

Barrett, C. J. (1992). Will Rogers' humor: A study in "communicative reciprocity." Unpublished doctoral dissertation, Ohio University.

Barrick, A., Hutchinson, R., & Deckers, L. (1990). Humor, aggression, and aging. *Gerontologist, 30*, 675–678.

Barrick, M. (1970). Racial riddles and the Polack joke. *Keystone Folklore Quarterly, 15*, 3–15.

Barron, F. (1982). Creativity. In D. J. Treffinger, S. G. Isaksen, & R. L. Firestien (Eds.), *Handbook of creative learning*. (Vol. 1). Williamsville, NY: Center for Creative Learning.

Barron, M. (1950). A content analysis of intergroup humor. *American Sociological Review, 15*, 88–94.

Barry, H. (1928). The role of subject-matter in individual differences in humor. *The Pedagogical Seminary and Journal of Genetic Psychology, 35*, 112–128.

Barry, P. (1999). It's no joke: Humor heals. *AARP Bulletin, 40*, 14–17.

Bartholomew, A. (1984). Wit and accuracy. *Australian and New Zealand Journal of Psychiatry, 18*, 193.

Basso, B., & Klosek, J. (1991). *This job should be fun!* Holbrook, MA: B. Adams.

Bateson, G. (1953). The role of humor in human communication. In H. Von Foerster (Ed.), *Cybernetics*. New York: Macy Foundation.

Bauer, M., & Geront, M. (1999). The use of humor in addressing the sexuality of elderly nursing home residents. *Sexuality and Disability, 17,* 147–155.

Behrens, R. (1974). On creativity and humor: An analysis of "Easy Street." *Journal of Creative Behavior, 8,* 227–238.

Bell, N., McGhee, P. E., & Duffey, N. (1986). Interpersonal competence, social assertiveness and the development of humor. *British Journal of Developmental Psychology, 4,* 51–55.

Bendelac, A. (1988). Humor and affectivity in Jaquetia, the Judeo-Spanish language of northern Morocco. *Humor: International Journal of Humor Research, 1,* 177–186.

Bender, J. (1994). Gender differences in the recall of humorous advertising material. *Dissertation Abstracts International, 54 (11–A),* 4178.

Bennett, C. E. (1996). An investigation of clients' perception of humor and its use in therapy. Unpublished doctoral dissertation, Texas Woman's University.

Berg, D. H. (1980). Humor and orientation as factors in the creative performance of gifted students. Unpublished doctoral dissertation, Indiana University.

Bergen, D. (1998). Development of the sense of humor. In W. Ruch (Ed.), *The sense of humor: Explorations of a personality characteristic.* Berlin: Mouton de Gruyter.

Berger, A. A. (1988). Humor and behavior: Therapeutic aspects of comedic techniques and other considerations. In B. D. Ruben (Ed.), *Information and behavior.* (Vol. 2). New Brunswick, NJ: Transaction.

Berger, A. A. (1995). *Blind men and elephants: Perspectives on humor.* New Brunswick, NJ: Transaction.

Berger, A., & Wildavsky, A. (1994). Who laughs at what? *Society, 31,* 82–86.

Bergmann, M. (1986). How many feminists does it take to make a joke? Sexist humor and what's wrong with it. *Hypatia, 1,* 63–82.

Bergson, H. (1911). *Laughter: An essay on the meaning of the comic.* New York: Macmillan.

Berk, L., Tan, S., Fry, W., Napier, B., Lee, J., Hubbard, R., Lewis, J., & Eby, W. (1989). Neuroendocrine and stress hormone changes during mirthful laughter. *The American Journal of the Medical Sciences, 298,* 390–396.

Berk, L., Tan, S., Napier, B., & Eby, W. (1989). Eustress of mirthful laughter modifies natural killer cell activity. *Clinical Research, 37,* 115A.

Berk, L., Tan, S., Nehlsen-Cannarella, S., Napier, B., Lewis, J., Lee, J., Eby, W., & Fry, W. (1988). Humor associated laughter decreases cortisol and increases spontaneous lymphocyte blastogenesis. *Clinical Research, 36,* 435A.

Berk, R. (2000). Does humor in course tests reduce anxiety? *College Teaching, 48,* 151–163.

Berk, R., & Nanda, J. (1998). Effects of jocular instructional methods on attitudes, anxiety, and achievement in statistics courses. *Humor: International Journal of Humor Research, 11,* 383–409.

Berkowitz, L. (1962a). *Aggression: A social psychological analysis.* New York: McGraw-Hill.

Berkowitz, L. (1962b). Aggressive stimuli, aggressive responses, and hostility catharsis. Symposium presented at American Association for the Advancement of Science—Academy of Psychoanalysis, December, 1962. Philadelphia, PA.

Berkowitz, L. (1965). Some aspects of observed aggression. *Journal of Personality and Social Psychology, 2*, 359–369.

Berkowitz, L. (1970a). Aggressive humor as a stimulus to aggressive responses. *Journal of Personality and Social Psychology, 16*, 710–717.

Berkowitz, L. (1970b). Experimental investigations of hostility catharsis. *Journal of Consulting and Clinical Psychology, 35*, 1–7.

Berkowitz, M. (1954). A study of some relationships between anxiety and the humor response. Unpublished doctoral dissertation, Pennsylvania State College.

Berlyne, D. E. (1960). *Conflict, arousal, and curiosity.* New York: McGraw-Hill.

Berlyne, D. E. (1969). Laughter, humor, and play. In G. Lindzey & E. Aronson (Eds.), *The handbook of social psychology* (Vol. 3). Reading, MA: Addison-Wesley.

Berlyne, D. E. (1972). Humor and its kin. In J. H. Goldstein & P. E. McGhee (Eds.), *The psychology of humor: Theoretical perspectives and empirical issues.* New York: Academic Press.

Bernstein, D. (1986). Development of humor: Implications for assessment and intervention. *Topics in Language Disorders, 6*, 65–71.

Bier, J. (1968). *The rise and fall of American humor.* New York: Holt, Rinehart & Winston.

Bier, J. (1976). Modern American humor. *Studies in American Humor, 3*, 22–32.

Bier, J. (1988). The problem of the Polish joke in derogatory American humor. *Humor: International Journal of Humor Research, 1*, 135–141.

Bihrle, A., Brownell, H., & Powelson, J. (1986). Comprehension of humorous and nonhumorous materials by left- and right-brain damaged patients. *Brain and Cognition, 5*, 399–411.

Birbilis, J. M. (1990). The relationship of sense of humor and hostility to the Type A Behavior Pattern. Unpublished doctoral dissertation, Oklahoma State University.

Birnbaum, M. (1971). On the language of prejudice. *Western Folklore, 30*, 247–268.

Bischoff, R. A. (1990). Humor, stress, and coping: Does laughing mean living? Unpublished doctoral dissertation, The University of Southern Mississippi.

Bizi, S., Keinan, G., & Beit-Hallahmi, B. (1988). Humor and coping with stress: A test under real-life conditions. *Personality and Individual Differences, 9*, 951–956.

Bjorkqvist, K., & Helenelund, K. (1985). Humorous and realistic presentation of film violence and its effects on behaviour. *Aggressive Behaviour, 11*, 148.

Bjorkqvist, K., & Lagerspetz, K. (1985). Children's experiences of three types of cartoon at two age levels. *International Journal of Psychology, 20*, 77–93.

Black, D. (1982). Pathological laughter: A review of the literature. *Journal of Nervous and Mental Diseases, 170*, 67–71.

Black, K. (1994). Pathological laughing and crying. *American Journal of Psychiatry, 151*, 456.

Blackburn, R. W. (1984). Leadership and laughter. Unpublished doctoral dissertation, The Union for Experimenting Colleges and Universities.

Blair, W. (1937). *Native American humor (1800–1900)*. New York: American Book Company.

Blair, W. (1987). *Tall tale America: A legendary history of our humorous heroes.* Chicago: University of Chicago Press.

Blair, W., & Hill, H. (Eds.) (1978). *America's humor: From Poor Richard to Doonesbury.* New York: Oxford University Press.

Blanch, A. (1974). The problem of feminine masochism. *Cornell Journal of Social Relations, 9,* 1–15.

Blank, A., Tweedale, M., Cappelli, M., & Ryback, D. (1983). Influence of trait anxiety on perception of humor. *Perceptual and Motor Skills, 57,* 103–106.

Blatner, A. (1988). *The art of play.* New York: Human Sciences Press.

Bleedorn, B. (1982). Humor as an indicator of giftedness. *Roeper Review, 4,* 33–34.

Bleustein, G. (1981). It only hurts when we laugh: Ethnic jokes and the international theme. *Thalia: Studies in Literary Humor, 4,* 10–13.

Bliss, S. (1915). The origin of laughter. *American Journal of Psychology, 26,* 236–246.

Bloch, S., Browning, S., & McGrath, G. (1983). Humour in group psychotherapy. *British Journal of Medical Psychology, 56,* 89–97.

Bloomfield, I. (1980). Humor in psychotherapy and analysis. *International Journal of Social Psychiatry, 26,* 135–141.

Blumenfeld, E., & Alpern, L. (1994). *Humor at work.* Atlanta, GA: Peachtree.

Blyth, R. (1959). *Oriental humor.* Tokyo, Japan: Hokuseido Press.

Boatright, M. (1949). *Folk laughter on the American frontier.* New York: Macmillan.

Bobo, J. W. (1989). Personality differences in the appreciation of humor. *Dissertation Abstracts International, 49 (7–B),* 2907.

Boman, J. A. (1996). Effective use of humor in nursing practice: Analysing the discourse of nurses known for making it happen. Unpublished doctoral dissertation, University of Alberta, Canada.

Booth-Butterfield, S., & Booth-Butterfield, M. (1991). Individual differences in the communication of humorous messages. *Southern Communication Journal, 56,* 205–218.

Borges, M., Barrett, P., & Fox, J. (1980). Humor ratings of sex stereotyped jokes as a function of gender of actor and gender of rater. *Psychological Reports, 47,* 1135–1138.

Bosker, G. (1995). *Medicine is the best laughter.* St. Louis, MO: Mosby.

Boskin, J. (1986). *Sambo: The rise and demise of an American jester.* New York: Oxford University Press.

Boskin, J. (1997). *Rebellious laughter: People's humor in American culture.* Syracuse, NY: Syracuse University Press.

Boskin, J., & Dorinson, J. (1985). Ethnic humor: Subversion and survival. *American Quarterly, 37,* 81–97.

Bourhis, R., Gadfield, N., Giles, H., & Tajfel, H. (1977). Context and ethnic humour in intergroup relations. In A. J. Chapman & H. C. Foot (Eds.), *It's a funny thing, humour.* Oxford, UK: Pergamon Press.

Boverie, P., Hoffman, J., Klein, D., McClelland, M., & Oldknow, M. (1994). Humor in human resources development. *Human Resource Development Quarterly, 5*, 75–91.

Boyd, R. K. (1991). The efficacy of humor in improving the quality of life on residents of long-term care facilities: An exploratory study. Unpublished doctoral dissertation, Clemson University.

Boyer, J. M. (1981). The relationship among personality, sex, and humor appreciation. Unpublished doctoral dissertation, Georgia State University.

Brackett, C. (1933). Laughing and crying of preschool children. *Journal of Experimental Education, 2*, 119–226.

Brackett, C. (1934). Laughing and crying of preschool children: A study of the social and emotional behavior of young children as indicated by laughing and crying. *Child Development Monographs*, No. 14.

Bradford, A. (1964). The place of humor in teaching. *Peabody Journal of Education, 9*, 67–70.

Bradley, S. (1937). Our native humor. *North American Review, 242*, 351–362.

Bradney, P. (1957). The joking relationship in industry. *Human Relations, 10*, 179–187.

Braham, J. (1988). Lighten up. *Industry Week, 3*, 49–52.

Brennanparkes, K., Goddard, M., & Wilson, W. (1991). Sex differences: Smiling as measured in a picture-taking task. *Sex Roles, 24*, 5–6; 375–382.

Brill, A. (1940). The mechanism of wit and humor in normal and psychopathic states. *Psychiatric Quarterly, 14*, 731–749.

Brisland, S., Castle, R., & Dann, J. (1977). Laughter in the basement. In A. J. Chapman & H. C. Foot (Eds.), *It's a funny thing, humour*. Oxford, UK: Pergamon Press.

Broden, S. (1994). The therapeutic use of humor in the treatment of eating disorders; or, there is life even after fat thighs. In B. P. Kinoy (Ed.), *Eating disorders: New directions in treatment and recovery*. New York: Columbia University Press.

Brody, M. (1950). The meaning of laughter. *Psychoanalytic Quarterly, 19*, 192–201.

Brodzinsky, D. (1977). Conceptual tempo as an individual difference variable in children's humour development. In A. J. Chapman & H. C. Foot (Eds.), *It's a funny thing, humour*. Oxford, UK: Pergamon Press.

Brodzinsky, D., Barnet, K., & Aiello, J. (1981). Sex of subject and gender identity as factors in humor appreciation. *Sex Roles, 7*, 561–573.

Brodzinsky, D., & Rightmyer, J. (1980). Individual differences in children's humour development. In P. E. McGhee & A. J. Chapman (Eds.), *Children's humour*. New York: Wiley.

Brodzinsky, D., & Rubien, J. (1976). Humor production as a function of sex of subject, creativity, and cartoon content. *Journal of Consulting and Clinical Psychology, 44*, 597–600.

Brooks, R. (1994). Humor in psychotherapy: An invaluable technique with adolescents. In E. S. Buckman (Ed.), *The handbook of humor: Clinical applications in psychotherapy*. Malabar, FL: Krieger.

Brown, I. (1991). Response to cartoon and riddle humour by three levels of developmentally disabled adults. Unpublished doctoral dissertation, University of Toronto, Canada.

Brown, I. (1993). Young children's explanations of pictorial humor: A preliminary study. *Early Child Development and Care, 93*, 35–40.

Brown, I. (1994). Perception of humor in cartoon riddles by adults with intellectual disability. *Perceptual and Motor Skills, 78*, 817–818.

Brown, P. E. (1980). Effectiveness of humorous confrontation in facilitating positive self-exploration by clients in an analogue study of therapy. Unpublished doctoral dissertation, University of Kentucky.

Brown, T. G. (1915). Note on the physiology of the basal ganglia and midbrain of the anthropoid ape, especially in reference to the act of laughter. *Journal of Physiology, 49*, 195–207.

Brownell, H., & Gardner, H. (1988). Neuropsychological insights into humour. In J. Durant & J. Miller (Eds.), *Laughing matters: A serious look at humour*. London: Longman Scientific and Technical.

Brownell, H., Michel, D., & Powelson, J. (1983). Surprise but not coherence: Sensitivity to verbal humor in right hemisphere patients. *Brain Language, 18*, 20–27.

Brownlee, C. (1992). The differential effects between humor treatments in computer-assisted instruction when predicting achievement and anxiety. Unpublished doctoral dissertation, The Univeristy of Akron.

Brumbaugh, F. (1939). Stimuli which cause laughter in children. Unpublished doctoral dissertation, New York University.

Bruner, J., & Postman, L. (1949). On the perception of incongruity: A paradigm. *Journal of Personality, 18*, 206–233.

Bruner, M. (1988). The effects of humor, creative problem-solving, and relaxation on divergent thinking. *Dissertation Abstracts International, 48 (10–A)*, 2575.

Bruno, R., Johnson, J., & Simon, J. (1987). Perception of humor by regular class students and students with learning disabilities or mild mental retardation. *Journal of Learning Disabilities, 20*, 568–570.

Bruno, R., Johnson, J., & Simon, J. (1988). Perception of humor by learning disabled, mildly retarded, and nondisabled students. *Learning Disabilities Focus, 3*, 114–123.

Bryant, J. (1977). Degree of hostility in squelches as a factor in humor appreciation. In A. J. Chapman & H. C. Foot (Eds.), *It's a funny thing, humour*. Oxford, UK: Pergamon Press.

Bryant, J., Brown, D., Silberberg, A., & Elliott, S. (1981). Effects of humorous illustrations in college textbooks. *Human Communication Research, 8*, 43–57.

Bryant, J., Comisky, P., & Zillmann, D. (1979). Teachers' humor in the college classroom. *Communication Education, 28*, 110–118.

Bryant, J., Crane, J., Comisky, P., & Zillmann, D. (1980). Relationship between college teachers' use of humor in the classroom and students' evaluations of their teachers. *Journal of Educational Psychology, 72*, 511–519.

Bryant, J., Gula, J., & Zillmann, D. (1980). Humor in communication textbooks. *Communication Education, 29*, 125–134.

Bryant, J., Hezel, R., & Zillmann, D. (1979). Humor in children's educational television. *Communication Education, 28,* 49–59.

Bryant, J., & Meyer, T. (1977). A developmental analysis of children's favourite jokes. In A. J. Chapman & H. C. Foot (Eds.), *It's a funny thing, humour.* Oxford, UK: Pergamon Press.

Bryant, J., & Zillmann, D. (1988). Using humor to promote learning in the classroom. *Journal of Children in Contemporary Society, 20,* 49–77.

Buckman, E. S. (1980). The use of humor in psychotherapy. Unpublished doctoral dissertation, Boston University.

Buckman, E. S. (1994a). *Handbook of humor: Clinical applications in psychotherapy.* Malabar, FL: Krieger.

Buckman, E. S. (1994b). Humor as a communication facilitator in couples' therapy. In E. S. Buckman (Ed.), *The handbook of humor: Clinical applications in psychotherapy.* Malabar, FL: Krieger.

Buckman, E. S. (1994c). Review of the literature: Historical and theoretical perspectives. In E. S. Buckman (Ed.), *The handbook of humor: Clinical applications in psychotherapy.* Malabar, FL: Krieger.

Buffum, M. (1992). Burden and humor: Relationships to mental health in spouse caregivers of Alzheimer's disease. Unpublished doctoral dissertation, University of California, San Francisco.

Burbach, H., & Babbitt, C. (1993). Exploration of the social functions of humor among college students in wheelchairs. *Journal of Rehabilitation, 59,* 6–9.

Burbridge, R. (1978). The nature and potential of therapeutic humor. Unpublished doctoral dissertation, Institute of Asian Studies, San Francisco.

Burke, K., Peterson, D., & Nix, C. (1995). The effect of the coaches' use of humor on female volleyball players' evaluation of their coaches. *Journal of Sport Behavior, 18,* 83–90.

Burma, J. (1946). Humor as a technique in race conflict. *American Sociological Review, 11,* 710–715.

Burns, C. A. (1996). Comparative analysis of humor versus relaxation training for the enhancement of immunocompetence. Unpublished doctoral dissertation, Rosemead School of Psychology, Biola University.

Burns, W., & Tyler, J. (1976). Appreciation of risque cartoon humor in male and female repressors and sensitizers. *Journal of Clinical Psychology, 32,* 315–321.

Burrs, V. L. (1967). The influence of peer reactions on children's humor preferences: An observational learning approach. Unpublished doctoral dissertation, Indiana University.

Bushnell, D., & Scheff, T. (1979). The cathartic effects of laughter on audiences. In H. Mindess & J. Turek (Eds.), *The study of humor.* Los Angeles: Antioch University Press.

Butland, M., & Ivy, D. (1990). The effects of biological sex and egalitarianism on humor appreciation: Replication and extension. *Journal of Social Behavior and Personality, 5,* 353–366.

Byrne, D. (1956). The relationship between humor and the expression of hostility. *Journal of Abnormal and Social Psychology, 53,* 84–89.

Byrne, D. (1958). Drive level, response to humor, and the cartoon sequence effect. *Psychological Reports, 4,* 439–442.

Byrne, D. (1961). Some inconsistencies in the effect of motivation arousal on humor preference. *Journal of Abnormal and Social Psychology, 62,* 158–160.

Byrne, D., Terrill, J., & McReynolds, P. (1961). Incongruency as a predictor of response to humor. *Journal of Abnormal and Social Psychology, 62,* 435–438.

Cade, B. (1982). Humor and creativity. *Journal of Family Therapy, 4,* 35–42.

Cade, B. (1986). The uses of humour in therapy. *Family Therapy Collections, 19,* 64–76.

Cade, J. R. (1992). The relationship between counselor use of interpersonal humor and counselor burnout. Unpublished doctoral dissertation, University of South Florida.

Calvert, J. F. (1968). An exploration of some of the relationships between sense of humor and creativity in children. Unpublished doctoral dissertation, Syracuse University.

Cantor, J. R. (1976). What is funny to whom? The role of gender. *Journal of Communication, 26,* 164–172.

Cantor, J. R., Bryant, J., & Zillmann, D. (1974). Enhancement of humor appreciation by transferred excitation. *Journal of Personality and Social Psychology, 30,* 812–821.

Cantor, J. R., & Venus, P. (1980). The effect of humor on recall of a radio advertisement. *Journal of Broadcasting, 24,* 13–22.

Cantor, J. R., & Zillmann, D. (1973). Resentment toward victimized protagonists and severity of misfortunes they suffer as factors in humor appreciation. *Journal of Experimental Research in Personality, 6,* 321–329.

Cantor, J. R., Zillmann, D., & Bryant, J. (1975). Enhancement of experienced sexual arousal in response to erotic stimuli through misattribution of unrelated residual excitation. *Journal of Personality and Social Psychology, 32,* 69–75.

Capelli, C., Nakagawa, N., & Madden, C. (1990). How children understand sarcasm: The role of context and intonation. *Child Development, 61,* 1824–1841.

Carlson, P. M. (1990). Teachers' perceptions of the use of humor as an intervention with students exhibiting behavior and/or academic problems. Unpublished doctoral dissertation, The University of Nebraska-Lincoln.

Carozza, P. (1986). Humor in psychotherapy: A phenomenological study of the experience of humor in therapy for the therapist. *Dissertation Abstracts International 47 (5–B),* 2152.

Carpenter, R. (1922). Laughter, a glory in sanity. *American Journal of Psychology, 33,* 419–422.

Carpenter, W. (1925). Experiments on the comic. *American Journal of Psychology, 36,* 309–310.

Carrell, A. (1994). Audience/community, situation, and language: A linguistic/rhetorical theory of verbal humor. *Dissertation Abstracts International, 54 (9–A),* 3418.

Carroll, J. L. (1989). Changes in humor appreciation of college students in the last twenty-five years. *Psychological Reports, 65,* 863–866.

Carroll, J. L. (1990). The relationship between humor appreciation and perceived physical health. *Psychology: A Journal of Human Behavior, 27*, 34–37.

Carroll, J. L., & Shmidt, J. (1992). Correlation between humorous coping style and health. *Psychological Reports, 70*, 402.

Carruthers, M., & Taggart, P. (1973). Vagotonicity of violence: Biochemical and cardiac responses to violent films and television programmes. *British Medical Journal, 3*, 384–389.

Casertano, M. A. (1992). Sense of humor and the severity of hassles among elementary school children. Unpublished doctoral dissertation, Virginia Polytechnic Institute and State University.

Casper, R. (1999). Laughter and humor in the classroom: Effects on test performance. *Dissertation Abstracts International, 60 (6–B)*, 3014.

Cassell, J. (1974). The function of humor in the counseling process. *Rehabilitation Counseling Bulletin, 17*, 240–245.

Castell, P. J., & Goldstein, J. H. (1977). Social occasions for joking: A cross-cultural study. In A. J. Chapman & H. C. Foot (Eds.), *It's a funny thing, humour*. Oxford, UK: Pergamon Press.

Cattell, R. B., & Luborsky, L. B. (1946). Measured response to humor as an indicator of personality structure. *American Psychologist, 1*, 257–258.

Cattell, R. B., & Luborsky, L. B. (1947). Personality factors in response to humor. *Journal of Abnormal and Social Psychology, 42*, 402–421.

Cattell, R. B., & Tollefson, D. (1963). *Handbook for the IPAT Humor Test of Personality*. Champaign, IL: Institute for Personality and Ability.

Celso, B. G. (1999). The relationships between health status, humor as a coping strategy, and life satisfaction among institutionalized older adults. *Dissertation Abstracts International, 59 (10–B)*, 5596.

Cerf, B. (Ed.) (1954). *Encyclopaedia of modern American humor*. Garden City, NY: Doubleday.

Cetola, H. (1980). The effect of mood, self-esteem, and direct experience with the thematic content of jokes on humor appreciation. Unpublished doctoral dissertation, Wayne State University.

Chafe, W. (1987). Humor as a disabling mechanism. *American Behavioral Scientist, 30*, 16–26.

Chandler, M. (1988). Healthy irreverence: Humor in stories of illness. *Humor: International Journal of Humor Research, 1*, 299–306.

Chapman, A. J. (1973). Social facilitation of laughter in children. *Journal of Experimental Social Psychology, 9*, 528–541.

Chapman, A. J. (1974). An experimental study of socially facilitated "humorous laughter." *Psychological Reports, 35*, 727–734.

Chapman, A. J. (1975a). Eye-contact, physical proximity, and laughter: A re-examination of the equilibrium model of social intimacy. *Social Behavior and Personality, 3*, 143–155.

Chapman, A. J. (1975b). Humorous laughter in children. *Journal of Personality and Social Psychology, 31*, 42–49.

Chapman, A. J. (1976). Social aspects of humorous laughter. In A. J. Chapman & H. C. Foot (Eds.), *Humour and laughter: Theory, research, and applications*. London: Wiley.

Chapman, A. J. (1983a). Humor. In R. Harre & R. Lamb (Eds.), *The encyclopedic dictionary of psychology*. Cambridge, MA: M. I. T. Press.

Chapman, A. J. (1983b). Humor and laughter in social interaction and some implications for humor research. In P. E. McGhee & J. H. Goldstein (Eds.), *Handbook of humor research* (Vol. 1, *Basic issues*). New York: Springer-Verlag.

Chapman, A. J., & Chapman, W. (1974). Responsiveness to humor: Its dependency upon a companion's humorous smiling and laughter. *Journal of Psychology, 88*, 245–252.

Chapman, A. J., & Chapman-Santana, M. (1995). The use of humor in psychotherapy. *Arquivos de Neuro-Psiquiatria, 53*, 153–156.

Chapman, A. J., & Crompton, P. (1978). Humorous presentation of material and presentations of humorous material: A review of the humor and memory literature and two experimental studies. In M. Gruneberg, P. Morris, & R. Sykes (Eds.), *Practical aspects of memory*. London: Academic Press.

Chapman, A. J., & Gadfield, N. (1976). Is sexual humor sexist? *Journal of Communication, 26*, 141–153,

Chapman, A. J., Smith, J., & Foot, H. C. (1980). Humour, laughter, and social interaction. In P. E. McGhee & A. J. Chapman (Eds.), *Children's humour*. London: Wiley.

Chapman, A. J., & Speck, L. (1977). Birth order and humour responsiveness in young children. In A. J. Chapman & H. C. Foot (Eds.), *It's a funny thing, humour*. Oxford, UK: Pergamon Press.

Chapman, A. J., & Wright, D. (1976). Social enhancement of laughter: An experimental analysis of some companion variables. *Journal of Experimental Child Psychology, 21*, 201–218.

Charney, M. (1983). Comic creativity in plays, films, and jokes. In P. E. McGhee & J. H. Goldstein (Eds.), *Handbook of humor research* (Vol. 2, *Applied studies*). New York: Springer-Verlag.

Chasseguet-Smirgel, J. (1988). The triumph of humor. In H. P. Blum & Y. Kramer (Eds.), *Fantasy, myth, and reality: Essays in honor of Jacob A. Arlow, M. D.* Madison, CT: International Universities Press.

Chatterji, N. (1952). Laughter in schizophrenia and psychotic disorders. *Samiksa, 6*, 32–37.

Childs, A. (1975). A tale of two groups: An observational study of targeted humor. Unpublished doctoral dissertation, University of Tennessee.

Christie, G. (1994). Some psychoanalytic aspects of humor. *International Journal of Psychoanalysis, 75*, 479–489.

Chubb, R. (1995). Humour: A valuable laugh skill. *Journal of Child and Youth Care, 10*, 61–66.

Chun, S. (Ed.) (1977). *Humor in Korean literature*. Seoul, Korea: International Cultural Foundation Press.

Clabby, J. (1979). Humor as a preferred activity of the creative and humor as a facilitator of learning. *Psychology, A Quarterly Journal of Human Behavior, 16,* 5–12.

Clabby, J. (1980). The wit: A personality analysis. *Journal of Personality Assessment, 44,* 307–310.

Clark, W., & Schultz, B. (1981). Pupillary and skin-conductance responses to jokes. *Psychophysiology, 18,* 187–188.

Clark, W., & Turner, W. (Eds.) (1984). *Critical essays on American humor.* Boston: G. Hall.

Cleary, H. P. (1991). Exploring personal constructions of humor. Unpublished doctoral dissertation, Chicago School of Professional Psychology.

Cleese, J. (1990). The really serious business of humor. Seriously. *Creative Living, 2,* 21–24.

Cleland, R. S. (1957). An investigation of the relationship between creative humor and authoritarianism. Unpublished doctoral dissertation, The University of Florida.

Clements, W. (1969). The types of the Polack jokes. *Folklore Forum: Bibliographic and Special Series, 3.* Bloomington: Folklore Institute, Indiana University.

Clements, W. (1979). Cueing for stereotype: The verbal strategies of ethnic jokes. *New York Folklore, 5,* 53–61.

Clements, W. (1986). The ethnic joke as a mirror of culture. *New York Folklore, 12,* 87–97.

Clinton, T. A. (1994). An experimental study of the effects of humor and a conventional lesson on the divergent thinking of undergraduate students. *Dissertation Abstracts International, 55 (8–A),* 2322.

Clouse, R., & Spurgeon, K. (1995). Corporate analysis of humor. *Psychology: A Journal of Human Behavior, 32,* 1–24.

Cogan, R., Cogan, D., Waltz, W., & McCue, M. (1987). Effects of laughter and relaxation on discomfort thresholds. *Journal of Behavioral Medicine, 10,* 139–143.

Cohen, G. D. (1995). Humor and aging: Methuselah and Thalia as close friends. *American Journal of Geriatric Psychiatry, 3,* 93–95.

Cohen, S. B. (1978). *Comic relief: Humor in contemporary American literature.* Detroit, MI: Wayne State University Press.

Colell, C., & Domino, G. (1980). Humor preferences and creativity. *Journal of Creative Behavior, 14,* 215.

Collins, M. C. (1988). Humor: An informal channel of communication used by institutionalized aged to express feelings of aggression due to personal deficits in power and status. *Dissertation Abstracts International, 49 (5–B),* 1619.

Collinson, D. (1988). "Engineering humor": Masculinity, joking, and conflict in shop-floor relations. *Organization Studies, 9,* 181–199.

Cong, D. (1986). *Wit and humour from ancient China.* Beijing: New World Press.

Conkell, C. (1994). The effects of humor on communicating fitness concepts to high school students. *Dissertation Abstracts International, 54 (11–A),* 4028.

Connelly, M., & Kronenberger, E. (1984). Effects of sex and serial position on appreciation of humor. *Psychological Reports, 55,* 499–502.

Consalvo, C. (1986). Humor in task-oriented management meetings. Unpublished doctoral dissertatiion, University of Vermont.

Consalvo, C. (1989). Humor in management: No laughing matter. *Humor: International Journal of Humor Research, 2,* 285–297.

Cook, W. (1985). Change the joke and slip the yoke: Traditions of Afro-American satire. *Journal of Ethnic Studies, 13,* 109–134.

Corbett, L. H. (1990). Effect of bilingualism on humor and creativity. Unpublished doctoral dissertation, Hofstra University.

Coriat, I. (1939). Humor and hypomania. *Psychiatric Quarterly, 13,* 681–688.

Cornelius, G., & Casler, J. (1991). Enhancing creativity in young children: Strategies for teachers. *Early Childhood Development and Care, 72,* 99–106.

Cornett, C. (1986). *Learning through laughter: Humor in the classroom.* Bloomington, IN: Phi Delta Kappa Educational Foundation.

Coser, R. (1959). Some social functions of laughter. *Human Relations, 12,* 171–182.

Coser, R. (1960). Laughter among colleagues. *Psychiatry, 23,* 81–89.

Cousins, N. (1977). Anatomy of an illness. *Saturday Review, 28,* 4–15.

Cousins, N. (1979a). *The anatomy of an illness as perceived by a patient.* New York: Norton.

Cousins, N. (1979b). Why laughter is good medicine. In H. Mindess & J. Turek (Eds.), *The study of humor.* Los Angeles: Antioch University Press.

Cousins, N. (1982). Back to Hippocrates. *Saturday Review, 33,* 12.

Cousins, N. (1985). Therapeutic value of laughter. *Integrative Psychiatry, 3,* 112–114.

Couturier, L., Mansfield, R., & Gallagher, J. (1981). Relationship between humor, formal operational ability, and creativity in eighth graders. *Journal of Genetic Psychology, 139,* 221–226.

Cox, J., Read, R., & VanAuken, P. (1990). Male-female differences in communicating job-related humor: An exploratory study. *Humor: International Journal of Humor Research, 3,* 287–295.

Craik, K., Lampert, M., & Nelson, A. (1993). *Research manual for the Humorous Behavior Q-sort Deck.* Berkeley: University of California, Institute of Personality and Social Research.

Craik, K., Lampert, M., & Nelson, A. (1996). Sense of humor and styles of everyday humorous conduct. *Humor: International Journal of Humor Research, 9,* 273–302.

Craik, K., & Ware, A. (1998). Humor and personality in everyday life. In W. Ruch (Ed.), *The sense of humor: Explorations of a personality characteristic.* Berlin: Mouton de Gruyter.

Crawford, M. (1989). Humor in conversational context: Beyond biases in the study of gender and humor. In R. K. Unger (Ed.), *Representations: Social constructions of gender.* Amityville, NY: Baywood.

Crawford, M. (1992). Just kidding: Gender and conversational humor. In R. Barreca (Ed.), *New perspectives on women and comedy.* Philadelphia, PA: Gordon & Breach.

Crawford, M. (2000). Only joking: Humor and sexuality. In C. B. Travis & J. W. White (Eds.), *Sexuality, society, and feminism*. Washington, DC: American Psychological Association.

Crawford, M., & Gressley, D. (1991). Creativity, caring, and context: Women's and men's accounts of humor preferences and practices. *Psychology of Women Quarterly, 15,* 217–231.

Creusere, M. (2000). A developmental test of theoretical perspectives on the understanding of verbal irony: Children's recognition of allusion and pragmatic insincerity. *Metaphor and Symbol, 15,* 29–45.

Cunningham, A. (1962). Relation of sense of humor to intelligence. *Journal of Social Psychology, 57,* 143–147.

Cupchik, G., & Leventhal, H. (1974). Consistency between expressive behavior and the evaluation of humorous stimuli: The role of sex and self-observation. *Journal of Personality and Social Psychology, 30,* 429–442.

Curran, F. W. (1973). A developmental study of cartoon humor appreciation and its use in facilitating learning. Unpublished doctoral dissertation, The Catholic University of America.

Czwartkowski, L., & Whissell, C. (1986). Children's appreciation and understanding of humorous cartoon drawings. *Perceptual and Motor Skills, 63,* 1199–1202.

D'Adamo, M. (1989). Use of subliminal symbiotic stimulation and humorous depiction of oral aggression as adjuncts in the inpatient treatment of anorexia and bulimia. *Dissertation Abstracts International, 49* (8–B), 3434.

Dale, J. A., Hudak, M., & Wasikowski, P. (1991). Effects of dyadic participation and awareness of being monitored on facial action during exposure to humor. *Perceptual and Motor Skills, 73,* 984–986.

Dana, R. (1994). Humor as a diagnostic tool in child and adolescent groups. In E. S. Buckman (Ed.), *The handbook of humor: Clinical applications in psychotherapy*. Malabar, FL: Krieger.

Dance, D. (1977). Wit and humor in the slave narratives. *Journal of Afro-American Issues, 5,* 125–134.

Daniels, A., & Daniels, R. (1964). The social function of the career fool. *Psychiatry, 27,* 218–229.

D'Antonio, I. (1988). The use of humor with children in hospital settings. *Journal of Children in Contemporary Society, 20,* 157–169.

Danzer, A., Dale, J., & Klions, H. (1990). Effect of exposure to humorous stimuli on induced depression. *Psychological Reports, 66,* 1027–1036.

Darmstadter, H. (1964). The effects of ego strength, motivation, and stimulus content on the humor response. Unpublished doctoral dissertation, University of Pennsylvania.

Datan, N. (1986). The last minority: Humor, old age, and marginal identity. In L. Nahemow, A. McCluskey-Fawcett, & P. E. McGhee (Eds.), *Humor and aging*. Orlando, FL: Academic Press.

Davidson, C. (1987). Ethnic jokes: An introduction to race and nationality. *Teaching Sociology, 15,* 296–302.

Davidson, I., & Brown, W. (1989). Using humour in counseling mentally retarded clients: A preliminary study. *International Journal for the Advancement of Counseling, 12*, 93–104.

Davies, A. (1977). Humor as a facilitator of learning in primary school children. In A. J. Chapman & H. C. Foot (Eds.), *It's a funny thing, humour*. Oxford, UK: Pergamon Press.

Davies, A., & Apter, M. (1980). Humor and its effect on learning in children. In P. E. McGhee & A. J. Chapman (Eds.), *Children's humour*. London: Wiley.

Davies, C. (1982). Ethnic jokes, moral values, and social boundaries. *British Journal of Sociology, 33*, 383–403.

Davies, C. (1987). Language identity and ethnic jokes about stupidity. *International Journal of the Sociology of Language, 65*, 39–52.

Davies, C. (1988). The Irish joke as a social phenomenon. In J. Durant & J. Miller (Eds.), *Laughing matters: A serious look at humour*. New York: Wiley.

Davies, C. (1990). *Ethnic humor around the world: A comparative analysis*. Bloomington: Indiana University Press.

Davies, C. (1991a). Ethnic humor, hostility, and aggression: A reply to Elliott Oring. *Humor: International Journal of Humor Research, 4*, 415–422.

Davies, C. (1991b). Fooltowns: Traditional and modern, local, regional, and ethnic jokes about stupidity. In G. Bennett (Ed.), *Spoken in jest*. Sheffield, UK: Academic Press.

Davies, C. (1998a). *Jokes and their relation to society*. Berlin: Mouton de Gruyter.

Davies, C. (1998b). The dog that didn't bark in the night: A new sociological approach to the cross-cultural study of humor. In W. Ruch (Ed.), *The sense of humor: Explorations of a personality characteristic*. Berlin: Mouton de Gruyter.

Davies, L. (1977). Attitudes toward old age and aging as shown by humor. *Gerontologist, 17*, 220–225.

Davis, E. M. (1983). Effects of self-monitoring, need for social approval, and sex on the occurrence of constructive humor. Unpublished doctoral dissertation, The University of Nebraska-Lincoln.

Davis, J. M. (1966). Appreciation of hostile humor: Some relationships to motivational and personality variables. Unpublished doctoral dissertation, University of Connecticut.

Davis, J., & Farina, A. (1970). Humor appreciation as social communication *Journal of Personality and Social Psychology, 15*, 175–178.

Deaner, S., & McConatha, J. (1993). The relationship of humor to depression and personality. *Psychological Reports, 72*, 755–763.

Decker, W. (1987). Managerial humor and subordinate satisfaction. *Social Behavior and Personality, 15*, 225–232.

Decker, W. (1996). Humor: A managerial tool for both genders? In R. Ebert (Ed.), *1996 Proceedings of the Decision Sciences Institute* (Vol. 1). Atlanta, GA: DSI.

Decker, W., & Rotondo, D. (1999). Use of humor at work: Predictors and implications. *Psychological Reports, 84*, 961–968.

Deckers, L. (1998). Influence of mood on humor. In W. Ruch (Ed.), *The sense of humor: Explorations of a personality characteristic.* Berlin: Mouton de Gruyter.

Deckers, L., & Carr, D. (1986). Cartoons varying in low-level pain ratings, not aggression ratings, correlate positively with funniness ratings. *Motivation and Emotion, 10,* 207–216.

Demos, V., & Jache, A. (1981). When you care enough: An analysis of attitudes toward aging in humorous birthday cards. *Gerontologist, 21,* 209–215.

Deneire, M. (1995). Humor and foreign language teaching. *Humor: International Journal of Humor Research, 8,* 285–298.

Deren, V. (1989). Funny to some, not to others: An analysis of some adolescent responses to Australian humor literature. *Humor: International Journal of Humor Research, 2,* 55–72.

Derks, P. (1987). Humor production: An examination of three models of creativity. *Journal of Creative Behavior, 21,* 325–326.

Derks, P., & Arora, S. (1993). Sex and salience in the appreciation of cartoon humor. *Humor: International Journal of Humor Research, 6,* 57–69.

Derks, P., & Hervas, D. (1988). Creativity in humor production: Quantity and quality in divergent thinking. *Bulletin of the Psychonomic Society, 26,* 37–39.

Derks, P., Leichtman, H., & Carroll, P. (1975). Production and judgment of "humor" by schizophrenics and college students. *Bulletin of the Psychonomic Society, 6,* 300–302.

Derks, P., Staley, R., & Haselton, M. (1998). "Sense" of humor: Perception, intelligence, or expertise? In W. Ruch (Ed.), *The sense of humor: Explorations of a personality characteristic.* Berlin: Mouton de Gruyter.

Deutsch, F. (1990). Status, sex, and smiling: The effect of role on smiling in men and women. *Personality and Social Psychology Bulletin, 16,* 531–540.

Dewane, C. (1978). Humor in therapy. *Social Work, 23,* 508–510.

Dews, S., Kaplan, J., & Winner, E. (1995). Why not say it directly? The social functions of irony. *Discourse Processes, 19,* 347–367.

Dienstbier, R. (1995). The impact of humor on energy, tension, task choices, and attributions: Exploring hypotheses from toughness theory. *Motivation and Emotion, 19,* 225–267.

Dillon, K., Minchoff, B., & Baker, K. (1986). Positive emotional states and enhancement of the immune system. *International Journal of Psychiatry in Medicine, 15,* 13–18.

Dillon, K., & Totten, M. (1989). Psychological factors, immunocompetence, and health of breast-feeding mothers and their infants. *Journal of Genetic Psychology, 150,* 155–162.

Dimmer, S. (1993). The effect of humor on creative thinking and personal problem-solving in college students. Unpublished doctoral dissertation, Central Michigan University.

Dimmer, S., Carroll, J., & Wyatt, G. (1990). Uses of humor in psychotherapy. *Psychological Reports, 66,* 795–801.

Ding, G., & Jersild, A. (1932). A study of laughing and smiling in preschool children. *Journal of Genetic Psychology, 40,* 452–472.

Dixon, N. F. (1980). Humor: A cognitive alternative to stress? In I. Sarason & C. D. Spielberger (Eds.), *Stress and anxiety* (Vol. 7). New York: Hemisphere.

Dixon, P., Willingham, W., Strano, D., & Chandler, C. (1989). Sense of humor as a mediator during incidental learning of humor-related material. *Psychological Reports, 64,* 851–855.

Docking, K., Jordan, F., & Murdoch, B. (1999). Interpretation and comprehension of linguistic humour by adolescents with head injury: A case-by-case analysis. *Brain Injury, 13,* 953–972.

Docking, K., Murdoch, B., & Jordan, F. (2000). Interpretation and comprehension of linguistic humour by adolescents with head injury: A group analysis. *Brain Injury, 14,* 89–108.

Dollard, J., & Miller, N. (1939). *Frustration and aggression.* New Haven, CT: Yale University Press.

Dooley, L. (1941). Relation of humor to masochism. *Psychoanalytic Review, 28,* 37–46.

Dorinson, J., & Boskin, J. (1988). Racial and ethnic humor. In L. E. Mintz (Ed.), *Humor in America: A research guide to genres and topics.* Westport, CT: Greenwood Press.

Doris, J., & Fierman, E. (1956). Humor and anxiety. *Journal of Abnormal and Social Psychology, 53,* 59–62.

Dormon, J. (1985). Ethnic stereotyping in American popular culture. *American Studies, 30,* 489–507.

Doskoch, P. (1996). Happily ever laughter. *Psychology Today, 29,* 32–35.

Dowd, E., & Milne, C. (1986). Paradoxical interventions in counseling psychology. *The Counseling Psychologist, 14,* 237–282.

Downs, V., Javidi, M., & Nussbaum, J. (1988). An analysis of teachers' verbal communication within the college classroom: Use of humor, self-disclosure, and narratives. *Communication Education, 37,* 127–141.

Draitser, E. (1998). *Taking penguins to the movies: Ethnic humor in Russia.* Detroit, MI: Wayne State University Press.

Dresser, J. (1967). Two studies on the social function of joking as an outlet for aggression. *Dissertation Abstracts, 28 (2–A),* 778–779.

Driscoll, R. (1987). Humor in pragmatic psychotherapy. In W. Fry & W. Salameh (Eds.), *Handbook of humor and psychotherapy.* Sarasota, FL: P. R. E.

Dritz, C. A. (1983). The role of humor in teaching. Unpublished doctoral dissertation, Brigham Young University.

Droz, M., & Ellis, L. (1996). *Laughing while learning: Using humor in the classroom.* Longmont, CO: Sopris West.

Druckman, R., & Chao, D. (1957). Laughter in epilepsy. *Neurology, 7,* 26–36.

Duchowny, M. (1983). Pathological disorders of laughter. In P. E. McGhee & J. H. Goldstein (Eds.), *Handbook of humor research* (Vol. 2, *Applied studies*). New York: Springer-Verlag.

Dumas, G. (1923). *Traite de psychologie.* Paris: Alcan

Duncan, W. J. (1982). Humor in management: Prospects for administrative practice and research. *Academy of Management Review, 7,* 136–142.

Duncan, W. J. (1985). The superiority theory of humor at work: Joking relationships as indicators of formal and informal status patterns in small, task-oriented groups. *Small Group Behavior, 16,* 556–564.

Duncan, W. J., & Feisal, J. P. (1989). No laughing matter: Patterns of humor in the workplace. *Organizational Dynamics, 17,* 18–30.

Duncan, W. J., Smeltzer, L., & Leap, T. (1990). Humor and work: Applications of joking behavior to management. *Journal of Management, 16,* 255–278.

Dundes, A. (1971). A study of ethnic slurs: The Jew and the Polack in the United States. *Journal of American Folklore, 84,* 186–203.

Dundes, A. (1975). Slurs international: Folk comparisons of ethnicity and national character. *Southern Folklore Quarterly, 39,* 15–38.

Dundes, A., & Hauschild, T. (1983). Auschwitz jokes. *Western Folklore, 42,* 249–260.

Dunkelbau, E. (1987). That'll be five cents, please!: Perceptions of psychotherapy in jokes and humor. In W. Fry & W. Salameh (Eds.), *Handbook of humor and psychotherapy.* Sarasota, FL: P. R. E.

Dunn, J. R. (1975). The effect of cognitive and aggressive humor stimuli and grade point average on self-disclosure and creativity. Unpublished doctoral dissertation, Mississippi State University.

Dupont, R., & Prentice, N. (1988). Relation of defensive style and thematic content to children's enjoyment and comprehension of joking riddles. *American Journal of Orthopsychiatry, 58,* 249–259.

Dworkin, E., & Efran, J. (1967). The angered: Their susceptibility to varieties of humor. *Journal of Personality and Social Psychology, 2,* 233–236.

Dwyer, T. (1991). Humor, power, and change in organizations. *Human Relations, 44,* 1–19.

Earls, P. (1972). Humorizing learning. *Elementary Education, 49,* 107–108.

Easthope, A. (2000). The English sense of humor? *Humor: International Journal of Humor Research, 13,* 59–75.

Egner, F. (1932). Humor und witz unter strukturpsychologischen standpunkt. *Archiv fur die Gesamte Psychologie, 84,* 330–371.

Ehrenberg, T. (1995). Female differences in creation of humor relating to work. *Humor: International Journal of Humor Research, 8,* 349–362.

Ehrlich, H. (1979). Observations on ethnic and intergroup humor. *Ethnicity, 6,* 383–398.

Eisenman, R. (1992). Using humor in psychotherapy with a sex offender. *Psychological Reports, 71,* 994.

Ekman, P., & Davidson, R. (1993). Voluntary smiling changes regional brain activity. *Psychological Science, 4,* 342–345.

Elbert, S. (1961). Humor preferences related to authoritarianism. Unpublished doctoral dissertation, New York University.

Elitzur, A. (1990a). Biomimesis: Humor, play, and neurosis as life mimicries. *Humor: International Journal of Humor Research, 3,* 159–175.

Elitzur, A. (1990b). Humor, play, and neurosis: The paradoxical power of confinement. *Humor: International Journal of Humor Research, 3,* 17–35.

Ellermeier, P. A. (1991). The humorous professor: A comparative study of teacher humor and the adult learner. Unpublished doctoral dissertation, Seattle University.

Elliott, S. H. (1989). Handling chronic illness when you're old: Relationships of purpose in life, emotional sensitivity, anxiety, neuroticism, and humor to health care utilization in an advanced age population. *Dissertation Abstracts International, 49 (8–A),* 2350.

Ellis, A. (1977). Fun as psychotherapy. *Rational Living, 12,* 2–6.

Ellis, A. P. (1991). The relationship between nursing education administrators' use of humor, and their leadership effectiveness as perceived by faculty. Unpublished doctoral dissertation, University of Maine.

Emerson, J. P. (1963). Social functions of humor in a hospital setting. Unpublished doctoral dissertation, University of California, Berkeley.

Enders, A. (1927). A study of the laughter of the preschool child in the Merrill-Palmer Nursery School. *Papers of the Michigan Academy of Science, Arts, and Letters, 8,* 341–356.

Endlich, E. (1993). Teaching the psychology of humor. *Teaching of Psychology, 20,* 181–183.

Epstein, B. H. (1996). The use of humor in cognitive-behavioral therapy with outpatient depressed male adolescents. Unpublished doctoral dissertation, California School of Professional Psychology at Berkeley/Alameda.

Epstein, S., & Smith, R. (1956). Repression and insight as related to reaction to cartoons. *Journal of Consulting Psychology, 20,* 391–395.

Escarpit, R. (1969). Humorous attitudes and scientific creativity. *Impact of Science on Society, 19,* 253–258.

Eysenck, H. J. (1942). Appreciation of humor—An experimental and theoretical study. *British Journal of Psychology, 32,* 295–309.

Eysenck, H. J. (1943). An experimental analysis of five tests of "appreciation of humor." *Educational and Psychological Measurement, 3,* 191–214.

Eysenck, H. J. (1944). National differences in "sense of humor": Three experimental and statistical studies. *Character and Personality, 13,* 37–54.

Eysenck, H. J. (1947). *Dimensions of personality.* London: Routledge.

Fabian, E., & Vonbulow, G. (1994). Significance of humor in psychotherapy. *Dynamische Psychiatrie, 27,* 245–251.

Fabrizi, M. (1982). A naturalistic study of humor in a third, seventh, and eleventh grade classroom. Unpublished doctoral dissertation, The University of Tennessee.

Fabrizi, M., & Pollio, H. (1987a). Are funny teenagers creative? *Psychological Reports, 61,* 751–761.

Fabrizi, M., & Pollio, H. (1987b). Laughing and smiling in third, seventh, and eleventh grade children. *Merrill-Palmer Quarterly, 33,* 107–128.

Falk, D., & Hill, C. (1992). Counselor interventions preceding client laughter in brief therapy. *Journal of Counseling Psychology, 39,* 39–45.

Farling, U. (1996). Parents' use of humor with their adolescent children: A grounded theory perspective. Unpublished doctoral dissertation, The Florida State University.

Farrelly, F., & Lynch, M. (1987). Humor in provocative therapy. In W. Fry & W. Salameh (Eds.), *Handbook of humor and psychotherapy: Advances in the clinical use of humor.* Sarasota, FL: P. R. E.

Farrelly, F., & Matthews, S. (1981). Provocative therapy. In R. J. Corsini (Ed.), *Handbook of innovative psychotherapies.* New York: Wiley.

Farzen, M. (1973). *Another way of laughter: A collection of Sufi humor.* New York: Dutton.

Feinberg, L. (1971). *Asian laughter: An anthology of Oriental satire and humor.* New York: Weatherhill.

Feingold, A. (1992). Gender differences in mate selection preferences: A test of the parental investment model. *Psychological Bulletin, 112,* 125–139.

Feingold, A., & Mazzella, R. (1991). Psychometric intelligence and verbal humor ability. *Personality and Individual Differences, 12,* 427–435.

Feleky, A. (1916). Influence of emotions on respiration. *Journal of Experimental Psychology, 1,* 218–246.

Felker, D., & Hunter, D. (1970). Sex and age differences in response to cartoons depicting subjects of different ages and sex. *Journal of Psychology, 76,* 19–21.

Fern, T. (1989). Identifying the gifted child humorist: An exploration of the relationships among cognitive, conative, and socioaffective factors in the child's ability to create a joking relationship. *Dissertation Abstracts International, 50 (3–A),* 610–611.

Ferraro, T. J. (1981). The role of empathetic arousal in children's cartoon appreciation. Unpublished doctoral dissertation, State University of New York at Stony Brook.

Ferris, D. (1972). Humor and creativity: Research and theory. *Journal of Creative Behavior, 6,* 75–79.

Ferris, W. (1970). Racial stereotypes in White folklore. *Keystone Folklore Quarterly, 15,* 188–198.

Ferro-Luzzi, G. (1990). Tamil jokes and the polythetic-prototype approach to humor. *Humor: International Journal of Humor Research, 3,* 147–158.

Ferro-Luzzi, G. (1992). *Taste of laughter: Aspects of Tamil humor.* Wiesbaden, Germany: Harrasowitz.

Fichtenbaum, J. (1993). Humor and conceptual flexibility in later life. Unpublished doctoral dissertation, Columbia University.

Fine, E. (1976). Obscene joking across cultures. *Journal of Communication, 26,* 134–140.

Fine, G. A. (1975). Components of perceived sense of humor ratings of self and others. *Psychological Reports, 36,* 793–794.

Fine, G. A. (1983). Sociological approaches to the study of humor. In P. E. McGhee & J. H. Goldstein (Eds.), *Handbook of humor research* (Vol. 1, *Basic issues*). New York: Springer-Verlag.

Fine, G. A., & Martin, D. D. (1990). A partisan view: Sarcasm, satire, and irony as voices in Erving Goffman's–I Asylums. *Journal of Contemporary Ethnography, 19,* 89–115.

Fink, E., & Walker, B. (1977). Humorous responses to embarrassment. *Psychological Reports, 40,* 475–486.

Fischman, J. (1999). The brain's humor zone: The impact of frontal lobe injury on the brain's perception of humor. *U. S. News & World Report, 126*, 49.

Fisher, G. M. (1962). Response to aggressive humor by depressive, sociopathic, and normal persons. Unpublished doctoral dissertation, University of Utah.

Fisher, R., & Fisher, S. (1987). Therapeutic strategies with the comic child. In W. Fry & W. Salameh (Eds.), *Handbook of humor and psychotherapy*. Sarasota, FL: P. R. E.

Fisher, S., & Fisher, R. (1981). *Pretend the world is funny and forever: A psychological analysis of comedians*. Hillsdale, NJ: Erlbaum.

Fisher, S., & Fisher, R. (1983). Personality and psychopathology in the comic. In P. E. McGhee & J. H. Goldstein (Eds.), *Handbook of humor research* (Vol. 2, *Applied studies*). New York: Springer-Verlag.

Flaherty, M. (1990). Two conceptions of the social situation: Some implications of humor. *Sociological Quarterly, 31*, 93–106.

Flugel, J. C. (1954). Humor and laughter. In G. Lindzey (Ed.), *Handbook of social psychology* (Vol. 2). Reading, MA: Addison-Wesley.

Foot, H. C., & Chapman, A. J. (1976). The social responsiveness of young children in humorous situations. In A. J. Chapman & H. C. Foot (Eds.), *Humour and laughter: Theory, research, and applications*. London: Wiley.

Foot, H. C., Smith, J., & Chapman, A. J. (1977). Sex differences in children's responses to humour. In A. J. Chapman & H. C. Foot (Eds.), *It's a funny thing, humour*. Oxford, UK: Pergamon Press.

Forabosco, G. (1998). The ill side of humor: Pathological conditions and sense of humor. In W. Ruch (Ed.), *The sense of humor: Explorations of a personality characteristic*. Berlin: Mouton de Gruyter.

Forabosco, G., & Ruch, W. (1994). Sensation seeking, social attitudes, and humor appreciation in Italy. *Personality and Individual Differences, 16*, 515–528.

Forbes, R. E. (1997). Humor as a teaching strategy to decrease anger in the classroom of students who are emotionally handicapped or severely emotionally disturbed. Unpublished doctoral dissertation, The Union Insitutue.

Ford, T. (2000). Effects of sexist humor on tolerance of sexist events. *Personality and Social Psychology Bulletin, 26*, 1094–1096.

Forsythe, J. (1985). Drug therapy for pathologic laughing and weeping. *Psychology Today, 19*, 76–77.

Foster, J. (1978). Humor and counseling: Close encounters of another kind. *Personnel and Guidance Journal, 57*, 46–49.

Foster, J., & Reid, J. (1983). Humor and its relationship to students' assessments of the counselor. *Canadian Counselor, 17*, 124–129.

Francis, L., Monahan, K., & Berger, C. (1999). A laughing matter? The uses of humor in medical interactions. *Motivation and Emotion, 23*, 155–174.

Francisco, S. M. (1990). Roy's Modes of Adaptation and use of humor related to family functioning. *Dissertation Abstracts International, 50 (7–B)*, 2843–2844.

Frankl, V. (1966). *Man's search for meaning*. New York: Washington Square Press.

Franzini, L., & Haggerty, S. (1994). Humor assessment of corporate managers and humor seminar and personality students. *Humor: International Journal of Humor Research, 7*, 341–350.

Frauenglass, W. (1967). A study of attitudes toward woman suffrage found in popular humor magazines, 1911–1920. Unpublished doctoral dissertation, New York University.

Frecknall, P. (1988). Good humor: A phenomenological investigation into the uses of humor in everyday life. *Dissertation Abstracts International, 49 (5–B)*, 1930.

Freedman, J., & Perlick, D. (1979). Crowding, contagion, and laughter. *Journal of Experimental Social Psychology, 15*, 295–303.

Freud, S. (1905/1916). *Wit and its relation to the unconscious*. New York: Moffat Ward.

Freud, S. (1950). Creative writers and day dreaming. In J. Strachey (Ed.), *Standard edition of the complete psychological works of Sigmund Freud*. London: Hogarth Press.

Frey, W. (1980). Not so idle tears. *Psychology Today, 14*, 91–92.

Friedman, H., Tucker, J., Tomlinson-Keasey, C., Schwartz, J., Wingard, D., & Criqui, M. (1993). Does childhood personality predict longevity? *Journal of Personality and Social Psychology, 65*, 176–185.

Frio, T. P. (1991). The impact of stress on the relationship between interpersonal awareness, humor generation, and behavioral competence. Unpublished doctoral dissertation, Seton Hall University, School of Education.

Fry, P. (1995). Perfectionism, humor, and optimism as moderators of health outcomes and determinants of coping styles of women. *Genetic, Social, and General Psychology Monographs, 121*, 211–245.

Fry, W. (1963). *Sweet madness: A study of humor*. Palo Alto, CA: Pacific Books.

Fry, W. (1971). Laughter: Is it the best medicine? *Stanford M. D., 10*, 16–20.

Fry, W. (1986). Humor, physiology, and the aging process. In L. Nahemow, A. McCluskey-Fawcett, & P. E. McGhee (Eds.), *Humor and aging*. Orlando, FL: Academic Press.

Fry, W. (1987). Humor and paradox. *American Behavioral Scientist, 30*, 42–71.

Fry, W. (1992a). Humor and chaos. *Humor: International Journal of Humor Research, 5*, 219–232.

Fry, W. (1992b). The physiological effects of humor, mirth, and laughter. *Journal of the American Medical Association (JAMA), 267*, 1857–1858.

Fry, W. (1994). The biology of humor. *Humor: International Journal of Humor Research, 7*, 111–126.

Fry, W., & Allen, M. (1975). *Make 'em laugh: Life studies of comedy writers*. Palo Alto, CA: Science and Behavior Books.

Fry, W., & Rader, C. (1977). The respiratory components of mirthful laughter. *Journal of Biological Psychology, 19*, 39–50.

Fry, W., & Salameh, W. (Eds.) (1987). *Handbook of humor and psychotherapy: Advances in the clinical use of humor*: Sarasota, FL: P. R. E.

Fry, W., & Salameh, W. (Eds.) (1993). *Advances in humor and psychotherapy*. Sarasota, FL: P. R. E.

Fry, W., & Stoft, P. (1971). Mirth and oxygen saturation levels of peripheral blood. *Psychotherapy and Psychosomatics, 19*, 76–84.

Fuller, R., & Sheehy-Skeffington, A. (1974). Effects of group laughter on responses to humorous material: A replication and extension. *Psychological Reports, 35*, 531–534.

Furman, B., & Ahola, T. (1988). The use of humour in brief therapy. *Journal of Strategic and Systemic Therapies, 7*, 3–20.

Gadfield, N. (1977). Sex differences in humour appreciation: A question of conformity. In A. J. Chapman & H. C. Foot (Eds.), *It's a funny thing, humour*. Oxford, UK: Pergamon Press.

Gadfield, N., Giles, H., Bourhis, R., & Tajfel, H. (1979). Dynamics of humor in ethnic group relations. *Ethnicity, 6*, 373–382.

Galinkin, M. B. (2000). The spontaneous humor production of four intellectually precocious preschoolers: A window into the mind. *Dissertation Abstracts International, 60 (7-A)*, 2361.

Gall, S. (1996). Humor. In S. Gall (Ed.), *The Gale encyclopedia of psychology*. Detroit, MI: Gale.

Gallagher, H., Happe, F., Brunswick, N., Fletcher, P., Frith, U., & Frith, C. (2000). Reading the mind in cartoons and stories: An fMRI study of "theory of the mind" in verbal and nonverbal tasks. *Neuropsychologia, 38*, 11–21.

Gallivan, J. (1991). Is there a sex difference in lateralization for processing of humorous materials? *Sex Roles, 24*, 525–530.

Gallivan, J. (1992). Group differences in appreciation of feminist humor. *Humor: International Journal of Humor Research, 5*, 369–374.

Gallivan, J. (1994). Lateralization in humor appreciation—Sex difference versus stimulus effects. *Canadian Psychology—Psychologie Canadienne, 35*, 68.

Gallivan, J. (1997). Lateralization in appreciation of humor: Sex differences versus stimulus effects. *Perceptual and Motor Skills, 85*, 528–530.

Gallivan, J. (1999). Gender and humor: What makes a difference? *North American Journal of Psychology, 1*, 307–318.

Gallois, C., & Callan, V. (1985). Influence of ethnocentrism and ethnic label on the appreciation of disparagment jokes. *International Journal of Psychology, 20*, 63–76.

Galloway, G. (1994). Psychological studies of the relationship of sense of humor to creativity and intelligence: A review. *European Journal for High Ability, 5*, 133–144.

Ganim, R. (1992). An examination of the relationship between creativity and humor. Unpublished master's thesis. State University of New York College at Buffalo.

Gardiner, H. (1972). The use of human figure drawings to assess a cultural value: Smiling in Thailand. *Journal of Psychology, 80*, 203–204.

Gardner, H. (1981). How the split brain gets a joke. *Psychology Today, 15*, 74–78.

Gardner, H., Ling, P., Flamm, L., & Silverman, J. (1975). Comprehension and appreciation of humorous material following brain damage. *Brain, 98*, 399–412.

Gascon, G., & Lombrosco, C. (1971). Epileptic (gelastic) laughter. *Epilepsia, 12*, 63–76.

Gavanski, I. (1986). Differential sensitivity of humor ratings and mirth responses to cognitive and affective components of the humor response. *Journal of Personality and Social Psychology, 51*, 209–214.

Gelazis, R. (1994). Humor, care, and well-being of Lithuanian Americans: An ethnonursing study using Leininger's theory of culture care diversity and universality. *Dissertation Abstracts International, 55 (4–B)*, 1377.

Gelkopf, M., Kreitler, S., & Sigal, M. (1993). Laughter in a psychiatric ward: Somatic, emotional, social, and clinical influences on schizophrenic patients. *Journal of Nervous and Mental Diseases, 181*, 283–295.

Gelkopf, M., & Sigal, M. (1995). It is not enough to have them laugh: Hostility, anger, and humor-coping in schizophrenic patients. *Humor: International Journal of Humor Research, 8*, 273–284.

Gelkopf, M., Sigal, M., & Kramer, R. (1994). Therapeutic use of humor to improve social support in an institutionalized schizophrenic inpatient community. *Journal of Social Psychology, 143*, 175–182.

Geller, L. S. (1981). Children's humorous language: A curriculum for developing mastery of verbal skills. Unpublished doctoral dissertation, New York University.

Getzels, J., & Jackson, P. (1962). *Creativity and intelligence.* New York: Wiley.

Giachin, M. (1989). Child humor: An explorative study on narrative and graphic production in a group of children. *Eta Evolutiva, 34*, 33–50.

Gibson, D. (1994). Humor consulting: Laughs for power and profit in organizations. *Humor: International Journal of Humor Research, 7*, 403–428.

Gilbert, M. G. (1990). Cognitive development and humor comprehension with implications for teaching methodology. Unpublished doctoral dissertation, Illinois State University.

Giles, H., & Oxford, G. (1970). Towards a multidimensional theory of laughter causation and its social implications. *Bulletin of the British Psychological Society, 23*, 97–105.

Gill, R. L. (1976). The effects of cartoon characters as motivators of pre-school disadvantaged children. Unpublished doctoral dissertation, University of Massachusetts.

Gillikin, L., & Derks, P. (1991). Humor appreciation and mood in stroke patients. *Cognitive Rehabilitation, 9*, 30–35.

Gilliland, H., & Mauritsen, H. (1971). Humor in the classroom. *Reading Teacher, 24*, 753–756.

Giora, R., & Fein, O. (1999). Irony comprehension: The graded salience hypothesis. *Humor: International Journal of Humor Research, 12*, 425–436.

Godkewitsch, M. (1976). Physiological and verbal indices of arousal in rated humor. In A. J. Chapman & H. C. Foot (Eds.), *Humour and laughter: Theory, research, and applications.* London: Wiley.

Golan, G., Rosenheim, E., & Jaffe, Y. (1988). Humour in psychotherapy. *British Journal of Psychotherapy, 4*, 393–400.

Goldin, E., & Bordan, T. (1999). The use of humor in counseling: The laughing cure. *Journal of Counseling and Development, 77*, 405–410.

Goldin, L. (1994). Anxiety reduction through humorous audiotapes in pediatric dental patients. *Dissertation Abstracts International, 54 (9–B)*, 4918.

Goldsmith, L. (1979). Adaptive regression humor and suicide. *Journal of Consulting and Clinical Psychology, 47*, 628–630.

Goldstein, J. H. (1970a). Humor and time to respond. *Psychological Reports, 27*, 445–446.

Goldstein, J. H. (1970b). Repetition, motive arousal, and humor appreciation. *Journal of Experimental Research in Personality, 4*, 90–94.

Goldstein, J. H. (1977). Cross-cultural researcher: Humour here and there. In A. J. Chapman & H. C. Foot (Eds.), *It's a funny thing, humour*. Oxford, UK: Pergamon Press.

Goldstein, J. H. (1982). A laugh a day: Can mirth keep disease at bay? *The Sciences, 22*, 21–25.

Goldstein, J. H. (1987). Therapeutic effects of laughter. In W. Fry & W. Salameh (Eds.), *Handbook of humor and psychotherapy: Advances in the clinical use of humor*. Sarasota, FL: P. R. E.

Goldstein, J. H., Mantell, M., Pope, B., & Derks, P. (1988). Humor and the coronary-prone behavior pattern. *Current Psychology: Research and Review, 7*, 115–121.

Goldstein, J. H., & McGhee, P. E. (Eds.) (1972). *The psychology of humor: Theoretical perspectives and empirical issues*. New York: Academic Press.

Gollob, H., & Levine, J. (1967). Distraction as a factor in the enjoyment of aggressive humor. *Journal of Personality and Social Psychology, 5*, 368–372.

Golub, R. (1979). An investigation of the effect of use of humor in counseling. Unpublished doctoral dissertation, Purdue University.

Good, L. (1977). Perceived value of personality characteristics. *Perceptual and Motor Skills, 44*, 590.

Goodchilds, J. (1959). Effects of being witty on position in the social structure of a small group. *Sociometry, 22*, 261–272.

Goodchilds, J. (1972). On being witty: Causes, correlates, and consequences. In J. H. Goldstein & P. E. McGhee (Eds.), *The psychology of humor: Theoretical perspectives and empirical issues*. New York: Academic Press.

Goodchilds, J., & Smith, E. (1964). The wit and his group. *Human Relations, 17*, 23–31.

Goode, S. (1996). Physicist with sense of humor spoofs earnest cultural critics. *Insight on the News, 12*, 38.

Gordon, W. (1961). *Synectics*. New York: Harper & Row.

Gorham, J., & Christophel, D. (1990). The relationship of teachers' use of humor in the classroom to immediacy and student learning. *Communication Education, 39*, 46–62.

Gottschalk, L. (1986). Hope and other deterrents to illness. *American Journal of Psychotherapy, 39*, 110–124.

Graham, E. (1995). The involvement of sense of humor in the development of social relationships. *Communication Reports, 8*, 158–169.

Graham, L. (1958). The maturation factor in humor. *Journal of Clinical Psychology, 14*, 326–328.

Grant, E. (1987). It only hurts when I don't laugh. *Psychology Today, 21*, 21.

Gravley, N. J. (1983). Relationships of sex-role identification, self-esteem, and attitudes toward women to responses on a scale of sexist humor. Unpublished doctoral dissertation, North Texas State University.

Green, R. (1977). Magnolias grow in dirt: The bawdy lore of Southern women. *Southern Exposure, 4*, 29–33.

Greenberg, A. (1972). Form and function of the ethnic joke. *Keystone Folklore Quarterly, 27*, 144–161.

Greenberg, M. (1979). Sexual humor appreciation and its relationship to gender, sex-role attitude, and sexist humor type. Unpublished doctoral dissertation, California School of Professional Psychology, Los Angeles.

Greenberg, M.-J. (1995). Therapeutic humor as a process of caring within the nurse-client relationship: Perspectives of three professional nurses and clients in an acute care hospital setting. *Dissertation Abstracts International, 56 (4–B)*, 1935.

Greenwald, H. (1975). Humor in psychotherapy. *Journal of Contemporary Psychotherapy, 7*, 113–116.

Greenwald, H. (1977). Humor in psychotherapy. In A. J. Chapman & H. C. Foot (Eds.), *It's a funny thing, humour*. Oxford, UK: Pergamon Press.

Greenwald, H. (1987). The humor decision. In W. Fry & W. Salameh (Eds.), *Handbook of humor and psychotherapy: Advances in the clinical use of humor*. Sarasota, FL: P. R. E.

Gregg, A. (1928). An observational study of humor in three-year olds. Unpublished master's thesis, Columbia University.

Gregg, A., Miller, M., & Linton, E. (1929). Laughter situations as an indication of social responsiveness in young children. In D. Thomas (Ed.), *Some new techniques for studying social behavior*. New York: Teacher's College.

Grieg, D. H. (1985). Humor processing by aphasic subjects. Unpublished doctoral dissertation, New York University.

Griffit, W., & Kaiser, D. (1978). Affect, quiet, gender, and the rewarding-punishing effects of erotic stimuli. *Journal of Personality and Social Psychology, 36*, 850–858.

Griffith, N. (1989). *Humor of the old Southwest: An annotated bibliography of primary and secondary sources*. Westport, CT: Greenwood Press.

Groch, A. S. (1974a). Generality of response to humor and wit in cartoons, jokes, stories, and photographs. *Psychological Reports, 35*, 835–838.

Groch, A. S. (1974b). Joking and appreciation of humor in nursery school children. *Child Development, 45*, 1098–1102.

Grossman, S. (1966). A study of the relationships between humor and individual problem areas. Unpublished doctoral dissertation, Yeshiva University.

Grossman, S. (1977). The use of jokes in psychotherapy. In A. J. Chapman & H. C. Foot (Eds.), *It's a funny thing, humour*. Oxford, UK: Pergamon Press.

Grotjahn, M. (1957). *Beyond laughter: A psychoanalytic approach to humor*. New York: McGraw-Hill.

Grotjahn, M. (1970). Laughter in psychotherapy. In W. Mendel (Ed.), *Celebration of laughter*. Los Angeles: Mara.

Grotjahn, M. (1971). Laughter in psychotherapy. *International Journal of Group Psychotherapy, 21*, 234–238.

Grotjahn, M. (1972). Sexuality and humor: Don't laugh! *Psychology Today, 7*, 51–53.

Grove, M., & Eisenman, R. (1970). Personality correlates of complexity-simplicity. *Perceptual and Motor Skills, 31*, 387–391.

Grow, M. L. (1991). Laughter for spirits, a vow fulfilled: The comic performance of Thailand's *lakhon chatri* dance-drama. Unpublished doctoral dissertation, The University of Wisconsin-Madison.

Grumet, G. (1989). Laughter: Nature's epileptoid catharsis. *Psychological Reports, 65*, 1059–1078.

Gruner, C. R. (1967). Effect of humor on speaker ethos and audience information gain. *Journal of Communication, 17*, 228–233.

Gruner, C. R. (1970). The effect of speaker ethos and audience information gain of humor in dull and interesting speeches. *Central States Speech Journal, 21*, 160–165.

Gruner, C. R. (1978). *Understanding laughter: The workings of wit and humor.* Chicago: Nelson Hall.

Grziwok, R., & Scodel, A. (1956). Some psychological correlates of humor preferences. *Journal of Consulting Psychology, 20*, 42.

Guilford, J. P. (1956). The structure of intellect. *Psychological Bulletin, 53*, 267–293.

Guilford, J. P. (1959). Traits of creativity. In H. H. Anderson (Ed.), *Creativity and its cultivation.* New York: Harper.

Gutman, J. (1967). The effects of justice, balance, and hostility on mirth. Unpublished doctoral dissertation, University of Southern California.

Gutman, J., & Priest, R. (1969). When is aggression funny? *Journal of Personality and Social Psychology, 12*, 60–65.

Hackman, M. (1988). Audience reactions to the use of direct and personal disparaging humor in informative public address. *Communication Research Reports, 5*, 126–130.

Haggard, E. (1942). A projective technique using comic strip characters. *Character and Personality, 10*, 289–295.

Haig, R. (1986). Therapeutic uses of humor. *American Journal of Psychotherapy, 40*, 543–553.

Haig, R. (1988a). Some sociocultural aspects of humour. *Australian and New Zealand Journal of Psychiatry, 22*, 418–422.

Haig, R. (1988b). *The anatomy of humor: Biopsychosocial and therapeutic perspectives.* Springfield, IL: Thomas.

Haig, R. (1990). *The anatomy of grief: Biopsychosocial and therapeutic perspectives.* Springfield, IL: Thomas.

Halberstadt, A., Hayes, C., & Pike, K. (1988). Gender and gender role differences in smiling and communication consistency. *Sex Roles, 19*, 9–10; 589–604.

Haley, J. (1963). *Strategies of psychotherapy.* New York: Grune and Stratton.

Hall, E. (1993). Smiling, deferring, and flirting: Doing gender by giving good service. *Work and Occupations, 20*, 452–471.

Hammes, J. (1962). Suggestibility and humor evaluation. *Perceptual and Motor Skills, 15*, 530.

Hammes, J., & Wiggins, S. (1962). Manifest anxiety and appreciation of humor involving emotional content. *Perceptual and Motor Skills, 14*, 291–294.

Hampes, W. (1993). Relation between humor and generativity. *Psychological Reports, 73*, 131–136.

Hampes, W. (1999). The relationship between humor and trust. *Humor: International Journal of Humor Research, 12*, 253–259.

Hampton, M. P. (1973). Perceptual differences in humor among children from four different socioeconomic environments. Unpublished doctoral dissertation, Saint Louis University.

Hancks, M. D. (1980). Sense of humor, level of moral development, and related variables. Unpublished doctoral dissertation, University of Kansas.

Harms, E. (1943). The development of humor. *Journal of Abnormal and Social Psychology, 38*, 351–369.

Harrelson, R., & Stroud, P. (1967). Observations of humor in chronic schizophrenics. *Mental Hygiene, 51*, 458.

Harrington, D. (1990). The ecology of human creativity: A psychological perspective. In M. Runco & R. Albert (Eds.), *Theories of creativity*. Newbury Park, CA: Sage.

Harrison, L., Carroll, D., Burns, V., Corkill, A., Harrison, C., Ring, C., & Drayson, M. (2000). Cardiovascular and secretory immunoglobin-A reactions to humorous, exciting, and didactic film presentations. *Biological Psychology, 52*, 113–126.

Harwood, J., & Giles, H. (1992). Don't make me laugh: Age representations in a humorous context. *Discourse and Society, 3*, 403–436.

Hassett, J., & Houlihan, J. (1979). Different jokes for different folks. *Psychology Today, 12*, 64–71.

Hauck, W., & Thomas, J. (1972). The relationship of humor to intelligence, creativity, and intentional and incidental learning. *Journal of Experimental Education, 40*, 52–55.

Hay, J. (2000). Functions of humor in the conversations of men and women. *Journal of Pragmatics, 32*, 709–742.

Hayworth, D. (1928). The social origin and function of laughter. *Psychological Review, 35*, 367–384.

Heath, R. L. (1999). Humor following cerebrovascular accident. *Dissertation Abstracts International, 60 (3–A)*, 788.

Hehl, F.-J. (1990). Relationships between somatic complaints and sense of humor. *Zeitschrift fuer Klinische Psychologie, Psychopathologie und Psychotherapie, 38*, 362–368.

Hehl, F.-J., & Ruch, W. (1985). Location of sense of humor within comprehensive personality spaces: An exploratory study. *Personality and Individual Differences, 6*, 703–715.

Heim, A. (1936). An experiment in humor. *British Journal of Psychology, 27*, 148–161.

Hemmasi, M., Graf, L., & Russ, G. (1994). Gender-related jokes in the workplace: Sexual humor or sexual harassment? *Journal of Applied Social Psychology, 24*, 1114–1128.

Henkin, B., & Fish, J. (1986). Gender and personality differences in the appreciation of cartoon humor. *Journal of Psychology, 120,* 157–175.

Herring, R., & Meggert, S. (1994). The use of humor as a counselor strategy with Native American Indian children. *Elementary School Guidance and Counseling, 29,* 67–76.

Hertzler, J. (1970). *Laughter: A socio-scientific analysis.* New York: Exposition Press.

Herzog, T. (1999). Gender differences in humor appreciation revisited. *Humor: International Journal of Humor Research, 12,* 411–423.

Herzog, T., & Bush, B. (1994). The prediction of preference for sick humor. *Humor: International Journal of Humor Research, 7,* 323–340.

Herzog, T., & Hager, A. (1995). The prediction of preference for sexual cartoons. *Humor: International Journal of Humor Research, 8,* 385–405.

Herzog, T., & Karafa, J. (1998). Preferences for sick versus nonsick humor. *Humor: International Journal of Humor Research, 11,* 291–312.

Hetherington, E. M. (1964). Humor preferences in normal and physically handicapped children. *Journal of Abnormal and Social Psychology, 69,* 694–696.

Hetherington, E. M., & Wray, N. P. (1964). Aggression, need for social approval, and humor preferences. *Journal of Abnormal and Social Psychology, 68,* 685–689.

Hetherington, E. M., & Wray, N. P. (1966). Effects of need aggression, stress, and aggressive behavior on humor preferences. *Journal of Personality and Social Psychology, 4,* 229–233.

Heuscher, J. (1980). The role of humor and folklore themes in psychotherapy. *American Journal of Psychiatry, 137,* 1546–1549.

Heuscher, J. (1993). Kierkegaard's humor and its implications for indirect humorous communication in psychotherapy. In W. Fry & W. Salameh (Eds.), *Advances in humor and psychotherapy.* Sarasota, FL: P. R. E.

Hibbs, S. (1995). The effects of nonhumorous and humorous teaching methods on anxiety and performance of beginning riflery students. *Dissertation Abstracts International, 56 (4–A),* 1286.

Hickson, J. (1976). Humor appreciation as an indicator of the counselor's facilitative ability. *Dissertation Abstracts International, 37, (3–A),* 1306.

Hickson, J. (1977a). Differential responses of male and female counselor trainees to humor stimuli. *Southern Journal of Educational Research, 11,* 1–8.

Hickson, J. (1977b). Humor as an element in the counseling relationship. *Psychology: A Journal of Human Behavior, 14,* 60–68.

Highet, G. (1954). *The anatomy of satire.* Princeton, NJ: Princeton University Press.

Hill, C. (1996). Ego development, creative humour and play, in a "good enough" mothering experience: An infant observational study. *Australian Journal of Psychotherapy, 15,* 82–91.

Hill, D. (1988). *Humor in the classroom: A handbook for teachers (and other entertainers!).* Springfield, IL: Thomas.

Hindman, M. L. (1994). Humor and field energy in older adults. *Dissertation Abstracts International, 54 (12–B),* 6133.

Hirdes, S. (1988). The use of humor and guided imagery in the enhancement of self-disclosure. *Dissertation Abstracts International, 48 (7–A)*, 1709.

Hirt, M., & Genshaft, J. (1982). Effects of incongruity and complexity on the perception of humor. *Personality and Individual Differences, 3*, 453–455.

Hogman, F. (1969). Effects of hostility arousal and manifest hostility on the appreciation of aggressive humor. Unpublished doctoral dissertation, New York University.

Holden, R. (1993). *Laughter: The best medicine.* London: Thorsons.

Holmes, D. S. (1969). Sensing humor: Latency and amplitude of response related to MMPI profiles. *Journal of Consulting and Clinical Psychology, 33*, 296–301.

Holt, D. (1994). Humor as a coping mechanism: Dealing with manifestations of stress associated with children identified as gifted and talented. *Dissertation Abstracts International, 54 (7–A)*, 2513.

Holt, D., & Willard-Holt, C. (1995). An exploration of the relationship between humor and giftedness in students. *Humor: International Journal of Humor Research, 8*, 257–271.

Holzberg, J., Bursten, B., & Santiccioli, A. (1955). The reporting of aggression as an indication of aggressive tension. *Journal of Abnormal and Social Psychology, 50*, 12–18.

Hom, G. (1966). Threat of shock and anxiety in the perception of humor. *Perceptual and Motor Skills, 23*, 535–538.

Honeycutt, J., & Brown, R. (1998). Did you hear the one about?: Typological and spousal differences in the planning of jokes and sense of humor in marriage. *Communication Quarterly, 46*, 342–346.

Hoppe, R. (1976). Artificial humor and uncertainty. *Perceptual and Motor Skills, 42*, 1051–1056.

Horgan, D. (1989). Learning to tell jokes: A case study of metalinguistic abilities. *Journal of Child Language, 8*, 217–224.

Horowitz, L. (1957). Attitudes of speech defectives toward humor based on speech defects. *Speech Monographs, 24*, 46–55.

Horowitz, M., & Horowitz, L. (1949). An examination of the social psychological situations of the physically disabled as it pertains to humor. *American Psychologist, 4*, 256–257.

Houndoumadi, A. (1977). Humor as a facilitator in the learning and retention of written instructional material. Unpublished doctoral dissertation, University of Oregon.

Huber, A. (1974). The effect of humor on client discomfort in the counseling interview. Unpublished doctoral dissertation, Lehigh University.

Hudak, D., Dale, J., Hudak, M., & DeGood, D. (1991). Effects of humorous stimuli and sense of humor on discomfort. *Psychological Reports, 69*, 779–786.

Hughes, L. (Ed.) (1966). *Book of Negro humor.* New York: Dodd, Mead.

Humke, C., & Schaefer, C. (1996). Sense of humor and creativity. *Perceptual and Motor Skills, 82*, 544–546.

Hummel, K. J. (1992). Children's humor appreciation: A study of its potential relation to moral level, gender, intentionality, and damage level. Unpublished doctoral dissertation, California School of Professional Psychology-San Diego.

Hunt, A. (1993). Humor as a nursing intervention. *Cancer Nursing, 16*, 34–39.

Hunter, E. G. (1978). Humor in the pulpit. Unpublished doctoral dissertation, School of Theology at Claremont.

Hunter, J. M. (1991). The effects of teaching strategy and cognitive style on student interpretations of editorial cartoons. Unpublished doctoral dissertation, Virginia Polytechnic Institute and State University.

Husband, C. (1988a). Mass media and the functions of ethnic humour in a racist Britain. In A. J. Chapman & H. C. Foot (Eds.), *It's a funny thing, humour*. Oxford, UK: Pergamon Press.

Husband, C. (1988b). Racist humour and racist ideology in British television, or I laughed till you cried. In C. Powell & G. Paton (Eds.), *Humour in society: Resistance and control*. Basingstoke, UK: Macmillan Press.

Hutchison, S. (1976). Humor: A link to life. In C. Knuse & H. Wilson (Eds.), *Current perspectives in psychiatric nursing: Issues and trends*. St. Louis, MO: Mosby.

Iapoce, M. (1988). *A funny thing happened on the way to the boardroom*. New York: Wiley.

Idar, I. (1984). Humor in the bilingual television series, "Que Pasa U. S. A.?" Unpublished doctoral dissertation, Georgetown University.

Ingrando, D. (1980). Sex differences in response to absurd, aggressive, profeminist, sexual, sexist, and racist jokes. *Psychological Reports, 46*, 368–370.

Ironside, R. (1956). Disorders of laughter due to brain lesions. *Brain, 79*, 589–609.

Isajiw, W. (1974). Definitions of ethnicity. *Ethnicity, 1*, 111–124.

Isaksen, S., & Murdock, M. (1990). Outlook for the study of creativity: Emerging discipline. *Studia Psychologica, 32*, 53–77.

Issar, N., Tsang, S., LaFave, L., Guilmette, A., & Issar, K. (1977). Ethnic humour as a function of social-normative incongruity and ego-involvement. In A. J. Chapman & H. C. Foot (Eds.), *It's a funny thing, humour*. Oxford, UK: Pergamon Press.

Itami, J., Nobori, M., & Teshima, H. (1994). Laughter and immunity. *Japanese Journal of Psychosomatic Medicine, 34*, 565–571.

Ivan, T., & Franco, K. (1994). Poststroke pathological laughing and crying. *American Journal of Psychiatry, 151*, 290–291.

Jablonski, C., & Zillmann, D. (1995). Humor's role in the trivialization of violence. *Medienpsychologie:Zeitschrift fuer Individual-Massenkommunikation, 7*, 122–133.

Jackson, H., & King, N. (1982). Therapeutic management of an autistic child's phobia using laughter as the anxiety inhibitor. *Behavioral Psychotherapy, 10*, 364–369.

Jacoby, L. B. (1988). Humorous students in the sixth grade: A comparison study with studious and athletic students. *Dissertation Abstracts International, 49 (6–A)*, 1374.

Jaffe, J. (1995). Age-related changes in comprehension and appreciation of humor in the elderly. *Dissertation Abstracts International, 56 (5–B)*, 2899.

Janes, L., & Olson, J. (2000). Jeer pressure: The behavioral effects of observing ridicule of others. *Personality and Social Psychology Bulletin, 26*, 474–476.

Janus, S. (1975). Great comedians: Personality and other factors. *American Journal of Psychoanalysis, 35*, 169–174.

Janus, S. (1981). Humor, sex, and power in American society. *American Journal of Psychoanalysis, 41*, 161–167.

Jaret, C. (1999). Attitudes of Whites and Blacks towards ethnic humor: A comparison. *Humor: International Journal of Humor Research, 12*, 385–409.

Javidi, M., & Long, L. (1989). Teachers' use of humor, self-disclosure, and narrative activity as a function of experience. *Communication Research Reports, 6*, 47–52.

Johnson, A. M. (1990a). A study of humor and the right hemisphere. *Perceptual and Motor Skills, 70*, 995–1002.

Johnson, A. M. (1990b). Speed of mental rotation as a function of problem-solving strategies. *Perceptual and Motor Skills, 71*, 803–806.

Johnson, A. M. (1991). Sex differences in the jokes college students tell. *Psychological Reports, 68*, 851–854.

Johnson, A. M. (1992). Language ability and sex affect humor appreciation. *Perceptual and Motor Skills, 75*, 571–581.

Johnson, C. A. (1997). Schizoid defenses, transitional phenomena and humor in bureaucratic corporate life. Unpublished doctoral dissertation, The Wright Institute.

Johnston, R. (1990). Humor: A preventive health strategy. *International Journal for the Advancement of Counselling, 13*, 257–265.

Jones, J. M. (1970). Cognitive factors in the appreciation of humor: A theoretical and experimental analysis. Unpublished doctoral dissertation, Yale University.

Jordan, D. K. (1988). Esperanto: The international language of humor: or What's funny about Esperanto? *Humor: International Journal of Humor Research, 1*, 143–157.

Juni, S. (1982). Humor preference as a function of preoedipal fixation. *Social Behavior and Personality, 10*, 63–64.

Juni, S. (1985). Jokes and the Freudian unconscious. *Psychology, 22*, 20–27.

Kahn, W. (1989). Toward a sense of organizational humor: Implications for organizational diagnosis and change. *Journal of Applied Behavioral Science, 25*, 45–63.

Kambouropoulou, P. (1926). Individual differences in the sense of humor. *American Journal of Psychology, 37*, 268–278.

Kambouropoulou, P. (1930). Individual differences in the sense of humor and their relation to temperamental differences. *Archives of Psychology, 121*, 1–83.

Kamei, T., Kumano, H., & Masumura, S. (1997). Changes of immunoregulatory cells associated with psychological stress and humor. *Perceptual and Motor Skills, 84*, 1296–1298.

Kane, T., Suls, J., & Tedeschi, J. (1977). Humour as a tool of social interaction. In A. J. Chapman & H. C. Foot (Eds.), *It's a funny thing, humour*. Oxford, UK: Pergamon Press.

Kaneko, S. (1971). The role of humor in psychotherapy. Unpublished doctoral dissertation, Smith College.

Kant, O. (1942). Inappropriate laughter and "silliness" in schizophrenia. *Journal of Abnormal and Social Psychology, 37*, 398–402.

Kao, G. (1946). *Chinese wit and humor*. New York: Sterling.

Kaplan, R., & Pascoe, G. (1977). Humorous lectures and humorous examples: Some effects upon comprehension and retention. *Journal of Educational Psychology, 69*, 61–65.

Katz, J. (1996). Families and funny mirrors: A study of the social construction and personal embodiment of humor. *American Journal of Sociology, 101*, 1194–1237.

Kaufman, B. (1995). Sense of humor, job stress, and work related outcomes: An empirical analysis. Unpublished master's thesis, Concordia University, Montreal, Quebec, Canada.

Kaupins, G. (1989). What's fo funny about training? *Training and Development Journal, 43*, 27–30.

Kawasaki, T., Shimizu, A., & Kawasaki, M. (1982). Polygraphic study of laughing in normals and schizophrenic patients. *Electroencephalography and Clinical Neurophysiology, 54*, 26.

Kaywell, J. (1984). Our readers write: Examples of classroom humor. *English Teacher, 73*, 49–50.

Keavney, M. F. (1993). Humor: Medicine for the mind. Unpublished doctoral dissertation, Stanford University.

Keith-Spiegel, P. (1972). Early conceptions of humor: Varieties and issues. In J. H. Goldstein & P. E. McGhee (Eds.), *The psychology of humor: Theoretical perspectives and empirical issues*. New York: Academic Press.

Kelling, G. (1971). Empirical investigations of Freud's theory of jokes. *Psychoanalytic Review, 58*, 473–485.

Kelly, L., Knox, V., & Gekoski, W. (1987). Age related humor as an indicator of attitudes and perceptions. *Journal of Social Psychology, 127*, 245–250.

Kendall, J. E. (1984). Communicating with humor: Identification and analysis of organizational subgroups and their perspectives on humor in the work environment. Unpublished doctoral dissertation, The University of Nebraska-Lincoln.

Kenderine, M. (1931). Laughter in the preschool child. *Child Development, 2*, 228–230.

Kennedy, A. (1970). An experimental study of the effect of humorous message content upon ethos and persuasiveness. Paper presented at the annual meeting of the Speech Communication Associaton, Chicago, IL.

Kennedy, L. (1991). Humor in group psychotherapy. *Group, 15*, 234–241.

Kenny, D. (1955). The contingency of humor appreciation on the stimulus-confirmation of joke-ending expectations. *Journal of Abnormal and Social Psychology, 51*, 644–648.

Keough, W. (1990). *Punchlines: The violence of American humor.* New York: Paragon House.

Kerrigan, J. (1983). The perceived effect of humor on six facilitative therapeutic conditions. *Dissertation Abstracts International, 44 (6–A),* 1694.

Khoury, R. (1977). Sex and intelligence differences in humor appreciation: A re-examination. *Social Behaviour and Personality, 5,* 377–382.

Khoury, R. (1978). The demythologization of humor. *Psychology: A Quarterly Journal of Human Behavior, 15,* 48–50.

Killinger, B. (1977). The place of humor in adult psychotherapy. In A. J. Chapman & H. C. Foot (Eds.), *It's a funny thing, humour.* Oxford, UK: Pergamon Press.

Killinger, B. (1987). Humor in psychotherapy: A shift to a new perspective. In W. Fry & W. Salameh (Eds.), *Handbook of humor and psychotherapy.* Sarasota, FL: P. R. E.

Kimmel, M. (1987). Healthy laugh. *Psychology Today, 21,* 5.

Kimmins, C. W. (1928). *The springs of laughter.* London: Methuen.

King, C. M. (1995). The influence of humor in violent action films on audience distress: Effects of hero humor, villain humor, and respondent gender on evaluations of fictional and non-fictional violence. Unpublished doctoral dissertation, The University of Alabama.

King, P., & King, J. (1973). A children's humor test. *Psychological Reports, 33,* 632.

Kinnosuke, A. (1927). What makes Japan laugh? *Outlook, 146,* 49–51.

Kizner, B. (1994). Use of humor in the treatment of people with cancer. In E. S. Buckman (Ed.), *The handbook of humor: Clinical applications in psychotherapy.* Malabar, FL: Krieger.

Klapp, O. (1950). The fool as a social type. *American Journal of Sociology, 55,* 157–162.

Klein, A. (1989). *Healing power of humor: Techniques for getting through loss, setbacks, upsets, disappointments, difficulties, trials, tribulations, and all that not-so-funny stuff.* Los Angeles: Tarcher.

Klein, D., Bryant, J., & Zillmann, D. (1982). Relationship between humor in introductory textbooks and students' evaluations of the texts' appeal and effectiveness. *Psychological Reports, 50,* 235–241.

Klein, J. (1974). The use of humour in counseling. *Canadian Counselor, 8,* 233–237.

Klein, J. (1976). Rationality and humour in counseling. *Canadian Counselor, 11,* 28–32.

Klein, M. A. (1992). The effects of exposure to positive humor on reducing public speaking apprehension among college undergraduate students. Unpublished doctoral dissertation, University of Maryland-College Park.

Kleinke, C., & Taylor, C. (1991). Evaluation of opposite-sex person as a function of gazing, smiling, and forward lean. *Journal of Social Psychology, 131,* 451–453.

Kline, L. W. (1907). The psychology of humor. *American Journal of Psychology, 18,* 421–441.

Kline, P. (1977a). Individual differences in humour: Discussion. In A. J. Chapman & H. C. Foot (Eds.), *It's a funny thing, humour.* Oxford, UK; Pergamon Press.

Kline, P. (1977b). The psychoanalytic theory of humour and laughter. In A. J. Chapman & H. C. Foot (Eds.), *It's a funny thing, humour.* Oxford, UK: Pergamon Press.

Klymasz, R. (1970). The ethnic joke in Canada today. *Keystone Folklore Quarterly, 15,* 167–173.

Knutson, R. L. (1989). Political partisanship, ideological identification, and rhetorical community: Attitudes and preferences in the use of political humor. *Dissertation Abstracts International, 49 (10–A),* 2861–2862.

Koelin, J. M. (1988). A phenomenological investigation of humor in psychotherapy. *Dissertation Abstracts International, 49 (4–B),* 1391.

Koestler, A. (1961). Some aspects of the creative process. In S. Farber & R. Wilson (Eds.), *Man and civilization: Control of the mind.* New York: McGraw-Hill.

Koestler, A. (1964). *The act of creation.* New York: Macmillan.

Konig, K. (1995). Humor in group therapy. *Gruppenpsychotherapie und Gruppendynamik, 31,* 16–22.

Koppel, M. (1969). The effects of humor on induced anxiety. Unpublished doctoral dissertation, Northwestern University.

Koppel, M., & Sechrest, L. (1970). A multitrait-multimethod matrix analysis of sense of humor. *Educational and Psychological Measurement, 30,* 77–85.

Korb, L. (1988). Humor: A tool for the psychoanalyst. *Ego Psychology, 11,* 45–54.

Korotkov, D., & Belicki, K. (1989). Relationships among humor appreciation, nightmare disturbance, and other dream phenomena. *Perceptual and Motor Skills, 69,* 786.

Kotthoff, H. (2000). Gender and joking: On the complexities of women's image politics in humorous narratives. *Journal of Pragmatics, 32,* 55–80.

Kovac, T. (1999a). Creativity and humor. *Vyskumny Ustav Detskij Psychologie a Patopsychologie, 34,* 346–350.

Kovac, T. (1999b). Humor and creativity in intrapsychological bonds (Empiric probe). *Studia Psychologica, 41,* 360–362.

Kramer, H. (1954). Laughing spells in patients after lobotomy. *Journal of Nervous and Mental Disease, 119,* 517–522.

Kravitz, S. (1977). London jokes and ethnic stereotypes. *Western Folklore, 36,* 275–301.

Krents, E. J. (1982). The humor response of deaf children: An exploratory study. Unpublished doctoral dissertation, Columbia University.

Kris, W. (1952). *Psychoanalytic explorations in art.* New York: International University Press.

Krogh, S. (1988). Role of humor in children's sharing. *Early Child Development and Care, 30,* 205–212.

Kronik, A., & Kronik, E. (1989). Diagnosis of satisfaction in significant relationships. *Voprosy Psikhologii, 5,* 112–121.

Kropiunigg, U. (1985). Why does psychotherapy work? *Zeitschrift fur Individual Psychologie, 10,* 57–71.

Kubie, L. (1971). The destructive potential of humor in psychotherapy. *American Journal of Psychiatry, 127,* 861–866.

Kuhlig, R. E. (1983). Socialization as a function of classroom humor. Unpublished doctoral dissertation, The University of Connecticut.

Kuhlman, T. (1984). *Humor and psychotherapy*. Homewood, IL: Dorsey.

Kuhlman, T. (1988). Gallows humor for a scaffold setting: Managing aggressive patients on a maximum-security forensic unit. *Hospital and Community Psychiatry, 39*, 1085–1090.

Kuhlman, T. (1993). Humor in stressful milieus. In W. Fry & W. Salameh (Eds.), *Advances in humor and psychotherapy*. Sarasota, FL: P. R. E.

Kuiper, N., & Martin, R. A. (1993). Humor as self-concept. *Humor: International Journal of Humor Research, 6*, 251–270.

Kuiper, N., & Martin, R. A. (1998). Is sense of humor a positive personality characteristic? In W. Ruch (Ed.), *The sense of humor: Explorations of a personality characteristic*. Berlin: Mouton de Gruyter.

Kuiper, N., Martin, R. A., & Dance, K. (1992). Sense of humour and enhanced quality of life. *Personality and Individual Differences, 13*, 1273–1283.

Kuiper, N., Martin, R. A., & Olinger, L. (1993). Coping humour, stress, and cognitive appraisals. *Canadian Journal of Behavioural Science, 25*, 81–96.

Kuiper, N., Martin, R. A. Olinger, L., Kazarian, S., & Jette, J. (1998). Sense of humor, self-concept, and psychological well-being in psychiatric inpatients. *Humor: International Journal of Humor Research, 11*, 357–381.

Kuiper, N., McKenzie, S., & Belanger, K. (1995). Cognitive appraisals and individual differences in sense of humor: Motivational and affective implications. *Personality and Individual Differences, 19*, 359–372.

Kuipers, G. (2000). The difference between a Surinamese and a Turk: Ethnic jokes and the position of ethnic minorities in the Netherlands. *Humor: International Journal of Humor Research, 13*, 141–175.

Kushner, M. (1990). *The light touch: How to use humor for business success*. New York: Simon & Schuster.

Kuznetsova, N. F. (1990). Creative abilities as a determinant of sense of humor at different ages. *Novye Issledovaniya v Psihologii i Vozrastnoji Fiziologii, 2*, 52–55.

Kwandt, J. (1992). The use of humor to relieve stress in psychiatric nurses. Unpublished doctoral dissertation, The College of William and Mary.

Labott, S., & Martin, R. B. (1987). Stress-moderating effects of weeping and humor. *Journal of Human Stress, 13*, 159–164.

Labrentz, H. (1973). The effects of humor on the initial client-counselor relationship. Unpublished doctoral dissertation, University of Southern Mississippi.

Lacroix, M. (1974). Humorous drawings and directed reverie therapy of children. *Etudes Psychotherapiques, 15*, 17–27.

LaFave, L. (1961). Humor judgments as a function of reference groups: An experimental study. Doctoral dissertation, University of Oklahoma.

LaFave, L. (1972). Humor judgments as a function of reference groups and identification classes. In J. H. Goldstein & P. E. McGhee (Eds.), *The psychology of humor: Theoretical perspectives and empirical issues*. New York: Academic Press.

LaFave, L. (1977). Ethnic humor: From paradoxes towards principles. In A. J. Chapman & H. C. Foot (Eds.), *It's a funny thing, humour*. Oxford, UK: Pergamon Press.

LaFave, L., Haddad, J., & Maesen, W. (1976). Superiority, enhanced self-esteem, and perceived incongruity humour theory. In A. J. Chapman & H. C. Foot (Eds.), *Humour and laughter: Theory, research, and applications*. London: Wiley.

LaFave, L., Haddad, J., & Marshall, N. (1974). Humor judgments as a function of identification classes. *Sociology of Social Research, 58*, 184–194.

LaFave, L., & Mannell, R. (1976). Does ethnic humor serve prejudice? *Journal of Communication, 26*, 116–123.

LaFave, L., McCarthy, K., & Haddad, J. (1973). Humor judgments as a function of identification classes: Canadian versus American. *Journal of Psychology, 85*, 53–59.

Laffal, J., Levine, J., & Redlich, F. C. (1953). An anxiety-reduction theory of humor. *American Psychologist, 8*, 383.

LaGaipa, J. J. (1957). An analysis of authoritarian submission and hostility toward authority by the use of humor as a semi-projective technique. Unpublished doctoral dissertation, The American University.

LaGaipa, J. J. (1968). Stress, authoritarianism, and the enjoyment of different kinds of hostile humor. *Journal of Psychology, 70*, 3–8.

Laing, A. (1939). The sense of humor in childhood and adolescence. *British Journal of Educational Psychology, 9*, 201.

Lamb, C. (1968). Personality correlates of humor enjoyment following motivational arousal. *Journal of Personality and Social Psychology, 9*, 237–241.

Lamb, C. (1980). Use of paradoxical intention: Self-management through laughter. *Personnel and Guidance Journal, 59*, 217–219.

Lampert, M. (1996). Studying gender differences in conversational humor of adults and children. In D. I. Slobin & J. Gerhardt (Eds), *Social interaction, social context, and language: Essays in honor of Susan Ervin-Tripp*. Mahwah, NJ: Erlbaum.

Lampert, M., & Ervin-Tripp, S. (1993). Structured coding for the study of language and social interaction. In J. A. Edwards & M. D. Lampert (Eds.), *Talking data: Transcription and coding in discourse research*. Hillsdale, NJ: Erlbaum.

Lampert, M., & Ervin-Tripp, S. (1998). Exploring paradigms: The study of gender and sense of humor near the end of the 20th century. In W. Ruch (Ed.), *The sense of humor: Explorations of a personality characteristic*. Berlin: Mouton de Gruyter.

Lampton, W. (1971). The effect of humor in a persuasive sermon. Paper presented at the annual meeting of the Speech Communication Association, Chicago, IL.

Landis, C., & Ross, J. (1933). Humor and its relation to other personality traits. *Journal of Social Psychology, 4*, 156–174.

Landy, D., & Mettee, D. (1969). Evaluation of an aggressor as a function of exposure to cartoon humor. *Journal of Personality and Social Psychology, 12*, 66–71.

Langevin, R., & Day, H. (1972). Physiological correlates of humor. In J. H. Goldstein & P. E. McGhee (Eds.), *The psychology of humor: Theoretical perspectives and empirical issues*. New York: Academic Press.

LaPointe, L., Mowrer, D., & Case, J. (1990). Comparative acoustic analysis of the laugh responses of 20–year old and 70–year old males. *International Journal of Aging and Human Development, 31*, 1–9.

Larkin, R. (Ed.) (1975). *The international joke book*. New York: Leisure.

LaRossa, R., Jaret, C., Gadgil, M., & Wynn, G. R. (2000). The changing culture of fatherhood in comic-strip families: A six-decade analysis. *Journal of Marriage and the Family, 62*, 375–387.

Leacock, S. (Ed.) (1936). *Greatest pages of American humor*. New York: Doubleday.

Leak, G. (1974). Effects of hostility arousal and aggressive humor on catharsis and humor preference. *Journal of Personality and Social Psychology, 30*, 736–740.

Lederman, S. (1988). "Humor: A tool for the psychoanalyst": Comment. *Ego Psychology, 11*, 55–59.

Lee, J., & Griffith, R. (1960). Forgetting of humor: Repression? *American Psychologist, 15*, 436.

Lee, J., & Griffith, R. (1963). Forgetting jokes: A function of repression? *Journal of Individual Psychology, 19*, 213–215.

Leekman, S., & Prior, M. (1994). Can autistic children distinguish lies from jokes? A second look at second-order belief attribution. *Journal of Child Psychology and Psychiatry and Allied Disciplines, 35*, 901–915.

Lefcourt, H. (1996). Perspective-taking humor and authoritarianism as predictors of anthropocentrism. *Humor: International Journal of Humor Research, 9*, 57–72.

Lefcourt, H., Antrobus, P., & Hogg, E. (1974). Humor response and humor production as a function of locus of control, field dependence, and type of reinforcements. *Journal of Personality, 42*, 632–651.

Lefcourt, H., & Davidson, K. (1991). The role of humor and the self. In C. Snyder & D. Forsyth (Eds.), *Handbook of Social and Clinical Psychology*. New York: Pergamon Press.

Lefcourt, H., Davidson, K., Shepherd, R., Phillips, M., Prkachin, K., & Mills, D. (1995). Perspective-taking humor: Accounting for stress moderation. *Journal of Social and Clinical Psychology, 14*, 373–391.

Lefcourt, H., Davidson-Katz, K., & Kueneman, K. (1990). Humor and immune-system functioning. *Humor: International Journal of Humor Research, 3*, 305–321.

Lefcourt, H., Gronnerud, P., & McDonald, P. (1973). Cognitive activity and hypothesis formation during a double entendre word association test as a function of locus of control and field dependence. *Canadian Journal of Behavioral Science, 5*, 161–173.

Lefcourt, H., & Martin, R. A. (1986). *Humor and life stress: Antidote to adversity*. New York: Springer-Verlag.

Lefcourt, H., & Shepherd, R. (1995). Organ donation, authoritarianism, and perspective-taking humor. *Journal of Research in Personality, 29*, 121–138.

Lefcourt, H., Sordoni, C., & Sordoni, C. (1974). Locus of control and the expression of humor. *Journal of Personality, 42,* 130–143.

Lefcourt, H., & Thomas, S. (1998). Humor and stress revisited. In W. Ruch (Ed.), *The sense of humor: Explorations of a personality characteristic.* Berlin: Mouton de Gruyter.

Legman, G. (1968). *The rationale of the dirty joke: An analysis of sexual humor.* New York: Grove.

Lehman, K. M. (1995). A reformulation on the study of the stress-moderating effects of productive humor. Unpublished doctoral dissertation, Northern Illinois University.

Leitner, K. (1992). Children's recognition of double meanings. Unpublished doctoral dissertation, Columbia University.

Lemma, A. (1999). *Humour on the couch: Exploring humour in psychotherapy and everyday life.* London: Whurr.

Leventhal, H., & Cupchik, G. (1975). The informational and facilitative effects of an audience upon expression and evaluation of humorous stimuli. *Journal of Experimental Social Psychology, 11,* 363–380.

Leventhal, H., & Safer, M. (1977). Individual differences, personality, and humor appreciation. Introduction to symposium. In A. J. Chapman & H. C. Foot (Eds.), *It's a funny thing, humour.* Oxford, UK: Pergamon Press.

Levi, L. (1965). The urinary output of adrenalin and noradrenalin during pleasant and unpleasant emotional states: A preliminary report. *Psychosomatic Medicine, 27,* 80–85.

Levin, M. (1957). Wit and schizophrenic thinking. *American Journal of Psychiatry, 113,* 917–923.

Levine, J. (1976). The feminine routine. *Journal of Communication, 26,* 173–175.

Levine, J. (1977). Humor as a form of therapy. In A. J. Chapman & H. C. Foot (Eds.), *It's a funny thing, humour.* Oxford, UK: Pergamon Press.

Levine, J. (1980). The clinical use of humor in work with children. In P. E. McGhee & A. J. Chapman (Eds.), *Children's humour.* London: Wiley.

Levine, J., & Abelson, R. (1959). Humor as a disturbing stimulus. *Journal of General Psychology, 60,* 191–200.

Levine, J., & Rakusin, J. (1959). The sense of humor of college students and psychiatric patients. *Journal of General Psychology, 60,* 183–190.

Levine, J., & Redlich, F. C. (1955). Failure to understand humor. *Psychoanalytic Quarterly, 24,* 560–572.

Levine, J., & Redlich, F. C. (1960). Intellectual and emotional factors in the appreciation of humor. *Journal of General Psychology, 62,* 25–35.

Levinson, D. (1962). The psychotherapist's contribution to the patient's treatment career. In H. Strupp & L. Luborsky (Eds.), *Research in psychotherapy* (Vol. 2). Washington, DC: American Psychological Association.

Lewin, P. G. (1980). Effects of sex-role and temporary group membership on men's appreciation of sexist humor. Unpublished doctoral dissertation, New York University.

Lieber, D. (1986). Laughter and humor in critical care. *Dementia and Critical Care Nursing, 5,* 162–170.

Lieberman, J. (1965). Playfulness and divergent thinking: An investigation of their relationship at the kindergarten level. *Journal of Genetic Psychology, 107,* 219–224.

Lieberman, J. (1977). *Playfulness: Its relationship to imagination and creativity.* New York: Academic Press.

Lindsey, D., & Benjamin, J. (1979). Humor in the emergency room. In H. Mindess & J. Turek (Eds.), *The study of humor.* Los Angeles: Antioch University.

Linneman, W. (1974). Immigrant stereotypes: 1800–1900. *Studies in American Humor, 1,* 28–39.

Linneman, W. (1984). Will Rogers and the Great Depression. *Studies in American Humor, 3,* 173–186.

Linstead, S. (1985). Joker's wild: The importance of humour in the maintenance of organizational culture. *Sociological Review, 33,* 741–767.

Lippold, G. A. (1977). The relationship of personalization, encouragement, and humor to student attitudes and post-test performance on a computer-assisted instructional program. Unpublished doctoral dissertation, University of Northern Colorado.

Lloyd, E. (1938). The respiratory mechanism in laughter. *Journal of General Psychology, 19,* 179–189.

Locke, K. (1996). A funny thing happened! The management of consumer emotions in service encounters. *Organization Science, 7,* 40–59.

Lodico, C. A. (1997). An investigation of the efficacy of a stress-management intervention that utilizes humor as a central aspect of the program. Unpublished doctoral dissertation, Bowling Green State University.

Loewald, E. (1976). The development and uses of humour in a four-year-old's treatment. *International Review of Psycho-Analysis, 3,* 209–221.

Long, P. (1987). Laugh and be well. *Psychology Today, 21,* 28–29.

Loomis, D., & Kolberg, K. (1993). *The laughing classroom: Everyone's guide to teaching with humor and play.* Tiburon, CA: H. J. Kramer.

Lorenz, K. (1963). *On aggression.* New York: Harcourt.

Losco, J., & Epstein, S. (1975). Humor preference as a subtle measure of attitudes toward the same and opposite sex. *Journal of Personality, 43,* 321–334.

Lott, H. M. (1990). An experiment in the initial effects of humor on immediate and delayed recall. *Dissertation Abstracts International, 50 (8–A),* 2372.

Love, A. M., & Deckers, L. (1989). Humor appreciation as a function of sexual, aggressive, and sexist content. *Sex Roles, 20,* 649–654.

Lowe, J. (1986). Theories of ethnic humor: How to enter laughing. *American Quarterly, 38,* 439–460.

Luborsky, L. B., & Cattell, R. B. (1947). The validation of personality factors in humor. *Journal of Personality, 15,* 283–291.

Lundell, T. (1993). An experiential exploration of why men and women laugh. *Humor: International Journal of Humor Research, 6,* 299–317.

Lundy, D. E. (1999). The role of different types of humor and physical attractiveness in heterosexual romantic preferences. *Dissertation Abstracts International, 59 (9–B),* 5169.

Lundy, D., & Tan, J. (1994). Gender differences in opposite-sex attraction: The role of physical attractiveness and humor. *Canadian Psychology—Psychologie Canadienne, 35*, 155.

Lynch, T. D. (1987). Quantitative analysis of the use of humor in psychotherapy: The strategic humor model of Ericksonian psychotherapy. Unpublished doctoral dissertation, The Union for Experimenting Colleges and Universities.

Lynn, R. (Ed.) (1981). *Dimensions of personality: Papers in honour of Hans-Jurgen Eysenck*. Oxford, UK: Pergamon Press.

MacAdam, B. (1985). Humor in the classroom: Implications for the bibliographic instruction librarian. *College of Research Libraries, 46*, 327–333.

MacHovec, F. J. (1988). *Humor: Theory, history, applications*. Springfield, IL: Thomas.

Mackoff, B. (1990). *What Mona Lisa knew: A woman's guide to getting ahead in business by lightening up*. Los Angeles: Lowell House.

Madanes, C. (1987). Humor in strategic family therapy. In W. Fry & W. Salameh (Eds.), *Handbook of humor and psychotherapy*. Sarasota, FL: P. R. E.

Mager, M., & Cabe, P. (1990). Effect of death anxiety on perception of death-related humor. *Psychological Reports, 66*, 1311–1314.

Maher, M. (1993). Humor in substance abuse treatment. In W. Fry & W. Salameh (Eds.), *Advances in humor and psychotherapy*. Sarasota, FL: P. R. E.

Mahony, D., & Mann, V. (1992). Using children's humor to clarify the relationship between linguistic awareness and early reading ability. *Cognition, 45*, 163–186.

Mahrer, A., & Gervaize, P. (1984). Integrative review of strong laughter in psychotherapy: What it is and how it works. *Psychotherapy: Theory, Research, and Practice, 21*, 510–516.

Maier, N. R. F. (1932). A Gestalt theory of humor. *British Journal of Psychology, 23*, 69–74.

Malone, P. (1980). Humor: A double-edged tool for today's managers? *Academy of Management Review, 5*, 357–360.

Malpass, L., & Fitzpatrick, E. (1959). Social facilitation as a factor in reaction to humor. *Journal of Social Psychology, 50*, 295–303.

Malrieu, P. (1967). *La construction de l'imaginaire*. Bruxelles: Dessart.

Mango, C., & Richman, J. (1990). Humor and art therapy. *American Journal of Art Therapy, 28*, 111–114.

Manke, B. (1995). The nature and nurture of adolescent humor: Links between childhood family environment and adolescent humor. *Dissertation Abstracts International, 56 (6–B)*, 3478.

Manke, B. (1998). Genetic and environmental contributions to children's interpersonal humor. In W. Ruch (Ed.), *The sense of humor: Explorations of a personality characteristic*. Berlin: Mouton de Gruyter.

Mannell, R. C. (1977a). Vicarious superiority, injustice, and aggression in humour: The role of the playful judgmental set. In A. J. Chapman & H. C. Foot (Eds.), *It's a funny thing, humour*. Oxford, UK: Pergamon Press.

Mannell, R. C. (1977b). When attitudes toward interpersonal aggression and injustice fail to modify humour judgements of humorous fantasy depicting human violence and injustice. Unpublished doctoral dissertation, University of Windsor, Canada.

Marcus, N. (1990). Treating those who fail to take themselves seriously: Pathological aspects of humor. *American Journal of Psychotherapy, 44*, 423–432.

Marek, W. (1989). A study on the correlation between expressive and receptive humor and between sense of humor and intelligence. *Dissertation Abstracts International, 50 (5–A)*, 1255.

Marini, I. D. (1992). The use of humor to modify attitudes, decrease interaction anxiety, and increase desire to interact with persons of differing abilities. Unpublished doctoral dissertation, Auburn University.

Markiewicz, D. (1972). The effects of humor on persuasion. Doctoral dissertation, The Ohio State University.

Markiewicz, D. (1974). Effects of humor on persuasion. *Sociometry, 37*, 407–422.

Marlowe, L. (1984–1985). A sense of humor. *Imagination, Cognition, and Personality, 4*, 265–275.

Martin, J. F. (1983). Humor in therapy: An observational study. Unpublished doctoral dissertation, The University of Tennessee.

Martin, J. P. (1950). Fits of laughter (sham mirth) in organic cerebral disease. *Brain, 70*, 453–464.

Martin, R. A. (1984). The sense of humor as a moderator of the relation between stressors and moods. Unpublished doctoral dissertation, University of Waterloo, Canada.

Martin, R. A. (1988). Humor and the mastery of living: Using humor to cope with the daily stresses of growing up. *Journal of Children in Contemporary Society, 20*, 135–154. (Note: Also see Martin, 1989.)

Martin, R. A. (1989). Humour and the mastery of living: Using humour to cope with the daily stresses of growing up. In P. E. McGhee (Ed.), *Humour and children's development: A guide to practical applications.* New York: Haworth Press. (Note: Also, see Martin, 1988.)

Martin, R. A. (1996). The Situational Humor Response Questionnaire (SHRQ) and Coping Humor Scale (CHS): A decade of research findings. *Humor: International Journal of Humor Research, 9*, 251–272.

Martin, R. A. (1998). Approaches to the sense of humor: A historical review. In W. Ruch (Ed.), *The sense of humor: Explorations of a personality characteristic.* Berlin: Mouton de Gruyter.

Martin, R. A. (2000). Humor and laughter. In A. E. Kazdin (Ed.), *Encyclopedia of psychology.* Washington, DC: American Psychological Association; New York: Oxford University Press.

Martin, R. A., & Dobbin, J. (1988). Sense of humor, hassles, and immunoglobin A: Evidence for a stress-modulating effect of humor. *International Journal of Psychiatry in Medicine, 18*, 93–105.

Martin, R. A., & Kuiper, N. (1999). Daily occurrence of laughter: Relationships with age, gender, and Type A personality. *Humor: International Journal of Humor Research, 12*, 355–384.

Martin, R. A., Kuiper, N., Olinger, L., & Dance, K. (1993). Humor, coping with stress, self-concept, and psychological well-being. *Humor: International Journal of Humor Research, 6,* 89–104.

Martin, R. A., Kuiper, N., & Westra, H. (1989). Cognitive and affective components of the Type A behavior pattern: Preliminary evidence for a self-worth contingency model. *Personality and Individual Differences, 10,* 771–784.

Martin, R. A., & Lefcourt, H. (1983). Sense of humor as a moderator of the relation between stressors and moods. *Journal of Personality and Social Psychology, 45,* 1313–1324.

Martin, R. A., & Lefcourt, H. (1984). Situation humor response questionnaire: Quantitative measure of sense of humor. *Journal of Personality and Social Psychology, 47,* 145–155.

Martineau, W. (1972). A model of the social functions of humor. In J. H. Goldstein & P. E. McGhee (Eds.), *The psychology of humor: Theoretical perspectives and empirical issues.* New York: Academic Press.

Martinez, J. J. (1989). The role of empathic humor in counteracting burnout and promoting renewal: The development and implementation of a personal growth workshop. Unpublished doctoral dissertation, University of Massachusetts.

Maslow, A. (1954). *Motivation and personality.* New York: Harper & Row.

Masten, A. (1989). Humor appreciation in children: Individual differences and response sets. *Humor: International Journal of Humor Research, 2,* 365–384.

Mayes, L., Klin, A., & Cohen, D. (1994). The effect of humour on children's developing theory of mind. *British Journal of Developmental Psychology, 12,* 555–561.

Mazick, B. S. (1990). Children's production of humor: The influence of concrete operational thought and anxiety. Unpublished doctoral dissertation, University of Detroit.

McBrien, R. (1993). Laughing together: Humor as encouragement in couples' counseling. *Individual Psychology: The Journal of Adlerian Theory, Research, and Practice, 49,* 419–427.

McCauley, C., Woods, K., Coolidge, C., & Kulick, W. (1983). More aggressive cartoons are funnier. *Journal of Personality and Social Psychology, 44,* 817–823.

McClelland, D., & Cheriff, A. (1997). The immunoenhancing effects of humor on secretory IgA and resistance to respiratory infections. *Psychology and Health, 12,* 329–344.

McClure, J. (1989). The similarities and differences between intellectually retarded and nonretarded children's humor appreciation. *Dissertation Abstracts International, 50 (2-A),* 394.

McComas, H. C. (1923). The origin of laughter. *Psychological Review, 30,* 45–55.

McCrae, R. (1984). Situational determinants of coping responses: Loss, threat, and challenge. *Journal of Personality and Social Psychology, 46,* 919–928.

McCullough, L. (1993). A cross-cultural test of the two-part typology of humor. *Perceptual and Motor Skills, 76,* 1275–1281.

McDonald, P., & Wooten, S. (1988). The influence of incompatible responses on the reduction of aggression: An alternative explanation. *Journal of Social Psychology, 128,* 401–406.

McDowell, J. (1979). *Children's riddling.* Bloomington: Indiana University Press.

McFadden, S. H. (1984). The wisdom and humor of aging persons: Perspectives on transformed narcissism in later life. Unpublished doctoral dissertation, Drew University.

McGhee, P. E. (1968). Cognitive development and children's comprehension of humor. Doctoral dissertation, Ohio State University.

McGhee, P. E. (1971a). Development of the humor response: A review of the literature. *Psychological Bulletin, 76,* 328–348.

McGhee, P. E. (1971b). Role of operational thinking in children's comprehension and appreciation of humor. *Child Development, 42,* 734–744.

McGhee, P. E. (1972). On the cognitive origins of incongruity humor: Fantasy assimilation versus reality assimilation. In J. H. Goldstein & P. E. McGhee (Eds.), *The psychology of humor: Theoretical perspectives and empirical issues.* New York: Academic Press.

McGhee, P. E. (1974). Cognitive mastery and children's humor. *Psychological Bulletin, 81,* 721–730.

McGhee, P. E. (1976). Sex differences in children's humor. *Journal of Communication, 26,* 176–189.

McGhee, P. E. (1977a). A model of the origins and early development of incongruity-based humour. In A. J. Chapman & H. C. Foot (Eds.), *It's a funny thing, humour.* Oxford, UK: Pergamon Press.

McGhee, P. E. (1977b). Children's humour: Review of current research trends. In A. J. Chapman & H. C. Foot (Eds.), *It's a funny thing, humour.* Oxford, UK: Pergamon Press.

McGhee, P. E. (1979). *Humor: Its origin and development.* San Francisco: Freeman.

McGhee, P. E. (1980a). Development of the creative aspects of humor. In P. E. McGhee & A. J. Chapman (Eds.), *Children's humour.* London: Wiley.

McGhee, P. E. (1980b). Development of the sense of humor in childhood: A longitudinal study. In P. E. McGhee & A. J. Chapman (Eds.), *Children's humour.* London: Wiley.

McGhee, P. E. (1980c). Toward the integration of entertainment and educational functions of television: The role of humor. In P. Tannenbaum (Ed.), *The entertainment functions of television.* Hillsdale, NJ: Erlbaum.

McGhee, P. E. (1983a). Humor development: Toward a life span approach. In P. E. McGhee & J. H. Goldstein (Eds.), *Handbook of humor research* (Vol. 1, *Basic issues*). New York: Springer-Verlag.

McGhee, P. E. (1983b). The role of arousal and hemispheric lateralization in humor. In P. E. McGhee & J. H. Goldstein (Eds.), *Handbook of humor research* (Vol. 1, *Basic issues*). New York: Springer-Verlag.

McGhee, P. E. (1986). Humor across the life span: Sources of developmental change and individual differences. In L. Nahemow, A. McCluskey-Fawcett, & P. E. McGhee (Eds.), *Humor and aging.* Orlando, FL: Academic Press.

McGhee, P. E. (1988). Contribution of humor to children's social development. *Journal of Children in Contemporary Society, 20,* 119–134.

McGhee, P. E. (Ed.) (1989). *Humor and children's development: A guide to practical applications.* New York: Haworth.

McGhee, P. E. (1991). *The laughter remedy: Health, healing, and the amuse system.* Montclair, NJ: The Laughter Remedy.

McGhee, P. E., Bell, N., & Duffey, N. (1986). Generational differences in humor and correlates of humor development. In L. Nahemow, A. McCluskey-Fawcett, & P. E. McGhee (Eds.), *Humor and aging.* Orlando, FL: Academic Press.

McGhee, P. E., & Duffey, N. (1983a). Children's appreciation of humor victimizing different racial-ethnic groups: Racial-ethnic differences. *Journal of Cross-Cultural Psychology, 14,* 29–40.

McGhee, P. E., & Duffey, N. (1983b). The role of identity of the victim in the development of disparagement humor. *Journal of General Psychology, 108,* 257–270.

McGhee, P. E., & Kach, J. (1981). Development of humor in Black, Mexican-American, and White pre-school children. *Journal of Research and Development in Education, 14,* 81–90.

McGhee, P. E., & Lloyd, S. (1982). Behavioral characteristics associated with the development of humor in young children. *Journal of Genetic Psychology, 141,* 253–259.

McGhee, P. E., Ruch, W., & Hehl, F.-J. (1990). A personality-based model of humor development during adulthood. *Humor: International Journal of Humor Research, 3,* 119–146.

McGuire, F. (1992). *Therapeutic humor with the elderly.* New York: Haworth.

McKiernan, J. (1993). Humor and spirituality in psychotherapy. In W. Fry & W. Salameh (Eds.), *Advances in humor and psychotherapy.* Sarasota, FL: P. R. E.

McMorris, R., Urbach, S., & Connor, M. (1985). Effects of incorporating humor in test items. *Journal of Educational Measurement, 22,* 147–155.

McNamara, S. G. (1980). Responses of fourth and seventh grade students to satire as reflected in selected contemporary picture books. Unpublished doctoral dissertation, Michigan State University.

McNinch, G., & Gruber, E. (1995). Humor in the elementary classroom. *College Student Journal, 29,* 340–343.

Mealyea, R. (1989). Humor as a coping strategy in the transition from tradesperson to teacher. *British Journal of the Sociology of Education, 10,* 311–333.

Meerloo, J. (1966). The biology of laughter. *Psychoanalytic Review, 53,* 189–208.

Megdell, J. (1984). Relationship between counselor-initiated humor and client's self-perceived attraction in the counseling inteview. *Psychotherapy, 21,* 517–523.

Meguiar, T. M. (1988). Humor and families: A hermeneutic phenomenological investigation. *Dissertation Abstracts International, 49 (4–B),* 1395.

Meissler-Daniels, S. (1990). Burnout, humor, and narcissism in psychologists. Unpublished doctoral dissertation, St. John's University.

Meyer, J. (2000). Humor as a double-edged sword: Four functions of humor in communication. *Communication Theory, 10*, 310–331.

Middleton, R. (1959). Negro and White reactions to racial humor. *Sociometry, 22*, 175–183.

Middleton, R., & Moland, J. (1959). Humor in Negro and White subcultures: A study of jokes among university students. *American Sociological Review, 24*, 61–69.

Mikes, G. (1970). *Humor: In memoriam*. London: Routledge & Kegan Paul.

Miles, E. A. (1989). The relationship of sense of humor to life satisfaction, functional health, death anxiety, and self-esteem in the elderly. *Dissertation Abstracts International, 49 (9–B)*, 4015.

Miller, G., & Bacon, P. (1971). Open- and closed-mindedness and recognition of visual humor. *Journal of Communication, 21*, 150–159.

Miller, H. D. (1956). The relative appropriateness of responses to humor in schizophrenia. Unpublished doctoral dissertation, Louisiana State University.

Minasian, B. J. (1990). Investigating the use of humor as a stress moderator. Unpublished doctoral dissertation, The Union Institute.

Minden, P. (1994). Humor: A corrective emotional experience. In E. S. Buckman (Ed.), *The handbook of humor: Clinical applications in psychotherapy*. Malabar, FL: Krieger.

Mindess, H. (1971). *Laughter and liberation*. Los Angeles: Nash Publishing.

Mindess, H. (1976). The use and abuse of humour in psychotherapy. In A. J. Chapman & H. C. Foot (Eds.), *Humour and laughter: Theory, research, and applications*. London: Wiley.

Mintz, L. E. (1977a). American humor and the spirit of the times. In A. J. Chapman & H. C. Foot (Eds.), *It's a funny thing, humour*. Oxford, UK: Pergamon Press.

Mintz, L. E. (1977b). Ethnic humor: Discussion. In A. J. Chapman & H. C. Foot (Eds.), *It's a funny thing, humour*. Oxford, UK: Pergamon Press.

Mintz, L. E. (Ed.) (1988). *Humor in America: A research guide to genres and topics*. Westport, CT: Greenwood Press.

Mishkinsky, M. (1977). Humor as a "courage mechanism." *Israel Annals of Psychiatry and Related Disciplines, 15*, 352–363.

Mitchell, C. (1977). The sexual prerogative in the appreciation and interpretation of jokes. *Western Folklore, 36*, 303–329.

Mitchell, C. (1978). Hostility and aggression toward males in female joke-telling. *Frontiers, 3*, 19–23.

Modlin, J. B. (1988). Political cartoons and the perception of Arab-Israeli conflict. *Dissertation Abstracts International, 48 (12–B)*, 3728.

Mones, L. (1939). Intelligence and a sense of humor. *Journal of the Exceptional Child, 5*, 150–153.

Monson, D. L. (1966). Children's responses to humorous situations in literature. Unpublished doctoral dissertation, University of Minnesota.

Moody, R. (1978). *Laugh after laugh: The healing power of humor*. Jacksonville, FL: Headwaters Press.

Mooney, N. (2000). The therapeutic use of humor. *Orthopaedic Nursing, 19*, 88–93.

Moore, M. L. (1992). A proposed model for describing marital humor: A content analysis of married partners' descriptions about their humor. Unpublished doctoral dissertation, Bowling Green State University.

Moore, W. M. (1992). Health locus-of-control and humor: Their role on reported illness behavior. Unpublished doctoral dissertation, University of Arkansas.

Moran, C. (1996). Short-term mood change, perceived funniness, and the effect of humor stimuli. *Behavioral Medicine, 22*, 32–38.

Moran, C., & Massam, M. (1999). Differential influences of coping humor and humor bias on mood. *Behavioral Medicine, 25*, 36–43.

More, D., & Roberts, A. (1957). Societal variation in humorous responses to cartoons. *Journal of Social Psychology, 45*, 233–243.

Morkes, J. (1999). Effects of successful and unsuccessful attempts at humor in human-computer interaction and computer-mediated communication. *Dissertation Abstracts International, 59 (10–B)*, 5446.

Morkes, J., Kernal, H., & Nass, C. (1999). Effects of humor in task-oriented human-computer interactions and computer-mediated communication: A direct test of SRCT theory. *Human-Computer Interaction, 14*, 395–435.

Morreall, J. (1991). Humor and work. *Humor: International Journal of Humor Research, 4*, 359–373.

Morreall, J. (1994). Gossip and humor. In R. F. Goodman & A. Ben-Ze'ev (Eds.), *Good gossip*. Lawrence: University Press of Kansas.

Morris, E. E. (1996). The relationship between humor and empathy among counselors-in-training. Unpublished doctoral dissertation, Auburn University.

Morris, R. (1991). Cultural analysis through semiotics. *Canadian Review of Sociology and Anthropology, 28*, 225–254.

Morse, C. (1982). College yearbook pictures: More females smile than males. *Journal of Psychology, 110*, 3–6.

Mosak, H. (1987). *Ha Ha and aha: The role of humor in psychotherapy*. Muncie, IN: Accelerated Development.

Mosak, H., & Maniacci, M. (1993). Adlerian approach to humor and psychotherapy. In W. Fry & W. Salameh (Eds.), *Advances in humor and psychotherapy*. Sarasota, FL: P. R. E.

Mosher, D. (1973). Sex differences, sex experience, sex guilt, and explicitly sexual material. *Journal of Social Issues, 29*, 95–112.

Mougenot, T. (1999). Humorousness and job success among adults with schizophrenia. *Dissertation Abstracts International, 59 (10–A)*, 3745.

Mowrer, D., & D'Zamko, M. (1990). A comparison of humor and directive language in Head Start classrooms. *Humor: International Journal of Humor Research, 3*, 297–304.

Mueller, C., & Donnerstein, E. (1977). The effects of humor-induced arousal upon aggressive behavior. *Journal of Research in Personality, 11*, 73–82.

Mueller, S. (1988). The relationship between sense of humor, life event stress, coping ability, academic aptitude, and gender in freshmen college students. *Dissertation Abstracts International, 48 (7–B)*, 2091–2092.

Muir, H. (2000). Family fun. *New Scientist, 165*, 13–15.

Mulkay, M. (1988). *On humour: Its nature and its place in modern society.* Oxford, UK: Basil Blackwell.

Mullaly, M. J. (1981). The structure and process of humor within adult sister relationships. Unpublished doctoral dissertation, California School of Professional Psychology, Berkeley.

Mundorf, N., Bhatia, A., Zillmann, D., Lester, P., & Robertson, S. (1988). Gender differences in humor appreciation. *Humor: International Journal of Humor Research, 1,* 231–243.

Murdock, M., & Ganim, R. (1993). Creativity and humor: Integration and incongruity. *Journal of Creative Behavior, 27,* 57–70.

Murgatroyd, S. (1987). Humour as a tool in counseling and psychotherapy: A reversal-theory perspective. *British Journal of Guidance and Counseling, 15,* 225–236.

Murray, H. A. (1934). The psychology of humor. 2. Mirth responses to disparagement jokes as a manifestation of an aggressive disposition. *Journal of Abnormal and Social Psychology, 29,* 66–81.

Murray, K. (1997). A cross-cultural comparison of cartoon perception. *Australian Journal of Comedy, 3,* 43–51.

Murstein, B., & Brust, R. (1985). Humor and interpersonal attraction. *Journal of Personality Assessment, 49,* 637–640.

Muthayya, B., & Mallikarjunan, M. (1969). Measure of humor and its relation to intelligence. *Journal of Psychological Researches, 13,* 101–105.

Mutuma, H., LaFave, L., Mannell, R., & Guilmette, A. (1977). Ethnic humour is no joke. In A. J. Chapman & H. C. Foot (Eds.), *It's a funny thing, humour.* Oxford, UK: Pergamon Press.

Myers, S., Ropog, B., & Rodgers, R. (1997). Sex differences in humor. *Psychological Reports, 81,* 221–222.

Nagaraja, J. (1985). Humour in psychotherapy. *Child Psychiatry Quarterly, 18,* 30–34.

Nahemow, L. (1986). Humor as a database for the study of aging. In L. Nahemow, A. McCluskey-Fawcett, & P. E. McGhee (Eds.), *Humor and aging.* Orlando, FL: Academic Press.

Nahemow, L., McCluskey-Fawcett, K., & McGhee, P. E. (Eds.) (1986). *Humor and aging.* Orlando, FL: Academic Press.

Nahemow, L., & Raymon, A. (1986). Performers' views of humor and aging. In L. Nahemow, A. McCluskey-Fawcett, & P. E. McGhee (Eds.), *Humor and aging.* Orlando, FL: Academic Press.

Neitz, M. (1980). Humor, hierarchy, and the changing status of women. *Psychiatry, 43,* 211–221.

Nelson, R. L. (1974). Responses of sixth-grade students to two types of humor present in fiction for children, and an investigation of the types of humor found in books for the middle grade reader. Unpublished doctoral dissertation, Michigan State University.

Nerhardt, G. (1977). Operationalization of incongruity in humour research: A critique and suggestions. In A. J. Chapman & H. C. Foot (Eds.), *It's a funny thing, humour.* Oxford, UK: Pergamon Press.

Ness, M. E. (1989). The use of humorous journal articles in counselor training. *Counselor Education and Supervision, 29*, 35–43.

Neto, D. (1984). The use of humor as a defense against anxiety in group analytic psychotherapy. *Alter Journal de Estudos Psicondinamicos, 14*, 37–44.

Neuliep, J. (1987). Gender differences in the perception of sexual and nonsexual humor. *Journal of Social Behaviour and Personality, 2*, 345–351.

Nevo, O. (1980). Humor responses as an expression of aggression by Jews and Arabs in Israel: Emphasis on different aspects of humor creation, appreciation, and report. Doctoral dissertation, Hebrew University.

Nevo, O. (1984). Appreciation and production of humor as an expression of aggression: A study of Jews and Arabs in Israel. *Journal of Cross-Cultural Psychology, 15*, 181–198.

Nevo, O. (1985). Does one ever really laugh at one's own expense? The case of Jews and Arabs in Israel. *Journal of Personality and Social Psychology, 49*, 799–807.

Nevo, O., Aharonson, H., & Klingman, A. (1998). The development and evaluation of a systematic program for improving sense of humor. In W. Ruch (Ed.), *The sense of humor: Explorations of a personality characteristic*. Berlin: Mouton de Gruyter.

Nevo, O., Keinan, G., & Teshimovsky-Arditi, M. (1993). Humor and pain tolerance. *Humor: International Journal of Humor Research, 6*, 71–88.

Nevo, O., & Nevo, B. (1983). What do you do when asked to answer humorously? *Journal of Personality and Social Psychology, 44*, 188–194.

Nevo, O., & Shapira, J. (1988). The use of humor by pediatric dentists. *Journal of Children in Contemporary Society, 20*, 171–178.

Nevo, O., & Shapira, J. (1989). The use of humor by pediatric dentists. In P. E. McGhee (Ed.), *Humor and children's development: A guide to practical applications*. New York: Haworth.

Newman, I., & Fiordalis, J. (1985). Humor as it relates to predictor of self-concept, depression, and creativity. *Ohio Journal of Science, 85*, 70.

Newton, G. (1988). Effect of client sense of humor and paradoxical intervention on anxiety. *Dissertation Abstracts International, 48 (7–B)*, 2104.

Newton, G., & Dowd, E. (1990). Effect of client sense of humor and paradoxical interventions on test anxiety. *Journal of Counseling and Development, 68*, 668–672.

Newton, J. K. (1993). The importance of life events, humor, and problem-solving to depression in undergraduate and graduate students. Unpublished doctoral dissertation, Kansas State University.

Nezu, A., Nezu, C., & Blissett, S. (1988). Sense of humor as a moderator of the relation between stressful events and psychological distress: A prospective analysis. *Journal of Personality and Social Psychology, 54*, 520–525.

Nias, D., & Wilson, G. (1977a). A genetic analysis of humour preferences. In A. J. Chapman & H. C. Foot (Eds.), *It's a funny thing, humour*. Oxford, UK: Pergamon Press.

Nias, D., & Wilson, G. (1977b). Female responses to chauvinist humour. In A. J. Chapman & H. C. Foot (Eds.), *It's a funny thing, humour*: Oxford, UK: Pergamon Press.

Nickels, C. (1993). *New England humor: From the Revolutionary War to the Civil War*. Knoxville: University of Tennessee Press.

Nickels, S., & Kallas, H. (1973). *Finland: An introduction*. London: Allen & Unwin.

Niethammer, T. (1983). Does man possess a laughter center? Laughing gas used in a new approach. *New Ideas in Psychology, 1*, 67–69.

Nilsen, D. (1988). Importance of tendency: An extension of Freud's concept of tendentious humor. *Humor: International Journal of Humor Research, 1*, 335–347.

Nilsen, D. (1991). Ethnic humor. *New Mexico English Journal, 6*, 20–25.

Nilsen, D. (1993). *Humor scholarship: A research bibliography*. Westport, CT: Greenwood Press.

Nilsen, D. (1996). *Humor in Irish literature: A reference guide*. Westport, CT: Greenwood Press.

Nilsen, D. (1997). *Humor in British literature from the Middle Ages to the Restoration: A reference guide*. Westport, CT: Greenwood Press.

Nilsen, D. (1998). *Humor in eighteenth- and nineteenth-century British literature: A reference guide*. Westport, CT: Greenwood Press.

Nilsen, D., & Nilsen, A. (1987). Parenting creative children: The role and evolution of humor. *Creative Child and Adult Quarterly, 12*, 53–61.

Nilsen, D., Nilsen, A., & Donelson, K. (1988). Humor in the United States. In A. Ziv (Ed.), *National styles of humor*. New York: Greenwood Press.

Nolan, M. (1986). Success can be a laughing matter. *Data Management, 24*, 28–29.

Noriega, V. (1995). Humor, health, and happiness: The use of humor in coping with cancer. *Dissertation Abstracts International, 55 (7–B)*, 3021.

Nosanchuk, T., & Lightstone, J. (1974). Canned laughter and public and private conformity. *Journal of Personality and Social Psychology, 29*, 153–156.

Nussbaum, K., & Michaux, W. (1963). Response to humor in depression: A predictor and evaluator of patient change? *Psychiatric Quarterly, 37*, 527–539.

Nwokah, E., & Fogel, A. (1993). Laughter in the mother-infant emotional communication. *Humor: International Journal of Humor Research, 6*, 137–162.

Obrdlik, A. (1942). Gallows humor: A sociological phenomenon. *American Journal of Sociology, 47*, 709–716.

O'Connell, W. E. (1960). The adaptive function of wit and humor. *Journal of Abnormal and Social Psychology, 61*, 263–270.

O'Connell, W. E. (1964a). Multidimensional investigation of Freudian humor. *Psychiatric Quarterly, 38*, 1–12.

O'Connell, W. E. (1964b). Resignation, humor, and wit. *Psychoanalytic Review, 51*, 49–56.

O'Connell, W. E. (1969). Creativity in humor. *Journal of Social Psychology, 78*, 237–241.

O'Connell, W. E. (1976). Freudian humour: The eupsychia of everyday life. In A. J. Chapman & H. C. Foot (Eds.), *Humour and laughter: Theory, research, and applications*. London: Wiley.

O'Connell, W. E. (1977). Sense of humour: Actualizer of persons and theories. In A. J. Chapman & H. C. Foot (Eds.), *It's a funny thing, humour*. Oxford, UK: Pergamon Press.

O'Connell, W. E. (1981). Natural high therapy. In R. J. Corsini (Ed.), *Handbook of innovative psychotherapies*. New York: Wiley.

O'Connell, W. E., & Peterson, P. (1964). Humor and repression. *Journal of Existential Psychology, 4*, 309–316.

Oertel, M. J. (1990). The relationship between stress and humor in mental health professionals. *Dissertation Abstracts International, 50 (7–B)*, 3171.

Olin-Jarvis, B. (1990). The use of humor as a moderator variable in the onset and course of post-traumatic stress disorder in Vietnam theatre veterans. *Dissertation Abstracts International, 50 (7–B)*, 3139.

Olson, H. (1976). The use of humor in psychotherapy. *Individual Psychologist, 13*, 34–37.

Olson, J. (1992). Self-perception of humor: Evidence for discounting and augmentation effects. *Journal of Personality and Social Psychology, 62*, 369–377.

Olson, J., & Roese, N. (1995). Perceived funniness of humorous stimuli. *Personality and Social Psychology Bulletin, 21*, 908–913.

Olson, L. K. (1996). Humor in therapy: An analysis of its uses and its benefits. Unpublished doctoral dissertation, California School of Professional Psychology at Berkeley/Alameda.

O'Maine, R. A. (1994). A training program to acquaint clinicians with the use of humor in psychotherapy. *Dissertation Abstracts International, 55 (4–B)*, 1675.

Omwake, L. (1937). A study of sense of humor: Its relation to sex, age, and personal characteristics. *Journal of Applied Psychology, 21*, 688–704.

Omwake, L. (1939). Factors influencing the sense of humor. *Journal of Social Psychology, 10*, 95–104.

Omwake, L. (1942). Humor in the making. *Journal of Social Psychology, 15*, 265–279.

O'Neill, R., Greenberg, R., & Fisher, S. (1992). Humor and anality. *Humor: International Journal of Humor Research, 5*, 283–291.

O'Quin, K., & Aronoff, J. (1981). Humor as a technique of social influence. *Social Psychology Quarterly, 44*, 349–357.

Oring, E. (1984). Humor and the individual: Introduction. *Western Folklore, 43*, 7–9.

Oring, E. (1988). Folklore methodology and American humor research. In L. E. Mintz (Ed.), *Humor in America: A research guide to genres and topics*. Westport, CT: Greenwood Press.

Oring, E. (1991). Sociology of the ethnic joke: A review essay. *Humor: International Journal of Humor Research, 4*, 109–114.

Oring, E. (1994). Humor and the suppression of sentiment. *Humor: International Journal of Humor Research, 7*, 7–26.

Osborn, A. (1953). *Applied imagination*. New York: Scribners.

Oshima, K. (2000). Ethnic jokes and social function in Hawai'i. *Humor: International Journal of Humor Research, 13*, 41–57.

Overholser, J. C. (1992). Sense of humor when coping with life stress. *Personality and Individual Differences, 13*, 799–804.

Overlade, D. (1954). Humor perception as abstraction ability. Unpublished doctoral dissertation, Purdue University.

Owens, H., & Hogan, J. (1983). Development of humor in children: Roles of incongruity, resolution, and operational thinking. *Psychological Reports, 53*, 477–478.

Palmer, C. (1993). Anger, aggression, and humor in Newfoundland floor hockey: An evolutionary analysis. *Aggressive Behavior, 19*, 167–173.

Palmer, J. (1994). *Taking humor seriously.* New York: Routledge.

Palmore, E. (1986). Attitudes toward aging shown by humor: A review. In L. Nahemow, A. McCluskey-Fawcett, & P. E. McGhee (Eds.), *Humor and aging.* Orlando, FL: Academic Press.

Panzer, M., & Mellow, A. (1992). Anti-depressant treatment of pathological laughing or crying in elderly stroke patients. *Journal of Geriatric Psychiatry and Neurology, 5*, 195–199.

Parisi, R., & Kayson, W. (1988). Effects of sex, year in school, and type of cartoon on ratings of humor and likability. *Psychological Reports, 62*, 563–566.

Park, R. (1977). A study of children's riddles using Piaget-derived definitions. *Journal of Genetic Psychology, 130*, 57–67.

Parnes, S. (1967). *Creative behavior guidebook.* New York: Scribners.

Parse, R. (1994). Laughing and health: A study using the Parse research method. *Nursing Science Quarterly, 7*, 55–64.

Parsons, N. P. (1989). An exploration of the relationship between occupational stress and sense of humor among middle-level managers. *Dissertation Abstracts International, 49 (8–A)*, 2119–2120.

Paskind, H. (1932). Effects of laughter on muscle tone. *Archives of Neurology and Psychiatry, 28*, 623–628.

Pasquali, G. (1987). Some notes on humor in psychoanalysis. *International Review of Psychoanalysis, 14*, 231–236.

Paton, G., Powell, C., & Wagg, S. (Eds.) (1996). *The social faces of humour: Practices and issues.* Brookfield, VT: Arena/Ashgate.

Paulson, T. (1989). *Making humor work: Take your job seriously and yourself lightly.* Los Altos, CA: Crisp.

Pauluk, W. (1999). Humor and its therapeutic application to psychotherapy with schizophrenics. *Dissertation Abstracts International, 60 (5–B)*, 2359.

Pearson, J., Miller, G., & Senter, M. (1983). Sexism and sexual humor: A research note. *Central States Speech Journal, 34*, 257–259.

Pearson, P. (1982). Personality characteristics of cartoonists. *Personality and Individual Differences, 4*, 227–228.

Pelusi, N. (1991). Effects of profanity and humor on perceived counselor expertness, attractiveness, and trustworthiness, and behavioral compliance. Unpublished doctoral dissertation, Hofstra University.

Perlini, A., Nenonen, R., & Lind, D. (1999). Effects of humor on test anxiety and performance. *Psychological Reports, 84*, 1203–1213.

Peterson, J. (1980). The communicative intent of laughter in group psychotherapy. Unpublished doctoral dissertation, University of Tennessee.

Peterson, J., & Pollio, H. (1982). Therapeutic effectiveness of differentially targeted humorous remarks in group psychotherapy. *Group, 6*, 39–50.

Petry, S., & Meyer, G. (1987). Subjective contours of humor. *Perception, 16*, 223–224.

Pfeifer, D. L. (1992). Humor and aging: A comparison between a younger and an older group. Unpublished doctoral dissertation, University of Miami.

Philbrick, K. D. (1989). The use of humor and effective leadership styles. Unpublished doctoral dissertation, University of Florida.

Phillips, M. L. (1992). Humour as a moderator of negative affect experienced within an evaluative context. Unpublished doctoral dissertation, University of Waterloo, Canada.

Piaget, J. (1947). *La psychologie de l'intelligence*. Paris: Leclerc et Cie.

Pickering, E., Pickering, A., & Buchanan, R. (1987). Learning-disabled and nonhandicapped boys' comprehension of cartoon humor. *Learning Disability Quarterly, 10*, 45–51.

Pien, D., & Rothbart, M. K. (1976). Incongruity and resolution in children's humor. *Child Development, 47*, 966–971.

Pien, D., & Rothbart, M. K. (1977). Measuring the effects of incongruity and resolution in children's humour. In A. J. Chapman & H. C. Foot (Eds.), *It's a funny thing, humour*. Oxford, UK: Pergamon Press.

Pierson, P. R. (1990). Analysis of elementary principals' use of humor in their interpersonal communications with teachers. *Dissertation Abstracts International, 50 (7–A)*, 1884.

Pinegar, P. W. (1984). Client self-exploration and humor in psychotherapy. *Dissertation Abstracts International, 44 (10–A)*, 3018.

Pines, L. (1964). Laughter as an equivalent of epilepsy. *Soviet Psychology and Psychiatry, 2*, 33–38.

Piret, A. (1940). Recherches genetiques sur le comique. *Acta Psychologica, 2*, 103–142.

Pita, D. G. (1984). Effects of age and type of visual incongruity on humor responses of preschool children. Unpublished doctoral dissertation, Fordham University.

Poland, W. (1971). The place of humor in psychotherapy. *American Journal of Psychiatry, 128*, 635–637.

Poland, W. (1990). The gift of laughter: On the development of a sense of humor in clinical analysis. *Psychoanalytic Quarterly, 59*, 197–225.

Pollio, D. (1995). Use of humor in crisis intervention. *Families in Society, 76*, 376–384.

Pollio, H. (1988). Development of laughing and smiling in nursery school children. *Child Development, 62*, 53–59.

Pollio, H., Edgerly, J., & Jordan, R. (1972). Comedians' world: Some tentative mappings. *Psychological Reports, 30*, 387–391.

Pollio, H., & Mers, R. (1974). Predictability and the appreciation of comedy. *Bulletin of the Psychonomic Society, 4*, 229–232.

Pollio, H., Mers, R., & Lucchesi, W. (1972). Humor, laughter, and smiling. Some preliminary observations of funny behaviors. In J. H. Goldstein & P. E.

McGhee (Eds.), *The psychology of humor: Theoretical perspectives and empirical issues.* New York: Academic Press.

Poole, A. (1991). *You will never die laughing: The healing effect of laughter and humor on the mind and body.* Colorado Springs, CO: Pulpit Rock Press.

Porcella, J. E. (1979). Children's adaptation to humorous material under varying stimulus conditions. Unpublished doctoral dissertation, St. John's University.

Porterfield, A. (1987). Does sense of humor moderate the impact of life stress on psychological and physical well-being? *Journal of Research in Personality, 21,* 306–317.

Potter, R., & Goodman, N. (1983). Implementation of laughter as a therapy facilitator with adult aphasics. *Journal of Communication Disorders, 16,* 41–48.

Pratt, S. B. (1996). Razzing: Ritualized uses of humor as a form of identification among American Indians. In H. B. Mokro (Ed.), *Interaction and identity.* New Brunswick, NJ: Transaction.

Praver, F., DiGiuseppe, R., Pelcovitz, D., Mandel, F., & Gaines, R. (2000). A preliminary study of a cartoon measure for children's reactions to chronic trauma. *Child Maltreatment: Journal of the American Professional Society on the Abuse of Children, 5,* 273–285.

Prentice, N., & Fatham, R. (1975). Joking riddles: A developmental index of children's humor. *Developmental Psychology, 11,* 210–216.

Prerost, F. (1975). The indication of sexual and aggressive similarities through humor appreciation. *Journal of Psychology, 91,* 283–288.

Prerost, F. (1976). Reduction of aggression as a function of related content of humor. *Psychological Reports, 38,* 771–777.

Prerost, F. (1980a). Developmental aspects of adolescent sexuality as reflected in the reactions to sexually explicit humor. *Psychological Reports, 46,* 543–548.

Prerost, F. (1980b). The relationship of male and female sexual activity and satisfaction to the appreciation of related humor content. In H. Mindess & J. Turek (Eds.), *The study of humor.* Los Angeles: Antioch Press.

Prerost, F. (1981). The application of humorous imagery situations in psychotherapy. In E. Klinger (Ed.), *Imagery: Concepts, results, and applications.* New York: Plenum.

Prerost, F. (1982). The development of the mood-inhibiting effects of crowding during adolescence. *The Journal of Psychology, 110,* 197–202.

Prerost, F. (1983a). Changing patterns in the response to humorous sexual stimuli: Sex roles and expression of sexuality. *Social Behavior and Personality, 11,* 23–28.

Prerost, F. (1983b). Locus of control as a factor in the aggression inhibiting effects of aggressive humor appreciation. *Journal of Personality Assessment, 47,* 294–299.

Prerost, F. (1984a). Evaluating the systematic use of humor in psychotherapy with adolescents. *Journal of Adolescence, 7,* 267–276.

Prerost, F. (1984b). Reactions to humorous sexual stimuli as a function of sexual activeness and satisfaction. *Psychology, A Quarterly Journal of Human Behavior, 21,* 23–27.

Prerost, F. (1985). A procedure using imagery and humor in psychotherapy: Case application with longitudinal assessment. *Journal of Mental Imagery, 9*, 67–76.

Prerost, F. (1987). Health locus of control, humor, and reduction in aggression. *Psychological Reports, 61*, 887–896.

Prerost, F. (1988). The use of humor and guided imagery in therapy to alleviate stress. *Journal of Mental Health Counselling, 10*, 16–22.

Prerost, F. (1989). Intervening during crises of life transitions: Promoting a sense of humor as a stress moderator. *Counseling Psychology Quarterly, 2*, 475–480.

Prerost, F. (1993a). Presentation of humor and facilitation of a relaxation response among internal and external scorers on Rotter's scale. *Psychological Reports, 72*, 1248–1250.

Prerost, F. (1993b). Relationship of sexual desire to the appreciation of related humor content and mood state. *Journal of Social Behavior and Personality, 8*, 529–536.

Prerost, F. (1995a). Humor preferences among angered males and females—Associations with humor content and sexual desire. *Psychological Reports, 77*, 227–234.

Prerost, F. (1995b). Sexual desire and the dissipation of anger arousal through humor appreciation: Gender and content issues. *Social Behaviour and Personality, 23*, 45–52.

Prerost, F., & Brewer, R. (1974). The common elements of sex and aggression as reflected in humor preferences. *Personality and Social Psychology Bulletin, 1*, 189–191.

Prerost, F., & Brewer, R. (1977). Humor content preferences and the relief of experimentally aroused aggression. *Journal of Social Psychology, 103*, 225–231.

Prerost, F., & Ruma, C. (1987). Exposure to humorous stimuli as an adjunct to muscle relaxation training. *Psychology: A Journal of Human Behavior, 24*, 70–74.

Pretorius, E. J. (1990). Humor as defeated discourse expectations: Conversational exchange in a Monty Python text. *Humor: International Journal of Humor Research, 3*, 259–276.

Priest, R. (1972). Sexism, intergroup conflict, and joking. American Psychological Association, J. S. A. S., *Catalog of Selected Documents in Psychology, 2*, 15.

Priest, R., & Wilhelm, P. (1974). Sex, marital status, and self-actualization as factors in the appreciation of sexist jokes. *Journal of Social Psychology, 92*, 245–249.

Prigatano, G., & Pribram, K. (1981). Humor and episodic memory following frontal versus posterior brain lesions. *Preceptual and Motor Skills, 53*, 999–1006.

Pritzker, S. (1999). The effect of Groucho Marx glasses on depression, and other benefits of humor in psychology. *Psychology Today, 32*, 88.

Prosser, B. (1997). The use of humor among adult educators in a formal classroom setting. Unpublished doctoral dissertation, North Carolina State University.

Radcliffe-Brown, A. R. (1940). On joking relationships. *Africa, 13*, 195–210.

Radcliffe-Brown, A. R. (1949). A further note on joking relationships. *Africa, 19*, 133–140.

Raeithel, G. (1988). Aggressive and evasive humor in Hemingway's letters. *Humor: International Journal of Humor Research, 1*, 127–134.

Raniseski, J. M. (1998). Exploring the relationship between humor and marital well-being. *Dissertation Abstracts International, 59 (6–B)*, 3124.

Ransohoff, R. (1975). Some observations on humor and laughter in young adolescent girls. *Journal of Youth and Adolescence, 4*, 155–170.

Ransohoff, R. (1977). Development aspects of humour and laughter in young adolescent girls. In A. J. Chapman & H. C. Foot (Eds.), *It's a funny thing, humour*. Oxford, UK: Pergamon Press.

Rapp, A. (1949). A phylogenetic theory of wit and humor. *Journal of Social Psychology, 30*, 81–96.

Ravella, N. (1988). The serious business of humor in therapy. *Journal of Strategic and Systemic Therapies, 7*, 35–40.

Rayl, A. (2000). Humor: A mind-body connection. *The Scientist, 14*, 1–6.

Redlich, F. C. (1960). Intellectual and emotional factors in appreciation of humor. *Journal of General Psychology, 62*, 25–35.

Redlich, F. C., Levine, J., & Sohler, T. (1951). A mirth response test: Preliminary report on a psychodiagnostic technique utilizing dynamics of humor. *American Journal of Orthopsychiatry, 21*, 717–734.

Reece, C. (1998). Male and female managers' self-reported uses of humor-oriented downward influence strategies and tactics. *Dissertation Abstracts International, 59 (6–A)*, 1835.

Reik, T. (1962). *Jewish wit*. New York: Gamut Press.

Reutener, D., & Kazak, A. (1976). Effect of cognitive task difficulty on humor ratings of captioned cartoons. *Bulletin of the Psychonomic Society, 7*, 275–276.

Reynes, R., & Allen, A. (1987). Humor in psychotherapy: A view. *American Journal of Psychotherapy, 41*, 260–270.

Reynolds, C. M. (1989). The enhancement and diminishment of humorous creativity. *Dissertation Abstracts International, 49 (10–B)*, 4607.

Richman, J. (1995). The life-saving function of humor with the depressed and suicidal elderly. *Gerontologist, 35*, 271–277.

Ridley, D., & Harrison, B. (1996). Comments on "Sense of humor and longevity" by Yoder and Haude. *Psychological Reports, 78*, 254.

Rim, Y. (1988). Sense of humour and coping styles. *Personality and Individual Differences, 9*, 559–564.

Rim, Y. (1990). Optimism and coping styles. *Personality and Individual Differences, 11*, 89–90.

Rinder, I. (1965). A note on humor as an index of minority group morale. *Phylon, 26*, 117–121.

Ritz, S. E. (1996). Survivor humor in disasters: Implications for public health training and practice. Unpublished doctoral dissertation, University of Hawaii.

Roback, A. (1944). *A dictionary of international slurs (ethnophaulisms)*. Cambridge, UK: Sci-Art.

Roberts, A. F. (1958). Some relationships between personality and humor. Unpublished doctoral dissertation, Michigan State University.

Roberts, A. K. (1994). The effects of imagery, group therapy, or laughter/humor on quality of life in cancer patients. *Dissertation Abstracts International, 54 (10–B)*, 5401.

Roberts, A., & Johnson, D. (1957). Some factors related to the perception of funniness in humor stimuli. *Journal of Social Psychology, 46*, 57–63.

Robinson, R., Parikh, R., & Lipsey, J. (1993). Pathological laughing and crying following a stroke: Validation of a measurement scale and a double-blind treatment. *American Journal of Psychiatry, 150*, 286–293.

Robinson, V. (1977). *Humor and the health professions*. Thorofare, NJ: Slack.

Robinson, V. (1983). Humor and health. In P. E. McGhee & J. H. Goldstein (Eds.), *Handbook of humor research* (Vol. 2, *Applied studies*). New York: Springer-Verlag.

Rodrigues, S., & Collinson, D. (1995). "Having fun?": Humour as resistance in Brazil. *Organization Studies, 16*, 739–768.

Rogers, M., Gittes, R., Dawson, D., & Reich, P. (1982). Giggle incontinence. *Journal of the American Medical Association (JAMA), 247*, 1446–1448.

Rose, G. (1969). King Lear and the use of humor in treatment. *Journal of the American Psychoanalytic Association, 12*, 927–940.

Rosen, M. (Ed.) (2000). *Mirth of a nation: The best contemporary humor*. New York: Harper Perennial.

Rosen, V. (1963). Varieties of comic caricature and their relationship to obsessive phenomena. *Journal of the American Psychoanalytic Association, 11*, 704–724.

Rosenberg, B., & Shapiro, G. (1959). Marginality and Jewish humor. *Midstream, 4*, 70–80.

Rosenberg, L. (1990). An exploratory investigation of the use of humor as a coping strategy for dealing with stress among paramedics. Unpublished doctoral dissertation, Loyola University of Chicago.

Rosenfeld, P., Giacalone, R., & Tedeschi, J. (1983). Humor and impression management. *Journal of Social Psychology, 121*, 59–63.

Rosenheim, E. (1974). Humor in psychotherapy: An interactive experience. *American Journal of Psychotherapy, 28*, 584–591.

Rosenheim, E., & Golan, G. (1986). Patients' reactions to humorous interventions in psychotherapy. *American Journal of Psychotherapy, 40*, 110–124.

Rosenheim, E., Tecucianu, F., & Dimitrovsky, L. (1989). Schizophrenics' appreciation of humorous therapeutic interventions. *Humor: International Journal of Humor Research, 2*, 141–152.

Rosenthal, F. (1956). *Humor in early Islam*. Philadelphia: University of Pennsylvania Press.

Rosenwald, G. (1964). The relation of drive discharge to the enjoyment of humor. *Journal of Personality, 32*, 682–698.

Rosin, S., & Cerbus, G. (1984). Schizophrenics' and college students' preference for, and judgment of, schizophrenic versus normal humorous captions. *Journal of Psychology, 118*, 189–195.

Ross, B. (1989). *Laugh, lead, and profit: Building productive workplaces with humor*. San Diego, CA: Arrowhead.

Rossel, R. (1981). Chaos and control: Attempts to regulate the use of humor in self-analytic therapy groups. *Small Group Behavior, 12*, 195–219.

Rothbart, M. K. (1973). Laughter in young children. *Psychological Bulletin, 80,* 247–256.

Rothbart, M. K. (1976). Incongruity, problem-solving and laughter. In A. J. Chapman & H. C. Foot (Eds.), *Humour and laughter: Theory, research, and applications.* London: Wiley.

Rotton, J. (1992). Trait humor and longevity: Do comics have the last laugh? *Health Psychology, 11,* 262–266.

Rotton, J., & Shats, M. (1996). Effects of state humor, expectancies, and choice on postsurgical mood and self-medication: A field experiment. *Journal of Applied Social Psychology, 26,* 1775–1794.

Roubicek, J. (1946). Laughter in epilepsy, with some general introductory notes. *Journal of Mental Science, 92,* 734–755.

Rouff, L. L. (1975). Creativity and sense of humor. *Psychological Reports, 37,* 1022.

Rourke, C. (1931). *American humor: A study of the national character.* Garden City, NY: Doubleday.

Rowe, K. (1995). *The unruly woman: Gender and the genres of laughter.* Austin, TX: University of Texas Press.

Roy, D. (1960). Banana time: Job satisfaction and informal interaction. *Human Organization, 18,* 158–168.

Rubin, L. (1983). *Comic imagination in American literature.* New Brunswick, NJ: Rutgers University Press.

Rubinstein, A. M. (1965). The relationship between hostile attitudes and the appreciation of hostile jokes. Unpublished doctoral dissertation, Columbia University.

Ruch, W. (1988). Sensation seeking and the enjoyment of structure and content of humor: Stability of findings across four samples. *Personality and Individual Differences, 9,* 861–871.

Ruch, W. (1992). Assessment of appreciation of humor: Studies with the 3WD humor test. In C. D. Spielberger & J. N. Butcher (Eds.), *Advances in personality assessment* (Vol. 9). Hillsdale, NJ: Erlbaum.

Ruch, W. (1994). Temperament, Eysenck's PEN system, and humor-related traits. *Humor: International Journal of Humor Research, 7,* 209–244.

Ruch, W. (Ed.) (1998). *The sense of humor: Explorations of a personality characteristic.* Berlin: Mouton de Gruyter.

Ruch, W., Accoce, J., Ott, C., & Bariaud, F. (1991). Cross-national comparison of humor categories: France and Germany. *Humor: International Journal of Humor Research, 4,* 391–414.

Ruch, W., Busse, P., & Hehl, F.-J. (1996). Relationship between humor and proposed punishment for crimes: Beware of humorous people. *Personality and Individual Differences, 20,* 1–12.

Ruch, W., & Deckers, L. (1993). Do extroverts like to laugh? An analysis of the situational humor response questionnaire. *European Journal of Personality, 7,* 211–220.

Ruch, W., & Forabosco, G. (1996). A cross-cultural study of humor appreciation: Italy and Germany. *Humor: International Journal of Humor Research, 9,* 5–22.

Ruch, W., & Hehl, F.-J. (1983). Intolerance of ambiguity as a factor in the appreciation of humor. *Personality and Individual Differences, 4,* 443–449.

Ruch, W., & Hehl, F.-J. (1987). Personal values as facilitating and inhibiting factors in the appreciation of humor content. *Journal of Social Behavior and Personality, 2,* 453–472.

Ruch, W., & Hehl, F.-J. (1988). Attitudes to sex, sexual behavior, and enjoyment of humour. *Personality and Individual Differences, 9,* 983–994.

Ruch, W., & Hehl, F.-J. (1998). A two-mode model of humor appreciation: Its relation to aesthetic appreciation and simplicity-complexity of personality. In W. Ruch (Ed.), *The sense of humor: Explorations of a personality characteristic.* Berlin: Mouton de Gruyter.

Ruch, W., & Kohler, G. (1998). A temperament approach to humor. In W. Ruch (Ed.), *The sense of humor: Explorations of a personality characteristic.* Berlin: Mouton de Gruyter.

Ruch, W., McGhee, P. E., & Hehl, F.-J. (1990). Age differences in the enjoyment of incongruity-resolution and nonsense humor during adulthood. *Psychology and Aging, 5,* 348–355.

Runco, M. (Ed.) (1996). *Creativity research handbook* (Vol. 1). Cresskill, NJ: Hampton Press.

Russell, A., & Calvacca, L. (1991). Should you be funny at work? *Working Woman, 3,* 74–75, 126–128.

Russo, C. (1987). Laughter: A creative muse. *Psychology Today, 21,* 21.

Rust, J., & Goldstein, J. (1989). Humor in marital adjustment. *Humor: International Journal of Humor Research, 2,* 217–223.

Rutherford, K. (1994). Humor in psychotherapy. *Individual Psychology: The Journal of Adlerian Theory, Research, and Practice, 50,* 207–222.

Ruvelson, L. (1988). The empathic use of sarcasm: Humor in psychotherapy from a self psychological perspective. *Clinical Social Work Journal, 16,* 297–305.

Ryan, E., Kennaley, D., Pratt, M., & Shumovich, M. (2000). Evaluations by staff, residents, and community seniors of patronizing speech in the nursing home: Impact of passive, assertive, or humorous responses. *Psychology and Aging, 15,* 272–285.

Sackett, R. (1987). Images of the Jew: Popular joke-telling in Munich on the eve of World War I. *Theory and Society, 16,* 527–563.

Sadowski, C., Gulgoz, S., & LoBello, S. (1994). An evaluation of the use of content-relevant cartoons as a teaching device. *Journal of Instructional Psychology, 21,* 368–370.

Safranek, R. (1981). Humor as a moderator for the effects of stressful life events. Unpublished doctoral dissertation, Southern Illinois University at Carbondale.

Safranek, R., & Schill, T. (1982). Coping with stress: Does humor help? *Psychological Reports, 51,* 222.

Salameh, W. (1983). Humor in psychotherapy: Past outlooks, present status, and future frontiers. In P. E. McGhee & J. H. Goldstein (Eds.), *Handbook of humor research* (Vol. 2, *Applied studies*). New York: Springer-Verlag.

Salameh, W. (1987a). Humor in integrative short-term psychotherapy (ISTP). In W. Fry & W. Salameh (Eds.), *Handbook of humor and psychotherapy*. Sarasota, FL: P. R. E.

Salameh, W. (1987b). *Psychotherapeutic humor: Applications in practice*. New York: P. R. E.

Salameh, W. (1993). Comprehensive research and clinical bibliography on humor and psychotherapy. In W. Fry & W. Salameh (Eds.), *Advances in humor and psychotherapy*. Sarasota, FL: P. R. E.

Salameh, W., & Fry, W. (Eds.) (2001). *Humor and wellness in clinical intervention*. Westport, CT: Praeger.

Salisbury, W. (1990). A study of humor in counseling among Adlerian therapists: A statistical research project. *Dissertation Abstracts International, 50 (11–B)*, 5301.

Salmons, J. (1988). On the social function of some southern Indiana German-American dialect stories. *Humor: International Journal of Humor Research, 1*, 159–175.

Sandberg, D. (1992). An exploratory study of the concept of bisociation applied to psychotherapist-initiated humor within redecision psychotherapy. Unpublished doctoral dissertation, The Fielding Institute.

Sanders, D. M. (1983). Dimensions of humor: The production and appreciation of humor by deaf children. Unpublished doctoral dissertation, University of Illinois at Urbana-Champaign.

Sanders, D. M. (1986). Sign language in the production and appreciation of humor by deaf children. *Sign Language Studies, 50*, 59–72.

Sands, S. (1983). The psychology of humor. *Dissertation Abstracts International, 43 (8–B)*, 2715.

Sands, S. (1984). The use of humor in psychotherapy. *Psychoanalytic Review, 71*, 441–460.

Saper, B. (1987). Humor in psychotherapy: Is it good or bad for the client? *Professional Psychology: Research and Practice, 18*, 360–367.

Saper, B. (1988). Humor in psychiatric healing. *Psychiatric Quarterly, 59*, 306–317.

Saper, B. (1991). A cognitive behavioral formulation of the relationship between the Jewish joke and anit-Semitism. *Humor: International Journal of Humor Research, 4*, 41–59.

Satterfield, M. G. (1988). The effect of topic-related, non-hostile humor upon retention of information in an instructional message delivered by videotape. Unpublished doctoral dissertation, Oklahoma State University.

Savell, H. E. (1983). The effects of humor on depression in chronic emotionally disturbed adults. Unpublished doctoral dissertation, The University of Mississippi.

Schachter, S., & Wheeler, L. (1962). Epinephrine, chlorpromazine, and amusement. *Journal of Abnormal and Social Psychology, 65*, 121–128.

Schaier, A., & Cicirelli, V. (1976). Age differences in humor comprehension and appreciation in old age. *Journal of Gerontology, 31*, 577–582.

Schechter, W. (1970). *History of Negro humor in America.* New York: Fleet Press.

Schienberg, P. (1979). Therapists' predictions of patients' responses to humor as a function of therapists' empathy regression in the service of the ego. Unpublished doctoral dissertation, California School of Professional Psychology, Los Angeles.

Schill, T., & O'Laughlin, S. (1984). Humor preference and coping with stress. *Psychological Reports, 55*, 309–310.

Schimel, J. (1993). Reflections on the function of humor in psychotherapy, especially with adolescents. In W. Fry & W. Salameh (Eds.), *Advances in humor and psychotherapy.* Sarasota, FL: P. R. E.

Schnarch, D. (1990). Therapeutic uses of humor in psychotherapy. *Journal of Family Psychotherapy, 1*, 75–86.

Schoel, D., & Busse, T. (1971). Humor and creative abilities. *Psychological Reports, 29*, 34.

Schulman, N. (1992). Laughing across the color barrier: In living color—satirizing the stereotypes. *Journal of Popular Film and Television, 20*, 2–7.

Schutz, C. (1989). The sociability of ethnic jokes. *Humor: International Journal of Humor Research, 2*, 165–177.

Schwarz, B. (1974). Telepathic humoresque. *Psychoanalytic Review, 61*, 591–606.

Scogin, F., & Merbaum, M. (1983). Humorous stimuli and depression: An examination of Beck's premise. *Journal of Clinical Psychology, 38*, 165–169.

Scogin, F., & Pollio, H. (1980). Targeting and the humorous episode in group process. *Human Relations, 33*, 831–852.

Scott, E. M. (1989). Humor and the alcoholic patient: A beginning study. *Alcoholism Treatment Quarterly, 6*, 29–39.

Sears, R. N. (1934). Dynamic factors in the psychology of humor. Unpublished doctoral dissertation, Harvard University.

Seligson, M., & Peterson, K. (Eds.) (1992). *AIDS prevention and treatment: Hope, humor, and healing.* New York: Hemisphere.

Seltzer, M. (1986). Timing: The significant common variable in both humor and aging. In L. Nahemow, A. McCluskey-Fawcett, & P. E. McGhee (Eds.), *Humor and aging.* Orlando, FL: Academic Press.

Senf, R., Houston, P., & Cohen, B. (1956). Use of comic cartoons for the study of social comprehension in schizophrenia. *American Journal of Psychiatry, 113*, 45–51.

Sev'er, A., & Ungar, S. (1997). No laughing matter: Boundaries of gender-based humor in the classroom. *Journal of Higher Education, 68*, 87–105.

Shade, R. (1990). A comparison of response to and comprehension of verbal humor between gifted students and students from the general population. *Dissertation Abstracts International, 50 (7–A)*, 2018.

Shade, R. (1991). Verbal humor in gifted students and students in the general population: A comparison of spontaneous mirth and comprehension. *Journal for the Education of Gifted Children, 14*, 134–150.

Shaeffer, M., & Hopkins, D. (1988). Miss Nelson, knock-knocks, and nonsense: Connecting through humor. *Childhood Education, 65,* 88–93.

Shaibani, A., Sabbagh, M., & Doody, R. (1994). Laughter and crying in neurologic disorders. *Neuropsychiatry, Neuropsychology, and Behavioral Neurology, 7,* 243–250.

Shakun, L. A. (1995). The funny bone project: A psychoeducational model using humor to facilitate adolescent-senior intergenerational relationships. *Dissertation Abstracts International, 56 (6–B),* 3463.

Shammi, P., & Stuss, D. (1999). Humour appreciation: A role of the right frontal lobe. *Brain, 122,* 657–666.

Shannon, D. M. (1993). Children's responses to humor in fiction. *Dissertation Abstracts International, 54 (12–A),* 4381.

Shapiro, D. E. (1995). Fledgling therapist disorder and fledgling therapist with supervisoraphobia disorder: Proposed DSM-IV categories. *Journal of Mental Health and Counseling, 17,* 456–461.

Shapiro, E., Biber, B., & Minichin, P. (1957). Cartoon test: A semi-structured technique for assessing aspects of personality pertinent to the teaching process. *Journal of Projective Techniques, 21,* 172–184.

Shaughnessy, M. (1984). Humor in logotherapy. *International Forum for Logotherapy, 7,* 106–111.

Shaughnessy, M., & Wadsworth, T. (1992). Humor in counseling and psychotherapy: A 20-year retrospective. *Psychological Reports, 70,* 755–762.

Shepherd, R. (1990). What's so funny about death? Sense of humor, mood disturbance, and beliefs as predictors of willingness to confront mortality. Unpublished doctoral dissertation, University of Waterloo, Canada.

Sheppard, A. (1977a). Developmental levels in explanations of humour from childhood to late adolescence. In A. J. Chapman & H. C. Foot (Eds.), *It's a funny thing, humour.* Oxford, UK: Pergamon Press.

Sheppard, A. (1977b). Sex-role attitudes, sex differences, and comedians' sex. In A. J. Chapman & H. C. Foot (Eds.), *It's a funny thing, humour,* Oxford, UK: Pergamon Press.

Sheppard, A. (1981). Response to cartoons and attitudes toward aging. *Journal of Gerontology, 36,* 122–126.

Sherman, L. (1977). Ecological determinants of gleeful behaviors in two nursery school environments. In A. J. Chapman & H. C. Foot (Eds.), *It's a funny thing, humour.* Oxford, UK: Pergamon Press.

Sherman, L. (1985). Humor and social distance. *Perceptual and Motor Skills, 61,* 1274.

Sherman, L. (1988). Humor and social distance in elementary school children. *Humor: International Journal of Humor Research, 1,* 389–404.

Shibles, W. (1979). How to teach creatively through humor and metaphor: A philosopher looks at creativity. *Creative Child and Adult Quarterly, 4,* 243–251.

Shimizu, A., Kawasaki, T., & Kawasaki, M. (1986). Psychophysiological study of laughing in schizophrenic patients. *International Journal of Neuroscience, 31,* 208–209.

Shirley, R., & Gruner, C. (1989). Self-perceived cynicism, sex, and reaction to gender-related satire. *Perceptual and Motor Skills, 69*, 1048–1050.

Shlien, R., & Wachs, A. (2000). Knock knock. Who's there? Cancer! *Psychology Today, 33*, 30–32.

Shultz, T. (1970). Cognitive factors in children's appreciation of cartoons: Incongruity and its resolution. Doctoral dissertation, Yale University.

Shultz, T. (1972). The role of incongruity and resolution in children's appreciation of cartoon humor. *Journal of Experimental Child Psychology, 13*, 456–477.

Shultz, T. (1974). Order of cognitive processing in humor appreciation. *Canadian Journal of Psychology, 28*, 409–420.

Shultz, T. (1977). A cross-cultural study of the structure of humour. In A. J. Chapman & H. C. Foot (Eds.), *It's a funny thing, humour.* Oxford, UK: Pergamon Press.

Shultz, T., & Horibe, F. (1974). Development of the appreciation of verbal jokes. *Developmental Psychology, 10*, 13–20.

Shultz, T., & Robillard, J. (1980). Development of linguistic humour in children: Incongruity through role violation. In P. E. McGhee & A. J. Chapman (Eds.), *Children's humour.* London: Wiley.

Shurte, P. (1992). The perception of the therapist utilizing three conditions of clinical humor as analyzed by dimensions of gender. Unpublished doctoral dissertation, Tulane University, School of Social Work.

Siegel, J. (1995). How to get a laugh in Fijian: Code-switching and humor. *Language in Society, 24*, 95–110.

Siegel, M. (1987). *Laughing matters: The comic tradition of India.* Chicago: University of Chicago Press.

Siegel, R., & Hirschman, A. (1985). Hashish and laughter: Historical notes and translations of early French investigations. *Journal of Psychoactive Drugs, 17*, 87–91.

Signer, S. (1988) Pathological crying and laughter. *American Journal of Psychiatry, 145*, 278.

Sikov, E. K. (1986). Laughing hysterically: American screen comedies of the 1950s. Unpublished doctoral dissertation, Columbia University.

Silberman, I. N. (1987). Humor and health: An epidemiological study. *American Behavioral Scientist, 30*, 100–112.

Silverman, S. R. (1995). An exploratory study of the effects of humor on depression and hopelessness of incarcerated males. *Dissertation Abstracts International, 55 (12–A)*, 4000.

Simmons, D. (1963). Protest humor: Folkloristic reaction to prejudice. *American Journal of Psychiatry, 120*, 567–570.

Simon, J. (1988). Therapeutic humor: Who's fooling who? *Journal of Psychosocial Nursing, 26*, 9–12.

Simon, J. (1990). Humor and its relationship to perceived health, life satisfaction, and morale in older adults. *Issues in Mental Health Nursing, 11*, 17–31.

Simons, C., & McCluskey-Fawcett, K. (1986). Theoretical and functional perspectives on the development of humor during infancy, childhood, and adolescence. In L. Nahemow, A. McCluskey-Fawcett, & P. E. McGhee (Eds.), *Humor and aging*. Orlando, FL: Academic Press.

Singer, D. (1964). The cathartic function of humor. Unpublished doctoral dissertation, Yale University.

Singer, D. (1968). Aggression arousal, hostile humor, catharsis. *Journal of Personality and Social Psychology Monograph Supplement, 8*, 1–14.

Singer, D., & Berkowitz, L. (1972). Differing "creativities" in the wit and the clown. *Perceptual and Motor Skills, 35*, 3–6.

Singer, D., Gollob, H., & Levine, J. (1967). Mobilization of inhibition and the enjoyment of aggressive humor. *Journal of Personality, 35*, 562–569.

Sinnott, J., & Ross, B. (1976). Comparison of aggression and incongruity as factors in children's judgments of humor. *Journal of Genetic Psychology, 128*, 241–249.

Sletta, O., Sobstad, F., & Valas, H. (1995). Humor, peer acceptance, and perceived social competence in preschool and school-aged children. *British Journal of Educational Psychology, 65*, 179–195.

Sloshberg, S. (1996). Counselor perceptions of humor within the counseling context. Unpublished doctoral dissertation, The University of Connecticut.

Smeltzer, L., & Leap, T. (1988). An analysis of individual reactions to potentially offensive jokes in work settings. *Human Relations, 41*, 295–304.

Smith, D. (1994). An age-based comparison of humor in selected musical compositions. *Journal of Music Therapy, 31*, 206–219.

Smith, E., & Goodchilds, J. (1963). The wit in large and small established groups. *Psychological Reports, 13*, 273–274.

Smith, E., & White, H. (1965). Wit, creativity, and sarcasm. *Journal of Applied Psychology, 49*, 131–134.

Smith, K. (1996). Laughing at the way we see: The role of visual organizing principles in cartoon humor. *Humor: International Journal of Humor Research, 9*, 19–38.

Smith, R., Ascough, J., Ettinger, R., & Nelson, D. (1971). Humor, anxiety, and task performance. *Journal of Personality and Social Psychology, 19*, 243–246.

Smith, W., Harrington, K., & Neck, C. (2000). Resolving conflict with humor in a diversity context. *Journal of Managerial Psychology, 15*, 606–621.

Smyth, M., & Fuller, R. (1972). Effects of group laughter on responses to humorous material. *Psychological Reports, 30*, 132–134.

Sobol, H. L. (1999). The impact of humor on early adolescents' emotional and behavioral response to events. *Dissertation Abstracts International, 59 (9–B)*, 5152.

Socha, T., & Kelly, B. (1994). Children making "fun": Humorous communication, impression management, and moral development. *Child Study Journal, 24*, 237–252.

Solomon, J. (1996). Humor and aging well: A laughing matter or a matter of laughing. *American Behavioral Scientist, 39*, 249–271.

Sordoni, C. (1980). Experiments in humor: Creativity, locus of control, and their relationship to two dimensions of humor. *Dissertation Abstracts International, 40 (9–B)*, 4512.

Spector, C. (1990). Linguistic humor comprehension of normal and language-impaired adolescents. *Journal of Speech and Hearing Disorders, 55*, 533–541.

Spector, C. (1992). Remediating humor comprehension deficits in language-impaired students. *Language, Speech, and Hearing Services in Schools, 23*, 20–27.

Spector, C. (1996). Children's comprehension of idioms in the context of humor. *Language, Speech, and Hearing Services in Schools, 27*, 307–313.

Spencer, G. (1989). Analysis of JAP-baiting humor on the college campus. *Humor: International Journal of Humor Research, 2*, 329–348.

Spiegel, D., Brodkin, S., & Keith-Spiegel, P. (1969). Unacceptable impulses, anxiety, and the appreciation of cartoons. *Journal of Projective Techniques and Personality Assessment, 33*, 154–159.

Spiegel, D., Keith-Spiegel, P., Abrahams, J., & Kranitz, L. (1969). Humor and suicide: Favorite jokes of suicidal patients. *Journal of Consulting and Clinical Psychology, 33*, 504–505.

Spindle, D. (1989). College instructor use of humor in the classroom: Interaction of instructor gender, type of condition of humor with instructor competence and sociability. *Dissertation Abstracts International, 50 (6–A)*, 1484.

Sprafkin, J., & Gadow, K. (1987). The immediate impact of aggressive cartoons on emotionally disturbed and learning disabled children. *Journal of Genetic Psychology, 149*, 35–44.

Spruill, T. E. (1993). Sense of humor as a mediator of the effects of stress on physical health and psychological well-being. *Dissertation Abstracts International, 53 (12–B)*, 6575.

Squier, H. (1995). Humor in the doctor-patient relationship. *Family Systems Medicine, 13*, 101–107.

St. James, P., & Tagerflusberg, H. (1994). Observational study of humor in autism and Down-syndrome. *Journal of Autism and Developmental Disorders, 24*, 603–617.

Starer, E. (1961). Reactions of psychiatric patients to cartoons and verbal jokes. *Journal of General Psychology, 65*, 301–304.

Stephenson, R. (1951). Conflict and control functions of humor. *American Journal of Sociology, 56*, 569–574.

Stern, W., & Brown, W. (1957). Pathological laughter. *Journal of Neurosurgery, 14*, 129–139.

Stillion, J., & White, H. (1987). Feminist humor: Who appreciates it and why? *Psychology of Women Quarterly, 11*, 219–232.

Stopsky, F. (1992). *Humor in the classroom: A new approach to critical thinking.* Lowell, MA: Discovery Enterprises.

Strean, H. (Ed.) (1994). *The use of humor in psychotherapy.* Northvale, NJ: Aronson.

Streff, C. (1994). Humor in family therapy: Laughter in the crucible. In E. S. Buckman (Ed.), *The handbook of humor: Clinical applications in psychotherapy.* Malabar, FL: Krieger.

Strickland, J. (1959). The effect of motivational arousal on humor preferences. *Journal of Abnormal and Social Psychology, 59*, 278–281.

Stuart, W., & Rosenfeld, L. (1994). Student perceptions of teacher humor and classroom climate. *Communication Research Reports, 11,* 87–92.

Stump, N. F. (1939). Sense of humor and its relationship to personality, scholastic aptitude, emotional maturity, height, and weight. *Journal of General Psychology, 20,* 25–32.

Stypulkowska, J. (2000). Humor and other aspects of drawing performance in a creativity test. *Psychologia Wychowawcza, 43,* 221–226.

Sullivan, J. F. (1992). Effects of humor on children's information acquisition. Unpublished doctoral dissertation, State University of New York at Albany.

Suls, J. (1972). A two-stage model for the appreciation of jokes and cartoons: An information-processing analysis. In J. H. Goldstein & P. E. McGhee (Eds.), *The psychology of humor: Theoretical perspectives and empirical issues.* New York: Academic Press.

Suls, J. (1975). Role of familiarity in the appreciation of humor. *Journal of Personality, 43,* 335–345.

Suls, J., & Miller, R. (1976). Humor as an attributional index. *Personality and Social Psychology Bulletin, 2,* 256–259.

Sumners, A. (1988). Humor: Coping in recovery from addiction. *Issues in Mental Health Nursing, 9,* 169–179.

Sutherland, J. (1982). The effect of humor on advertising credibility and recall. Paper presented at the annual meeting of the Association for Education in Journalism, Athens, OH. (ERIC Document Reproduction Service No. 218, 627).

Svebak, S. (1975a). Respiratory patterns as predictors of laughter. *Psychophysiology, 12,* 62–65.

Svebak, S. (1975b). Styles of humor and social self image. *Scandinavian Journal of Psychology, 16,* 79–84.

Svebak, S. (1977). Some characteristics of resting respiration as predictors of laughter. In A. J. Chapman & H. C. Foot (Eds.), *It's a funny thing, humour.* Oxford, UK: Pergamon Press.

Svebak, S. (1982). The effect of mirthfulness upon amount of discordant right-left occipital EEG alpha. *Motivation and Emotion, 6,* 133–147.

Svebak, S. (1994). More evidence for the moderating effects of sense of humor upon the relation between stress and psychosomatic illness. *Psychosomatic Medicine, 56,* 178.

Swartz, L. (1995). Building relationships through humor. Unpublished doctoral dissertation, Case Western Reserve University.

Swash, M. (1972). Released involuntary laughter after temporal lobe infarction. *Journal of Neurology, Neurosurgery, and Psychiatry, 35,* 108–113.

Sykes, A. (1966). Joking relationships in an industrial setting. *American Anthropologist, 68,* 188–193.

Szafran, A. (1981). Humor, creativity, and psychotherapy. *Annales Medico-Psychologiques, 139,* 11–19.

Tait, P. (1986). Visual impairment, verbal humor, and conversation. *Journal of Genetic Psychology, 147,* 107–111.

Tait, P., & Ward, M. (1982). Comprehension of verbal humor by visually impaired children. *Journal of Visual Impairment and Blindness, 76,* 144–147.

Tamaoka, K., & Takahashi, T. (1994). Understanding humor from another culture: Comprehension of parental brain twisters by Japanese university students learning English as a second language. *Psychologia: An International Journal of Psychology in the Orient, 37,* 150–157.

Tamashiro, R. (1979). Children's humor: A developmental view. *Elementary School Journal, 80,* 68–75.

Tamborini, R., & Zillmann, D. (1981). College students' perception of lecturers using humor. *Perceptual and Motor Skills, 52,* 427–432.

Tanner, S. (1989). E. B. White and the theory of humor. *Humor: International Journal of Humor Research, 2,* 43–53.

Tansey, M. K. (1989). Male adolescent's perceptions of humor: A phenomenological study. *Dissertation Abstracts International, 49 (8–B),* 3110.

Taubman, M. (1980). Humor and behavioral matching and their relationship to child care worker evaluation and delinquency in group home treatment programs. Unpublished doctoral dissertation, University of Kansas.

Taylor, P. (1964). The effectiveness of humor in informative speaking. *Central States Speech Journal, 15,* 295–296.

Taylor, P. M. (1971). The role of listener-defined supportive humor in speeches of information. Unpublished doctoral dissertation, Indiana University.

Taylor, P. M. (1972). The relationship between humor and retention. Paper presented at the annual meeting of the Speech Communication Association, Chicago, IL.

Tennison, J. M. (1994). Cognitive development and humor of young adolescents: A content analysis of jokes. *Dissertation Abstracts International, 54 (8–A),* 2975.

Terry, R., & Ertel, S. (1974). Exploration of individual differences in preferences for humor. *Psychological Reports, 34,* 1031–1037.

Terry, R., & Woods, M. (1975). Effects of humor on the test performance of elementary school children. *Psychology in the Schools, 12,* 182–185.

Teslow, J. L. (1995a). An evaluation of humor as a motivational, cognitive, and affective enhancement to lean feedback and remediation strategies in computer-based instruction. Unpublished doctoral dissertation, University of Colorado at Denver.

Teslow, J. L. (1995b). Humor me: A call for research. *Education Technology Research and Development, 43,* 6–28.

Thomas, D., Shea, J., & Rigby, R. (1971). Conservatism and response to sexual humor. *British Journal of Social and Clinical Psychology, 10,* 185–186.

Thomas, P. (1986). Anatomy of coping: Medicine's funny bone. *Medical World News, 27,* 42–66.

Thompson, T., & Zerbinos, E. (1995). Gender roles in animated cartoons: Has the picture changed in 20 years? *Sex Roles, 32,* 651–673.

Thompson, T., & Zerbinos, E. (1997). Television cartoons: Do children notice it's a boy's world? *Sex Roles, 37,* 415–432.

Thorson, J. (1985). A funny thing happened on the way to the morgue: Some thoughts on humor and death, and a taxonomy of the humor associated with death. *Death Studies, 9,* 201–216.

Thorson, J., & Powell, F. (1992). A revised Death Anxiety Scale. *Death Studies, 16*, 507–521.

Thorson, J., & Powell, F. (1993a). Development and validation of a multidimensional sense of humor scale. *Journal of Clinical Psychology, 48*, 13–23.

Thorson, J., & Powell, F. (1993b). Relationship of death anxiety and sense of humor. *Psychological Reports, 72*, 1364–1366.

Thorson, J., & Powell, F. (1993c). Sense of humor and dimensions of personality. *Journal of Clinical Psychology, 48*, 799–809.

Thorson, J., & Powell, F. (1994). Depression and sense of humor. *Psychological Reports, 75*, 1473–1474.

Thorson, J., & Powell, F. (1996). Women, aging, and sense of humor. *Humor: International Journal of Humor Research, 9*, 169–186.

Thorson, J., Powell, F., Sarmany-Schuller, I., & Hampes, W. (1997). Psychological health and sense of humor. *Journal of Clinical Psychology, 53*, 605–619.

Thurston, R. (1991). Social dimensions of Stalinist rule: Humor and terror in the USSR 1935–1941. *Journal of Social History, 24*, 541–562.

Titze, M. (1987). Conspiritive method: Applying humoristic inversion in psychotherapy. In W. Fry & W. Salameh (Eds.), *Handbook of humor and psychotherapy*. Sarasota, FL: P. R. E.

Toda, S., & Fogel, A. (1993). Infant response to the still face situation at three and six months. *Developmental Psychology, 29*, 532–538.

Tollefson, D. L. (1961). Differential responses to humor and their relation to personality and motivation measures. Unpublished doctoral dissertation, University of Illinois.

Torrance, E. P. (1974). *The Torrance test of creative thinking*. Lexington, MA: Ginn.

Tower, R., & Singer, J. (1980). Imagination, interest, and joy in early childhood: Some theoretical considerations and empirical findings. In P. E. McGhee & A. J. Chapman (Eds.), *Children's humour*. London: Wiley.

Townsend, J., Torrance, E., & Wu, T. (1981). Role of creative ability and style in the production of humor among adults. *Journal of Creative Behavior, 15*, 280–281.

Townsend, M., & Mahoney, P. (1981). Humor and anxiety: Effects of class test performance. *Psychology in the Schools, 18*, 228–234.

Treadwell, Y. (1970). Humor and creativity. *Psychological Reports, 26*, 55–58.

Trice, A. (1985). Alleviation of helpless responding by a humorous experience. *Psychological Reports, 57*, 474.

Trutt, S. D. (1983). Psychological correlates of humor preferences in oncology patients. Unpublished doctoral dissertation, Texas A & M University.

Turcotte, G. (1989). Alternative traditions: An introduction to Australian humor. *Thalia: Studies in Literary Humor, 10*, 3–6.

Turek, J. S. (1992). The relationship between self-generated humor and psychological health and pathology. Unpublished doctoral dissertation, United States International University.

Turner, R. (1980). Self-monitoring and humor production. *Journal of Personality, 48*, 163–172.

Tuttman, S. (1991). On utilizing humor in group psychotherapy. *Group, 15*, 246–256.

Ullian, J. (1976). Joking at work. *Journal of Communications, 26*, 129–133.

Ullmann, L., & Lim, D. (1962). Case history material as a source of the identification of patterns of response to emotional stimuli in a study of humor. *Journal of Consulting Psychology, 26*, 221–225.

Valett, R. (1981). Developing the sense of humor and divergent thinking. *Academic Therapy, 17*, 35–42.

VanBourgondien, M., & Mesibov, G. (1987). Humor in high functioning autistic adults. *Journal of Autism and Developmental Disorders, 17*, 417–424.

Vance, C. M. (1981). The development and test of a prescriptive strategy for the use of incongruity humor in the design of instruction. Unpublished doctoral dissertation, Syracuse University.

Vance, C. M. (1987). A comparative study on the use of humor in the design of instruction. *Instructional Science, 16*, 79–100.

VanGiffen, K. (1990). Influence of professor gender and perceived use of humor on course evaluations. *Humor: International Journal of Humor Research, 3*, 65–74.

VanGiffen, K., & Maher, K. (1995). Memorable humorous incidents: Gender, themes, and setting effects. *Humor: International Journal of Humor Research, 8*, 39–50.

VanGundy, A. (1982). *Training your creative mind.* Englewood Cliffs, NJ: Prentice-Hall.

VanGundy, A. (1984). *Managing group creativity.* New York: American Management Association.

Vardi, J., Finkelstein, Y., Zlotogorski, Z., & Hod, I. (1994). L'homme qui rit: Inappropriate laughter and release phenomena of the frontal subdominant lobe. *Behavioral Medicine, 20*, 44–46.

Varga, D. (2000). Hyperbole and humor in children's language play. *Journal of Research in Childhood Education, 14*, 142–152.

Ventis, W. (1973). Case history: The use of laughter as an alternative response in systematic desensitization. *Behavior Therapy, 4*, 120–122.

Ventis, W. (1987). Humor and laughter in behavior therapy. In W. Fry & W. Salameh (Eds.), *Handbook of humor and psychotherapy.* Sarasota, FL: P. R. E.

Ventis, W., & Ventis, D. (1988). Guidelines for using humor in therapy with children and young adolescents. *Journal of Children in Contemporary Society, 20*, 179–197.

Vergeer, G., & Macrae, A. (1993). Therapeutic use of humor in occupational therapy. *American Journal of Occupational Therapy, 47*, 678–683.

Verinis, J. (1970a). Inhibition of humor: Differential effects with traditional diagnostic categories. *Journal of General Psychology, 82*, 157–163.

Verinis, J. (1970b). Inhibition of humor enjoyment: Effects of sexual content and introversion-extroversion. *Psychological Reports, 26*, 167–170.

Vinton, K. (1989). Humor in the workplace: Is it more than telling jokes? *Small Group Behavior, 20*, 151–166.

Viti, R. (1995). Developing a professional workshop on patients' use of humor and laughter to manage chronic pain. *Dissertation Abstracts International, 56 (6–B)*, 3468.

Vitulli, W. (1978). Humor is human, healthy, and handy. *Aim Magazine, 5,* 21–23.

Vitulli, W., & Barbin, J. (1991). Humor-value assessment as a function of sex, age, and education. *Psychological Reports, 69,* 1155–1164.

Vitulli, W., & Parman, D. (1996). Elderly persons' perceptions of humor as a gender-linked characteristic. *Psychological Reports, 78,* 83–89.

Vitulli, W., & Tyler, K. (1988). Sex related attitudes towards humor among high school and college students. *Psychological Reports, 63,* 616–618.

Vogel, B. (1958). Humor and personality: A study of the relationship between certain selected aspects of personality and the preference for aggressive or non-aggressive written humor. Unpublished doctoral dissertation, New York University.

Volcek, M. (1994). Humor and the mental health of the elderly. In E. S. Buckman (Ed.), *The handbook of humor: Clinical applications in psychotherapy.* Malabar, FL: Krieger.

VonWormer, K. (1986). Aspects of humor in alcoholism counseling. *Alcoholism Treatment Quarterly, 3,* 25–32.

Wagoner, J., & Sullenberger, C. (1978). Pupillary size as an indicator of preference in humor. *Perceptual and Motor Skills, 47,* 779–782.

Wakshlag, J., Day, K., & Zillmann, D. (1981). Selective exposure to educational television programs as a function of differently paced humorous inserts. *Journal of Educational Psychology, 73,* 27–32.

Wakshlag, J., Reitz, R., & Zillmann, D. (1982). Selective exposure to and acquisition of information from educational television programs as a function of appeal and tempo of background music. *Journal of Educational Psychology, 74,* 666–677.

Walker, N., & Dresner, Z. (Eds.) (1988). *Redressing the balance: American women's literary humor from Colonial times to the 1980s.* Jackson: University of Mississippi Press.

Wallach, M., & Kogan, N. (1965). *Modes of thinking in young children: A study of the creativity-intelligence distinction.* New York: Holt, Rinehart & Winston.

Wallas, G. (1926). *The art of thought.* New York: Harcourt & Brace.

Wallis, W. (1922). Why do we laugh? *Scientific Monthly, 15,* 343–347.

Walsh, J. (1928). *Laughter and health.* New York: Appleton.

Walter, G. (2000). The psychiatric patient in American cartoons, 1941–1990. *Humor: International Journal of Humor Research, 13,* 7–17.

Wanzer, M., Booth-Butterfield, M., & Booth-Butterfield, S. (1996). Are funny people popular? An examination of humor orientation, loneliness, and social attraction. *Communication Quarterly, 44,* 42–52.

Warners-Kleverlaan, N., Oppenheimer, L., & Sherman, L. (1996). To be or not to be humorous: Does it make a difference? *Humor: International Journal of Humor Research, 9,* 117–141.

Weaver, J., Masland, J., Kharazmi, S., & Zillmann, D. (1985). Effects of alcohol intoxication on the appreciation of different types of humor. *Journal of Personality and Social Psychology, 49,* 781–787.

Weaver, J., & Zillmann, D. (1994). Effect of humor and tragedy on discomfort tolerance. *Perceptual and Motor Skills, 78,* 632–634.

Weaver, J., Zillmann, D., & Bryant, J. (1988). Effects of humorous distortions on children's learning from educational television: Further evidence. *Communication Education, 37,* 181–187.

Weaver, R., & Cotrell, H. (1987). Ten specific techniques for developing humor in the classroom. *Education, 108,* 167–179.

Webb, E. (1915). Character and intelligence. *British Journal of Psychology Monographs Supplement;* No. 3.

Weil, A., Nosik, W., & Demmy, N. (1958). Electroencephalographic correlation of laughing fits. *American Journal of the Medical Sciences, 235,* 301–308.

Weinberg, M. (1973). The interactional effect of humor and anxiety on academic performance. Unpublished doctoral dissertation, Yeshiva University.

Weiner, M. A. (1981). Appreciation of humor in adults with unilateral lesions due to cerebrovascular accident. Unpublished doctoral dissertation, University of Pittsburgh.

Weisberg, P., & Springer, K. (1961). Environmental factors in creative function. *Archives of General Psychiatry, 5,* 554–564.

Weise, R. (1996). Partisan perceptions of political humor. *Humor: International Journal of Humor Research, 9,* 199–207.

Weisenberg, M., Tepper, I., & Schwarzwald, R. (1995). Humor as a cognitive technique for increasing pain tolerance. *Pain, 63,* 207–212.

Weiss, H. (1984). Humor and imagination. *Hakomi Forum, 1,* 25–28.

Welander-Hass, M. (1990). Sense of humor as a coping strategy for stress created by the person-environment incongruence. *Dissertation Abstracts International, 50 (9-A),* 2845–2846.

Welch, K. J. (1999). Substance use in HIV-infected patients and humor as a treatment approach. *Dissertation Abstracts International, 60 (6-B),* 2642.

Welker, W. (1977). Humor in education: A foundation for wholesome living. *College Student Journal, 11,* 252–254.

Wells, D. (1974). The relationship between the humor of elementary school teachers and the perception of students. Unpublished doctoral dissertation, United States International University, San Diego.

Wells, H. (1971). *Traditional Chinese humor: A study in art and literature.* Bloomington: Indiana University Press.

Wells, M. (1983). Implicit frame crashing: A comprehensive psychological theory of humor and its application to a psychotherapy model. *Dissertation Abstracts International, 44,* 932.

Wells, R. (1934). A study of tastes in humorous literature among pupils of junior and senior high schools. *Journal of Educational Research, 28,* 81–91.

Wender, R. (1996). Humor in medicine. *Primary Care, 23,* 141.

Wessell, M. (1975). Use of humor by an immobilized adolescent girl during hospitalization. *Maternal-Child Nursing Journal, 4,* 35–48.

Westcott, R. (1983). Self-generated humor as an alternative in identifying potentially gifted, talented, and creative high school students: An exploratory study. Unpublished doctoral dissertation, University of Georgia.

Whaley, D. B. (1991). Humor as a moderator of negative stress responses in incarcerated adolescent males. Unpublished doctoral dissertation, Clemson University.

Whisonant, R. (1999). The effects of humor on cognitive learning in a computer-based environment. *Dissertation Abstracts International, 59 (10–A)*, 3796.

Whissell, C. (1998). Objective analysis of text: II. Using an emotional compass to describe the emotional tone of situation comedies. *Psychological Reports, 82*, 643–646.

Whitaker, C. (1975). Psychotherapy of the absurd: With a special emphasis on the psychotherapy of aggression. *Family Process, 14*, 1–16.

White, C. L. (1988). Liberating laughter: An inquiry into the nature, content, and functions of feminist humor. In B. Bate & A. Taylor (Eds.), *Women communicating: Studies of women's talk*. Norwood, NJ: Ablex.

White, S., & Camarena, P. (1989). Laughter as a stress reducer in small groups. *Humor: International Journal of Humor Research, 2*, 73–79.

White, S., & Winzelberg, A. (1992). Laughter and stress. *Humor: International Journal of Humor Research, 5*, 343–355.

Whitt, J., & Prentice, N. (1982). Development of children's enjoyment and comprehension of thematic riddles. *American Journal of Orthopsychiatry, 52*, 92–101.

Wiberg, T. R. (1993). A comparison of the effectiveness of instructional use of introductory and integrated modes of humor on short-term and long-term recall. Unpublished doctoral dissertation, University of Maryland, College Park.

Wickberg, D. (1993). The sense of humor in American culture, 1850–1960. Unpublished doctoral dissertation, Yale University.

Wickberg, D. (1998). *The senses of humor: Self and laughter in modern America*. Ithaca, NY: Cornell University Press.

Wicker, F. (1985). A rhetorical look at humor as creativity. *Journal of Creative Behavior, 19*, 175–184.

Wicker, F., Thorelli, I., Barron, W., & Ponder, M. (1981). Relationships among affective and cognitive factors in humor. *Journal of Research in Personality, 15*, 359–370.

Wicker, F., Thorelli, I., Barron, W., & Willis, A. (1981). Studies of mood and humor appreciation. *Motivation and Emotion, 5*, 47–59.

Wigginton, S. E. (1992). The use of humor in pastoral counseling with adolescents. Unpublished doctoral dissertation, The Southern Baptist Theological Seminary.

Wiklinski, B. (1994). Has humor a meaning for persons adapting to a cancer experience? A phenomenological question. *Dissertation Abstracts International, 54 (12–B)*, 6137.

Wilde, L. (1973a). *The official Italian joke book*. New York: Pinnacle.

Wilde, L. (1973b). *The official Polish joke book*. New York: Pinnacle.

Wilde, L. (1983). *The complete book of ethnic humor*. New York: Pinnacle.

Wilder, D. S. (1995). Stress, coping, and AIDS: Is there a relationship with humor? *Dissertation Abstracts International, 55 (10–B)*, 4596.

Williams, A. J. (1979). Effects of sex and sex role differences in appreciation of cross-gender aggressive humor. Unpublished doctoral dissertation, University of Georgia.

Williams, C., & Cole, D. (1964). The influence of experimentally induced inadequacy feelings upon the appreciation of humor. *Journal of Social Psychology, 64,* 113–117.

Williams, H. (1986). Humor and healing: Therapeutic effects in geriatrics. *Gerontion, 1,* 14–17.

Williams, J. M. (1945). An experimental and theoretical study of humor in children. Unpublished doctoral dissertation, London University.

Williams, K. E. (1997). The humor matrix: A calculus of the entry and intensity variable in friend and mate relationships within a marginalized community. Unpublished doctoral dissertation, The Ohio State University.

Williams, M. H. (1993). The relationships among humor, divergent thinking, and coping with retirement in older adults. Unpublished doctoral dissertation, The University of Texas at Austin.

Wilson, C. (1931). A study of laughter situations among young children. Unpublished doctoral dissertation, University of Nebraska.

Wilson, D., & Molleston, J. (1981). Effects of sex and type of humor on humor appreciation. *Journal of Personality Assessment, 45,* 90–96.

Wilson, G., Nias, D., & Brazendale, A. (1975). Vital statistics, perceived sexual attractiveness, and response to risque humor. *Journal of Social Psychology, 95,* 201–205.

Wilson, G., & Patterson, J. (1969). Conservatism as a predictor of humor preferences. *Journal of Consulting and Clinical Psychology, 33,* 271–274.

Wilson, G., Rust, J., & Kasriel, J. (1977). Genetic and family origins of humor preferences: A twin study. *Psychological Reports, 41,* 659–660.

Wilson, K. (1927). Sense of humor. *Contemporary Review, 131,* 628–633.

Wilson, M. P. (1968). The relation of sense of humor to creativity, intelligence, and achievement. Unpublished doctoral dissertation, University of Southern California.

Wilson, W. (1975). Sex differences in response to obscenities and bawdy humor. *Psychological Reports, 37,* 1074.

Wimmer, A. (1994). The jolly mediator: Some serious thoughts about humor. *Negotiation Journal, 10,* 193–199.

Winkel, M. (1993). Autonomic differentiation of temporal components of sexist humor. *Humor: International Journal of Humor Research, 6,* 27–42.

Winner, E. (1988). *Point of words: Children's understanding of metaphor and irony.* Cambridge, MA: Harvard University Press.

Wise, B. D. (1989). Comparison of immune response to mirth and to distress in women at risk for recurrent breast cancer. *Dissertation Abstracts International, 49 (7–B),* 2918.

Witztum, E., Briskin, S., & Lerner, V. (1999). The use of humor with chronic schizophrenic patients. *Journal of Contemporary Psychotherapy, 29,* 223–234.

Wolfenstein, M. (1954). *Children's humor: A psychological analysis.* Glencoe, IL: Free Press.

Wolff, H., Smith, C., & Murray, H. (1934). The psychology of humor: 1. A study of responses to race-disparagement jokes. *Journal of Abnormal and Social Psychology, 28,* 341–365.

Wong-Leonard, C. (1992). Effects of wildlife cartoons on children's perceptions of wildlife and their use of conservation education material. Unpublished doctoral dissertation, Michigan State University.

Wood, R. (1985). *The modern handbook of humor.* New York: McGraw-Hill.

Word, C. E. (1960). Freudian theories of wit and humor as applied to certain theories of social conflict. Unpublished doctoral dissertation, Boston University School of Theology.

Wright, D. (1977). Children's humour: Discussion. In A. J. Chapman & H. C. Foot (Eds.), *It's a funny thing, humour.* Oxford, UK: Pergamon Press.

Wyer, R., Weatherly, D., & Terrell, G. (1965). Social role, aggression, and academic achievement. *Journal of Personality and Social Psychology, 1,* 645–649.

Wynn-Jones, L. (1927). The appreciation of wit. *Report of the British Association of the Advancement of Science, 10,* 373.

Wynn-Jones, L. (1934). *Theory and practice of psychology.* London: Macmillan.

Yarnold, J., & Berkeley, M. (1954). An analysis of the Cattell-Luborsky humor test into homogeneous scales. *Journal of Abnormal and Social Psychology, 49,* 543–546.

Yoder, M., & Haude, R. (1995). Sense of humor and longevity: Older adults' self-ratings compared with ratings for deceased siblings. *Psychological Reports, 76,* 945–946.

Yoder, S. M. (1989). Selected humorous and non-humorous videos as a means of reducing pre-examination anxiety in Mathematics I day students attending Delaware Technical and Community College. *Dissertation Abstracts International, 49 (7–A),* 1779.

Yorukoglu, A. (1974). Children's favorite jokes and their relation to emotional conflicts. *Journal of Child Psychiatry, 45,* 677–690.

Yorukoglu, A. (1993). Favorite jokes and their use in psychotherapy with children and parents. In W. Fry & W. Salameh (Eds.), *Advances in humor and psychotherapy.* Sarasota, FL: P. R. E.

Young, F. (1988). Three kinds of strategic humor: How to use and cultivate them. *Journal of Strategic and Systemic Therapies, 7,* 21–34.

Young, M. M. (1989). Humor and social competence in middle childhood. *Dissertation Abstracts International, 50 (5–B),* 2182.

Young, R., & Frye, M. (1966). Some are laughing; some are not—why? *Psychological Reports, 18,* 747–754.

Youngman, H. (1981). *Henny Youngman's 500 all-time greatest one-liners.* New York: Pinnacle Books.

Yovetich, N., Dale, J., & Hudak, M. (1990). Benefits of humor in reduction of threat-induced anxiety. *Psychological Reports, 66,* 51–58.

Yuill, N. (1996). A funny thing happened on the way to the classroom: Jokes, riddles, and metalinguistic awareness in understanding and improving poor comprehension in children. In C. Cornoldi & J. Oakhill (Eds.), *Reading comprehension difficulties: Processes and intervention.* Hillsdale, NJ: Erlbaum.

Zajdman, A. (1995). Humorous face-threatening acts: Humor as strategy. *Journal of Pragmatics, 23*, 325–339.

Zalis, T. (1980). The incidence and role of humor in hypomanic reactions. Unpublished doctoral dissertation, Long Island University.

Zall, D. (1994). Ya get it?: Children, humor, and psychotherapy. In E. S. Buckman (Ed.), *The handbook of humor: Clinical applications in psychotherapy.* Malabar, FL: Krieger.

Zapinsky, R. D. (1978). Comic style and the comedian's world: Phenomenological and interpersonal dimensions of humor. Unpublished doctoral dissertation, The University of Tennessee.

Zavala, L. (1989). Humor in Pre-columbian and contemporary Meso American languages. *Latin American Indian Literatures Journal, 5*, 81–91.

Zelvys, V. (1990). Obscene humor: What the hell? *Humor: International Journal of Humor Research, 3*, 323–332.

Zenner, W. (1970). Joking and ethnic stereotyping. *Anthropological Quarterly, 43*, 93–113.

Ziegler, V. F. (1982). A study of the relationship of principals' self-report humor scores and their leadership styles as perceived by teachers. Unpublished doctoral dissertation, University of New Orleans.

Ziff, S. S. (1982). An investigation of the written expression of humor by sixth-grade gifted children. Unpublished doctoral dissertation, Virginia Polytechnic Institute and State University.

Zigler, E., Levine, J., & Gould, L. (1966a). Cognitive processes in the development of children's humor appreciation. *Child Development, 37*, 505–518.

Zigler, E., Levine, J., & Gould, L. (1966b). The humor response of normal, institutionalized retarded, and noninstitutionalized retarded children. *American Journal of Mental Deficiencies, 71*, 472–480.

Zigler, E., Levine, J., & Gould, L. (1967). Cognitive challenge as a factor in children's humor appreciation. *Journal of Personality and Social Psychology, 6*, 332–336.

Zilberg, N. (1995). In-group humor of immigrants from the former Soviet Union to Israel. *Israel Social Science Research, 10*, 1–22.

Zillmann, D. (1980). Anatomy of suspense. In P. H. Tannenbaum (Ed.), *The entertainment functions of television*. Hillsdale, NJ: Erlbaum.

Zillmann, D. (1983). Disparagement humor. In P. E. McGhee & J. H. Goldstein (Eds.), *Handbook of humor research* (Vol. 1, *Basic issues*). New York: Springer-Verlag.

Zillmann, D., & Bryant, J. (1983). Uses and effects of humor in educational ventures. In P. E. McGhee & J. H. Goldstein (Eds.), *Handbook of humor research* (Vol. 2, *Applied studies*). New York: Springer-Verlag.

Zillmann, D., & Bryant, J. (1988). Guidelines for the effective use of humor in children's educational television programs. *Journal of Children in Contemporary Society, 20*, 201–221.

Zillmann, D., Bryant, J., & Cantor, J. R. (1974). Brutality of assault in political cartoons affecting humor appreciation. *Journal of Research in Personality, 7*, 334–345.

Zillmann, D., & Cantor, J. R. (1972). Directionality of transitory dominance as a communication variable affecting humor appreciation. *Journal of Personality and Social Psychology, 24,* 191–198.

Zillmann, D., & Cantor, J. R. (1976). A disposition theory of humour and mirth. In A. J. Chapman & H. C. Foot (Eds.), *Humour and laughter: Theory, research, and applications.* London: Wiley.

Zillmann, D., Masland, J., & Weaver, J. (1984). Effects of humorous distortions on children's learning from educational television. *Journal of Educational Psychology, 76,* 802–812.

Zillmann, D., Rockwell, S., Schweitzer, K., & Sundar, S. (1993). Does humor facilitate coping with physical discomfort? *Motivation and Emotion, 17,* 1–21.

Zillmann, D., & Stocking, H. (1976). Putdown humor. *Journal of Communication, 26,* 154–163.

Zillmann, D., Williams, B., Bryant, J., Boynton, K., & Wolf, M. (1980). Acquisition of information from educational television programs as a function of differently paced humorous inserts. *Journal of Educational Psychology, 72,* 170–180.

Zinger, D. (1988). Humor in child care: The double-edged sword. *Child and Youth Care Quarterly, 17,* 268–274.

Zink, T. C. (1989). A psychological process by which parents incorporate humor into their relationships with their children, aged birth to six. *Dissertation Abstracts International, 49 (9–A),* 2828.

Zippin, D. (1966). Sex differences and the sense of humor. *Psychoanalytic Review, 53,* 209–219.

Zirlott, C. (1999). The formative relationship of the dispositions of humor and humility for reforming false life strategies. *Dissertation Abstracts International, 59 (12–B),* 6511.

Ziv, A. (1976). Facilitating effects of humor on creativity. *Journal of Educational Psychology, 68,* 318–322.

Ziv, A. (1979). Sociometry of humor: Objectifying the subjective. *Perceptual and Motor Skills, 38,* 431–432.

Ziv, A. (1980). Humor and creativity. *Creative Child and Adult Quarterly, 5,* 159–170.

Ziv, A. (1981). *The psychology of humor.* Tel Aviv: Yahdav.

Ziv, A. (1983). The influence of humorous atmosphere on divergent thinking. *Contemporary Educational Psychology, 8,* 68–75.

Ziv, A. (1984). *Personality and sense of humor.* New York: Springer.

Ziv, A. (1987). The effect of humor on aggression catharsis in the classroom. *Journal of Psychology, 121,* 359–364.

Ziv, A. (Ed.) (1988a). *National styles of humor.* Westport, CT: Greenwood Press.

Ziv, A. (1988b). Teaching and learning with humor: Experiment of replication. *Journal of Experimental Education, 57,* 5–15.

Ziv, A. (1988c). Using humor to develop creative thinking. *Journal of Children in Contemporary Society, 20,* 99–116.

Ziv, A. (1992). Struggling with identity through humor. *Humor: International Journal of Humor Research, 5,* 183–186.

Ziv, A., & Gadish, O. (1989). Humor and marital satisfaction. *Journal of Social Psychology, 129*, 759–768.

Ziv, A., & Gadish, O. (1990a). Humor and giftedness. *Journal for the Education of Gifted Children, 13*, 332–345.

Ziv, A., & Gadish, O. (1990b). The disinhibiting effects of humor: Aggressive and affective responses. *Humor: International Journal of Humor Research, 3*, 247–257.

Ziv, A., & Zajdman, A. (Eds.) (1993). *Semites and stereotypes: Characteristics of Jewish humor.* Westport, CT: Greenwood Press.

Zolten, J. J. (1982). The use of premeditated humor in interpersonal relationships. Unpublished doctoral dissertation, The Pennsylvania State University.

Zuk, G. (1964). Further study of laughter in family therapy. *Family Process, 3*, 77–89.

Zuk, G. (1966). On the theory and pathology of laughter in psychotherapy. *Psychotherapy: Theory, Research, and Practice, 3*, 97–101.

Zuk, G., Boszormenyi-Nagy, L., & Heiman, E. (1963). Some dynamics of laughter during family therapy. *Family Process, 2*, 302–314.

Zwerling, I. (1955). The favorite joke technique in diagnostic and therapeutic interviewing. *Psychoanalytic Quarterly, 24*, 104–115.

Methodological and Futuristic Aspects of Humor

SCIENTIFIC METHODOLOGY AND HUMOR RESEARCH

It would be presumptuous to suppose that any satisfactory explanation or classification of the causes and nature of humor can be easily achieved. Nevertheless, the need for attempting to obtain some kind of order or unity out of apparent chaos is one that is constantly and inevitably felt.
—J. C. Flugel, 1954

Along with the insufficient amount of attention devoted to the nature of the stimulus situation in humor research, many investigators have also failed to give serious consideration to the dependent variables used and to factors that might influence performance on those measures . . . Before theories of humor may be satisfactorily tested, a number of basic methodological issues must be settled . . . Once we have achieved a better understanding of the independent and dependent variables used in research on humor, the study of (children's) humor might progress more rapidly upon the development of a standardized test (or tests), which might be available to all experimenters.
—P. E. McGhee, 1971

To me the most basic characteristic of a science is answers: large principles that enable us to understand many situations. I do not feel that experimental psychologists who have studied humor and laughter have yet arrived at such principles.
—N. Holland, 1982

Many of the great minds of history have brought their powers of concentration to bear on the mystery of humor, but their conclusions are so contradictory and ephemeral that they cannot possibly be classified as scientific.

—S. Allen and J. Wollman, 1987

The wide variety of seemingly unrelated situations which often provoke laughter have in common certain elements and a structure which can be represented by a formula . . . laughter is the result of a particular mix of basic perceptual and response patterns and not the result of a separately evolved trait with a specific function.

—R. E. Russell, 1996

The position advanced in this book, and most directly expressed in this chapter, is that the phenomenon of humor (i.e., the *psychology* of humor) should be treated as any other topic or issue that is examined by scientific principles and methods (cf: Russell, 1996, p. 54, who observes that "laughter is not an epiphenomenon; it springs from the same basic psychological processes that give rise to other human behavior"; and Russell's, 2000, p. 219, dictum that "one objective of a scientific inquiry is to establish some connection between an effect and its cause by eliminating nonessential elements that may obscure this connection"). That is, in particular, humor may most effectively be studied by employment of two of the hallmarks of the scientific approach: the *empirical* method, and the determination of *causality*. [Note: Discussions of the major characteristics of science—empiricism, determinism, generalization, hypotheses, theories, models, analysis, and reductionism—and their application to the science of psychology are provided by Abra (1998), Elmes, Kantowitz, & Roediger (1995), Goodwin (1998), and Kantowitz, Roediger, & Elmes (1997).]

Perhaps, arguably, one of the most significant, visible, and accessible developments in the last decade for revitalization of, and interest in, the *scientific* study of the psychology of humor vis-à-vis methodology, measurement, and diversity of coverage is the trend toward the *interdisciplinary* study of humor (cf: Apte, 1988). This development is exemplified by the publication of a journal (*Humor: International Journal of Humor Research*, or here, simply, *Humor*) since 1988 that is devoted exclusively to humor research and study (cf: Cohen, 1989). The editorial policy of *Humor* states that it was established as an international interdisciplinary forum for the publication of high-quality research papers on humor that draws from a wide range of academic disciplines including anthropology, biology, computer science, education, family science, film studies, history, linguistics, literature, mathematics, medicine, philosophy, physiology, psychology, and sociology.

Within the discipline of *psychology*, currently two of the most active proponents—among others—of the scientific study of the psychology of humor (whose approaches, it may be said, are more toward the "empirical/measurement" perspective than toward the "causal-deterministic/experimental" one) are Willibald Ruch (e.g., Ruch, 1993, 1994, 1995, 1996, 1997, 1998) and Rod Martin (e.g., Martin, 1996, 1998, 2000). Recently, Ruch and his colleagues (e.g., Kohler & Ruch, 1996; Ruch & Carrell, 1998; Ruch & Deckers, 1993; Ruch & Hehl, 1986a,b, 1987, 1988, 1993, 1998; Ruch & Kohler, 1998; Ruch, Kohler, & VanThriel, 1996, 1997; Ruch & Rath, 1993), and Martin and his colleagues (e.g., Kuiper & Martin, 1993, 1998; Kuiper, Martin, & Dance, 1992; Kuiper, Martin, & Olinger, 1993; Lefcourt & Martin, 1986; Martin & Gray, 1996; Martin, Kuiper, Olinger, & Dance, 1993; Martin & Lefcourt, 1983, 1984), have made major impacts on the scientific study of humor, especially within the psychological areas of personality/factor analysis/traits/measurement (cf: Eysenck, 1942, 1943, 1947, 1952, 1953). Some of Ruch's and Martin's work on the psychology of humor is discussed in more detail later in this chapter, most specifically in the section "Measurement of Humor."

In 1877 the American philosopher C. S. Peirce compared the scientific way of knowing a phenomenon with three nonscientific methods of developing beliefs (i.e., a priori, authority, and tenacity methods). In his analysis, Peirce asserts that the scientific methods are superior over nonscientific approaches in that scientific approaches fix belief about a phenomenon on the basis of experience wherein a repeatable and self-correcting process occurs within the framework of *empirical* observation. The term *empirical* derives from an early Greek word meaning *experience* (it means literally "that which is sensed"), and the current usage of *empirical* (when associated with research methods, it refers to procedures and techniques involving sensory experience) includes the systematic collection of observable data to publicly fix belief about an event or phenomenon under study. Thus, *empirical* observation has the great advantage of making scientific data open to public, and repeatable, verification.

Another important characteristic of scientific methodology is the determination of *causality*. While the term *cause* itself may be unpopular among contemporary scientists for various reasons (e.g., see Elmes, Kantowitz, & Roediger, 1995, p. 184), it is suggested here that the use of psychological *experiments* in studying the topic of humor may lead to valid *causal* inferences that yield strong scientific support for, and understanding of, the phenomenon. In general terms, although scientific psychologists may recognize the tentative nature of explanations for behavior (such as the humor response) gained through experimentation, they are willing to conclude that *A* "causes" *B* to occur if an experiment is conducted in which *A* (sometimes called the *independent variable*) is systematically varied (where all other "extraneous" or outside factors are controlled) and it is observed that *B* (sometimes called the *dependent variable*) occurs with some probability greater than chance and where variations of *B* are predictable from the variations in *A* (cf: Goodwin, 1998, p. 22).

In this way, *A* and *B* are said to "covary" (or occur together), and because *A* occurs first it may confidently be said that *A* is the *cause* of *B*.

Also, one may refer to the "functional relationship(s)" between two sets of variables, where the manipulated independent variable(s) "cause" the measured dependent variable(s). Thus, within this terminological frame of reference, and for present purposes, all *experiments* (i.e., causal determination strategy/design involving manipulation of independent variables, control of extraneous or "nuisance" variables, and measurement of dependent variables) are assumed to be *empirical* in nature, but not all *empirical* studies (e.g., those involving *only* description, observation, and/or collection of data) are assumed to be *experimental* in nature (cf: Allen, 1984; Greenberg, 1984; Lampert & Ervin-Tripp, 1998; Merenda, 1984).

In a major review written over 40 years ago on humor research, Flugel (1954) reports on the cognitive, conative, and affective aspects of humor and laughter (cf: Eysenck, 1947) that have emerged principally from the more systematic or a priori considerations found in humor studies up to the mid-1950s. Flugel (1954, p. 709) observes that in the 20th century the experimental method has "thrown considerable light upon the many aspects of humor and laughter, although it has done little toward explaining the ultimate nature of the phenomena concerned," and notes that experimentation on the topic of humor and laughter generally has taken the form of the presentation of "humorous" stimuli, auditory or visual, under conditions in which the participant is asked to rank the items in order of funniness or to give them marks in accordance with a predetermined scale. Also, several "tests" of humor have been devised and applied, and the results have been subjected sometimes to more or less elaborate statistical treatment. Other quasi-systematic approaches have required children or adults to report or record humorous experiences, to draw "something funny," to supply humorous captions to pictures, and so forth.

In reading Flugel's (1954) early account of the literature on humor, one readily gains an overall impression of the lack of discussion regarding *empirical/experimental* variables and foundations (save for some references to a very few correlational and factor analytical studies), and of the absence of the application of *experimental* methodologies to the study of humor and laughter. [Notes: This circumstance relates to the distinction in psychology between the terms *nomothetic* and *idiographic* where *nomothetic* refers to *general* scientific laws/principles that apply to *all* individuals and are discoverable especially via empirical/experimental methodologies, and where *idiographic* refers to the single-case/unique/individualistic approach to understanding a phenomenon and is discernible especially via nonexperimental methods, in particular the case study method (cf: Keith-Spiegel, 1972, pp. 24–25; Roeckelein, 1998, pp. 250–251). Perhaps, in these terms, investigators prior to about the middle and late 1960s—that is, prior to a significant increase in published *experimen-*

tal research on humor—had a keener interest in the nonexperimental/individual case approach toward humor for various theoretical reasons, presuppositions, assumptions, or prejudices (e.g., Hellyar, 1927, asserts that both the emotional and perceptual aspects of mind combine to make laughter a completely *individual* affair).]

Most of the material that Flugel (1954) presents (approximately 92 percent) is of a philosophical, interpretative, literary, historical, and/or psychoanalytic nature. Also, based on an analysis of Flugel's references, only about 8 percent of the studies are experimental in nature or content (e.g., see Ghosh, 1939; Heim, 1936; Hollingworth, 1911; Perl, 1933a; Williams, 1945). Writing 15 years later, Berlyne (1969, p. 808) provides a similar assessment of the state of the art concerning the application of experimentation to humor research (cf: McGhee, 1971; Treadwell, 1967):

The quantity of experimental work on humor during the three decades since Perl's (1933a) article was published has been scarcely greater than during the preceding three . . .Many so-called experiments have actually examined correlations between expressions of preference and other forms of behavior or personality traits, rather than the effects on reactions to humor of experimentally manipulated independent variables.

In the present work, it is suggested that the phenomenon of humor may fundamentally and optimally (i.e., "scientifically") be understood best by analysis of those research studies on humor having *empirical* and/or *experimental* bases or methodologies. Goldstein & McGhee (1972, pp. 264–267) provide some interesting statistics (via Tables 1–4) reflecting their survey of *methodology* in *empirical* studies for the period 1950–1971. In one case (Table 1), "type of experimental design" in two decades (1950–1960 versus 1961–1971) shows a comparison between usage of correlational versus experimental designs. Goldstein & McGhee state that the renewed interest in various aspects of humor has been accompanied by an increase in *methodological* sophistication and, if the transition from a correlational to experimental approach may be accepted as an index of improved methodology, their data (Table 1) indicate such a shift in methodology. That is, not only did the total number of *empirical* studies on humor sharply increase in the second half of the period (1961–1971), but the percentage of *experimental* studies also increased greatly. However, Goldstein & McGhee caution that while the increasing concern with the effect of specific *experimental* manipulations on humor has generated a greater understanding of the effect of various stimulus, personal, and social aspects upon humor, many studies have failed to relate their results to theory (correlational studies have been even less frequently derived from theory). Goldstein & McGhee suggest that while the trend in their survey data is promising, future research may make major contributions by developing *theoretically based experimental* studies; cf: O'Connell's (1984/1994) recommendation that one way out of "our perennial ignorance" concerning our limited scientific knowledge of humor is to conduct large-scale longitudinal studies of identified humorists for the initial purpose of gaining empirical facts as well as generating further experimental questions (e.g., Fisher & Fisher, 1981); O'Connell also cautions that we must be wary of generalizations across researchers' work because of the different definitions of humor that are used as well as the different measurement devices used to assess humor. Accordingly, in this chapter, primary consideration and importance are given to studies on humor that contain *empirical* and/or *experimental* characteristics and, thus, genuinely reflect the scientific attitudes of empiricism and causal determination.

Selected Early Psychological Humor Studies (1890–1959)

In this section, a number of selected "early" psychological studies of humor published during the period 1890–1959 are discussed. In the following section, selected "modern" psychological studies of humor published during the period 1960–2000 are examined. The rationale here for the temporal break/cut off between the "early" and "modern" periods (i.e., the break between 1959 and 1960) is one of intuition, personal choice, and convenience, and is based on the respective publication dates of two major review articles in the psychological literature on humor, i.e., Flugel (1954) and Berlyne (1969). It is suggested here that the transition period between these two publication events in psychology roughly marks the end of an "early" period (or "pre-experimental" period) defined by minimal use of empirical/experimental methodologies in humor research, and the beginning of a "modern" period characterized by a large increase in the number of publications on humor containing empirical/experimental emphases, procedures, and methods.

Of course, there may be exceptions to the observation or "rule" suggested here vis-à-vis number of empirical/experimental articles on humor (and particular articles), but it *is* certain—regarding the pre-1960s versus the post-1960s—that by the 1970s, psychology demonstrated its strong acceptance and advocacy of the empirical/experimental methods in the study of the phenomenon of humor (e.g., Chapman, 1983; Chapman & Foot, 1976, 1977; Goldstein & McGhee, 1972; McGhee, 1971; Ruch, 1993). [Note: Another longitudinal perspective or assessment of the history of humor study is provided by Goldstein, Harman, McGhee, & Karasik (1975); these researchers—writing from the perspective of the mid-1970s—note that the history of the psychological analysis of humor has gone through three fairly distinct phases: phase one—which lasted until about 1940—was characterized by *observational* (nonexperimental) studies without much theoretical basis, resulting in a number of disparate *descriptive* studies; phase two—focused on Freud's (1905/1916) work and where *psychoanalytically oriented* research makes up the bulk of data on humor (cf: Levine, 1969), and which is the first approach to be specifically theoretical; and phase three—emphasizes *cognitive* and *physiological* approaches, and evolved as the credibility of the psychoanalytic framework diminished, and as alternative and more parsimonious theoretical explanations of humor appeared (cf: Goldstein & McGhee, 1972; Ruch, 1993, p. 1, states that since the publication of Goldstein & McGhee's book in 1972, "humor has become a more established field of psychological inquiry").]

One of the earliest research studies on humor (in which *empirical* data were collected, but does not constitute an *experimental* study because there was no manipulation of independent variables) was conducted by Hall and Allin (1897) who proposed that theories of humor or laughter should go beyond mere speculation and be founded on empirical data. Hall and Allin received responses from about 3,000 people (on approximately 4,000 items) on a *questionnaire* they sent out requesting a description of all situations which individuals considered to be humorous, and included questions on tickling and its effects at various ages, causes of laughter in children, laughter in animals, fun in the theater, spontaneous laughter, laughter at calamities, and the best jokes in each class including puns, repartee, and practical jokes (cf: Perl, 1933a; Berlyne, 1969, pp. 807–808).

Briefly, the questionnaire consisted of the following 11 initial questions (each of the initial questions actually was followed by a series of six or more related questions in each category—making for a rather lengthy and extensive questionnaire overall): Just how would you tickle a child, physically. Describe individual cases of giggling, simpering, smiling, tittering, grinning, convulsive and hysterical laughter. Recall a few cases of great laughter in children and describe its cause, stories, jokes, funny mishaps, buffooneries, mimicry. What have you ever seen or heard of that seemed as if any animals laughed? Recall a few cases where you have laughed hardest and tell what caused it. Kindly consider carefully and write the best you ever heard of each of the following: a pun; repartee; practical joke; the funniest dinner or club story or social anecdote; the drollest, queerest, oddest story; describe the funniest character you ever saw or ever read of. What do you like best or dislike most in: burlesque, caricatures, satire, droll or silly "carryings on," quaint or humorous, naïve, eccentric traits, etc. Describe any case of purely spontaneous laughing in self or others. What peculiarities have you noticed in the wit and humor or stories or laughter of old people? Describe cases of laughter and joy at the calamity of others. Miscellaneous: Have you anything, or do you know of any helpful literature on this subject?

Following data collection, Hall and Allin (1897) classified laughs, gave a resume of theories of laughter, and concluded (p. 40) that "all current theories are utterly inadequate and speculative, and there are few more promising fields for psychological research" (than that of humor); moreover, Hall and Allin suggest that what is needed next is the application of all the resources of "instantaneous photography" to collect laughs and smiles in all their stages in men and women, children and adults; they assert that such behaviors are so evanescent that there are differences "as marked as those found in the gait of the horse" (p. 41). Additionally, in their proposed research agenda, Hall and Allin suggest that the resources of the "phonograph" should be applied to the vocal utterances of laughter, that a collection be made of thousands of the best ancient and modern jests for "inductive" classification purposes, and that an exhaustive review be made of humorous literature, proverbs, etc. for "analytic" purposes.

In a very ambitious study (84 journal pages), L. Martin (1905) pioneered the application of several early *experimental* methods to the study of humor (her stimulus materials consisted largely of pictures). Among her measurement tools were "undirected introspection," experimental/psychophysical judgments (including the methods of impression with serial judgments, constant differences, averages, choice, gradual variation, and expression), and "directed introspection." Based on participants' responses using the "undirected introspective" method, Martin concluded the following: a smiling face or an animal in a picture suggests funniness even if the picture in other respects is not humorous; there is a carry-over effect of humor from one picture to the next; a person's judgment of humor is influenced greatly by her or his physical condition; and on repeated viewing, pictures get stale, trite, or even cause a feeling of unpleasantness in the participant. Based on participants' responses on a questionnaire (16 multiple-item questions that included the requirement of incorporating the classical theories of humor in giving responses) using the method of "directed introspection," Martin concluded that laughter and funniness are intimately tied together, and that restraining the laughter decreases the overall feeling of fun in the participants.

The series of experiments in which Martin (1905) applied the psychophysical methods [cf: Woodworth & Poffenberger's (1920) assertion—via Perl, 1933a, p. 762—that the "experimental aesthetics" and methods used in humor research are "fundamentally the same as those used in psychophysics"] yielded results (p. 83) which show that participants' judgments of humor depend, in part, upon the length of time the stimulus materials (pictures) are exposed; also, the degree of funniness and the "fun duration" varied directly with the complexity of the pictures or the number of "fun centers" in each. Moreover, in her experiments, Martin found "fun fatigue" for a long series of pictures, and "fun accumulation" for a short series of pictures; and she observed an element of suggestion in her participants where a sad "fore-picture," or sad music, made funny pictures seem less funny.

Hollingworth (1911) notes that only two *empirical/experimental* studies of humor had been conducted (i.e., Hall & Allin, 1897; Martin, 1905) up to the time of his paper. Hollingworth (1911, p. 132) begins his report by saying, "Re-

actions to comic situations are notoriously dependent on individual temperament, mood, and circumstance. So much is this true that few attempts to control
these variable factors experimentally or to measure in any way the subjective
element in the response to the comic have been reported." Further,
Hollingworth asserts that one of the most striking things about reactions to
comic situations is the important role played by adaptation to the stimulus;
there is a marked change in the reaction whenever the climax is in any way
remembered or anticipated. Hollingworth notes that the mere fact that these
factors are subjective, or highly variable, is no reason why they should not submit to measurement by appropriate methods. Hollingworth suggests that the
variable elements in judgments of the comic fall into two chief groups:
variabilities in the *observer* due to experience, present attitude, emotional com-
plexes, and even racial differences; and variabilities in the *comic situation*
including speed of presentation, number of repetitions, and degree of adaptation that has occurred.

Hollingworth's method required each of 10 participants (all of whom were
women students) to arrange 39 jokes into 10 stacks/categories according to perceived "funniness"; the "order of merit" method (e.g., Cattell, 1903, 1906;
Sumner, 1898; Thorndike, 1910) was used to compute the average ratings, and
each participant arranged the joke cards five times with one week separating
each arrangement.

Hollingworth's results are treated under three headings: judgment of the
comic (including individual differences, variability of the same participant
from time/period to time/period, average variability of one observer compared
with that of the group, correlation of consistency with agreement with group
average, and relation of quality of motivation to variability); psychology of
adaptation to the comic (including decrease in fun with repetition, relative
decrease in fun among various types of jokes, and waxing-waning, and static
jokes); and with respect to the contributions to the theory of the comic.

Hollingworth found that four discriminations of merit are all that can accurately be made by groups or individuals when judging jokes in his procedure;
initially, participants agree more closely on the good than on the poor jokes, but
with repeated presentation, this difference disappears. Moreover, the same person was, on the average, more certain of judgments in the lower section than in
the upper section of the stimulus list; also, there was nothing to indicate that an
individual whose judgments were variable in one experiment were variable in
another experiment; those participants whose personal consistency was least in
judgments of humor correlated most closely with the group. Hollingworth suggests the existence in his procedure of the "waxing and waning" of the jokes:
upon repetition, the funniness of the list as a whole falls, but the relative positions of the jokes change (cf: Perl, 1933a, p. 754). In sum, Hollingworth's
results point to a theory of the comic which suggests that the comic is the suc-

cess of a "trick as play activity," and that there is an objective-comic and a sub-jective-comic aspect which is parallel to the phenomena of the waxing and waning, respectively, of joke judgments and joke appreciation (cf: Schauer, 1910, p. 410).

In testing for the perception of the comic, Walker and Washburn (1919) employed a *picture-completion task* (i.e., they obtained responses on the "Healy-Fernald Picture Completion Test"). In this approach, for each of the vacant squares on the test board, three picture squares/conditions are selected; one of these squares is the appropriate one that logically completes the picture; one forms an incongruous combination with the picture; and one is intended to appeal to a more "intellectual" sense of humor (i.e., by an aspect of appropriate-ness in the midst of incongruity). The participants (consisting of 80 young women college students, 18 seventh-grade boys and girls, and 18 fourth-grade boys and girls) rated the conditions on a five-point scale, attempting to indicate which of the three completed conditions gives the most humorous picture. Results in Walker and Washburn's study indicate that the intensity of the reac-tion to the comic is greatest in the fourth-grade children and least in the adult participants; also, the pictures in their appropriate context were considered to be funnier to the fourth-grade children than to the other groups. On the other hand, the incongruity condition was markedly funnier to the seventh-grade children than to either the fourth-grade children or adults.

In a series of early studies conducted by graduate students at Columbia Uni-versity as fulfillment of their Master's Degree requirements, Scofield (1921), Hester (1924), Lange (1927), Gregg (1928), and Allentuck (1929) investigated various aspects of humor and laughter. Scofield (1921) used a combined method of *order of merit* and a *rating* scale to study the effect of jokes and pic-tures in her participants who were tested individually to avoid the influence of group laughter. Participants ranked the jokes (10 jokes varying in equal steps from "most funny" to "least funny") on a four-point scale before making them over into an order of merit series. Scofield recorded the participants' breathing rates and found that the final respiration value was greatest for forced laughter, next for pictures, next for normal breathing, and lowest for the jokes—where, theoretically, thought inhibits normal respiration; she also found that the reac-tion time for the jokes was longer than for the pictures used, and suggested that the longer the preparation period for the stimulus materials, the less hearty is the laughter.

Hester (1924) asked her participants (three different age groups: preschool children, girls who were 7–10 years old, and young college women) to *tell* the "funniest thing" they knew. The preschool children indicated the surprise aspect of humor as the most salient; physical situations and calamities were also prevalent in their responses. The 7–10 year old girls also showed that phys-ical situations and calamities were significant in their responses and, also, suggestion (via "diffusion" among the participants) played a large part in their accounts; moreover, the linguistic aspect of humor, "play on words," did not seem to be a type of joke situation for the girls under 10 years of age. In addition to recounting the funniest thing they knew, the college women also graded (on a five-point scale) a list of 40 jokes of various types ranging from good to bad; these participants ranked the "naïve" jokes the highest. Hester also found that a sense of humor among "normal" persons is unrelated to their level of intelligence.

Lange (1927) studied the reactions of separate *crowds/audiences* to humor (in the play "Iolanthe") in the theater (in both professional and amateur productions); she found that there was never a variation of more than one second for the four studied audiences for each laugh concerning the professional performance, but the amateur performance indicated audience laughter that was less constant. Among her other results, Lange observed that the duration of the crowd laughter tended to increase in direct proportion to the style/practice of the actors. Lange also compared her audiences' results (professional performance) against some "daily laughter diary" results of Kambouropoulou (1926, 1930). [Note: For a more complete account of Kambouropoulou's study, as well as other information on early studies by Barry (1928) and Landis & Ross (1933), see my Chapter 4 section, "Individual, Personality, and Gender Differences".] Lange found notable crowd and audience laughter (in order of frequency) in the top three categories (ranked, respectively, from higher to lower frequency) of: "objective physical cause," "incongruity in situations," and "mental inferiority of another"; whereas Kambouropoulou indicates a different frequency order (concerning "daily life laughter"): in the first three places, she shows "mental inferiority of another," "objective physical cause," and "incongruity in situations."

Gregg (1928) conducted an *observational* study of the laughter of 22 three-year old children for a period of 40 hours over a three-month period; she found that 93 percent of all the children's laughter occurred when they were in a group setting; most of the remaining 7 percent of the child's laughter (when alone) occurred in connection with movement of some sort. Overall, the factor of motion entered into 73 percent of all laughs, the factor of sound into 13 percent, the factor of incongruity into 12 percent, and the factors of self-achievement, stories, and pictures into the remaining 2 percent. Based on these and other results, Gregg concludes that laughter is more a matter of temperament than I.Q. scores; also, laughter is not equivalent to the pleasurable: children often were very pleased apparently, but did not necessarily laugh.

In one of the first humor studies employing a true *experimental* approach (i.e., the manipulation, measurement, and control of classes of variables), Allentuck (1929) used a simple experimental design (experimental versus control groups) in his study of the effect of suggestion on humor (cf: Hammes,

1962); both an experimental group (participants rated high in suggestibility) and the control/standard group (nonsuggestible individuals) rated a series of jokes. Jokes were presented from least- to most-funny, and the degree of humor was graded by the length of a line drawn to represent it. Allentuck's results indicate that the experimental group and control group ratings of jokes were virtually identical when the experimental group was in the "normal" (i.e., "nonsuggestible") condition; even when the experimental group was in a "suggestible" (but not humor condition) state (involving the carrying out of "nonhumor" suggestions regarding pendulum swinging and falling backward behaviors), its judgments did not differ from those of the control group. However, when positive suggestions regarding humor (the humor condition) were provided to the experimental group in its suggestible state, it showed large differences in joke-ratings as compared to the standard/control group; moreover, individual differences in participants in the experimental group in the "humor-suggestible" state—that is, under the humor condition of receiving positive suggestions regarding humor—lessened markedly.

Barry (1928) studied the role of subject matter in participants' *individual differences* in humor. [Note: Barry used only two participants—graduate students—in his study which leaves it open to an experimenter's related criticisms of the lack of external validity and generalization of results from sample to general population.] Barry's participants were asked to rate jokes according to humorousness; he found that different types of jokes were rated funny by each individual (one person most-liked jokes about violence, the other person enjoyed alcohol-related jokes most). Barry also gave his two participants other tests and tasks in his procedure, and concluded that there are great individual differences in the appreciation of humor, and humor may be classified into topics according to meaningful content where topics capable of eliciting a humorous reaction in a person seem to be related often for that person with an unpleasant emotional affect. Accordingly, Barry suggests that humor is due to the *change* of the affective tone of the original perception from unpleasant to neutral or pleasant, and that the perception of the unreality in the situation is what causes a potentially humorous stimulus heavily infused with emotion to become humorous.

In their early study on the laughing and smiling in preschool children, Ding and Jersild (1932, p. 455) state that "no *experimental* factor was introduced" (italics added) in their procedure, but they did *observe* (across 276 hours), and record, the laughs and smiles that occurred during the free play and normal activities of 59 Chinese children in a combined kindergarten and nursery school (cf: Enders, 1927; Washburn, 1929); they attempted to study the relationship between laughing/smiling and various factors such as age, sex, and intelligence, and to analyze individual differences among participants. More specifically, Ding and Jersild collected categorical data on the children concerning the following behaviors/situations/materials: presentation of pictures, speaking and being spoken to, child's own motor activity, motor activity of others, presentation of stories, vocal sounds, nonvocal sounds, moving things, laughing/crying/smiling persons, nonverbal social contacts, frequency of being alone and passive, music and motor activity, music and songs, frequency of showing awkwardness/clumsiness, and child being "funny" or "clownish."

Based on their results, Ding and Jersild conclude the following, among other observations: laughter and smiling occur most frequently in association with general motor activity; the three-year-old children respond somewhat less frequently than the children of ages two, four, and five years; smiling occurs approximately seven times more frequently than laughing; laughing/smiling occurring when the child is physically active at play outnumbers the responses observed in all other situations combined; and the older child responds somewhat more frequently to social contacts and to music than does the younger child. Moreover, Ding and Jersild found marked individual differences in frequency of laughter/smiling, and the frequencies had no significant relationship to age, intelligence, nutritional status, height, weight, or socioeconomic status. From a theoretical perspective, they also found no evidence to support the view that laughter represents a feeling of superiority or of derision; and no evidence that tickling, release from repression, perception of the incongruous—or other special factors stressed in the prominent theories of laughter—played a salient role in humor appreciation. In summary, according to Ding and Jersild, laughing and smiling in children from two to five years of age occur predominantly in connection with general physical activity and serve, in large part, as a motor outlet in response to many different forms of stimulation; the fact that the child responds more frequently when in the company of others than when alone arises most likely from early social conditioning and from the increased stimulation to general activity afforded by the presence of others.

Landis and Ross (1933) devised a *humor test* of sorts in their attempt to study individual differences (among male and female college students, and female delinquents) in rating and classifying jokes. They found no significant relations between participants' scores on the devised humor test and on the personality and intelligence tests that were administered also to the participants; in one case, however, they found that men seemed to value the stimulus materials (jokes) more highly than did women of the same age and social status [Note: The fact that the jokes were picked originally by men may help to explain this finding!]

Perl (1933b) studied whether jokes presented under certain *social conditions* are judged quantitatively to be more or less funny than equally humorous jokes presented under different social conditions (cf: Asch, 1955; Moore, 1921; Wheeler & Jordan, 1929). Initially, Perl collected three lists of jokes that were equated for funniness; these lists were then presented to 40 graduate students who graded the jokes (on a five-point scale) under various conditions: one list was presented in mimeographed form and was graded by the students in the privacy of their homes; a second list was read to the students as a group while they graded them; and a third list was presented to the group visually by slides. Perl's results indicate the following: the jokes presented visually were judged to be funnier than those jokes rated privately; the visually presented jokes were also funnier than the jokes presented vocally; jokes rated in private were the least funny; and the phenomenon of social facilitation seemed to have more influence in raising the scores of the poor jokes than it had in raising the scores of the good jokes (cf: Malpass & Fitzpatrick, 1959, who employed a methodology involving a good *experimental* control measure where three different types of social condition—large group, small group, individual—had their *order counterbalanced* across presentations of humor tests for different participants). Concerning the last finding, Perl suggests that perhaps *all* of the poor jokes are socially facilitated while only *some* of the good jokes are facilitated and others are inhibited.

In her review of "experiments" on humor, Perl (1933a) suggests that one might profitably examine the techniques used in some of the earlier studies on humor (e.g., Allentuck, 1929; Barry, 1928; Gregg, 1928; Hall & Allin, 1897; Hester, 1924; Hollingworth, 1911; Kambouropoulou, 1926, 1930; Landis & Ross, 1933; Lange, 1927; L. Martin, 1905; Scofield, 1921; Walker & Washburn, 1919). The methods of ranking and rating are used extensively, and methods involving questionnaires, diaries, physiological measures, and observations are often used by themselves. Perl notes that there seems to be no uniformity in the procedures employed, some experimenters using the order of merit, some using a graphic rating scale, and some using a three-, four-, or five-point scale. She also observes that a great deal of discussion of rating methods has appeared in the psychological literature where most of the emphasis has been on rating people/traits rather than on rating ideas or jokes. Perl indicates the controversial nature of using the rating and ranking methods, and examines a few of the sensitive points concerning this issue (e.g., Symonds, 1924, 1925, suggests that a seven-point scale is preferable in this context to other types of scale; cf: Allentuck, 1929; Freyd, 1923; Hollingworth, 1911).

In her conclusions concerning the early research studies on humor, Perl (1933a) states that tremendous individual differences in humor have been observed in the studies where neither intelligence nor personality type seems to be closely connected with appreciation of humor in general, but categories of jokes that are preferred appear to be influenced by these factors. Moreover, college students appreciate naïve jokes or those based on the mental inferiority of another person, while the surprise element ranks high with young children; extraverts seem to prefer jokes based on superiority (or the exposure of unrevealed thoughts), while introverts seem to prefer jokes having to do with repressions such as sex or fear; individual differences in affective tone and emotional connections influence humor judgments; physiological states seem to influence, and be influenced by, humor; and suggestion—no matter whether given to suggestible persons in the form of positive suggestions of humor or given to normal participants by the social facilitation in a group situation—seems to play a salient role in judgments of humor.

Murray (1934) and Wolff, Smith, and Murray (1934) conducted a series of *experiments* on mirth/humor responses to disparaging, derisive, and aggressive jokes. Regarding the methodology used by Wolff et al. (1934, p. 363) to record participant's responses, they report that mirth responses may be evoked in the laboratory and measured on the following functional levels: the autonomic level via the psychogalvanometer; the expressive action level (laughter) via a motion picture camera; the level of immediate apperception via "indeliberate" verbal appraisals; and the level of postreflective apperception via "deliberate" verbal appraisals after an analysis of the presented material is made. Wolff et al. found that when presented with jokes at the expense of Jews, the Gentile and Jewish participants differentiated themselves on all levels—particularly in their deliberate appraisals after analysis of the jokes—by the intensity of their mirth responses (i.e., the Gentiles laughed more heartily at Jew-disparagement jokes than did the Jews). Moreover, when the Jewish names in the racial jokes were changed to Scotch names, these same jokes were given relatively higher ratings by a second group of Jewish participants (however, even these higher ratings were less than the ratings assigned by a group of Gentile participants; in accounting for these results, it was suggested that the Jews may have mentally affiliated themselves with the Scots and may have apperceived the jokes as also disparaging to themselves); and female participants estimated more highly than male participants the jokes on men, and vice versa.

In the research conducted by Murray (1934), rank-difference *correlations* between participants' scores (regarding self-reliance, aggressive-assertive disposition) and their affective responses/appraisals of disparagement jokes are reported. [Note: One must keep in mind, when assessing data based on methodologies involving *correlation coefficients*, that "correlational studies" are not equivalent to "causal determination" statements. That is, as Ray (2000, pp. 262–263) points out, "correlation does not imply causality," and that "with correlational designs, no variables are manipulated and, thus, there are no independent and dependent variables"; also, when a significant correlation *is* found between variables, the *possibility* of causality exists, but when there is a *lack* of correlation between variables the possibility of causality is ruled out (i.e., "there is no causality without correlation, but there may be correlation without causality".] Based upon his results, Murray (1934) concludes—among other things—that participants with strong, self-assertive trends who assume a critical, hostile, world-derogatory/misanthropic attitude towards their fellow humans are those who most intensely enjoy the disparagement type of jokes and, consequently, the response to such jokes may be used as criteria of specific sentiments towards particular objects of general aggressive attitudes; Murray also suggests that intense enjoyment of derisive/disparaging jokes is an indication of repressed malice (which is in accord with Freud's, 1905/1916, theory of "tendency wit," i.e., excessive laughter following the stimulus of a disparaging joke is due to the release of a repressed, unconscious—usually sexual or aggressive—impulse), and is a sign of an unconscious desire or need for destruction.

Heim (1936) conducted an "experiment" on humor consisting of two parts: the presentation of materials (jokes) to discover rules/tendencies that people use during laughter (employing methods of introspection and joke-ratings using the five categories of Not Funny, Slightly Funny, Funny, Very Funny, and Extremely Funny), and the recall of stimulus materials after time intervals ranging from two to 24 weeks (employing the method of written responses, e.g., "write down as many of the jokes as you can remember, in the order in which you originally received them"). The main conclusion of Heim's (1936) study is

to make one exceedingly chary of setting up any rules on the subject of humour, and to allay the great temptation of classifying types of humour and senses of humour. At the present stage it looks as if this would merely involve a listing of individual jokes and individual people . . . an informal discussion on the subject always leaves one with the same impression of lack of objectivity. (p. 161)

Furthermore, Heim provides comments that may be construed as constituting constructive criticism for the future *experimental* study of humor. For example, "there are obvious objections to applying experimental procedures to a study of humour" (p. 156). "It is risky to draw conclusions from one set of subjects and of jokes—the experiment has at least shown the impossibility of one individual's accounting for objective differences . . . in the goodness of jokes" (p. 156). "All the usual drawbacks to experimental conditions such as the effect of suggestion, change in what is to be observed as the result of observation, variation in mood of experimenter and so on, are present, and some are augmented; for instance, introspection of amusement is notoriously one of the hardest and most untrustworthy kinds of introspection, and the social element in laughter is perhaps its most essential factor. It seems probable that the number and kind of companions of the laughing individual determine his reaction, to a far greater extent than does the joke which he thinks is stimulating his laughter" (p. 156). "The self-conscious attitude and artificial atmosphere inevitably present can be dispelled during the course of the experiment only to some extent, since the presence of the stop-watch, the repeated request for a judgement and the hurried scribbling of the experimenter continue till the end"

(p. 156). "There are, on the other hand, one or two advantages in the experimental procedure . . . the laugh of politeness is almost entirely eliminated since the subjects feel for the most part that it is not offensive to show no sign of amusement at an 'experimental joke' and also since they are asked not to laugh if possible" (p. 157). "The experimental method must be supplemented by observations, both of individuals and of groups of varying sizes and composition, in social situations . . . experimentation has at least demonstrated the futility of forming plausible and attractive theories based on unverified assumptions" (p. 161).

Young (1937) employed the methodology of a *test-retest* (with a 16–day interval) design with that of a combined *questionnaire* and *rating scale* to his study of laughing/weeping and cheerfulness/depression in 240 college students. Results are reported in terms of frequency of, and reasons for, weeping; frequency of, and reasons for, laughing; duration of weeping and laughing periods; mood self-ratings; factors which determine moods, variability of moods, laughing/cheerful moods, and affective reactions and moods. Among Young's conclusions are the following: weeping both in female and male college students is a relatively infrequent experience (occurring on the average about once in 20–21 days); laughing in college students, both sexes, occurs so frequently that participants had to resort to guessing when attempting to estimate its frequency (occurring on the average of about 19.6 times per day, or more than 400 times that of weeping); the causes of weeping are 80–90 percent due to the social environment, while the remaining percent is due to organic causes (e.g., fatigue, nervousness, bodily injury, etc.); the causes of laughing are 98 percent due to the social environment; and college students rate their prevailing mood as cheerful 4.6 times as frequently as they rate it depressed.

In his "experimental" study of humor (originally a doctoral dissertation at the University of London), Ghosh (1939) employed four different methods of data collection: experimental, incidental observations, clinical observations, and questionnaires. The experimental method consisted in taking introspections and judgments (via a six-point scale from "Not Funny" to "Extremely Funny") from 51 participants on 50 jokes. [Note: Once again, as in most of the early so-called experimental studies of humor, the term experimental does *not* refer specifically to the use of a "causal determination" methodology in which independent variables are manipulated, extraneous variables are controlled, and dependent variables are measured.] Based upon his results, Ghosh concludes that the common inferences from the four methods are the following: humor serves as an escape from reality and an expression of aggression; failure of humor is attended by unpleasant consequences, namely, the arousal of pity, anger, annoyance, and sympathy; the search for humor is a very common activity; humor affords a cover for the expression of many socially tabooed wishes;

sexual jokes are best enjoyed in the company of equals; and humor may make aggression, retaliation, and humiliation innocuous.

In an empirical and theoretical study of humor, Eysenck (1942) employed the methodology of *factorial analysis* (cf: Andrews, 1943; Eysenck, 1943) to investigate three questions: What is the relative generality/objectivity of humor appreciation? What are the different types of appreciation involved in responses to humorous stimuli? and What is the influence of temperamental factors on humor appreciation? Eysenck introduced an innovative measure (relative to other early "experiments" on humor) into the humor tests he gave to his participants: the incorporation of two "controls" (or "jokers") into the sets of humorous stimuli in order to test certain assumptions regarding the extraneous influence of the "behavioral field"; these controls—while similar in form to the other items in the humor tests—were made up in such a way that they were not funny at all, but quite meaningless (for example, in the "humorous drawings with captions" type of stimulus item, the captions were cut off two of the drawings and replaced by quite unrelated captions).

Among Eysenck's conclusions (based on his methodology of administering to 16 participants a test of temperament and administering three tests of humor involving the ranking of 189 jokes of various kinds, where the resulting rankings were correlated and the tables of correlations were factor analyzed) are the following: a positive, general factor emerged that accounted for over 19 percent of the variance, as well as the extraction of several bipolar factors (these factors divided the participants into types according to the three principles of classification of "liking for *sexual* versus *nonsexual* jokes," "liking for *complex* versus *simple* jokes," and "liking for *personal* versus *impersonal* jokes"); and extraverts were found to prefer sexual and simple jokes, while introverts prefer complex and nonsexual jokes. Moreover, Eysenck's analyses of the jokes he used led him to a theory of humor that stresses the complex nature of the phenomenon: on the "orectic" (conative/affective) side, his results support the view that laughter is due to the joyful consciousness of superior adaptation, while on the "cognitive" (knowing) side the conditions responsible for the emergence of laughter may be summarized under rubrics that emphasize the sudden/insightful integration of contradictory/incongruous ideas, attitudes, or sentiments that are experienced objectively. Eysenck suggests that the distinction between the "orectic" and the "cognitive" aspects of laughter is useful in *theory*, but warns that the distinction should not be carried too far because in *practice* both factors are usually operative in varying proportions.

In an "experimental" and theoretical study of humor in children (originally a master's thesis at the University of London), Williams (1945) attempted to devise tests of humor for use with children and to assess their diagnostic value. Williams employed the method of survey/questionnaire with 294 children (boys and girls, aged 7–12 years) as participants. [Note: Accordingly, based upon the use of a methodology involving "surveys" and "questionnaires," and involving nonmanipulation of variables, perhaps a better characterization of Williams' study is "empirical" rather than "experimental"—as indicated in the original title of the work.] Analysis of data regarding children's humorous experiences revealed that laughter is largely an instinctive outlet for superfluous emotional energy, when *any* primitive instinct has been aroused, and when the individual so stimulated is intelligent enough to suppress overt expression of the instinct in its primitive form (cf: Burt, 1945).

Based upon collected data, Williams was able to construct three humor appreciation tests (with 30 items in each test) consisting, respectively, of: pictures with no words, humorous pictures with verbal captions, and jokes in words with no pictorial illustrations. Williams' other results, based on ratings made on the tests, indicate that children with a high appreciation of humor are extraverts rather than introverts, are intelligent rather than dull, and are emotional rather than unemotional; also, Williams found both a general factor that appears to represent the typical appreciation of humor found in children of this age, and a bipolar factor (personal versus impersonal) as distinguishing two opposite types of humor appreciation.

In an *experiment* reported by Kenny (1955), the methodology employed did include an aspect of variable/stimulus manipulation (i.e., a set of jokes was divided into three levels—low, moderate, and high—of varying stimulus-confirmation of joke-ending expectancy). The aim of Kenny's study was to determine the influence of different levels of stimulus-confirmation of joke-ending expectancies upon humor ratings (predictions were made on the basis of the *incongruity* hypothesis of humor and the *discrepancy* hypothesis of hedonic arousal). Kenny initially had a group of 55 judges (university students) rate jokes regarding how expected or unexpected were the endings. Next, a larger group of different participants (114 university students) then rated the same jokes for humor; the intention was to test the hypothesis that humor depends on incongruity, equated with unexpectedness of ending.

Kenny found that—in direct opposition to the prediction—a positive relation occurred between perceived humor and expectedness (i.e., the degree of humor appreciation increases with the degree to which the joke-ending expectancy is confirmed). Kenny suggested that this finding might be due to the fact that many of the jokes with expected endings involved extrinsic motives which turned them into instances of what Freud (1905/1916) called "tendency wit"; as to why tendency wit jokes should be regarded as funnier than "harmless wit" jokes, Kenny suggests that one can only speculate (e.g., the most parsimonious supposition is that the participants like jokes better which confirm their expectancies; however, Kenny asserts that such post hoc explanations are surely only gratuitous interpretations of the obtained data). Kenny notes that clarification of such findings awaits further experimental study where the tendency dimensions of jokes are varied *systematically* in relation to the stimulus-confirming properties of their endings. Kenny concludes that, regarding humor as an affective response, any theoretical account of humor appreciation must take into consideration not only the stimulus-confirmation of joke-ending expectancy, but also the dynamic "tendency," i.e., wit content of jokes (cf: Frankel, 1953; Sumno, 1958).

Byrne (1956) conducted an *experiment* to investigate the relationships among behavior ratings of expression of hostility, the extent to which hostile cartoons are judged to be amusing, and the ability to recognize that the cartoons contain hostility (Freudian theory would seem to predict a negative correlation between expression of hostility and finding hostile cartoons amusing while previous research findings tend to suggest a positive correlation). Byrne's methodology initially involved having five psychologists and psychology graduate students judge over 230 cartoons as to their expression, and nonexpression, of interpersonal hostility; from this procedure, 32 cartoons (16 characterized as having "hostile" content, and 16 as having "nonhostile" content) were used as stimulus materials. Participants were 45 male neuropsychiatric patients who were classified in one of three groups by hospital workers (psychiatrist, head nurse, chief attendant) as being "overtly hostile," "covertly hostile," or "nonhostile"; thus, there were 45 "experimental" participants in Byrne's study, 15 in each of three groups concerning rated hostility level. Based upon his findings, Byrne reports that previous experimental results are corroborated, and that psychoanalytic theory is contradicted in that a positive relationship was obtained between the type of humor found amusing and overt personality characteristics.

Regarding methodology, Byrne gives a word of caution about his *experimental* results: it is desirable to present any experimental findings simultaneously with cross-validation material; at the very least, there should be some assurance from the researcher that the measures which she or he is using show some stability over time [cf: Byrne's (1958) methodology in which participants were placed in one of four "treatment" conditions: Control Group—participants rated cartoons under the same neutral conditions as they did in a previous session; High (Unpleasant) Drive Level Group—participants rated cartoons first, followed by a difficult midsemester exam; High (Pleasant) Drive Level Group—participants rated cartoons, followed by a classroom party; and Low Drive Level Group—a midsemester exam was given first, followed by the cartoon-rating activity. In this study, Byrne tested the hypothesis that response to humor is tension-reducing by having 150 participants rate cartoons under conditions of neutral, increased, and decreased drive level; he found that cartoon ratings were not significantly influenced by drive level, but that a "cartoon-sequence effect" was present whereby cartoons are rated as increasingly funny from beginning to end in a 22–item series of cartoons; cf: Lee & Griffith

(1962) who found a similar "sequence effect" in a cartoon series, and who relate the phenomenon both to the "negative time error" frequently found in psychophysical experiments, and to Berlyne's (1960) "arousal jag" concept]. Levine and Abelson (1959) employed an *experimental* method (involving two experimental groups and one control group of participants) in their study designed to test one aspect of the assumed relationship between humor and anxiety—that the more anxiety a humor stimulus produces the greater is the likelihood that it will evoke a painful, rather than a gratifying, response. They used the 31 cartoons of the Mirth Response Test as the humorous stimuli which were given to three separate groups of participants (24 naval submarine enlistees who demonstrated an absence of overt anxiety, 45 hospitalized schizophrenic patients who had good contact and no major deterioration, and 27 acute hospitalized psychiatric patients who were diagnosed as having anxiety). Each participant was asked to sort the cartoons into those he liked, those he disliked, and those eliciting indifference. The cartoons were rated subsequently by 10 judges (psychiatrists) on a seven-point scale of "disturbingness"; the average disturbingness rating was used as a measure of the potential anxiety-arousing properties of that cartoon, and the cartoons were ranked in order from least disturbing (low rank position) to most disturbing (high rank position).

The responses of each participant were tabulated on the basis of overt mirth responses, and the cartoons sorted as liked and disliked; cartoons were classified according to their "disturbingness rank" and a mean score of "disturbingness" was obtained; each participant was assigned a score which was called "vulnerability to disturbingness,"—that is, the tendency to dislike cartoons which had been specifically adjudged to be potentially disturbing. Results indicate—when the participants' dislikes for the cartoons were examined—that psychiatric patients respond differently than do normal controls concerning the kinds of humorous stimuli they enjoy; in terms of the overt mirth responses, as well as deliberate choices of cartoons liked and disliked, the patients showed a preference for those cartoons which were rated by the judges as "minimally disturbing" (the control group of participants showed no such preferences: they enjoyed the more disturbing cartoons equally as well as the less disturbing ones). Thus, in summary, Levine and Abelson found that the hospitalized patients were more vulnerable to disturbing cartoons than were participants in the control ("normal") group.

Strickland (1959) employed an *experimental* methodology in his study of the effect of motivation arousal on humor preferences, and in which participants (students) rated 33 cartoons that were divided equally into "aggressive," "sexual," and "neutral/nonsensical" categories. Strickland randomly assigned 25 participants to each of three experimental groups: Hostile Group—the experimenter showed displeasure toward the participant; Sexual Group—prior to taking the humor test, the participant was shown photographs of nude female models; and Control Group—participants immediately took the humor test after being brought into the experimental situation. Each participant was tested individually to obtain a measure of his humor preference. Strickland's results indicate that a treatment designed to arouse hostility (Hostile Group) raised subsequent appreciation of aggressive cartoons, and that a sexually arousing treatment (Sexual Group) made cartoons with sexual content more appealing (cf: Byrne, 1961, who failed to confirm Strickland's findings; however, Byrne did find that sexual arousal—instigated by participants' reading of sexually inciting literary passages—reduced the appeal of cartoons that were dependent on ridicule for their humor). [Notes: For another motive-arousal/humor appreciation study in which sexual arousal as an *independent variable* was manipulated via presentation of photographs of nude female models, see Goldstein (1970b); for a study whose *dependent variables* included humor ratings of, and time to respond to, cartoons of varying content and complexity, see Goldstein (1970a); and for a study whose *dependent variables* included the physiological measures of heart rate and skin conductance during a test of hypotheses based on cognitive problem-solving models of humor, see Goldstein, Harman, McGhee, & Karasik (1975); cf: Langevin & Day (1972) who found that galvanic skin response amplitude and heart rate correlate positively with humor ratings of cartoons, and Godkewitsch (1976) who found that heart rate and skin conductance increase with the presentation of "punch lines" in jokes. For other studies that used physiological indices as their *dependent variable* measures, see Sekeres & Clark (1980) who recorded heart rate and skin conductance responses to sexual cartoons; and Wagoner & Sullenberger (1978) who employed pupillary size measures as an indicator of humor preferences.]

Selected Modern Psychological Humor Studies (1960–2000)

In this section, I examine a number of selected, representative "modern" (post-1959) *empirical/experimental* studies of humor which give an indication of the novelty, diversity, and breadth of methodological approaches (as well as investigators' particular humor interests) which characterize contemporary scientific humor research. In Chapter 6, other studies conducted in the period 1970–2001 and which employ empirical and/or experimental methodologies are discussed, also, via an annotated bibliographic format.

Byrne (1961) reports on some inconsistencies in the effect of motivation arousal on humor preferences, in particular on the similarities and differences regarding *methodology* between his and a similar study by Strickland (1959). Byrne presents a table showing the comparison of the methods used in the two experiments (Strickland versus Byrne); the following methodological issues are cited: definition of cartoon content; cartoons used; judges' ratings; criterion of cartoon acceptance; number of cartoons; administration of cartoons; rating scales of funniness; aggression-arousal procedure; and sex-arousal procedure. Byrne asserts that any one, or a combination, of these methodological differences could conceivably account for the divergence of results between his and Strickland's study. Byrne's attempts to relate drive-arousal to humor response yielded negative results (as did Hetherington & Wray, 1966; O'Connell, 1960; and Singer, 1968), while Strickland's results were positive regarding the motivational-arousal/humor preference relationship (cf: Rosenwald, 1964; and Lamb, 1968, p. 240, whose findings "constitute a replication of Strickland's, 1959, study").

Hammes and Wiggins (1962) tested the prediction that individuals having high manifest anxiety would appreciate humor material involving emotions of worry, tension, and depression less than would low-anxiety persons. Their methodology involved the creation of two *experimental* groups—32 low-anxious participants (16 men, 16 women), and 32 high-anxious participants (16 women, 16 men)—based upon participants' scores on an improved version of the Taylor Manifest Anxiety Scale (cf: Doris & Fierman, 1956; Hedberg, 1963; Hom, 1966; and Smith, Ascough, Ettinger, & Nelson, 1971, for other humor/anxiety experiments employing manipulations/measures of the independent variable of "anxiety"). Hammes and Wiggins' prediction was verified with regard to male participants only; thus, according to these results, appreciation of humor ("light" humor inasmuch as the comic strip *Peanuts* was used as humor stimuli) involving certain emotional components appears to be a function of an interaction between the participant's characteristics of manifest anxiety and sex/gender.

Williams and Cole (1964) investigated the relevance of a tension-inducing *social situation* upon an individual's appreciation of humor; specifically, the *experiment* examined the effect of (created) social experiences designed to instill a sense of inadequacy upon the participants' perception of humor. In the past, empirical studies of the tension-reduction theory of humor have sometimes involved the use of correlational studies of the relationship of other variables to humor preference (e.g., Doris & Fierman, 1956; Murray, 1934; Redlich, 1960; Redlich, Levine, & Sohler, 1951), and other studies have investigated the relationship of *experimentally* induced sets/conditions on humor appreciation (e.g., Byrne, 1956; Strickland, 1959; for experiments on humor in which various *alcohol* manipulations/conditions/levels served as the *independent variable*, see Hetherington & Wray, 1964; Lowe & Taylor, 1993, 1997; Weaver, Masland, Kharazmi, & Zillmann, 1985).

The study by Williams and Cole reflects the *experimental* mode of the investigation of humor appreciation; they employed a methodology involving the administration of different lists of jokes to four subgroups of participants: two experimental groups (in which "plants" or confederates performed), and two control groups; in this procedure, the "created social presumption" during the joke-rating phase of the study was that the experimental participants were confronted with the situation of hearing their "peers" (actually, confederates) present elaborate and seemingly sophisticated explanations of the "humor" in "jokes" they themselves did not understand, while at the same time feeling that they might be called upon a moment later to make a similar explanation of some other "joke"; immediately following this treatment or experience (the independent variable), the experimental participants were asked to rate the jokes (the dependent variable) on a legitimate list of jokes they had not seen previously. Williams and Cole found that individuals who had been placed in an inadequacy-inducing situation rated jokes (in which the main subject is depicted as inadequate, or as in an ego-deflating situation) with an increase of appreciation and preference over those individuals (controls) who were not exposed to the experimental treatment.

Young and Frye (1966) conducted three studies that explored the relative importance of various *experimental* manipulations of the *social environment* upon humor appreciation in college men. Young and Frye's (1966) experimental manipulations included the following treatment conditions: hostility-arousal, individual versus group administration, and a laughing versus nonlaughing confederate. Young and Frye found that overt laughter was more responsive to manipulation than was the rating of jokes; also, the conditions of group administration of humor stimuli, and laughter by the confederate, resulted in social facilitation of responsiveness to humor, while the conditions of hostility-arousal, and the confederate's embarrassment at sex jokes, decreased participants' ratings of humor appreciation. In essence, Young and Frye found that when participants heard jokes both alone and in a group, overt laughter significantly increased under group conditions. Young and Frye suggest that more research attention be given to the environmental factors influencing humor, and recommend the consideration of one additional experimental factor: because participants are sometimes influenced by the experimenter's hypothesis (and the participants' perceptions of the experimenter's "demands"—which in experiments of the present type may be more important in determining participants' responses than the humor per se), it is wise to hire the experimenters ostensibly as "actors" (as Young and Frye did) and not as "experimenters," and where such "actors" are not informed of the actual hypotheses of the study, even though they carry out the procedures of the study. [Notes: For other humor studies in which *social* variables are manipulated and serve as *independent variables*, see: Smyth & Fuller (1972)—effects on humor responses of conditions with and without group laughter; Chapman (1973), Fuller (1977), Fuller & Sheehy-Skeffington (1974), Nosanchuk & Lightstone (1974), and Porterfield, Mayer, Dougherty, Kredich, Kronberg, Marsee, & Okazaki (1988)—effects of dubbed/canned laughter on humor responses; Chapman (1972, 1975), Chapman & Chapman (1974), Chapman & Wright (1976)—effects on humor of a companion's laughing behavior (cf: Brown, Brown, & Ramos, 1981; Brown, Wheeler, & Cash, 1980; Calvert, 1949; Foot, Chapman, & Smith, 1977; Malpass, 1955; Malpass & Fitzpatrick, 1959; Martin & Gray, 1996; Olson, 1992; Perl, 1933b; Pistole & Shor, 1979; Rosenfeld, Giacalone, & Tedeschi, 1983); also, cf: Morrison (1940)—a *correlational* study reporting positive correlations between size of audience and number of laughs per performance, and Kaplan & Pascoe (1977)—a study in which a control group (students given a "serious" lecture) and three levels of a classroom humorous lecture ("concept humor"; "nonconcept humor"; and "mixed humor") are manipulated as *independent variables*. For studies in which experimental manipulation/arousal of participants' anger/aggression and hostile disposition served as an *independent variable*, and included a control group of nonangered/nonaggressive/nonhostile participants, see: Baron (1978a,b), Baron & Ball (1974), Berkowitz (1970), Leak (1974), Mueller & Donnerstein (1977), Prerost (1975, 1976, 1993, 1995), Prerost & Brewer (1977), and Singer (1968); cf: Baron & Bell (1977), Donnerstein, Donnerstein, & Evans (1975), and Zillmann (1971); for *independent variables* involving experimental manipulation of "hedonic tone" (positive and negative), and "excitatory potential" (low and high), see Cantor, Bryant, & Zillmann (1974); for a study that controls for the objects and agents of aggression in humorous materials, and investigates the effects of experimentally-induced *stress* on the appreciation of hostile humor in authoritarian personalities, see LaGaipa (1968); cf: Elbert (1961); and for a study that employed a methodology involving physiological/chemical substances as the *independent variables* (i.e., injections of epinephrine, chlorpromazine, or a placebo before participants rated a slapstick comedy film, see Schachter & Wheeler (1962)—in this study, epinephrine increased humor appreciation and chlorpromazine decreased it.]

   Deckers, Jenkins, and Gladfelter (1977) conducted three *experiments*—which employed weight-judgment tasks with the psychophysical method of constant stimuli—to examine the incongruity and tension-relief hypotheses of humor. According to the incongruity hypothesis, humor is a function of the degree of discrepancy between an expected and an actual outcome (e.g., Deckers, Edington, & VanCleave, 1981; Deckers & Kizer, 1974, 1975; Deckers & Winters, 1986; Gerber & Routh, 1975; and Nerhardt, 1970, 1977, found that participants who laughed and smiled the most upon lifting a weight were responding to conditions in which the weight was most divergent from a series of prior lifted weights). According to the relief hypothesis, humor is the result of relief or release from tension created by some task or situation [e.g., Rothbart (1973); cf: Shurcliff (1968) who employed three experimental treatments of different degrees of tension/anxiety—participants initially were told to: (a) hold a rat for five seconds; (b) to get a small sample of blood from a rat; or (c) to extract 2cm. of blood from a rat—where, subsequently, there was a relief-from-tension phase in which the participants discovered, upon opening the animal cage, that the rat was, in fact, a *toy* rat; Shurcliff found that—prior to the relief phase—treatment (c) produced the most anxiety/tension, and treatment (a) the least; also, discovery of the toy rat was rated *most* funny in treatment (c), and *least* funny in treatment (a). Shurcliff concluded that his results support a relief hypothesis of humor because greater tension/anxiety resulted in greater relief and, consequently, in greater funniness ratings.]

The lifted-weight experiments by Deckers et al. were designed to test and compare the incongruity and tension-relief hypotheses of humor inasmuch as many of the results from previous studies in this area may be explained by reference to either of the two hypotheses. In their first two experiments, Deckers et al. found that incongruity, but not tension-relief manipulations, influenced their dependent variables (i.e., participants' facial expressions and their ratings of humor); their third experiment on lifted weights (which varied participants' expectations about the heaviness of the final comparison weight) indicated incongruity, but not tension, expectancies, and where the expectancy manipulations influenced facial expressions and humor ratings. Thus, the results of all three of Deckers' et al. experiments support the incongruity, but not the tension-relief, hypothesis of humor (cf: Deckers & Salais, 1983).

Zillmann, Williams, Bryant, Boynton, and Wolf (1980) conducted an *experiment* in education that employed five experimental communications levels as the *independent variable*: humorous segments—interspersed at a slow pace, humorous segments—interspersed at a fast pace, no humorous inserts, slow-paced nonhumorous inserts, and fast-paced nonhumorous inserts. Zillmann et al. attempted to determine the particular effects of the involvement of humor—specifically of the pacing of humor—in educational programs for children on information acquisition and on hedonic aspects of the learning experience. They found that humor conditions produced results that are superior to those of any one of the several nonhumor control conditions employed; fast pacing of humorous inserts produced the facilitatory effect on information acquisition more rapidly than slow pacing; also, no significant sex differences concerning the experimental tasks were observed in the (child) participants. [Note: For another experiment in which the *independent variable* consisted of manipulations of humorous inserts in educational television programs (i.e., no humor; humor at a slow pace; humor at an intermediate pace; and humor at a fast pace), and the *dependent variable* consisted of children's choices/duration of exposure time to the differently paced humorous inserts, see Wakshlag, Day, & Zillmann (1981).]

In an *empirical* study of laughter and humor within a "reversal theory" context, Svebak & Apter (1987) used scores on the Telic Dominance Scale (TDS) to assign participants to two separate personality-type groups: the "telic" (serious-minded) and the "paratelic" (playful). Reversal theory (Apter, 1979, 1982, 1984; Apter, Fontana, & Murgatroyd, 1985; Apter & Smith, 1977), vis-à-vis humor, suggests that to experience humor the person needs to be in a particular "state of mind" (or "metamotivational state"); if the individual is not already in this state of mind, then the "comedy" material/stimuli will need to induce it for humor to be experienced. Moreover, when a person is in this state of mind, the greater the arousal in response to humorous material the more intensely the humor or pleasure is experienced. Svebak and Apter (1987) examined such aspects of the reversal theory account of humor—that is, the "state of mind" aspect, and the "arousal-humor" relationship. One of the basic notions in reversal theory is that there are a number of pairs of metamotivational states that operate whereby one or the other of each pair is always operating during waking life, and a switch, or reversal, from one to the other may be manifested under a variety of conditions with the result that individuals tend to switch back and forth between these states during their daily experiences.

Further, one of the metamotivational pairs consists of the "telic" and "paratelic" states, the former being a serious goal-oriented state of mind and the latter a more playful state in which the person is involved with the immediate enjoyment of an experience (where goals are "excuses" for the current behavior, rather than the genuine reason for the behavior). Theoretically, when a person is in the "telic state," high arousal is experienced as unpleasant and the accompanying anxiety is avoided, while low arousal is felt to be pleasant and relaxing; in contrast, for a person in the "paratelic state," high arousal is experienced as pleasant and exciting, while low arousal/boredom is unpleasant. Participants in Svebak and Apter's study were individually exposed to television comedy material and their ratings were recorded regarding their felt/preferred level of arousal and for "telic" and "paratelic" states. Analysis of the data (in which one of the *dependent variables*, laughter, was operationally defined via polygraph recordings of respiration rate) indicated that humorous material tends to induce the "paratelic state," even in "telic state-dominant" participants, and frequency of laughter in the "paratelic state" is positively correlated with degree of perceived arousal and with arousal preference (which confirms a linear, rather than a ditonic, relation of hedonic tone to perceived arousal in the "paratelic state").

White and Camarena (1989) employed a *repeated-measures* experimental design in their investigation of the effectiveness of laughter as a stress reducer (cf: White & Winzelberg, 1992). Ninety-three participants were assigned randomly to one of three treatment (independent variable) groups: control group, laughter group, relaxation training group. The dependent variable measures of stress included the physiological indices of heart rate and blood pressure, and the subjective measures of mood and anxiety; pre- and posttreatment measurements (i.e., a "within-participants" design) were taken to be able to assess any reduction in the pretreatment measures; also, the posttreatment measures were repeated ("post-post") within 10 minutes to assess the duration of any stress-reducing effects. Participants met in their respective groups weekly for one and one-half hours for six consecutive weeks. Results indicate that there were no significant differences in stress-reduction in the three groups in terms of pre- and posttreatment group scores for the physiological measures, and while the laughter group did not experience significantly reduced stress, it did show consistent decreases in stress levels for the two psychological measures as compared to the control group.

White and Camarena suggest that although there appears to be a groundswell of support for the adage "laughter is the best medicine," the veracity of this notion has not yet been established with scientific certainty; their study did find only marginal support for the contention that laughter reduces psychological stress. White and Camarena offer recommendations for future research involving good *experimental* practice and procedure in this area: the use of *continuous* physiological monitoring of participants (their procedure made only intermittent measures); the use of *additional* psychological measurements (they used only two—a mood-adjective checklist and a state-trait anxiety inventory); the use of a procedure whereby there is *uniform* stressing of participants for the purpose of establishing standard *baselines* of stress levels (cf: the use by Yovetich, Dale, & Hudak, 1990, of an anticipation of shock—a stressor design to bring about an increase in anxiety, and measured by heart rate and self-reports of stress/anxiety); and the *standardization* of amounts of treatment to more accurately compare the effects of the laughter treatment condition with that of the relaxation training condition. White and Camarena suggest, also, that further research should evaluate the long-term effects on individuals who engage in, or increase their use of, laughter.

In a study with well-defined independent and dependent variables, Butland and Ivy (1990) conducted an investigation of the dispositional theory of humor. Employing a "two-by-two-by-two" design, Butland and Ivy's independent variables were biological sex, sex role attitudes, and manipulations of disparaged roles in four jokes, and their dependent variables were participants' humor appreciation for each of the four jokes. In their replication and extension of Cantor's (1976) research, Butland and Ivy found, among other results, that the data for male participants supports the dispositional theory of humor, and for one of the jokes, "traditional" male participants (rated as "traditional" via a sex-role attitude scale) had significantly greater appreciation for female-disparaging humor than did "traditional" female participants.

Zillmann, Rockwell, Schweitzer, and Sundar (1993) *experimentally* explored the mediation of superior coping with physical discomfort after humorous stimulation was given. In brief, their experimental procedure consisted of the following: the thresholds for physical discomfort (via blood-pressure cuff inflation) were determined for all participants (50 male and 50 female university students) who were able to release the cuff pressure when their own personal discomfort threshold was reached; following this determination of basal thresholds, participants were exposed to one of five programs shown on a television monitor—standup comedy, situation comedy, serious drama, tragedy, or instructional material (this last treatment group was employed as a neutral, control condition). Immediately following this exposure, participants' discomfort thresholds were measured again, and their perceptions also were recorded concerning how they reacted to the various treatments (programs). Essentially, the experimental design was an "A1–B–A2" type where "A1" was a pretreatment measure, "B" was the treatment (television program), and "A2" involved posttreatment measures. Among their conclusions, Zillmann et al. suggest that exposure to comedy is capable of elevating an individual's threshold for physical discomfort; compared against the control condition, the two types of comedy (standup and situation) showed this effect (cf: the laughter/discomfort threshold study by Cogan, Cogan, Waltz, & McCue, 1987, who report similar—and stronger—effects).

Zillmann et al. also found, unexpectedly, that participants' thresholds for physical discomfort after exposure to the tragedy program treatment/condition was elevated and equivalent to that produced by exposure to the comedy programs treatments/conditions [cf: the endocrinological research by Levi (1965), and Carruthers & Taggart (1973), which suggests that *both* comedy and tragedy material may produce comparable increments in sympathetic activity, e.g., high release levels of catecholamine]. In terms of *experimental refinement* for future research in this area, Zillmann et al. suggest that a behavioral assessment of amusement might prove superior to one of retrospection in which participants' evaluative apprehensions may act as contaminants to valid quantification of responses; also, ratings of arousal from exposure to entertaining programs are known to be problem-laden (cf: Zillmann, 1991); for example, the arousal-ratings are blind to specific excitatory reactions, such as increased activity in the brain-stem reticular formation or heightened sympathetic responding occurring in participants' peripheral structures.

Cann, Holt, and Calhoun (1999) employed an *experimental* methodology in their assessment of sense of humor and a humorous external event as factors affecting individuals' emotional responses to a stressor. Their procedure included the following phases: measurement of participant's anxiety level and affective state before, and after, observing a stress-arousing segment of a film (the movie *Alive* in which the reactions are shown of a group of passengers on an airplane just before, and just after, the plane crashes); following the administration of this stressor, participants received a treatment which involved viewing either a humorous videotape, a nonhumorous videotape, or waiting without distraction (control condition), before providing a final measure of anxiety and affect.

Among other findings, Cann et al. found results which indicate that the stressor elevated anxiety, and lowered positive affect; moreover, the humor treatment condition successfully reduced anxiety, and raised positive affect as compared to the waiting (control) condition; and the nonhumorous treatment condition also reduced anxiety, but it did not increase positive affect (cf: a similar study by White & Winzelberg, 1992, who assessed only anxiety, not affect, and found no differences in reported post-stressor anxiety between groups exposed to a humor videotape, a relaxation audiotape, or a control videotape). Cann, et al. provide a valuable ancillary/supplemental analysis in their study concerning sense of humor relationships: nine measures of sense of humor were used in regression analyses to predict anxiety and affect at each point in their procedure (pre-stressor, post-stressor, post-treatment); the most useful predictor across the different measures of anxiety and affect was Svebak's (1974b, 1993, 1996) "Metamessage Sensitivity" scale on his "Sense of Humor Questionnaire."

Olson, Maio, and Hobden (1999) conducted three *experiments* to test whether exposure to disparaging humor produces either more extreme stereotypes/attitudes or more accessible stereotypes/attitudes regarding the disparaged group. Their experimental procedure vis-à-vis independent variables/treatments was as follows: participants were exposed to disparaging humor about men (women participants in two experiments) or lawyers (both men and women in one experiment); in the control conditions, individuals were exposed to nondisparaging humor (all three experiments), nonhumorous disparaging information (two experiments), or nothing at all (two experiments). Olson et al. employed the dependent variable measures of the ratings of the target (disparaged) group on stereotypic attributes, of attitudes toward the target group, of interpretations of ambiguous behaviors made by members of the target group, and of the latencies of attitudinal/stereotypic judgments about the target group. Based upon a total of 83 analyses, across three experiments, Olson et al. found consistent results (save one analysis that was in the predicted direction) that there was no (null) evidence that disparaging humor yields any reliable effects. Olson et al. (1999, pp. 215–216) provide an "experimentally healthy" discussion in an attempt to cover some simple methodological explanation for their null results; for example, perhaps their choices of disparaging humor were not funny enough or not of sufficient duration to have an effect; perhaps their dependent measures were not sensitive enough; maybe their findings were constrained by the laboratory setting in which they were obtained; and perhaps the delay between exposure to the disparaging humor and measurement of stereotypes/attitudes was too long for any effects to persist; cf: Hobden & Olson, 1994).

In summary, for this section on scientific methodology and humor research, it may be observed—when comparing collectively the nature and quality of the "early" (1890–1959) studies against the "modern" (1960–2000) studies—that great strides in methodology have been made recently in the design of humor experiments which are in accord with sound scientific principles and practices (that are characteristic, also, of the other more advanced and mature sciences), and that involve more sophisticated data collection activities in the *empirical* studies, the proper manipulation of independent variables, the control of extraneous variables (to eliminate alternative explanations of observed results), and the more accurate and precise measurement of more diverse dependent variables in the *experimental* studies. Further examples of, and discussion of, modern empirical and experimental studies on humor may be found in Chapter 6.

MEASUREMENT OF HUMOR

It is generally agreed, among psychologists as well as among laymen, that "sense of humor" is an important and valuable personality trait. It has been equated with "insight" . . . it has been ascribed to various nations and races in varying proportions . . . it has been used as an aid in classifying and diagnosing mental illness . . . it has been correlated with personality and temperament, as well as with scholastic aptitude, emotional maturity, height, and weight. Yet in spite of these manifold uses of the term, scientific measurement of the trait has lagged seriously behind.

—H. J. Eysenck, 1943

At some stage in most humour studies, it becomes necessary to assess the degree of amusement experienced by the subject. Naturally, any measure used should be reliable, objective, and capable of fairly precise quantification . . . if we want to quantify and compare various degrees of amusement, there is no doubt that the issues in measurement will have to be clarified.

—A. Sheehy-Skeffington, 1977

Measuring humor is an important part of understanding it. In order to evaluate the variables that contribute to humor, an estimate of the intensity of the response is necessary.

—P. Derks, 1992

Humor can provide a method of coping with a variety of stressful situations. Unfortunately, the scientific measurement of humor has suffered from many methodological problems, including low reliability and social desirability bias.

—J. C. Overholser, 1992

There has been a renaissance of research interest in the "sense of humor" in recent years, partly as an attempt to define the concept but more strenuously to provide instruments for its measurement.

—W. Ruch, 1996

Merenda (1984) discusses empirical research methods and notes the importance of the precision of *measurement* for scientific psychology. According to Merenda, in using psychometrics the investigator is confronted with at least two serious issues: the crudeness of even the most sophisticated and reliable instruments available for obtaining measures on independent and dependent variables; and the fact that all psychological measurement is indirect rather than direct (that is, no psychological attribute can ever be measured directly—only its assumed manifestation in behavior is measured).

In his review of the literature on the measurement of humor, R. A. Martin (1996) notes that most of the measures that have been developed could best be described as tests of humor *appreciation* (cf: Ruch, 1996); in such types of scales, participants are presented with a large number of jokes and/or cartoons and are instructed to rate how funny they find each of them. Subsequently, the ratings of humor stimuli typically are factor analyzed, resulting in the identification of a number of types of humor (e.g., aggressive, nonsense, sexual, etc.). Next, participants' funniness ratings are summed across the jokes in each factor and yields scores that gauge the degree to which participants enjoy one type of humor as compared to another type. Additionally, an overall humor appreciation score may be computed by summing all the funniness ratings across the various factors.

While some psychologists employ this factor analytic approach to humor measurement (e.g., Ruch, 1992), Martin's (1996) particular research interests and purposes indicate to him the use of a somewhat different measurement strategy. Martin is interested in the potential stress-buffering effects of humor, and is not concerned with the *types* of humor that individuals prefer but, rather, with the *degree* to which they find humor in their daily lives regardless of the content/nature of that humor. Martin is concerned, also, that the traditional humor appreciation tests might have little to do with the actual daily experience of humor; for instance, the observation that a person shows preference for one joke over another does not mean necessarily that the individual tends to perceive, create, and enjoy humor in daily living experiences (cf: Babad, 1974, who found no relation between participants' scores on such scales and their sense of humor as rated by their peers). Moreover, Martin suggests that the existing humor appreciation tests are outdated, containing cartoons and jokes that may have been funny a few decades ago, but are now more odd or quaint than humorous. Consequently, Martin and his associates take a different measurement approach than the traditional one in developing their self-report measure of sense of humor (see Martin & Lefcourt, 1984).

This brief introduction to the measurement of humor shows that it is a vital and lively area of research (cf: the current debate in the literature between Ruch, 1999, and Paolillo, 1998) with a history of psychologist's attempts to develop humor appreciation tests and to devise new materials in response to particular research needs and interests. [Note: Ruch (1998, pp. 405–411, *Appendix: Humor Measurement Tools*) provides a nonevaluative, but nonetheless useful and valuable, list of five and one-half dozen *historical* and *current* instruments for the assessment of humor traits and states in children and adults, as well as the variables measured by the instruments. Ruch gives the *name* of each test, the *developer(s)* of each test, and the *traits* to be measured by each test; the following eight categories are used (with the corresponding number of tests included in each category): Informal Surveys, Joke-Telling Techniques, or Diary Method (n=8); Joke and Cartoon Tests (n=18); Questionnaires, Self-Report Scales (n=14); Peer-Reports (n=7); State Measures (n=1); Children-Humor Tests (n=5); Humor Scales in General Instruments (n=6); and Miscellaneous/Unclassified (n=7).] In this section, I discuss some selected studies (chronologically arranged) in the history of the *measurement* of humor and indicate, where possible and appropriate in a few cases, various methodological criticisms, shortcomings, and limitations of some of the studies.

In the first half of the 20th century, a number of studies involving the measurement of humor were conducted. In their use and examination of the Healy-Fernald Picture Completion Test (H-FPCT), Walker and Washburn (1919) decided that the test may be useful as a test of the perception of the comic when the items on the test are administered in a modified way different from the originally intended way. That is, when the puzzle/test is used as originally intended, the problem for the child tested is to find (from among a number of blocks that are supplied), and put in place, the proper object/block for each episodic picture in a series of 10 episodes (e.g., in the blank space between the boys whose pictures show that they are playing football the child must fit the square block bearing the picture of a football). Walker and Washburn discovered that in some of the episodes on the test the effect is quite funny if a wrong object is substituted, and this suggested to them the use of the puzzle as a test of the comic, and constitutes, most likely, one of the earliest humor tests developed and reported in the psychological literature.

In their modified use of the test, Walker and Washburn (1919, p. 305) themselves selected three picture squares for each of the vacant squares on the test board: one was the "appropriate" one (which logically completed the episodic picture); one formed a "merely incongruous combination" with the picture; and one was intended "to appeal by an element of appropriateness in the midst of incongruity to a more intellectual sense of humor." Walker and Washburn

(1919, p. 305) gave the following directions to their participants: "I am going to put three blocks successively in each of these squares, and I want you to assign a numerical value, from 1 to 5, with 5 being the highest, for the degree of funniness of each of the blocks."

Further description and the results of Walker and Washburn's use of the H-FPCT are given earlier in this chapter under "Selected Early Psychological Humor Studies (1890–1959)." However, for present purposes, a few comments are provided concerning Walker and Washburn's study: first, they base their rationale for using the H-FPCT as a humor test on the following statement (which, today, would most likely be debated by various theorists; cf: Bergler, 1956, pp. 1–41; Brown & Keegan, 1999, p. 67; Martin, 2000, pp. 202–203): "Now all authorities agree that a situation to be comic must involve an element of incongruity" (p. 304); and second, in their presentation of the three blocks for each episodic picture, the *order* used by Walker and Washburn was the *same* throughout the test (i.e., the "appropriate" block was given first, the "really funny" block was second, and the "merely incongruous" block was third) which, procedurally, may have introduced a response-order bias, and could have been corrected by *counterbalancing* the order of presentation of the blocks across trials.

Davenport and Craytor (1923) measured the degree of humor in persons of different nationalities (German, Irish, Italian, Austrian, Russian, Jewish) in their study of the comparative social traits of various races (other measured traits included leadership, pertinacity, frankness, suspiciousness, sympathy, loyalty, generosity, obtrusiveness, and coolness). The purpose of Davenport and Craytor's (1923, p. 127) study was "to replace opinion as to race differences in social traits by quantitative estimates." Their method of data collection consisted of analyzing the independent judgments of one to three teachers concerning 10 traits of each of 102 students (in a New York City high school). Their results concerning the trait of humor indicate that the German children rank first and the Irish rank second; the difference between these two nationalities is not great, though, and is also not differentiated from the Austrians/Jews in general; however, the difference between these groups and the Italians demonstrates a probable real difference in respect to national humor. Davenport and Craytor admit that the interpretation of the differences in averages of the 10 measured traits is not easy: it may indicate a difference in the intrinsic variability of the traits or a difference in the ease or certainty of estimating them.

A methodological shortcoming in Davenport and Craytor's (1923, see footnote, p. 132) study is the fact that the probable errors and the standard deviations upon which they are based are probably influenced to some extent by the procedure whereby different teachers rated the different students, and where one set of teachers rated a larger proportion of the German students than another set which treated a larger proportion of the Irish, and so on; thus, the different sets of raters did *not* play an *equal* role in determining the average rating of persons belonging to different nationalities. Such a potential error may be overcome through the use of larger numbers of students who are rated, and having the different pairs of teachers rate an equal proportion of persons of the different nationalities.

Bird (1925) describes an "objective humor test for children" which consists of 20 pictures of absurd situations that are easily comprehended by elementary school children (cf: the 5–item/drawings humor test for children by King & King, 1973). The pictures represent an ascending scale of difficulty ranging from "zero humor," through obvious absurdity, up to situations requiring a considerable degree of interpretation. The pictures are arranged in pairs and the child is asked to indicate the funnier picture of each pair, making 10 choices in all. The score value attached to each "correct" choice in each pair of pictures is determined by the number of individuals in that grade who selected that picture as the more amusing of the two; the norm of each school grade is the median score attained by that grade; the norms are based upon the decisions of 500 children ranging in age from 3 to 16, in each school grade from kindergarten to the eighth grade. The favorite pictures among the tested children show themes of: unusual antics of persons or animals, discomfiture of an individual, and various types of contests or pursuits. Bird found a high correlation (.89) between "success" in the humor test and IQ score. The aim of Bird's (1925, p. 138) test is "to determine objectively to what extent a child's 'sense of humor' deviates from the norm of his associates, with a view to discovering the underlying reason, thereby making one more contribution to the various methods of diagnosis."

Andrews (1943) constructed a "sense-of-humor" test as part of a larger empirical program designed to determine whether or not humor is a single unit quality of a general nature, or whether it consists of several different identifiable qualities; the test was intended, also, to serve as a diagnostic tool in the area of personality measurement and assessment. Andrew's initial procedure involved the collection of 200 jokes, 175 puns, 200 limericks, and 71 cartoons, and also involved the use of the psychophysical method of equal-appearing intervals (in order to obtain relative scale values of the humor values of each item). Participants (university students) rated the items by sorting them into nine piles according to how funny they seemed. Eighteen judges rated the jokes, 18 rated the puns, 18 rated the limericks, and eight rated the cartoons. Altogether, the final humor test consists of 90 items (18 cartoons, and 24 each of jokes, puns, and limericks); below each item on the test, a five-number rating scale was printed for use in rating the degree of humor of each item. Next, Andrews' "Sense-of-Humor Test" was administered to 300 persons, their ratings tallied and recorded, and 24 items were chosen subsequently to be intercorrelated and factor analyzed; statistical analyses were carried out until six factors (accounting for all the significant relationships) had been extracted from the data.

Andrews provides a primary conclusion based upon the results of his rotated factor matrix: there is no *general* or *universal* factor involved in the comic material; although the data fail to indicate the presence of a factor that is common to all the humor items, they do reveal the presence of six common factors which are relatively independent from each another (Andrews reluctantly suggests the following terms/names for these factors: derision-superiority, reaction to debauchery, subtlety, play on words and ideas, sexual, and ridiculous wisecracks). Andrews asserts that an important aspect of his study is that the six humor factors he identified are based on empirical, experimental, and statistical evidence rather than on the anecdotal and rational methods employed by the layman or philosopher; he also maintains that the approach to the study of personality using the methodology of factor analysis tends to realize, partially, the goal of scientific objectivity via the *operational definition* of personality traits.

Yarnold and Berkeley (1954, p. 543) state that Andrews accomplished the first large-scale statistical analysis of a sample of humor items—his factor analysis of a 24–item matrix demonstrated that humor response was not of an entirely general nature as maintained by certain early theorists (e.g., Eastman, 1921); additionally, Andrews' study indicates that the specific item structure, whether it be cartoon, joke, or limerick, is not of primary importance. On the other hand, Yarnold and Berkeley maintain that while this latter information is important, it should be noted that Andrews' factors would have little utility as actual measures of humor response.

Eysenck (1943) cites the following methods (none of which, he asserts, can escape serious criticisms on the theoretical level, and none of which can be said to have gained wide acceptance) as the only ones that appear to have been employed (to date) in an attempt to quantify the elusive trait of humor: determination of a person's "humor" by comparing his or her ranking of humorous items with that of a standard group (e.g., Roback, 1939); by comparing the absolute judgments of funniness of various humorous items with a standard derived from a large group (e.g., Almack, 1928; Bird, 1925); by requiring the participant to select the funniest ending for a joke with several different endings being provided, or by presenting the participant with a cartoon, and asking her or him to produce a funny caption for it, or with an unfinished joke, which he or she is required to finish (e.g., Claparede, 1934; Harrower, 1932).

Eysenck suggests that the first two "appreciation" methods involve two different principles (the third method has been shown to provide a good test of intelligence but shows little evidence of any specific "humor" factor; see Thorndike & Stein, 1937); one principle emphasizes the *cognitive* agreement between the participant and the criterion group (determining the number of times the individual's judgment regarding the goodness or badness of a joke agrees with that of the standard group); the other principle stresses the *affective* score of the participant (i.e., determination of whether the participant finds very many or very few jokes to be funny). According to Eysenck, the first method is better adapted to deal with *cognitive* agreement, and the second method is better adapted to deal with *affective* scores. Eysenck suggests that the virtues of both methods can be realized by combination of both, and having the participants rank the items and by asking them at the same time how many items they find amusing or funny (cf: Eysenck, 1942).

Eysenck (1943) examines five tests of "appreciation of humor," each consisting of 12 items to be ranked in order of "funniness"; participants were 50 women and 50 men who represented a sample of the population equated in terms of social class, age, and such; the number of items known and the number of items found funny were noted for each test and for each participant. Next, scores were established for each person in each test by correlating the participants' rankings with the average ranking. The items in each of three tests were intercorrelated, and the resulting matrices factorized to discover group factors; the five tests were intercorrelated both for scores and for "number of items liked" in order to find whether there were any factors common to all tests. Among his conclusions, Eysenck gives the following: there was as much divergence of opinion on the "funniness" of the items in one of the tests as there was on that of the items in any of the other tests; on the whole, about 35 percent of the items were found to be amusing; men and women did not differ on the number of items liked; the rankings of the women intercorrelated on the average higher than those of the men; the validity of the average rankings was very high (.96); there were no significant correlations between the scores of the 100 participants in the five tests used; three group factors were found in an analysis of the intercorrelations of the items in three tests ("clever" versus "funny" jokes; "situational" versus "character" humor; and "clever" versus "funny" limericks); the results of this experiment confirm the theoretical analysis of "sense of humor" as developed by Eysenck (1942).

Cattell and Luborsky (1946) describe their research on humor; in particular, they indicate their concerns for: how far humor appreciation is constant for the individual over a fairly long period of time; what groupings of responses are to be found expressed in humor reactions; in what way humor responses are affected by familiarity with the joke; and in what way humor responses are related to personality (cf: Luborsky & Cattell, 1947b). They gave 100 jokes (which varied in subject matter and apparent dynamic content) to 100 selected participants who made ratings of their enjoyment of each joke; the participants also estimated the number of jokes with which they were familiar. Six months later, the same participants were given the same jokes to rate; split-half and repeat reliabilities were obtained; also, a correlation cluster analysis of the responses was carried out which yielded 13 clusters; most of these clusters had some readily recognizable psychological unity. Then, the 13 clusters were treated as separate measures, each participant being given a score for each cluster, and the clusters were factor analyzed (cf: J. H. Campbell, 1967). Five factors were extracted with Cattell and Luborsky's statistical procedure.

In a follow-up study, Cattell and Luborsky (1947b) also developed response clusters, but according to a critique by Yarnold and Berkeley (1954) the clusters were developed with a too-lenient criterion for including an item in a cluster, resulting in measures with low reliabilities. Also, a later study by Cattell, Luborsky, and Hicks (1950) was concerned with the factor analysis of a sample of humor items; the factor tests resulting from this analysis also failed to meet the minimum qualifications for an adequate set of scales, and the "psychological meaning" involved also seems to be overly complex (cf: Tollefson & Cattell, 1963–1964). Thus, according to criticisms by Yarnold and Berkeley (1954), the research of Cattell and others have yielded little in terms of sufficiently homogeneous and independent humor measurement devices.

Raley (1946) notes that while there have been many attempts to define and explain psychologically the phenomenon of humor, little has been done (to date) to *measure* scientifically the humor experience. Raley proposed the construction of a four-point attitude scale—using the methods of rank order and rating scales—as an objective instrument for measuring the trait of humor; she used captioned cartoons as the humorous stimuli (which were selected and submitted by girls ranging in age from 10 to 18 years inclusive); the ratings of 140 girls from these age groups were taken as the bases for the scale construction. Next, ratings were obtained from 738 girls to standardize two comparable forms of the scale, each form including 32 cartoons; these cartoons comprised eight different categories (i.e., men, women, romance, children, cars, animals, sports, and soldiers) of four cartoons each. Raley then attempted to discover whether or not there was a differential response from age to age when the eight cartoons which represented the separate categories were ranked. Raley's results include the following: a test-retest correlation (.98) indicates that the scale—when used with the appropriate age group—is reliable; the four scale positions were maintained consistently whether the cartoons were ranked by the older or by the younger girls; there are signs that the categories were ranked differently at the several age levels (the change appears regularly at age 15 years); there is some evidence that the variations in responses from year to year are dependent upon the classifications of the pictures (cf: Raley, 1942; Raley & Ballmann, 1957). Of course, Raley's (1946) use of only female participants in her study opens the issue of a possible sex bias and gender differences in her scaling effects concerning humor.

More than 10 years following Raley's (1942) original study, an investigation by Ballmann (1954) used the same cartoons as standardized by Raley (1942), but in this case with boys as well as girls serving as participants. Ballmann's

(1954) study was designed primarily to examine sex differences in humor preferences, and she found such sex differences when 224 participants (16 of each sex at each year interval from ages 11 to 17 years, covering grades six to twelve inclusive) were given the "classification ranking" procedure (i.e., the cartoons from the eight categories were ranked one against the other) of the humor scale. Raley and Ballmann (1957) conclude that in the matter of humor—as well as nearly all other personality traits—there are definite and well-defined differences that occur and are, in this case, due to adolescent development. Moreover, by using scaling as a technique and cartoons as a medium of humor expression, Raley and Ballmann assert that it is possible to offer an *objective* method for *measuring* the trait of humor (cf: Ziv's, 1979, "sociometry of humor test" useful in the classroom situation and on adolescent participants).

On the basis of their perceptions concerning the scaling deficiencies of the humor clusters and factors derived from previous attempts at empirical classification of humor items, Yarnold and Berkeley (1954) set out to derive an unspecified number of homogeneous scales from a hetergeneous pool of humor items. Their overall research design was organized as follows: selection of the first item set; selection of the participant sample; test administration; analysis into tentative scales; selection of the second item set; analysis into final scales; comparison of the tentative and final tests; and psychological interpretations of the final scales. Yarnold and Berkeley conclude that their analysis of both Form A and Form B of the Cattell-Luborsky Humor Test (Cattell & Luborsky, 1947a; Cattell, Luborsky, & Hicks, 1950) by a cluster method of analysis resulted in their construction of seven scales which appear to be superior (at least statistically) to the scales previously derived for this test. Additionally, Yarnold and Berkeley's analysis of reactions to humor stimuli are consistent with the notion that *humor* provides a potentially effective and subtle means for the *measurement* of *personality* where research on validation measures is an ongoing process.

Levine (1956) and his colleagues (cf: Levine & Redlich, 1955, 1960; Redlich, Levine, & Sohler, 1951) developed a humor measurement device called The Mirth Response Test which utilizes a set of 20 cartoons; in the test the response of the participant is recorded by the examiner on the following six-category "mirth spectrum": negative response, no response, half-smile, smile, chuckle, laugh. Levine's test is based on the Freudian theory that humor gives pleasure by permitting the momentary gratification of some hidden and forbidden wish and, at the same time, reducing the anxiety that normally inhibits the fulfillment of the wish. By treating the forbidden impulse lightly, or by treating it as trivial or universal, a cartoon or joke may serve to release one's inner tension; the sudden release of tension comes as a pleasant surprise, while the unconscious source of the person's tension is so disguised in the cartoon or joke that it usually is not disturbing. According to this theoretical approach, a joke or cartoon seems to be funny only if it arouses anxiety and, at the same time, relieves it.

Based on this theory, Levine asserts that there are three types of reaction to a joke, cartoon, or humorous event: if it evokes no anxiety at all in a person (either because the individual has no conflict over the subject or because his or her conflict is too deeply repressed) she or he will be indifferent to the joke; if the humorous stimulus elicits anxiety and immediately dispels it, the person will find it funny; if the humorous stimulus arouses anxiety without dissipating it, the individual will react to the humorous material with disgust, horror, embarrassment, or shame. A common criticism against such an analysis of humor based on the Freudian/psychoanalytic perspective is that it ultimately involves *circular reasoning* concerning the anxiety-laugh relationship: if the person laughs (or doesn't laugh) at humorous material it is because there was (or wasn't) anxiety present; if there was (or there wasn't) anxiety present, the person's reaction to a humorous stimulus is to laugh (or not to laugh). That is, why does the individual laugh (or doesn't laugh)? Because there is anxiety (or no anxiety) present. Is the person anxious (or not anxious)? Yes (or no), because the person laughs (or doesn't laugh).

Nevertheless, Levine and others have used The Mirth Response Test to practical advantage in the psychiatric setting where mental health workers have found that they can predict pretty reliably which cartoons on the test will disturb their patients. [Note: For another application of a humor measurement tool to a practical situation, see Kole & Henderson's (1966) development of a "cartoon reaction scale" (involving cartoon driving situations) to test the hypothesis that problem and nonproblem drivers would respond differentially to the humor test; out of an original pool of 150 cartoons, 34 cartoons achieved discriminatory ability regarding individual's problem driving behavior; however, the predictive ability of Kole & Henderson's humor test has not yet been shown.] For psychiatric patients, Levine found that the most-often-disturbing cartoons are those that contain themes or content regarding undisguised sex, gruesome aggression, extreme prankishness, or irreverence toward accepted authority; also, individuals whose sexual problems are close to the surface of awareness are likely to laugh boisterously (too loudly and too readily) at humor material dealing with sexual matters (also see: Levine & Abelson, 1959; Levine & Rakusin, 1959; cf: Lee & Griffith, 1962, who suggest that judgments of humorous material are influenced by other than motivational factors of the type proposed by the Freudian psychoanalysts; they cite the factor of "time error" which often complicates classical psychophysical experiments, and also focus on the variable of "practice effects" which are potential contaminants in contexts involving continued exposure to stimuli).

Holmes' (1969) contribution to the measurement of humor involves the use of two behavioral "immediate reaction measures" (i.e., *latency* of response—that is, the *time* between the presentation of a cartoon and the participant's reaction to it; and *amplitude* of response—that is, the *distance* the manipulandum/knob was turned by the participant between two poles of a continuum from "0" for "not funny" to "80" for "very funny") in participants' responses to 40 hostile-content cartoons, 40 sexual-content cartoons, 30 nonsense-content cartoons, and 10 "nonfunny, out-of-context" cartoon-like stimuli. [Notes: For other behavioral/physiological indices concerning the measurement of humor, see Pollio, Mers, & Lucchesi (1972, p. 216) who recorded simultaneously the duration and amplitude of participants' laughter; see Wagoner & Sullenberger (1978) who investigated changes in *pupil size* in relation to different levels of humor as judged by participants' preferences; their hypothesis—confirmed by data—was that participants' pupils dilate while looking at stimuli perceived as humorous; and Deckers, Kuhlhorst, & Freeland's (1987) study of the relationship between facial reactions/facial feedback hypotheses and surprise/humor ratings; their results indicate that the facial feedback hypothesis may not be testable in the humor context; cf: Ellsworth & Tourangeau (1981). Also note Thorson's (1990) caution to researchers *not* to assume that a single behavioral measure of humor, e.g., laughter, is equivalent to an assessment of the multidimensional construct of sense of humor.]

Holmes maintains that instead of relying totally on the traditional/judgmental rating responses of humor preference, his measures more closely approximate the *perceptual* process of "humor-being-sensed" (cf: Feingold's, 1982, 1983, "Humor Perceptiveness Test" and "Humor Achievement Test" which are based on his notion of "humor perception" defined as the ability to absorb and retain humor from the environment, and on one's "humor knowledge"; also, see Feingold & Mazzella, 1991; and Russell, 1996, 2000). Holmes found that his participants (48 male psychiatric technicians and trainees) readily accepted the special apparatus in the "immediate reaction" situation and paid the appropriate attention to the humorous stimuli rather than to the measuring technique/apparatus itself; thus, it appears that neither elaborate warm-up procedures nor "special" laboratory environments are necessary to obtain reasonable measures of "humor-being-perceived" (cf: Holmes, 1955).

Holmes concludes that the type of measures (i.e., latency and amplitude) used in his "immediate reaction" method lend themselves well to systematic laboratory-like study by means of tightly controlled manipulation of stimulus, environment, and participant variables. For instance, stimuli might be varied in their complexity, content, and subtlety; the social environment might be varied by introducing the illusory presence of other participants through tape- and video-recordings; and emotional states might be manipulated by visual and/or auditory presentation of nonhumorous material. The measures of "humor-being-perceived" also possess the potential for various applications: as a measure of *emotional* functioning, latency might reveal perceptual sensitization or blocking concerning conflict or vulnerability in the participant; as a measure of *intellectual* functioning, latency might reveal speed of cognitive-processing as a function of stimulus complexity (and, thereby, identify the "wit" aspect of humor); and as a measure of *preference*, the amplitude measures might indicate the degree of participants' preference for different humorous stimuli.

Koppel and Sechrest's (1970) approach to the measurement of humor was to determine the degree to which appreciation of humor, intelligence, humor creation, and introversion-extraversion can be distinguished as traits. Their methodology consists of the use of the "multitrait-multimethod matrix" (e.g., D. Campbell, 1960; Campbell & Fiske, 1959) which results in data concerning convergent and discriminant validities. [Note: For another application of the multitrait-multimethod validation procedure to a humor study, see Arlin & Hills (1974) who found that elementary-grade students greatly prefer cartoon-over verbal-versions of the same material, and where no differences were found between the validities of the two types of material formats.] The four traits (intelligence, extraversion, sense of humor, and humor creation/joke-making) studied by Koppel and Sechrest were assessed by self- and peer-ratings and by objective measures from 62 student participants. The humor measures involved both rating the humorousness of 20 cartoons and making up captions for cartoons which were rated, subsequently, by 20 other judges (psychology graduate students). The results of Koppel and Sechrest's study generally support the hypothesis that the four traits they examined may be conceptualized as distinct and measurable; moreover, the relatively high validities obtained tend to support the notion that humor *appreciation* and humor *creation* are distinct, as well as useful, concepts.

In a series of studies, Svebak (1974a,b,c, 1975) presents a theory of sense of humor and a *measurement* approach toward humor appreciation (cf: Svebak, 1996). Svebak (1974c) used factorization in an exploratory study on the predictive validity of some attitude scores in relation to laughter and found three dimensions that fit his theory (Svebak, 1974a) regarding the distribution of content over those items that were the best predictors. Svebak's (1974b) revised Sense-of-Humor Questionnaire (SHQ) [consisting of 21 items, and based on his proposed three-dimensional theory (there is one "laughter-activating" dimension which taps into the individual's habitual sensitivity to humorous messages, and two "laughter-inhibiting" dimensions which tap into the individual's habitual tendencies to suppress laughter, and by the person's defense strategems against emotional impulses of joy)] was given to female and male students in the social and physical sciences to test its construct validity. He found positive significant correlations between the laughter-activating dimension and each of the two laughter-inhibiting dimensions (with a zero correlation between the latter two dimensions). Svebak (1974b) concludes that compared with the questionnaire used in his previous study on predictive validity of dimension scores (Svebak, 1974c), his present data on covariance indicate improved construct validity of the SHQ; also, his present data suggest that men and women in the *social* sciences are equally expressive regarding "emotional dispositions," while men and women in the *physical* sciences are equally expressive regarding "interpersonal sentiment relations" (cf: Svebak's, 1975, study which indicates a sex difference in developmental patterns of styles in humor as shown by his "social self-image" data; however, Svebak notes that the observed developmental trends may be spurious due to a potential bias in the selective recruitment of his participants). All of Svebak's (1974b) results are in agreement with his sense of humor theory (Svebak, 1974a).

In an overview of the humor measurement area, and in an attempt to clarify measurement issues, Sheehy-Skeffington (1977) notes that two general methods are commonly employed in studies of the measurement of humor appreciation: either the participant is observed to see if she or he shows signs of amusement, or the participant is asked (usually via a five-point scale of "funniness") if she or he is amused. By the first method, certain characteristics of the overt mirth response (including both laughs and smiles) are measured; the amplitude or the frequency of the response may be measured, but reliable quantification of these variables is difficult technically (cf: Holmes, 1969). The most common practice is to record the total duration of the mirth response over an experimental session. According to Sheehy-Skeffington, the overt mirth response appears to be influenced by variables other than the humor content of the material (e.g., the presence of others who are laughing—or are merely present; the use of "canned laughter"; or the presence of alcohol in the bloodstream); he suggests that although the "strength" of the overt mirth response is a simple and obvious measure of amusement, it is yet a fairly crude one, and a more reliable measure is needed. Sheehy-Skeffington asserts that researchers cannot yet be confident about the quantitative aspects of *any* measure of amusement. One of the biggest problems is that individuals tend to use overt expressions of mirth and verbal behavior about equally as indicators of amusement; the trouble is that the best answer to the question "What sort of thing is amusing?" is still "The sort of thing that people laugh and smile at." Inasmuch as it seems virtually impossible to define one aspect (stimulus) satisfactorily without some reference to the other aspect (response), there is some degree of *circular reasoning* present in the attempt to define humor stimuli or humor responses.

Sheehy-Skeffington offers some experimental strategies in the measurement of humor that may help, eventually, to skirt some of these more logical/theoretical considerations and serve to advance more the "heuristic" research on humor (e.g., in one case, he suggests the value of an operant paradigm involving the use of "concurrent schedules of reinforcement" to piece out the relative preferences between reinforcers, say, for the reinforcing values of a humorous recording with added "canned" laughter and the same recording without the added stimulation; another suggestion is to use an operant "titration schedule" which is a procedure that is useful in determining the level of intensity of a reinforcer/stimulus that is preferred by a participant). Sheehy-Skeffington advances the notion that a systematic investigation of the operation of discriminative stimuli in the context of humor appreciation situations is possible using operant techniques (cf: Main & Schillace, 1968; Roeckelein, 1968, 1969).

In their psychophysical scaling emphasis on humor measurement, Derks, Lewis, and White (1981) observe that the evaluation/measurement of humor usually takes the form of a category scale to assess the amount of humor in a cartoon, joke, or comedy routine; such category scales range from a simple "laugh-no laugh" dichotomy to as many as 100 category units. [Note: For a humor experiment employing a scaling technique based on the "law of comparative judgment" (Torgerson, 1958), see Godkewitsch (1972, pp. 150–152).] A five-category scale with obvious category names or labels is a popular format: "not at all funny," "slightly funny," "moderately funny," "very funny," and "extremely funny." The correlations and relations among these various category scale formats of humor measurement have been reasonably good; however, the use of category scales for measuring effect has been criticized as an incomplete estimate of the humor response.

A preferred alternative to the category scale approach has been the use of ratio scales based on magnitude estimations because they give additional information about the relative magnitude of sensations and attitudes (cf: Stevens, 1966; Stevens & Galanter, 1957). In the area of psychophysical scaling, there are many instances where category scales are concave downward when plotted against ratio scales; one reason for this discrepancy is the decreasing ability of the participant to discriminate differences between more intense stimuli (i.e., "Weber's law"). According to Derks et al., the result of this "sliding" scale of discrimination is that more stimuli are "misclassified" in the "intense" categories where discrimination is poor, and relatively fewer stimuli are placed in the "faint" categories where discrimination is good. Such a finding appears clearly in experiments on brightness and loudness; moreover, concerning experiments on humor, asking participants on a ratio scale to say how funny one event is compared to another (e.g., "twice as funny," "half as funny," etc.) may give more information than simply categorizing the events.

Derks et al. suggest that the phenomenon of humor seems intuitively to be a "prothetic continuum" (see Stevens & Galanter, 1957): it appears to grow additively (e.g., a joke is "more" or "less" funny) and such judgments apparently represent a change in the quantity, rather than the kind, of humor. They also suggest that if such an intuition regarding humor is accurate, then category scales of humor should be concave downward relative to ratio scales, and variability of judgment should increase with increased magnitude; however, if a qualitative rationale is more appropriate, the scales should match one another. Based upon the results of two experiments where 190 participants judged the funniness of the punch lines of recorded comedy routines, Derks et al. found that category judgments (category scales) and magnitude estimations (ratio scales) were isomorphic and demonstrate approximately equivalent discrimination over the range of humor presented. Moreover, they found that the occasional discriminability gained with ratio scales does not seem sufficient to warrant their use over category scales in measuring humor, that any difference which has been demonstrated with a category scale could be replicated with a ratio scale, and that ratio scales do not show promise of revealing aspects of humor that would be lost to a reasonably gauged category scale [cf: the development of a new humor scale, the Humor Response Scale (HRS), by Lowis & Nieuwoudt (1995) and their use of a cartoon rating scale containing the numbers 0 through 6, with the anchors of "not funny" at 0, "moderately funny" at 3, and "very funny" at 6; the application by Thorson, Brdar, & Powell (1997) of their Multidimensional Sense of Humor Scale (Thorson & Powell, 1993)—which uses a four-point anchored rating scale across 24 items—in a cultural or national setting; and McGhee's (1996) construction of a Sense of Humour Scale (SHS) which is a 40–item questionnaire with a four-point anchored answer format (1 is "strongly disagree," and 4 is "strongly agree")]. Derks et al. conclude that category-type scales are adequate to measure humor, and suggest that humor judgments and participants' appreciation of humor involve reactions to quality rather than to quantity (cf: Derks, 1992).

In their systematic approach toward humor measurement where various personality traits/variables (e.g., rigidity, conservatism, dogmatism) are related to humor appreciation, Ruch and Hehl (1983) examine differences between participants who prefer resolution-related types of jokes with those who prefer incongruity-related types of jokes in regard to the concept of "intolerance of ambiguity" as a predictor—that is, the classification of individuals according to the intensity of their experience of ambiguous (that is, new, unsolvable, and complex) stimuli as a source of threat. Ruch and Hehl suggest that resolution of incongruity/ambiguity should be more reinforcing for "intolerant" individuals than for a group of "tolerant" persons. According to their predictions, "intolerant" people should prefer jokes whose incongruity is solvable, while rejecting the nonsolvable types of nonsense jokes. Based upon their results from 134 male student participants who rated 120 jokes according to "funniness" and "rejection," both their hypotheses were confirmed. Among Ruch and Hehl's conclusions is that an individual's "sense of humor" depends on the way she or he deals with ambiguous and uncertain stimuli or material.

In their discussion of the development of a quantitative measure of sense of humor (the "Situational Humor Response Questionnaire," or SHRQ), Martin and Lefcourt (1984) assert that the traditional paper-and-pencil tests of humor developed so far are inadequate for researching humor for two reasons: they focus on various *types* of humor (e.g., sexual, aggressive, or nonsense)—rather than measuring a generalized propensity toward humor (a "generalized humor construct")—regardless of the type of humor involved; and they are concerned primarily with self-reported humor appreciation rather than the production of humor in daily life. Martin and Lefcourt suggest the need for more valid measures of sense of humor than the traditional measures afford, and advocate the development of measures that emphasize two of Eysenck's (1972) definitions of "sense of humor" (i.e., the *productive* and *quantitative* definitions that emphasize, respectively, the extent to which the individual *tells* funny stories and amuses other people, and the *frequency* with which a person laughs and smiles and how easily she or he is amused; Eysenck's other definition/type of sense of humor is the *conformist* type which stresses the degree of similarity between people's appreciation of humorous material).

Martin and Lefcourt (1984) found support in each of three studies for the validity of their SHRQ as a quantitative measure of sense of humor for university students (see their Table 1, pp. 148–150, for the 21 items contained on the SHRQ). For male participants, the SHRQ was found to be significantly correlated with the following: the frequency and duration of laughter measured during an interview phase; peers' ratings of their sense of humor; a measure of positive moods; the number of witty remarks produced in an impromptu comedy routine; the rated humorousness of this routine; and the rated humorousness of a narrative produced while watching a stressful film. Similar correlational results were found for the female participants with the exception of the ratings of the comedy routine. According to Martin and Lefcourt, the SHRQ possesses several advantages over other measures of humor: it emphasizes a *quantitative* definition of humor (how *often* the person smiles and laughs), rather than the "conformist" definition (the degree to which the person agrees with others about what is funny) used in previous humor scales; it taps into the *productive* aspect of humor (the degree to which the individual amuses others); and it focuses on behaviors related to humor and mirth that are *not* closely identified with a particular theory concerning the underlying processes in humor and, thus, it affords a greater degree of generality among many different theoretical orientations concerning humor appreciation.

Hehl and Ruch (1985) attempt to define sense(s) of humor as personality concepts (cf: Ruch & Kohler, 1998), and place them within already existing and comprehensive personality systems. Hehl and Ruch note that there are many ways to establish humor categories and there have been numerous attempts to establish a taxonomy empirically and/or theoretically. Ruch and his colleagues used the method of factor analysis and found a three-dimensional system (e.g., Hehl & Ruch, 1983; Ruch, 1981, 1984; Ruch & Hehl, 1984) in which jokes and cartoons differ with respect to two properties, *structure* and *content*, and in which two basic structural dimensions are formed by combinations of the two most fundamental ingredients in jokes—incongruity and resolution. There are jokes that contain punch lines which are incongruent and surprise the recipient, but can be completely resolved subsequently (incongruity-resolution jokes); the other type of joke is characterized by impossible incongruities that cannot be resolved or not resolved completely (nonsense jokes). According to Hehl and Ruch, these two factors are heterogeneous with regard to content, whereas a third category (sex jokes) is dominated by a common theme.

Hehl and Ruch employed a sense of humor inventory, called "3 WD (*Witz-Dimensionen*)-K" (Ruch, 1983), to determine how their proposed dimensions of sense of humor relate to other personality traits; questionnaires which cover the whole domain of personality (temperament) were given to 200 participants (male and female university students), and their humor scores on the "3WD-K" were related to the temperament dimensions to ascertain what traits influence sense of humor. Based on correlations between personality traits and types of humor, a positioning of each type of humor in a "personality space" then was attempted. [Notes: also, see Ruch & Hehl (1986b) who examined the trait of "conservatism" as a predictor variable in locating sense of humor in a comprehensive "attitude space"; cf: Wilson (1973); Hehl & Ruch (1990) who suggest a potential link between humor and "psychosomatic disturbances"; Ruch, Kohler, & VanThriel (1997) who examine the relevance of the temperamental states of cheerfulness, seriousness, and bad mood for research on the emotion of "exhilaration"; and Ruch & Carrell (1998) who hypothesize in a cross-cultural study that the traits of cheerfulness, seriousness, and bad mood form the temperamental basis of the sense of humor.]

Results of Hehl and Ruch's (1985) study give evidence for the notion that humor is related to temperamental variables (cf: Hehl & Ruch, 1990; Ruch, 1984; and Ruch & Hehl, 1983, 1986a,b, who found that "conservatism" as well as "intolerance of ambiguity" correlate positively with funniness ratings of jokes containing incongruity-resolution structures); several significant predictors were found for each of six humor scales. The validity of Hehl and Ruch's taxonomy was supported, also, because the different humor categories (i.e., "funniness" and "rejection") were shown to be located at different places in the "personality space."

Korotkov (1991) attempted to determine if the "sense of humor" personality construct—as assessed by seven, presumed distinct, self-report measures—could be represented more parsimoniously through factor analysis. The following four tests, given to 90 participants (female and male university students), were included initially in Korotkov's statistical procedure: The Coping

Humour Scale (CHS; Martin & Lefcourt, 1983), The Situational Humour Response Questionnaire (SHRQ; Martin & Lefcourt, 1984), The Humour Initiation and Responsiveness Measure (HIRM; Bell, McGhee, & Duffey, 1986), and Svebak's Sense of Humor Questionnaire (SSHQ; Svebak, 1974b). [Notes: For another study that employed *multiple* sense of humor inventories/tests, see Kohler & Ruch (1996); for a discussion of the development, and updated version, of Svebak's SSHQ, see Svebak (1996); and for a recent "status report" of Martin & Lefcourt's (1983, 1984) SHRQ and CHS inventories, see R. A. Martin (1996).]

Because of differences in face validity, two of the tests (HIRM and SSHQ) were broken down into subscales, resulting in a final factor analysis involving seven variables. Korotkov's factor analytic results indicate that there are two aspects/factors involved in the sense of humor personality construct: laughter responsiveness, and general self- and others-beliefs about humor. Korotkov suggests that his results need to be replicated with a wider range of humor tests, as well as with a larger sample size that represents a more heterogeneous population than he used in order to reduce the standard error of the correlations and to confirm his present analysis.

A study similar in methodology to that of Korotkov (1991) was conducted by Thorson and Powell (1991) who had a larger heterogeneous sample of 365 participants complete three humor scales (Svebak's Sense of Humor Questionnaire—SSHQ, Coping Humor Scale—CHS; and Situational Humor Response Questionnaire—SHRQ) in which data were factor analyzed subsequently to assess the personal construct of sense of humor. Thorson and Powell conclude that the SSHQ lacks face validity, has an unacceptably low scale reliability, and has "attitudes toward humor" assessment questions not "personal sense of humor" questions; the SHRQ measures the questionable behavioral response of likelihood to laugh which may not have a valid relationship to "true" sense of humor (cf: Deckers & Ruch, 1992); and the CHS appears to measure only the single aspect of a coping mechanism in humor (cf: Overholser, 1992). Thorson and Powell suggest that the use of any, or a combination of all, of the three scales examined by them does not give an accurate picture of sense of humor in the broadest sense, and the personal construct of sense of humor is not a unidimensional, but rather a multidimensional, construct (cf: Thorson & Powell, 1993). They propose that sense of humor, as a multidimensional phenomenon, contains at least the following elements: humor *production* (the creative ability of the person to amuse others); a sense of *playfulness* (the person's ability to have a good time, to be whimsical, and to be good-natured); the achievement of *social goals* by the use of humor (the individual's ability to use humor to ease a tense social situation, to enforce social norms, to enhance the solidarity of the ingroup, or to deflate the pompous and pretentious individual); the personal *recognition* of humor (including life's absurdities, and recognition of the self as humorous); the personal *appreciation* of humor (in other people and in humorous situations); and the use of humor as an *adaptive/coping* mechanism (to be able to laugh at problems, and to master difficult situations via the uses of humor).

In a humor measurement methodology involving the use of a "similarity-between-jokes" rating procedure, Ruch, Attardo, and Raskin (1993) attempted to verify empirically the General Theory of Verbal Humor (GTVH) (cf: Attardo & Raskin, 1991), formerly known as the Semantic Script Theory of Humor (SSTH) (cf: Raskin, 1985). Participants (534 university students) were given three sets of jokes, each consisting of an anchor joke and comparison jokes in which variations in one of six "knowledge resources" (that is, the six variables of script opposition, logical mechanism, situation, target, narrative strategy, and language) occurred, and participants rated the degree of "similarity" between the anchor joke and the six comparison jokes. The results found by Ruch et al. support the hypothesis that the degree to which the participants' judgment of joke similarity is affected depends on the particular types of the "knowledge of resources" that are manipulated; variations in some "knowledge resources" make the joke pairs more dissimilar than variations in others. Another result is the confirmation of a prediction of a decreasing trend in the perception of similarity between the variables of "language" and "script opposition"; the general decrease in similarity for this case was reflected in all three sets of jokes as well as in average scores. A further finding is that variation in "narrative strategy" makes a joke less similar to the anchor joke than variations in the variable of "language." Overall, Ruch et al. conclude that the perception of similarity across the "knowledge resources" variables is as predicted by the GTVH with minor exceptions (e.g., the variable of "logical mechanism"). [Note: For another study whose methodology includes the GTVH, see Attardo, (1998).]

Ruch et al. suggest a possible limitation to their study: they considered "similarity" to be a unidimensional construct, but participants may actually use more dimensions to portray the similarity between the jokes. What is needed, according to Ruch et al., is a complete comparison between all possible pairs of jokes and application of multidimensional scaling techniques that allow for the determination of the nature and number of the dimensions involved. Another potential limitation in Ruch's et al. study is the untested assumption that *any* variation in a "knowledge resource" variable leads to the same amount of dissimilarity from the anchor joke.

Kohler and Ruch (1996) examined the relationship of several self-report inventories of "sense of humor" and behavioral measures of humor, as well as their location in the Eysenckian "PEN" system (see Ruch, 1994). Participants (110 adult women and men, ages 17–83 years) were given the following inventories to complete: Martin and Lefcourt's (1984) SHRQ, Ziv's (1981) SHQZ,

Svebak's (1993) revised SHQ-3, Martin and Lefcourt's (1983) CHS, Thorson and Powell's (1993) MSHS, Bell, McGhee, and Duffey's (1986) HIS, Ruch's (1983) 3WD-K, Kohler and Ruch's (1993) CPPT, Murgatroyd, Rushton, Apter, and Ray's (1978) TDS, Ruch, Freiss, and Kohler's (1993) STCI-T, and Eysenck, Eysenck, and Barrett's (1985) EPQ-R. Kohler and Ruch (1996) obtained reliability data for the humor scales and determined the convergent and discriminant validity of equivalent scales of humor appreciation/humor creation. They found that the behavioral measures of self-report instruments yielded only meager correlations. Moreover, humor appreciation and humor creation could not be discriminated validly in the self-reports even though they did form distinct traits in the behavioral measures. The self-report data—when subjected to factor analysis—resulted in the appearance of the two orthogonal dimensions of "seriousness" and "cheerfulness." Other findings are that high scores on the "psychoticism" dimension (composed of traits such as aggression, coldness, egocentrism, impersonal, impulsivity, antisocial, creative, and tough-minded) are associated with low seriousness, high wit, and high *quality* of humor production, and that high scores on the "extraversion" dimension (composed of traits such as sociability, liveliness, activity, assertiveness, sensation-seeking, carefree, dominance, and venturesome) are predictive of high cheerfulness, low seriousness, and large *quantity* of humor production.

Based upon their results, Kohler and Ruch conclude that humor studies must pay closer attention to the *methodological* issues involved in the *measurement/assessment* of the sense of humor. They maintain that it is *not* sufficient to rely on implicit assumptions concerning the sense of humor construct, to do some brainstorming and write up a list of items, to label the resulting questionnaire a "sense of humor" inventory, and to go into validation studies using only small-sized samples. Kohler and Ruch suggest that humor research should be focused on at least two goals: theoretical and empirical work aimed at a more *precise* outline and definition of the sense of humor construct (i.e., identification of the nature and number of validly distinguishable components), and application of a more *sophisticated* technology for constructing instruments for the measurement and assessment of the construct of sense of humor and its components.

An interesting and instructive exchange/debate in the humor literature has developed between Paolillo (1998) and Ruch (1999). Paolillo notes that the *Far Side* cartoons of Gary Larson have been claimed to illustrate the "nonsense" humor type of the 3WD humor taxonomy (Kohler & Ruch, 1994) where the "nonsense" humor is characterized as having a structure in which there is no resolution. Paolillo asserts that close examination of that proposition reveals three main difficulties with Kohler and Ruch's (1994) approach: the cartoon sample size used; the participants' cultural background; and the interpretation of the 3WD as a comprehensive taxonomy.

Paolillo conducted a structural analysis of 800 *Far Side* cartoons, using the GTVH (Attardo & Raskin, 1991). His results indicate that three distinct resolution types are present in the sample ("full," "part," and "none"), and that the full range of resolution types is unlikely to be represented in Kohler and Ruch's (1994) sample where their German participants most likely lacked critical aspects of the "cultural knowledge" for properly assessing *Far Side* cartoons. Consequently, Paolillo offers an alternative interpretation of Kohler and Ruch's results in which "cultural knowledge" plays different roles in processing and assessing *Far Side* cartoons containing different resolution types.

Subsequently, in a rebuttal to Paolillo's (1998) study, Ruch (1999) points out that Paolillo's conclusions are based on misrepresentation and misunderstanding of Kohler and Ruch's general approach as well as of their intended goals. Following a review of his own taxonomy of humor (i.e., 3WD), and his reminder that the basis of his 3WD inventory is on a particular model ("Model C") of the taxonomy of humor (i.e., it considers the participants' cognitive-emotional responses to the stimuli, and "is a taxonomy of humor as seen through the eyes of lay persons and systematized by a personality researcher"; p. 74), Ruch (1999) attempts to meet Paolillo's (1998) critical points, one by one, in the following sets of questions (along with Ruch's corresponding answers that are briefly indicated):

Is nonsense humor NONsense? (No. It was never assumed by Ruch that the nonsense category of stimulus materials consists exclusively of cartoons/jokes containing no resolution).

Does nonsense humor cover partial resolutions? (Yes. Ruch discovered that some of the nonsense cartoons lying on the margins of the nonsense factor sometimes also have a low positive loading on "incongruity-resolution," and still, when correlating these cartoons with personality variables, they behaved like the others in the NON category, and different—often with opposite signs—than those in the "incongruity-resolution" category; and, so it is obvious to leave them in the nonsense category).

Why study *Far Side* humor? (There might be at least three reasons for this strategy: researchers may use the humor they themselves like in their studies—however, it is advisable to use the work of *different* cartoonists and different representatives of a comprehensive taxonomy of humor to balance out the different tastes of the research participants; the cartoons may represent something special that is well-suited for one's research purpose and which other humor does not provide—however, one should try to relate them to existing similar humor and locate them in a comprehensive framework such as a taxonomy of humor; the cartoons may reflect the use of the method of the case study of an artist—in this case, according to Ruch, one should be more interested in studying the *complete* works of the artist. The poster exhibited by Kohler and Ruch, 1994, was aimed at raising awareness of such problems, rather than pursuing any one of these aims in detail; they argued that if one decides to use a newly emerged cartoon series the researcher should try to locate this new kind of humor in existing taxonomies of humor so that one can compare findings, provide standardized bases, and accumulate knowledge in humor research).

Is *Far Side* humor something new? (Yes and no. *Far Side* humor is unique in some ways, e.g., the format, the drawing style, the characters, etc.; however, *Far Side* humor is also comparable to what existed previously, and Kohler and Ruch conclude that while the *Far Side* cartoons do enrich the pool of nonsense cartoons, they do not challenge the comprehensiveness of their 3WD taxonomy and do not require the expansion of that taxonomy).

Is *Far Side* NONsense? (No.). Does *Far Side* fall under the nonsense humor factor? (Yes, but . . . Kohler and Ruch do not claim that *Far Side* cartoons are NONsense, as in making no sense at all, and the 3WD taxonomy does not even foresee such a category).

What is the evidence that *Far Side* also goes under "incongruity-resolution" humor? (Ruch notes that Paolillo uses two sources of evidence here: the significant correlations between aversiveness of the *Far Side* cartoons and the rated aversiveness of the 3WD categories, and the finding that 16 percent of the *Far Side* cartoons Paolillo analyzed fell into his "full" category concerning "incongruity-resolution" humor). In his rebuttal article, Ruch (1999) provides further detailed discussion concerning the following issues: "Paolillo's findings (what is new is not true, and what is true is not new)"; "On claims and untested hypotheses"; "On raising and not clarifying problems"; "How to improve the 3WD taxonomy?"; "What exactly is wrong with the 3WD studies?" [Note: In this section, Ruch asserts that his humor studies have shifted the direction of personality-based humor research away from considering only *content* to studying, also, the *structural* properties of humor; Ruch states that it is ironic that not many have made this move yet and current studies still try to predict *content* variables without controlling for the major variance which—Ruch maintains—is *structure*-related.] Ruch (1999) concludes that Paolillo seems to be reluctant to accept the fact that there are different approaches to a taxonomy and that in an *empirically* derived approach the definition of the dimensions is secondary, whereas in a *rationally* derived taxonomy the definition of the dimensions comes first; also, Paolillo builds up a straw man by distorting how he (Ruch) understands the notion of nonsense humor and consequently tries to destroy the straw man by bringing his deliberately changed understanding of nonsense humor into conflict with what he claims to have found. Further, Ruch notes that Paolillo does not acknowledge that even his (Paolillo's) analysis confirms Kohler and Ruch's (1994) conclusions as being correct: the *Far Side* cartoons do fit well into the boundaries of the 3WD taxonomy, even if perhaps not *all* cartoons fall under "nonsense," and where, perhaps, "incongruity-resolution" needs to be considered as well. Finally, Ruch states that he fails to see the rationale and logic in Paolillo's analysis of 800 *Far Side* cartoons as a basis for making comments on the taxonomy underlying the 3WD.

In summary, the extended discussion concerning the debate between Paolillo (1998) and Ruch (1999) provided here is for the purpose of indicating the current vitality and controversy in the area of humor measurement and research, and points out the general need for further research toward the understanding of humor appreciation, production, and taxonomy.

FUTURE FACES OF HUMOR

As researchers take a more comprehensive look at all the factors that play a part in the enjoyment of humor, we are likely to see a major shift in the current paradigms for how we view the differences between men and women.

—M. D. Lampert and S. M. Ervin-Tripp, 1998

The future of humor research will no doubt witness the continued application of behavioral genetic methodologies. One does not need to be a behavioral geneticist in order to address behavioral genetic research questions about the origins of individual differences in humor.

—B. Manke, 1998

A considerable amount of work is still needed in order to bring research on sense of humor to the same level of sophistication as established personality constructs such as extraversion or intelligence.

—R. A. Martin, 1998

It needs to be emphasized that the development of a valid taxonomy of humor appreciation should be seen as an inter-disciplinary and cross-national endeavor. Both interdisciplinary research and cross-cultural studies have only begun.

—W. Ruch and F.-J. Hehl, 1998

In concluding his historical review of the approaches to the *sense of humor*, Martin (1998) discusses some issues related to the directive, "Where we need to go (from here)" (cf: McGhee & Goldstein, 1972, pp. 243–257, for an earlier "future faces of humor" discussion). Martin suggests that we still need a comprehensive, agreed-upon definition of the construct of *sense of humor* and identification of its structure, or component dimensions, that are psychometrically sound; measures of the construct and its dimensions are still largely lacking. Theoretical models concerning the dynamics of the various aspects of *sense of humor* are needed, also, and would allow the researcher to derive hypotheses from the model rather than simply gain information and data from everyday or anecdotal observations. Martin proposes a three-dimensional model of humor based on Eysenck's (1942) tripartite framework; although Eysenck's model was meant originally to categorize the themes of jokes and cartoons, it might also be useful in conceptualizing the major dimensions of *sense of humor* in terms of *cognitive, emotional*, and *conative* (motivational) components. Martin observes that one possible limitation of this framework for humor is that it does not readily lend itself to categorizations of the *content* of humor that the individual enjoys (such as sexual, ethnic, or sick humor); this aspect has been the focus of much past research on humor and, according to Martin, it needs to be included in any future comprehensive model of *sense of humor.*

In answering the question, "Are there any recommendations for future approaches to the *measurement* of the "sense of humor?," Ruch (1996, pp. 249–250) is in agreement with Martin (1998) on various points. Ruch maintains that the field of humor research does not necessarily need more new scales, but it does need more theoretical and empirical work on the definition/foundation of the concepts. However, according to Ruch, deriving the construct, constructing the scale, and attempting to validate it in one single step, or even in one sample of participants, doesn't seem to be all that fruitful (each stage needs greater attention). Moreover, if new measurement instruments are developed, they may well focus on certain construct areas not yet explored (e.g., there are not yet instruments that explicitly study aspects such as humor vis-à-vis a "benevolent world view" which tolerates and accepts the shortcomings of life and humankind; also, instruments that predict "destructive" forms of humor may be welcomed). Ruch asserts that researchers in the future should broaden their range of methodological approaches once again; recently, in the last few years, there has been too much focus on the self-report types of scales at the expense of behavioral observations, performance tests, peer-nominations/peer-evaluations, and biographical data. Most important of all, according to Ruch, is the development or achievement of a *comprehensive* definition of the *sense of humor*, a supreme goal of humor research that has not yet been attained.

Provine (1996, 2000a, b) describes his research on the humor-related behavior of *laughter* in terms of its properties as a social stimulus and as a motor act, and indicates some future directions for further study of the social aspects, gender differences, and the speech/sonic spectra of human laughter. For example, the phenomenon of "pathological laughter" is a frequent, but only vaguely described, medical symptom that requires further investigation. Damage to a wide variety of brain areas produces abnormal or modified laughter; such laughter is especially mystifying to both patient and clinician as the behavior occurs in sudden bursts that are neither associated with a feeling of mirth, nor with an environmental stimulus. [Note: Also see Shammi & Stuss, 1999, who found that damage to the right frontal lobe disrupts patients' ability to appreciate humor and causes diminished laughing and smiling in the individual; cf:

Fischman, 1999.] Provine suggests that with the development of more improved descriptive tools, it may be possible to specify more precisely what is "abnormal," "pathological," or "inappropriate" about such cases, and the dynamics of the behavior may be determined as due to sonic structure, placement in speech, social/contextual and adaptive patterns (cf: Grumet, 1989), contagion sensitivity, or perception of humor; new "laugh-related syndromes" may even be discovered.

Another area for future research is the issue of laughter-related substances; for instance, do alcohol (cf: Meer, 1986), "laughing gas," and other drugs—known to increase laughter—simply lower one's threshold for laughter, or do they actually alter its pattern or quality? Yet another area for study is cerebral structure/activity (e.g., while the left cerebral hemisphere has a specialized role in language, is this also the case for the perception and/or production of laughter?). Provine (1996, 2000a) identifies various other issues for future research: *developmental* questions remain unanswered [e.g., laughter typically appears in human babies during the first three to four months of age, but little is known about the actual developmental process (cf: Bergen, 1998); Do babies have to hear their own laughter or the laughter of others for laughter to develop and mature? Is there a "critical period" for the development of laughter? How does laughter develop in hearing-impaired children as compared to normal children? Do different "types" of laughter develop in certain families, indicating a genetic component to laughter—or is it a learned behavior developed in the family context? (cf: Manke, 1998).] Questions concerning comparisons across *species* may be studied, also (e.g., Do the great apes show the sexually dimorphic or contagious laughter found in human beings? Do animals other than the great apes produce laugh-like vocalizations? How do the neurobehavioral mechanisms of laugh production differ between species? Can one "tickle" nonhuman species—as one may tickle humans; cf: Pfeifer, 1997; Wheeler, 1997—and produce laughter in those "lower" animals?). Provine asserts that research on laughter is still in its infancy and suggests that such research is a visible reminder that not all science concerns narrow or arcane problems involving expensive or complex laboratory equipment and facilities.

At the conclusion of a discussion of their "person-environment" approach to the study of humor, Craik and Ware (1998) suggest that future researchers should seek programmatically to establish an "ultimate framework" for the complex and multifaceted phenomenon of humor. Such a framework would require a complex person-environment formulation that incorporates both reputational factors within the individual's community and self-reflexive purposive aspects of the person as an agent of action. According to Craik and Ware, because such a task would be overwhelming for any single study, one sensible goal or strategy for humor researchers is to work toward this "ultimate framework" by exploring several more limited frameworks, testing their functional-ity, discarding the inappropriate, and build bridges between them linking the separate structures to a larger whole (cf: Ruch, 1996). Craik and Ware assert that the "community-oriented reputational" approach in studying personality and humor has been largely neglected by researchers in the field, even though this approach represents an exciting unexplored way of conceptualizing humor. For example, perceptions and influences within the social environment on an individual's humorousness are issues that need study; also, continued development is needed of the more clearly articulated "purposive-cognitive system" approaches, as well as investigation of the links between emotions (such as exhilaration and amusement) and the more cognitive construct of humor comprehension.

Ruch and Hehl (1998) examine some "open questions" and "possible future developments" concerning their two-mode model of humor appreciation. One question involves the issue of the most appropriate structural model to use in accounting for humor appreciation data; that is, should there be a movement from uni- to multimodal models? Ruch and Hehl maintain, curiously enough—against all evidence, that extant taxonomies of humor generally are stuck in serial/unimodal classifications rather than bi- or multimodal models; such a neglect of bimodal thinking in taxonomizing humor stimuli is evident, moreover, in factor analytic studies which typically attempt to achieve "simple structure"—that is, to attach each joke onto one and only one factor. According to Ruch and Hehl, if both *content* and *structure* are important in an analysis, a joke should have two loadings: one on a structural factor and one on a content factor (such as has been found for sexual humor). Such an approach, however, is not compatible with the conventional exploratory factor analytic procedures but requires target rotations—with each joke having two assignments in the hypothesis matrix—and/or the use of structural equations modeling techniques. Thus, Ruch and Hehl suggest that the first step in future humor studies should be a theoretical analysis of thematic *and* schematic properties of the pool of humor items to be taxonomized, and the second empirical step should be the testing of different structural models against each other with the goal of retaining the one with the best goodness of fit index regarding the data.

Other questions and issues raised by Ruch and Hehl, and others, that may be examined in future humor research include the following: the identification of further *content* classes (the present taxonomy of humor appreciation is very limited); the further study of *disparagement/superiority* humor (intercorrelations among the humor categories for this genre are needed); the *revision* of the two-step model (this model initially involves the detection of incongruity, followed by resolution of incongruity; a new three-step model, or a revised two-step model, may postulate that after resolving the incongruity a set of cognitive meta-processes are activated); the study of the *origins* of individual differences in humor appreciation (to what extent are they due to environmental and heredity factors; can one improve one's sense of humor? cf: Nevo, Aharonson, & Klingman, 1998; are the strong age-related differences observed in humor appreciation across the whole life-span due to genuine developmental changes or are they merely cross-generational cohort differences?); the study of whether humor preference can be changed by long-term *intervention* programs (is there a clear "order" of humor components—and the positive versus negative affects of humor—as regards psychic and somatic well-being?; can the use of humor in stressful situations have positive effects in alleviating distress? cf: Lefcourt & Thomas, 1998; do "trait-cheerful" individuals have a better "psychological immune system" that protects them against the negative impact of the stresses, annoyances, and mishaps encountered in everyday life? cf: Ruch & Kohler, 1998); the study of *pathological* conditions vis-à-vis humor (in what cases, and to what extent, is the impairment of humor a "local" condition—involving a limited aspect, such as type of humor material, production of humor versus appreciation of humor, etc.—as opposed to a "global" condition? what changes in humor parallel the evolution of a mental or physical disorder? cf: Forabosco, 1998); the study of the effects of *mood* on humor (such studies will depend, most likely, on the reliability and validity of mood induction procedures and the measurement of mood; is the individual more likely to interpret events as amusing when in a good mood than when in a bad mood? are physiological, expressive, and amusement variables equally affected by mood states, whether positive or negative? cf: Deckers, 1998).

In addition to an expected increase in psychological humor research containing empirical and experimental designs in the future, and in more practical contexts and applications concerning the "future faces of humor," it is likely that humor will continue to make its appearance on television (via new "sitcoms"—with and without "canned laughter," and even "action" shows; see Littleton, 1997), on the Internet (via new "dot-coms"), and in medicine as an immunological and therapeutic variable in hospital and clinical settings. In the future, also, it is expected that one may find an increase in various resources dealing with humor and humor-related issues. For example, in the area of publications/printed material, it is likely that academic journals such as *Humor: International Journal of Humor Research* will continue to flourish and publish original contributions in the form of empirical observational studies, theoretical discussions, presentations of experimental research, short notes, reactions/replies to recent articles, book reviews, interdisciplinary humor research, studies of humor technology, and studies of humor research methodologies. In the areas of organizations, conferences, newsletters, newspapers, magazines, courses, programs, and "registered scholars" dedicated to humor—in both professional and nonprofessional settings—it is expected that one will observe continued, and new, growth in terms of attendance, interest, recruitment, and number of participants. [Note: For a useful list of such humor resources, see Nilsen (1993, pp. 315–331).]

As of *this* writing (things change *quickly* on the "net"), regarding humor resources available on the Internet, the following list represents a small sample of Internet addresses dedicated to humorous material (look for more such Web sites in the future):

www.aath.org (American Association for Therapuetic Humor)

www.humorproject.com (Comedy Connection) (cf: www.goofyface.com)

www.allenklein.com/ (Allen Klein: The Jollytologist)

www.cypla.com/hum/index.htm (World Humor/Laugh Center)

www.stoplaughing.com.au/ (National Cartoon Competition)

www.jocularity.com/ (Journal of Nursing Jocularity)

www.les.man.ac.uk/cric/Jason_Rutter/HumourResearch/search.htm (Centre for Research on Innovation & Competition)

www.degruyter.de/journals/humor/index.html (Homepage of *Humor: International Journal of Humor Research*)

www.subatomichumor.com (A weekly humor column)

www.netfunny.com/rhf/ (The net's oldest and most popular comedy publication)

www.workingdogweb.com/Cartoons.htm (Dog stuff) (cf: www.pethumor.com)

www.elsop.com/wrc/humor/net_hist.htm (True history of the net)

http://www.weddinghumor.com/ (List of wedding jokes and humor)

http://www.SowingSeedsofFaith.com (A Christian humor site)

http://www.mel.org/libraries/LIBS-humor.html (Humor and culture in libraries)

http://www.anekdot.ru/ (Humor and anecdotes from Russia)

http://www.infidels.org/misc/humor/ (Internet infidels humor collection)

http://www.eggzone.com (A humor magazine dedicated to absolutely nothing!)

http://www.action-electronics.com/fun/fun45.htm (Action-electronics humor)

http://www.timsample.com/ (Maine humorist's Web site)

http://www.necronom.com/humor.htm (Black humor sites)

http://www.fallingdream.com (A weekly web comic strip in color)

http://www.geocities.com/SunsetStrip/Amphitheatre/7277/index.html ("1960's")

http://www.metroline-online.com/metrozone (Reader's contributions)

http://www.suite101.com/welcome.cfm/womens_humor (Women's humor)

http://www.inforserv.com/sfp/index_1134.html (Cookbooks with humor)

http://www.geocities.com/Heartland/Meadows/6033/humor.html (Rabbit jokes)

http://www.eff.org/pub/Net_culture/Folklore/Humor/ ("Net culture-humor")

http://www.jokesandhumor.com/top/index.html (Top 25 humor sites) www.psych.upenn.edu/humor.html (Psychology humor)

http://www.psychotherapistresources.com (Psychotherapeutic humor)

http://www.stressdoc.com/ (Online psychohumorist)

http://www.communitypsychology.net/humor/ (Psychology-related humor)

http://www.rorschach-analyzer.com/fun/ (Pop psychology humor)

http://www.humormatters.com (Therapeutic humor)

http://mentalhelp.net/humor/joke.htm (Mental health humor/jokes)

http://www.quincyweb.net/quincy/psychology.html (Humorous links to tests)

http://www.psychhumor.com/samples.html (*Journal of Polymorphous Perversity*)

http://users.erols.com/geary/psychology/ (Pop psychology humor)

http://www.fortunecity.com/campus/psychology/781/psycholo.htm (Try it!)

www.cartoonbank.com (The URL tells it all) (cf: www.politicalcartoons.com)

www.funtrivia.com/jokes.html (A catalog of jokes and one-liners)

REFERENCES

Abra, J. (1998). *Should psychology be a science? Pros and cons.* Westport, CT: Praeger.

Allen, M. (1984). Scientific method. In R. J. Corsini (Ed.), *Encyclopedia of psychology.* (Vol. 3). New York: Wiley.

Allen, S., & Wollman, J. (1987). *How to be funny: Discovering the comic you.* New York: McGraw-Hill.

Allentuck, S. (1929). The effect of suggestion on humor. Unpublished master's essay/thesis, Columbia University.

Almack, J. (1928). *Sense of Humor Test (Form 1).* Cincinnati, OH: Gregory.

Andrews, T. G. (1943). A factorial analysis of responses to the comic as a study in personality. *Journal of General Psychology, 28*, 209–224.

Apte, M. (1988). Disciplinary boundaries in humorology: An anthropologist's ruminations. *Humor: International Journal of Humor Research, 1*, 5–25.

Apter, M. (1979). Human action and the theory of psychological reversals. In G. Underwood & R. Stevens (Eds.), *Aspects of consciousness* (Vol. 1, *Psychological issues*). London: Academic Press.

Apter, M. (1982). *The experience of motivation: The theory of psychological reversals.* London: Academic Press.

Apter, M. (1984). Reversal theory and personality: A review. *Journal of Research in Personality, 18*, 265–288.

Apter, M., Fontana, D., & Murgatroyd, S. (Eds.) (1985). *Reversal theory: Applications and developments.* Cardiff, UK: University College Cardiff Press.

Apter, M., & Smith, K. (1977). Humour and the theory of psychological reversals. In A. J. Chapman & H. C. Foot (Eds.), *It's a funny thing, humour.* Oxford, UK: Pergamon Press.

Arlin, M., & Hills, D. (1974). Comparison of cartoon and verbal methods of school attitude assessment through multitrait-multimethod validation. *Educational and Psychological Measurement, 34*, 989–995.

Asch, S. (1955). Opinions and social pressure. *Scientific American, 193*, 31–35.

Attardo, S. (1998). The analysis of humorous narratives. *Humor: International Journal of Humor Research, 11*, 231–260.

Attardo, S., & Raskin, V. (1991). Script theory revis(it)ed: Joke similarity and joke representation model. *Humor: International Journal of Humor Research, 4*, 293–347.

Babad, E. (1974). A multimethod approach to the assessment of humor: A critical look at humor tests. *Journal of Personality, 42*, 618–631.

Ballmann, C. (1954). A study of adolescent sex differences in humor response. Unpublished master's thesis, Saint Louis University.

Baron, R. (1978a). Aggression-inhibiting influence of sexual humor. *Journal of Personality and Social Psychology, 36*, 189–197.

Baron, R. (1978b). The influence of hostile and nonhostile humor upon physical aggression. *Personality and Social Psychology Bulletin, 4*, 77–80.

Baron, R., & Ball, R. (1974). The aggression-inhibition influence of nonhostile humor. *Journal of Experimental Social Psychology, 10*, 23–33.

Baron, R., & Bell, P. (1977). Sexual arousal and aggression by males: Effects of type of erotic stimuli and prior provocation. *Journal of Personality and Social Psychology, 35*, 79–87.

Barry, H. (1928). The role of subject matter in individual differences in humor. *Journal of General Psychology, 35*, 112–127.

Bell, N., McGhee, P. E., & Duffey, N. (1986). Interpersonal competence, social assertiveness, and the development of humour. *British Journal of Developmental Psychology, 4*, 51–55.

Bergen, D. (1998). Development of the sense of humor. In W. Ruch (Ed.), *The sense of humor: Explorations of a personality characteristic.* Berlin: Mouton de Gruyter.

Bergler, E. (1956). *Laughter and the sense of humor.* New York: Intercontinental Medical Book Corporation.

Berkowitz, L. (1970). Aggressive humor as a stimulus to aggressive responses. *Journal of Personality and Social Psychology, 16*, 710–717.

Berlyne, D. E. (1960). *Conflict, arousal, and curiosity.* New York: McGraw-Hill.

Berlyne, D. E. (1969). Laughter, humor, and play. In G. Lindzey & E. Aronson (Eds.), *The handbook of social psychology.* (Vol. 3). Reading, MA: Addison-Wesley.

Bird, G. (1925). An objective humor test for children. *Psychological Bulletin, 22*, 137–138.

Brown, G., Brown, D., & Ramos, J. (1981). Effects of a laughing versus a nonlaughing model on humor responses in college students. *Psychological Reports, 48*, 35–40.

Brown, G., Wheeler, K., & Cash, M. (1980). The effects of a laughing versus a nonlaughing model on humor responses in preschool children. *Journal of Experimental Child Psychology, 29*, 334–339.

Brown, R., & Keegan, D. (1999). Humor in the hotel kitchen. *Humor: International Journal of Humor Research, 12*, 47–70.

Burt, C. (1945). The psychology of laughter. *Health Education Journal, 3*, 101–105.

Butland, M., & Ivy, D. (1990). The effects of biological sex and egalitarianism on humor appreciation: Replication and extension. *Journal of Social Behavior and Personality, 5*, 353–366.

Byrne, D. (1956). The relationship between humor and the expression of hostility. *Journal of Abnormal and Social Psychology, 53*, 84–89.

Byrne, D. (1958). Drive level, response to humor, and the cartoon sequence effect. *Psychological Reports, 4*, 439–442.

Byrne, D. (1961). Some inconsistencies in the effect of motivation arousal on humor preferences. *Journal of Abnormal and Social Psychology, 62*, 158–160.

Calvert, W. (1949). The effect of the social situation on humor. Unpublished master's thesis, Stanford University.

Campbell, D. (1960). Recommendations for APA test standards regarding trait or discriminant validity. *American Psychologist, 15*, 546–555.

Campbell, D., & Fiske, D. (1959). Convergent and discriminant validation by the multitrait-multimethod matrix. *Psychological Bulletin, 56*, 81–105.

Campbell, J. H. (1967). A message system analysis: Variable subsystems in cartoon humor. Unpublished doctoral dissertation, Michigan State University.

Cann, A., Holt, K., & Calhoun, L. (1999). The roles of humor and sense of humor in responses to stressors. *Humor: International Journal of Humor Research, 12*, 177–193.

Cantor, J. R. (1976). What is funny to whom? The role of gender. *Journal of Communication, 26*, 164–172.

Cantor, J. R., Bryant, J., & Zillmann, D. (1974). Enhancement of humor appreciation by transferred excitation. *Journal of Personality and Social Psychology, 30*, 812–821.

Carruthers, M., & Taggart, P. (1973). Vagotonicity of violence: Biochemical and cardiac responses to violent films and television programmes. *British Medical Journal, 3*, 384–389.

Cattell, J. M. (1903). Statistics of American psychologists. *American Journal of Psychology, 14*, 310–328.

Cattell, J. M. (1906). A statistical study of American men of science. *Science, 24* (Nov. & Dec.).

Cattell, R. B., & Luborsky, L. (1946). Measured response to humor as an indicator of personality structure. I. Analysis of humor. *American Psychologist, 1*, 257–258.

Cattell, R. B., & Luborsky, L. (1947a). *Handbook for the C-L Humor Test of Personality*. Champaign, IL: Institute for Personality and Ability Testing.

Cattell, R. B., & Luborsky, L. (1947b). Personality factors in response to humor. *Journal of Abnormal and Social Psychology, 42*, 402–421.

Cattell, R. B., Luborsky, L., & Hicks, V. (1950). *Revised handbook for the C-L Humor Test of Personality*. Champaign, IL: Institute for Personality and Ability Testing.

Chapman, A. J. (1972). Some aspects of the social facilitation of "humorous laughter" in children. Doctoral dissertation, University of Leicester, UK. (Also see: Social facilitation of laughter in children. *Journal of Experimental Social Psychology*, 1973, *9*, 528–541).

Chapman, A. J. (1973). Funniness of jokes, canned laughter, and recall performance. *Sociometry, 36*, 569–578.

Chapman, A. J. (1975). Humorous laughter in children. *Journal of Personality and Social Psychology, 31*, 42–49.

Chapman, A. J. (1983). Humor and laughter in social interaction and some implications for humor research. In P. E. McGhee & J. H. Goldstein (Eds.), *Handbook of humor research* (Vol. 1, *Basic issues*). New York: Springer-Verlag.

Chapman, A. J., & Chapman, W. (1974). Responsiveness to humor: Its dependency upon a companion's humorous smiling and laughter. *Journal of Psychology, 88*, 245–252.

Chapman, A. J., & Foot, H. C. (Eds.) (1976). *Humour and laughter: Theory, research, and applications*. London: Wiley.

Chapman, A. J., & Foot, H. C. (Eds.) (1977). *It's a funny thing, humour*. Oxford, UK: Pergamon Press.

Chapman, A. J., & Wright, D. (1976). Social enhancement of laughter: An experimental analysis of some companion variables. *Journal of Experimental Child Psychology, 21*, 201–218.

Claparede, E. (1934). La genese de l'hypothese. *Archives de Psychologie, 24*, 1–154.

Cogan, R., Cogan, D., Waltz, W., & McCue, M. (1987). Effects of laughter and relaxation on discomfort thresholds. *Journal of Behavioral Medicine, 10*, 139–144.

Cohen, D. (1989). Laugh? You must be joking. *New Scientist, 123*, 74.

Craik, K. H., & Ware, A. P. (1998). Humor and personality in everyday life. In W. Ruch (Ed.), *The sense of humor: Explorations of a personality characteristic*. Berlin: Mouton de Gruyter.

Davenport, C., & Craytor, L. (1923). Comparative social traits of various races, second study. *Journal of Applied Psychology, 7*, 127–134.

Deckers, L. (1998). Influence of mood on humor. In W. Ruch (Ed.), *The sense of humor: Explorations of a personality characteristic*. Berlin: Mouton de Gruyter.

Deckers, L., Edington, J., & VanCleave, G. (1981). Mirth as a function of incongruities in judged and unjudged dimensions of psychophysical tasks. *Journal of General Psychology, 105*, 225–233.

Deckers, L., Jenkins, S., & Gladfelter, E. (1977). Incongruity versus tension relief hypotheses of humor. *Motivation and Emotion, 1*, 261–272.

Deckers, L., & Kizer, P. (1974). A note on weight discrepancy and humor. *Journal of Psychology, 86*, 309–312.

Deckers, L., & Kizer, P. (1975). Humor and the incongruity hypothesis. *Journal of Psychology, 90*, 215–218.

Deckers, L., Kuhlhorst, L., & Freeland, L. (1987). The effects of spontaneous and voluntary facial reactions on surprise and humor. *Motivation and Emotion, 11*, 403–412.

Deckers, L., & Ruch, W. (1992). The Situational Humour Response Questionnaire (SHRQ) as a test of "sense of humour": A validity study in the field of humour appreciation. *Personality and Individual Differences, 13*, 1149–1152.

Deckers, L., & Salais, D. (1983). Humor as a negatively accelerated function of the degree of incongruity. *Motivation and Emotion, 7*, 357–363.

Deckers, L., & Winters, J. (1986). Surprise and humor in response to discrepantly short and/or heavy stimuli in a psychophysical task. *Journal of General Psychology, 113*, 57–63.

Derks, P. (1992). Category and ratio scaling of sexual and innocent cartoons. *Humor: International Journal of Humor Research, 5*, 319–329.

Derks, P., Lewis, D., & White, R. (1981). A comparison of ratio and category scales of humour. *Canadian Journal of Behavioural Science, 13*, 226–237.

Ding, G., & Jersild, A. (1932). A study of the laughing and smiling of preschool children. *Pedagogical Seminary and Journal of Genetic Psychology, 40*, 452–472.

Donnerstein, E., Donnerstein, M., & Evans, R. (1975). Erotic stimuli and aggression: Facilitation or inhibition. *Journal of Personality and Social Psychology, 32*, 237–244.

Doris, J., & Fierman, E. (1956). Humor and anxiety. *Journal of Abnormal and Social Psychology, 53*, 59–62.

Eastman, M. (1921). *The sense of humor.* New York: Scribner's.

Elbert, S. (1961). Humor preferences related to authoritarianism. Unpublished doctoral dissertation, New York University.

Ellsworth, P., & Tourangeau, R. (1981). On our failure to disconfirm what nobody ever said. *Journal of Personality and Social Psychology, 40*, 363–369.

Elmes, D., Kantowitz, B., & Roediger, H. (1995). *Research methods in psychology.* St. Paul, MN: West.

Enders, A. (1927). A study of the laughter of the preschool child in the Merrill-Palmer Nursery School. *Papers of the Michigan Academy of Science, Arts, and Letters, 8*, 341–356.

Eysenck, H. J. (1942). The appreciation of humour: An experimental and theoretical study. *British Journal of Psychology, 32*, 295–309.

Eysenck, H. J. (1943). An experimental analysis of five tests of "appreciation of humor." *Educational and Psychological Measurement, 3*, 191–214.

Eysenck, H. J. (1947). *Dimensions of personality.* London: Routledge & Kegan Paul.

Eysenck, H. J. (1952). *The scientific study of personality.* London: Routledge & Kegan Paul.

Eysenck, H. J. (1953). *The structure of human personality.* London: Methuen.

Eysenck, H. J. (1972). Foreword. In J. H. Goldstein & P. E. McGhee (Eds.), *The psychology of humor: Theoretical perspectives and empirical issues.* New York: Academic Press.

Eysenck, S., Eysenck, H. J., & Barrett, P. (1985). A revised version of the psychoticism scale. *Personality and Individual Differences, 6*, 21–29.

Feingold, A. (1982). Measuring humor: A pilot study. *Perceptual and Motor Skills, 54*, 986.

Feingold, A. (1983). Measuring humor ability: Revision and construct validating of the Humor Perceptiveness Test. *Perceptual and Motor Skills, 56,* 159–166.

Feingold, A., & Mazzella, R. (1991). Psychometric intelligence and verbal humor ability. *Personality and Individual Differences, 12,* 427–435.

Fischman, J. (1999). The brain's humor zone. *U.S. News & World Report, 126,* 49.

Fisher, S., & Fisher, R. (1981). *Pretend the world is funny and forever: A psychological analysis of comedians, clowns, and actors.* Hillsdale, NJ: Erlbaum.

Flugel, J. C. (1954). Humor and laughter. In G. Lindzey (Ed.), *Handbook of social psychology.* (Vol. 2). Reading, MA: Addison-Wesley.

Foot, H. C., Chapman, A. J., & Smith, J. (1977). Friendship and social responsiveness in boys and girls. *Journal of Personality and Social Psychology, 35,* 401–411.

Forabosco, G. (1998). The ill side of humor: Pathological conditions and sense of humor. In W. Ruch (Ed.), *The sense of humor: Explorations of a personality characteristic.* Berlin: Mouton de Gruyter.

Frankel, E. (1953). An experimental study of psychoanalytic theories of humor. Unpublished doctoral dissertation, University of Michigan.

Freud, S. (1905/1916). *Der witz und seine beziehung zum unbewussten.* Leipzig: Deuticke.

Freyd, M. (1923). The graphic rating scale. *Journal of Educational Psychology, 14,* 83–102.

Fuller, R. (1977). Uses and abuses of canned laughter. In A. J. Chapman & H. C. Foot Eds.), *It's a funny thing, humour.* Oxford, UK: Pergamon Press.

Fuller, R., & Sheehy-Skeffington, A. (1974). Effects of group laughter on responses to humorous material: A replication and extension. *Psychological Reports, 35,* 531–534.

Gerber, W., & Routh, D. (1975). Humor response as related to violation of expectancies and to stimulus intensity in a weight-judgment task. *Perceptual and Motor Skills, 41,* 673–674.

Ghosh, R. (1939). An experimental study of humour. *British Journal of Educational Psychology, 9,* 98–99.

Godkewitsch, M. (1972). The relationship between arousal potential and funniness of jokes. In J. H. Goldstein & P. E. McGhee (Eds.), *The psychology of humor: Theoretical perspectives and empirical issues.* New York: Academic Press.

Godkewitsch, M. (1976). Physiological and verbal indices of arousal in rated humour. In A. J. Chapman & H. C. Foot (Eds.), *Humour and laughter: Theory, research, and applications.* London: Wiley.

Goldstein, J. H. (1970a). Humor appreciation and time to respond. *Psychological Reports, 27,* 445–446.

Goldstein, J. H. (1970b). Repetition, motive arousal, and humor appreciation. *Journal of Experimental Research in Personality, 4,* 90–94.

Goldstein, J. H., Harman, J., McGhee, P. E., & Karasik, R. (1975). Test of an information-processing model of humor: Physiological response changes during problem- and riddle-solving. *Journal of General Psychology, 92,* 59–68.

Goldstein, J. H., & McGhee, P. E. (Eds.) (1972). *The psychology of humor: Theoretical perspectives and empirical issues.* New York: Academic Press.

Goodwin, C. J. (1998). *Research in psychology: Methods and design*. New York: Wiley.

Greenberg, M. (1984). Galilean/Aristotelian thinking. In R. J. Corsini (Ed.), *Encyclopedia of psychology*. (Vol. 2). New York: Wiley.

Gregg, A. (1928). An observational study of laughter in three-year-olds. Unpublished master's essay/thesis, Columbia University.

Grumet, G. (1989). Laughter: Nature's epileptoid catharsis. *Psychological Reports, 65*, 1059–1078.

Hall, G. S., & Allin, A. (1897). The psychology of tickling, laughing, and the comic. *American Journal of Psychology, 9*, 1–41.

Hammes, J. (1962). Suggestibility and humor evaluation. *Perceptual and Motor Skills, 15*, 530.

Hammes, J., & Wiggins, S. (1962). Manifest anxiety and appreciation of humor involving emotional content. *Perceptual and Motor Skills, 14*, 291–294.

Harrower, M. (1932). Organization of higher mental processes. *Psychologische Forschung, 17*, 56–120.

Hedberg, A. (1963). Response to humor stimuli as a function of anxiety and a success or failure experience. Unpublished master's thesis, Northern Illinois University.

Hehl, F.-J., & Ruch, W. (1983). Where can sense of humor be located in personality/attitude space? Paper presented at the First Meeting of ISSID (July 6–9). London. ISSID.

Hehl, F.-J., & Ruch, W. (1985). The location of sense of humor within comprehensive personality spaces: An exploratory study. *Personality and Individual Differences, 6*, 703–715.

Hehl, F.-J., & Ruch, W. (1990). Conservatism as a predictor of responses to humour. III. The prediction of appreciation of incongruity-resolution based humour by content saturated attitude scales in five samples. *Personality and Individual Differences, 11*, 439–445.

Heim, A. (1936). An experiment on humor. *British Journal of Psychology, 27*, 148–161.

Hellyar, R. (1927). Laughter and jollity. *Contemporary Review, 132*, 757–763.

Hester, M. (1924). Variations in the sense of humor according to age and mental condition. Unpublished master's essay/thesis, Columbia University.

Hetherington, E. M., & Wray, N. (1964). Aggression, need for social approval, and humor preferences. *Journal of Abnormal and Social Psychology, 68*, 685–689.

Hetherington, E. M., & Wray, N. (1966). Effects of need aggression, stress, and aggressive behavior on humor preferences. *Journal of Personality and Social Psychology, 4*, 229–233.

Hobden, K., & Olson, J. (1994). From jest to antipathy: Disparagement humor as a source of dissonance-motivated attitude change. *Basic and Applied Social Psychology, 15*, 239–249.

Holland, N. (1982). *Laughing: A psychology of humor*. Ithaca, NY: Cornell University Press.

Hollingworth, H. (1911). Experimental studies in judgment: Judgments of the comic. *Psychological Review, 18*, 132–156.

Holmes, D. S. (1955). The development of measures of the sensing of humor. *California Mental Health Research Digest, 3*, 27–28.

Holmes, D. S. (1969). Sensing humor: Latency and amplitude of response related to MMPI profiles. *Journal of Consulting and Clinical Psychology, 33*, 296–301.

Hom, G. (1966). Threat of shock and anxiety in the perception of humor. *Perceptual and Motor Skills, 23*, 535–538.

Kambouropoulou, P. (1926). Individual differences in the sense of humor. *American Journal of Psychology, 37*, 268–278.

Kambouropoulou, P. (1930). Individual differences in the sense of humor and their relation to temperamental differences. *Archives of Psychology, 121*, 1–83.

Kantowitz, B., Roediger, H., & Elmes, D. (1997). *Experimental psychology: Understanding psychological research*. St. Paul, MN: West.

Kaplan, R., & Pascoe, G. (1977). Humorous lectures and humorous examples: Some effects upon comprehension and retention. *Journal of Educational Psychology, 69*, 61–65.

Keith-Spiegel, P. (1972). Early conceptions of humor: Varieties and issues. In J. H. Goldstein & P. E. McGhee (Eds.), *The psychology of humor: Theoretical perspectives and empirical issues*. New York: Academic Press.

Kenny, D. (1955). The contingency of humor appreciation on the stimulus-confirmation of joke-ending expectations. *Journal of Abnormal and Social Psychology, 51*, 644–648.

King, P., & King, J. (1973). A children's humor test. *Psychological Reports, 33*, 632.

Kohler, G., & Ruch, W. (1993). The Cartoon Punchline Production Test (CPPT). Unpublished manuscript, Department of Psychology, University of Dusseldorf, Dusseldorf, Germany.

Kohler, G., & Ruch, W. (1994). Testing the comprehensiveness of the 3WD taxonomy of humor: Does Gary Larson's *Far Side* Gallery fit in? Poster session poster presented at the *International Society of Humor Studies Conference* (June 22–26). Ithaca College, New York.

Kohler, G., & Ruch, W. (1996). Sources of variance in current sense of humor inventories: How much substance, how much method variance? *Humor: International Journal of Humor Research, 9*, 363–397.

Kole, T., & Henderson, H. (1966). Cartoon reaction scale with special reference to driving behavior. *Journal of Applied Psychology, 50*, 311–316.

Koppel, M., & Sechrest, L. (1970). A multitrait-multimethod matrix analysis of sense of humor. *Educational and Psychological Measurement, 30*, 77–85.

Korotkov, D. (1991). An exploratory factor analysis of the sense of humour personality construct: A pilot project. *Personality and Individual Differences, 12*, 395–397.

Kuiper, N., & Martin, R. A. (1993). Humor and self-concept. *Humor: International Journal of Humor Research, 6*, 251–270.

Kuiper, N., & Martin, R. A. (1998). Is sense of humor a positive personality characteristic? In W. Ruch (Ed.), *The sense of humor: Explorations of a personality characteristic*. Berlin: Mouton de Gruyter.

Kuiper, N., Martin, R. A., & Dance, K. (1992). Sense of humor and enhanced quality of life. *Personality and Individual Differences, 13*, 1273–1283.

Kuiper, N., Martin, R. A., & Olinger, L. (1993). Coping humour, stress, and cognitive appraisals. *Canadian Journal of Behavioural Science, 25*, 81–96.

LaGaipa, J. (1968). Stress, authoritarianism, and the enjoyment of different kinds of hostile humor. *Journal of Psychology, 70*, 3–8.

Lamb, C. (1968). Personality correlates of humor enjoyment following motivational arousal. *Journal of Personality and Social Psychology, 9*, 237–241.

Lampert, M., & Ervin-Tripp, S. (1998). Exploring paradigms: The study of gender and sense of humor near the end of the 20th century. In W. Ruch (Ed.), *The sense of humor: Explorations of a personality characteristic*. Berlin: Mouton de Gruyter.

Landis, C., & Ross, W. (1933). Humor and its relation to other personality traits. *Journal of Social Psychology, 4*, 156–175.

Lange, F. (1927). A statistical analysis of crowd laughter. Unpublished master's essay/thesis, Columbia University.

Langevin, R., & Day, H. (1972). Physiological correlates of humor. In J. H. Goldstein & P. E. McGhee (Eds.), *The psychology of humor: Theoretical perspectives and empirical issues*. New York: Academic Press.

Leak, G. (1974). Effects of hostility arousal and aggressive humor on catharsis and humor preference. *Journal of Personality and Social Psychology, 30*, 736–740.

Lee, J., & Griffith, R. (1962). Time error in the judgment of humor. *Psychological Reports, 11*, 410.

Lefcourt, H., & Martin, R. A. (1986). *Humor and life stress: Antidote to adversity*. New York: Springer-Verlag.

Lefcourt, H., & Thomas, S. (1998). Humor and stress revisited. In W. Ruch (Ed.), *The sense of humor: Explorations of a personality characteristic*. Berlin: Mouton de Gruyter.

Levi, L. (1965). The urinary output of adrenalin and noradrenalin during pleasant and unpleasant emotional states: A preliminary report. *Psychosomatic Medicine, 27*, 80–85.

Levine, J. (1956). Responses to humor. *Scientific American, 194*, 31–35.

Levine, J. (Ed.) (1969). *Motivation in humor*. New York: Atherton.

Levine, J., & Abelson, R. (1959). Humor as a distracting stimulus. *Journal of General Psychology, 60*, 191–200.

Levine, J., & Rakusin, J. (1959). The sense of humor of college students and psychiatric patients. *Journal of General Psychology, 60*, 183–190.

Levine, J., & Redlich, F. (1955). Failure to understand humor. *Psychoanalytic Quarterly, 24*, 560–572.

Levine, J., & Redlich, F. (1960). Intellectual and emotional factors in the appreciation of humor. *Journal of General Psychology, 62*, 25–35.

Littleton, C. (1997). Humor is where the action is. *Broadcasting & Cable, 127*, 52–53.

Lowe, G., & Taylor, S. (1993). Relationship between laughter and weekly alcohol consumption. *Psychological Reports, 72*, 1210.

Lowe, G., & Taylor, S. (1997). Effects of alcohol on responsive laughter and amusement. *Psychological Reports, 80*, 1149–1150.

Lowis, M., & Nieuwoudt, J. (1995). The use of a cartoon rating scale as a measure of the humor construct. *Journal of Psychology, 129*, 133–144.

Luborsky, L., & Cattell, R. B. (1947). The validation of personality factors in humor. *Journal of Personality, 15*, 283–291.

Main, D., & Schillace, R. (1968). Aversive stimulation and the laughter response. *Psychonomic Science, 13*, 241–242.

Malpass, L. (1955). Social facilitation as a factor in reaction to humor. *American Psychologist, 10*, 360.

Malpass, L., & Fitzpatrick, E. (1959). Social facilitation as a factor in reaction to humor. *Journal of Social Psychology, 50*, 295–303.

Manke, B. (1998). Genetic and environmental contributions to children's interpersonal humor. In W. Ruch (Ed.), *The sense of humor: Explorations of a personality characteristic*. Berlin: Mouton de Gruyter.

Martin, G. N., & Gray, C. (1996). The effects of audience laughter on men's and women's responses to humor. *Journal of Social Psychology, 136*, 221–231.

Martin, L. (1905). Psychology of aesthetics: Experimental prospecting in the field of the comic. *American Journal of Psychology, 16*, 35–118.

Martin, R. A. (1996). The Situational Humor Response Questionnaire (SHRQ) and Coping Scale (CHS): A decade of research findings. *Humor: International Journal of Humor Research, 9*, 251–272.

Martin, R. A. (1998). Approaches to the sense of humor: A historical review. In W. Ruch (Ed.), *The sense of humor: Explorations of a personality characteristic*. Berlin: Mouton de Gruyter.

Martin, R. A. (2000). Humor and laughter. In A. E. Kazdin (Ed.), *Encyclopedia of psychology*. (Vol. 4). Washington, DC: American Psychological Association; New York: Oxford University Press.

Martin, R. A., Kuiper, N., Olinger, L., & Dance, K. (1993). Humor, coping with stress, self-concept, and psychological well-being. *Humor: International Journal of Humor Research, 6*, 89–104.

Martin, R. A., & Lefcourt, H. (1983). Sense of humor as a moderator of the relation between stressors and moods. *Journal of Personality and Social Psychology, 45*, 1313–1324.

Martin, R. A., & Lefcourt, H. (1984). Situational Humor Response Questionnaire: Quantitative measure of the sense of humor. *Journal of Personality and Social Psychology, 47*, 145–155.

McGhee, P. E. (1971). Development of the humor response: A review of the literature. *Psychological Bulletin, 76*, 328–348.

McGhee, P. E. (1996). *The laughter remedy: Health, healing, and the amuse system*. Dubuque, IA: Kendall-Hunt.

McGhee, P. E., & Goldstein, J. H. (1972). Advances toward an understanding of humor: Implications for the future. In J. H. Goldstein & P. E. McGhee (Eds.),

The psychology of humor: Theoretical perspectives and empirical issues. New York: Academic Press.

Meer, J. (1986). In vino comedia? *Psychology Today, 20,* 16.

Merenda, P. (1984). Empirical research methods. In R. J. Corsini (Ed.), *Encyclopedia of psychology.* (Vol. 1). New York: Wiley.

Moore, H. (1921). The comparative influence of majority and expert opinion. *American Journal of Psychology, 32,* 16–20.

Morrison, J. (1940). A note concerning investigations in audience laughter. *Sociometry, 3,* 179–185.

Mueller, C., & Donnerstein, E. (1977). The effects of humor-induced arousal upon aggressive behavior. *Journal of Research in Personality, 11,* 73–82.

Murgatroyd, S., Rushton, C., Apter, M., & Ray, C. (1978). The development of the Telic Dominance Scale. *Journal of Personality Assessment, 42,* 519–528.

Murray, H. (1934). The psychology of humor. II. Mirth responses to disparagement jokes as a manifestation of an aggressive disposition. *Journal of Abnormal and Social Psychology, 29,* 66–81.

Nerhardt, G. (1970). Humor and inclinations to laugh: Emotional reactions to stimuli of different divergence from a range of expectancy. *Scandinavian Journal of Psychology, 11,* 185–195.

Nerhardt, G. (1977). Operationalization of incongruity in humour research: A critique and suggestions. In A. J. Chapman & H. C. Foot (Eds.), *It's a funny thing, humour.* Oxford, UK: Pergamon Press.

Nevo, O., Aharonson, H., & Klingman, A. (1998). The development and evaluation of a systematic program for improving sense of humor. In W. Ruch (Ed.), *The sense of humor: Explorations of a personality characteristic.* Berlin: Mouton de Gruyter.

Nilsen, D. (1993). *Humor scholarship: A research bibliography.* Westport, CT: Greenwood Press.

Nosanchuk, T., & Lightstone, J. (1974). Canned laughter and public and private conformity. *Journal of Personality and Social Psychology, 29,* 153–156.

O'Connell, W. E. (1960). The adaptive function of humor. *Journal of Abnormal and Social Psychology, 61,* 263–270.

O'Connell, W. E. (1984/1994). Humor. In R. J. Corsini (Ed.), *Encyclopedia of psychology.* (Vol. 2). New York: Wiley.

Olson, J. (1992). Self-perception of humor: Evidence for discounting and augmentation effects. *Journal of Personality and Social Psychology, 62,* 369–377.

Olson, J., Maio, G., & Hobden, K. (1999). The (null) effects of exposure to disparagement humor on stereotypes and attitudes. *Humor: International Journal of Humor Research, 12,* 195–219.

Overholser, J. C. (1992). Sense of humor when coping with life stress. *Personality and Individual Differences, 13,* 799–804.

Paolillo, J. (1998). Gary Larson's *Far Side*: Nonsense? Nonsense! *Humor: International Journal of Humor Research, 11,* 261–290.

Peirce, C. S. (1877). The fixation of belief. *Popular Science Monthly, 12,* 1–15.

Perl, R. (1933a). A review of experiments on humor. *Psychological Bulletin, 30,* 752–763.

Perl, R. (1933b). The influence of a social factor upon the appreciation of humor. *American Journal of Psychology, 45*, 308–312.

Pfeifer, K. (1997). Laughter, freshness, and titillation. *Inquiry: An Interdisciplinary Journal of Philosophy, 40*, 307–322.

Pistole, D., & Shor, R. (1979). A multivariate study of the effect of repetition on humor appreciation as qualified by two social influence factors. *Journal of General Psychology, 100*, 43–51.

Pollio, H., Mers, R., & Lucchesi, W. (1972). Humor, laughter, and smiling: Some preliminary observations of funny behaviors. In J. H. Goldstein & P. E. McGhee (Eds.), *The psychology of humor: Theoretical perspectives and empirical issues.* New York: Academic Press.

Porterfield, A., Mayer, F.S., Dougherty, K., Kredich, K., Kronberg, M., Marsee, K., & Okazaki, Y. (1988). Private self-consciousness, canned laughter, and responses to humorous stimuli. *Journal of Research in Personality, 22*, 409–423.

Prerost, F. (1975). The indication of sexual and aggressive similarities through humor appreciation. *Journal of Psychology, 91*, 283–288.

Prerost, F. (1976). Reduction of aggression as a function of related content of humor. *Psychological Reports, 38*, 771–777.

Prerost, F. (1993). The relationship of sexual desire to the appreciation of related humor content and mood state. *Journal of Social Behavior and Personality, 8*, 529–536.

Prerost, F. (1995). Humor preferences among angered males and females: Associations with humor content and sexual desire. *Psychological Reports, 77*, 227–234.

Prerost, F., & Brewer, R. (1977). Humor content preferences and the relief of experimentally-aroused aggression. *Journal of Social Psychology, 103*, 225–231.

Provine, R. (1996). Laughter. *American Scientist, 84*, 38–47.

Provine, R. (2000a). *Laughter: A scientific investigation.* New York: Viking Penguin.

Provine, R. (2000b). The science of laughter. *Psychology Today, 33*, 58–62.

Raley, A. (1942). Responses of girls to the humor of cartoons. Unpublished doctoral dissertation, Fordham University.

Raley, A. (1946). A psychometric study of humor. *American Psychologist, 1*, 265.

Raley, A., & Ballmann, C. (1957). Theoretical implications for a psychology of the ludicrous. *Journal of Social Psychology, 45*, 19–23.

Raskin, V. (1985). *Semantic mechanisms of humor.* Dordrecht: Reidel.

Ray, W. (2000). *Methods toward a science of behavior and experience.* Belmont, CA: Wadsworth/Thomson Learning.

Redlich, F. (1960). Intellectual and emotional factors in appreciation of humor. *Journal of General Psychology, 62*, 25–35.

Redlich, F., Levine, J., & Sohler, T. (1951). A mirth response test: Preliminary report on a psychodiagnostic technique utilizing dynamics of humor. *American Journal of Orthopsychiatry, 21*, 717–734.

Roback, A. (1939). *Sense of Humor Test.* Cambridge, MA: Sci-Art.

Roeckelein, J. E. (1968). The effects of "canned" laughter on adult humor responses. Unpublished manuscript, Arizona State University.

Roeckelein, J. E. (1969). Auditory stimulation and cartoon ratings. *Perceptual and Motor Skills, 29,* 772.

Roeckelein, J. E. (1998). *Dictionary of theories, laws, and concepts in psychology.* Westport, CT: Greenwood Press.

Rosenfeld, P., Giacalone, R., & Tedeschi, J. (1983). Humor and impression management. *Journal of Social Psychology, 121,* 59–63.

Rosenwald, G. (1964). The relation of drive discharge to the enjoyment of humor. *Journal of Personality, 32,* 682–698.

Rothbart, M. (1973). Laughter in young children. *Psychological Bulletin, 80,* 247–256.

Ruch, W. (1981). Witzbeurteilung und personlichkeit: Eine trimodale analyse. *Zeitschrift fur Differentielle und Diagnostische Psychologie, 2,* 253–273.

Ruch, W. (1983). Humor-Test 3WD (Form A, B, and K). Unpublished manuscript, Department of Psychology, University of Dusseldorf, Germany.

Ruch, W. (1984). Konservativismus und witzbeurteilung: Konvergenz gegenstandsbereichsinterner und ubergreifender variabilitat. *Zeitschrift fur Differentielle und Diagnostische Psychologie, 5,* 221–245.

Ruch, W. (1992). Assessment of appreciation of humor: Studies with the 3WD humor test. In C. D. Spielberger & J. N. Butcher (Eds.), *Advances in personality assessment.* (Vol. 9). Hillsdale, NJ: Erlbaum.

Ruch, W. (1993). Introduction: Current issues in psychological humor research. *Humor: International Journal of Humor Research, 6,* 1–7.

Ruch, W. (1994). Temperament, Eysenck's PEN system, and humor-related traits. *Humor: International Journal of Humor Research, 7,* 209–244.

Ruch, W. (1995). Will the real relationship between facial expression and affective experience please stand up: The case of exhilaration. *Cognition and Emotion, 9,* 33–58.

Ruch, W. (1996). Measurement approaches to the sense of humor: Introduction and overview. *Humor: International Journal of Humor Research, 9,* 239–250.

Ruch, W. (1997). State and trait cheerfulness and the induction of exhilaration: A FACS-study. *European Psychologist, 2,* 328–341.

Ruch, W. (Ed.) (1998). *The sense of humor: Explorations of a personality characteristic.* Berlin: Mouton de Gruyter.

Ruch, W. (1999). The sense of nonsense lies in the nonsense of sense. Comment on Paolillo's (1998) "Gary Larson's *Far Side:* Nonsense? Nonsense!" *Humor: International Journal of Humor Research, 12,* 71–93.

Ruch, W., Attardo, S., & Raskin, V. (1993). Toward an empirical verification of the General Theory of Verbal Humor. *Humor: International Journal of Humor Research, 6,* 123–136.

Ruch, W., & Carrell, A. (1998). Trait cheerfulness and the sense of humour. *Personality and Individual Differences, 24,* 551–558.

Ruch, W., & Deckers, L. (1993). Do extraverts "like to laugh?" : An analysis of the Situational Humor Response Questionnaire (SHRQ). *European Journal of Personality, 7,* 211–220.

Ruch, W., Freiss, M., & Kohler, G. (1993). The State-Trait Cheerfulness Inventory (STCI). Preliminary manual. Unpublished manuscript, Department of General Psychology, Heinrich-Heine-University, Dusseldorf, Germany.

Ruch, W., & Hehl, F.-J. (1983). Intolerance of ambiguity as a factor in the appreciation of humour. *Personality and Individual Differences, 4*, 443–449.

Ruch, W., & Hehl, F.-J. (1984). Individual differences in sense of humor: A factor analytic approach. Paper presented at the Fourth International Congress on Humor (June, 10–15). Tel Aviv.

Ruch, W., & Hehl, F.-J. (1986a). Conservatism as a predictor of responses to humour. I. A comparison of four scales. *Personality and Individual Differences, 7*, 1–14.

Ruch, W., & Hehl, F.-J. (1986b). Conservatism as a predictor of responses to humour. II. The location of sense of humour in a comprehensive attitude space. *Personality and Individual Differences, 7*, 861–874.

Ruch, W., & Hehl, F.-J. (1987). Personal values as facilitating and inhibiting factors in the appreciation of humor content. *Journal of Social Behavior and Personality, 2*, 453–472.

Ruch, W., & Hehl, F.-J. (1988). Attitudes to sex, sexual behaviour, and enjoyment of humour. *Personality and Individual Differences, 9*, 983–994.

Ruch, W., & Hehl, F.-J. (1993). Humor appreciation and needs: Evidence from questionnaire, self- and peer-rating data. *Personality and Individual Differences, 15*, 433–445.

Ruch, W., & Hehl, F.-J. (1998). A two-mode model of humor appreciation: Its relation to aesthetic appreciation and simplicity-complexity of personality. In W. Ruch (Ed.), *The sense of humor: Explorations of a personality characteristic*. Berlin: Mouton de Gruyter.

Ruch, W., & Kohler, G. (1998). A temperament approach to humor. In W. Ruch (Ed.), *The sense of humor: Explorations of a personality characteristic*. Berlin: Mouton de Gruyter.

Ruch, W., Kohler, G., & VanThriel, C. (1996). Assessing the "humorous temperament": Construction of the facet and standard trait forms of the State-Trait-Cheerfulness-Inventory (STCI). *Humor: International Journal of Humor Research, 9*, 303–339.

Ruch, W., Kohler, G., & VanThriel, C. (1997). To be in good or bad humour: Construction of the state form of the State-Trait-Cheerfulness-Inventory (STCI). *Personality and Individual Differences, 22*, 477–491.

Ruch, W., & Rath, S. (1993). The nature of humor appreciation: Toward an integration of perception of stimulus properties and affective experience. *Humor: International Journal of Humor Research, 6*, 363–384.

Russell, R. (1996). Understanding laughter in terms of basic perceptual and response patterns. *Humor: International Journal of Humor Research, 9*, 39–55.

Russell, R. (2000). Humor's close relatives. *Humor: International Journal of Humor Research, 13*, 219–233.

Schachter, S., & Wheeler, L. (1962). Epinephrine, chlorpromazine, and amusement. *Journal of Abnormal and Social Psychology, 65*, 121–128.

Schauer, O. (1910). Ueber das wesen der komik. *Archiv fur die Gesamte Psychologie, 18*, 410.

Scofield, H. (1921). The psychology of laughter. Unpublished master's essay/thesis, Columbia University.

Sekeres, R., & Clark, W. (1980). Verbal, heart rate, and skin conductance responses to sexual cartoons. *Psychological Reports, 47*, 1227–1232.

Shammi, P., & Stuss, D. (1999). Humour appreciation: A role of the right frontal lobe. *Brain, 122*, 657–666.

Sheehy-Skeffington, A. (1977). The measurement of humour appreciation. In A. J. Chapman & H. C. Foot (Eds.), *It's a funny thing, humour*. Oxford, UK: Pergamon Press.

Shurcliff, A. (1968). Judged humor, arousal, and the relief theory. *Journal of Personality and Social Psychology, 8*, 360–363.

Singer, D. (1968). Aggression arousal, hostile humor, catharsis. *Journal of Personality and Social Psychology Monograph Supplement, 8*, 1–14.

Smith, R., Ascough, J., Ettinger, R., & Nelson, D. (1971). Humor, anxiety, and task performance. *Journal of Personality and Social Psychology, 19*, 243–246.

Smyth, M., & Fuller, R. (1972). Effects of group laughter on responses to humorous material. *Psychological Reports, 30*, 132–134.

Stevens, S. S. (1966). A metric for the social consensus. *Science, 151*, 530–541.

Stevens, S. S., & Galanter, E. (1957). Ratio scales and category scales for a dozen perceptual continua. *Journal of Experimental Psychology, 54*, 377–411.

Strickland, J. (1959). The effect of motivation arousal on humor preferences. *Journal of Abnormal and Social Psychology, 59*, 278–281.

Sumner, F. (1898). A statistical study of belief. *Psychological Review, 5*, 616–631.

Sumno, A. (1958). Humor in review. *Journal of Social Therapy, 4*, 201–208.

Svebak, S. (1974a). A theory of sense of humor. *Scandinavian Journal of Psychology, 15*, 99–107.

Svebak, S. (1974b). Revised questionnaire on the sense of humor. *Scandinavian Journal of Psychology, 15*, 328–331.

Svebak, S. (1974c). Three attitude dimensions of sense of humor as predictors of laughter. *Scandinavian Journal of Psychology, 15*, 185–190.

Svebak, S. (1975). Styles in humour and social self-images. *Scandinavian Journal of Psychology, 16*, 79–84.

Svebak, S. (1993). Sense of Humor Questionnaire—Revised (SHQ-3). Unpublished manuscript, University of Bergen, Norway.

Svebak, S. (1996). The development of the Sense of Humor Questionnaire: From SHQ to SHQ-6. *Humor: International Journal of Humor Research, 9*, 341–361.

Svebak, S., & Apter, M. (1987). Laughter: An empirical test of some reversal theory hypotheses. *Scandinavian Journal of Psychology, 28*, 189–198.

Symonds, P. (1924). On the loss in reliability in ratings due to coarseness of the scale. *Journal of Experimental Psychology, 7*, 456–461.

Symonds, P. (1925). Notes on rating. *Journal of Applied Psychology, 9*, 188–195.

Thorndike, E. L. (1910). Handwriting. *Teachers College Record, 11*, 57.

Thorndike, R., & Stein, S. (1937). An evaluation of the attempts to measure social intelligence. *Psychological Bulletin, 34*, 275–285.

Thorson, J. (1990). Is propensity to laugh equivalent to sense of humor? *Psychological Reports, 66*, 737–738.

Thorson, J., Brdar, I., & Powell, F. (1997). Factor analytic study of sense of humor in Croatia and the USA. *Psychological Reports, 81*, 971–977.

Thorson, J., & Powell, F. (1991). Measurement of sense of humor. *Psychological Reports, 69*, 691–702.

Thorson, J., & Powell, F. (1993). Development and validation of a multidimensional sense of humor scale. *Journal of Clinical Psychology, 49*, 13–23.

Tollefson, D., & Cattell, R. B. (1963–1964). *Handbook for the IPAT Humor Test of Personality*. Champaign, IL: Institute for Personality and Ability Testing.

Torgerson, W. (1958). *Theory and methods of scaling*. New York: Wiley.

Treadwell, Y. (1967). Bibliography of empirical studies of wit and humor. *Psychological Reports, 20*, 1079–1083.

Wagoner, J., & Sullenberger, C. (1978). Pupillary size as an indicator of preference in humor. *Perceptual and Motor Skills, 47*, 779–782.

Wakshlag, J., Day, K., & Zillmann, D. (1981). Selective exposure to educational television programs as a function of differently paced humorous inserts. *Journal of Educational Psychology, 73*, 27–32.

Walker, M., & Washburn, M. (1919). The Healy-Fernald Picture Completion Test as a test of the perception of the comic. *American Journal of Psychology, 30*, 304–307.

Washburn, R. (1929). A study of the smiling and laughing of infants in the first year of life. *Genetic Psychology Monographs, 6*, 397–535.

Weaver, J., Masland, J., Kharazmi, S., & Zillmann, D. (1985). Effect of alcoholic intoxication on the appreciation of different types of humor. *Journal of Personality and Social Psychology, 49*, 781–787.

Wheeler, D., & Jordan, H. (1929). Change of individual opinion to accord with group opinion. *Journal of Abnormal and Social Psychology, 24*, 203–207.

Wheeler, M. (1997). The ten fingers of Dr. H: The saga of a psychologist who tortures volunteers in an effort to understand tickling. *Discover, 18*, 32–34.

White, S., & Camarena, P. (1989). Laughter as a stress reducer in small groups. *Humor: International Journal of Humor Research, 2*, 73–79.

White, S., & Winzelberg, A. (1992). Laughter and stress. *Humor: International Journal of Humor Research, 5*, 343–355.

Williams, C., & Cole, D. (1964). The influence of experimentally-induced inadequacy feelings upon the appreciation of humor. *Journal of Social Psychology, 64*, 113–117.

Williams, J. (1945). An experimental and theoretical study of humour in children. *British Journal of Educational Psychology, 16*, 43–44.

Wilson, G. (1973). Conservatism and response to humour. In G. Wilson (Ed.), *The psychology of conservatism*. London: Academic Press.

Wolff, H., Smith, C., & Murray, H. (1934). The psychology of humor. I. A study of responses to race-disparagement jokes. *Journal of Abnormal and Social Psychology, 28*, 341–365.

Woodworh, R. S., & Poffenberger, A. T. (1920). Text book of experimental psychology. Unpublished manuscript. Columbia University.

Yarnold, J., & Berkeley, M. (1954). An analysis of the Cattell-Luborsky Humor Test into homogeneous scales. *Journal of Abnormal and Social Psychology, 49,* 543–546.

Young, P. (1937). Laughing and weeping, cheerfulness and depression: A study of moods among college students. *Journal of Social Psychology, 8,* 311–334.

Young, R., & Frye, M. (1966). Some are laughing; some are not—why? *Psychological Reports, 18,* 747–754.

Yovetich, N., Dale, J., & Hudak, M. (1990). Benefits of humor in reduction of threat-induced anxiety. *Psychological Reports, 66,* 51–58.

Zillmann, D. (1971). Excitation transfer in communication-mediated aggressive behavior. *Journal of Experimental Social Psychology, 7,* 419–434.

Zillmann, D. (1991). Television viewing and physiological arousal. In J. Bryant & D. Zillmann (Eds.), *Responding to the screen: Reception and reaction processes.* Hillsdale, NJ: Erlbaum.

Zillmann, D., Rockwell, S., Schweitzer, K., & Sundar, S. (1993). Does humor facilitate coping with physical discomfort? *Motivation and Emotion, 17,* 1–21.

Zillmann, D., Williams, B., Bryant, J., Boynton, K., & Wolf, M. (1980). Acquisition of information from educational television programs as a function of differently paced humorous inserts. *Journal of Educational Psychology, 72,* 170–180.

Ziv, A. (1979). Sociometry of humor: Objectifying the subjective. *Perceptual and Motor Skills, 49,* 97–98.

Ziv, A. (1981). The self concept of adolescent humorists. *Journal of Adolescence, 4,* 187–197.

Annotated Bibliography of Humor
Studies in Psychology (1970–2001)

The material for the selected annotated bibliography on the psychology of humor in this chapter is organized around the following ten rubrics: Aggression and Humor; Application of Humor; Bibliographies and Literature Reviews of Humor; Cognition and Humor; Humor as Comedy/Jokes/Puns/Riddles/Satire/Irony; Humor as Laughter and Wit; Individual and Group Differences in Humor; Methodology and Measurement of Humor; Nature of the Humorous Stimulus; Social Aspects of Humor.

Due to the large number of humor studies available in the psychological literature, and to the limited page space here, when a choice had to be made concerning the inclusion of a particular humor study in this selected bibliography, the criterion of "empirical" and/or "experimental" methodology was applied. That is, a humor study containing data collection (empirical) and/or manipulation and measurement, respectively, of independent and dependent variables (experimental) is selected for inclusion in this bibliography over another study that does not possess such methodological features. Moreover, an attempt is made here *not* to duplicate references to studies that have already been described and discussed in previous chapters; however, in the few cases where this does occur, the purpose is to provide further information and more detail—than was given previously—concerning the important study in question.

Accordingly, across the ten rubrics, this chapter contains over 380 annotated entries concerning humor research conducted in psychology from 1970 to 2001. [Notes: The general *format* for most entries in this chapter includes the following information (where appropriate): a statement concerning the participants and materials used, the results of the study, and any conclusions, suggestions, or implications of the study. Also, the use of a single asterisk (*) at the end of an annotation indicates that the study mainly employed an *empirical* (data collection) methodology, while the use of a double asterisk (**) at the end of an annotation denotes that the study employed an *experimental* (causal determination) methodology. See Chapter 5 for further discussion of scientific research and methodology.]

AGGRESSION AND HUMOR

1. Byars, B. (1970). Aggressive humor as a stimulus to aggressive behavior. Unpublished doctoral dissertation, University of California, Los Angeles. Reports data from 96 college women that support the following predictions: aggressive humor stimulates aggressive behavior among nonaroused persons, and anger and drive-reduction—based in the vicarious catharsis provided by aggressive humor—occur in participants. **

2. Davidson, E. S. (1975). Effects of aggressive, neutral, and antiaggressive cartoons on children's tolerance of aggression by others. Unpublished doctoral dissertation, State University of New York at Stony Brook. Reports data from 60 third-graders offering only *weak* support for the following hypotheses: children in an antiaggressive cartoon group respond more quickly than those children in an aggressive cartoon group, and gender differences occur where girls respond more quickly and more often than boys. **

3. Decker, W. (1986). Sex conflict and impressions of managers' aggressive humor. *The Psychological Record, 36*, 483–490. In this study, 384 students evaluated aggressive humor used by a hypothetical manager in an organizational context. Results indicate that males judge the humor funnier and more contextually appropriate than do females; some of the evidence reported here supports the "intergroup-conflict" theory of humor. **

4. Deleanu, M. (1983). The role of aggression and conflict about aggression on humor appreciation. Unpublished doctoral dissertation, The University of Tennessee. Among the results reported, it was found for 64 college students that both aggression and conflict about aggression influence humor appreciation; that aggressive, conflicted persons enjoy humor most and nonaggressive, nonconflicted persons enjoy humor least; that aggressive persons tend to prefer emotionally vivid humor that is laden with sexuality and aggression, and that compared to males, females tend to prefer gallows humor. *

5. Edelman, C. (1987). Attitudes toward violence: The subculture of violence revisited; Conflict and control functions of sexual humor. Unpublished doctoral dissertation, The University of Arizona. This three-part study suggests the following notions, among others: middle- and upper-class whites are more proviolence than lower-class blacks; and in a functional analysis of sexual humor it was found that sexual humor has much in common with racial and ethnic humor because all three forms distinguish dominant from subordinate groups

and exaggerate the weaknesses of the out-group and the strengths of the in-group. *

6. Fathman, R. (1971). Aggressive humor in normal and delinquent adolescents. Unpublished doctoral dissertation, The University of Texas at Austin. Presents data from 90 seventh-graders to support the hypotheses that an experimental group of normal boys and girls will have lower enjoyment ratings of aggressive jokes when such jokes fail to serve as a release for repressed aggression, and that there are no differences between control and experimental groups of delinquent boys in their ratings of aggressive jokes because delinquents tend to act out, rather than repress, their impulses. **

7. Grody, G. (1976). The effects of exposing derisive humor to juvenile delinquent males as a cathartic tool to reduce aggressive impulse strength. Unpublished doctoral dissertation, United States International University. In this "test-retest" study, 45 participants from a juvenile residence were assigned randomly to one of three treatment groups: Group 1—received derisive humor; Group 2—received neutral humor; and Group 3—control (no treatment modality given). Results indicate significant differences between Group 1 and Group 3, and between Group 2 and Group 3, on both a first and a second administration of an aggression scale derived from a personal orientation inventory. Within a psychoanalytic theory of humor context, it is concluded that humor, though not necessarily derisive humor, is effective in reducing aggressive impulse strength. **

8. Hauenstein, L. (1970). Anger, salience and the appreciation of hostile humor. Unpublished doctoral dissertation, The University of Michigan. Under conditions of posthypnotic suggestion, three participants experienced various states of anger, and then rated hostile and nonhostile cartoons; they also rated the cartoons again in a normal waking state. Findings indicate that there are large individual differences in cartoon enjoyment, and that hostile thoughts alone do not lead to the greatest hostile-humor appreciation; support is shown for the "salience hypothesis" of hostile-humor appreciation. **

9. Hoffman, H. (1975). The relationship between defensive style, hostility arousal, humor preference and humor production. Unpublished doctoral dissertation, New York University. Experimental results from college students indicate that "sensitizer" participants do not have a higher preference for hostile jokes, nor a greater number of humor productions, as compared to "repressor" participants. It was found, also, that a motivation arousal technique was ineffective in influencing humor preference or production. There was no support for the hypothesis that the prediction to tendency for hostile humor—on the basis of defensive style and motivation arousal—is greater for hostile joke preference than for hostile humor production. **

10. Lockton, D. (1985). Age and sex differences in the preference, appreciation, and comprehension of aggressive and non-aggressive humor in children.

Unpublished doctoral dissertation, University of Southern California. Reports that no sex differences were found in boys and girls—aged three and a half to seven and a half—for their preference of aggressive over nonaggressive cartoon humor. Age differences were found in interpersonal aggressive cartoons where younger children preferred nonaggressive cartoons; this suggests that it is not aggression itself that may be problematic for younger children but only an "interpersonal" type of aggression. **

11. McCauley, C., Woods, K., Coolidge, C., & Kulick, W. (1983). More aggressive cartoons are funnier. *Journal of Personality and Social Psychology, 44*, 817–823. Provides results from six studies involving six different sets of cartoons and six different groups of participants (total *n* =136)—including both children and adults, high and low socioeconomic status persons, and foreign-born and native-born persons. High correlations found between humor and aggressiveness ratings of participants are consistent with the arousal, superiority, and Freudian theories of humor. However, the finding that individuals higher in socioeconomic status were *not* more appreciative of aggressive humor than persons lower in socioeconomic status failed to support the Freudian theory of humor. *

12. Prerost, F. (1987). Health locus of control, humor, and reduction in aggression. *Psychological Reports, 61*, 887–896. Examines the role of "health locus of control" in the relationship between humor appreciation and positive mood states. Participants were 144 college women who were classified initially as either "internal" or "external" scorers on the "health locus of control" scale and who experienced subsequently either an arousal of aggression, or a neutral, nonarousing procedure. Participants were presented, also, with three stimulus conditions: neutral humor, aggressive humor, or nonhumorous material, and then assessed for mood state. Results indicate that "internal" scorers—when angered—show the most enjoyment of aggressive humor; scores on the "health locus of control" scale appear to be related to the effective use of humor to reduce anger and the scale may be important in college women's capacity to regulate mood via humor. **

13. Prerost, F. (1995). Humor preferences among angered males and females: Associations with humor content and sexual desire. *Psychological Reports, 77*, 227–234. The variable of anger was induced experimentally in 180 women and 180 men who indicated sexual desire before being exposed to humor with sexual, sexist, and neutral content. Results indicate that angered men and women prefer sexual and sexist humor when they report high sexual desire; the appreciation of such humor content appears to enable the person to reduce and/or release his or her hostile mood state and to experience, subsequently, a positive happy condition. **

14. Ross, L. (1972). The effect of aggressive cartoons on the group play of children. Unpublished doctoral dissertation, Miami University. This study em-

ployed a 2 x 2 x 3 factorial design with the independent variables of sex of child, group size (two or four children), and cartoon condition (aggressive cartoons, nonaggressive cartoons, and no cartoons). Results from factor analyses of the dependent measures for 96 kindergarten-aged children identified four major factors: normative play/normative aggression, transgressive-aggression, and two factors composed of time of play measures. Conclusions are that aggression is *not* a single class of behavior, and that the effect of viewing aggressive models is *not* to reduce inhibitions against aggression in preschool children. **

15. Shindelman, H. (1987). The appreciation of hostile targeted humor as a moderator of event-specific and global perceived stress. Unpublished doctoral dissertation, City University of New York. Reports—for 144 college students—that neither the level of appreciation for hostile targeted jokes nor level of favorability toward nonhostile, nontargeted jokes improve the predictability of illness beyond the information provided by scores taken for the types of stress that were measured; also, the magnitude of the relationship between level of event-specific, or global, stress and illness outcome was unaffected by the level of appreciation for either hostile or nonhostile, nontargeted jokes. *

16. Sinnott, J., & Ross, B. (1976). Comparison of aggression and incongruity as factors in children's judgments of humor. *The Journal of Genetic Psychology, 128,* 241–249. Participants were 230 boys and girls from ages three to eight who each made six paired comparison judgments of the funniness of two brief incidents involving hand puppets manipulated by the experimenter. Results indicate that children at all the age levels tested preferred aggressive and incongruous incidents to neutral incidents. Conclusions are that aggression is an early occurring and potent factor in children's humor, and that employment of the methodology of cognitive choice in assessing humor in preschoolers is as useful as traditional observational measures such as laughing and smiling. **

17. Sprafkin, J., & Gadow, K. (1987). The immediate impact of aggressive cartoons on emotionally disturbed and learning disabled children. *The Journal of Genetic Psychology, 149,* 35–44. Participants were 15 emotionally disturbed (ED) and 23 learning disabled (LD) children between the ages of 5 and 10 years who viewed either an aggressive or a comparison cartoon, and then played a "help-hurt" game. Results showed that both ED and LD children exposed to an aggressive cartoon program were more willing to hurt another child than were those children who viewed a nonaggressive cartoon; also, responses of the ED children indicated longer durations for hurting another child than those of the LD children. **

18. Sprafkin, J., Gadow, K., & Grayson, P. (1988). Effect of cartoons on emotionally disturbed children's social behavior in school settings. *Journal of Child Psychology and Psychiatry and Allied Disciplines, 1,* 91–99. Four classes of emotionally disturbed boys and girls (*n* = 38) were exposed to aggressive and nonaggressive/control cartoons. Direct observations of the children's behaviors were made during lunch and recess periods. Results indicate that more nonphysical aggression occurred following the control cartoons, and more physical aggression followed the aggressive cartoons. *

19. Summers, D. (1974). The effects of aggressive humor stimuli upon measured hostility in male adolescent delinquents. Unpublished doctoral dissertation, University of Maryland. Participants in this study were 48 male adolescent delinquents incarcerated in a correctional facility. In a repeated measurement design, the experimental group of boys were shown an anger-arousal videotape or a nonarousal videotape, and then given an aggressive humor scale; two control groups of boys were given an identical procedure as the experimental group but with a nonsensical humor scale substituted for the aggressive humor scale. The following results, among others, are reported: aggressive and nonsensical humor stimuli are cathartically effective in reducing measured hostility only under anger-arousal conditions; and measured hostility scores are higher after exposure to aggressive or nonsensical humor stimuli under conditions of nonarousal of anger where aggressive humor stimuli show comparatively higher posthostility scores. **

20. Toney, K. (1973). The function of locus of control in the appreciation of aggressive humor. Unpublished doctoral dissertation, University of Massachusetts. Participants in this study were 120 male college students who—based on their scores on two scales of locus of control and one scale of aggression—were placed into the following four groups of 30 persons each: high aggression-internals, high aggression-externals, low aggression-internals, and low aggression-externals. Three instructional sets given to participants constituted the different levels of control of the outcome of the study; following this, participants rated the funniness of 60 cartoons on a ten-point scale of humor. Findings here indicate that an individual's appreciation of aggressive humor depends upon at least two factors: his level of "felt control"—the extent to which one's expectations of control are consistent with the available external control cues; and the levels of aggressive humor to which one may respond. Conclusions are that as "felt control" increases, a person is more likely to express aggressive feelings directly via a preference for highly aggressive humor material, and as "felt control" decreases, one is more likely to express aggressive feelings indirectly via a preference for only mildly aggressive humor material. **

21. Wieriman, J. (1970). A "displacement-defense" model of humor. Unpublished doctoral dissertation, The University of Texas at Austin. To test "displacement-defense" model predictions of humor response (i.e., how a person acts in becoming hostile—such as retaliatory, masochistic, or avoidant—and how this transfers to his or her enjoyment of humor—such as identifying either with the aggressor or the victim, or preferring "nonsense" humor), a miniature classroom was set up in which participants played the roles of textbook, teacher, and pupil. The variable of hostility was manipulated in pupils via the use of an unjust punishment (shock or verbal) of a teacher of the opposite sex during a "line-judging" task; response to hostility was measured via the pupil's choice to play, subsequently, either the teacher (retaliation), the textbook (avoidance), or the pupil (masochism). Later, humor ratings of jokes involving antimale, antifemale, and nonsense materials were collected. Results of this study are largely negative, and do *not* support the hypotheses based on the "displacement-defense" model; that is, "retaliators" do *not* prefer "hostile/other sex" jokes, "masochists" do *not* prefer "hostile/same sex" jokes, and "avoiders" do *not* prefer "nonsense" jokes. **

22. Williams, A. (1979). Effects of sex and sex role differences in appreciation of cross-gender aggressive humor. Unpublished doctoral dissertation, University of Georgia. Participants in this study were 122 men and women who rated the funniness of cartoons that consisted of male-to-female aggressive cartoons, female-to-male aggressive cartoons, and neutral, nonaggressive cartoons. Results indicate that—based upon participants' earlier scores on sex-role attitude scales—both "traditional" and "nontraditional" males, and "traditional" females, prefer antifemale humor; also, "nontraditional" females appreciate antifemale humor less, and antimale humor more, than the three former groups. The "intergroup-conflict" theory of humor is used to interpret these results. *

23. Ziv, A. (1987). The effect of humor on aggression catharsis in the classroom. *The Journal of Psychology, 121*, 359–364. Reports on two studies designed to measure the cathartic effects of humor on aggressive responses in adolescents (total $n = 268$): in the first study, students' aggressive responses were measured following a frustrating task; in the second study, two videotapes were shown to students—a humorous tape to some students, and a neutral tape to other students. Subsequently, a frustration test was administered a second time to students to obtain aggressivity scores. Results indicate that frustrated students who viewed the humorous videotape had lower aggression scores than did those students who viewed the neutral videotape. **

APPLICATION OF HUMOR

24. Abel, M. (1998). Interaction of humor and gender in moderating relationships between stress and outcomes. *The Journal of Psychology, 132*, 267–276. Participants were 131 women and men college students who completed self-report scales measuring perceived stress, humor, and symptomology. Results from regression analyses of this data indicate a moderating effect for humor—found only for men—between stress and anxiety; and no gender differences were found for a moderating effect of humor between stress and physical symptoms. Generally, when humor is high, there is

no relationship between stress and anxiety, or between stress and physical symptoms. *

25. Allespach-Stanley, H. (1996). The role of humor and social support in recovery from substance abuse. Unpublished doctoral dissertation, California School of Professional Psychology, Los Angeles. This study employed a correlational design having a longitudinal component in which 13 women and 18 men—who had enrolled in a substance abuse treatment program—were given two measures of humor and eight measures of social support. The dependent variable of continued abstinence included measures of urinalyses and self-reports of alcohol consumption over a 90–day period. At the end of the three-month period—depending on the scores and data collected—participants were assigned to either an "abstainers" or a "relapsers" group. Results indicate that coping humor is associated with instrumental support in substance abusers, and support for communication problems is predictive of continued abstinence, although humor in this case shows no relationship to the dependent variable. *

26. Angell, J. (1970). The effects of social success and social failure on the humor productions of wits. Unpublished doctoral dissertation, University of Nevada. Based on the scores obtained by 75 college students on a humor use questionnaire, "high" wits and "low" wits were identified and assigned to experimental and control groups. Each participant simulated a party situation with four other persons for 12 minutes; also, each participant rated the others on an interpersonal judgment scale and feedback was given concerning "social success," "mild failure," or "severe failure"; a second conversation among participants was arranged, subsequently. Observers recorded the number of "attempts-to-be-funny" (ATBF) and also recorded the time spent talking. Results indicate that "mild failure" wits had a lower ATBF rate than "severe failure" wits in the second conversation. Findings support the notion that interpersonal judgments—within a context involving the concepts of depression and anxiety about lack of approval and the interaction of such feelings with clear ("severe failure") and ambiguous ("mild failure") messages—affect the use of humor. **

27. Bentley, L. (1991). The use of humor as a stress coping mechanism for college student perceived stresses in the college environment. Unpublished doctoral dissertation, Claremont Graduate School. Participants in this study were 220 college students who completed four self-report instruments: a social readjustment scale, a situational humor response questionnaire, a coping humor scale, and a student stressor inventory. Results indicate the following: situational humor and actual stress are the highest predictors of perceived stress; college students use humor to cope with stress in the college environment; students who use situational humor have lower perceived stress; there are no gender differences between college males and females in usage of humor or in their perception of stress; and major student stressors are test anxiety, grades, girl- and boy-friend problems, and speaking in public. *

28. Bradley, M. (1972). An exploratory study of children's responses to humorous stimuli as related to health indices. Unpublished doctoral dissertation, University of Maryland. Examines the relationship between humor and physical health. Data from 30 boys and 30 girls, ages 7–11, were collected concerning their health (e.g., height, weight, motor coordination, posture, etc.) and their level of humor appreciation (e.g., responses of smile, chuckle, and laugh to a film loop humorous stimulus). Results were negative concerning a direct relationship between humor and health; however, a sex-by-age interaction for humor and health was obtained with humor as the main contributor. *

29. Brown, I. (1994). Perception of humor in cartoon riddles by adults with intellectual disability. *Perceptual and Motor Skills, 78*, 817–818. Reports findings which indicate that 30 young adults of intellectual disability (i.e., with IQs between 40 and 75) do find humor in cartoon riddles but that they most often respond to the visual aspects of the stimuli rather than to the linguistic/auditory aspects; thus, the behavior here of such individuals shows that they do not integrate visual and auditory perceptual features in optimal ways. *

30. Brueggeman, C. (1985). The effects of humor on anxiety and divergent thinking in normal and emotionally disturbed adolescents. Unpublished doctoral dissertation, California School of Professional Psychology, San Diego. Participants in this study were 144 persons: 84 "normals," and 60 "seriously disturbed emotionally," who were assigned randomly to a humorous or a nonhumorous test condition; following this exposure, participants completed a state anxiety questionnaire and a divergent thinking task. Results indicate partial confirmation of the hypotheses that humor decreases anxiety and increases divergent thinking. **

31. Bullock, M. (1983). The effects of humor on anxiety and divergent thinking in children. Unpublished doctoral dissertation, California School of Professional Psychology, San Diego. Participants were 94 boys and girls, average age of 11 years, who assigned randomly to a humorous or a nonhumorous treatment condition based on a pretest trait-anxiety level; following this treatment, participants completed a state-trait anxiety inventory and a test of divergent thinking. Results show that children exposed to humorous material have lower state anxiety compared to children exposed to nonhumorous material, and that children with low levels of trait anxiety perform better on a divergent thinking measure of flexibility but not on measures of fluency or originality. **

32. Danzer, A., Dale, J. A., & Klions, H. (1990). Effect of exposure to humorous stimuli on induced depression. *Psychological Reports, 66*, 1027–1036. Female college students ($n = 38$) were shown depressive slides involving mood statements and then assigned to one of three groups: exposure to a humorous audiotape, exposure to a nonhumorous tape, or no tape exposure/waiting control; participants' heart rate and smile/frown recordings were made during the slide and tape presentations. A "multiple affect adjective checklist"—given before and after the slide and tape presentations—showed depression induction to be successful. Results indicate that only the humor group decreased depression scores to a preexperimental baseline level, although both the humor and waiting/control groups had decreases in depression scores after the treatment; smiling responses and heart rates were elevated in the humorous treatment condition. **

33. Deaner, S., & McConatha, J. (1993). The relation of humor to depression and personality. *Psychological Reports, 72*, 755–763. Participants were 91 female and 38 male college students who completed five self-report questionnaires consisting of humor, depression, and personality scales. Results indicate that persons scoring low on the depression scale tend to score high on humor and extraversion/neuroticism personality scales. It is suggested that the personality factors of introversion and neuroticism be employed in the identification of a predisposition toward depression. *

34. Ecker, J., Levine, J., & Zigler, E. (1973). Impaired sex-role identification in schizophrenia expressed in the comprehension of humor stimuli. *The Journal of Psychology, 83*, 67–77. Three tests of sex-role identification were given to 20 female and 20 male schizophrenics, and to 10 female and 10 male "normals." Results indicate no differences between schizophrenics and "normals" on the "role preference" and "body-parts satisfaction" tests; however, on the humor test, the schizophrenics showed less comprehension of cartoons depicting persons engaged in ambiguous and/or "abnormal" sex roles than did the "normals." Moreover, the schizophrenics showed *no* such deficit in their comprehension of cartoons depicting non-sex-role or "normal" sex-role behaviors; these findings confirm the results of other studies which suggest that schizophrenics are disturbed concerning their sexual identification. *

35. Fay, R. (1983). The defensive role of humor in the management of stress. Unpublished doctoral dissertation, United States International University. Employing a correlational design, this study recorded the stress and anxiety levels of 101 adult participants; also, assessments were made of participants' appreciation of humor in relation to their ability to cope with stress. Results show that persons who are most effective in coping with life's stresses have the greatest capacity for humor appreciation, and those who are least effective in coping with stress show less ability for humor appreciation. Findings are interpreted within the psychoanalytic theory of humor which suggests that humor functions as a defense mechanism protecting the ego from internal and external stress. *

36. Fetzek, M. (1981). The impact of counselor humor on secondary students perception of facilitative conditions. Unpublished doctoral dissertation, University of Cincinnati. Participants were 54 students, grades 9 through 12, who were assigned randomly to one of three videotape groups: joke-telling hu-

mor, integrated humor, or no humor—each in a counseling interaction situation. Following viewing of the tape, participants were asked to give their perceptions of the taped counselor. Results indicate that the joke-telling condition yielded higher perceptions of regard level, congruence, and unconditional positive regard in girls but not in boys; on the other hand, the integrated humor condition increased positive perceptions in boys but not in girls. **

37. Fry, P. S. (1995). Perfectionism, humor, and optimism as moderators of health outcomes and determinants of coping styles of women executives. *Genetic, Social, and General Psychology Monographs, 121,* 211–245. Reports on four studies with 104 female executives as participants. Three studies indicate how perfectionism, humor, and optimism moderate the deleterious effects of "daily hassles" on self-esteem, burnout, and physical health. A fourth study reports on the use of different coping strategies and orientations; in one analysis, high levels of humor and optimism are associated with strategies that involve practical social support; also, in another analysis, humor is associated with existential coping orientations. *

38. Fulbright, B. (1996). The use of humor and its mediation of depression in cancer patients and primary caregivers. Unpublished doctoral dissertation, The University of North Carolina, Greensboro. Proposes a path model predicting the relationships between symptom distress, daily-living activities, humor use, and depression. Participants were 73 cancer patients and 37 caregivers who completed six self-report measures, two of which were humor scales, two were depression scales, and two were stress scales. Results from path analyses via linear regression data support the notion that humor is a mediator from cancer patient symptom distress to cancer patient depression; also, path analysis showed that humor is a mediator from cancer patient daily-living activities to cancer patient depression, but not to primary caregiver depression. *

39. Gelkopf, M., Sigal, M., & Kramer, R. (1994). Therapeutic use of humor to improve social support in an institutionalized schizophrenic inpatient community. *The Journal of Social Psychology, 134,* 175–182. In this study, two groups of 17 chronic schizophrenic patients each were compared in their functioning before and after the intensive presentation of video movies during a three-month period; the experimental group was exposed *only* to comedies, and the control group was exposed to an assortment of topics with only 15 percent comedies. Based upon data given by patients on a social support questionnaire, results indicate that humor affects the therapeutic alliance between staff and patients but it does not affect other social networks due to the regressed nature of schizophrenics' social relationships. **

40. Gibbs, F. (1996). Humor as experienced by hearing impaired women. Unpublished doctoral dissertation, The University of Arizona. Participants were nine hearing impaired women who provided over 600 statements for analysis and categorization in this descriptive and phenomenological research de-

sign. Overall results indicate that the women's perceptions of their impairment influenced their ability to experience humor. *

41. Gidynski, C. (1972). Associative shift, peer rejection, and humor response in children: An exploratory study. Unpublished doctoral dissertation, Columbia University. Examines an assumption from psychoanalytic humor theory that high levels of anxiety decrease responsiveness to tension-relevant humor; also attempts to determine the combined effects of anxiety, peer rejection, and associative shift flexibility on humor appreciation and its comprehension among preadolescent boys. Based upon cartoon ratings and self-report questionnaires concerning peer acceptance and flexibility in associative shift, results confirmed the expectation that the boys' associative shift flexibility facilitates the appreciation and comprehension of all types of humor studied. *

42. Golan, G., Rosenheim, E., & Jaffe, Y. (1988). Humour in psychotherapy. *British Journal of Psychotherapy, 4*, 393–400. Examines the responsiveness of 60 female depressive, hysterical, or obsessive patients, aged 21–49 years, to interventions by therapists in which humorous or nonhumorous materials were used. Based upon participants' reactions to the interventions, results indicate that nonhumorous types of interventions are preferred over humorous ones, and this preference depends on the relationship between type of humor used and the individual's personality type. *

43. Goldsmith, L. (1979). Adaptive regression, humor, and suicide. *Journal of Consulting and Clinical Psychology, 47*, 628–630. Based on data collected for her 1973 doctoral dissertation at The City University of New York, this researcher examines the relationship between the capacity for adaptive regression, its manifestation in humor, and the potential for suicide in a group of 31 female psychiatric in-patients. Results on self-report measures of adaptiveness, humor, and suicide potentiality show a negative relationship between suicidality and both adaptive regression and ego strength, and a positive relationship between ego strength and humor. *

44. Goldstein, J., Mantell, M., Pope, B., & Derks, P. (1988). Humor and the coronary-prone behavior pattern. *Current Psychology: Research and Reviews, 7*, 115–121. Participants in this study were 52 college students and 23 coronary heart disease patients (ages 41–80 years) who completed an activity survey, and also rated aggressive and nonaggressive jokes for funniness. Results show that hostile humor was appreciated generally over nonhostile humor across all participants, that those individuals *less* prone to coronary heart disease appreciate both hostile and nonhostile humor, and that coronary heart disease patients, Type B, prefer nonhostile humor. *

45. Golub, R. (1979). An investigation of the effect of use of humor in counseling. Unpublished doctoral dissertation, Purdue University. Participants here included 48 female volunteers (16 counselors, 16 clients, and 16 secretaries/technicians) who were shown a videotape of a simulated counselor-client session. One half of the participants in each of the three groups were shown a tape employing humor, while the other half viewed the same tape in which humor excerpts were edited out. Following this, all persons rated the tape and completed an anxiety inventory. Results showed no differences between participants' evaluations of counselors when humor was, and was not, used; anxiety was related to participants' responses both linearly and quadratically. *

46. Goodkind, R. (1976). Some relationships between humor preferences and trait anxiety. Unpublished doctoral dissertation, The University of New Mexico. Tested a model which proposed that humor is caused by the arousal of anxiety by a humor stimulus which is followed subsequently by a decrease in anxiety arousal. Participants were 100 male and female college students who initially took an ink blot test and a coping style inventory to establish baseline levels of anxiety and coping skills; later, they rated hostile, incongruous, and sexual cartoons for humor content. Results indicate a positive correlation between anxiety level and hostile humor appreciation. *

47. Goren, K. (1992). Humor use as a stress moderator: Immediate versus delayed coping with small and large events. Unpublished doctoral dissertation, Arizona State University. Participants were 262 college students who completed two measures of situational humor and a humor-use scale; they also recorded their daily television comedy viewing for two weeks. Participants' "small life-events," "large life-events," and "moods" were reported at the beginning, midpoint, and end of the study. Results show that neither situational, nor delayed, humor-use has a stress-moderating effect; also, television comedy viewing appears to be unrelated to stress. *

48. Harrison, L., Carroll, D., Burns, V., Corkill, A., Harrison, C., Ring, C., & Drayson, M. (2000). Cardiovascular and secretory immunoglobin A reactions to humorous, exciting, and didactic film presentations. *Biological Psychology, 52*, 113–126. Cardiovascular activity and secretory immunoglobin A (sIgA) in the saliva of 30 healthy graduate students were measured at rest and in response to film extracts differing in affective content. Films were classified as humorous, didactic, or exciting in content and elicited distinct patterns of cardiovascular autonomic activity. The humorous film was related to participants' reduction in beta-adrenergic drive as shown by reduced cardiac output and a lengthening of pre-ejection period. However, the sIgA secretion rate—while enhanced by exposure to the films—did not vary with film content; this finding is contrasted with previous research that reports a rise in sIgA during exposure to humorous stimuli. **

49. Hirdes, S. (1987). The use of humor and guided imagery in the enhancement of self-disclosure. Unpublished doctoral dissertation, Northern Arizona University. Based on their scores on a trait anxiety inventory, 53 female and male college students were identified as being low or high in social anxiety and assigned to a control group or to one of two treatment groups: guided imagery with humor, or humor only. Participants also gave responses on a self-disclosure questionnaire. Results show no differences in the treatment groups concerning willingness to self-disclose; however, a supplemental analysis indicated an interaction effect between gender and sexual level of self-disclosure where females were less willing than males to self-disclose sexual information. **

50. Kelly, K. (1985). Humor preference as a means of assessing children's resentment of parents. Unpublished doctoral dissertation, United States International University. Examines children's reactions to humorous cartoons whose content ranges from animal-, parental-, and child-disparagement, as well as nondisparagement/neutral, humor. Results indicate that children most enjoy humor that disparages the object of his or her resentment, specifically the parents; also, older children harbor more resentment than do younger children; moreover, the marital status of the child's parents influences resentment and its reflection through the child's humor preference. *

51. Kridler, K. (1987). The relationship of sense of humor presence and use to stress, adaptivity, pathology, and prognosis for treatment in a combined substance abuse/psychiatric hospitalized sample. Unpublished doctoral dissertation, The University of Akron. Participants in this study—44 patients from a psychiatric hospital and 66 patients from a substance abuse facility—completed a personality inventory, and two humor scales. Findings in this ex post facto study failed to show any significant relationships between humor and stress, adaptivity, pathology, and prognosis for treatment for either of the two groups of patients. *

52. Labrentz, H. (1973). The effects of humor on the initial client-counselor relationship. Unpublished doctoral dissertation, University of Southern Mississippi. Eighty male and female college students were assigned randomly to a control group or to one of three precounseling treatment groups: humor/cartoon ratings, filler/geometric design ratings, or matched time/waiting period with no prescribed activity; the control group had no precounseling treatment or waiting time. Based on data from an interviewing session and a "relationship" questionnaire, results indicate those persons receiving humor prior to the initial counseling interview tended to rate the counseling relationship higher than did those participants in the other three groups; also, a gender difference was observed in the "relationship" scores where women gave higher scores than did the men. **

53. Mager, M., & Cabe, P. (1990). Effect of death anxiety on perception of death-related humor. *Psychological Reports, 66,* 1311–1314. Reports that humor ratings differ significantly among three groups of college students ($n = 98$) who scored low, medium, and high on a "death-anxiety" scale; also, participants scoring high in death-anxiety give lower humor ratings, overall, than do the medium or low death-anxiety scorers. *

54. Maiman, J. (1977). Response to humor stimuli as a function of the obsessional defense. Unpublished doctoral dissertation, California School of Professional Psychology, Los Angeles. Based on questionnaire data from 117 female and male college students, this study supports the psychoanalytic supposition that the topics of time, dirt, and money are capable of providing a source of enjoyment via humor appreciation to obsessional persons much as sexual and aggressive humor achieve for the "normal" population. *

55. Martin, R. A., & Lefcourt, H. (1983). Sense of humor as a moderator of the relation between stressors and moods. *Journal of Personality and Social Psychology, 45*, 1313–1324. Describes three studies in which a negative-life-events checklist is used to predict stress scores on a measure of mood disturbance. Data from sense of humor measures, self-report scales, and behavioral assessments of ability to produce humor under nonstressful and stressful conditions were collected from college male and female students ($n = 159$). Results indicate that five of the six humor scales employed show a moderating effect on the relation between negative life events and mood disturbance; thus, support is given for the hypothesis that humor reduces the impact of stress in daily life. *

56. McCleary, R., & Zucker, E. (1991). Higher trait- and state-anxiety in female law students than male law students. *Psychological Reports, 68*, 1075–1078. Reports on a humor-rating task (completed by 86 students) and on the observed elevated anxiety and stress levels among preprofessional women—found to be significantly higher than those of preprofessional men—and suggests the need for stress-management interventions for law students. *

57. McCray, J. (1985). A study of relationships among text anxiety, taking academic responsibility, and humor. Unpublished doctoral dissertation, University of Missouri, Kansas City. Participants were 140 fourth- and fifth-grade students who completed inventories of test anxiety and academic locus of control, and also made ratings of other students' sense of humor. Results indicate very little relationship between perception of a child's sense of humor and the amount of test anxiety that the child experiences. *

58. Megdell, J. (1981). Relationship between counselor-initiated humor and client's self-perceived attraction in the counseling interview. Doctoral dissertation, California School of Professional Psychology, San Diego. Based upon data—from 30 clients in two alcoholism counseling agencies—that were collected via counseling sessions, ratings of counselor attraction, and ratings of counselor-initiated "shared" and "non-shared" humor, results here support the assertion that counselor-initiated humor in an initial counseling session enhances the clients' attraction for the counselor. **

59. Mueller, S. (1987). The relationship between sense of humor, life event stress, coping ability, academic aptitude, and gender in freshman college stu-

dents. Unpublished doctoral dissertation, University of Cincinnati. Participants were 58 male and 92 female college freshman students who provided
academic aptitude scores, and who also completed a situational humor scale
and a life experience survey. Results show no gender differences on sense of
humor; also, no relationships were found between sense of humor and the factors of ability to cope, stressfulness, or academic aptitude. *

   60. Murray, S. (1986). The effect of gender on the perception of therapists
who incorporate humor in psychotherapy. Unpublished doctoral dissertation,
Saint Louis University. Participants in this study were 80 female and 80 male
students at a pharmacy college who were assigned randomly to one of eight
treatment conditions involving either a humorous or nonhumorous approach
taken by an audiotaped therapist, and all possible gender combinations of therapist and client. Following exposure to a treatment condition, each participant
completed a "level of regard/relationship" scale. Results indicate no difference
between the presence versus absence of humor and the participants' perception
of the rapport created by the therapist, regardless of the participants' sex. **

   61. Napora, J. (1984). A study of the effects of a program of humorous activity on the subjective well-being of senior adults. Unpublished doctoral dissertation, University of Maryland-Baltimore Professional Schools. Employing a
quasi-experimental, pretest-posttest design, one group of senior adults engaged
in a program of mirthful activity while another group of seniors comprised a
control group; measures of "subjective well-being" were given before and after
the six-week program. Results show that seniors' mood levels elevated in the
activity condition, notably with the humorous materials; however, no support
was found for a positive association between the humorous activity and the
more enduring aspects of the construct of "subjective well-being."**

   62. Nemeth, P. (1979). An investigation into the relationship between humor
and anxiety. Unpublished doctoral dissertation, United States International
University. Seventy-five participants awaiting treatment at a hospital were divided into three groups—a "humorous silent comedy film," a "nonhumorous
film," and a "nonactivity/no film" group—and given a "before-and-after" testing on an anxiety scale. Results indicate that the "comedy film" group showed
reduced levels of anxiety in the hospital setting. *

   63. Newman, M. (1992). Does humor production moderate the effects of experimentally induced stress? Unpublished doctoral dissertation, State University of New York at Stony Brook. Forty participants high in measured trait
humor and 40 persons low in trait humor were asked to generate a humorous
monologue, as well as a serious monologue to a silent stressful film. Physiological measures were taken of the participants before, during, and after their presentations. Results show that—compared to the production of a serious
narrative—humor production is related to a lower negative affect, lower ten-

sion, and reduced physiological reactivity for both the low- and high-trait-humor groups. **

64. Newton, G. (1987). Effect of client sense of humor and paradoxical intervention on anxiety. Unpublished doctoral dissertation, The University of Nebraska-Lincoln. Participants were 53 college students—who were self-identified as "test anxious" and who were divided into "high" and "low" sense of humor groups—experienced two interviews in which they received either a "paradoxical directive" or a "nonparadoxical directive." Results based on scores from an anxiety scale, a counselor rating form, and a "clients' perceptions" rating scale indicate that participants with a low sense of humor had lower anxiety—than those with a high sense of humor—after receiving a "paradoxical directive"; also, overall anxiety was decreased in participants in both the "paradoxical" and "nonparadoxical" conditions. **

65. Nicholson, S. (1973). Relationship between certain measures of mental health and a cartoon measure of humor in fifth-grade children. Unpublished doctoral dissertation, University of Maryland. A sample size of 379 fifth grade children in 16 classrooms from 11 schools completed the following measures: a health opinion survey, a mental symptomatology test, and a humor inventory consisting of a cartoon-humor appreciation test yielding scores for aggressive, nonsensical, incongruous, and cognitive types of humor; in addition, teachers' evaluations of the students' adjustment were obtained. Results show that while there is no significant relationship between the health opinion scores and the humor inventory scores, a significant relationship was found between students' appreciation of aggressive and nonsensical humor and the teachers' ratings for "negative adjustment." *

66. Nies, D. (1982). A role of humor in psychotherapy: Reduction of dating anxiety in males. Unpublished doctoral dissertation, Fuller Theological Seminary, School of Psychology. Participants were 14 dating-anxious men assigned to one of two treatment groups: a cognitive restructuring (CR) group and a cognitive restructuring approach infused with humor group (CRH). Results based on 15 dependent variable measures show that both groups improved, including anxiety reduction; also, the CRH group showed greater improvement than the CR group on four of the dependent variables. **

67. Perlini, A., Nenonen, R., & Lind, D. (1999). Effects of humor on test anxiety and performance. *Psychological Reports, 84,* 1203–1213. Following their completion of anxiety, coping-humor, and sense of humor scales and inventories, 34 college women and 26 college men were given achievement tests under one of three conditions: low-humor, moderate-humor, or no-humor. Results indicate that humor frequency does not improve the test performance of highly test-anxious participants under either low (quiz) or high (examination) outcome-value conditions. It is suggested that the hypothesized moderating effect of item humor on anxiety-performance may be overstated. **

68. Perlman, G. (1972). The ameliorative effects of humor on induced anxiety in a black and white population. Unpublished doctoral dissertation, The University of Tennessee. Participants were black and white male college students who were subjected initially to insulting and disparaging remarks made by both black and white examiners, and then asked to rate humorous cartoons containing both black- and white-featured individuals. Results indicate that humor ameliorated feelings of anxiety and anger in participants, and was explained in terms of catharsis in which the humor tasks permitted gratification of a repressed impulse forbidden to the participant. **

69. Prerost, F. (1975). A cross-sectional investigation of coping with crowding: Humor appreciation and preferences. Unpublished doctoral dissertation, De Paul University. Participants in this study included three age groups: preadolescents, early adolescents, and young adults who were exposed to three types of jokes (aggressive, sexual, and neutral/innocent) in either high or low density/crowding situations. Results show that—contrary to prediction—greater humor appreciation occurred in the low-density condition, and no switches in humor preference occurred as a function of density. **

70. Prerost, F. (1985). A procedure using imagery and humor in psychotherapy: Case application with longitudinal assessment. *Journal of Mental Imagery, 9,* 67–76. Employs the case study method and describes the development of a "humorous imagery situation technique" for the purpose of utilizing humor in a systematic fashion during therapy. *

71. Priddy, M. (1990). The role of client sense of humor on therapeutic outcome. Unpublished doctoral dissertation, University of Southern California. Participants in this "pretest/posttest outcomes" study were 31 female and male clients who were receiving psychotherapy at a university counseling clinic, and who completed a situational humor response questionnaire. Findings were that clients with a high sense of humor spend less time in therapy as compared to clients with a low sense of humor; also, gender differences were observed where women had higher sense of humor scores than men, and women spent less time in therapy than did the men. **

72. Remington, M. (1985). Relationship between the use of humor by nursing education administrators and organizational climate. Unpublished doctoral dissertation, University of Idaho. Participants were 211 nursing program faculty members who completed a questionnaire measuring the nursing education administrator's use of humor and the program's organizational climate. Results show a significant positive correlation between the perceived use of humor by nursing education deans and department heads and a presupposed ideal level concerning organizational/work climate. *

73. Rosin, S., & Cerbus, G. (1984). Schizophrenics' and college students' preference for and judgment of schizophrenic versus normal humorous captions. *The Journal of Psychology, 118,* 189–195. Participants were 20 male hospitalized schizophrenics and 20 male college students who ranked the funniness of two sets of photograph captions that were provided previously by independent groups of college students and schizophrenics. Results indicate that the schizophrenic judges rank the schizophrenic captions as being more humorous than do the student judges, and that the student judges rank the student captions as being more humorous than do the schizophrenic judges; also, the student judges are better evaluators of "normal" humor than are the schizophrenic judges. **

74. Schienberg, P. (1979). Therapists' predictions of patients' responses to humor as a function of therapists' empathy and regression in the service of the ego. Unpublished doctoral dissertation, California School of Professional Psychology, Los Angeles. Ten female and 15 male therapists completed scales for cognitive and emotional empathy, a questionnaire for "ego-service regression," and ratings of three versions of the same set of 18 cartoons differing in rating instructions. Partial results are that therapists' ability to empathize is negatively associated with their accuracy in predicting their own patients' funniness ratings of the cartoons; also, male therapists tend to rely on cognitive empathy in making accurate predictions while female therapists employ emotional empathy. *

75. Shocket, S. (1985). The use of humor in the treatment of an anger response. Unpublished doctoral dissertation, Old Dominion University. Participants in this pretest/posttest study were 32 college psychology students who experienced anger related to driving a car, and who composed a hierarchy of driving anger scenes. In the study's experimental design, humorous imagery was compared with systematic desensitization and a no-treatment control group under the hypothesis that the treatment groups would show a greater decrease in skin conductance and self-reported anger following treatment than the control group; however, results failed to support the hypothesis. **

76. Smith, R., Ascough, J., Ettinger, R., & Nelson, D. (1971). Humor, anxiety, and task performance. *Journal of Personality and Social Psychology, 19*, 243–246. Participants were 106 female and 109 male college students who differed in test anxiety level and who were given a course exam where half of the students received a form of the exam containing one-third humorous test items, and the other half received a nonhumorous form of the same exam. Results show that high-test-anxious students who received the nonhumorous exam scored lower than did low- or moderate-test-anxious students and, also, that they scored lower than did the high-test-anxious students who received the humorous form of the exam. **

77. Stevens, G. (1986). Selected aspects of humorous interaction among elderly participants and staff caregivers in community based health support programs of the adult day care type. Unpublished doctoral dissertation, University of Maryland-Baltimore Professional Schools. In this exploratory, field methodology, and case-study investigation, data were generated via observations and interviews concerning the humorous interactions between the elderly and staff in an adult day care center. Results show that humorous interaction seems to enhance the elasticity of personal and interpersonal boundaries of the elderly. *

78. Stratil, M. (1971). A theory of philosophical humor: The effects of humor on optimism and emotional involvement. Unpublished doctoral dissertation, The University of Florida. Describes a laboratory experiment designed to test hypotheses derived from the author's theory of philosophical humor which involves the stimulus qualities of condensation, playfulness, make-believe, discovery, harm symbols, reinterpretation, and drive content. Partial results indicate that humor appreciation is positively related to emotional involvement, and adaptive regression is positively related to the effect of humor exposure on optimism but not on emotional involvement. **

79. Taubman, M. (1980). Humor and behavioral matching and their relationship to child care worker evaluation and delinquency in group home treatment programs. Unpublished doctoral dissertation, University of Kansas. Based on the observation and recording of four humor-related behaviors during dinnertime—followed by three questionnaires—at 13 group-home treatment programs for delinquent males, it was suggested that high evaluation and low delinquency are found in programs in which youths imitate the socially appropriate behaviors—such as humor responses—of teaching-parents. *

80. Thomson, B. (1985). Appropriate and inappropriate uses of humor in psychotherapy as perceived by certified reality therapists: A Delphi study. Unpublished doctoral dissertation, University of Georgia. Participants were 56 certified reality therapists who responded to four rounds of questionnaires, employing the Delphi method, and identified 243 items for inclusion in a two-section—appropriate and inappropriate uses of humor in psychotherapy—questionnaire for final rounds of the study. Based on this approach, six recommendations were offered concerning the uses of humor in reality psychotherapy. *

81. Thorson, J., & Powell, F. (1994). Depression and sense of humor. *Psychological Reports, 75,* 1473–1474. This is a follow-up on a previous study regarding the issue of the "relation of humor to depression and personality." Reports partial confirmation of a negative relationship between depression and sense of humor; it is suggested that depression decreases as sense of humor increases. *

82. Weinberg, M. (1973). The interactional effect of humor and anxiety on academic performance. Unpublished doctoral dissertation, Yeshiva University. Participants were 140 college students who were tested during one class period where two classes heard a lecture interspersed with humor, two classes heard a lecture without humor, and three classes served as controls, either hearing a lecture without examples, or no lecture at all. Following the treatment condition, rating scales of humor, anxiety, and intelligence were administered to all participants. Results indicate that low-anxious students of high intelligence benefit from humor, and high-anxious students of lower intelligence do not benefit from humor, as measured by test performance on presented material. **

83. Weise, R. (1996). Quality of life and sense of humor in college students. Unpublished doctoral dissertation, University of Maryland-College Park. Participants were 117 college students who completed three self-report scales: "quality of life," "sense of humor," and "affect balance." Results indicate a positive correlation between quality of life and sense of humor for female—but not for male—students, and also suggest that the relation of quality of life to sense of humor is mediated for women by situational happiness. *

84. Zalis, T. (1980). The incidence and role of humor in hypomanic reactions. Unpublished doctoral dissertation, Long Island University, The Brooklyn Center. Participants were 90 adults—an experimental group of 30 outpatient manic-depressives who were maintained on lithium, and a control group of 60 volunteers with no history of mania or lithium treatment. Measures were made of humor production (laughs, smiles, jokes) and depressive behavior (tears, sighs, dysphoria) occurring during interviews, and of humor appreciation via a mirth test. Among the results are that manics—while appreciating humorous stimuli—produce relatively less humor than "normal" controls, and that humor may function in a defensive/adaptive role in maintaining psychological equilibrium. *

BIBLIOGRAPHIES AND LITERATURE REVIEWS OF HUMOR

85. Berger, A. A. (1995). *Blind men and elephants: Perspectives on humor.* New Brunswick, NJ: Transaction. Employs case histories to indicate how scholars from different disciplines have attempted to describe and understand humor. Topics include: making sense of humor; humor and communication theory; philosophical approaches to humor; the techniques used in humor; semiotics, literary theory, and humor; sociological aspects of humor, a cultural theory of humor preferences; psychology and humor; and visual aspects of humor.

86. Boverie, P., Hoffman, J., Klein, D., McClelland, M., & Oldknow, M. (1994). Humor in human resources development. *Human Resource Development Quarterly, 5,* 75–91. Discusses and reviews the humor literature relating to the adult learner, including the psychological and physiological benefits of humor, the effect of humor in the educational environment, and the applications of humor in training programs.

87. Buckman, E. S. (Ed.) (1994). *The handbook of humor: Clinical applications in psychotherapy.* Malabar, FL: Krieger. Contents include a review of the literature on humor in the therapeutic setting, children's humor from a developmental perspective, the use of humor as a diagnostic tool, humor and the adolescent child, humor as a communication facilitator in couples' therapy, humor in family therapy, the technique of paradoxical intention, humor as a mental health tool for the elderly, humor as a corrective emotional experience, and the use of humor in cancer treatment. Provides a useful 29–page bibliography and index on the therapeutic use of humor.

88. Dimmer, S., Carroll, J., & Wyatt, G. (1990). Uses of humor in psychotherapy. *Psychological Reports, 66,* 795–801. Reviews various studies that indicate some uses, and potential misuses, of humor in psychotherapy, and suggests new directions for research and practical applications.

89. Evans, J. (1987). *Comedy: An annotated bibliography of theory and criticism.* Metuchen, NJ: Scarecrow Press. Contents include comic theory before 1900 (classical, medieval, Renaissance, neoclassical, 19th century), comic theory after 1900, comic literature (Greek, Roman, Italian, Spanish, French, German, English, Irish, Russian, American), and comic film and other media (including the topics of caricature, humor, laughter, jokes, parody, satire, irony, farce, fools, clowns, and tricksters).

90. Fry, W., & Salameh, W. (Eds.) (1987). *Handbook of humor and psychotherapy: Advances in the clinical use of humor.* Sarasota, FL: P.R.E. Contents include the following issues and topics: the role of humor in psychotherapy; the uses and misuses of humor in various types of psychotherapy; how to apply humor in therapy; and an historical perspective of positive and negative views of the therapeutic value of laughter and humor.

91. Fry, W., & Salameh, W. (Eds.) (1993). *Advances in humor and psychotherapy.* Sarasota, FL: P. R. E. Provides a collection of essays on humor and psychotherapy, including examples and suggestions by therapists who exhibit a wide variety of approaches, issues, and perspectives—such as gallows humor; humor as religious experience; Kierkegaardian existential implications of humor; the uses of humor with hyperaggressive patients; advantages of humor use for therapists under extremely stressful conditions; the use of the favorite-joke technique with children; Freudian notions regarding laughter and humor; and the effective integration of humor into psychotherapy.

92. Galloway, G. (1994). Psychological studies of the relationship of sense of humor to creativity and intelligence: A review. *European Journal of High Ability, 5,* 133–144. This review suggests that the relationship of sense of humor to intelligence and creativity is affected by the manner in which the relevant variables are operationalized, the characteristics of the experimental participants, and the factors concerning the broader experimental context.

93. Galloway, G., & Cropley, A. (1999). Benefits of humor for mental health: Empirical findings and directions for further research. *Humor: International Journal of Humor Research, 12*, 301–314. This literature review looks at the effects of humor on psychological conditions and examines how humor may influence mental health in beneficial ways. Discusses the relationships between humor and mental health vis-à-vis individual difference variables such as personality, gender, negative life-events experiences, and the nature of humor appreciation concerning humorous stimuli in the experimental context.

94. Haig, R. (1988). *The anatomy of humor: Biopsychosocial and therapeutic perspectives.* Springfield, IL: Thomas. Contents include the following: theories of humor; biological aspects of humor; mental disorders, mood, personal attributes, and humor; cognitive strategies, incongruity, culture, and humor; persuasion, education, therapy, and humor; paradoxical intention, child-, behavior-, cognitive-, provocative-, and natural high-therapy.

95. McGhee, P. E. (1971). Development of the humor response: A review of the literature. *Psychological Bulletin, 76*, 328–348. This review focuses on children's humor and summarizes the theoretical views and empirical findings in the psychological literature up to 1971. It discusses the methodological problems and unresolved issues that confront a developmental approach to humor research, and covers the arousal, classical psychoanalytic, and gestalt theories of humor while advancing a developmental theory of cognitive humor. Emphases in the review are placed on age and sex differences in humor responsiveness, language and children's humor, the relationship between intellectual development and children's humor, the humor of the exceptional and preschool child, the importance of the dependent variables used in research on children's humor, and the social-contextual aspects of the humor response.

96. McGhee, P. E. (1974). Cognitive mastery and children's humor. *Psychological Bulletin, 81*, 721–730. This review covers the theoretical perspectives and research concerning the cognitive aspects of children's humor, and suggests that a Piagetian approach is very promising regarding an understanding of the relationship between cognitive mastery and the child's appreciation and comprehension of humor. In particular, emphasis is placed on the operation of the principle of cognitive congruency in the development of children's humor.

97. McGhee, P. E. (1988). Introduction: Recent developments in humor research. *Journal of Children in Contemporary Society, 20*, 1–12. Presents an overview of developments in humor research from the 1970s to 1988. Bibliographies are given for three areas: conferences and books on humor, research on children's humor, and the relationship between humor and children's play activities.

98. McGhee, P. E., & Goldstein, J. H. (Eds.) (1983). *Handbook of humor research.* (Vol. 1, *Basic issues*). (Vol. 2, *Applied studies*). New York: Springer-Verlag. Summarizes the current and classical literature on laughter and humor. Literature reviews in these handbooks emphasize the theories of the nature of humor, the relationship of humor to language, cognition, and social functioning, the physiological and biological factors of humor, and the presence, use, and effects of humor in a number of settings. The books contain theoretical integrations, philosophical speculations, and methodological suggestions concerning humor and humor-related areas.

99. Muskat, L. (1989). Making magic: Verbal humor creation and individual differences. Unpublished doctoral dissertation, University of Pennsylvania. Presents a comprehensive review and critique of the psychological theories of humor, and concludes that humor research has been restricted by three issues: a lack of theoretical integration; a disproportionately large focus on humor appreciation to the neglect of the topic of humor creation/production; and a systematic bias caused by "male hegemony" that has resulted in the development of theories and methodologies that ignore individual differences.

100. Nilsen, D. (1993). *Humor scholarship: A research bibliography.* Westport, CT: Greenwood Press. This interdisciplinary reference source on humor includes material, and bibliographies, concerning the psychology of humor under the rubrics "humor and the individual," "humor, maturity, and education," and "humor theory and epistemology"; other contents are: the humor of personal interactions, language play and rhetorical devices, humor and the media, national styles of humor, humor and ethnicity, humor in mythology and religion, and humor and the fine arts.

101. Rothbart, M. (1973). Laughter in young children. *Psychological Bulletin, 80,* 247–256. Reviews research studies of laughter in children and describes a model concerning the eliciting conditions for laughter, and related, behavior in children. Proposes, generally, that laughter occurs following conditions of heightened tension or arousal when—at the same time—there is a judgment that the situation is inconsequential or is safe. Suggests that laughter serves the function of signaling to a caretaker that a particular stimulus is within the child's arousal limits.

102. Ruch, W. (Ed.) (1998). *The sense of humor: Explorations of a personality characteristic.* Berlin: Mouton de Gruyter. Contents in this book on the concept of sense of humor at a trait level include the following: a historical review of the sense of humor; theoretical issues; major new models of different aspects of the sense of humor and research on current approaches; national and group differences in sense of humor; developmental changes and intraindividual variation in sense of humor; and some causes of inter- and intraindividual differences in sense of humor. Includes a useful appendix on humor measurement tools/tests, and a very extensive bibliography on sense of humor.

103. Rutter, J. (1998). Laughingly referred to: An interdisciplinary bibliography of published work in the field of humour studies and research. *Salford Papers in Sociology, 21,* University of Salford, UK. Contains bibliographic information on the following subjects and interdisciplinary areas: age, applications, culture, ethnicity, gender, health and physical aspects, individual differences, language, media, and theory. Claims to contain over 3,700 individual references on humor across a wide range of topics—a noteworthy bibliographic effort, in my estimation, and one of the largest bibliographies on humor research in the literature; however, beware of a number of inaccuracies and incomplete entries concerning citations/authors.

104. Shaughnessy, M., & Wadsworth, T. (1992). Humor in counseling and psychotherapy: A 20-year retrospective. *Psychological Reports, 70,* 755–762. Selectively reviews the literature on humor in counseling/psychotherapy from 1970 through 1990, and discusses the topics of: the controversy regarding appropriateness/effectiveness of humor in therapy; the various modes of therapy; the need for training in the area; the definitions, guidelines, and techniques of humor in therapy; and the relevance of clinical data; a 67–item bibliography is included.

105. Solomon, J. (1996). Humor and aging well: A laughing matter or a matter of laughing? *American Behavioral Scientist, 39,* 249–271. Discusses the issues surrounding the use of humor and its positive physical, psychological, and social fitness functions; in particular, emphasis is placed on the proposition that humor helps people to age well because it provides ways of coping with losses to the aged. Includes a 97–item bibliography on the relationship between humor and aging.

106. Suls, J. (1976). Misattribution and humor appreciation: A comment on "Enhancement of humor appreciation by transferred excitation." *Journal of Personality and Social Psychology, 34,* 960–965. Reviews the misattribution-excitation transfer account of humor appreciation, and concludes that the theory of collative motivation may account for data just as well as the misattribution account of humor appreciation.

107. Svebak, S. (1974). A theory of sense of humor. *Scandinavian Journal of Psychology, 15,* 99–107. Proposes a conceptual scheme for the prediction of laughter based on the following three dimensions of the comic situation: the humorous message, the interpersonal likings, and the permissiveness towards actual laughter; the corresponding personal dispositions in this scheme depend on the habitual sensitivity to such messages, the habitual tendency to favor comical situations and persons, and the habitual need for emotional-impulse control.

108. Wicki, W. (1992). The psychology of humor: A survey. *Schweizerische Zeitschrift fur Psychologie, 51,* 151–163, Examine˜ the theories of, and research on, the psychology of humor published in the 15 years from 1978 to 1992, and describes the use of humor in education and psychotherapy, as well as covering the various functions of humor—as a regulatory mechanism in interpersonal relations, as a personality trait, and as a personal resource for coping with stress. Identifies the concept of incongruity as the fundamental cognitive principle of humor.

109. Wycoff, E. (1999). Humor in academia: An international survey of humor instruction. *Humor: International Journal of Humor Research, 12,* 437–456. Reviews the current status of humor instruction at the college level in a survey involving 34 domestic and nine foreign institutions of higher learning. In one case, it is noted that there is a widespread antipathy toward humor instruction and courses among administrators; in another case, however, it is noted that a strong majority of instructors design whole courses around the topic and focus attention on the research aspect of humor study.

110. Zillmann, D. (2000). Humor and comedy. In D. Zillmann & P. Vorderer (Eds.), *Media entertainment: The psychology of its appeal.* Mahwah, NJ: Erlbaum. Presents the major theories of humor/comedy enjoyment within a discussion of the issue of what it is that causes people to laugh, smile, chuckle, and giggle. Includes an examination of the merits of humor as an antidote for physical and emotional ailments.

COGNITION AND HUMOR

111. Barnett, L., & Kleiber, D. (1982). Concomitants of playfulness in early childhood: Cognitive abilities and gender. *The Journal of Genetic Psychology, 141,* 115–127. Participants were 92 preschool children who were rated on five components of playfulness, and then given a battery of verbal intelligence and divergent-thinking-ability tests. Results indicate gender differences with girls showing a positive relationship between play and divergent thinking, while boys show an inverse relationship between play and divergent thinking. *

112. Barron, W. (1980). The role of imaginal processing in humor. Unpublished doctoral dissertation, The University of Texas at Austin. Participants were 115 female college students who were asked to rate the funniness of two types of jokes—10 high- and 10 low-imagery, and two types of cartoons—10 captioned and 10 captionless. Among the results of this study are that participants with higher scores on visual imagery scales prefer jokes over cartoons more than those women with lower scores on the imagery scales, and that the product of funniness, surprise, and resolution ratings correlate negatively with joke recall across all participants. **

113. Brodzinsky, D. (1974). The role of conceptual tempo in the child's comprehension and appreciation of various types of cartoon humor. Unpublished doctoral dissertation, State University of New York at Buffalo. Among the results reported are that cartoons containing highly salient incongruity and/or resolution elements yield higher levels of comprehension for boys, ages 6–10 years old, than cartoons in which such structural elements are of an abstract or conceptual nature. **

114. Cooper, J., Fazio, R., & Rhodewalt, F. (1978). Dissonance and humor: Evidence for the undifferentiated nature of dissonance arousal. *Journal of Personality and Social Psychology, 36,* 280–285. Participants were 33 college students who were committed to showing counterattitudinal behavior under low- or high-choice conditions; some students first watched—and then rated—a cartoon, and also completed a posttreatment attitude measure, while other students first completed the attitude measure and then viewed the cartoon. Results indicate that the attitude and humor ratings of high-choice participants were more affected by the order-manipulation of tasks than were the ratings of low-choice participants. Results suggest that the arousal created by an induced compliance-manipulation is a general and undifferentiated state that can be attributed to any reasonable source, and question the popular notion that the arousal produced by dissonance-manipulations is intrinsically aversive. ******

115. Czwartkowski, L., & Whissell, C. (1986). Children's appreciation and understanding of humorous cartoon drawings. *Perceptual and Motor Skills, 63,* 1199–1202. Participants were 116 children, aged 4–9 years old, who rated, and explained, the funniness of five cartoons depicting each of three types of humor—incongruous, body, and aggressive. Results show that humor appreciation increases with age and types of humor; for these children, incongruous and body humor were rated higher than aggressive humor. ******

116. Deckers, L., & Salais, D. (1983). Humor as a negatively accelerated function of the degree of incongruity. *Motivation and Emotion, 7,* 357–363. Reports that as incongruity in stimulus materials increases, humor increases to some asymptotic value, after which further increases fail to produce a decline in humor—as predicted from an inverted-U relation. It is suggested that the change in incongruity accounts for the increase and subsequent decrease in humor in studies showing an inverted-U relation. ******

117. Feingold, A., & Mazzella, R. (1991). Psychometric intelligence and verbal humor ability. *Personality and Individual Differences, 12,* 427–435. Participants were 36 graduate students, 59 college students, and 52 adult volunteers (not attending school at the time) who were given a battery of cognitive tests of "verbal humor ability" and other traditional verbal tests. Results show evidence for two broad aspects of convergent humor behavior—humor *cognition* and humor *memory*—where humor cognition is more strongly related to general verbal ability than is humor memory. *****

118. Foreman, M.-L. (1981). An investigation of third graders' listening comprehension and appreciation of humorous children's literature and the effects of their reading attitudes. Unpublished doctoral dissertation, University of Georgia. Participants were 67 third-grade students (31 girls and 36 boys) who were presented with tape-recorded humorous picture books comprising nine categories of humor, and measurements of the children's attitudes and humor appreciation were recorded. Results indicate that the humor categories of exaggeration, slapstick, and the absurd are appreciated significantly more than the categories of defiance, violence, and surprise; there were *no* gender differences concerning the humor appreciation ratings of the nine categories of humor. *

119. Fox, F. (1982). Humor responses in children's reactions to a tone series. Unpublished doctoral dissertation, The Pennsylvania State University. Participants were 120 elementary school children who were tested in an experiment in which a series of tones were presented—where a final tone violated the child's auditory stimulus expectancy—and which confirmed the hypothesis that the experiencing of humor is a function of perceiving a discrepant or incongruent event in the place of an expected event. **

120. Gavanski, I. (1986). Differential sensitivity of humor ratings and mirth responses to cognitive and affective components of the humor response. *Journal of Personality and Social Psychology, 51,* 209–214. Participants were 40 male and female college students who rated, and reacted to, cartoon stimuli presented from one to five times. Results indicate that cartoon repetition reduced amusement for all participants according to self-report data; however, repetition reduced humor *ratings* only for women who received "amusement" instructions, while mirth *behavior* decreased with cartoon repetition for all participants. It is suggested that future humor studies employ both measures—humor *evaluation* scales and humor *appreciation* scales—in their methodologies. **

121. Gerber, W., & Routh, D. (1975). Humor response as related to violation of expectancies and to stimulus intensity in a weight-judgment task. *Perceptual and Motor Skills, 41,* 673–674. Participants were 60 female and male college students who judged weights in a psychophysical task that was disguised as a study of humor. Results support the incongruity theory of humor where the greater the discrepancy between a weight given to a participant and that expected, the more intense the elicited humor response. **

122. Hirt, M., & Genshaft, J. (1982). The effects of incongruity and complexity on the perception of humor. *Personality and Individual Differences, 3,* 453–455. Describes a study that examines the relationship between participants' style/preference for cognitive complexity and the influence of incongruity and complexity on humor perception. Results—based on the responses of adult women—indicate that the simpler, and less incongruous, stimulus materials (cartoons) are perceived to be the most humorous. *

123. Huffman, J. (1984). The development of humor during the sensorimotor period. Unpublished doctoral dissertation, University of Virginia. Participants were 24 infants placed into three age groups—4–8 months, 9–13 months, and 14–18 months; they were exposed to three trials of eight randomly-presented humor stimuli. Based upon judges' assessments of the infants' humor responses to the stimuli, results indicate that infants at different stages of development laugh/smile at different things, and that there is an age/stage-related developmental pattern related to sequence of infant responses to humor stimuli during the sensorimotor period of cognitive development. *

124. Johnson, A. M. (1990a). A study of humor and the right hemisphere. *Perceptual and Motor Skills, 70*, 995–1002. Participants were 130 college students who rated 32 jokes for funniness, and who also solved 14 visually displayed mental-rotation (MR) problems. Results indicate that those individuals with faster MR times tend to rate jokes as funnier than those with slower MR times—a finding that is consistent with other studies that implicate the right hemisphere in humor processing. *

125. Johnson, A. M. (1990b). Humor and the hemispheres. Unpublished doctoral dissertation, University of Missouri—Columbia. Based upon the responses of 126 college students to a "style of thinking/learning" scale and a humor appreciation scale, this study reports the following results: speed of mental rotation predicts humor ratings which indicates that right hemisphere input and spatial ability are involved in humor processing; men prefer sexual and aggressive humor while women prefer subtle verbal humor; and gender differences in humor ratings may arise partly from differences in lateralized cognitive functions. *

126. Jones, J. M. (1970). Cognitive factors in the appreciation of humor: A theoretical and experimental analysis. Unpublished doctoral dissertation, Yale University. Reports on a series of experiments designed to aid in the development of a model of the cognitive aspects of humor enjoyment, to develop a methodology for experimental investigations of theoretical notions derived from the model, and to show empirical relationships between elements in the model and humor responses. In general, the model proposes that the core of humor consists of an incongruity that is constructed in the participant—in this case, in grade-school children. **

127. Klein, A. (1983). Concept development in relation to humor comprehension and humor appreciation in kindergarten children. Unpublished doctoral dissertation, Boston University School of Education. Results based upon the testing of 59 kindergarten children's humor comprehension and humor appreciation indicate that a majority of the children fully comprehended, and were able to resolve, the comic incongruity presented to them; these data fail to support theories which hypothesize that young children have little awareness of the information needed to resolve comic incongruity. *

128. Knowles, A., & Nixon, M. (1989). Children's comprehension of expressive states depicted in a television cartoon. *Australian Journal of Psychology, 41*, 17–24. Describes three experiments that examine children's (ages 6–13 years old) comprehension of expressive states as presented on television programs. Partial longitudinal results indicate that accuracy in labeling expressive states is stable—over a period of two years—in children of 6–10 years. It is suggested that the poor comphrehension of television often seen in young children may be attributed to their inability to identify correctly the program's discrete elements—such as the characters' expressions. **

129. Kuiper, N., McKenzie, S., & Belanger, K. (1995). Cognitive appraisals and individual differences in sense of humor: Motivational and affective implications. *Personality and Individual Differences, 19,* 359–372. Describes two studies that examine how sense of humor relates to persons' cognitive appraisals. Results indicate that more humorous persons change their perspective more often—than nonhumorous persons—for stressful events; also, higher levels of task motivation and positive affect are found in individuals with a greater sense of humor. *

130. Madden, T. (1982). Humor in advertising: Applications of a hierarchy of effects paradigm. Unpublished doctoral dissertation, University of Massachusetts. Describes an experiment employing a 2 x 2 x 3 factorial design—two products (new versus mature), two program contexts (humorous versus nonhumorous), and three commercials (product-related humor, product-unrelated humor, and nonhumor). Each college-level participant was exposed to one of 12 experimental treatments and his or her attention, comprehension, retention, product attitude, and reaction to the commercial were recorded. Overall results are supportive of the use of humor in advertising, and suggest that advertising messages should be compared in terms of persuasion itself and not the separate cognitive factors which comprise persuasion. **

131. Mahony, D., & Mann, V. (1992). Using children's humor to clarify the relationship between linguistic awareness and early reading ability. *Cognition, 45,* 163–186. Participants were 48 second-grade children who were tested on various "phoneme/morpheme" and "control" riddles. Results show that reading ability is related to correct resolution of the "phoneme/morpheme" riddles, but not to correct resolution of the "control" riddles. It is suggested that while intelligence is related to the resolution of riddles in general, reading ability has a special relation to riddles that manipulate morphemes and phonemes, a notion that is consistent with the morphophonological structure of English. *

132. Merz, K. (1979). Cognitive set and humor appreciation. Unpublished doctoral dissertation, Indiana University. Attempts to confirm and expand an experiment conducted by Goldstein, Suls, and Anthony (1972) concerning the influence of cognitive set, or salience, on participants' preferences for humor stimuli; present results fail to confirm those found in the Goldstein et al. study. ** [Note: For the Goldstein et al study, see "Enjoyment of specific types of humor content: Motivation or salience?" in J. H. Goldstein & P. E. McGhee (Eds.), *The psychology of humor.* New York: Academic Press, 1972: pp. 159–171.]

133. Middleton, D. (1986). The effect of actor-observer perspective differences on the ability to perceive humor: An attributional analysis. Unpublished doctoral dissertation, California School of Professional Psychology, Los Angeles. Reports data that support the hypothesis that persons form different attributions about the causes of funny and non-funny cartoons, and that an attributional perspective shift occurs to help the individual comprehend and appreciate humor that requires incongruity resolution. **

134. Mollica, M. (1984). Paradox recognition: A proposed common cognitive process between creativity and humor. Unpublished doctoral dissertation, De Paul University. Based upon the responses of college students on humor and creativity measures, this study reports that—contrary to other published results in the literature—there was no significant relationship between humor and creativity. It was concluded that neither "paradox recognition" nor any other cognitive process could be confirmed as a common factor underlying both creativity and humor. *

135. Nerhardt, G. (1970). Humor and inclination to laugh: Emotional reactions to stimuli of different divergence from a range of expectancy. *Scandinavian Journal of Psychology, 11*, 185–195. Describes an experiment that confirms the hypothesis—based on the incongruity theory of humor—that the experience of humor, and the inclination to laugh, is a function of the divergence of a perceived stimulus set from an expected set, using lifted weights as stimuli. **

136. Nerhardt, G. (1975). Rated funniness and dissimilarity of figures. *Scandinavian Journal of Psychology, 16*, 156–166. Describes three experiments that tested successfully the hypothesis that the perceived funniness of a stimulus (involving combinations of two moving, successive, nonrepresentational figures projected onto two screens) is a function of the divergence from expectancy in regard to the stimulus as a member of different classes. **

137. Owens, H., & Hogan, J. (1983). Development of humor in children: Roles of incongruity, resolution, and operational thinking. *Psychological Reports, 53*, 477–478. Participants were 87 grade-school children who gave responses to five cartoons and nine jokes in a study designed to test a two-stage model of humor appreciation. Results failed to confirm the model; comprehension of humorous material was related to grade-level and conservation ability, but neither of these factors related to humor appreciation. *

138. Perry, A. (1982). Influence of problem solving and creative thinking ability on production and appreciation of humor. Unpublished doctoral dissertation, Fordham University. Participants were 233 adolescents who were given problem-solving, creativity, and ambiguity-tolerance tasks, as well as humor appreciation and humor production tests. Multiple regression analyses of the data yielded the conclusion that while problem-solving ability is a necessary condition in the prediction of appreciation of incongruity-resolution humor, it may not be a sufficient condition. *

139. Rouff, L. (1973). The relation of personality and cognitive structure to humor appreciation. Unpublished doctoral dissertation, Bryn Mawr College. Participants were 117 college students who rated a set of 20 cartoons—differing in factors such as incongruity and emotional salience—on four humor scales involving the variables of surprise, centrality, offensiveness, and funniness. Results show that participants' humor comprehension scores are negatively related to dogmatism scales, and positively related to creativity scores; such findings—among others reported here—support the general hypothesis that individuals differing in aspects of cognitive structure and personality respond in predictable ways to humor materials. *

140. Schwager, I. (1983). The relationship between operational level and children's comprehension, appreciation, and memory for cognitive humor. Unpublished doctoral dissertation, City University of New York. Eighty children, ages 6–12, were presented with jokes based on class-inclusion and weight-conservation discrepancies, and their expressive and evaluative appreciation and comprehension of the humor was recorded. Results of this study provide partial confirmation of the hypotheses that operational level is predictive of humor comprehension, appreciation, and recall of humor materials. **

141. Scragg, M. (1984). The effects of prosody and humor on ambiguity awareness in preadolescent children. Unpublished doctoral dissertation, Wayne State University. Participants in this experiment were 90 sixth-grade students who were asked to give their impressions of various sentences differing in prosodic cues, ambiguity, and humor content. Results indicate that humor has a potentially facilitative effect on students' emerging language capabilities in ambiguity-detection at syntactic levels. **

142. Shammi, P., & Stuss, D. (1999). Humour appreciation: A role of the right frontal lobe. *Brain, 122,* 657–666. Participants were 21 patients, aged 18–70 years old, who had focal damage in various parts of the brain, and 10 non-damaged controls. In response to humor stimuli—and as compared with the controls—patients with damage to the right frontal lobe showed the most disrupted ability to appreciate humor, and they also demonstrated less physical and emotional (e.g., smiling and laughter) responsivity. **

143. Shirley, R., & Gruner, C. R. (1989). Self-perceived cynicism, sex, and reaction to gender-related satire. *Perceptual and Motor Skills, 68,* 1048–1050. Reports that men and women college students ($n = 137$) show no gender differences in the understanding, or appreciation, of sex-related satires. *

144. Shultz, T. R. (1970). Cognitive factors in children's appreciation of cartoons: Incongruity and its resolution. Doctoral dissertation, Yale University. Reports on two experiments designed to test predictions based on a structural theory of humor that involves factors of incongruity and resolution. Results based on data from grade-school children indicate that there is a tendency for the child first to identify an incongruity in cartoons and then to make an attempt to resolve the incongruity in each of the humor stimuli. **

145. Suls, J. (1973). In search of a reduction of inhibitions or discounting cue in attitude attribution. Unpublished doctoral dissertation, Temple University. Reports on three experiments designed to examine how observers use provided information concerning whether an actor is drunk, upset, or telling a joke. Among the findings are that drunken behavior is given less weight than sober behavior (thus supporting a "discounting cue" hypothesis); and that humor does *not* function as a reduction of inhibitions cue. **

146. Tait, P. (1986). Visual impairment, verbal humor, and conservation. *The Journal of Genetic Psychology, 147*, 107–111. Describes the behavior of 51 visually impaired and 51 sighted children, aged 7–15 years old, on joke-comprehension and conservation of weight tasks. Results indicate that although age and intelligence level influence joke comprehension, the ability to conserve is not a significant factor. It is suggested that the issue of cerebral hemispheric specialization be considered when studying the language and cognitive abilities of visually impaired children. *

147. Tsang, S. (1981). Irony of ironies: Interfacing vicarious superiority and interactive incongruity humour theories. Unpublished doctoral dissertation, University of Windsor-Canada. Participants in this study were 256 college students who were assigned randomly to one of eight experimental conditions involving various combinations of relationships (friend versus enemy), degree of realism (realistic versus unrealistic), and degree of insult (extreme versus mild). The findings of this study provide a link between the vicarious-superiority humor theory and the interactive-incongruity humor theory; one result is that participants correctly do perceive an extreme insult as more insulting than a mild insult—yet when the extreme insult is paired with a friendly relationship and an unrealistic assigned attribute, the persons' judgments are reversed, and in this way, theoretically, persons may believe themselves to be amused at their own expense. **

148. Waxler, M. (1976). The role of ambiguity and ambiguity tolerance in the appreciation of humor. Unpublished doctoral dissertation, University of Maryland. Participants were 124 college students who rated the funniness of 50 randomly ordered uncaptioned cartoons that had been judged previously on the basis of degree of ambiguity. Results *failed* to confirm the following hypotheses: the more ambiguous the humor materials are, the greater is the perceived funniness of the materials; the more ambiguity-intolerant that participants are, the greater is the perceived funniness of "equally" ambiguous humor materials; and the amount of ambiguity in humor materials and the degree of ambiguity-intolerance of participants combine to produce a heightened perceived funniness. *

149. Westburg, N. (1999). Hope and humor: Using the Hope Scale in outcome studies. *Psychological Reports, 84*, 1014–1020. Participants were 80 college students who were assigned randomly to one of four treatment conditions (two "humor condition" groups that were given a sorting task involving the funniness of comics, and two "control" groups that sorted neutral stimuli involving geometric shapes) in a pretest/posttest procedure designed to assess the Hope Scale. Results indicate that scores on the Hope Scale do not differ from pretest to posttest, and the Hope Scale seems to be a suitable measure to use in conducting outcome studies in clinical/research settings without having to control for possible sensitization from a pretest. **

150. Whitt, J. (1976). Cognitive and affective factors in children's development of humor enjoyment and comprehension. Unpublished doctoral dissertation, The University of Texas at Austin. Reports results—based on riddle-enjoyment data from 90 boys at kindergarten, second-, and fourth-grade levels—that support the following hypotheses: comprehension of logical incongruity riddles increases with grade-level; and enjoyment of logical incongruity riddles increases relative to illogical incongruity appreciation as a function of grade-level. *

151. Wicker, F., Barron, W., & Willis, A. (1980). Disparagement humor: Dispositions and resolutions. *Journal of Personality and Social Psychology, 39*, 701–709. Participants were 66 female college students who rated written "retaliation" jokes on a funniness scale and on eight other scales. Partial results show that jokes with disliked victims are rated as both funnier and higher in resolution than are jokes with neutral or liked victims; results support a proposed synthesis of disparagement theories with incongruity-resolution theories of humor appreciation. **

152. Wierzbicki, M., & Young, R. D. (1978). The relation of intelligence and task difficulty to appreciation of humor. *The Journal of General Psychology, 99*, 25–32. Participants were 165 male college students who viewed cartoons in each of two conditions: captioned cartoons that were rated for funniness, and selection of one of four captions with rating of the combination for funniness. Results indicate that participants' intelligence quotient is related positively to cartoon comprehension, and that both positive and negative relationships between cartoon appreciation and task difficulty depend on how task difficulty is defined. **

153. Wilson, T. D., Lisle, D., Kraft, D., & Wetzel, C. (1989). Preferences as expectation-driven inferences: Effects of affective expectations on affective experience. *Journal of Personality and Social Psychology, 56*, 519–530. Presents a pilot study and two experiments based on a model which asserts that affect and emotion are formed often in an expectation-driven fashion. Results indicate that when the value of a stimulus is consistent with an affective expectation, individuals form evaluations of cartoons relatively rapidly. **

154. Winchell, D. (1977). Children's humor and the acquisition of qualitative identity. Unpublished doctoral dissertation, Arizona State University. Based upon the responses of school children, aged 4–6 years old, on the measures of cartoon comprehension, cartoon funniness ratings, and spontaneous mirth responses, results indicate that the most incongruous cartoons produce the maximum humor appreciation. *

155. Wolosin, R. (1975). Cognitive similarity and group laughter. *Journal of Personality and Social Psychology, 32*, 503–509. Laughter in groups of female and male college students was examined as a function of cognitive similarity of group members. Based on the behavior of group members in telling one another funny stories, jokes, and anecdotes, it was found—for male participants—that groups containing a greater number of dyads that were cognitively similar yielded more frequent laughter than the groups containing fewer cognitively similar dyads. It is suggested that laughter in informal groups is associated with communication efficiency. **

HUMOR AS COMEDY/JOKES/PUNS/RIDDLES/SATIRE/IRONY

156. Alford, R. (1979). Humor, and the structures of responsibility and play. Unpublished doctoral dissertation, University of Pittsburgh. Following a review of the humor literature, this study describes a cross-cultural survey of humor in 75 preindustrial societies. Among the topics discussed are the structure of responsibility activity, play activity, and humor (the perception of a non-serious violation of salient expectations); also, the relation of humor to social structure and culture is examined, including the emergence of comic specialists and the range of cultural variation in humor expression. *

157. Dews, S., Kaplan, J., & Winner, E. (1995). Why not say it directly? The social functions of irony. *Discourse Processes, 19*, 347–367. Describes three experiments in which participants rated examples of irony. Findings show that ironic comments are rated as more amusing than literal-type comments; also, when irony is directed at one's poor performance, it may protect the individual's esteem by softening the criticism. **

158. Dupont, R. (1981).Thematic factors in children's enjoyment and comprehension of humor. Unpublished doctoral dissertation, The University of Texas at Austin. Participants were 60 children, ages 8–11 years old, who were assigned to one of three groups (constricted, normal, and impulsive) based on their earlier responses to aggressive/frustrating situations. Results from data on the children's appreciation and comprehension of riddles show that affective factors, such as an aggressive theme in riddles, influence the appreciation and comprehension of such riddles. **

159. Fouts, G., & Burggraf, K. (1999). Television situation comedies: Female body images and verbal reinforcements. *Sex Roles, 40,* 473–481. Examines 28 prime-time television situation comedies concerning the factors of female body weight and verbal behaviors concerning females' weight. Concludes that a combination of modeling the "thin ideal" and the verbal reinforcements associated with such modeling in the comedies may affect young female viewers and put them at risk for developing eating disorders. *

160. Fouts, G., & Burggraf, K. (2000). Television situation comedies: Female weight, male negative comments, and audience reactions. *Sex Roles, 42,* 925–932. Analyzes 18 prime-time television situation comedies concerning the issues of females' body weights, the negative comments made by males on the programs, and audience reactions/laughter following the negative comments. Results show that the situation comedies typically present derogatory remarks by males about heavier women's weights and bodies in a context in which such behavior is reinforced by audience reactions/laughter. *

161. Gruner, C. R. (1988). Prior attitude and perception of satirical theses. *Perceptual and Motor Skills, 67,* 677–678. Describes data from 90 college students concerning their attitudes about government power and labor unions. Results indicate that students' prior attitude is not independent of their ability to recognize a thesis regarding the "work rule" satire; also, it is suggested that prior attitude, ability to perceive satiric theses, and persuasion by satire are variables that interact differently according to the satire topic. *

162. Gruner, C. R. (1989). A quasiexperimental study of the effect of humor preference and other variables on understanding/appreciation of editorial satire. *Psychological Reports, 65,* 967–970. College student participants ($n = 42$) gave their humor preference (philosophical versus nonsense), and other personal data, on seven variables, and then evaluated three satirical editorials, including giving a rating of the funniness of each satire. Results show that students' funniness/interestingness scores support the notion of a general factor of "appreciation of satire" by college students. *

163. Gruner, C. R. (1990). "Humor style" and understanding of editorial satire. *Perceptual and Motor Skills, 71,* 1053–1054. Participants were 106 college students who completed a "humor style" scale and also evaluated three editorial satires. Results indicate that separate ratings of the funniness and interestingness of satires are related and, thus, give evidence of a general factor of "satire appreciation" in college students. *

164. Gruner, C. R. (1996). Appreciation and understanding of satire: Another quasi-experiment. *Psychological Reports, 78,* 194. Participants were 85 college students who provided data on a sense of humor questionnaire as well as giving their assessments of three satirical editorials. Results show that sense of humor is *not* correlated with understanding of the satires; however, the measures of "funniness" and "interestingness" of the satires were related positively. *

165. Gulbranson, B. (1972). Audience response during the performance of comedy in relation to tempo and delivery of initial comic lines. Unpublished doctoral dissertation, Columbia University. Describes a study in which the first third of a play was directed at two different tempos, with the actors receiving different instructions in the two situations. Results show that a decrease in tempo during the first third of the play is associated with an increase in the number/loudness of audience responses throughout the play. *

166. Heilbronn, L. (1986). Domesticating social change: The situation comedy as social history. Unpublished doctoral dissertation, University of California, Berkeley. Examines every situation comedy which aired on a network between 1947 and 1982, and outlines the various subgenres of the comedies. Such analyses provide a record of what issues the public finds most problematic and for which the most comic relief is required. *

167. Hunt, J., & Pollio, H. (1995). What audience members are aware of when listening to the comedy of Whoopi Goldberg. *Humor: International Journal of Humor Research, 8,* 135–154. Participants were 200 college students who gave responses to four comedy routines by Whoopi Goldberg consisting of taboo and nontaboo material presented in both nonnarrative and narrative styles. Results indicate that listeners make a distinction between two modes of comic routine: one centering on present experience via nonnarrative style, and another centering on imaginary contexts via narrative routines. *

168. Lampert, M. (1989). The appreciation and comprehension of ironic humor from nine to eighteen. Unpublished doctoral dissertation, University of California, Berkeley. Participants were fourth-, eighth-, and twelfth-graders who were given stories to evaluate in which a protagonist's unsuspecting nature towards some unseen event was portrayed throughout—and revealed at the end of—the story. Partial results show that twelfth-graders are more likely than fourth- and eighth-graders to explain their amusement at a protagonist's remarks by stating that they knew something the protagonist did not and, thus, indicate recognition of dramatic irony; twelfth-graders also showed appreciation for both verbal and situational irony. *

169. Leslie, L. (1986). Audience perceptions of five types of radio humor. Unpublished doctoral dissertation, The University of Tennessee. Participants were 160 adults who rated 15 humorous radio segments, as well as the announcer's delivery style, in which humorous themes included sexual, ethnic, political, alcohol, and body type issues. Results show that liking of the announcer's style related highly to appreciation of each of the five humor types; gender was significant in ethnic humor, and age was significant in humor containing sexual, ethnic, or alcohol themes. *

170. Lippman, L., & Dunn, M. (2000). Contextual connections within puns Effects on perceived humor and memory. *Journal of General Psychology, 127* 185–197. Participants were high school and college students who judged 2 "Tom Swifties" in which the variables of pun and context were manipulated Results indicate that the punning relationship is responsible mainly for the per ception of humor and cleverness, as well as greater memory strength. It is sug gested that a coherent context facilitates humor appreciation in more lengthy forms of punning (e.g., "shaggy dog" stories). **

171. Longobardi, P. (1975). Comprehension of joke humor in schizophre nia. Unpublished doctoral dissertation, The University of Wisconsin—Madi son. Participants were 32 patients diagnosed as schizophrenic who were exposed to two kinds of humorous materials (double-meaning verbal jokes and other verbal "control" jokes). Results show that the schizophrenics have more accurate understanding of double-meaning jokes than of either control jokes o nonjoke control items; also, they do not differ significantly from normal partic ipants on double-meaning jokes, thus suggesting that schizophrenics are no deficient globally in humor comprehension. **

172. Medoff, N. (1979). The avoidance of comedy by persons in a negative affective state: A further study in selective exposure. Unpublished doctoral dis sertation, Indiana University. Female and male adult participants were placed in neutral, failure, and failure-plus-insult conditions and then given the oppor tunity to view privately a television comedy program differing in high-ridicule or low-ridicule content. Results indicate that participants in the fail ure-plus-insult condition avoided viewing comedy that was high in ridicule. **

173. Park, R. (1977). A study of children's riddles using Piaget-derived defi nitions. *The Journal of Genetic Psychology, 130*, 57–67. Participants were 8 kindergarten and grade-school children, aged 5–14 years old, who gave inter action data concerning the structure, function, and content of riddles; riddle categories were based on Piaget's three general reasoning classes of logical causal, and psychological relations. Results show that a cogni tive-developmental view of children's humor evolves in which riddles are re garded as a form of cognitive organization and adaptation following a stage-type development. *

174. Powell, J. (1975). Ego involvement: A mediating factor in satirical per suasion. Unpublished doctoral dissertation, The University of Florida. Partici pants were 220 college students who were assigned to one of three treatmen groups: experimental-direct, experimental-satirical, or control, and given satir ical-content, or nonsatirical, materials for evaluation. Partial results indicate that the element of satire is susceptible to distortion on the basis of selective perception, and that satirical treatment is more effective than direct treatment in inoculation against counterpersuasion. **

175. Shade, R. (1989). A comparison of response to and comprehension of verbal humor between gifted students and students from the general population. Unpublished doctoral dissertation, University of Northern Colorado. Participants were 120 gifted and "normal" fourth-, sixth-, and eighth-grade students who gave mirth responses and comprehension ratings to riddles, jokes, puns, satire selections, and nonhumorous items. Results show that the gifted students have higher mirth response and comprehension scores than the general population of students, especially on the pun and satire items. *

176. Verstaendig, J. (1984). The retention of jokes as it relates to defensive style, joke type, and joke disguise. Unpublished doctoral dissertation, St. John's University. Participants were 80 young adults, aged 18–35 years old, who were exposed to, and tested on retention of, sexual, aggressive, and neutral jokes; they also gave scores on a scale measuring defensive styles of repression and sensitization. Results indicate that participants retained significantly more neutral jokes than either sexual or aggressive jokes, and that one's defensive style seems *not* to be a critical factor in retention of humorous material. *

177. Yalisove, D. (1975). The effect of riddle-structure on children's comprehension and appreciation of riddles. Unpublished doctoral dissertation, New York University. Describes two studies in which participants were 554 children in grades 1–10 who provided, and responded to, riddles. Results led to a proposed three-stage model of comprehension and appreciation of riddles in which stage 1 reflects the child's orientation toward silly and what appears silly is considered funny; stage 2 indicates that the child attempts to justify a riddle's answer at all costs without acknowledging the incongruity of the riddle; and stage 3 shows that the child can acknowledge the riddle's incongruity and also appreciate the resolution of the riddle. *

HUMOR AS LAUGHTER AND WIT

178. Arthur, R. (1974). A serious look at laughing and smiling. Unpublished doctoral dissertation, The University of Tennessee. Describes the development of a reliable method of oscillographically showing observer scorings of televised individuals laughing and smiling to discrete punch lines by comedians in the context of group laughter. *

179. Beckerman, D. (1995). What's so funny? A test of Freud's theory of wit. Unpublished doctoral dissertation, California School of Professional Psychology at Berkeley/Alameda. Participants were 65 male and female college students who rated two matched cartoon sets—containing harmless, low aggressive, and high aggressive themes—for funniness, one before and one after an intervening task. Results indicate that the high aggression cartoons are most affected by the experimental condition in which participants rate the same set of cartoons in terms of underlying aggressive content, following an initial funniness rating of those same cartoons—thus supporting Freud's model of wit. **

180. Carey, C. (1993). Mature humor or immature wit? The interaction effects of laughter, humor production, humor appreciation, and defensive coping strategies on emotional and physical stress symptoms. Unpublished doctoral dissertation, University of Maryland, College Park. Participants were 2,000 employees of a university who were surveyed on an emotional coping scale to assess laughter and humor production, and a stress mediators inventory to measure mature coping and immature defense strategies. Partial results show that men score higher than women on three components of humor, that humor appreciation and laughter—but not humor production—are related to emotional stress, that those participants with higher humor scores have lower stress scores, and that those participants with high demand, and low control, jobs have higher stress scores. *

181. Claiborne, J. (1971). A Freudian theory of laughter. Unpublished doctoral dissertation, The University of Tennessee. Analyzes wit into a component of tendency that corresponds to psychological inhibitions, and a component of technique that corresponds to autistic thought styles. According to the gestalt principle of confusion of sources, the shift from inhibition of tendency to expression of it, and the shift from reality-orientation to autistic thinking, leads—via a combination of the two—to the potential release of surplus cathexis in the form of laughter.

182. Grumet, G. (1989). Laughter: Nature's epileptoid catharsis. *Psychological Reports, 65,* 1059–1078. Describes laughter as a symbolically triggered release mechanism that unleashes instinctive drive energies related to survival and, in the process, lowers personal anxiety. Suggests that the ability to laugh, much like other adaptive behavioral traits, may have evolved in response to environmental stresses and favors reproduction among those individuals who adapt successfully; laughter is viewed as a mechanism for maintaining emotional homeostasis amidst the demands and repressions of an increasingly complex world.

183. Harris, C., & Christenfeld, N. (1997). Humour, tickle, and the Darwin-Hecker hypothesis. *Cognition and Emotion, 11,* 103–110. Participants—in a study designed to examine the proposition that laughter induced by tickle and by humor share common underlying mechanisms—consisted of 72 college students who were tickled before and after viewing comedy and control videotapes. Findings indicate *no* evidence that comedy-induced laughter increased subsequent laughter to tickle or that ticklish laughter increased subsequent laughter to comedy material. **

184. Kerrigan, J. (1983). The perceived effect of humor on six facilitative therapeutic conditions. Unpublished doctoral dissertation, The University of Arizona. Participants were 72 college students who viewed, and rated, six excerpts illustrating different levels of humor use in psychotherapy. Results of the ratings—based on the dimensions of empathy, warmth, respect, genuineness, concreteness, and self-disclosure—indicate that only the dimension of respect yielded significant differences across humor levels. *

185. McCarthy, J. (1980). An exploratory investigation of the appreciation of humor and hostile wit among adolescents with emphasis on psychoanalytic conceptualization. Unpublished doctoral dissertation, University of Massachusetts. Participants were 90 junior and senior high school students who rated the funniness of humor and hostile wit cartoons, and who also gave scores on personality adjustment and intelligence measures. Partial results show that adolescents prefer hostile wit to humor, that hostile wit presenting a woman as the butt of aggressive/insulting joking is preferred to hostile wit presenting a man in this same role, and that—for humor—cartoons presenting a man using light-hearted jest to overcome a stressful situation is preferred to humor presenting a woman in this same role. *

186. Schneyer, B. (1981). Mothering is a ticklish situation, or the contributions of a sense of humor to mothering. Unpublished doctoral dissertation, The Union for Experimenting Colleges and Universities. Participants were five women and their young children who provided data regarding audible laughter and various maternal behaviors via the methods of naturalistic observation, in-depth interviews, and projective testing. Results support the assumption that humor serves as an adaptive mechanism in the developmental process of separation-individuation; also, the mothers who had the most and least interest in humor demonstrated, respectively, the most and least effective parenting. *

187. Speier, H., & Jackall, R. (1998). Wit and politics: An essay on laughter and power. *The American Journal of Sociology, 103,* 1352–1401. This essay includes material from a wide range of epochs and societies in analyzing the intricacies, uses, and paradoxes of wit in various levels of political relationships. Among the topics covered are the following: wit as a weapon; the element of surprise; the uses of nonsense; the laughter of both the weak and the mighty; jokes in totalitarian regimes; and death and wit. A recurrent theme is the presence of similar forms of political humor and joking across different centuries and different societies.

188. Svebak, S. (1974). Three attitude dimensions of sense of humor as predictors of laughter. *Scandinavian Journal of Psychology, 15,* 185–190. Describes a theory of sense of humor that distinguishes between three dimensions of a comical situation and the related personality equivalents: "sensitivity to humorous messages"; "personal likings of comical situations," and "need for emotional control." Participants were 25 female and male college students whose laughter in an entertainment situation was observed and recorded. Results indicate that laughter in men is predicted by the "personal likings" variable, and in women by the "need for emotional control" variable. *

INDIVIDUAL AND GROUP DIFFERENCES IN HUMOR

189. Andonov, N. (1973). Differential humor response by two generations. Unpublished doctoral dissertation, California School of Professional Psychology, Los Angeles. Participants were 43 fathers, 33 sons, and 11 daughters who gave responses on an intelligence test and a humor test. Results indicate a significant difference in the response to selected categories of humor between the older and the younger groups; also, the younger generation has a significant preference for "sick humor," the "generation-gap" humor is viewed as funnier by the older generation, and the "nonsense" type of humor is appreciated equally by the two generations. *

190. Barrick, A. (1986). Aging and emotion: Ratings of cartoons and the survey of the quality of life of adult men and women. Unpublished doctoral dissertation, Ball State University. Participants were 61 noninstitutionalized men and women, and 93 male and female college students who completed a quality-of-life survey, and gave ratings of 38 cartoons for funniness, pain, and hostility content. Results show that cartoon ratings of aged males are higher on negative emotion than are those of younger males, and for positive emotion, males give higher cartoon ratings than do females. *

191. Bennett, P. (1982). Humorous children's literature and divergent thinking. Unpublished doctoral dissertation, University of South Florida. Participants were 144 fifth-grade students who gave reactions to children's literature passages regarding humorous and nonhumorous material, low- and high-divergent passages, and routine, dramatic, and taped readings of the passages. Partial results indicate that listening to humorous literature does *not* lead to significantly higher divergent responses in the children than does listening to nonhumorous literature. **

192. Bleakley, M. (1977). The effect of the sex of the main character in selected mystery, humor, and adventure stories on the interest and comprehension of fifth-grade children. Unpublished doctoral dissertation, University of Colorado at Boulder. Participants were 540 fifth-grade students, each of whom read one selected short story (involving adventure, mystery or humor content) and responded to corresponding interest and comprehension measures. Partial results show a significant reader/sex by main character/sex interaction on the interest measure with boys preferring stories with male main characters and girls preferring stories with female main characters; also, mystery stories are most interesting to children, followed by adventure and humor stories. **

193. Borges, M., Barrett, P., & Fox, J. (1980). Humor ratings of sex-stereotyped jokes as a function of gender of actor and gender of rater. *Psychological Reports, 47,* 1135–1138. Participants were 108 college students who rated the humor of 30 disparaging jokes depicting gender-stereotypic behaviors. Results show that both sexes rated jokes as *less* humorous when men blundered in female roles than in their "appropriate" male roles, but even *more* humorous when women blundered in male roles than in their "appropriate" female roles. *

194. Boyer, J. (1981). The relationship among personality, sex, and humor appreciation. Unpublished doctoral dissertation, Georgia State University. Participants were 168 female and male college students who gave responses on a personality inventory and also rated their humor appreciation of 40 sexual, aggressive, nonsense, and disparaging jokes. Results confirm the psychoanalytic notion that persons who exhibit less superego control prefer sexual humor and, thus, allow more direct impulse expression; however, this hypothesis was not supported regarding aggressive humor. *

195. Breme, F. (1975). Humor and its relationship to needs. Unpublished doctoral dissertation, University of Missouri—Columbia. Participants were 276 college students who gave measures of their humor preference and needs. Results indicate the presence of gender differences in humor preferences as well as in need patterns. *

196. Brodzinsky, D., & Rubien, J. (1976). Humor production as a function of sex of subject, creativity, and cartoon content. *Journal of Consulting and Clinical Psychology, 44,* 597–600. Participants were 168 female and male college students who were categorized as high or low in creativity, and were asked to produce humorous captions to cartoons containing aggressive, sexual, or neutral themes. Results indicate that creativity is related positively to humor production, and that men generate funnier captions than do women to sexual and aggressive cartoons but not to neutral-theme stimuli. *

197. Bruner, M. (1987). The effects of humor, creative problem solving, and relaxation on divergent thinking. Unpublished doctoral dissertation, Mississippi State University. Based on the results of a 2 x 3 factorial study involving three treatments (exposure to humor, creative problem solving, and relaxation), participants who were presented with creative problem solving tasks scored significantly higher on a creativity-thinking test than did participants presented with humor or relaxation conditions. **

198. Cantor, J., Bryant, J., & Zillmann, D. (1974). Enhancement of humor appreciation by transferred excitation. *Journal of Personality and Social Psychology, 30,* 812–821. Participants were 120 female and male college students who were exposed to humorous communications after reading one of four written communications varying in positive or negative hedonic tone, and high or low excitatory potential. Results indicate that under conditions of both positive and negative hedonic tone, previous exposure to highly arousing communications is related to higher funniness ratings of later-presented cartoons/jokes than is previous exposure to lesser-arousing communications. **

199. Carroll, J. (1989). Changes in humor appreciation of college students in the last twenty-five years. *Psychological Reports, 65,* 863–866. Participants were 79 college students who were given a humor test of personality that was

developed in 1963. Results show *no* differences between men and women regarding their humor appreciation scores; however, when compared with a sample from the 1963 population norms, college students of both sexes appear to
have changed in humor appreciation during the last 25 years on factors such as
gruesomeness, low anxiety, theatricalism, evasion of responsibility, and aggression toward women *

200. Cassell, J. (1974). Relation of threat of personal disablement to reactions to humor stimuli and attitudes toward disabled persons. Unpublished doctoral dissertation, University of Kansas. Participants were 162 college students
who were separated into three groups (high, medium, low) according to their
scores on an "attitudes-toward-personal-disability" scale; also, equal numbers
of persons from each of the three groups were assigned to one of three experimental (disability-related stress, nondisability stress, and nonstressful) conditions. Following the experimental manipulations, participants rated the
funniness of cartoons. Results give tentative support for the hypothesis that humor serves to reduce anxiety; also, disabled humor elicits differing reactions
from persons who differ in their level of "threat of personal disability." **

201. Clabby, J. (1977). Humor as a preferred activity of the creative and humor as a facilitator of learning. Doctoral dissertation, University of Southern
Mississippi. Participants were 180 college students who were given a creativity
test, and a "quick word" test, and who also were exposed to a task involving humorous cartoons. Partial results show that "low-creative experimental" participants recognize more humorous captions than nonhumorous captions; also,
humor does not seem to help either "low-creative experimental" or
"high-creative experimental" students in an incidental learning task. *

202. Connelly, M. D., & Kronenberger, E. (1984). Effects of sex and serial
position on appreciation of humor. *Psychological Reports, 55*, 499–502. Participants were 100 female and male college students who rated the funniness of
a series of 20 jokes—in which one "target" joke was placed at various positions
in the series. Results show that the position of the "target" joke in the series does
not affect its humorousness rating. **

203. Couturier, L., Mansfield, R., & Gallagher, J. (1981). Relationships between humor, formal operational ability, and creativity in eighth graders. *The
Journal of Genetic Psychology, 139*, 221–226. Participants were 117
eighth-graders who completed two tests of humor, two creativity tests, and one
formal-operations test. Results support the hypothesis that the understanding
of verbal humor (word-play and jokes) is associated with the attainment of for-
mal-operational thinking ability. *

204. Cupchik, G., & Leventhal, H. (1974). Consistency between expressive
behavior and the evaluation of humorous stimuli: The role of sex and
self-observation. *Journal of Personality and Social Psychology, 30*, 429–442.
Describes two experiments in which 150 college men and women were partici-

pants and who rated the funniness of cartoons under canned-laughter and no canned-laughter conditions, and under informal-set and formal-set conditions. Results indicate that feedback from mirth reactions (via canned laughter) directly influences funniness ratings in female, but not in male, participants; also, support is given for the hypothesis that making participants (especially the women) aware of their mirth—by asking them to self-observe and rate their own smiling and laughing—reduces the mirth reactions' influence upon evaluations of funniness. **

205. Deckers, L., Kuhlhorst, L., & Freeland, L. (1987). The effects of spontaneous and voluntary facial reactions on surprise and humor. *Motivation and Emotion, 11*, 403–412. Describes two studies—a correlational design with 61 college students and an experimental design with 128 college student participants—dealing with the relationship between facial reactions and surprise/humor ratings as suggested by the facial feedback hypothesis. Results show a positive correlation between participants' spontaneous facial reactions and their funniness ratings for 36 cartoons; however, in the experimental portion of the study, surprise and funniness ratings vary with facial reactions but are unaffected when those reactions are voluntarily amplified or inhibited. It is suggested that facial reactions may only correlate with emotional experience, and present experimental data do *not* support the facial feedback hypothesis. **

206. Deckers, L., & Ruch, W. (1992). Sensation seeking and the Situational Humour Response Questionnaire (SHRQ): Its relationship in American and German samples. *Personality and Individual Differences, 13*, 1051–1054. Participants were 206 United States and 159 German college students who completed a sensation-seeking scale and a humor scale. Results show that in both groups all sensation-seeking subscales and the total scale correlate positively with the humor scale; the "thrill and adventure-seeking" scale gave the highest correlation. *

207. Derks, P., & Hervas, D. (1988). Creativity in humor production: Quantity and quality in divergent thinking. *Bulletin of the Psychonomic Society, 26*, 37–39. Participants were 38 college students who produced humorous captions for still pictures from old movies. Results show that average caption funniness improves with output order, and indicates—in a task involving divergent responses—that quantity can lead to quality. *

208. Dienstbier, R. (1995). The impact of humor on energy, tension, task choices, and attributions: Exploring hypotheses from toughness theory. *Motivation and Emotion, 19*, 255–267. Participants were 81 female and male college students who were assigned randomly to watch a video of a comedy routine or to watch a nonhumorous control video analyzing the comedy routine; participants also engaged in a boring/proofreading task and completed a moods-checklist and an entertainment-preference scale. Results show that the humor condition is associated with increases in feelings of energy but not of tension; other results confirm hypotheses derived from toughness theory. **

209. Doyle, P. (1988). Effect of gender, sex role, aggression, and socioeconomic status on cartoon humor perception of male and female college students. *Dissertation Abstracts International, 48 (10–A)*, 2578. Participants were 150 male and female college students who were given a cartoon test composed of male-disparaging, female-disparaging, and neutral cartoons, a sex-role inventory, an aggression scale, and a "social position" index. Results indicate that all students rate female-disparaging and neutral cartoons as funnier than male-disparaging cartoons; the assumption that women and men would prefer humor disparaging the opposite sex over humor disparaging their own sex was not supported. *

210. Duffey, N. (1983). The relationship between women's self-concepts and sex-role orientations and disparagement humor appreciation. Unpublished doctoral dissertation, Texas Tech University. Participants were 214 college female students who completed several self-concept, and sex-role orientation, measures. Partial results indicate that both high- and low-self-identity, and low social self-concept, women appreciate opposite-sex disparagement jokes significantly more than they do self-disparagement jokes. *

211. Elders, M. (1989). An investigation of the expression and appreciation of humor and hostile wit and ego identity status in male and female college students. Unpublished doctoral dissertation, Columbia University. Participants were 176 college students who gave appreciation, production, and creation of humor scores. Partial results show that there are significant differences between the sexes in the appreciation and production of humor and hostile wit where men are more appreciative of hostile wit and women are more appreciative of humor. *

212. Ellsworth, J. (1985). The perception of cartoon humor as a function of depressive and aggressive personality types. Unpublished doctoral dissertation, Saybrook Institute. Participants were 60 adult men and women who were divided equally into groups according to gender and personality type (aggressive, depressed, and control), and were given a mirth-response test. Findings suggest that depressed persons have significantly lower humor appreciation ratings than aggressive or control participants, and that the control individuals have significantly higher humor ratings than the other two groups; no significant gender differences were observed. *

213. Erickson, J. (1977). A study of the verbal productive humor of preschool children. Unpublished doctoral dissertation, University of Illinois at Urbana-Champaign. Participants were 28 male and female preschool children who provided productive humor data within a naturalistic observation research design. Based upon a total of 552 samples of productive humor, a taxonomy of verbal productive humor was generated and included three types ("prescribed format"—riddles, jokes, knock-knocks; "spontaneous"—teasing or sarcastic wit, joking wit, idiosyncratic one-liners; and "drawing" humor). *

214. Fine, G. A. (1975). Components of perceived sense of humor ratings of self and other. *Psychological Reports, 36,* 793–794. Participants were 120 college students who rated themselves and their same-sex best friend on sense of humor, and several other humor-related measures. Results indicate that the sense of humor ratings are high for both self and one's best friend; one's own sense of humor is determined mostly by the quality of the jokes one appreciates, while the best friend's sense of humor is determined by the quality of the jokes that he or she tells. *

215. Forabosco, G., & Ruch, W. (1994). Sensation seeking, social attitudes, and humor appreciation in Italy. *Personality and Individual Differences, 16,* 515–528. Participants were 148 male and female adult Italians who completed a humor test, a sensation-seeking scale, and a conservatism scale. Partial results indicate that funniness of incongruity-resolution humor correlates positively with the factors of conservatism, age, and female sex, and negatively with sensation-seeking; funniness of nonsense humor correlates positively with experience-seeking, sensation-seeking, and male sex, and negatively with conservatism; and funniness of sexual humor correlates positively with the factors of male sex, disinhibition, boredom susceptibility, and toughmindedness. *

216. Franzini, L. R. (1996). Feminism and women's sense of humor. *Sex Roles, 35,* 811–819. Participants were 175 college women who completed various humor, and women's attitudes, scales, as well as providing self-ratings concerning their attitudes on women's issues, their own sense of humor, and how often others typically laugh at their humor. Results show that there are significant positive correlations between the humor scale and the participants' perception of their own sense of humor and how often others laugh at their humor. It is concluded—based on other data and results in this study—that there is no relationship between feminism/attitudes toward women and sense of humor. *

217. Friedman, H., Tucker, J., Tomlinson-Keasey, C., Schwartz, J., Wingard, D., & Criqui, M. (1993). Does childhood personality predict longevity? *Journal of Personality and Social Psychology, 65,* 176–185. Participants were 1,178 children from a larger sample that was studied originally in the Terman Life-Cycle Study from 1921 to 1986, and on whom personality, health, and longevity data were available. Results based on analyses of variables representing major dimensions of personality indicate that conscientiousness in childhood relates to survival in middle to old age; also, contrary to prediction, the trait of cheerfulness (optimism and sense of humor) is inversely related to longevity. *

218. Gallivan, J. (1991). Is there a sex difference in lateralization for processing of humorous materials? *Sex Roles, 24,* 525–530. Participants were 120 female and male college students who rated the funniness of 35 monaurally presented comedy excerpts, with half of the participants receiving input to each ear. Results *fail* to confirm previous findings in which women rate items funnier with left-ear input, while men give higher ratings with right-ear input. **

219. Gilbert, C. (1977). Humor, creativity, conceptual tempo, and IQ in first grade children. Unpublished doctoral dissertation, University of Oregon. Participants were 112 male and female first-graders who completed creative-thinking, familiar-figures, cartoon, and intelligence tests. Partial results show that there is no relationship between humor appreciation and creativity, but there is a significant relationship between humor comprehension and creativity; also, "reflective" children have the greatest comprehension of humor, as well as demonstrating the most creativity. *

220. Grote, B., & Cvetkovich, G. (1972). Humor appreciation and issue involvement. *Psychonomic Science, 27,* 199–200. Participants were 36 female college students who were involved personally with women's rights issues, and who were exposed to one of the experimental conditions (relevant humor, nonrelevant humor, nonhumorous material). Results—based on a behavioral measure of participant's change in personal involvement with the relevant issue, and on subjective evaluations—show that the women appreciate the relevant humor but do not experience decreased involvement with the women's rights theme. It is suggested that the intellectual appreciation of humor may occur in the absence of emotional or cognitive reinterpretation of the material; findings confirm the notion that simple distraction may be a key variable in reducing issue involvement following humor. *

221. Grove, M., & Eisenman, R. (1970). Personality correlates of complexity-simplicity. *Perceptual and Motor Skills, 31,* 387–391. Participants were 61 college students who completed a battery of personality measures, and some of whom were exposed to an authoritarian speech as a treatment condition. Results show that—although the authoritarian speech does *not* influence humor preferences—the personality correlates of complexity-simplicity preferences are consistent with previous research. **

222. Hampes, W. (1992). Relation between intimacy and humor. *Psychological Reports, 71,* 127–130. Participants were 103 college students who completed measures of psychosocial development/intimacy and a situational humor response questionnaire. Results show that high-intimacy students have higher humor scores than low-intimacy students. It is suggested that humor helps people succeed in intimate relationships because it allows them to deal with the stress occurring within those relationships. *

223. Hampes, W. (1993). Relation between humor and generativity. *Psychological Reports, 73,* 131–136. Participants were 56 college students who completed measures of psychosocial development/generativity, and two humor tests. Results show that students scoring high on generativity (i.e., promoting the welfare of other people) score significantly higher on both measures of humor (situational and coping humor) than those students scoring low on generativity. *

224. Hehl, F.-J., & Ruch, W. (1990). Conservatism as a predictor of responses to humour. III. The prediction of appreciation of incongruity-resolution based humour by content saturated attitude scales in five samples. *Personality and Individual Differences, 11,* 439–445. Participants were 663 male and female adults—including school teachers and college students—who comprised five samples and who completed a battery of attitudes-scales, conservatism scales, and a humor test. Results confirm the notion that appreciation of the incongruity-resolution structure in humor is mainly related to the dimension of conservatism and is the main factor in the attitude domain. *

225. Henkin, B. (1984). The appreciation of cartoon humor: Effects of sex differences and selected personality characteristics. Unpublished doctoral dissertation, St. John's University. Participants were 120 college students who rated the humor of six sexual, six aggressive, and six absurd cartoons; there were two identical sets of sexual and aggressive cartoons with only the genders of cartoon "aggressors/victors" and "objects" reversed. Results show that there are no differences in humor appreciation between men and women and, contrary to reference-group theory predictions, there is no difference between men's and women's appreciation of male- and female-oriented humor. **

226. Honeycutt, J., & Brown, R. (1998). Did you hear the one about?: Typological and spousal differences in the planning of jokes and sense of humor in marriage. *Communication Quarterly, 46,* 342–346. Describes the results of a survey/questionnaire dealing with humor in marriage and showing a 66% response/return rate—containing a sample of 76 matched-pair husband/wife married couples. Results indicate support for the hypothesis that gender differences in telling jokes in marriage reflect husbands *telling* jokes with wives reinforcing the jokes by *laughing* at the jokes; thus, the notion is reinforced via data in this study that humor is primarily a masculine trait in marriage while humor appreciation is a feminine trait. *

227. Ingrando, D. P. (1980). Sex differences in response to absurd, aggressive, pro-feminist, sexual, sexist, and racial jokes. *Psychological Reports, 46,* 368–370. Participants were 100 college students who completed a questionnaire containing 30 jokes to be rated and 20 biographical items. Results—contrary to previous studies—show no significant differences between the sexes on use of humor and on feminist attitudes. *

228. Jaffe, J. (1995). Age-related changes in comprehension and appreciation of humor in the elderly. Unpublished doctoral dissertation, California School of Professional Psychology, San Diego. Participants were 92 older adults, ages 60–89, who rated 12 jokes differing on three dimensions: incongruity, incongruity-resolution, or nonjoke control; they were given, also, a battery of cognitive-ability tests. Partial results show that there are appreciation differences among types of jokes, but there is no interaction with age; also, support is given for the cognitive-congruency theory of humor where humor appreciation increases with age, while humor comprehension decreases. *

229. Johnson, A. M. (1992). Language ability and sex affect humor appreciation. *Perceptual and Motor Skills, 75,* 571–581. Participants were 126 male and female college students who completed a humor appreciation scale and 20 trials on a word-recognition task using a divided visual field condition. Results indicate that greater liking for specific types of humor are associated with basic language abilities; also, data support the notion of sex differences in humor preferences. However, it is concluded that there is *no* evidence that hemispherically lateralized language abilities interact with sex in predicting appreciation of various types of humor. *

230. Kelly, F. D., & Osborne, D. (1999). Ego states and preference for humor. *Psychological Reports, 85,* 1031–1039. Participants were 77 male and female college students who gave scores on a sense of humor inventory and on an ego states scale. Results indicate that the "critical parent" ego state has a strong negative evaluation of nonsense humor, the "free child" and "adapted child" ego states are strong predictors of negative evaluation of ethnic humor; and the "critical parent" and "adapted child" ego states are the strongest predictors of positive preference for sexual humor. *

231. Knutson, R. (1988). Political partisanship, ideological identification and rhetorical community: Attitudes and preferences in the use of political humor. Unpublished doctoral dissertation, University of Minnesota. Examines the attitudes surrounding the use of political humor via small and large survey sample methods of data collection, and that give evidence for the proposition that political humor may be used to identify and describe groups of political partisans; it is concluded that attitudes and preferences for political humor differ with political partisanship and ideological identification. *

232. Kuiper, N., Martin, R. A., & Dance, K. (1992). Sense of humour and enhanced quality of life. *Personality and Individual Differences, 13,* 1273–1283. Participants were 39 college students who completed a battery of humor tests, social role-related and life experiences measures, and positive/negative affective measures. Overall results give empirical support for the notion that greater humor facilitates a more positive orientation towards life. *

233. Lachance, A. (1972). A study of the correlation between humor and self-concept in fifth-grade boys and girls. Unpublished doctoral dissertation, University of Maryland. Participants were 119 fifth-grade children who wrote humor booklets that were collected and categorized according to three humor themes: taboos, hostility, and sophistication; also, a self-concept test was given to all participants. Partial results indicate that *no* significant relationships occur between a positive self-concept score and humor events relating to the sophistication theme, and *no* significant relationships between a low self-concept score and humor instances relating to the taboo theme; also, boys report a higher proportion of hostility themes/items than do girls. *

234. Lammers, H. B. (1991). Moderating influence of self-monitoring and gender on responses to humorous advertising. *The Journal of Social Psychology, 131*, 57–69. Participants were 111 female and male college students who gave their reactions to a new advertisement in a 2 x 2 x 2 factorial design (high versus low self-monitoring; humorous versus serious advertisement; men versus women). Results indicate that self-monitoring interacts significantly with audience gender in moderating responses to advertising. **

235. Masten, A. (1982). Humor and creative thinking in stress-resistant children. Unpublished doctoral dissertation, University of Minnesota. Participants were 93 fifth- to eighth-grade children who provided three aspects of humor scores via cartoons (appreciation-mirth-funniness ratings, generation, and comprehension), as well as divergent-thinking, competency, stress, and intelligence scores. Results show that divergent-thinking is related to competence, primarily via shared variance with intelligence, and that divergent-thinking and humor are related beyond shared variance with intelligence. *

236. McGhee, P. E. (1973). Birth order and social facilitation of humor. *Psychological Reports, 33*, 105–106. Participants were 64 college students who viewed cartoons either alone/individually or with four other persons in a group. Results indicate that first-borns have greater humor appreciation in the group situation, while later-borns find the cartoons funnier in the individual-viewing situation. **

237. McGhee, P. E., & Duffey, N. (1983). Children's appreciation of humor victimizing different racial-ethnic groups: Racial-ethnic differences. *Journal of Cross-Cultural Psychology, 14*, 29–40. Participants were 281 children, ages 3–6 years old, who were from varied racial-ethnic and socioeconomic backgrounds, and who responded to the funniness of a series of drawings—differing in racial-ethnic content—accompanied by a story. Results provide support for the identification/disposition theory of humor, and suggest that as soon as children begin to develop a strong positive sense of racial-ethnic identity, they are likely to find greater enjoyment in seeing other racial-ethnic groups disparaged in some way rather than in seeing their own group disparaged. **

238. McGhee, P. E., & Grodzitsky, P. (1973). Sex-role identification and humor among preschool children. *The Journal of Psychology, 84*, 189–193. Participants were 17 three- to five-year-old boys who gave responses on the "It Scale" and were shown drawings of children engaged in sex-appropriate, or inappropriate, behavior whose outcome was either positive or negative. Results show that inappropriate and negative outcomes are viewed as funnier than appropriate and positive ones; also, when inappropriate positive outcomes are pitted against appropriate negative ones, the boys who choose the former as funnier than the latter are those individuals with higher sex-role identity scores. **

239. McGhee, P. E., & Lloyd, S. (1982). Behavioral characteristics associated with the development of humor in young children. *The Journal of Genetic Psychology, 141,* 253–259. Participants were 60 children, ages 38–75 months old, who provided laughter-frequency data, as well as data on behavioral and verbal attempts to initiate humor, during observed free play sessions in a university child development center. Results indicate that the amount of time spent in *social* play accounts for the greatest amount of variance in amount of laughter, and humor initiation, shown by the child; only limited support is given for the notion that humor rechannels aggressive behavior into more socially-acceptable forms of behavior. *

240. Medanich, C. (1973). The effects of arousal and sex guilt upon judgments of sex-relevant humor by males and females. Unpublished doctoral dissertation, Baylor University. Participants were 72 male and female college students who completed a sex guilt scale and then viewed one of three films whose sexual content served to elicit changes in arousal; following this, participants rated the degree of humor of 12 cartoons. Partial results indicate that low sex guilt persons rate the cartoons as being more humorous than do the high sex guilt individuals after the presentation of each film. **

241. Menahem, S. (1976). The effect of role playing on the creation of humor. Unpublished doctoral dissertation, United States International University. Participants were 120 college students who gave scores on creativity, cartoons, and remote-associations tests presented in a pretest/posttest design, and they also reacted to a role-playing-instructions condition. Results indicate that role-playing instructions have a significant effect in stimulating creativity as measured by the cartoons test. **

242. Michalowski-Bragg, K. (1977). A test of Maslow's hypothesis regarding self-actualization level and philosophical humor preference. Unpublished doctoral dissertation, United States International University. Participants were 304 female and male adults who completed a personal-orientation inventory, a demographic information sheet, and a humor test. Results indicate that there is *no* significant difference in the philosophical humor preferences of high and low self-actualizing individuals. *

243. Mones, A. (1974). Humor and its relation to field dependence-independence and open mindedness-closed mindedness. Unpublished doctoral dissertation, Long Island University. Participants were 60 college students working in 30 dyad units on a problem-solving task designed to elicit the spontaneous creation of verbal and nonverbal humor; also, measures were taken concerning the speed of humor comprehension that involved the realignment of scrambled cartoon sequences. Results give support for the conceptualization of a two-stage model of humor that involves both perceptual analysis and perceptual synthesis. *

244. Moran, C., & Massam, M. (1999). Differential influences of coping humor and humor bias on mood. *Behavioral Medicine, 25,* 36–42. Participants were 32 male and female social work college students who provided mood-scale, and sense-of-humor scale, data. Partial results indicate that mood is altered significantly in a negative direction after exposure to sad cartoons; also, coping humor is associated with less negative mood ratings after exposure to sad cartoons, and humor bias is associated with more positive mood ratings after exposure to humorous cartoons; it is suggested that attentional bias toward humor serves as a protective psychological mechanism by helping the individual focus on mood-enhancing environmental stimuli. The study includes a useful 42–item references section. **

245. Myers, S., Ropog, B., & Rodgers, R. P. (1997). Sex differences in humor. *Psychological Reports, 81,* 221–222. Participants were 136 college students who completed two self-report scales with reference to their general use of humor in their lives. Results show that men report a greater frequency of attempts at humor than do women, that such attempts are perceived by men as more effective than those perceived by women, and that men use humor for negative affect more often than do women. *

246. Nevo, O. (1985). Does one ever really laugh at one's own expense? The case of Jews and Arabs in Israel. *Journal of Personality and Social Psychology, 49,* 799–807. Describes two studies in which 390 Jewish and Arab male high-school participants rated the funniness of different jokes, as well as producing humor, with either a Jewish butt or an Arab butt in the content. Partial results indicate that Jews prefer jokes with an Arab butt, as do Arabs who feel positively toward Israel (but not those Arabs whose attitude is negative); in the humor production task, both Jews and Arabs express more aggression toward an Arab butt; also, Jews tend to use a kind of self-aimed humor in which aggression is turned inward but the situation is denied and the participant finds a humorous way to benefit from it. **

247. Newman, J. (1986). Perceptions of aging in an older sample: Life satisfaction, evaluations of old age, and responses to cartoons about old people. Unpublished doctoral dissertation, The University of Arizona. Participants were 86 community residents, aged 53–85 years old, who gave responses on life satisfaction, and attitudes-toward-aging, scales, as well as making ratings of aging-related cartoons. Results show that all participants rate cartoons which portray a negative view of aging as less funny, and more negative, than cartoons which portray a more ambivalent view of aging. *

248. Neyhart, M. (1991). Motivational and cognitive components of self-presentation in humor and embarrassment: A multi-measure approach. Unpublished doctoral dissertation, University of New Hampshire. Describes

three studies—employing different methodologies—that examine the role of situational variables and personality factors on participants' feelings of threat and their response time to complete self-directed humorous or embarrassing situations. Partial results show that participants take longer to complete embarrassing than humorous situations, take longer to complete humorous situations when they are with high-threat women and low-threat men, and that they perform fewer reversals when they are with low-threat women. **

249. Ofman, P. (1988). Effects of sexual and aggressive subliminal stimulation on response to sexual and aggressive humor. *Dissertation Abstracts International, 48 (7–B),* 2105. Reports on an unsuccessful attempt to employ subliminal psychodynamic activation to raise the unconscious sexual and aggressive motivation of male college students involving a limericks-rating task. **

250. Olson, J. (1992). Self-perception of humor: Evidence for discounting and augmentation effects. *Journal of Personality and Social Psychology, 62,* 369–377. Participants were 60 college women who read two equally funny sets of jokes where a laugh track was played in their headphones for one of the two sets. Although the laugh track had no impact on participants' mirth, they were told that it would facilitate, inhibit, or not affect their laughter and smiling. Results show that participants who were told the laugh track *increased* mirth spent the most time reading the book whose jokes were *not* accompained by laughter—a discounting effect, whereas participants who were told the laugh track *decreased* mirth spent the most time reading the book whose jokes were accompanied by laughter—an augmentation effect; other participants who were told that the laugh track does *not* affect mirth spent an equal amount of time reading each of the two books. **

251. Parisi, R., & Kayson, W. (1988). Effects of sex, year in school, and type of cartoon on ratings of humor and likability. *Psychological Reports, 62,* 563–566. Participants were 80 college students who rated cartoons for funniness and likability. Results show that *Far Side* cartoons are funnier and more likable than *Family Circus* cartoons, and that men are more extreme in their ratings of cartoons than are women. *

252. Pearson, P. (1983). Personality characteristics of cartoonists. *Personality and Individual Differences, 4,* 227–228. A personality questionnaire was mailed to members of the Cartoonists Club of Great Britain; out of 180 members, 62 returned "usable" surveys. Results show that scores on psychoticism and neuroticism scales are higher for the cartoonists than for those individuals in the normal population. *

253. Powell, L., & Kitchens, J. (1999). Sex and income as factors associated with exposure to jokes about the Clinton-Lewinsky controversy. *Psychological Reports, 84,* 1047–1050. Participants were 800 registered voters in Missouri who were surveyed via a telephone interview consisting of 55 questions regarding state and local issues, and including a question about the number of jokes heard by the participant concerning the Clinton sex scandal. Results show that men report hearing more jokes on the issue than do women, and that voters in higher income brackets heard more jokes than those individuals at middle- or lower-income levels. *

254. Prerost, F. (1980). Developmental aspects of adolescent sexuality as reflected in reactions to sexually explicit humor. *Psychological Reports, 46,* 543–548. Participants were 180 male and female adolescents—representing early-, middle-, and late-adolescent groups—who rated the funniness of sexual-humor cartoons. Results show that age, gender of participant, and sexual content explicitness of humor material are significant factors influencing adolescents' enjoyment of sexual humor. **

255. Prerost, F. (1993a). Presentation of humor and facilitation of a relaxation response among internal and external scorers on Rotter's scale. *Psychological Reports, 72,* 1248–1250. Participants were 80 male and female college students who were categorized as internal or external in orientation on the locus of control dimension, and who were measured for relaxation following exposure to humorous or nonhumorous materials. Results show that internal scorers demonstrate enhanced relaxation during subsequent biofeedback measurements. **

256. Prerost, F. (1993b). The relationship of sexual desire to the appreciation of related humor content and mood state. *Journal of Social Behavior and Personality, 8,* 529–536. Participants were 180 female college students who were categorized as expressing either high- or low-sexual desire, who were angered or nonangered, and who rated the humor of sexual, aggressive, or neutral jokes. Results indicate that high-sexual-desire women enjoy sexual humor and have a positive mood state after being angered, while low-sexual-desire women remain in a hostile mood state. **

257. Pustel, G., Sternlicht, M., & Siegel, L. (1972). The psychodynamics of humor, as seen in institutionalized retardates. *The Journal of Psychology, 80,* 69–73. Participants were 60 mildly mentally retarded institutionalized adolescents and adults who were asked to tell a joke to the interviewer. Results indicate that the participants prefer jokes that unconsciously reflect motives of irreverent rebelliousness; it is suggested that the humor of such retarded participants represents—psychodynamically—a striving for compensatory superiority due to feelings of lack of self-possession. *

258. Rubin, J. (1983). Levels of creativity and feedback and their relation to the creation of humor. Unpublished doctoral dissertation, Hofstra University. Participants' scores on a creativity test, their reactions to random feedback on it, and their scores on a mood questionnaire lead to the conclusion in this study that a social context adds to the enjoyment of humor independently of joke funniness; also, data suggests that different types of humor may elevate differentially mood states—a finding that has implications for the psychological treatment of affective disorders. *

259. Ruch, W. (1988). Sensation seeking and the enjoyment of structure and content of humour: Stability of findings across four samples. *Personality and Individual Differences, 9*, 861–871. Participants were 448 male and female German college students who comprised four separate samples, and who completed personality questionnaires and different versions of a humor test. Partial results show that "experience-seeking" and "boredom susceptibility" are predictive of low appreciation of humor in which the punch line is mildly surprising and the surprise overcome by incongruity resolution; also, "disinhibition" is correlated with funniness and low aversiveness of sexual humor. *

260. Ruch, W., Busse, P., & Hehl, F.-J. (1996). Relationship between humor and proposed punishment for crimes: Beware of humorous people. *Personality and Individual Differences, 20*, 1–11. Participants were 68 male college students who served as judges and stipulated what punishments would be proper for various crimes on a list of criminal acts; they also completed scales of humor appreciation, dogmatism, conservatism, and intolerance of ambiguity. Partial results indicate that funniness of incongruity-resolution humor relates positively with minimum and maximum punishments imposed. *

261. Ruch, W., & Carrell, A. (1998). Trait cheerfulness and the sense of humour. *Personality and Individual Differences, 24*, 551–558. Participants were 414 American and German male and female adults, and college students, who completed the "state-trait cheerfulness" inventory, as well as a sense of humor scale. Results show that "trait cheerfulness" accounts for most of the variance in the sense of humor scales with "trait seriousness" and "bad mood" accounting for other incremental variance. It is suggested that affective and mental factors and qualities be separated and distinguished in attempts to conceptualize fully the construct of sense of humor. *

262. Ruch, W., & Hehl, F.-J. (1983). Intolerance of ambiguity as a factor in the appreciation of humour. *Personality and Individual Differences, 4*, 443–449. Participants were 134 male German college students who completed an "intolerance of ambiguity" questionnaire, a conservatism scale, and a sense of humor test consisting of 120 jokes covering three joke types (incongruity-resolution, sexual, unsolvable incongruity/nonsense). Partial results indicate that "intolerant" participants prefer jokes whose incongruity is solvable, while rejecting the nonsolvable nonsense type of jokes. *

263. Ruch, W., & Hehl, F.-J. (1986). Conservatism as a predictor of responses to humour. II. The location of sense of humour in a comprehensive attitude space. *Personality and Individual Differences, 7*, 861–874. Participants were 115 female and male German college students who completed four conservatism scales/questionnaires, a "values" scale, two forms of a humor test, and various other subscales measuring factors such as toughmindedness, rigidity, and intolerance of ambiguity. Factor analyses of data show that the funniness of incongruity-resolution types of jokes are located/identified as conservative, while the funniness of nonsense jokes are located/identified as liberal. It is suggested that the factor of toughmindedness is a second dimension (in addition to the dimension of conservatism) of sense of humor in a comprehensive attitude space. *

264. Ruch, W., & Hehl, F.-J. (1987). Personal values as facilitating and inhibiting factors in the appreciation of humor content. *Journal of Social Behavior and Personality, 2*, 453–472. Describes two studies in which 115 German college students rated the funniness, and degree of "rejection," of jokes and cartoons of three types (incongruity-resolution, sex, and nonsense); also, measures of value orientation were given to participants. Results provide the basis for the development of a model specifying the inhibiting and facilitating effects of value orientation on the appreciation of humor content. *

265. Ruch, W., & Hehl, F.-J. (1988). Attitudes to sex, sexual behaviour, and enjoyment of humour. *Personality and Individual Differences, 9*, 983–994. Participants were 115 female and male German college students who gave responses on a questionnaire concerning attitudes toward sex, and who completed a sexual behavior inventory, and a humor test. Partial results indicate a positive correlation between appreciation of sexual humor and the sex scales examined (sexual libido, satisfaction, experience, and pleasure); also, low sexual satisfaction, low permissiveness, and prudishness are correlated with aversiveness of all types of humor. It is suggested that such variables are better predictors of sexual-humor enjoyment than the more general factors of conservatism and toughmindedness. *

266. Ruch, W., & Hehl, F.-J. (1993). Humour appreciation and needs: Evidence from questionnaire, self-, and peer-rating data. *Personality and Individual Differences, 15*, 433–445. Participants were 264 college students and adults who comprised two samples and who completed a humor test, and a needs-assessment inventory via a questionnaire, self-ratings, and peer-ratings. Results indicate that participants' need for order is related to humor structure where, in particular, the need for order correlates positively with funniness of the incongruity-resolution type of humor, and one's dislike for lack of order predicts aversiveness of the nonsense type of humor; also, certain aspects of the need for play are predictive of nonsense and sexual humor appreciation, but not of incongruity-resolution humor. *

267. Ruch, W., Kohler, G., & VanThriel, C. (1997). To be in good or bad humour: Construction of the state form of the state-trait-cheerfulness-inventory—STCI. *Personality and Individual Differences, 22*, 477–491. Describes the relevance of the states of "cheerfulness," "seriousness," and "bad mood" for study of the emotion of "exhilaration" and, also, describes the construction of the "trait-cheerfulness" inventory. A pilot study used over 800 participants who completed 40 items, and the subsequent standard state form with 10 items per scale was developed using the data from a sample of 595 participants. Results based on joint factor analyses of state and trait items yielded the factors of "cheerfulness," "seriousness," and "bad mood"—both as traits and states. *

268. Schaier, A. (1975). Humor appreciation and comprehension in the elderly. Unpublished doctoral dissertation, Purdue University. Participants were 96 older adults who resided at home, cared for themselves, and were categorized into three age groups: 50–59, 60–69, and 70–79; they were tested for their appreciation and comprehension of 24 conservation and nonconservation jokes, as well as giving responses on three Piagetian conservation tasks (mass, volume, and weight). Findings show that age is an important factor in both the appreciation and comprehension of both types of jokes where appreciation increases with age and comprehension decreases with age; also, appreciation scores are higher, and comprehension is greater, for conservation—than for nonconservation—jokes. *

269. Schoel, D., & Busse, T. (1971). Humor and creative abilities. *Psychological Reports*, *29*, 34. Participants were 16 college men and women identified by their teachers as "humorous" (i.e., "funny, amusing, comical, and droll"), and who were given creativity tests. Results indicate *no* relationship between humor and creativity in this study (employing teacher's ratings of student's humor) with this college sample—a finding that is contrary to previous studies with younger children that links humor to creativity. *

270. Schwartz, S. (1971). The effects of sexual arousal, sex guilt, and expectancy for censure on appreciation for varying degrees of sex-relevant humor. Unpublished doctoral dissertation, Syracuse University. Participants were 96 male college students—half of whom were rated as sex-guilty, and the other half as low on sex-guilt—assigned to one of four treatments in a factorial design. Participants were sexually stimulated, or not stimulated, by viewing either erotic photographs or landscapes; also, the experimenter engaged in fixed role-playing with an accomplice concerning high or low expectancy for censure for sexual behavior. Following this, participants rated the funniness of explicit and subtle sexual cartoons. Results show that under stimulating conditions, sex-guilt is unrelated to "displacement"; also, expectancies for censure have no effect on humor preferences; results are consistent with hypotheses derived from arousal theory. **

271. Shellberg, L. (1970). The effects of motivational arousal on humor appreciation. Unpublished doctoral dissertation, Claremont Graduate School and University Center. Participants were 388 college students who rated the funniness of 30 cartoons under various experimental conditions of arousal (relaxed; low-, moderate-, high-, and extreme-arousal); also, scores were obtained from participants on an anxiety scale and a "security-insecurity" test. Results show support for a hypothesized U-shaped relationship between motivational arousal and humor preference. **

272. Silvan, M. (1989). The role of the ego in the use of humor as a defense. *Dissertation Abstracts International, 49 (10–B)*, 4561. Participants were 80 college men who provided scores on a psychological inventory, on humor scales, on ego-function assessment scales, and on story/cartoon/picture tests. Partial results indicate that the picture test is a valid and reliable means of measuring the ability to use humor as a defense mechanism, and that the ability to use humor is related, also, to the capacity for "adaptive regression in the service of the ego," ego-strength level, and level of defense. *

273. Singer, D., & Berkowitz, L. (1972). Differing "creativities" in the wit and the clown. *Perceptual and Motor Skills, 35*, 3–6. Participants were 27 college men who completed two different types of creativity measures, and who provided sociometric ratings, and scholastic aptitude scores. Results show that students identified as "wits" have high scores on ideational creativity but not on adaptive regression, and "clowns" have high scores on adaptive regression but not on ideational creativity. *

274. Steinfeld, M. (1986). The relationship between adolescent humor perception and adaptive functioning. Unpublished doctoral dissertation, The Fielding Institute. Participants were 95 adolescent high school students who gave responses on a self-image questionnaire, a sense of humor inventory, and a personal data form. Results indicate that humor perception is a significant and positive aspect of adolescent personality and it relates to healthy adjustment in adolescents; also, the variable of sex/gender interacts with humor perception. *

275. Terry, R., & Ertel, S. (1974). Exploration of individual differences in preferences for humor. *Psychological Reports, 34*, 1031–1037. Participants were 39 college students who completed a personality inventory and also gave preference scores for hostile, sexual, and nontendentious cartoons. Results show that sexual cartoons are liked more by men (in particular, those men who are "tough" or group-dependent) than by women (especially by women with higher general intelligence); nonsense cartoons are liked more by women (especially by women with lower general intelligence). *

276. Townsend, J. (1982). Relationships among humor, creative thinking abilities, race, sex, and socioeconomic factors of advantagedness and disadvantagedness of a selected sample of high school students. Unpublished doctoral dissertation, University of Georgia. Participants were 110 high school juniors and seniors who gave responses on creative thinking, humor appreciation, and humor production tests. Results show a positive relationship between quantity of humor production—but not humor appreciation—and creative thinking. *

277. Treadwell, Y. (1970). Humor and creativity. *Psychological Reports, 26*, 55–58. Participants were 83 college students who completed two humor and three creativity tests. Results indicate that scores on all of the creativity measures correlate significantly with scores on a cartoons test; however—contrary to prediction—humor *appreciation* scores are correlated significantly with the cartoons test scores, while the humor *use* scores are not. *

278. Tucci, R. (1990). The effects of self-deprecating, aggressive, and neutral humor on depressive, acting-out, and normal adolescents. *Dissertation Abstracts International, 50 (8–B)*, 3718. Participants were 57 sixteen- and seventeen-year-old adolescents who rated self-deprecating, aggressive, and neutral cartoons; they also gave responses on affective, self-concept, social desirability, and defense mechanisms scales. Results show that all participants prefer aggressive humor to self-deprecating or neutral humor, that anxiety level is inversely related to self-deprecating and aggressive humor, and that depression and hostile mood levels are inversely related to all three types of humor. *

279. Vitulli, W., & Parman, D. (1996). Elderly persons' perceptions of humor as a gender-linked characteristic. *Psychological Reports, 78*, 83–89. Participants were 96 older men and women, ages 51–93 years old, who completed a humor rating scale that measures attitudes toward male- and female-oriented humor, and general humor values. Results show that older men and women agree on general humor values, and they both rate humor as an important quality for men on the male-oriented rating scale; however, there is a gender difference on the female-oriented scale in which older women perceive humor as an important quality for women, whereas older men do not. *

280. Vitulli, W., & Tyler, K. (1988). Sex-related attitudes toward humor among high-school and college students. *Psychological Reports, 63*, 616–618. Participants were 45 high school students and 33 college students who completed a humor scale dealing with various opinions of the importance of humor for women and men. Results show a significant difference between the groups, especially on the variable of male-oriented humor; data are interpreted in terms of "androgynous" social conditioning factors. *

281. Waterman, J. (1972). Humor in young children: Relationships of behavioral style and age with laughter and smiling. Unpublished doctoral dissertation, University of California, Los Angeles. Participants were 40 elementary school children who gave responses to a humorous television comedy program; their humor expressiveness (e.g., frequency and duration of laughter and smiling), and various cognitive measures, were recorded, also. Results indicate that humor responses devoted to smiling are higher for withdrawn individuals than for behavioral-problem children; it was concluded that "high smilers" accurately reflect their own humor response in cognitive ratings while the two types of measures are independent for "high laughers"; also, smiling seems to be related to understanding/comprehension, while laughing seems to be a social phenomenon. *

282. Weaver, J., Masland, J., Kharazmi, S., & Zillmann, D. (1985). Effect of alcoholic intoxication on the appreciation of different types of humor. *Journal of Personality and Social Psychology, 49*, 781–787. Participants were 36 male college students who were assigned to one of three intoxication conditions (no ethanol, low dose, high dose), and then exposed to humorous television program excerpts. At some point during intoxication, participants were exposed to material containing blunt/unsophisticated humor and to material containing subtle/sophisticated humor. Results indicate that the perceived funniness of blunt humor increases with ethanol intoxication; in contrast, for the subtle humor, perceived funniness decreases with intoxication. **

283. Wicker, F., Thorelli, I., Barron, W., & Willis, A. (1981). Studies of mood and humor appreciation. *Motivation and Emotion, 5*, 47–59. Describes two studies in which 189 college students rated jokes on funniness, and on other scales, following the rating of their own mood. Results indicate that three mood factors—vigor, elation, and surgency—predict reliably participants' joke appreciation in both studies. *

284. Wilson, G., & Maclean, A. (1974). Personality, attitudes, and humor preferences of prisoners and controls. *Psychological Reports, 34*, 847–854. Participants were 100 recidivists serving medium-term sentences in a London prison, and 100 trainee bus drivers, who completed measures of personality, social attitudes, and humor preferences. Results support other research findings showing that criminals tend to be more extraverted, psychotic, and neurotic than controls; also, on the attitude and humor tests, the prisoners are less favorable toward sexual stimuli than controls. *

285. Wilson, G., Nias, D., & Brazendale, A. (1975). Vital statistics, perceived sexual attractiveness, and response to risque humor. *The Journal of Social Psychology, 95*, 201–205. Participants were 200 female student teachers who rated the funniness of risque cartoons/postcards; also, measures of their social attitudes, and their perceived self-attractiveness, were taken. Results show that women who rate themselves as attractive view the cartoons as less funny than those rating themselves as unattractive; however, women who are "shapely," based on their bust/waist ratio, are more appreciative of the cartoons; neither of the measures of attractiveness relate to social attitude scores. *

286. Wilson, G., Rust, J., & Kasriel, J. (1977). Genetic and family origins of humor preferences: A twin study. *Psychological Reports, 41*, 659–660. Participants were 49 pairs of monozygotic and 52 pairs of dizygotic twins who rated a series of 48 cartoons containing nonsense, sexual, satirical, and aggressive content. Results indicate that there may be a genetic effect on reactions to aggressive humor, but family environment seems to be more important in determining individual differences concerning the appreciation of sexual, satirical, and nonsense humor. *

287. Wilson, W. (1975). Sex differences in response to obscenities and bawdy humor. *Psychological Reports, 37,* 1074. Participants in one study were 116 college students who answered a questionnaire concerning the usage of 121 obscenities. Results show that only a small number of expressions are used in equal accord by both sexes, with men being more familiar, and using more frequently, a greater range of obscenities. In a second study, 57 college students gave humor ratings of 10 bawdy stories, and showed that women—with wide variability—are stricter censors of such stories than are men. *

288. Zillmann, D., & Bryant, J. (1980). Misattribution theory of tendentious humor. *Journal of Experimental Social Psychology, 16,* 146–160. Participants were 90 college students who were treated rudely, or in a normal manner, by a female experimenter; they then witnessed the experimenter in one of three conditions: misfortune with innocuous humor cues; misfortune but no humor cues; and humor cues with no misfortune. Results show that there are no gender differences in participants' mirth responses measured during the experiment; also, participants' negative dispositions are associated with greater mirth responses to the misfortune, than to the neutral, condition whether or not humor cues are associated with that misfortune. Findings support the disposition theory of mirth. **

289. Ziv, A. (1976). Facilitating effects of humor on creativity. *Journal of Educational Psychology, 68,* 318–322. Participants were 282 tenth-graders who were divided into four groups according to a Solomon research design; they listened to a recording of a comedy routine that is popular with children, and they were given a verbal creativity test. Results indicate that those adolescents who listen to a humorous recording perform better on a creativity test than do control participants. **

290. Ziv, A., & Zajdman, A. (Eds.) (1993). *Semites and stereotypes: Characteristics of Jewish humor.* Westport, CT: Greenwood Press. Presents essays by writers from France, England, Denmark, Israel, Australia, and the United States who explore the characteristics of Jewish humor from a variety of disciplines, including religion, anthropology, literature, sociology, and psychology. Contents include the following: Jewish humor—a survey and a program; psychosocial characteristics of Jewish humor; black humor and the shtetl tradition; humor of Sholom Aleichem; the self-deprecating Jewish sense of humor; the politics of gallows humor; the origins and evolution of a classic Jewish joke; the humor of Philip Roth, Woody Allen, and Sigmund Freud; from Eve to the Jewish-American Princess; and Jewish marriage jokes and transactionalism.

291. Zussman, I. (1983). Rorschach test correlates of humor appreciation. Unpublished doctoral dissertation, United States International University. Participants were 60 graduate and undergraduate college students who gave scores on a sense of humor inventory and on the Rorschach Inkblot Test. Results support the hypotheses that tendentious humor is rated funnier than innocent humor, and that men and women do not generally show significant differences in humor appreciation. *

METHODOLOGY AND MEASUREMENT OF HUMOR

292. Deckers, L., & Kizer, P. (1975). Humor and the incongruity hypothesis. *The Journal of Psychology, 90,* 215–218. Describes the use of the classical method of constant stimuli in the investigation of the effects of an incongruity between an expected and an actual comparison weight on humor responses of female and male college students. Results indicate that humor increases as a function of the incongruity between the expected and the actual stimulus, and shows that the heaviness of the actual stimulus determines the degree of incongruity; also, it was found that humor increases with the number of judgments made prior to the presentation of the incongruous comparison stimulus. **

293. Deckers, L., & Ruch, W. (1992). The Situational Humour Response Questionnaire (SHRQ) as a test of "sense of humor": A validity study in the field of humour appreciation. *Personality and Individual Differences, 13,* 1149–1152. Participants were 206 college students who completed initially a well-known humor questionnaire/test, and then rated the funniness and aversiveness of one of two sets of 35 jokes and cartoons taken from another humor test developed by the second author. Results indicate that—contrary to expectations—the first humor test does not correlate with any level of the second humor test, suggesting that the two tests tap into totally different domains of humor. A hypothesis is proposed which suggests that the relationship between the first humor test and humor appreciation may be mediated by social factors, and that the second humor test may more completely measure the entire humor experience. *

294. Feingold, A. (1983). Measuring humor ability: Revision and construct validation of the Humor Perceptiveness Test. *Perceptual and Motor Skills, 56,* 159–166. Participants were 198 female and male college students who completed a humor-perceptiveness test, an intelligence scale, a self-report interest inventory, and a personality inventory. Results indicate that scores on the revised humor-perceptiveness test are related to humor appreciation and to intelligence scores; in particular, scores on the humor measure correlate only with intelligence for "dull" participants, but with both intelligence and humor appreciation for "brighter" participants. * [Note: Also see Feingold, A. (1982). Measuring humor: A pilot study. *Perceptual and Motor Skills, 54,* 986.]

295. Fiordalis, J. (1987). The construction and validation of the Sociometric Humor Measure. Unpublished doctoral dissertation, The University of Akron. Participants in a pilot study, and a validation study, were 120 female registered nurses who gave scores on a standard humor test, on a "burnout" inventory, and on the proposed Sociometric Humor Measure. Results indicate that the proposed humor test measures something different from the standard humor test, and that it is able to predict "burnout" in a health care setting. *

296. Froman, R. (1989). A sense of humor assessment instrument based on a theoretically- and empirically-derived taxonomy of humor. Unpublished doctoral dissertation, University of Wyoming. Describes a five-step research project designed to study a taxonomy of humor and which resulted in the development of a humor assessment instrument; the new instrument—containing two gender-specific forms, employing one-frame comics as stimulus materials, and requiring funniness ratings from participants—is an attempt to operationalize the concept of sense of humor. *

297. Guilmette, A. M. (1980). Psychophysical and psychosocial humour judgements as a function of interactive incongruity humour. Unpublished doctoral dissertation, University of Windsor, Canada. Examines, experimentally, the following five major hypotheses concerning interactive humor as a joint function of the stimulus situation and the mental experience of the individual: whether violation of belief expectancy occurs as a function of a range of expectation or as a means of expectation; whether heavy-to-light weights or light-to-heavy weights will generate contrast effect; whether participants respond differentially to the violation of a narrow range of belief expectancy as opposed to the violation of a broad range of expectancy; whether participants who are exposed frequently to beliefs respond differently from those who are infrequently exposed to beliefs; and whether a heavy discrepant weight will be judged more incongruous than a light discrepant weight. The use of five dependent measures (threat, amusement, playful, surprise, and discrepant), in conjunction with the five major hypotheses, generated 25 separate hypotheses that are tested and which receive varying degrees of support. **

298. Hampes, W. (1994). Relation between intimacy and the Multidimensional Sense of Humor Scale. *Psychological Reports, 74*, 1360–1362. Participants were 60 male and female college students who completed a multidimensional humor response scale, and a psychosocial development/intimacy scale. Results show that high scores on the intimacy scale are associated with high scores on the humor test. The discrepancy between results regarding the factor of intimacy for the present multidimensional humor test—which is characterized as a broad and comprehensive measure of humor—and another widely-used situational humor response test—which is characterized as a narrower measure of humor—may be explained by the social nature of the concept of intimacy and by differences that highlight the non-equivalent social aspects of the two tests of humor. *

299. Lowis, M., & Nieuwoudt, J. (1995). The use of a cartoon rating scale as a measure of the humor construct. *The Journal of Psychology, 129*, 133–144. Participants were 129 male and female White South Africans who completed a new humor-response scale based on the rating of newspaper cartoons. Results indicate that—although there is a significant and positive relationship between chronological age and funniness ratings on the new scale—there are no valid relationships with other life ("social readjustment," "affect balance," and "life satisfaction") measures or with scores on three other humor ("coping humor," "frequency of humor initiation," and "sense of humor questionnaire") scales. The study contains a useful 42–item reference section. *

300. Maase, S. (1986). Multidimensional scaling applied to the cognitive response to humor. Unpublished doctoral dissertation, University of Maryland, College Park. Participants were 210 college students who were exposed to two jokes in which the timing was manipulated between the joke segments (the joke body and the punchline), and in which participants' humor responses were measured. Two cognitive models are examined: a "feint" model which suggests that the joke body serves as a feint, or trick, to move concepts to the wrong place cognitively—a situation which is then corrected by the appearance of the joke punchline; and a "warp" model which proposes that humor results from a sudden warping, or dewarping, of the cognitive space that occurs as a result of the joke message. Results indicate that—while metric multidimensional scaling may be useful in describing the general humor process—specific joke content may be a primary determinant in observed cognitive-configuration changes. *

301. Powell, L. (1986). Items for evaluating humor. *Psychological Reports, 58*, 323–326. Participants were 64 female and male college students who read and evaluated via a semantic differential scale three different written satires. Results based on factor analyses of the data indicate that response dimensions vary with the different satirical messages, and only a *humor* factor is identified consistently for all three messages; it is suggested that responses to humor are based upon "collapsible" factors. *

302. Ruch, W. (1996). Measurement approaches to the sense of humor: Introduction and overview. *Humor: International Journal of Humor Research, 9*, 239–250. Based on the observation of a renaissance recently of research interest in the topic of humans' sense of humor, this study examines various questions related to humor research: "Is there a need for a unique personality construct regarding sense of humor?" "What is the research agenda concerning the study of humor?" "Is the term 'sense of humor' a good representative of humor at the trait level?" "What are the recommendations for future approaches to the measurement of the sense of humor?" The author also gives a brief review of the papers presented at a symposium called *Approaches to the Sense of Humor: Concepts and Measurement* that was organized for the International Society for Humor Studies Conference held in Ithaca, New York in 1994.

303. Sumners, F. A. (1986). The development of an instrument to measure attitudes of professional registered nurses toward humor. Unpublished doctoral dissertation, The University of Texas at Austin. Participants were 255 randomly selected registered nurses in a descriptive, and a pilot, study to develop an instrument capable of measuring the attitudes of nurses toward humor in the professional-work setting. Results based upon semantic differential ratings indicate that the attitude of registered nurses in Texas toward humor is positive, and shows significant differences between the personal-life setting and the professional-work setting with participants reflecting more positive attitudes in the personal life setting. *

NATURE OF THE HUMOROUS STIMULUS

304. Bolick, T., & Nowicki, S. (1984). The incidence of external locus of control in televised cartoon characters. *The Journal of Genetic Psychology, 144*, 99–104. Describes the content analysis of 33 half-hour Saturday morning program segments of network television. Employing operationalized definitions of "internal-" and "external-locus of control," in cartoon events, results show that Saturday morning programs often present an "external" view of the world in which the individual is at the mercy of luck, magic, or various powerful characters. Discusses the potential impact of such an external orientation upon the expectancies, or locus of control, of youthful television viewers. *

305. Burns, W. (1974). The rating of sexual and nonsexual cartoons as a function of repression-sensitization. Unpublished doctoral dissertation, The University of North Dakota. Participants were 60 male and female college students who rated the degree of humor in each of a series of 40 sexual and nonsexual cartoons; participants also provided scores on a social desirability scale which identifies "sensitizers," "nondefensive repressors," and "defensive repressors." Partial results show that women "defensive repressors" have lower humor ratings for sexual-, than for nonsexual, cartoons. **

306. Cann, A., Calhoun, L., & Nance, J. (2000). Exposure to humor before and after an unpleasant stimulus: Humor as a preventative or a cure. *Humor: International Journal of Humor Research, 13*, 177–191. Participants were 138 college students who watched a humorous videotape before and after exposure to an unpleasant videotape that aroused negative emotions in the participants; the humor condition was compared to a nonhumorous condition to determine if mood states and negative emotions are affected by humor. Results show that the humor condition has an effect regardless of the timing of the treatment on moods experienced as anger and depression; for emotions and moods experienced as anxiety, the humor intervention was most effective when presented before the unpleasant videotape; overall, results show that sense of humor is *not* related to reported emotional reactions, and humor may be either a cure or a preventative depending on particular emotion reactions and the timing of the humor intervention. **

307. Deckers, L., Buttram, R., & Winsted, D. (1989). The sensitization of humor responses to cartoons. *Motivation and Emotion, 13*, 71–81. Describes three experiments in which 184 college-student participants rated cartoons in an effort to determine if responding to cartoons with the same theme depends on the cartoon's serial position. Results show that participants' facial responses and funniness ratings increase over the first few cartoons and, thereby, reflect the effect of arousal or salience—apparently, the initial cartoons make the individual more sensitive to subsequent cartoons; it is suggested that cartoon researchers be aware of the effect of a cartoon's serial position on humor responses. **

308. Deckers, L., & Carr, D. (1986). Cartoons varying in low-level pain ratings, not aggression ratings, correlate positively with funniness ratings. *Motivation and Emotion, 10*, 207–216. Describes three studies in which 220 college-student participants rated cartoons for aggression, pain, and funniness in an effort to determine the relationships among these factors. Results indicate that pain correlates more reliably with funniness than does aggression, that funniness increases to asymptote within the first third of the pain dimension (low-level pain) and is unaffected by further pain increases, and that no downward trend is observed in funniness with increased pain ratings. **

309. Downs, A. C. (1990). Children's judgments of televised events: The real versus pretend distinction. *Perceptual and Motor Skills, 70*, 779–782. Participants were 36 children, ages 4–6 years old, who judged—via adult interviews of the children—the reality of specific televised events shown on videotape; events varied in format, aggressiveness, and type of character shown. Results indicate that children's judgments are dependent on the format (cartoon versus noncartoon) of the televised events rather than on other variables; no gender or age differences were observed in the study. **

310. Enter, R. (1972). The relationship of cartoon type, cartoon preference, and repression-sensitization, to retention of cartoon humor. Unpublished doctoral dissertation, Ohio University. Initial participants were 69 male and female college students who rated 120 cartoons of four types: tendentious-low preference, tendentious-high preference, nonsense-low preference, and nonsense-high preference. One-half of the cartoons were shown, subsequently, to 135 college students and, a week later, they were presented with the captions of these cartoons along with the captions of the cartoons not shown; the dependent measure was the number of cartoon captions shown that were recognized correctly; participants also completed a repression-sensitization scale. Results indicate that retention is best for high-preference cartoons and poorest for low-preference cartoons; also, retention is poorest for cartoons with a sexual or hostile theme which are *not* considered to be funny, while cartoons with a sexual or hostile theme that are considered to be funny have the best retention scores. **

311. Gerhart, D. (1990). The effect of humor on subjective appraisals of disturbance in response to aversive stimuli. *Dissertation Abstracts International,*

50 (7–A), 1985. Participants were 90 adults who viewed four aversive pictures that had been independently rated as moderately disturbing; in the experimental conditions, participants listened to a brief humorous tape-recording following each picture, while control participants listened to a serious tape-recording that was equivalent in content. Results are largely negative in that no differences in disturbance ratings occurred between participants who heard humorous- versus serious-content recordings, and no differences occurred between relevant-, irrelevant-, and no-content-humor conditions. It is suggested that while humor may have a transient effect upon immediate mood states, it does *not* alter cognitive appraisals concerning one's perceived disturbance of an aversive event. **

312. Godkewitsch, M. (1974). Verbal, exploratory, and physiological responses to stimulus properties underlying humour. Unpublished doctoral dissertation, University of Toronto, Canada. Describes six studies to assess the role of stimulus properties in responses indicative of experienced humor, as distinct from that of "receiver/situation-associated" variables; both "analytic-" and "synthetic-type" approaches, involving joke-ratings and other rating-scale measures, were employed. Results show that six humor measures (verbal ratings of humorousness, wittiness, and funniness, and three nonverbal measures) are positive linear functions of the semantic distance between the members of adjective-noun pairs; also, rated humorousness and funniness relate to a factor called "hedonic tone." The "analytic" studies show that content and collative properties interact to influence rated funniness, while the "synthetic" studies show that some verbal and nonverbal correlates of experienced humor may be evoked reliably by manipulated properties of adjective-noun pairs. **

313. Goldstein, J. (1970). Repetition, motive arousal, and humor appreciation. *Journal of Experimental Research in Personality, 4*, 90–94. Participants were 44 male college students who each were assigned randomly to one cell of a 2 x 2 factorial design that tested the factors of motive arousal (present or absent) and cartoon content (sexual or nonsexual); they each were presented with eight cartoons, repeated four times in a random sequence, and were asked to rate each cartoon on a humor scale. Results indicate that humor ratings decrease as a function of repetition, but repetition interacts with motive arousal where the decreased ratings for aroused participants was significantly less than for non-aroused participants. **

314. Gruner, C. R. (1993). Audience's response to jokes in speeches with and without recorded laughs. *Psychological Reports, 73*, 347–350. Participants were 64 college students who rated the interestingness and funniness of videotaped speeches containing humor before a live audience: in one presentation the audience laughed at the jokes and in the other there was no laughter; each participant saw one tape with the laughter, then the other tape without the

laughter. Results show that participants prefer the speaker who elicited the laughter, but a significant order effect makes the findings tentative. **

315. Hackman, M. (1986). Audience reactions to the use of self-disparaging humor by informative speakers. Doctoral dissertation, University of Denver. Participants were 204 college students who were exposed to audiotape recorded informative speeches concerning listening behavior; selected speeches contained examples of self-disparaging humor either related, or not directly related, to the topic of the speech; participants also rated their perception of the speaker's sense of humor. Partial results indicate that speakers who use self-disparaging humor are rated as having a better sense of humor than speakers who do not use humor in their speeches; also, speakers who use self-disparaging humor are viewed as *less* interesting than speakers who use *no* humor. **

316. Herzog, T., & Larwin, D. (1988). The appreciation of humor in captioned cartoons. *The Journal of Psychology, 122,* 597–607. Participants were 516 male and female college students who gave humor appreciation ratings for captioned cartoons varying in cartoon category and eight factors: complexity, difficulty, fit, depth, visual humor, artwork, vulgarity, and originality. Partial results based on factor analyses of humor appreciation ratings yield four dimensions: sexual, incongruity, social issues, and marriage-family; the *most* appreciated cartoons are the sexual and marriage-family categories, and social issues the *least* appreciated dimension. It is suggested that the kinds of cognitive processes involved in cartoon-humor appreciation are similar to those involved in preference reactions for environmental settings. *

317. Hoptman, M., & Levy, J. (1988). Perceptual asymmetries in left- and right-handers for cartoon and real faces. *Brain and Cognition, 8,* 178–188. Participants were 40 right- and 40 left-handed college students and community residents who completed two free-vision tests of face-processing (involving a chimeric face—consisting of a smiling half-face joined to either a neutral half-face/real face, or a sad half-face/cartoon face—and its mirror-image); participants judged which chimeric face appeared happier: the one with the smile to the left, or the one with the smile to the right. Results indicate that *right-handers* have a significant *leftward* attentional bias—based on the finding that chimeras with the smile to the left are judged as happier than those with the smile to the right. **

318. Jones, J. M., Fine, G. A., & Brust, R. (1979). Interaction effects of picture and caption on humor ratings of cartoons. *The Journal of Social Psychology, 108,* 193–198. Participants were 21 female and male college students who rated a set of 51 cartoons presented either in a complete mode, or with picture or caption missing. Results indicate that the humor of the cartoon picture is related positively to the humor rating of the entire cartoon, an effect that is particularly strong for highly humorous cartoons. Support is given to the incongruity notion

of cartoon structure by the observed interaction between picture and caption where there's a high correlation with humor ratings for the funny cartoons, but *not* for the less funny cartoons. **

319. Jorgensen, J. (1979). Facial expression, emotion attribution and self-reported experience of cartoon humor. Unpublished doctoral dissertation, The University of Nebraska. Examines the interactive effects of *mode* of manipulation (facial expression versus cognitive-attribution) and *type* of manipulation (consonant versus dissonant) on students' self-reported experience of cartoon humor. It was hypothesized that smiling participants will rate cartoons as funnier than frowning participants, and that those persons expecting non-humor-symptoms (from music) will rate cartoons as funnier than those individuals expecting humor-symptoms (from music). Results are generally negative, and fail to support the hypotheses: there is *no* significant interaction effect for *mode*-by-*type* of manipulation on mean ratings of five rated cartoons. It is concluded that the effectiveness of experimental manipulations varies with the type of characters, the visual features, the type of humor (aggressive versus innocent), and the degree of funniness of the cartoons. **

320. Lott, H. (1989). An experiment in the initial effects of humor on immediate and delayed recall. Unpublished doctoral dissertation, University of San Francisco. Participants were 66 senior nursing students who were divided randomly into three groups, each of which viewed one of three videotapes differing in humor content (concept-related humor, non-concept-related humor, no-humor); following exposure to the tapes, participants were tested on written recall of nine research concepts presented in the tapes. Results show that—under delayed conditions—concept-related humor as compared with non-concept-related humor is associated with greater recall of material; also, under delayed conditions, frequency among the first three concepts recalled is greater for those participants who receive concept-related humor than for those who receive non-concept-related humor. It is suggested that concept-related humor helps delayed recall in long-term learning. **

321. Mahoney, J. (1971). The effect of reality orientation and impulse control on the preference for frivolous, social, and existential humor. Unpublished doctoral dissertation, State University of New York at Buffalo. Participants were 144 female and male adults who rated 58 jokes consisting of 18 jokes each of three types of humor (frivolous, social, existential), including four buffer jokes. Results show no gender differences in humor perception or general preference for the different types of humor; however, when sexual jokes are considered alone, it was found that individuals low in "reality orientation" rate sexual jokes as significantly funnier than do participants high in "reality orientation." **

322. Maio, G., Olson, J., & Bush, J. (1997). Telling jokes that disparage social groups: Effects on the joke teller's stereotypes. *Journal of Applied Social*

Psychology, 27, 1986–2000. Participants were 95 female and male college students who recited humor that either disparaged Newfoundlanders (a relatively disadvantaged group in Canada) or recited nondisparaging humor; subsequently, participants completed a measure of their attitudes and stereotypes toward Newfoundlanders. Results show that those who recited disparaging humor report more negative stereotypes of Newfoundlanders than those participants who told jokes containing nondisparaging humor; however, attitudes toward the target group were not affected by the experimental manipulation. **

323. Mathews, R. M., & Dix, M. (1992). Behavior change in the funny papers: Feedback to cartoonists on safety belt use. *Journal of Applied Behavior Analysis, 25,* 769–775. Participants were eight nationally syndicated cartoonists who responded to a letter-writing campaign advocating the use of safety belts for motor vehicle occupants in comic strips. During a baseline measurement, the cartoonists depicted safety belt use in only 15% of their strips, but following receipt of a personal letter requesting safety belt use 41% of their strips depicted such use. Results are discussed within the context of advocacy efforts intended to increase prevention-message exposure in the media. *

324. McKay, T., & McKay, M. (1982). Captioned and non-captioned cartoons: Effects of structural properties on ratings of humor. *Perceptual and Motor Skills, 54,* 143–146. Participants were 80 male and female college students who rated noncaptioned cartoons for comparison with captioned cartoons and with independent ratings of the pictures and captions for whole-captioned cartoons. Partial results show that whole-captioned cartoons are rated as funnier than the independent ratings of pictures or captions; also, noncaptioned cartoons are *not* rated significantly different from pictures, captions, or whole-captioned cartoons. Results suggest the use of control measures for cartoons' structure in future studies of humor containing cartoon materials. **

325. O'Mahony, M., & Brown, M. (1977). The interstimulus humour effect. *European Journal of Social Psychology, 7,* 253–257. Participants were 480 young adults and adults, ages 13–69 years old, who were divided equally between two conditions: an "interstimulus humor" and a "neutral interstimulus" condition; in the former condition, participants were required to look at a series of 40 cartoons in which the humor was given by the caption, and rate every fourth "target" cartoon for humor; in the latter condition, a control condition, the cartoons between the target cartoons had their captions removed, rendering them merely pictures. Results show that the "interstimulus humor" group gives higher ratings to the cartoons; it is suggested that an interstimulus humor effect is strong in the data and—to generalize—an effect other than mere speed contributes to the success of the "quickfire" humor routines often used in theater performances. It is noted that the interstimulus humor effect runs counter to predictions made from a habituation or adaptation hypothesis that is a useful predictive framework in sensory psychophysics. **

326. Petry, A. (1978). Young children's response to three types of humor. Unpublished doctoral dissertation, The University of Connecticut. Participants were 60 children, ages 5–7 years old, who were exposed to three stories, each containing a distinctive type of humor (incongruity, exaggeration, nonsense); mirth responses of participants were observed, they rated the funniness of the stories, and they were interviewed following each story. Results show that the variable of age (followed, in order, by verbal ability and self-concept) is the most influential in explaining variations in humor comprehension; also, significant correlations are present between participants' overall humor comprehension scores and the ratings they give to humor stimuli. *

327. Porterfield, A., Mayer, F. S., Dougherty, K., Kredich, K., Kronberg, M., Marsee, K., & Okazaki, Y. (1988). Private self-consciousness, canned laughter, and responses to humorous stimuli. *Journal of Research in Personality, 22,* 409–423. Participants were 82 female and male college students who listened to humorous stimuli presented either with, or without, canned laughter; participants' funniness ratings and overt laughter were the dependent measures. Results indicate that private self-consciousness (self-focus) and funniness ratings are negatively correlated in the canned laughter group, but not correlated in the no-canned laughter group; however, for both groups, the overt laughter measure and private self-consciousness are correlated positively. Results are interpreted within a research context showing that funniness ratings represent affect-free evaluations of humor stimuli, whereas laughter represents amusement. **

328. Rozsa, J. (1975). The effects of difficulty and objective self awareness on the evaluation of cartoon humor. Unpublished doctoral dissertation, The University of Texas at Austin. Participants were 78 male college students who rated the funniness (low, medium, high) of nine sexual cartoons differing in level of difficulty (low, medium, high). Results show that moderate-difficulty cartoons are rated significantly funnier than low- or high-difficulty cartoons. A treatment involving the induction of feelings of negative self-worth in participants produced no differences in ratings. Another finding is that correlations between "understanding time" and "funniness" ratings yield a curvilinear function for low-difficulty jokes, and negative correlations for medium- and high-difficulty jokes. **

329. Schick, C., McGlynn, R., & Woolam, D. (1972). Perception of cartoon humor as a function of familiarity and anxiety level. *Journal of Personality and Social Psychology, 24,* 22–25. Participants were 203 college students who completed a manifest anxiety scale and a cartoon test (familiar and unfamiliar cartoon strips) in tests of the hypothesis that mere exposure enhances one's attitude toward a stimulus object, and of the optimal-level hypothesis of novelty response. Results show that familiar cartoons are preferred over unfamiliar cartoons, that unfamiliar cartoons increase in humor rating with repeated exposure (while the familiar cartoon ratings remain unchanged), and that the high-anxiety group rates the familiar cartoons higher, and the unfamiliar cartoons lower, than does the low-anxiety group. **

330. Schleicher, M. (1981). The use of humor in facilitating voluntary selective exposure to televised educational programs. Unpublished doctoral dissertation, University of Massachusetts. Describes a study in which a voluntary audience was exposed to educational television programs with humorous episodes inserted; the design included the following factors: level of difficulty of the educational message (easy, difficult), funniness of the humor (funny, not-so-funny), distribution of the humor (random, predictable), and density of the humor (intervals without humor ranged from two, four, and six minutes in length). Results show that the voluntary choice of viewing an educational message may be enhanced when the informative message consists of a mix of humor and education; also, the density (or pacing) of the humorous segments within the educational message is the single most reliable factor for inducing viewers to turn their eyes toward the screen during presentation of the educational material. **

331. Schmidt, S. (1994). Effects of humor on sentence memory. *Journal of Experimental Psychology: Learning, Memory, and Cognition, 20,* 953–967. College students participated in a memory test involving humorous and nonhumorous versions of sentences. Results show that humorous sentences are remembered better than nonhumorous sentences on both free- and cued-recall tests, and on measures of word recall and sentence recall; also, it was found that subjective-humor ratings affect memory in both within- and between-participants designs. It is suggested that humorous material be given increased attention and rehearsal in comparison with non-humorous material. **

332. Sewell, E. (1984). Appreciation of cartoons with profanity in captions. *Psychological Reports, 54,* 583–587. Participants were 210 male and female college students who rated a cartoon containing three levels of profanity in the captions. Results show that participants evaluate the cartoon with the mild profanity in the caption as funnier than either the strong or nonprofanity in the caption; also, with the nonprofane caption, there are no gender differences in funniness ratings, but when there is either mild or strong profanity in the caption, men find the cartoon funnier than do women. **

333. Sheppard, A. (1983). Effect of mode of representation on visual humor. *Psychological Reports, 52,* 299–305. Participants were 361 college students who rated 24 cartoons—redrawn from rated photographs—representing four types of humor (superiority, aggression, incongruity, and surprise). Results show that photographs are judged to be more humorous than cartoons with residual effects due to type of humor and gender factors. It is suggested that the belief of an event's actual occurrence (as found in photographs) is significant for effective use of visual humor. **

334. Stocking, S. H., & Zillmann, D. (1976). Effects of humorous disparagement of self, friend, and enemy. *Psychological Reports, 39*, 455–461. Participants were 72 male and female college students who were exposed to an audiotaped communication of five humorous stories. Treatment conditions regarding the target of humorous disparagement by a male figure included: the disparager himself, a male friend of the disparager, and a male enemy of the disparager. Results indicate that self-disparagement affects person-perception negatively where—compared to the person who disparages others—the self-disparager is perceived as *less* witty, intelligent, and confident; also, for humor appreciation, an interaction occurs between the target of disparagement and the gender of the respondent. Women find self-disparagement of a man funnier than do men, whereas men find disparagement of an enemy funnier than do women. In a second study—which varied the gender of the self-disparager with the gender of the respondent—120 college students gave data which rules out the possibility that the women's appreciation of self-disparaging humor in the first study is due to the disparagement-target being a man. **

335. Thommen, E., & Suchet, C. (1999). Humour and intentionality in children: Incongruity between human and animal properties. *Archives de Psychologie, 67*, 215–238. Participants were 60 female and male children and adults, ages 5–27 years old, who were asked to give humor responses to two types of drawings: those presenting abstract humorous stimuli related to the exchange of specific properties between humans and animals, and to the gain or loss of properties by the animals; and those drawings having no humorous content. Results show that all the drawings are viewed as "funny" by 5–year-old but not by 7–year-old children; it is suggested that the ability to appreciate and to explain humor begins to develop in children at approximately 9 years of age. **

336. Wakshlag, J., Day, K., & Zillmann, D. (1981). Selective exposure to educational television programs as a function of differently paced humorous inserts. *Journal of Educational Psychology, 73*, 27–32. Participants were 60 first- and second-grade boys and girls who were able to choose one of three television programs for viewing; of three educational programs, two contained either no humor or humor at a slow, intermediate, or fast pace. Results regarding the effect of pacing were derived from a factorial design varying the levels of pace with two educational programs; it was found that the presence of humor facilitates selective exposure to an educational television program where facilitation increases with the pacing of the humor inserted—fast-paced humor (the frequent placement of short humorous inserts) is the most effective condition in generating and maintaining selective exposure. **

337. Washington, L. (1980). The influence of age, gender, social context, and humor stimulus features in children's humor responses. Unpublished doctoral dissertation, Yale University. Participants were 160 preschool and elementary school children who were tested in same-sex dyads, or alone, in either a circus-decorated setting or an academic setting. Participants were exposed to 24 aggression and dependency cartoons of three difficulty levels, along with four noncartoon pictures; for each stimulus, the child's facial mirth response, cartoon comprehension, and cartoon funniness rating were recorded. Partial results show that both cartoon difficulty and theme are determinants of children's humor responses; all children prefer the aggression cartoons, and gender does not appear to influence cartoon preference or overall humor responsiveness. **

338. Welford, T. (1971). An experimental study of the effectiveness of humor used as a refutational device. Unpublished doctoral dissertation, The Louisiana State University, Agricultural and Mechanical College. Participants were 328 college students who rated the relative effectiveness of a tape-recorded political speech of refutation which used a humor, versus nonhumor condition. Results indicate that of four null hypotheses set up for test, only one was rejected without qualification; the finding, in this case, is that participants hearing the serious refutation and those hearing the humorous refutation differ in their ratings of the speaker's "ethos"; moreover, speaker authoritativeness and character are rated significantly higher by participants hearing the serious speech. **

339. Womach, J. (1974). Differential effects of two humor types on impression formation. Unpublished doctoral dissertation, Saint Louis University. Participants were 200 female and male college students who were assigned randomly to one of two treatment groups in which ratings were made of two paragraphs of positive and negative information about a hypothetical person: half of the participants received the material in a positive-negative order, and the other half in a negative-positive order; within the experimental groups each half received one of the two types of humor (self- or other-derogatory) inserted into the first paragraph. Results show *no* main effects for the humor variable, but there is a significant humor-by-trial interaction; results give partial support to a major hypothesis in which one of the two self-derogatory humor groups reaches a significant increase in a second character rating as compared to control group ratings. **

340. Zillmann, D., Williams, B., Bryant, J., Boynton, K., & Wolf, M. (1980). Acquisition of information from educational television programs as a function of differently paced humorous inserts. *Journal of Educational Psychology, 72,* 170–180. Participants were 70 female and male kindergarten and first-grade children who were first exposed to—and then tested for information acquisition of—an educational television program containing the following variations: humorous segments interspersed at a slow pace; the same segments interspersed at a fast pace; no humorous inserts; slow-paced nonhumorous inserts; or fast-paced nonhumorous inserts. Results indicate that information-acquisition for both humor conditions is superior to that of any one of the nonhumor control conditions; also, fast-paced humorous inserts produce information acquisition more rapidly than do slow-paced inserts. **

SOCIAL ASPECTS OF HUMOR

341. Askenasy, G. (1973). Humor, aggression, defense, and conservatism: Group characteristics and differential humor appreciation. Doctoral dissertation, University of California, Los Angeles. A broad sample of 14 groups of participants were selected for this study: paraplegics, clinical psychologists, career-military officers, female and male students, chronic alcoholics, famous cartoonists, stutterers, skidrowers, successful businessmen, women's libbers, teenage girls, and policemen—all of whom completed a conservatism scale, and a humor appreciation scale composed of nine joke categories (put-down of men, put-down of women, put-down of minorities, put-down of authority, nonsense, get-even, Freudian humor, "sick" humor, and sexual humor). Among the results are the following: a sense of humor in an individual is a measurable trait; a person's sense of humor correlates positively with the sense of humor of other members in a given group as defined by its social, cultural, and vocational aspects, and that such groups differ from one another in humor appreciation; and groups differ with regard to conservatism, and this dimension correlates with the sense of humor expressed in certain joke categories. *

342. Bates, L. (1984). The relational nature of humor. Unpublished doctoral dissertation, University of Colorado at Boulder. Participants were 21 task-oriented dyads of female and male college students who provided audio-recording- and interview-data of the dyads' meetings in an investigation of the transactional nature of humor in a dyadic context. Results of this study give support for the notion that humor is a transactional process, and that the nature of the relationship between the interactants is the most important factor in determining whether or not something is perceived as humorous; also, the functions of humor vary, depending on the nature of the relationship; and it was found that "put-down" humor is far less predominant in dyads than in small groups. *

343. Brown, G., Brown, D., & Ramos, J. (1981). Effects of a laughing versus a nonlaughing model on humor responses in college students. *Psychological Reports, 48*, 35–40. Participants were 48 male and female college students who were exposed to one of three conditions: no model present, a laughing model present, or a nonlaughing model, before reading cartoons alone in a room. Results show that students who observe a laughing model laugh *more* than those who observe a nonlaughing or no model. **

344. Brown, G., Dixon, P., & Hudson, J. D. (1982). Effect of peer pressure on imitation of humor response in college students. *Psychological Reports, 51*,

1111–1117. Participants were 20 male and 30 female college students who—in groups of three persons with one randomly selected to be a model and the others randomly assigned to either a "laughing" model group or a "nonlaughing" model group—rated a series of cartoons. Results show that students who observe laughing models laugh more than the students who observe nonlaughing models when reading magazine cartoons alone; also, the number of models present in the room has *no* effect on the amount of laughter or humor ratings. **

345. Burford, C. (1985). The relationship of principals' sense of humor and job robustness to school environment. Unpublished doctoral dissertation, The Pennsylvania State University. Participants were 50 principals—from 27 elementary and 23 secondary schools—who were matched against 225 teachers in a data-collection effort that included teachers' (and principals') perceptions of principals' sense of humor and the school environment, teachers' job satisfaction, loyalty, and perception of school effectiveness. Results indicate *no* significant relationship between principals' job robustness and teachers' perceptions of their environment, or between the principals' score on a humor perceptiveness test, the principals' own rated sense of humor, and teachers' perception of the school environment. However, a principal's sense of humor—as perceived by teachers—plays an important part in the environment of schools, especially teachers' loyalty to the principal and perceptions of school effectiveness. *

346. Chapman, A. J. (1975). Humorous laughter in children. *Journal of Personality and Social Psychology, 31,* 42–49. Participants were 140 girls and boys, ages 7–8 years old, who listened to humorous material via headphones, and were tested alone, in dyads, or in triads with confederates of the same gender. Results show that—in the triads condition—duration of laughter and smiling is inversely related to the amount that the confederates looked at one another; the laughter and smiling scores in this study support the notion that sharing the social situation is important in the facilitation of humorous laughter; also, a social-laughter theory is proposed that combines the social-facilitation drive theory and the tension-reduction features of humor theory. **

347. Chapman, A. J., & Chapman, W. (1974). Responsiveness to humor: Its dependency upon a companion's humorous smiling and laughter. *The Journal of Psychology, 88,* 245–252. Participants were 90 seven- and eight-year-old boys and girls who listened to a humorous story and a song with nine-year-old confederate-companions (same sex as the participants) who were trained to respond to prerecorded on-line directions; humorous material was presented via headphones, as well as the directions that varied systematically relative to smiling and laughter behavior. Results show that increases in the companions' laughter leads to enhanced laughter, smiling, and funniness ratings by participants who expect the companions to rate the material as funnier; also, increases in the companions' smiling behavior results in increased smiling from participants. **

348. Childs, A. (1975). A tale of two groups: An observational study of targeted humor. Unpublished doctoral dissertation, The University of Tennessee. Examines the role of humor for individuals in various group settings (an outpatient therapy group; a classroom growth group) in which teams of spotters, and coders, were used to identify, and classify, instances of humor. Results show that different groups use targeted and nontargeted humor differentially based on the composition and purposes of the group, and individual group members within different types of groups demonstrate different characteristic uses of humor; also, gender differences—in terms of amount of humor produced—occur where men are the predominant source of humor. *

349. Damico, S., & Purkey, W. (1978). Class clowns: A study of middle school students. *American Educational Research Journal, 15,* 391–398. Participants were 96 "class clowns" identified from a sample of 3,500 eighth-grade students using peer nominations on a sociometric scale; the class clowns were compared to a randomly selected sample of 237 nonclown classmates chosen via teacher ratings, student self-esteem measures, and school-attitude scales. Results show that class clowns are predominantly boys, and are viewed by their teachers as *higher* than nonclowns in the traits of assertiveness, unruliness, attention-seeking, leadership, and cheerfulness, while they are *lower* in the aspect of accomplishing goals; also, clowns reflect *lower* attitudes toward teacher and principal than do nonclowns, and they view themselves as being relatively vocal in expression of opinions and ideas in front of classmates. *

350. Davis, J., & Farina, A. (1970). Humor appreciation as social communication. *Journal of Personality and Social Psychology, 15,* 175–178. Participants were 60 male college students who rated 24 sexual-, hostile-, and other-content cartoons that were given by an attractive female experimenter. A 2 x 2 factorial design (two levels of arousal, two levels of communication) was used to assess, independently, the role of the arousal variable versus the communication variable. In testing the hypothesis that men use appreciation of sexual humor as a means of communicating sexual interest in a female experimenter, it was found that both independent variables—arousal and communication—are effective, with communication being the more potent factor. **

351. Fink, E., & Walker, B. (1977). Humorous responses to embarrassment. *Psychological Reports, 40,* 475–485. Participants were 60 male college students who were interviewed via telephone by female interviewers who asked them a series of embarrassing personal questions in a multiple-experimental-conditions design involving manipulation of interviewer status (low, equal, high) relative in participant's status, anticipated future interaction between interviewer and participant, and presence of others during the interview. Results indicate that there is *no* significant effect for the "anticipated interaction" condition, that more laughter occurs between persons of relatively equal status than between persons of unequal status, and that the larger the number of others present in the interview, the more laughter—and the less embarrassment—occurs. **

352. Fuller, R., & Sheehy-Skeffington, A. (1974). Effects of group laughter on responses to humourous material, a replication and extension. *Psychological Reports, 35,* 531–534. Describes a two-stage study in which participants were 51 male and female college students in a test of the validity of one interpretation of the notion of "social laughter"; that is, that the sound of others laughing increases the chances that a person will show overt expressions of amusement. Participants were observed under conditions in which group laughter was dubbed onto, or omitted from, verbal material varying in humor content. Results show that—with material of both high and low humor—the addition of dubbed laughter increases the frequency of the participants' overt expressions of amusement. Discussion includes the implications for the practice of dubbing laughter onto radio and television programs. ** [Note: cf: Smyth, M., & Fuller, R. (1972). Effects of group laughter on responses to humorous material. *Psychological Reports, 30,* 132–134.]

353. Graham, E. E. (1989). A multivariate analysis of humor and relationship development. *Dissertation Abstracts International, 49 (10–A),* 2861. Examines the role that sense of humor shares with relationship-development in a study in which 80 high- and low-sense-of-humor participants were paired with 80 moderate-sense of humor partners and instructed to interact socially for 30 minutes. Results show that sense of humor—along with perceptions of attraction, self-disclosure, and interpersonal competence—all predict "intent of interacting with the other individual" in the future; however, *specific* uses of humor are *not* predictive of relationship-development. Results support the notion of the facilitative nature of humor in the management of interpersonal relations. * [Note: cf: Graham, E. E. (1995). The involvement of sense of humor in the development of social relationships. *Communication Reports, 8,* 158–169.]

354. Grayson, P. (1979). Humor and intimacy: An exploratory study of couples. Unpublished doctoral dissertation, The University of North Carolina at Chapel Hill. Participants were 52 heterosexual couples who wrote down perceived attempts at humor during five 45–minute sessions at home; during a subsequent meeting with the experimenter, they completed humor rating forms for both their own, and their partners', humor, as well as other scales of dyadic satisfaction, ratings of influence, an adjective checklist, and a brief biographical data form. Results show that only one formally stated hypothesis is confirmed: relatively satisfied couples rate one another's humor as funnier than less-satisfied couples; however, another finding is that men rate higher than women on amount of humor, funniness, and positive notings (elevated humor) of partner, while women are perceived as emitting more putdowns, especially self-directed putdowns. *

355. Hawkins, K. (1977). Elementary school children's preferences for selected elements of humor in children's books as determined by sex and grade level. Unpublished doctoral dissertation, University of Georgia. Participants were 150 randomly selected second-, fourth-, and sixth-grade students who listened to, and rated the funniness of, taped recordings of eight picture books containing four types of humor (human predicament situations, absurdity, incongruity, and verbal humor). The following conclusions are drawn from the findings: there are no gender differences among the three grade levels concerning preference for the four types of humor; fourth- and sixth-grade children perceive verbal humor better than do second-grade children; there is a wide range and variety of humor preferences in children in the three grade levels; and it appears that humor preference is an individual trait in the children. *

356. Jacobs, E. (1985). The functions of humor in marital adjustment. Unpublished doctoral dissertation, New School for Social Research. Participants were 102 adult women, ages 25–66 years old and married from 2 to 43 years, who completed a humor questionnaire, an adjustment scale, a semistructured interview, a social desirability scale, and a biographical survey. Results based on factor analyses of data show that positive and negative functions of humor are differentiated; the positive functions are "intimacy regulation" and "conflict management," while the negative function is "expression of hostility/creation of distance"; it is suggested that most successful marital adjustment is related to a greater degree of positive humor use, especially "intimacy regulation." *

357. Jakobs, E., Manstead, A., & Fischer, A. (1999). Social motives, emotional feelings, and smiling. *Cognition and Emotion, 13*, 321–345. Participants were 94 female and male college students who listened to two stories—one moderately funny, and the other strongly funny—that were told ("social context" variable) by either a friend or a stranger (via a tape recorder, the telephone, or face-to-face/in person). Results indicate that the funnier of the two stories elicits more smiling from the participants, but it is *not* mediated by experienced affect; also, the variable of social context—mediated by social motives—influences participants' smiling behavior. **

358. Janes, L., & Olson, J. (2000). Jeer pressures: The behavioral effects of observing ridicule of others. *Personality and Social Psychology Bulletin, 26*, 474–476. Describes two experiments in which participants were 161 college students who observed videotapes containing "other-ridiculing" humor, "self-ridiculing" humor, or "nonridiculing"/no-humor materials; participants then completed creativity, conformity, and fear-of-failure tasks. Results indicate that participants who view ridicule of others are more conforming and more afraid of failure than those participants who view self-ridicule or no-ridicule materials; also, creativity is *not* affected by the humor manipulations. **

359. Kaplan, R., & Pascoe, G. (1977). Humorous lectures and humorous examples: Some effects upon comprehension and retention. *Journal of Educational Psychology, 69*, 61–65. Participants were 508 female and male college students who viewed either a serious lecture or one of three versions of a humorous lecture (concept humor, nonconcept humor, mixed concept/nonconcept humor). Results based on a test of comprehension and retention given twice (immediately after the lecture, and six weeks later) indicate that immediate comprehension is *not* facilitated by the use of humorous examples in the lecture; however, upon retesting, retention of concept humor material is improved significantly by viewing a lecture with humorous examples illustrating concepts. **

360. Khramtsova, I. (1996). College students' perceptions about sense of humor and about the use of humor in U.S. and Russian classrooms. Unpublished doctoral dissertation, Kansas State University. Participants were 494 U.S.- and Russian-college students who completed a multidimensional sense of humor scale and a "uses-of-humor" scale. Statistical tests—conducted to examine cross-cultural differences in terms of sense of humor—show that the multidimensional sense of humor scale scores are similar for both the U.S. and Russian samples; in terms of attitudes, both the U.S. and Russian students are positive concerning classroom humor and agree about its positive effects on them. *

361. Lerstrom, A. (1986). An analysis of the impact of psychological and relational dominance and sex on humor and social interaction. Unpublished doctoral dissertation, University of Kansas. Participants were 80 female and male college students who were classified as high- or low-dominant and who were assigned to groups of four—balanced for psychological dominance and gender—and videotaped in a social interaction discussion of a problem. Partial results show that there is a significant relationship between psychological dominance/gender and frequency of domineering statements, and there is a significant relationship between psychological dominance/gender and humor purpose as groups define situations through "accounts" and "alternative definitions"; also, the relationship between dominance score and domineering statements is significant for all participants and women, but not for men—when analyzed as a separate group; and all correlations between domineering-statements and humor-attempts are significant. *

362. Martin, G. N., & Gray, C. (1996). The effects of audience laughter on men's and women's responses to humor. *The Journal of Social Psychology, 136*, 221–231. Participants were 40 female and male college students who were exposed to a recording of radio-show comedy material under one of two conditions: audience laughter, or no-laughter, present; following this treatment, participants rated the funniness and level of enjoyment of the comedy material.

Results indicate that students who listen with the audience laughter present give higher ratings of the funniness and enjoyability of the material (as well as demonstrating more laughter and smiling in this condition) than those students in the no-laughter condition; also, *no* gender differences occur in this study. **

363. Murphy, B. (1975). Mood development and change in a humorous setting. Unpublished doctoral dissertation, The University of Tennessee. Examines the social factors that are important in setting, blocking, or terminating a humorous mood by exposing adult audiences to audio-taped recordings of comic routines; trained "claques" or "shills" were planted in the audiences with instructions to behave either in a manner that communicated enjoyment, or in a manner that communicated dislike for the comic routines; control groups were studied with no "claques" present. Results indicate that the "claques" are effective in altering the frequencies of laughing and smiling, as well as other hand/body movements, in audience members. **

364. O'Quin, K., & Aronoff, J. (1981). Humor as a technique of social influence. *Social Psychology Quarterly, 44*, 349–357. Participants were 120 male and 130 female college students who—in a dyadic-bargaining paradigm at a predetermined time in the negotiation—received an influence attempt from a confederate that differed in size and was administered in either a humorous or a nonhumorous manner. Results support the major hypothesis that humor leads to an increased financial concession in bargaining, and that the use of humor results in a more positive evaluation of the task (and self-reported tension), but does not increase the liking of the partner; also, consistent with other studies employing social tasks, women laugh and smile more than do men. **

365. Parrott, W. (1985). Cognitive and social factors underlying infants' smiling and laughter during the peek-a-boo game. Unpublished doctoral dissertation, University of Pennsylvania. Describes five experiments in which infants, 6–8 months of age, participated in a peek-a-boo game in which—on occasional "person-switch" (and "other-type" switches involving differing locations and times) trials—one adult hid and a second adult reappeared in his or her place. Among the results are the following: infants in all age groups smile *less* following the "person-switch" than the normal reappearances; smiling in infants decreases for "location-switches" as well as for "person-switches"; the use of different lengths of "disappearance times" (five seconds versus three seconds) does *not* affect infants' smiling; the presence of "animacy" (e.g., a puppet) affects infants' smiling and laughter; and infants smile *more* when there is eye contact during the reappearance than when there is no eye contact.**

366. Pistole, D., & Shor, R. (1979). A multivariate study of the effect of repetition on humor appreciation as qualified by two social influence factors. *The Journal of General Psychology, 100*, 43–51. Participants were 25 male and 39 female college students who gave smiling, subjective-amusement, and objective-funniness ratings to 25 recorded "bloopers" in which material varied according to one of four recorded laughter sequences presented in two sessions: with/with, with/without, without/with, and without/without. Results show that decreases in ratings as a function of repetition are more common in group, than individual, settings (with smiling more often affected than the other measures); also, only smiling ratings decrease with repetition in the individual setting, and only when recorded laughter does *not* accompany the second presentation. **

367. Rosenfeld, P., Giacalone, R., & Tedeschi, J. (1983). Humor and impression management. *The Journal of Social Psychology, 121*, 59–63. Participants were 30 male college students who were approached by an interviewer in a college cafeteria (and asked to rate the funniness of a cartoon) in one of three situations: person is alone, person is in the presence of a nonlaughing confederate, or person is in the presence of a laughing confederate. Results indicate an increase of humor ratings only in the presence of a laughing confederate—a finding that supports the notion that the facilitation of humor appreciation in the presence of others is due to impression-management factors. **

368. Smyth, M., & Fuller, R. (1972). Effects of group laughter on responses to humorous material. *Psychological Reports, 30*, 132–134. Participants were 40 male and female college students who listened to two humorous recordings: one with, and one without, the dubbed laughter of an audience. Results show that—in the condition of group/audience laughter—participants laugh more frequently, and for longer periods of time; they also rated the humorous material as more amusing in this condition than in the condition without the dubbed laughter of a group of people. ** [Note: cf: Fuller, R., & Sheehy-Skeffington, A. (1974). Effects of group laughter on responses to humourous material, a replication and extension. *Psychological Reports, 35*, 531–534.]

369. Snyder, A. (1970). The effects of demand characteristics upon conformity in judgments of humor. Unpublished doctoral dissertation, University of Southern California. Examines the effects of prestige, participants' gender, and the demand characteristics via the experimenter upon conformity behavior in three different experimental conditions all involving one actual participant and one female and one male confederate posing as participants in a conformity-test situation. Results indicate that there are *no* significant effects of either prestige or gender variables on the conformity behavior elicited in any of the experimental conditions; also, one condition (a "*laboratory*-room" setting without experimenter present) was found to be four times more effective in predicting conformity behavior than a "*waiting*-room-without-experimenter-present" condition or a "*laboratory*-room-with experimenter-present" condition. **

370. Socha, T., & Kelly, B. (1994). Children making "fun": Humorous communication, impression management, and moral development. *Child Study Journal, 24*, 237–252. Participants were 208 preschool, elementary, and secondary school children and adolescents, ages 4–14 years old, who provided hu-

morous messages whose contents were analyzed in terms of prosocial and antisocial themes. Results show an association between age, gender, target, and prosocial/antisocial humorous themes; children in preschool to the third grade produce mostly prosocial messages, while children in the fourth grade begin to produce proportionately more antisocial than prosocial humorous messages; also, boys produce more antisocial humorous messages than do girls, and they produce more antisocial humorous messages for their best friends than for teachers. *

371. Spindle, D. (1989). College instructor use of humor in the classroom: Interaction of instructor gender, type and condition of humor with instructor, competence, and sociability. Unpublished doctoral dissertation, The University of Oklahoma. Participants were 124 male and female college students who heard an audiotaped introduction that established an instructor as sociable and competent, and then viewed a videotaped presentation of either a female or male instructor teaching a lesson with one combination of "type" (tendentious versus nontendentious) and "condition" (related, or unrelated, to the educational point) of humor. Results indicate a significant three-way interaction between humor condition, humor type, and instructor gender for the "sociability" data; also, two of the main effects—type and instructor gender—are significant. It is concluded that when an instructor is unknown to students—under conditions of high credibility—the use of all combinations of "type" and "condition" of humor results in perceived decreased competence and sociability of both female and male instructors. **

372. Strombom, T. (1989). Humor and the problem-solving behavior of married couples. Unpublished doctoral dissertation, Virginia Polytechnic Institute and State University. Participants were 20 married couples who were assigned randomly to either a treatment or nontreatment group; the treatment condition involved the viewing of a humorous videotape before completing a marital conflict scale. Results indicate that couples who view the tape prior to a problem-solving task report higher levels of satisfaction with their decisions than couples not experiencing the humor treatment. **

373. Tamborini, R., & Zillmann, D. (1981). College students' perception of lecturers using humor. *Perceptual and Motor Skills, 52,* 427–432. Participants were 50 female and 50 male college students who—after exposure to an audiotaped lecture by a male or female professor in which conditions of humor content (no humor, sexual humor, other-disparaging humor, self-disparaging humor) were manipulated—gave their perceptions of the lecturer's intelligence and appeal. Results show there are significant interactions between sex of speaker and sex of respondent (for both sexual and self-disparaging humor) on the measures of appeal, where the use of *self-disparaging* humor leads to higher appeal ratings when the speaker and respondent are of the *same* sex; and, in contrast, the use of *sexual* humor leads to higher appeal ratings when the speaker and respondent are of *opposite* sex; also, it was found that the various conditions of humor content have *no* effect on the respondents' perceptions of the lecturer's intelligence. **

374. Wanzer, M., Booth-Butterfield, M., & Booth-Butterfield, S. (1996). Are funny people popular? An examination of humor orientation, loneliness, and social attraction. *Communication Quarterly, 44,* 42–52. Participants were 125 male and female college students who completed measures of humor orientation, loneliness, and verbal aggressiveness, and then had two acquaintances complete an "other-perceived" humor orientation scale, and a social-attractiveness scale, on them. Results show that higher humor orientation is associated with lower levels of loneliness, that acquaintances' perceptions of humor orientation and self-reported humor orientation are related positively, and people who are viewed as more humorous are seen, also, as socially attractive; also, persons high in verbal aggressiveness do not report more loneliness, but are perceived to be less socially attractive than individuals without aggressiveness. *

375. Warners-Kleverlaan, N., Oppenheimer, L., & Sherman, L. (1996). To be or not to be humorous: Does it make a difference? *Humor: International Journal of Humor Research, 9,* 117–141. Participants were 225 children and adolescents, aged 8–17 years old, who completed measures of humor, funniness, social distance, social status, and play and work preferences. Results show that the meaning and interpretation of humor and perceived humorousness in children is gender- and age-related; also, a good sense of humor helps to establish social-distance characteristics in participants and aids in the formation of their social status. *

376. Webber, J. (1974). The influence of racial group composition on racial-aggressive humor appreciation: A test of reference group theory. Unpublished doctoral dissertation, Michigan State University. Participants were 84 male college students (10 black and 74 white) who rated racial-theme cartoons and who also completed an inventory of the assessment of different kinds of hostility. Results show that reference-group theory is correct to the extent that blacks enjoy problack humor more than whites, while whites enjoy prowhite humor more than blacks; and two distinctly different attitudes are apparent between black and white participants regarding "hostility intensity" and racial humor (blacks display negative attitude, while whites display more indirect hostility). *

377. Wells, D. (1974). The relationship between the humor of elementary school teachers and the perceptions of students. Unpublished doctoral dissertation, United States International University. Participants were 300 elementary school students, grades 4–6, and their 10 classroom teachers, who interacted in eight 20–minute observation periods in each of the classrooms; each teacher completed a personality test, and an interviewing session. Results based on descriptive data show that teachers have preferred types of humor but do not employ such preferences in the classroom. Main conclusions include the following: spontaneous humor is viewed by students and teachers alike as a vital classroom ingredient; teacher humor is identifiable and may be categorized via observation and testing; teacher and student humor may be described meaningfully; the nature of classroom humor is usually a short, snappy retort; male teachers use more humor, and a greater variety of types, than female teachers; boys are more often the recipients of humor than are girls; teachers need humor in their daily routine for themselves as much as for their pupils; and other classroom variables—such as size of instructional group, academic area, and time of day—are *not* significantly related to teacher humor. *

378. Wuerffel, J. (1986). The relationship between humor and family strengths. Unpublished doctoral dissertation, The University of Nebraska. Responses were analyzed from 304 collected surveys that descriptively explored the use of humor in the family where family members were asked to report the amounts and effects of a variety of types and ways they use humor. Results indicate—via "family strength" scale scores—that stronger families use humor more often than weaker families to maintain a positive outlook on life, for entertainment, to reduce tension, to express warmth, to put others at ease, to facilitate conversations, to lessen anxiety, and to help cope with difficult situations; also, most families benefit more from the use of incongruity humor than of superiority humor. *

379. Yates, J., & Miller, R. (1982). Effects of seating orientation on appreciation of humor. *Psychological Reports, 51*, 567–576. Describes two experiments to test the notion that participants' preexisting arousal states influence their appreciation of humor. In one case, 18 female college students rated 10 jokes for humorousness while seated either side-by-side or face-to-face with a female stranger; as predicted, jokes in this situation are rated more humorous in the more arousing side-by-side condition. In another case, 32 female and 32 male college students rated the same 10 jokes while seated in either arrangement with a same-sex stranger; once again, according to prediction, *women* rate jokes as more humorous when side-by-side, but—contrary to prediction—so do the *men*. **

380. Zillmann, D., & Cantor, J. (1972). Directionality of transitory dominance as a communication variable affecting humor appreciation. *Journal of Personality and Social Psychology, 24*, 191–198. Participants were 40 female and male college students, and 40 male passengers traveling on a "luxury" train, who rated the humor of cartoons and jokes in which a protagonist and an antagonist were portrayed in various dominant-subordinate roles and exchanges. Results indicate that individuals with primarily subordinate experiences exhibit greater appreciation for humorous exchanges that show a subordinate temporarily dominating a superior than for those in which the superior dominates the subordinate, and that persons primarily occupying superior positions show the opposite preference. **

381. Ziv, A., & Gadish, O. (1989). Humor and marital satisfaction. *The Journal of Social Psychology, 129,* 759–768. Participants were 50 married Israeli couples who completed humor-creation and humor-appreciation tests, as well as a questionnaire assessing marital satisfaction. Results show that marital satisfaction is related to perception of the partner's humor more than the spouse's own humor; also, while there is a significant relationship for husbands between their humor appreciation scores and their marital satisfaction, *no* such relationship is found for wives' humor scores and their marital satisfaction. *

Name Index

Subject Index

About the Author

JON E. ROECKELEIN is a professor of psychology at Mesa Community College in Mesa, Arizona. A past Staff Intelligence Officer and research psychologist for the U.S. Army, he has taught and conducted psychological research for more than 30 years. He is the author of *Dictionary of Theories, Laws, and Concepts in Psychology* (Greenwood, 1998), and *The Concept of Time in Psychology* (Greenwood, 2000).